Investment Analysis and Portfolio Management

8th Edition

Investment Analysis and Portfolio Management

8th Edition

Frank K. Reilly
University of Notre Dame

Keith C. Brown
University of Texas at Austin

SOUTH-WESTERN
CENGAGE Learning™

Australia • Brazil • Japan • Korea • Mexico • Singapore • Spain • United Kingdom • United States

Investment Analysis and Portfolio Management, Eighth Edition

Frank K. Reilly and Keith C. Brown

VP/Editorial Director:
Jack W. Calhoun

Editor-in-Chief:
Alex von Rosenberg

Executive Editor:
Michael R. Reynolds

Senior Developmental Editor:
Elizabeth R. Thomson

Marketing Manager:
Heather MacMaster

Production Project Manager:
Amy Hackett

Manager of Technology, Editorial:
Vicky True

Technology Project Editor:
Christine Wittmer

Web Coordinator:
Karen Schaffer

Senior Manufacturing Coordinator:
Sandee Milewski

Production House:
Pre-Press Company, Inc.

Printer:
Quebecor World
Taunton, MA

Art Director:
Bethany Casey

Cover and Internal Designer:
Stratton Design

Cover Image:
PhotoDisc

Photo and Text Permissions Researcher:
James Reidel

To my best friend & wife,
Therese,
and the greatest gifts and
sources of our happiness,
Frank K. III, Charlotte, and Lauren
Clarence R. II, Michelle, and Sophie
Therese B., and Denise
Edgar B., Kayleigh, and Madison J. T.
F. K. R.

To Sheryl, Alexander, and Andrew
who make it all worthwhile
K. C. B.

Preface

The pleasure of authoring a textbook comes from writing about a subject that you enjoy and find exciting. As an author, you hope that you can pass on to the reader not only knowledge but also the excitement that you feel for the subject. In addition, writing about investments brings an added stimulant because the subject can affect the reader during his or her entire business career and beyond. We hope what readers derive from this course will help them enjoy better lives through managing their financial resources properly.

The purpose of this book is to help you learn how to manage your money so that you will derive the maximum benefit from what you earn. To accomplish this purpose, you need to learn about the investment alternatives that are available today and, what is more important, to develop a way of analyzing and thinking about investments that will remain with you in the years ahead when new and different investment opportunities become available.

Because of its dual purpose, the book mixes description and theory. The descriptive material discusses available investment instruments and considers the purpose and operation of capital markets in the United States and around the world. The theoretical portion details how you should evaluate current investments and future opportunities to develop a portfolio of investments that will satisfy your risk–return objectives.

Preparing this eighth edition has been challenging for two reasons. First, many changes have occurred in the securities markets during the last few years in terms of theory, new financial instruments, and trading practices. Second, as mentioned in prior editions, capital markets have become increasingly global in nature. Consequently, early in the book we present the compelling case for global investing. Subsequently, to ensure that you are prepared to function in a global environment, almost every chapter discusses how investment practice or theory is influenced by the globalization of investments and capital markets. This completely integrated treatment is to ensure that you develop a broad mindset on investments that will serve you well in the 21st century.

Intended Market

This text is addressed to both graduate and advanced undergraduate students who are looking for an in-depth discussion of investments and portfolio management. The presentation of the material is intended to be rigorous and empirical, without being overly quantitative. A proper discussion of the modern developments in investments and portfolio theory must be rigorous. The detailed discussion of numerous empirical studies reflects the belief that it is essential for alternative investment theories to be exposed to the real world and be judged on the basis of how well they help us understand and explain reality.

Key Features of the Eighth Edition

When planning the eighth edition of *Investment Analysis and Portfolio Management,* we wanted to retain its traditional strengths and capitalize on new developments in the investments area to make it the most comprehensive investments textbook available.

First, the current edition maintains its unparalleled international coverage. Investing knows no borders, and although the total integration of domestic and global investment opportunities may seem to contradict the need for separate discussions of international issues, it in fact makes the need for specific information on non-U.S. markets, instruments, conventions, and techniques even more compelling.

Second, today's investing environment includes derivative securities not as exotic anomalies but as standard investment instruments. We felt that *Investment Analysis and Portfolio Management* must reflect that reality. Consequently, our four chapters on derivatives have been revised and rearranged to provide an even more intuitive, clear discussion of the different instruments, their markets, valuation, trading strategies, and general use as risk management/ return enhancement tools.

Third, Chapter 24, "Professional Asset Management," has been significantly revised to include an extensive discussion of the hedge fund industry. In a very short period of time, hedge funds have emerged as one of the most important vehicles for attracting investment capital throughout the world. We provide a discussion of how the industry is structured and has evolved over the past decade, as well as a breakdown of the myriad portfolio strategies that hedge fund managers employ. We also contrast the salient characteristics of hedge funds with more traditional professional money management products, such as mutual funds.

Fourth, we have added many new questions and problems to the end-of-chapter material, including a significant number of CFA exercises through the 2004 exam, to provide more student practice on executing computations concerned with more sophisticated investment problems. These are designated by the CFA icon.

Fifth, we have added Thomson ONE: Business School Edition exercises in several end-of-chapter problem sets. Thomson ONE: BSE is a professional analytical package used by professionals world-wide. Our text allows one-year access for students to access Thomson ONE: BSE, containing information on firms, including financial statement comparisons with competitors, stock price information, and indexes for comparing firm performance against the market or sector. Thomson ONE: BSE is a great package for hands-on learning which rivals or exceeds those offered by other textbook publishers.

Web Site Listings

To reflect the growing use of the World Wide Web as a learning tool and a source of information, each chapter contains an annotated list of the Web sites that relate to the chapter's topic. Students will want to "surf the net" using these applications to gain further insight into the practice of investments and the textbook discussions.

Major Content Changes in the Eighth Edition

The text has been thoroughly updated for currency. In addition to these time-related revisions, we have also made the following specific changes to individual chapters:

Chapter 2 In this asset allocation chapter there is a discussion of several tax changes and how they impact the asset allocation decision. We also demonstrate the importance of investing early and regularly. We emphasize not only what should be done, but also some common mistakes by investors. Finally, we consider how the asset allocation differs among foreign countries and is changing.

Chapter 3 The updated evidence of returns (especially 2000–2004) continues to support the notion of global diversification. A new study of global assets also supports the use of a global measure of systematic risk to explain asset returns. Also, there is a consideration of new investment instruments available for global investors, including global index funds and, notably, exchange-traded funds (ETFs) for numerous countries that trade continuously.

Chapter 4 Because of the significant growth in trading volume experienced by the electronic communication networks (ECNs), this chapter was heavily rewritten to reflect the new and evolving secondary market for stocks. In addition, the corporate bond market also experienced major changes in how and when trades are reported. We also demonstrate that global markets and exchanges continue to consolidate.

Chapter 5 Contains an expanded discussion of growth and value style stock indexes and an updated analysis of the relationship among indexes.

Chapter 6 Considers new studies that both support the efficient market hypothesis but also provide new evidence of anomalies. The section that describes *behavioral finance* and discusses how it explains many of the anomalies is expanded and updated to include recent studies. There is an expanded discussion of the implications of the recent findings related to the efficient market hypothesis for both analysts and portfolio managers.

Chapter 9 The discussion of the theory and practice using multifactor models of risk and expected return has been updated and expanded. The connection between the Arbitrage Pricing Theory (APT) and empirical implementations of the APT continues to be stressed, both conceptually and with several new examples.

Chapter 10 Contains a detailed examination of alternative cash flow specifications that are used in valuation models and credit analysis. There is also a discussion of how to analyze operating leases and a demonstration of how the capitalization of these leases and the implied interest dramatically impacts the financial risk ratios for retail firms like Walgreens.

Chapter 11 Emphasizes the two alternative approaches to valuation (present value of cash flows and relative valuation). We discuss how and when they should be implemented and consider the estimation of the variables that are relevant for all valuation models.

Chapter 12 This is a new chapter that combines prior chapters 12 and 13 that considers both the macroeconomic variables that affect capital markets, and the microvaluation of these markets using the valuation concepts and models considered in Chapter 11.

Chapter 13 We reorganized the industry analysis presentation to increase the emphasis on the macroanalysis of an industry and concentrated this analysis in the early part of the chapter. This macroanalysis has a large impact on the subsequent microanalysis (valuation) of the industry.

Chapter 14 The stock of Walgreens was valued using the alternative techniques and emphasized a key point that an outstanding company like Walgreens can have a fully valued or overvalued stock. There is also an expanded discussion dealing with the importance of quarterly earnings estimates. We conclude the chapter with a consideration of several models that can be used to value true growth companies.

Chapter 16 Contains an expanded discussion of the relative merits of passive versus active management techniques for equity portfolio focusing on the important role of tracking error. Also includes enhanced analysis of equity portfolio investment strategies, including fundamental and technical approaches, as well as a detailed description of equity style analysis.

Chapter 17 The updated global bond market data considers the recent creation of the Euroland Sector.

Chapter 18 Contains a discussion of the calculation and use of empirical duration. We also consider the relationship between static yield spreads and option-adjusted spreads (OAS) and what variables affect the option-adjusted spreads.

Chapter 19 Contains a new discussion of the core-plus bond portfolio management technique and some of the "plus" strategies. There is an update and analysis of an expanded set of cumulative default rates for bonds across rating classes.

Chapter 20 Enhanced discussions of the "fundamentals" associated with using derivative securities (e.g., interpreting price quotations, basic payoff diagrams, basic strategies). Also provides updated examples of both basic and intermediate risk management applications using derivative positions.

Chapter 21 Updated examples and applications throughout the chapter, emphasizing the role that forward and futures contracts play in managing exposures to equity, fixed-income, and foreign exchange risk.

Chapter 22 Presents a revised discussion linking valuation and applications of call and put options in the context of investment management. The chapter contains both new and updated examples designed to illustrate how investors use options in practice.

Chapter 23 Includes a revised discussion of several advanced derivative applications (e.g., swap contracting, convertible securities, structured notes, real options), as well as updated examples and applications of each of these applications.

Chapter 24 Contains a completely revised and updated discussion of the organization and participants in the professional asset management industry. Of particular note is an extensive new examination of the structure and strategies employed by hedge funds. The discussion of ethics and regulation in the asset management industry that concludes the chapter has also been expanded considerably.

Chapter 25 Provides an updated and considerably expanded application of the performance measurement techniques that are introduced throughout the chapter. The discussion has been expanded to include a new section on the use of performance measurement tools that are based on an examination of the security holdings of a manager's portfolio, rather than the returns the portfolio generates.

Supplement Package

The preparation of the eighth edition provided the opportunity to enhance the supplement products offered to instructors and students who use *Investment Analysis and Portfolio Management.* The result of this examination is a greatly improved package that provides more than just basic answers and solutions. We are indebted to the supplement writers who devoted their time, energy, and creativity to making this supplement package the best it has ever been.

STOCK-TRAK® Thousands of students every year use STOCK-TRAK® to practice investment strategies, test theories, practice day trading, and learn about the various markets. This optional stock simulation access code can be bundled with the text to enhance the real-world experience with the text.

The Instructor's Manual and Test Bank The *Instructor's Manual*, written by Narendar Rao at Northeastern Illinois University, and *Test Bank*, written by Murli Rajan at the University of Scranton, contains a brief outline of each chapter's key concepts and equations that can be easily copied and distributed to students as a reference tool. The *Test Bank* includes an extensive set of new questions and problems and complete solutions to the testing material. For instructors who would like to prepare their exams electronically, there is a *Computerized Test Bank* as well as Test Bank in Word format that contains all the test questions found in the printed version.

The Solutions Manual This separate volume, which can be purchased by students if instructors wish, contains all the answers to the end-of-chapter questions and solutions to end-of-chapter problems. David Leahigh at King's College was ever diligent in the preparation of these materials, ensuring the most error-free solutions possible.

Lecture Presentation Software A comprehensive set of PowerPoint slides created by Narendar Rao at Northeastern Illinois University is available. Each chapter has a self-contained presentation that covers all the key concepts, equations, and examples within the chapter. The files can be used as is for an innovative, interactive class presentation. Instructors who have access to Microsoft PowerPoint can modify the slides in any way they wish, adding or deleting materials to match their needs.

Web Site The text's *Web Site* can be accessed through *academic.cengage.com/finance/reilly* and includes up-to-date teaching and learning aids for instructors and students. The *Instructor's Manual, Test Bank,* and PowerPoint slides are available to instructors for download. Instructors may post, on a password-protected site only, the PowerPoint presentation for their students if they choose to.

Acknowledgments

So many people have helped us in so many ways that we hesitate to list them, fearing that we may miss someone. Accepting this risk, we will begin with the University of Notre Dame and the University of Texas at Austin because of their direct support. Also, we must thank the Bernard J. Hank Family, who have endowed the Chair that helped bring Frank Reilly back to Notre Dame and that has provided support for our work.

Reviewers for this edition were:

Hsiu-lang Chen
University of Illinois at Chicago

Jimmy Senteza
Drake University

Shelly Howton
Villanova University

Lawrence S. Tai
Loyola Marymount College

Malek Lashgari
University of Hartford

Richard S. Warr
North Carolina State University

Iqbal Mansur
Widener University

Sheng-Ping Yang
Wayland Baptist University

Jonathan Ohn
Wagner College

We were fortunate to have the following excellent reviewers for earlier editions:

John Alexander
Clemson University

Paul Bolster
Northeastern University

Robert Angell
East Carolina University

Robert E. Brooks
University of Alabama

George Aragon
Boston College

Robert J. Brown
Harrisburg, Pennsylvania

Brian Belt
University of Missouri—Kansas City

Charles Q. Cao
Pennsylvania State University

Omar M. Benkato
Ball State University

Atreya Chakraborty
Brandeis University

Arand Bhattacharya
University of Cincinnati

Dosoung Choi
University of Tennessee

Carol Billingham
Central Michigan University

Robert Clark
University of Vermont

Susan Block
University of California—Santa Barbara

John Clinebell
University of Northern Colorado

Gerald A. Blum
Babson College

James D'Mello
Western Michigan University

Eugene F. Drzycimski
University of Wisconsin—Oshkosh

William Dukes
Texas Tech University

John Dunkelberg
Wake Forest University

Eric Emory
Sacred Heart University

Thomas Eyssell
University of Missouri—St. Louis

Heber Farnsworth
Washington University, St. Louis

James Feller
Middle Tennessee State University

Eurico Ferreira
Clemson University

Michael Ferri
John Carroll University

Greg Filbeck
University of Toledo

Joseph E. Finnerty
University of Illinois

Harry Friedman
New York University

R. H. Gilmer
University of Mississippi

Steven Goldstein
University of South Carolina

Steven Goldstein
Robinson-Humphrey/American Express

Keshav Gupta
Oklahoma State University

Sally A. Hamilton
Santa Clara University

Eric Higgins
Drexel University

Ronald Hoffmeister
Arizona State University

Ron Hutchins
Eastern Michigan University

A. James Ifflander
Arizona State University

Stan Jacobs
Central Washington University

Kwang Jun
Michigan State University

Jaroslaw Komarynsky
Northern Illinois University

Danny Litt
Century Software Systems/UCLA

Miles Livingston
University of Florida

Christopher Ma
Texas Tech University

Ananth Madhaven
University of Southern California

Davinder Malhotra
Philadelphia College of Textiles and Science

Stephen Mann
University of South Carolina

Iqbal Mansur
Widener University

Linda Martin
Arizona State University

George Mason
University of Hartford

John Matthys
DePaul University

Michael McBain
Marquette University

Dennis McConnell
University of Maine

Jeanette Medewitz
University of Nebraska—Omaha

Jacob Michaelsen
University of California—Santa Cruz

Nicholas Michas
Northern Illinois University

Thomas W. Miller Jr.
University of Missouri—Columbia

Lalatendu Misra
University of Texas—San Antonio

Michael Murray
LaCrosse, Wisconsin

Henry Oppenheimer
University of Rhode Island

John Peavy
Southern Methodist University

George Philippatos
University of Tennessee

George Pinches
University of Kansas

Rose Prasad
Central Michigan University

Laurie Prather
University of Tennessee at Chattanooga

George A. Racette
University of Oregon

Murli Rajan
University of Scranton

Narendar V. Rao
Northeastern Illinois University

Steve Rich
Baylor University

Bruce Robin
Old Dominion University

James Rosenfeld
Emory University

Stanley D. Ryals
Investment Counsel, Inc.

Katrina F. Sherrerd
Association of Investment Management and Research

Shekar Shetty
University of South Dakota

Frederic Shipley
DePaul University

Douglas Southard
Virginia Polytechnic Institute

Harold Stevenson
Arizona State University

Kishore Tandon
The City University of New York— Baruch College

Donald Thompson
Georgia State University

David E. Upton
Virginia Commonwealth University

E. Theodore Veit
Rollins College

Premal Vora
King's College

Bruce Wardrep
East Carolina University

Robert Weigand
University of South Florida

Russell R. Wermers
University of Maryland

Rolf Wubbels
New York University

Valuable comments and data support has come from my frequent co-author David Wright, University of Wisconsin—Parkside. Once more, we were blessed with bright, dedicated research assistants when we needed them the most. These includes Tom Boyd and Brandon Grinwis, who have been extremely careful, dependable, and creative.

Current and former colleagues have been very helpful: Yu-Chi Chang, Rob Batallio, Mike Hemler, Jerry Langley, and Paul Schultz, University of Notre Dame; and John M. Wachowicz, University of Tennessee. As always, some of the best insights and most stimulating comments continue to come during too-infrequent walks with a very good friend, Jim Gentry of the University of Illinois.

We are convinced that professors who want to write a book that is academically respectable and relevant, as well as realistic, require help from the "real world." We have been fortunate to develop relationships with a number of individuals (including a growing number of former students) whom we consider our contacts with reality.

The following individuals have graciously provided important insights and material:

Sharon Athey
Brown Brothers Harriman

Joseph Bencivenga
Bankers Trust

David G. Booth
Dimensional Fund Advisors, Inc.

Gary Brinson
GP Investments

David Chapman
Boston College

David Chapman
University of Texas

Dwight D. Churchill
Fidelity Management and Research

Abby Joseph Cohen
Goldman, Sachs and Company

Robert Conway
Goldman, Sachs and Company

Robert J. Davis
Crimson Capital Company

Philip Delaney Jr.
Northern Trust Bank

Sam Eisenstadt
Value Line

Frank J. Fabozzi
Journal of Portfolio Management

Kenneth Fisher
Forbes

John J. Flanagan Jr.
*Lawrence, O'Donnell, Marcus and
    Company*

H. Gifford Fong
Gifford Fong Associates

Martin S. Fridson
Fridson Vision, LLC

M. Christopher Garman
Merrill, Lynch, Pierce, Fenner & Smith

Khalid Ghayur
Morgan Stanley

William J. Hank
Moore Financial Corporation

Rick Hans
Walgreens Corporation

Lea B. Hansen
Greenwich Associates

W. Van Harlow
Fidelity Management and Research

Craig Hester
Hester Capital Management

Joanne Hill
Goldman, Sachs and Company

John W. Jordan II
The Jordan Company

Andrew Kalotay
Kalotay Associates

Luke Knecht
Dresdner RCM Capital Management

Warren N. Koontz Jr.
Loomis, Sayles and Company

Mark Kritzman
Windham Capital Management

Sandy Leeds
University of Texas

Martin Leibowitz
Morgan Stanley

Douglas R. Lempereur
Templeton Investment Counsel, Inc.

Robert Levine
Nomura Securities

Amy Lipton
Bankers Trust

George W. Long
Long Investment Management Ltd.

Scott Lummer
Lummer Investment Consulting

John Maginn
Maginn Associates

Scott Malpass
University of Notre Dame

Jack Malvey
Lehman Brothers

Andras Marosi
University of Alberta

Dominic Marshall
Wells Fargo Benson Associates

Frank Martin
Martin Capital Management

Todd Martin
Martin Capital Management

Joseph McAlinden
Morgan Stanley

Richard McCabe
*Merrill, Lynch, Pierce, Fenner &
  Smith*

Michael McCowin
*State of Wisconsin Investment
  Board*

Terrence J. McGlinn
McGlinn Capital Markets

Mitch Merin
Morgan Stanley

Kenneth Meyer
Lincoln Capital Management

Janet T. Miller
Rowland and Company

Brian Moore
U.S. Gypsum Corp.

Salvator Muoio
SM Investors, LP

Gabrielle Napolitano
Goldman, Sachs and Company

David Nelms
Morgan Stanley

George Noyes
*Standish Mellon Asset
  Management*

Ian Rossa O'Reilly
Wood Gundy, Inc.

Robert Parrino
University of Texas

Philip J. Purcell III
Morgan Stanley

Jack Pycik
Consultant

John C. Rudolf
Summit Capital Management

Guy Rutherford
Morgan Stanley

Ron Ryan
Asset Liability Management

Mark Rypzinski
Henry & Co.

Sean St. Clair
Lehman Brothers

Robert F. Semmens Jr.
Semmens Consultants

Brian Singer
UBS Global Asset Management

Clay Singleton
Rollins College

Donald J. Smith
Boston University

Fred H. Speece Jr.
Speece, Thorson Capital Group

Laura Starks
University of Texas

William M. Stephens
Husic Capital Management

James Stork
Uitermarkt & Associates

Kevin Terhaar
UBS Global Asset Management

William M. Wadden
LongShip Capital Management

Sushi Wadhwani
Goldman, Sachs and Company

Ken Wiles
Fulcrum Financial Group

Richard S. Wilson
Ryan Labs, Inc.

Robert Wilmouth
National Futures Association

Hong Yan
University of Texas

We continue to benefit from the help and consideration of the dedicated people who are or have been associated with the CFA Institute:, Tom Bowman, Whit Broome, Jeff Diermeier, Bob Johnson, Bob Luck, Sue Martin, Katie Sherrerd, and Donald Tuttle.

Professor Reilly would like to thank his assistant, Rachel Karnafel, who had the unenviable task of keeping his office and his life in some sort of order during this project.

As always, our greatest gratitude is to our families—past, present, and future. Our parents gave us life and helped us understand love and how to give it. Most important are our wives who provide love, understanding, and support throughout the day and night. We thank God for our children and grandchildren who ensure that our lives are full of love, laughs, and excitement.

Frank K. Reilly
Notre Dame, Indiana

Keith C. Brown
Austin, Texas

September 2005

About the Authors

Frank K. Reilly is the Bernard J. Hank Professor of Finance and former dean of the Mendoza College of Business at the University of Notre Dame. Holding degrees from the University of Notre Dame (B.B.A.), Northwestern University (M.B.A.), and the University of Chicago (Ph.D.), Professor Reilly has taught at the University of Illinois, the University of Kansas, and the University of Wyoming in addition to the University of Notre Dame. He has several years of experience as a senior securities analyst, as well as experience in stock and bond trading. A Chartered Financial Analyst (CFA), he has been a member of the Council of Examiners, the Council on Education and Research, the grading committee, and was Chairman of the Board of Trustees of the Institute of Charted Financial Analysts and Chairman of the Board of the Association of Investment Management and Research (AIMR) (now the CFA Institute). Professor Reilly has been president of the Financial Management Association, the Midwest Business Administration Association, the Eastern Finance Association, the Academy of Financial Services, and the Midwest Finance Association. He is or has been on the board of directors of the First Interstate Bank of Wisconsin, Norwest Bank of Indiana, the Investment Analysts Society of Chicago, UBS Brinson Global Funds (chairman), Fort Dearborn Income Securities (Chairman), Discover Bank, NIBCO, Inc., International Board of Certified Financial Planners, Battery Park High Yield Bond Fund, Inc., Morgan Stanley Trust FSB, the CFA Institute Research Foundation (Chairman), the Financial Analysts Seminar, and the Association for Investment Management and Research.

As the author of more than 100 articles, monographs, and papers, his work has appeared in numerous publications including *Journal of Finance, Journal of Financial and Quantitative Analysis, Journal of Accounting Research, Financial Management, Financial Analysts Journal, Journal of Fixed Income,* and *Journal of Portfolio Management.* In addition to *Investment Analysis and Portfolio Management,* Eighth Edition, Professor Reilly is the co-author of another textbook, *Investments,* Seventh Edition (South-Western, 2006) with Edgar A. Norton.

Professor Reilly was named on the list of *Outstanding Educators in America* and has received the University of Illinois Alumni Association Graduate Teaching Award, the Outstanding Educator Award from the M.B.A. class at the University of Illinois, and the Outstanding Teacher Award from the M.B.A. class and the Senior Class at Notre Dame. He also received from the Association of Investment Management and Research (AIMR) both the C. Stewart Sheppard Award for his contribution to the educational mission of the Association and the Daniel J. Forrestal III Leadership Award for Professional Ethics and Standards of Investment Practice. He was part of the inaugural group selected as a Fellow of the Financial Management Association International. He is editor of *Readings and Issues in Investments, Ethics and the Investment Industry,* and *High Yield Bonds: Analysis and Risk Assessment,* and is or has been a member of the editorial boards of *Financial Management, The Financial Review, International Review of Economics and Finance, Journal of Financial Education, Quarterly Review of Economics and Finance,* and the *European Journal of Finance.* He is included in the *Who's Who in Finance and Industry, Who's Who in America, Who's Who in American Education,* and *Who's Who in the World.*

Keith C. Brown holds the position of Fayez Sarofim Fellow and Professor of Finance at the McCombs School of Business, University of Texas. He received his B.A. in Economics from San Diego State University, where he was a member of the Phi Beta Kappa, Phi Kappa Phi, and Omicron Delta Epsilon honor societies. He received his M.S. and Ph.D. in Financial Economics from the Krannert Graduate School of Management at Purdue University. Since leaving school in 1981, he has specialized in teaching Investment Management, Portfolio Management and Security Analysis, Capital Markets, and Derivatives courses at the Undergraduate, MBA, and Ph.D. levels and has received more than a dozen awards for teaching innovation and excellence. In addition to his academic responsibilities, he has also served as President and Chief Executive Officer of The MBA Investment Fund, L.L.C., a privately funded investment company managed by graduate students at the University of Texas.

Professor Brown has published more than 40 articles, monographs, chapters, and papers on topics ranging from asset pricing and investment strategy to financial risk management. His publications have appeared in such journals as *Journal of Finance, Journal of Financial Economics, Review of Financial Studies, Journal of Financial and Quantitative Analysis, Review of Economics and Statistics, Financial Analysts Journal, Financial Management, Advances in Futures and Options Research, Journal of Fixed Income, Journal of Applied Corporate Finance,* and *Journal of Portfolio Management.* In addition to his contributions to *Investment Analysis and Portfolio Management,* Eighth Edition, he is a co-author of *Interest Rate and Currency Swaps: A Tutorial,* a textbook published in 1995 through the Association for Investment Management and Research (AIMR). He received a Graham and Dodd Award from the Financial Analysts Federation as an author of one of the best articles published by *Financial Analysts Journal* in 1990, and a Smith-Breeden Prize from the *Journal of Finance* in 1996.

In August 1988, Professor Brown received his charter from the Institute of Chartered Financial Analysts (ICFA). He has served as a member of AIMR's CFA Candidate Curriculum Committee and Education Committee, and on the CFA Examination Grading staff. For 5 years, he was the research director of the Research Foundation of the ICFA, from which position he guided the development of the research portion of the organization's worldwide educational mission. For several years, he was also associate editor for *Financial Analysts Journal* and currently holds that position for *Journal of Investment Management, Journal of Behavioral Finance,* and *Journal of Restructuring Finance.* In other professional service, Professor Brown has been a regional director for the Financial Management Association and has served as the applied research track chairman for that organization's annual conference.

Professor Brown is the co-founder and senior partner of Fulcrum Financial Group, a portfolio management and investment advisory firm located in Austin, Texas, and Atlanta, Georgia, that currently oversees portfolios holding a total of $60 million in fixed-income securities. From May 1987 to August 1988 he was based in New York as a senior consultant to the Corporate Professional Development Department at Manufacturers Hanover Trust Company. He has lectured extensively throughout the world on investment and risk management topics in the executive development programs for such companies as Fidelity Investments, JP Morgan Chase, BMO Nesbitt Burns, Merrill Lynch, Chase Manhattan Bank, Chemical Bank, Lehman Brothers, Union Bank of Switzerland, Shearson, Chase Bank of Texas, The Beacon Group, Motorola, and Halliburton. He is an Advisor to the Boards of the Texas Teachers Retirement System and the University of Texas Investment Management Company and serves on the Investment Committee of LBJ Asset Management Partners.

Contents in Brief

Contents

Part 1

The Investment Background

The chapters in this section will provide a background for your study of investments by answering the following questions:

- *Why do people invest?*
- *How do you measure the returns and risks for alternative investments?*
- *What factors should you consider when you make asset allocation decisions?*
- *What investments are available?*
- *How do securities markets function?*
- *How and why are securities markets in the United States and around the world changing?*
- *What are the major uses of security-market indexes?*
- *How can you evaluate the market behavior of common stocks and bonds?*
- *What factors cause differences among stock-and-bond market indexes?*

In the first chapter, we consider why an individual would invest, how to measure the rates of return and risk for alternative investments, and what factors determine an investor's required rate of return on an investment. The latter point will be important in subsequent analyses when we work to understand investor behavior, the markets for alternative securities, and the valuation of various investments.

Because the ultimate decision facing an investor is the makeup of his or her portfolio, Chapter 2 deals with the all-important asset allocation decision. This includes specific steps in the portfolio management process and factors that influence the makeup of an investor's portfolio over his or her life cycle.

To minimize risk, investment theory asserts the need to diversify. Chapter 3 begins our exploration of investments available to investors by making an overpowering case for investing globally rather than limiting choices to only U.S. securities. Building on this premise, we discuss several investment instruments found in global markets. We conclude the chapter with a review of the historical rates of return and measures of risk for a number of alternative asset groups.

In Chapter 4, we examine how markets work in general, and then specifically focus on the purpose and function of primary and secondary bond and stock markets. During the last 15 years, significant changes occurred in the operation of the securities market, including a trend toward a global market and electronic trading markets.

After discussing these changes and the rapid development of new capital markets around the world, we speculate about how global markets will continue to expand available investment alternatives.

Investors, market analysts, and financial theorists generally gauge the behavior of securities markets by evaluating the return and risk implied by various market indexes and evaluate portfolio performance by comparing a portfolio's results to an appropriate benchmark. In Chapter 5, we examine and compare a number of stock-market and bond-market indexes available for the domestic and global markets.

This initial section provides the framework for you to understand various securities, how to allocate among alternative asset classes, the markets where they are bought and sold, the indexes that reflect their performance, and how you might manage a collection of investments in a portfolio. Specific portfolio management techniques are described in later chapters.

The Investment Setting

After you read this chapter, you should be able to answer the following questions:

- Why do individuals invest?
- What is an investment?
- How do investors measure the rate of return on an investment?
- How do investors measure the risk related to alternative investments?
- What factors contribute to the rates of return that investors require on alternative investments?
- What macroeconomic and microeconomic factors contribute to changes in the required rates of return for investments?

This initial chapter discusses several topics basic to the subsequent chapters. We begin by defining the term *investment* and discussing the returns and risks related to investments. This leads to a presentation of how to measure the expected and historical rates of returns for an individual asset or a portfolio of assets. In addition, we consider how to measure risk not only for an individual investment but also for an investment that is part of a portfolio.

The third section of the chapter discusses the factors that determine the required rate of return for an individual investment. The factors discussed are those that contribute to an asset's *total* risk. Because most investors have a portfolio of investments, it is necessary to consider how to measure the risk of an asset when it is a part of a large portfolio of assets. The risk that prevails when an asset is part of a diversified portfolio is referred to as its *systematic risk*.

The final section deals with what causes *changes* in an asset's required rate of return over time. Changes occur because of both macroeconomic events that affect all investment assets and microeconomic events that affect the specific asset.

WHAT IS AN INVESTMENT?

For most of your life, you will be earning and spending money. Rarely, though, will your current money income exactly balance with your consumption desires. Sometimes, you may have more money than you want to spend; at other times, you may want to purchase more than you can afford. These imbalances will lead you either to borrow or to save to maximize the long-run benefits from your income.

When current income exceeds current consumption desires, people tend to save the excess. They can do any of several things with these savings. One possibility is to put the money under a mattress or bury it in the backyard until some future time when consumption desires exceed current income. When they retrieve their savings from the mattress or backyard, they have the same amount they saved.

Another possibility is that they can give up the immediate possession of these savings for a future larger amount of money that will be available for future consumption. This trade-off of *present* consumption for a higher level of *future* consumption is the reason for saving. What you do with the savings to make them increase over time is *investment*.[1]

Those who give up immediate possession of savings (that is, defer consumption) expect to receive in the future a greater amount than they gave up. Conversely, those who consume more than their current income (that is, borrow) must be willing to pay back in the future more than they borrowed.

The rate of exchange between *future consumption* (future dollars) and *current consumption* (current dollars) is the *pure rate of interest*. Both people's willingness to pay this difference for borrowed funds and their desire to receive a surplus on their savings give rise to an interest rate referred to as the *pure time value of money*. This interest rate is established in the capital market by a comparison of the supply of excess income available (savings) to be invested and the demand for excess consumption (borrowing) at a given time. If you can exchange $100 of certain income today for $104 of certain income one year from today, then the pure rate of exchange on a risk-free investment (that is, the time value of money) is said to be 4 percent (104/100 − 1).

The investor who gives up $100 today expects to consume $104 of goods and services in the future. This assumes that the general price level in the economy stays the same. This price stability has rarely been the case during the past several decades when inflation rates have varied from 1.1 percent in 1986 to 13.3 percent in 1979, with an average of about 5.2 percent a year from 1970 to 2004. If investors expect a change in prices, they will require a higher rate of return to compensate for it. For example, if an investor expects a rise in prices (that is, he or she expects inflation) at the rate of 2 percent during the period of investment, he or she will increase the required interest rate by 2 percent. In our example, the investor would require $106 in the future to defer the $100 of consumption during an inflationary period (a 6 percent nominal, risk-free interest rate will be required instead of 4 percent).

Further, if the future payment from the investment is not certain, the investor will demand an interest rate that exceeds the nominal risk-free interest rate. The uncertainty of the payments from an investment is the *investment risk*. The additional return added to the nominal, risk-free interest rate is called a *risk premium*. In our previous example, the investor would require more than $106 one year from today to compensate for the uncertainty. As an example, if the required amount were $110, $4 (4 percent) would be considered a risk premium.

Investment Defined

From our discussion, we can specify a formal definition of investment. Specifically, an **investment** is the current commitment of dollars for a period of time in order to derive future payments that will compensate the investor for (1) the time the funds are committed, (2) the expected rate of inflation, and (3) the uncertainty of the future payments. The "investor" can be an individual, a government, a pension fund, or a corporation. Similarly, this definition

---

[1]In contrast, when current income is less than current consumption desires, people borrow to make up the difference. Although we will discuss borrowing on several occasions, the major emphasis of this text is how to invest savings.

includes all types of investments, including investments by corporations in plant and equipment and investments by individuals in stocks, bonds, commodities, or real estate. This text emphasizes investments by individual investors. In all cases, the investor is trading a *known* dollar amount today for some *expected* future stream of payments that will be greater than the current outlay.

At this point, we have answered the questions about why people invest and what they want from their investments. They invest to earn a return from savings due to their deferred consumption. They want a rate of return that compensates them for the time, the expected rate of inflation, and the uncertainty of the return. This return, the investor's **required rate of return**, is discussed throughout this book. A central question of this book is how investors select investments that will give them their required rates of return.

The next section of this chapter describes how to measure the expected or historical rate of return on an investment and also how to quantify the uncertainty of expected returns. You need to understand these techniques for measuring the rate of return and the uncertainty of these returns to evaluate the suitability of a particular investment. Although our emphasis will be on financial assets, such as bonds and stocks, we will refer to other assets, such as art and antiques. Chapter 3 discusses the range of financial assets and also considers some nonfinancial assets.

MEASURES OF RETURN AND RISK

The purpose of this book is to help you understand how to choose among alternative investment assets. This selection process requires that you estimate and evaluate the expected risk-return trade-offs for the alternative investments available. Therefore, you must understand how to measure the rate of return and the risk involved in an investment accurately. To meet this need, in this section we examine ways to quantify return and risk. The presentation will consider how to measure both *historical* and *expected* rates of return and risk.

We consider historical measures of return and risk because this book and other publications provide numerous examples of historical average rates of return and risk measures for various assets, and understanding these presentations is important. In addition, these historical results are often used by investors when attempting to estimate the *expected* rates of return and risk for an asset class.

The first measure is the historical rate of return on an individual investment over the time period the investment is held (that is, its holding period). Next, we consider how to measure the *average* historical rate of return for an individual investment over a number of time periods. The third subsection considers the average rate of return for a *portfolio* of investments.

Given the measures of historical rates of return, we will present the traditional measures of risk for a historical time series of returns (that is, the variance and standard deviation).

Following the presentation of measures of historical rates of return and risk, we turn to estimating the *expected* rate of return for an investment. Obviously, such an estimate contains a great deal of uncertainty, and we present measures of this uncertainty or risk.

Measures of Historical Rates of Return

When you are evaluating alternative investments for inclusion in your portfolio, you will often be comparing investments with widely different prices or lives. As an example, you might want to compare a $10 stock that pays no dividends to a stock selling for $150 that pays dividends of $5 a year. To properly evaluate these two investments, you must accurately compare their historical rates of returns. A proper measurement of the rates of return is the purpose of this section.

When we invest, we defer current consumption in order to add to our wealth so that we can consume more in the future. Therefore, when we talk about a return on an investment, we are concerned with the *change in wealth* resulting from this investment. This change in wealth can be either due to cash inflows, such as interest or dividends, or caused by a change in the price of the asset (positive or negative).

If you commit $200 to an investment at the beginning of the year and you get back $220 at the end of the year, what is your return for the period? The period during which you own an investment is called its *holding period*, and the return for that period is the **holding period return (HPR)**. In this example, the HPR is 1.10, calculated as follows:

$$1.1 \qquad HPR = \frac{Ending\ Value\ of\ Investment}{Beginning\ Value\ of\ Investment}$$

$$= \frac{\$220}{\$200} = 1.10$$

This value will always be zero or greater—that is, it can never be a negative value. A value greater than 1.0 reflects an increase in your wealth, which means that you received a positive rate of return during the period. A value less than 1.0 means that you suffered a decline in wealth, which indicates that you had a negative return during the period. An HPR of zero indicates that you lost all your money.

Although HPR helps us express the change in value of an investment, investors generally evaluate returns in *percentage terms on an annual basis.* This conversion to annual percentage rates makes it easier to directly compare alternative investments that have markedly different characteristics. The first step in converting an HPR to an annual percentage rate is to derive a percentage return, referred to as the **holding period yield (HPY)**. The HPY is equal to the HPR minus 1.

$$1.2 \qquad\qquad HPY = HPR - 1$$

In our example:

$$HPY = 1.10 - 1 = 0.10$$
$$= 10\%$$

To derive an *annual* HPY, you compute an *annual* HPR and subtract 1. Annual HPR is found by:

$$1.3 \qquad\qquad Annual\ HPR = HPR^{1/n}$$

where:

n = number of years the investment is held

Consider an investment that cost $250 and is worth $350 after being held for two years:

$$HPR = \frac{Ending\ Value\ of\ Investment}{Beginning\ Value\ of\ Investment} = \frac{\$350}{\$250}$$

$$= 1.40$$

$$\text{Annual HPR} = 1.40^{1/n}$$
$$= 1.40^{1/2}$$
$$= 1.1832$$
$$\text{Annual HPY} = 1.1832 - 1 = 0.1832$$
$$= 18.32\%$$

If you experience a decline in your wealth value, the computation is as follows:

$$\text{HPR} = \frac{\text{Ending Value}}{\text{Beginning Value}} = \frac{\$400}{\$500} = 0.80$$

$$\text{HPY} = 0.80 - 1.00 = -0.20 = -20\%$$

A multiple year loss over two years would be computed as follows:

$$\text{HPR} = \frac{\text{Ending Value}}{\text{Beginning Value}} = \frac{\$750}{\$1,000} = 0.75$$

$$\text{Annual HPR} = (0.75)^{1/n} = 0.75^{1/2}$$

$$= 0.866$$

$$\text{Annual HPY} = 0.866 - 1.00 = -0.134 = -13.4\%$$

In contrast, consider an investment of $100 held for only six months that earned a return of $12:

$$\text{HPR} = \frac{\$112}{\$100} = 1.12 (n = 0.5)$$

$$\text{Annual HPR} = 1.12^{1/.5}$$

$$= 1.12^2$$

$$= 1.2544$$

$$\text{Annual HPY} = 1.2544 - 1 = 0.2544$$

$$= 25.44\%$$

Note that we made some implicit assumptions when converting the HPY to an annual basis. This annualized holding period yield computation assumes a constant annual yield for each year. In the two-year investment, we assumed an 18.32 percent rate of return each year, compounded. In the partial year HPR that was annualized, we assumed that the return is compounded for the whole year. That is, we assumed that the rate of return earned during the first half of the year is likewise earned on the value at the end of the first six months. The 12 percent rate of return for the initial six months compounds to 25.44 percent for the full year.[2] Because of the uncertainty of being able to earn the same return in the future six months, institutions will typically not compound partial year results.

Remember one final point: The ending value of the investment can be the result of a positive or negative change in price for the investment alone (for example, a stock going from $20

---

[2]To check that you understand the calculations, determine the annual HPY for a three-year HPR of 1.50. (Answer: 14.47 percent.) Compute the annual HPY for a three-month HPR of 1.06. (Answer: 26.25 percent.)

a share to $22 a share), income from the investment alone, or a combination of price change and income. Ending value includes the value of everything related to the investment.

Computing Mean Historical Returns

Now that we have calculated the HPY for a single investment for a single year, we want to consider **mean rates of return** for a single investment and for a portfolio of investments. Over a number of years, a single investment will likely give high rates of return during some years and low rates of return, or possibly negative rates of return, during others. Your analysis should consider each of these returns, but you also want a summary figure that indicates this investment's typical experience, or the rate of return you should expect to receive if you owned this investment over an extended period of time. You can derive such a summary figure by computing the mean annual rate of return for this investment over some period of time.

Alternatively, you might want to evaluate a portfolio of investments that might include similar investments (for example, all stocks or all bonds) or a combination of investments (for example, stocks, bonds, and real estate). In this instance, you would calculate the mean rate of return for this portfolio of investments for an individual year or for a number of years.

Single Investment   Given a set of annual rates of return (HPYs) for an individual investment, there are two summary measures of return performance. The first is the arithmetic mean return, the second is the geometric mean return. To find the **arithmetic mean (AM)**, the sum (Σ) of annual HPYs is divided by the number of years (n) as follows:

1.4 $$AM = \Sigma HPY/n$$

where:

  ΣHPY = the sum of annual holding period yields

An alternative computation, the **geometric mean (GM)**, is the nth root of the product of the HPRs for n years.

1.5 $$GM = [\pi HPR]^{1/n} - 1$$

where:

  π = the product of the annual holding period returns as follows:

$$(HPR_1) \times (HPR_2) \cdots (HPR_n)$$

To illustrate these alternatives, consider an investment with the following data:

Year	Beginning Value	Ending Value	HPR	HPY
1	100.0	115.0	1.15	0.15
2	115.0	138.0	1.20	0.20
3	138.0	110.4	0.80	−0.20

$$AM = [(0.15) + (0.20) + (-0.20)]/3$$
$$= 0.15/3$$
$$= 0.05 = 5\%$$

$$GM = [(1.15) \times (1.20) \times (0.80)]^{1/3} - 1$$
$$= (1.104)^{1/3} - 1$$
$$= 1.03353 - 1$$
$$= 0.03353 = 3.353\%$$

Investors are typically concerned with long-term performance when comparing alternative investments. GM is considered a superior measure of the long-term mean rate of return because it indicates the compound annual rate of return based on the ending value of the investment versus its beginning value.[3] Specifically, using the prior example, if we compounded 3.353 percent for three years, $(1.03353)^3$, we would get an ending wealth value of 1.104.

Although the arithmetic average provides a good indication of the expected rate of return for an investment during a future individual year, it is biased upward if you are attempting to measure an asset's long-term performance. This is obvious for a volatile security. Consider, for example, a security that increases in price from $50 to $100 during year 1 and drops back to $50 during year 2. The annual HPYs would be:

Year	Beginning Value	Ending Value	HPR	HPY
1	50	100	2.00	1.00
2	100	50	0.50	−0.50

This would give an AM rate of return of:

$$[(1.00) + (-0.50)]/2 = .50/2$$
$$= 0.25 = 25\%$$

This investment brought no change in wealth and therefore no return, yet the AM rate of return is computed to be 25 percent.

The GM rate of return would be:

$$(2.00 \times 0.50)^{1/2} - 1 = (1.00)^{1/2} - 1$$
$$= 1.00 - 1 = 0\%$$

This answer of a 0 percent rate of return accurately measures the fact that there was no change in wealth from this investment over the two-year period.

When rates of return are the same for all years, the GM will be equal to the AM. If the rates of return vary over the years, the GM will always be lower than the AM. The difference between the two mean values will depend on the year-to-year changes in the rates of return. Larger annual changes in the rates of return—that is, more volatility—will result in a greater difference between the alternative mean values.

An awareness of both methods of computing mean rates of return is important because published accounts of investment performance or descriptions of financial research will use both the AM and the GM as measures of average historical returns. We will also use both throughout this book. Currently most studies dealing with long-run historical rates of return include both AM and GM rates of return.

---

[3]Note that the GM is the same whether you compute the geometric mean of the individual annual holding period yields or the annual HPY for a three-year period, comparing the ending value to the beginning value, as discussed earlier under annual HPY for a multiperiod case.

A Portfolio of Investments   The mean historical rate of return (HPY) for a portfolio of investments is measured as the weighted average of the HPYs for the individual investments in the portfolio, or the overall change in value of the original portfolio. The weights used in computing the averages are the relative *beginning* market values for each investment; this is referred to as *dollar-weighted* or *value-weighted* mean rate of return. This technique is demonstrated by the examples in Exhibit 1.1. As shown, the HPY is the same (9.5 percent) whether you compute the weighted average return using the beginning market value weights or if you compute the overall change in the total value of the portfolio.

Although the analysis of historical performance is useful, selecting investments for your portfolio requires you to predict the rates of return you *expect* to prevail. The next section discusses how you would derive such estimates of expected rates of return. We recognize the great uncertainty regarding these future expectations, and we will discuss how one measures this uncertainty, which is referred to as the risk of an investment.

Calculating Expected Rates of Return

Risk is the uncertainty that an investment will earn its expected rate of return. In the examples in the prior section, we examined *realized* historical rates of return. In contrast, an investor who is evaluating a future investment alternative expects or anticipates a certain rate of return. The investor might say that he or she *expects* the investment will provide a rate of return of 10 percent, but this is actually the investor's most likely estimate, also referred to as a *point estimate*. Pressed further, the investor would probably acknowledge the uncertainty of this point estimate return and admit the possibility that, under certain conditions, the annual rate of return on this investment might go as low as -10 percent or as high as 25 percent. The point is, the specification of a larger range of possible returns from an investment reflects the investor's uncertainty regarding what the actual return will be. Therefore, a larger range of expected returns makes the investment riskier.

An investor determines how certain the expected rate of return on an investment is by analyzing estimates of expected returns. To do this, the investor assigns probability values to all

Exhibit 1.1	Computation of Holding Period Yield for a Portfolio

Investment	Number of Shares	Beginning Price	Beginning Market Value	Ending Price	Ending Market Value	HPR	HPY	Market Weight[a]	Weighted HPY
A	100,000	$ 10	$ 1,000,000	$ 12	$ 1,200,000	1.20	20%	0.05	0.01
B	200,000	20	4,000,000	21	4,200,000	1.05	5	0.20	0.01
C	500,000	30	15,000,000	33	16,500,000	1.10	10	0.75	0.075
Total			$ 20,000,000		$ 21,900,000				0.095

$$\text{HPR} = \frac{21,900,000}{20,000,000} = 1.095$$

$$\text{HPY} = 1.095 - 1 = 0.095$$

$$= 9.5\%$$

[a]Weights are based on beginning values.

possible returns. These probability values range from zero, which means no chance of the return, to one, which indicates complete certainty that the investment will provide the specified rate of return. These probabilities are typically subjective estimates based on the historical performance of the investment or similar investments modified by the investor's expectations for the future. As an example, an investor may know that about 30 percent of the time the rate of return on this particular investment was 10 percent. Using this information along with future expectations regarding the economy, one can derive an estimate of what might happen in the future.

The *expected* return from an investment is defined as:

$$\text{Expected Return} = \sum_{i=1}^{n} (\text{Probability of Return}) \times (\text{Possible Return})$$

1.6
$$E(R_i) = [(P_1)(R_1) + (P_2)(R_2) + (P_3)(R_3) + \cdots + (P_nR_n)]$$

$$E(R_i) = \sum_{i=1}^{n} (P_i)(R_i)$$

Let us begin our analysis of the effect of risk with an example of perfect certainty wherein the investor is absolutely certain of a return of 5 percent. Exhibit 1.2 illustrates this situation.

Perfect certainty allows only one possible return, and the probability of receiving that return is 1.0. Few investments provide certain returns. In the case of perfect certainty, there is only one value for P_iR_i:

$$E(R_i) = (1.0)(0.05) = 0.05$$

In an alternative scenario, suppose an investor believed an investment could provide several different rates of return depending on different possible economic conditions. As an example, in a strong economic environment with high corporate profits and little or no inflation, the investor might expect the rate of return on common stocks during the next year to reach as high as 20 percent. In contrast, if there is an economic decline with a higher-than-average rate of

---

Exhibit 1.2 | **Probability Distribution for Risk-Free Investment**

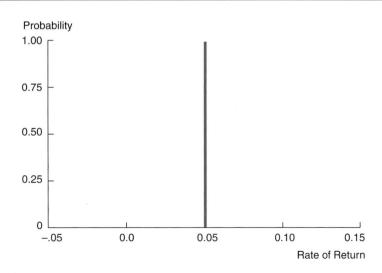

| **Exhibit 1.3** | **Probability Distribution for Risky Investment with Three Possible Rates of Return** |

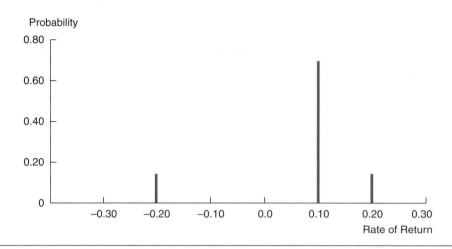

inflation, the investor might expect the rate of return on common stocks during the next year to be −20 percent. Finally, with no major change in the economic environment, the rate of return during the next year would probably approach the long-run average of 10 percent.

The investor might estimate probabilities for each of these economic scenarios based on past experience and the current outlook as follows:

Economic Conditions	Probability	Rate of Return
Strong economy, no inflation	0.15	0.20
Weak economy, above-average inflation	0.15	−0.20
No major change in economy	0.70	0.10

This set of potential outcomes can be visualized as shown in Exhibit 1.3.

The computation of the expected rate of return [$E(R_i)$] is as follows:

$$E(R_i) = [(0.15)(0.20)] + [(0.15)(-0.20)] + [(0.70)(0.10)]$$
$$= 0.07$$

Obviously, the investor is less certain about the expected return from this investment than about the return from the prior investment with its single possible return.

A third example is an investment with 10 possible outcomes ranging from −40 percent to 50 percent with the same probability for each rate of return. A graph of this set of expectations would appear as shown in Exhibit 1.4.

In this case, there are numerous outcomes from a wide range of possibilities. The expected rate of return [$E(R_i)$] for this investment would be:

$$E(R_i) = (0.10)(-0.40) + (0.10)(-0.30) + (0.10)(-0.20) + (0.10)(-0.10) + (0.10)(0.0)$$
$$+ (0.10)(0.10) + (0.10)(0.20) + (0.10)(0.30) + (0.10)(0.40) + (0.10)(0.50)$$

Exhibit 1.4	**Probability Distribution for Risky Investment with 10 Possible Rates of Return**

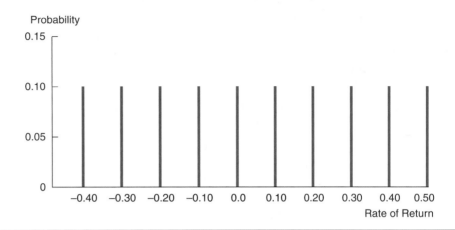

$$= (-0.04) + (-0.03) + (-0.02) + (-0.01) + (0.00) + (0.01) + (0.02) + (0.03)$$
$$+ (0.04) + (0.05)$$
$$= 0.05$$

The *expected* rate of return for this investment is the same as the certain return discussed in the first example; but, in this case, the investor is highly uncertain about the *actual* rate of return. This would be considered a risky investment because of that uncertainty. We would anticipate that an investor faced with the choice between this risky investment and the certain (risk-free) case would select the certain alternative. This expectation is based on the belief that most investors are **risk averse**, which means that if everything else is the same, they will select the investment that offers greater certainty (i.e., less risk).

Measuring the Risk of Expected Rates of Return

We have shown that we can calculate the expected rate of return and evaluate the uncertainty, or risk, of an investment by identifying the range of possible returns from that investment and assigning each possible return a weight based on the probability that it will occur. Although the graphs help us visualize the dispersion of possible returns, most investors want to quantify this dispersion using statistical techniques. These statistical measures allow you to compare the return and risk measures for alternative investments directly. Two possible measures of risk (uncertainty) have received support in theoretical work on portfolio theory: the *variance* and the *standard deviation* of the estimated distribution of expected returns.

In this section, we demonstrate how variance and standard deviation measure the dispersion of possible rates of return around the expected rate of return. We will work with the examples discussed earlier. The formula for variance is as follows:

1.7
$$\text{Variance } (\sigma^2) = \sum_{i=1}^{n} (\text{Probability}) \times \left(\begin{array}{c} \text{Possible} \\ \text{Return} \end{array} - \begin{array}{c} \text{Expected} \\ \text{Return} \end{array} \right)^2$$

$$= \sum_{i=1}^{n} (P_i)[R_i - E(R_i)]^2$$

Variance   The larger the **variance** for an expected rate of return, the greater the dispersion of expected returns and the greater the uncertainty, or risk, of the investment. The variance for the perfect-certainty (risk-free) example would be:

$$(\sigma^2) = \sum_{i=1}^{n} P_i[R_i - E(R_i)]^2$$

$$= 1.0(0.05 - 0.05)^2 = 1.0(0.0) = 0$$

Note that, in perfect certainty, there is *no variance of return* because there is no deviation from expectations and, therefore, *no risk* or *uncertainty*. The variance for the second example would be:

$$(\sigma^2) = \sum_{i=1}^{n} P_i[R_i - E(R_i)]^2$$

$$= [(0.15)(0.20 - 0.07)^2 + (0.15)(-0.20 - 0.07)^2 + (0.70)(0.10 - 0.07)^2]$$

$$= [0.010935 + 0.002535 + 0.00063]$$

$$= 0.0141$$

Standard Deviation   The **standard deviation** is the square root of the variance:

1.8   Standard Deviation $= \sqrt{\sum_{i=1}^{n} P_i[R_i - E(R_i)]^2}$

For the second example, the standard deviation would be:

$$\sigma = \sqrt{0.0141}$$

$$= 0.11874 = 11.874\%$$

Therefore, when describing this investment example, you would contend that you expect a return of 7 percent, but the standard deviation of your expectations is 11.87 percent.

A Relative Measure of Risk   In some cases, an unadjusted variance or standard deviation can be misleading. If conditions for two or more investment alternatives are not similar—that is, if there are major differences in the expected rates of return—it is necessary to use a measure of *relative variability* to indicate risk per unit of expected return. A widely used relative measure of risk is the **coefficient of variation (CV)**, calculated as follows:

1.9 $\dfrac{\text{Coefficieint of}}{\text{Variation(CV)}} = \dfrac{\text{Standard Deviation of Returns}}{\text{Expected Rate of Return}}$

$$= \frac{\sigma_i}{E(R)}$$

The *CV* for the preceding example would be:

$$CV = \frac{0.11874}{0.07000}$$

$$= 1.696$$

This measure of relative variability and risk is used by financial analysts to compare alternative investments with widely different rates of return and standard deviations of returns. As an illustration, consider the following two investments:

	Investment A	Investment B
Expected return	0.07	0.12
Standard deviation	0.05	0.07

Comparing absolute measures of risk, investment B appears to be riskier because it has a standard deviation of 7 percent versus 5 percent for investment A. In contrast, the *CV* figures show that investment B has less relative variability or lower risk per unit of expected return because it has a substantially higher expected rate of return:

$$CV_A = \frac{0.05}{0.07} = 0.714$$

$$CV_B = \frac{0.07}{0.12} = 0.583$$

Risk Measures for Historical Returns

To measure the risk for a series of historical rates of returns, we use the same measures as for expected returns (variance and standard deviation) except that we consider the historical holding period yields (HPYs) as follows:

1.10
$$\sigma^2 = \sum_{i=1}^{n}[\text{HPY}_i - E(\text{HPY})]^2/n$$

where:

σ^2 = the variance of the series
HPY_i = the holding period yield during period i
$E(\text{HPY})$ = the expected value of the holding period yield that is equal to the arithmetic mean of the series
n = the number of observations

The standard deviation is the square root of the variance. Both measures indicate how much the individual HPYs over time deviated from the expected value of the series. An example computation is contained in the appendix to this chapter. As is shown in subsequent chapters where we present historical rates of return for alternative asset classes, presenting the standard deviation as a measure of risk for the series or asset class is fairly common.

DETERMINANTS OF REQUIRED RATES OF RETURN

In this section, we continue our consideration of factors that you must consider when selecting securities for an investment portfolio. You will recall that this selection process involves finding securities that provide a rate of return that compensates you for: (1) the time value of

Exhibit 1.5	Promised Yields on Alternative Bonds						

Type of Bond	1998	1999	2000	2001	2002	2003	2004
U.S. government 3-month Treasury bills	4.78%	4.64%	5.82%	3.40%	1.61%	1.01%	1.37%
U.S. government long-term bonds	5.69	6.14	6.41	6.18	5.41	5.02	5.10
Aaa corporate bonds	6.53	7.05	7.62	7.08	6.49	5.66	5.63
Baa corporate bonds	7.22	7.88	8.36	7.95	7.80	6.76	6.39

Source: *Federal Reserve Bulletin*, various issues.

money during the period of investment, (2) the expected rate of inflation during the period, and (3) the risk involved.

The summation of these three components is called the *required rate of return*. This is the minimum rate of return that you should accept from an investment to compensate you for deferring consumption. Because of the importance of the required rate of return to the total investment selection process, this section contains a discussion of the three components and what influences each of them.

The analysis and estimation of the required rate of return are complicated by the behavior of market rates over time. First, a wide range of rates is available for alternative investments at any time. Second, the rates of return on specific assets change dramatically over time. Third, the difference between the rates available (that is, the spread) on different assets changes over time.

The yield data in Exhibit 1.5 for alternative bonds demonstrate these three characteristics. First, even though all these securities have promised returns based upon bond contracts, the promised annual yields during any year differ substantially. As an example, during 1999 the average yields on alternative assets ranged from 4.64 percent on T-bills to 7.88 percent for Baa corporate bonds. Second, the changes in yields for a specific asset are shown by the three-month Treasury bill rate that went from 4.64 percent in 1999 to 5.82 percent in 2000. Third, an example of a change in the difference between yields over time (referred to as a spread) is shown by the Baa–Aaa spread.[4] The yield spread in 1998 was 69 basis points (7.22−6.53), but the spread in 2002 was 131 basis points (7.80−6.49). (A basis point is 0.01 percent.)

Because differences in yields result from the riskiness of each investment, you must understand the risk factors that affect the required rates of return and include them in your assessment of investment opportunities. Because the required returns on all investments change over time, and because large differences separate individual investments, you need to be aware of the several components that determine the required rate of return, starting with the risk-free rate. The discussion in this chapter considers the three components of the required rate of return and briefly discusses what affects these components. The presentation in Chapter 11 on valuation theory will discuss the factors that affect these components in greater detail.

The Real Risk-Free Rate

The **real risk-free rate (RRFR)** is the basic interest rate, assuming no inflation and no uncertainty about future flows. An investor in an inflation-free economy who knew with certainty

---

[4]Bonds are rated by rating agencies based upon the credit risk of the securities, that is, the probability of default. Aaa is the top rating Moody's (a prominent rating service) gives to bonds with almost no probability of default. (Only U.S. Treasury bonds are considered to be of higher quality.) Baa is a lower rating Moody's gives to bonds of generally high quality that have some possibility of default under adverse economic conditions.

what cash flows he or she would receive at what time would demand the RRFR on an investment. Earlier, we called this the *pure time value of money*, because the only sacrifice the investor made was deferring the use of the money for a period of time. This RRFR of interest is the price charged for the risk-free exchange between current goods and future goods.

Two factors, one subjective and one objective, influence this exchange price. The subjective factor is the time preference of individuals for the consumption of income. When individuals give up $100 of consumption this year, how much consumption do they want a year from now to compensate for that sacrifice? The strength of the human desire for current consumption influences the rate of compensation required. Time preferences vary among individuals, and the market creates a composite rate that includes the preferences of all investors. This composite rate changes gradually over time because it is influenced by all the investors in the economy, whose changes in preferences may offset one another.

The objective factor that influences the RRFR is the set of investment opportunities available in the economy. The investment opportunities are determined in turn by the *long-run real growth rate of the economy*. A rapidly growing economy produces more and better opportunities to invest funds and experience positive rates of return. A change in the economy's long-run real growth rate causes a change in all investment opportunities and a change in the required rates of return on all investments. Just as investors supplying capital should demand a higher rate of return when growth is higher, those looking for funds to invest should be willing and able to pay a higher rate of return to use the funds for investment because of the higher growth rate. Thus, a *positive* relationship exists between the real growth rate in the economy and the RRFR.

Factors Influencing the Nominal Risk-Free Rate (NRFR)

Earlier, we observed that an investor would be willing to forgo current consumption in order to increase future consumption at a rate of exchange called the *risk-free rate of interest*. This rate of exchange was measured in real terms because the investor wanted to increase the consumption of actual goods and services rather than consuming the same amount that had come to cost more money. Therefore, when we discuss rates of interest, we need to differentiate between *real* rates of interest that adjust for changes in the general price level, as opposed to *nominal* rates of interest that are stated in money terms. That is, nominal rates of interest that prevail in the market are determined by real rates of interest, plus factors that will affect the nominal rate of interest, such as the expected rate of inflation and the monetary environment. It is important to understand these factors.

As noted earlier, the variables that determine the RRFR change only gradually over the long term. Therefore, you might expect the required rate on a risk-free investment to be quite stable over time. As discussed in connection with Exhibit 1.5, rates on three-month T-bills were *not* stable over the period from 1998 to 2004. This is demonstrated with additional observations in Exhibit 1.6, which contains yields on T-bills for the period 1983 to 2004.

Investors view T-bills as a prime example of a default-free investment because the government has unlimited ability to derive income from taxes or to create money from which to pay interest. Therefore, one could expect that rates on T-bills should change only gradually. In fact, the data show a highly erratic pattern. Specifically, there was an increase in yields from 8.61 percent in 1983 to 9.52 percent in 1984 before declining to less than 6 percent in 1987 and 3.33 percent in 1993. In sum, T-bill rates increased almost 23 percent in one year and then declined by almost 60 percent in six years. Clearly, the nominal rate of interest on a default-free investment is *not* stable in the long run or the short run, even though the underlying determinants of the RRFR are quite stable. The point is, two other factors influence the *nominal risk-free rate (NRFR):* (1) the relative ease or tightness in the capital markets, and (2) the expected rate of inflation.

Exhibit 1.6 | **Three-Month Treasury Bill Yields and Rates of Inflation**

Year	3-Month T-bills	Rate of Inflation	Year	3-Month T-bills	Rate of Inflation
1983	8.61%	3.20%	1994	4.25%	2.67%
1984	9.52	4.00	1995	5.49	2.54
1985	7.48	3.80	1996	5.01	3.32
1986	5.98	1.10	1997	5.06	1.70
1987	5.78	4.40	1998	4.78	1.61
1988	6.67	4.40	1999	4.64	2.70
1989	8.11	4.65	2000	5.82	3.40
1990	7.50	6.11	2001	3.40	1.55
1991	5.38	3.06	2002	1.61	2.49
1992	3.43	2.90	2003	1.01	1.87
1993	3.33	2.75	2004	1.37	3.39

Source: *Federal Reserve Bulletin*, various issues; *Economic Report of the President*, various issues.

Conditions in the Capital Market   You will recall from prior courses in economics and finance that the purpose of capital markets is to bring together investors who want to invest savings with companies or governments who need capital to expand or to finance budget deficits. The cost of funds at any time (the interest rate) is the price that equates the current supply and demand for capital. A change in the relative ease or tightness in the capital market is a short-run phenomenon caused by a temporary disequilibrium in the supply and demand of capital.

As an example, disequilibrium could be caused by an unexpected change in monetary policy (for example, a change in the growth rate of the money supply) or fiscal policy (for example, a change in the federal deficit). Such a change in monetary policy or fiscal policy will produce a change in the NRFR of interest, but the change should be short-lived because, in the longer run, the higher or lower interest rates will affect capital supply and demand. As an example, an increase in the federal deficit caused by an increase in government spending (easy fiscal policy) will increase the demand for capital and increase interest rates. In turn, this increase in interest rates (for example, the price of money) will cause an increase in savings and a decrease in the demand for capital by corporations or individuals. These changes in market conditions will bring rates back to the long-run equilibrium, which is based on the long-run growth rate of the economy.

Expected Rate of Inflation   Previously, it was noted that if investors expected the price level to increase during the investment period, they would require the rate of return to include compensation for the expected rate of inflation. Assume that you require a 4 percent real rate of return on a risk-free investment but you expect prices to increase by 3 percent during the investment period. In this case, you should increase your required rate of return by this expected rate of inflation to about 7 percent [$(1.04 \times 1.03) - 1$]. If you do not increase your required return, the $104 you receive at the end of the year will represent a real return of about 1 percent, not 4 percent. Because prices have increased by 3 percent during the year, what previously cost $100 now costs $103, so you can consume only about 1 percent more at the end of the year [($104/103) $-$ 1]. If you had required a 7.12 percent nominal return, your real consumption could have increased by 4 percent [($107.12/103) − 1]. Therefore, an investor's nominal required rate of return on a risk-free investment should be:

1.11   NRFR = (1 + RRFR) × (1 + Expected Rate of Inflation) − 1

Rearranging the formula, you can calculate the RRFR of return on an investment as follows:

1.12 $$RRFR = \left[\frac{(1 + NRFR\ of\ Return)}{(1 + Rate\ of\ Inflation)} \right] - 1$$

To see how this works, assume that the nominal return on U.S. government T-bills was 9 percent during a given year, when the rate of inflation was 5 percent. In this instance, the RRFR of return on these T-bills was 3.8 percent, as follows:

$$RRFR = [(1 + 0.09)/(1 + 0.05)] - 1$$
$$= 1.038 - 1$$
$$= 0.038 = 3.8\%$$

This discussion makes it clear that the nominal rate of interest on a risk-free investment is not a good estimate of the RRFR, because the nominal rate can change dramatically in the short run in reaction to temporary ease or tightness in the capital market or because of changes in the expected rate of inflation. As indicated by the data in Exhibit 1.6, the significant changes in the average yield on T-bills typically were caused by large changes in the rates of inflation.

The Common Effect   All the factors discussed thus far regarding the required rate of return affect all investments equally. Whether the investment is in stocks, bonds, real estate, or machine tools, if the expected rate of inflation increases from 2 percent to 6 percent, the investor's required rate of return for *all* investments should increase by 4 percent. Similarly, if a decline in the expected real growth rate of the economy causes a decline in the RRFR of 1 percent, the required return on all investments should decline by 1 percent.

Risk Premium

A risk-free investment was defined as one for which the investor is certain of the amount and timing of the expected returns. The returns from most investments do not fit this pattern. An investor typically is not completely certain of the income to be received or when it will be received. Investments can range in uncertainty from basically risk-free securities, such as T-bills, to highly speculative investments, such as the common stock of small companies engaged in high-risk enterprises.

Most investors require higher rates of return on investments if they perceive that there is any uncertainty about the expected rate of return. This increase in the required rate of return over the NRFR is the **risk premium (RP)**. Although the required risk premium represents a composite of all uncertainty, it is possible to consider several fundamental sources of uncertainty. In this section, we identify and discuss briefly the major sources of uncertainty, including: (1) business risk, (2) financial risk (leverage), (3) liquidity risk, (4) exchange rate risk, and (5) country (political) risk.

Business risk is the uncertainty of income flows caused by the nature of a firm's business. The less certain the income flows of the firm, the less certain the income flows to the investor. Therefore, the investor will demand a risk premium that is based on the uncertainty caused by the basic business of the firm. As an example, a retail food company would typically experience stable sales and earnings growth over time and would have low business risk compared to a firm in the auto industry, where sales and earnings fluctuate substantially over the business cycle, implying high business risk.

Financial risk is the uncertainty introduced by the method by which the firm finances its investments. If a firm uses only common stock to finance investments, it incurs only business risk. If a firm borrows money to finance investments, it must pay fixed financing charges (in the form of interest to creditors) prior to providing income to the common stockholders, so the uncertainty of returns to the equity investor increases. This increase in uncertainty because of fixed-cost financing is called *financial risk* or *financial leverage* and causes an increase in the stock's risk premium. For an extended discussion on this, see Brigham (2004).

Liquidity risk is the uncertainty introduced by the secondary market for an investment. When an investor acquires an asset, he or she expects that the investment will mature (as with a bond) or that it will be salable to someone else. In either case, the investor expects to be able to convert the security into cash and use the proceeds for current consumption or other investments. The more difficult it is to make this conversion, the greater the liquidity risk. An investor must consider two questions when assessing the liquidity risk of an investment: (1) How long will it take to convert the investment into cash? (2) How certain is the price to be received? Similar uncertainty faces an investor who wants to acquire an asset: How long will it take to acquire the asset? How uncertain is the price to be paid?[5]

Uncertainty regarding how fast an investment can be bought or sold, or the existence of uncertainty about its price, increases liquidity risk. A U.S. government Treasury bill has almost no liquidity risk because it can be bought or sold in minutes at a price almost identical to the quoted price. In contrast, examples of illiquid investments include a work of art, an antique, or a parcel of real estate in a remote area. For such investments, it may require a long time to find a buyer and the selling prices could vary substantially from expectations. Investors will increase their required rates of return to compensate for liquidity risk. Liquidity risk can be a significant consideration when investing in foreign securities depending on the country and the liquidity of its stock and bond markets.

Exchange rate risk is the uncertainty of returns to an investor who acquires securities denominated in a currency different from his or her own. The likelihood of incurring this risk is becoming greater as investors buy and sell assets around the world, as opposed to only assets within their own countries. A U.S. investor who buys Japanese stock denominated in yen must consider not only the uncertainty of the return in yen but also any change in the exchange value of the yen relative to the U.S. dollar. That is, in addition to the foreign firm's business and financial risk and the security's liquidity risk, the investor must consider the additional uncertainty of the return on this Japanese stock when it is converted from yen to U.S. dollars.

As an example of exchange rate risk, assume that you buy 100 shares of Mitsubishi Electric at 1,050 yen when the exchange rate is 115 yen to the dollar. The dollar cost of this investment would be about $9.13 per share (1,050/115). A year later you sell the 100 shares at 1,200 yen when the exchange rate is 130 yen to the dollar. When you calculate the HPY in yen, you find the stock has increased in value by about 14 percent (1,200/1,050), but this is the HPY for a Japanese investor. A U.S. investor receives a much lower rate of return, because during this period the yen has weakened relative to the dollar by about 13 percent (that is, it requires more yen to buy a dollar—130 versus 115). At the new exchange rate, the stock is worth $9.23 per share (1,200/130). Therefore, the return to you as a U.S. investor would be only about 1 percent ($9.23/$9.13) versus 14 percent for the Japanese investor. The difference in return for the Japanese investor and U.S. investor is caused by the decline in the value of the yen relative to the dollar. Clearly, the exchange rate could have gone in the other direction, the dollar

---

[5]You will recall from prior courses that the overall capital market is composed of the primary market and the secondary market. Securities are initially sold in the primary market, and all subsequent transactions take place in the secondary market. These concepts are discussed in Chapter 4.

weakening against the yen. In this case, as a U.S. investor, you would have experienced the 14 percent return measured in yen, as well as a gain from the exchange rate change.

The more volatile the exchange rate between two countries, the less certain you would be regarding the exchange rate, the greater the exchange rate risk, and the larger the exchange rate risk premium you would require. For an analysis of pricing this risk, see Jorion (1991).

There can also be exchange rate risk for a U.S. firm that is extensively multinational in terms of sales and components (costs). In this case, the firm's foreign earnings can be affected by changes in the exchange rate. As will be discussed, this risk can generally be hedged at a cost.

Country risk, also called *political risk*, is the uncertainty of returns caused by the possibility of a major change in the political or economic environment of a country. The United States is acknowledged to have the smallest country risk in the world because its political and economic systems are the most stable. Nations with high country risk include Russia, because of the several changes in the government hierarchy and its currency crises during 1998, and Indonesia, where there were student demonstrations, major riots, and fires prior to the resignation of President Suharto in May 1998. In both instances, the stock markets experienced significant declines surrounding these events, which are discussed in Gall (1998), Thornhill (1998), Chote (1998), and Thoenes (1998). Individuals who invest in countries that have unstable political economic systems must add a country risk premium when determining their required rates of return.

When investing globally (which is emphasized throughout the book), investors must consider these additional uncertainties. How liquid are the secondary markets for stocks and bonds in the country? Are any of the country's securities traded on major stock exchanges in the United States, London, Tokyo, or Germany? What will happen to exchange rates during the investment period? What is the probability of a political or economic change that will adversely affect your rate of return? Exchange rate risk and country risk differ among countries. A good measure of exchange rate risk would be the absolute variability of the exchange rate relative to a composite exchange rate. The analysis of country risk is much more subjective and must be based on the history and current environment of the country.

This discussion of risk components can be considered a security's *fundamental risk* because it deals with the intrinsic factors that should affect a security's standard deviation of returns over time. In subsequent discussion, the standard deviation of returns is referred to as a measure of the security's *total risk*, which considers the individual stock by itself—that is, it is not considered as part of a portfolio.

Risk Premium = f(Business Risk, Financial Risk, Liquidity Risk, Exchange Rate Risk, Country Risk)

Risk Premium and Portfolio Theory

An alternative view of risk has been derived from extensive work in portfolio theory and capital market theory by Markowitz (1952, 1959) and Sharpe (1964). These theories are dealt with in greater detail in Chapter 7 and Chapter 8 but their impact on the risk premium should be mentioned briefly at this point. These prior works by Markowitz and Sharpe indicated that investors should use an *external market* measure of risk. Under a specified set of assumptions, all rational, profit-maximizing investors want to hold a completely diversified market portfolio of risky assets, and they borrow or lend to arrive at a risk level that is consistent with their risk preferences. Under these conditions, the relevant risk measure for an individual asset is its *comovement with the market portfolio*. This comovement, which is measured by an asset's covariance with the market portfolio, is referred to as an asset's **systematic risk,** the portion of an individual asset's total variance attributable to the variability of the total market portfolio. In addition, individual assets have variance that is unrelated to the market portfolio (the asset's nonmarket variance) that is due to the asset's unique features. This nonmarket variance is called *unsystematic risk*, and it is generally considered unimportant because it is eliminated in a large, diversified portfolio. Therefore, under these assumptions, *the risk premium for an individual earning asset is a function of the asset's systematic risk with the aggregate market portfolio of risky assets.* The measure of an asset's systematic risk is referred to as its *beta:*

$$\text{Risk Premium} = f(\text{Systematic Market Risk})$$

Fundamental Risk versus Systematic Risk

Some might expect a conflict between the market measure of risk (systematic risk) and the fundamental determinants of risk (business risk, and so on). A number of studies have examined the relationship between the market measure of risk (systematic risk) and accounting variables used to measure the fundamental risk factors, such as business risk, financial risk, and liquidity risk. The authors of these studies (especially Thompson, 1976) have generally concluded that *a significant relationship exists between the market measure of risk and the fundamental measures of risk.* Therefore, the two measures of risk can be complementary. This consistency seems reasonable because, in a properly functioning capital market, the market measure of the risk should reflect the fundamental risk characteristics of the asset. As an example, you would expect a firm that has high business risk and financial risk to have an above average beta. At the same time, as we discuss in Chapter 8, it is possible that a firm that has a high level of fundamental risk and a large standard deviation of return on stock can have a lower level of systematic risk because its variability of earnings and stock price is not related to the aggregate economy or the aggregate market. Therefore, one can specify the risk premium for an asset as:

$$\text{Risk Premium} = f(\text{Business Risk, Financial Risk, Liquidity Risk, Exchange Rate Risk, Country Risk})$$

or

$$\text{Risk Premium} = f(\text{Systematic Market Risk})$$

Summary of Required Rate of Return

The overall required rate of return on alternative investments is determined by three variables: (1) the economy's RRFR, which is influenced by the investment opportunities in the economy (that is, the long-run real growth rate); (2) variables that influence the NRFR, which include short-run ease or tightness in the capital market and the expected rate of inflation (notably, these variables, which determine the NRFR, are the same for all investments); and (3) the risk premium on the investment. In turn, this risk premium can be related to fundamental factors, including business risk, financial risk, liquidity risk, exchange rate risk, and country risk, or it can be a function of an asset's systematic market risk (beta).

Measures and Sources of Risk In this chapter, we have examined both measures and sources of risk arising from an investment. The *measures* of risk for an investment are:

- Variance of rates of return
- Standard deviation of rates of return
- Coefficient of variation of rates of return (standard deviation/means)
- Covariance of returns with the market portfolio (beta)

The *sources* of risk are:

- Business risk
- Financial risk
- Liquidity risk
- Exchange rate risk
- Country risk

RELATIONSHIP BETWEEN RISK AND RETURN

Previously, we showed how to measure the risk and rates of return for alternative investments and we discussed what determines the rates of return that investors require. This section discusses the risk-return combinations that might be available at a point in time and illustrates the factors that cause *changes* in these combinations.

Exhibit 1.7 graphs the expected relationship between risk and return. It shows that investors increase their required rates of return as perceived risk (uncertainty) increases. The line that reflects the combination of risk and return available on alternative investments is referred to as the **security market line (SML)**. The SML reflects the risk-return combinations available for all risky assets in the capital market at a given time. Investors would select investments that are consistent with their risk preferences; some would consider only low-risk investments, whereas others welcome high-risk investments.

Beginning with an initial SML, three changes can occur. First, individual investments can change positions on the SML because of changes in the perceived risk of the investments. Second, the slope of the SML can change because of a change in the attitudes of investors toward risk; that is, investors can change the returns they require per unit of risk. Third, the SML can experience a parallel shift due to a change in the RRFR or the expected rate of inflation—that is, a change in the NRFR. These three possibilities are discussed in this section.

Movements along the SML

Investors place alternative investments somewhere along the SML based on their perceptions of the risk of the investment. Obviously, if an investment's risk changes due to a change in one of its risk sources (business risk, and such), it will move along the SML. For example, if a firm increases its financial risk by selling a large bond issue that increases its financial leverage, investors will perceive its common stock as riskier and the stock will move up the SML to a higher risk position. Investors will then require a higher rate of return. As the common stock

Exhibit 1.7	**Relationship between Risk and Return**

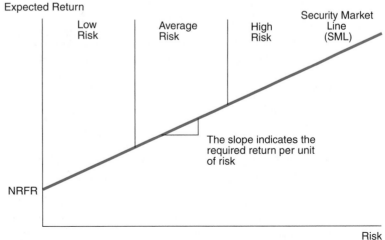

| Exhibit 1.8 | **Changes in the Required Rate of Return Due to Movements along the SML** |

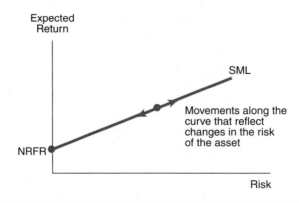

becomes riskier, it changes its position on the SML. Any change in an asset that affects its fundamental risk factors or its market risk (that is, its beta) will cause the asset to move *along* the SML as shown in Exhibit 1.8. Note that the SML does not change, only the position of assets on the SML.

Changes in the Slope of the SML

The slope of the SML indicates the return per unit of risk required by all investors. Assuming a straight line, it is possible to select any point on the SML and compute a risk premium (RP) for an asset through the equation:

1.13
$$RP_i = E(R_i) - \text{NRFR}$$

where:

RP_i = risk premium for asset i
$E(R_i)$ = the expected return for asset i
NRFR = the nominal return on a risk-free asset

If a point on the SML is identified as the portfolio that contains all the risky assets in the market (referred to as the *market portfolio*), it is possible to compute a market RP as follows:

1.14
$$RP_m = E(R_m) - \text{NRFR}$$

where:

RP_m = the risk premium on the market portfolio
$E(R_m)$ = the expected return on the market portfolio
NRFR = the nominal return on a risk-free asset

This market RP is *not constant* because the slope of the SML changes over time. Although we do not understand completely what causes these changes in the slope, we do know that there are changes in the *yield* differences between assets with different levels of risk even though the inherent risk differences are relatively constant.

Exhibit 1.9	**Plot of Monthly Bond Yield Spreads (Bbb–Aaa) with Series Mean and Standard Deviations (1973–2004)**

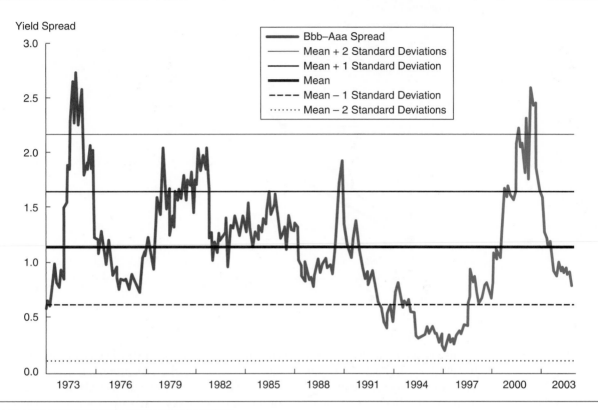

Source: Lehman Brothers data; computations by authors.

These differences in yields are referred to as **yield spreads**, and these yield spreads change over time. As an example, if the yield on a portfolio of Aaa-rated bonds is 7.50 percent and the yield on a portfolio of Baa-rated bonds is 9.00 percent, we would say that the yield spread is 1.50 percent. This 1.50 percent is referred to as a credit risk premium because the Baa-rated bond is considered to have higher credit risk—that is, it has a higher probability of default. This Baa–Aaa yield spread is *not* constant over time. For an example of changes in a yield spread, note the substantial changes in the yield spreads on Aaa-rated bonds and Baa-rated bonds shown in Exhibit 1.9.

Although the underlying risk factors for the portfolio of bonds in the Aaa-rated bond index and the Baa-rated bond index would probably not change dramatically over time, it is clear from the time-series plot in Exhibit 1.9 that the difference in yields (i.e., the yield spread) has experienced changes of more than 100 basis points (1 percent) in a short period of time (for example, see the yield spread increase in 1974 to 1975 and the dramatic yield spread decline in 2003 to 2004). Such a significant change in the yield spread during a period where there is no major change in the risk characteristics of Baa bonds relative to Aaa bonds would imply a change in the market RP. Specifically, although the risk levels of the bonds remain relatively constant, investors have changed the yield spreads they demand to accept this relatively constant difference in risk.

| Exhibit 1.10 | **Change in Market Risk Premium** |

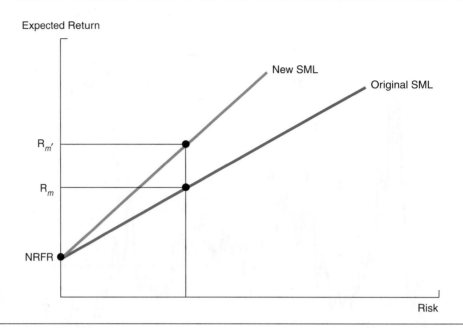

This change in the RP implies a change in the slope of the SML. Such a change is shown in Exhibit 1.10. The exhibit assumes an increase in the market risk premium, which means an increase in the slope of the market line. Such a change in the slope of the SML (the market risk premium) will affect the required rate of return for all risky assets. Irrespective of where an investment is on the original SML, its required rate of return will increase, although its individual risk characteristics remain unchanged.

Changes in Capital Market Conditions or Expected Inflation

The graph in Exhibit 1.11 shows what happens to the SML when there are changes in one of the following factors: (1) expected real growth in the economy, (2) capital market conditions, or (3) the expected rate of inflation. For example, an increase in expected real growth, temporary tightness in the capital market, or an increase in the expected rate of inflation will cause the SML to experience a parallel shift upward. The parallel shift occurs because changes in expected real growth or in capital market conditions or a change in the expected rate of inflation affect the economy's nominal risk-free rate (NRFR) that impacts all investments, no matter what their levels of risk are.

Summary of Changes in the Required Rate of Return

The relationship between risk and the required rate of return for an investment can change in three ways:
1. A movement *along* the SML demonstrates a change in the risk characteristics of a specific investment, such as a change in its business risk, its financial risk, or its systematic risk (its beta). This change affects only the individual investment.

| Exhibit 1.11 | **Capital Market Conditions, Expected Inflation, and the Security Market Line** |

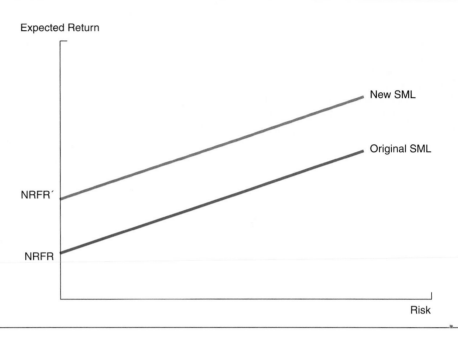

2. A change in the *slope* of the SML occurs in response to a change in the attitudes of investors toward risk. Such a change demonstrates that investors want either higher or lower rates of return for the same risk. This is also described as a change in the market risk premium (R_m − NRFR). A change in the market risk premium will affect all risky investments.
3. A *shift* in the SML reflects a change in expected real growth, a change in market conditions (such as ease or tightness of money), or a change in the expected rate of inflation. Again, such a change will affect all investments.

The Internet — Investments Online

Many Internet sites seek to assist the beginning or novice investor. Because they cover the basics, have helpful links to other Internet sites, and sometimes allow users to calculate items of interest (rates of return, the size of an investment necessary to meet a certain goal, and so on), these sites are useful for the experienced investor, too.

http://www.finpipe.com The Financial Pipeline is an excellent site for those just starting to learn about investments or who need a quick refresher. The site contains information and links on a variety of investment topics such as bonds, stocks, strategy, retirement, and consumer finance.

http://www.investorguide.com This is another site offering a plethora of information useful to both the novice and seasoned investor. It contains links to pages with market summaries, news research, and much more. It offers a glossary of investment terms. Basic investment education issues are taught in their "University" section. There are links to a number of personal financial help pages, including sites dealing with buying a home, or car, retirement, loans, and insurance. It offers links to a number of calculator functions to help users make financial decisions.

http://www.aaii.com This is the home page for the American Association of Individual Investors, a group dealing with investor education. Educational topics include mutual funds, stocks, bonds, dealing with a broker, and portfolio management issues. It offers a number of features for both the beginning and experienced investor.

http://fisher.osu.edu/fin/journal/ jofsites.htm Has links to numerous finance sites.

Many representatives of the financial press have Internet sites:

http://online.wsj.com *The Wall Street Journal*
http://www.ft.com *Financial Times*
http://www.economist.com *The Economist* magazine
http://www.fortune.com *Fortune* magazine
http://money.cnn.com *Money* magazine
http://www.forbes.com *Forbes* magazine
http://www.worth.com *Worth* magazine
http://www.smartmoney.com *SmartMoney* magazine
http://www.barrons.com *Barron's* newspaper

SUMMARY

The purpose of this chapter is to provide background that can be used in subsequent chapters. To achieve that goal, we covered several topics:

- We discussed why individuals save part of their income and why they decide to invest their savings. We defined *investment* as the current commitment of these savings for a period of time to derive a rate of return that compensates for the time involved, the expected rate of inflation, and the uncertainty.
- We examined ways to quantify historical return and risk to help analyze alternative investment opportunities. We considered two measures of mean return (arithmetic and geometric) and applied these to a historical series for an individual investment and to a portfolio of investments during a period of time.
- We considered the concept of uncertainty and alternative measures of risk (the variance, standard deviation, and a relative measure of risk—the coefficient of variation).
- Before discussing the determinants of the required rate of return for an investment, we noted that the estimation of the required rate of return is complicated because the rates on individual investments change over time, because there is a wide range of rates of return available on alternative investments, and because the differences between required returns on alternative investments (for example, the yield spreads) likewise change over time.

- We examined the specific factors that determine the required rate of return: (1) the real risk-free rate, which is based on the real rate of growth in the economy, (2) the nominal risk-free rate, which is influenced by capital market conditions and the expected rate of inflation, and (3) a risk premium, which is a function of fundamental factors, such as business risk, or the systematic risk of the asset relative to the market portfolio (that is, its beta).
- We discussed the risk-return combinations available on alternative investments at a point in time (illustrated by the SML) and the three factors that can cause changes in this relationship. First, a change in the inherent risk of an investment (that is, its fundamental risk or market risk) will cause a movement along the SML. Second, a change in investors' attitudes toward risk will cause a change in the required return per unit of risk—that is, a change in the market risk premium. Such a change will cause a change in the slope of the SML. Finally, a change in expected real growth, in capital market conditions, or in the expected rate of inflation will cause a parallel shift of the SML.

Based on this understanding of the investment environment, you are prepared to consider the asset allocation decision, which is discussed in Chapter 2.

QUESTIONS

1. Discuss the overall purpose people have for investing. Define investment.
2. As a student, are you saving or borrowing? Why?

3. Divide a person's life from ages 20 to 70 into 10-year segments and discuss the likely saving or borrowing patterns during each period.
4. Discuss why you would expect the saving-borrowing pattern to differ by occupation (for example, for a doctor versus a plumber).
5. *The Wall Street Journal* reported that the yield on common stocks is about 2 percent, whereas a study at the University of Chicago contends that the annual rate of return on common stocks since 1926 has averaged about 12 percent. Reconcile these statements.
6. Some financial theorists consider the variance of the distribution of expected rates of return to be a good measure of uncertainty. Discuss the reasoning behind this measure of risk and its purpose.
7. Discuss the three components of an investor's required rate of return on an investment.
8. Discuss the two major factors that determine the market nominal risk-free rate (NRFR). Explain which of these factors would be more volatile over the business cycle.
9. Briefly discuss the five fundamental factors that influence the risk premium of an investment.
10. You own stock in the Gentry Company, and you read in the financial press that a recent bond offering has raised the firm's debt/equity ratio from 35 percent to 55 percent. Discuss the effect of this change on the variability of the firm's net income stream, other factors being constant. Discuss how this change would affect your required rate of return on the common stock of the Gentry Company.
11. Draw a properly labeled graph of the security market line (SML) and indicate where you would expect the following investments to fall along that line. Discuss your reasoning.
    a. Common stock of large firms
    b. U.S. government bonds
    c. U.K. government bonds
    d. Low-grade corporate bonds
    e. Common stock of a Japanese firm
12. Explain why you would change your nominal required rate of return if you expected the rate of inflation to go from 0 (no inflation) to 4 percent. Give an example of what would happen if you did not change your required rate of return under these conditions.
13. Assume the long-run growth rate of the economy increased by 1 percent and the expected rate of inflation increased by 4 percent. What would happen to the required rates of return on government bonds and common stocks? Show graphically how the effects of these changes would differ between these alternative investments.
14. You see in *The Wall Street Journal* that the yield spread between Baa corporate bonds and Aaa corporate bonds has gone from 350 basis points (3.5 percent) to 200 basis points (2 percent). Show graphically the effect of this change in yield spread on the SML and discuss its effect on the required rate of return for common stocks.
15. Give an example of a liquid investment and an illiquid investment. Discuss why you consider each of them to be liquid or illiquid.

PROBLEMS

1. On February 1, you bought 100 shares of a stock for $34 a share and a year later you sold it for $39 a share. During the year, you received a cash dividend of $1.50 a share. Compute your HPR and HPY on this stock investment.
2. On August 15, you purchased 100 shares of a stock at $65 a share and a year later you sold it for $61 a share. During the year, you received dividends of $3 a share. Compute your HPR and HPY on this investment.
3. At the beginning of last year, you invested $4,000 in 80 shares of the Chang Corporation. During the year, Chang paid dividends of $5 per share. At the end of the year, you sold the 80 shares for $59 a share. Compute your total HPY on these shares and indicate how much was due to the price change and how much was due to the dividend income.
4. The rates of return computed in Problems 1, 2, and 3 are nominal rates of return. Assuming that the rate of inflation during the year was 4 percent, compute the real rates of return on these investments. Compute the real rates of return if the rate of inflation was 8 percent.

5. During the past five years, you owned two stocks that had the following annual rates of return:

Year	Stock T	Stock B
1	0.19	0.08
2	0.08	0.03
3	−0.12	−0.09
4	−0.03	0.02
5	0.15	0.04

   a. Compute the arithmetic mean annual rate of return for each stock. Which stock is most desirable by this measure?

   b. Compute the standard deviation of the annual rate of return for each stock. (Use Chapter 1 Appendix if necessary.) By this measure, which is the preferable stock?

   c. Compute the coefficient of variation for each stock. (Use the Chapter 1 Appendix if necessary.) By this relative measure of risk, which stock is preferable?

   d. Compute the geometric mean rate of return for each stock. Discuss the difference between the arithmetic mean return and the geometric mean return for each stock. Discuss the differences in the mean returns relative to the standard deviation of the return for each stock.

6. You are considering acquiring shares of common stock in the Madison Beer Corporation. Your rate of return expectations are as follows:

MADISON BEER CORP.	
Possible Rate of Return	Probability
−0.10	0.30
0.00	0.10
0.10	0.30
0.25	0.30

Compute the expected return $[E(R_i)]$ on your investment in Madison Beer.

7. A stockbroker calls you and suggests that you invest in the Lauren Computer Company. After analyzing the firm's annual report and other material, you believe that the distribution of expected rates of return is as follows:

LAUREN COMPUTER CO.	
Possible Rate of Return	Probability
−0.60	0.05
−0.30	0.20
−0.10	0.10
0.20	0.30
0.40	0.20
0.80	0.15

Compute the expected return $[E(R_i)]$ on Lauren Computer stock.

8. Without any formal computations, do you consider Madison Beer in Problem 6 or Lauren Computer in Problem 7 to present greater risk? Discuss your reasoning.

9. During the past year, you had a portfolio that contained U.S. government T-bills, long-term government bonds, and common stocks. The rates of return on each of them were as follows:

U.S. government T-bills	5.50%
U.S. government long-term bonds	7.50
U.S. common stocks	11.60

During the year, the consumer price index, which measures the rate of inflation, went from 160 to 172 (1982–1984 = 100). Compute the rate of inflation during this year. Compute the real rates of return on each of the investments in your portfolio based on the inflation rate.

10. You read in *BusinessWeek* that a panel of economists has estimated that the long-run real growth rate of the U.S. economy over the next five-year period will average 3 percent. In addition, a bank newsletter estimates that the average annual rate of inflation during this five-year period will be about 4 percent. What nominal rate of return would you expect on U.S. government T-bills during this period?

11. What would your required rate of return be on common stocks if you wanted a 5 percent risk premium to own common stocks given what you know from Problem 10? If common stock investors became more risk averse, what would happen to the required rate of return on common stocks? What would be the impact on stock prices?

12. Assume that the consensus required rate of return on common stocks is 14 percent. In addition, you read in *Fortune* that the expected rate of inflation is 5 percent and the estimated long-term real growth rate of the economy is 3 percent. What interest rate would you expect on U.S. government T-bills? What is the approximate risk premium for common stocks implied by these data?

SUGGESTED READINGS

Fama, Eugene F., and Merton H. Miller. *The Theory of Finance*. New York: Holt, Rinehart and Winston, 1972.

Fisher, Irving. *The Theory of Interest*. New York: Macmillan, 1930, reprinted by Augustus M. Kelley, 1961.

THOMSON ONE | Business School Edition

1. Read *A Guide to Using Thomson One: Business School Edition* by Rosemary Carlson, which was shrink-wrapped with your text. Thomson One: Business School Edition is a special version of a powerful data and analytical package used by many investment professionals. It will be useful to you in this and other classes you are taking this semester.

2. Follow the directions in section III "How do I find general overview information for a firm?" for Walgreens (stock symbol: WAG) and Wal-Mart (WMT), two firms in the retail industry (or try two firms in an industry of your choice). On what stock markets are the firms traded? How do their growth rates in sales and earnings compare? How have their stocks performed over the past few months? Are stock analysts recommending investors buy or sell each of the two firm's stocks?

APPENDIX
Chapter 1   Computation of Variance and Standard Deviation

Variance and standard deviation are measures of how actual values differ from the expected values (arithmetic mean) for a given series of values. In this case, we want to measure how rates of return differ from the arithmetic mean value of a series. There are other measures of dispersion, but variance and standard deviation are the best known because they are used in statistics and probability theory. Variance is defined as:

$$\text{Variance } (\sigma^2) = \sum_{i=1}^{n} (\text{Probability})(\text{Possible Return} - \text{Expected Return})^2$$

$$= \sum_{i=1}^{n} (P_i)[R_i - E(R_i)]^2$$

Consider the following example, as discussed in the chapter:

Probability of Possible Return (P_i)	Possible Return (R_i)	P_iR_i
0.15	0.20	0.03
0.15	−0.20	−0.03
0.70	0.10	0.07
		$\Sigma = 0.07$

This gives an expected return $[E(R_i)]$ of 7 percent. The dispersion of this distribution as measured by variance is:

Probability (P_i)	Return (R_i)	$R_i - E(R_i)$	$[R_i - E(R_i)]^2$	$P_i[R_i - E(R_i)]^2$
0.15	0.20	0.13	0.0169	0.002535
0.15	−0.20	−0.27	0.0729	0.010935
0.70	0.10	0.03	0.0009	0.000630
				$\Sigma = 0.014100$

The variance (σ^2) is equal to 0.0141. The standard deviation is equal to the square root of the variance:

$$\text{Standard Deviation } (\sigma^2) = \sqrt{\sum_{i=1}^{n} P_i[R_i - E(R_i)]^2}$$

Consequently, the standard deviation for the preceding example would be:

$$\sigma_i = \sqrt{0.0141} = 0.11874$$

In this example, the standard deviation is approximately 11.87 percent. Therefore, you could describe this distribution as having an expected value of 7 percent and a standard deviation of 11.87 percent.

In many instances, you might want to compute the variance or standard deviation for a historical series in order to evaluate the past performance of the investment. Assume that you are given the following information on annual rates of return (HPY) for common stocks listed on the New York Stock Exchange (NYSE):

Year	Annual Rate of Return
2006	0.07
2007	0.11
2008	−0.04
2009	0.12
2010	−0.06

In this case, we are not examining expected rates of return but actual returns. Therefore, we assume equal probabilities, and the expected value (in this case the mean value, R) of the series is the sum of the individual observations in the series divided by the number of observations, or 0.04 (0.20/5). The variances and standard deviations are:

Year	R_i	$R_i - \bar{R}$	$(R_i - \bar{R})^2$	
2006	0.07	0.03	0.0009	$\sigma^2 = 0.0286/5$
2007	0.11	0.07	0.0049	$= 0.00572$
2008	−0.04	−0.08	0.0064	
2009	0.12	0.08	0.0064	$\sigma = \sqrt{0.00572}$
2010	−0.06	−0.10	0.0110	$= 0.0756$
			$\Sigma = 0.0286$	

We can interpret the performance of NYSE common stocks during this period of time by saying that the average rate of return was 4 percent and the standard deviation of annual rates of return was 7.56 percent.

Coefficient of Variation

In some instances, you might want to compare the dispersion of two different series. The variance and standard deviation are *absolute* measures of dispersion. That is, they can be influenced by the magnitude of the original numbers. To compare series with greatly different values, you need a *relative* measure of dispersion. A measure of relative dispersion is the coefficient of variation, which is defined as:

$$\text{Coefficient of Variation } (CV) = \frac{\text{Standard Deviation of Returns}}{\text{Expected Rate of Return}}$$

A larger value indicates greater dispersion relative to the arithmetic mean of the series. For the previous example, the *CV* would be:

$$CV_1 = \frac{0.0756}{0.0400} = 1.89$$

It is possible to compare this value to a similar figure having a markedly different distribution. As an example, assume you wanted to compare this investment to another investment that had an average rate of return of 10 percent and a standard deviation of 9 percent. The standard deviations alone tell you that the second series has greater dispersion (9 percent versus 7.56 percent) and might be considered to have higher risk. In fact, the relative dispersion for this second investment is much less.

$$CV_1 = \frac{0.0756}{0.0400} = 1.89$$

$$CV_2 = \frac{0.0900}{0.1000} = 0.90$$

Considering the relative dispersion and the total distribution, most investors would probably prefer the second investment.

Problems

1. Your rate of return expectations for the common stock of Gray Disc Company during the next year are:

GRAY DISC CO.	
Possible Rate of Return	Probability
−0.10	0.25
0.00	0.15
0.10	0.35
0.25	0.25

a. Compute the expected return $[E(R_i)]$ on this investment, the variance of this return (σ^2), and its standard deviation (σ).
b. Under what conditions can the standard deviation be used to measure the relative risk of two investments?
c. Under what conditions must the coefficient of variation be used to measure the relative risk of two investments?

2. Your rate of return expectations for the stock of Kayleigh Computer Company during the next year are:

KAYLEIGH COMPUTER CO.	
Possible Rate of Return	Probability
−0.60	0.15
−0.30	0.10
−0.10	0.05
0.20	0.40
0.40	0.20
0.80	0.10

a. Compute the expected return $[E(R_i)]$ on this stock, the variance (σ^2) of this return, and its standard deviation (σ).
b. On the basis of expected return $[E(R_i)]$ alone, discuss whether Gray Disc or Kayleigh Computer is preferable.
c. On the basis of standard deviation (σ) alone, discuss whether Gray Disc or Kayleigh Computer is preferable.
d. Compute the coefficients of variation (CVs) for Gray Disc and Kayleigh Computer and discuss which stock return series has the greater relative dispersion.

3. The following are annual rates of return for U.S. government T-bills and U.K. common stocks.

Year	U.S. Government T-Bills	U.K. Common Stock
2006	.063	.150
2007	.081	.043
2008	.076	.374
2009	.090	.192
2010	.085	.106

a. Compute the arithmetic mean rate of return and standard deviation of rates of return for the two series.
b. Discuss these two alternative investments in terms of their arithmetic average rates of return, their absolute risk, and their relative risk.
c. Compute the geometric mean rate of return for each of these investments. Compare the arithmetic mean return and geometric mean return for each investment and discuss this difference between mean returns as related to the standard deviation of each series.

Chapter 2

The Asset Allocation Decision*

After you read this chapter, you should be able to answer the following questions:

- What is involved in the asset allocation process?
- What are the four steps in the portfolio management process?
- What is the role of asset allocation in investment planning?
- Why is a policy statement important to the planning process?
- What objectives and constraints should be detailed in a policy statement?
- How and why do investment goals change over a person's lifetime and circumstances?
- Why do asset allocation strategies differ across national boundaries?

The previous chapter informed us that *risk drives return.* Therefore, the practice of investing funds and managing portfolios should focus primarily on managing risk rather than on managing returns.

This chapter examines some of the practical implications of risk management in the context of asset allocation. **Asset allocation** is the process of deciding how to distribute an investor's wealth among different countries and asset classes for investment purposes. An **asset class** is comprised of securities that have similar characteristics, attributes, and risk/return relationships. A broad asset class, such as "bonds," can be divided into smaller asset classes, such as Treasury bonds, corporate bonds, and high-yield bonds. We will see that, in the long run, the highest compounded returns will most likely accrue to those investors with larger exposures to risky assets. We will also see that although there are no shortcuts or guarantees to investment success, maintaining a reasonable and disciplined approach to investing will increase the likelihood of investment success over time.

The asset allocation decision is not an isolated choice; rather, it is a component of a structured four-step portfolio management process that we present in this chapter. As we will see, the first step in the process is to develop an investment policy statement, or plan, that will guide all future decisions. Much of an asset allocation strategy depends on the investor's policy statement, which includes the investor's goals or objectives, constraints, and investment guidelines.

What we mean by an "investor" can range from an individual to trustees overseeing a corporation's multibillion-dollar pension fund, a university endowment, or invested premiums for

*The authors acknowledge the collaboration of Professor Edgar Norton of Illinois State University on this chapter.

an insurance company. Regardless of who the investor is or how simple or complex the invest-ment needs, he or she should develop a policy statement before making long-term investment decisions. Although most of our examples will be in the context of an individual investor, the concepts we introduce here—investment objectives, constraints, benchmarks, and so on—apply to any investor, individual or institutional. We'll review historical data to show the importance of the asset allocation decision and discuss the need for investor education, an important issue for individuals or companies who offer retirement or savings plans to their employees. The chapter concludes by examining asset allocation strategies across national borders to show the effect of market environment and culture on investing patterns; what is appropriate for a U.S.-based investor is not necessarily appropriate for a non-U.S.-based investor.

INDIVIDUAL INVESTOR LIFE CYCLE

Financial plans and investment needs are as different as each individual. Investment needs change over a person's life cycle. How individuals structure their financial plan should be related to their age, financial status, future plans, risk aversion characteristics, and needs.

The Preliminaries

Before embarking on an investment program, we need to make sure other needs are satisfied. No serious investment plan should be started until a potential investor has adequate income to cover living expenses and has a safety net should the unexpected occur.

Insurance Life insurance should be a component of any financial plan. Life insurance pro-tects loved ones against financial hardship should death occur before our financial goals are met. The death benefit paid by the insurance company can help pay medical bills and funeral ex-penses and provide cash that family members can use to maintain their lifestyle, retire debt, or invest for future needs (for example, children's education, spouse retirement). Therefore, one of the first steps in developing a financial plan is to purchase adequate life insurance coverage.

Insurance can also serve more immediate purposes, including being a means to meet long-term goals, such as retirement planning. On reaching retirement age, you can receive the cash or surrender value of your life insurance policy and use the proceeds to supplement your retirement lifestyle or for estate planning purposes.

Insurance coverage also provides protection against other uncertainties. *Health* insurance helps to pay medical bills. *Disability* insurance provides continuing income should you become unable to work. *Automobile and home* (or rental) insurances provide protection against acci-dents and damage to cars or residences.

Although nobody ever expects to use his or her insurance coverage, a first step in a sound financial plan is to have adequate coverage "just in case." Lack of insurance coverage can ruin the best-planned investment program.

Cash Reserve Emergencies, job layoffs, and unforeseen expenses happen, and good invest-ment opportunities emerge. It is important to have a cash reserve to help meet these occasions. In addition to providing a safety cushion, a cash reserve reduces the likelihood of being forced to sell investments at inopportune times to cover unexpected expenses. Most experts recom-mend a cash reserve equal to about six months' living expenses. Calling it a "cash" reserve does not mean the funds should be in cash; rather, the funds should be in investments you can easily convert to cash with little chance of a loss in value. Money market or short-term bond mutual funds and bank accounts are appropriate vehicles for the cash reserve.

Exhibit 2.1	Rise and Fall of Personal Net Worth over a Lifetime

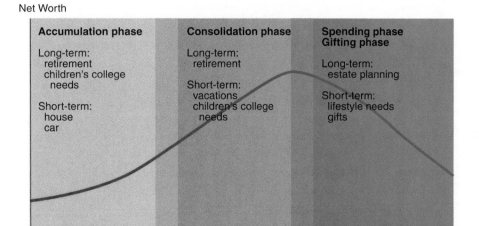

Net Worth

Accumulation phase

Long-term:
retirement
children's college
needs

Short-term:
house
car

Consolidation phase

Long-term:
retirement

Short-term:
vacations
children's college
needs

**Spending phase
Gifting phase**

Long-term:
estate planning

Short-term:
lifestyle needs
gifts

25   35   45   55   65   75   85
Age

Similar to the financial plan, an investor's insurance and cash reserve needs will change over his or her life. The need for disability insurance declines when a person retires. In contrast, other insurance, such as supplemental Medicare coverage or long-term care insurance, may become more important.

Life Cycle Net Worth and Investment Strategies

Assuming the basic insurance and cash reserve needs are met, individuals can start a serious investment program with their savings. Because of changes in their net worth and risk tolerance, individuals' investment strategies will change over their lifetime. In the following sections, we review various phases in the investment life cycle. Although each individual's needs and preferences are different, some general traits affect most investors over the life cycle. The four life cycle phases are shown in Exhibit 2.1 (the third and fourth phases—spending and gifting—are shown as concurrent) and described here.

Accumulation Phase   Individuals in the early-to-middle years of their working careers are in the **accumulation phase**. As the name implies, these individuals are attempting to accumulate assets to satisfy fairly immediate needs (for example, a down payment for a house) or longer-term goals (children's college education, retirement). Typically, their net worth is small, and debt from car loans or their own past college loans may be heavy. As a result of their typically long investment time horizon and their future earning ability, individuals in the accumulation phase are willing to make relatively high-risk investments in the hopes of making above-average nominal returns over time.

Here we must emphasize the wisdom of investing early and regularly in one's life. Funds invested in early life-cycle phases, with returns compounding over time, will reap financial benefits during later phases. Exhibit 2.2 shows growth from an initial $10,000 investment over 20, 30, and 40 years at assumed annual returns of 7 and 8 percent. The middle-aged person

Exhibit 2.2	**Benefits of Investing Early**

		The Future Value of an Initial $10,000 Investment	The Future Value of Investing $2,000 Annually	The Future Value of the Initial Investment Plus the Annual Investment
Interest rate	7.0%			
20 years		$38,696.84	$81,990.98	$120,687.83
30 years		$76,122.55	$188,921.57	$265,044.12
40 years		$149,744.58	$399,270.22	$549,014.80
Interest rate	8.0%			
20 years		$46,609.57	$91,523.93	$138,133.50
30 years		$100,626.57	$226,566.42	$327,192.99
40 years		$217,245.21	$518,113.04	$735,358.25

Source: Calculations by authors.

who invests $10,000 "when he or she can afford it" will only reap the benefits of compounding for 20 years or so before retirement. The younger person who saves will reap the much higher benefits of funds invested for 30 or 40 years. Regularly investing $2,000 a year reaps large benefits over time, as well. A person who has invested a total of $90,000—an initial $10,000 investment followed by $2,000 annual investments over 40 years—will have over half a million dollars accumulated from the 7 percent return. If the funds are invested more aggressively and earn the 8 percent return, the accumulation will be nearly three-quarters of a million dollars.

Consolidation Phase   Individuals in the **consolidation phase** are typically past the midpoint of their careers, have paid off much or all of their outstanding debts, and perhaps have paid, or have the assets to pay, their children's college bills. Earnings exceed expenses, so the excess can be invested to provide for future retirement or estate planning needs. The typical investment horizon for this phase is still long (20 to 30 years), so moderately high risk investments are attractive. At the same time, because individuals in this phase are concerned about capital preservation, they do not want to take very large risks that may put their current nest egg in jeopardy.

Spending Phase   The **spending phase** typically begins when individuals retire. Living expenses are covered by social security income and income from prior investments, including employer pension plans. Because their earning years have concluded (although some retirees take part-time positions or do consulting work), they seek greater protection of their capital. At the same time, they must balance their desire to preserve the nominal value of their savings with the need to protect themselves against a decline in the *real* value of their savings due to inflation. The average 65-year-old person in the United States has a life expectancy of about 20 years. Thus, although their overall portfolio may be less risky than in the consolidation phase, they still need some risky growth investments, such as common stocks, for inflation (purchasing power) protection.

The transition into the spending phase requires a sometimes difficult change in mindset; throughout our working life we are trying to save; suddenly we can spend. We tend to think that if we spend less, say 4 percent of our accumulated funds annually instead of 5, 6, or 7 percent, our wealth will last far longer. But a bear market early in our retirement can greatly reduce our accumulated funds. Fortunately, there are planning tools that can give a realistic view of what can happen to our retirement funds should markets fall early in our retirement years; this insight can assist in budgeting and planning to minimize the chance of spending (or losing) all the saved retirement funds. Annuities, which transfer risk from the individual to the annuity firm (most likely an insurance company), are another possibility. With an annuity, the recipient receives a guaranteed, lifelong stream of income. Options can allow for the annuity to continue until both a husband and wife die.

Gifting Phase   The **gifting phase** is similar to, and may be concurrent with, the spending phase. In this stage, individuals believe they have sufficient income and assets to cover their current and future expenses while maintaining a reserve for uncertainties. Excess assets can be used to provide financial assistance to relatives or friends, to establish charitable trusts, or to fund trusts as an estate planning tool to minimize estate taxes.

Life Cycle Investment Goals

During the investment life cycle, individuals have a variety of financial goals. **Near-term, high-priority goals** are shorter-term financial objectives that individuals set to fund purchases that are personally important to them, such as accumulating funds to make a house down payment, buy a new car, or take a trip. Parents with teenage children may have a near-term, high-priority goal to accumulate funds to help pay college expenses. Because of the emotional importance of these goals and their short time horizon, high-risk investments are not usually considered suitable for achieving them.

Long-term, high-priority goals typically include some form of financial independence, such as the ability to retire at a certain age. Because of their long-term nature, higher-risk investments can be used to help meet these objectives.

Lower-priority goals are just that—it might be nice to meet these objectives, but it is not critical. Examples include the ability to purchase a new car every few years, redecorate the home with expensive furnishings, or take a long, luxurious vacation. A well-developed policy statement considers these diverse goals over an investor's lifetime. The following sections detail the process for constructing an investment policy, creating a portfolio that is consistent with the policy and the environment, managing the portfolio, and monitoring its performance relative to its goals and objectives over time.

THE PORTFOLIO MANAGEMENT PROCESS

The process of managing an investment portfolio never stops. Once the funds are initially invested according to the plan, the real work begins in monitoring and updating the status of the portfolio and the investor's needs.

The first step in the portfolio management process, as seen in Exhibit 2.3, is for the investor, either alone or with the assistance of an investment advisor, to construct a **policy statement**. The policy statement is a road map; in it, investors specify the types of risks they are willing to take and their investment goals and constraints. All investment decisions are based on the policy statement to ensure they are appropriate for the investor. We examine the process of constructing a policy statement in the following section. Because investor needs change over time, the policy statement must be periodically reviewed and updated.

The process of investing seeks to peer into the future and determine strategies that offer the best possibility of meeting the policy statement guidelines. In the second step of the portfolio management process, the manager should study current financial and economic conditions and forecast future trends. The investor's needs, as reflected in the policy statement, and financial market expectations will jointly determine **investment strategy**. Economies are dynamic; they are affected by numerous industry struggles, politics, and changing demographics and social

Exhibit 2.3	The Portfolio Management Process

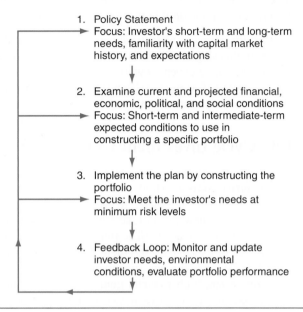

1. Policy Statement
   Focus: Investor's short-term and long-term needs, familiarity with capital market history, and expectations

2. Examine current and projected financial, economic, political, and social conditions
   Focus: Short-term and intermediate-term expected conditions to use in constructing a specific portfolio

3. Implement the plan by constructing the portfolio
   Focus: Meet the investor's needs at minimum risk levels

4. Feedback Loop: Monitor and update investor needs, environmental conditions, evaluate portfolio performance

attitudes. Thus, the portfolio will require constant monitoring and updating to reflect changes in financial market expectations. We examine the process of evaluating and forecasting economic trends in Chapter 12.

The third step of the portfolio management process is to **construct the portfolio**. With the investor's policy statement and financial market forecasts as input, the advisors implement the investment strategy and determine how to allocate available funds across different countries, asset classes, and securities. This involves constructing a portfolio that will minimize the investor's risks while meeting the needs specified in the policy statement. Financial theory frequently assists portfolio construction, as is discussed in Part 2. Some of the practical aspects of selecting investments for inclusion in a portfolio are discussed in Part 4 and Part 5.

The fourth step in the portfolio management process is the **continual monitoring** of the investor's needs and capital market conditions and, when necessary, updating the policy statement. Based upon all of this, the investment strategy is modified accordingly. A component of the monitoring process is to evaluate a portfolio's performance and compare the relative results to the expectations and the requirements listed in the policy statement. The evaluation of portfolio performance is discussed in Chapter 25. Once you have completed the four steps, it is important to recognize that this is continuous—it is essential to revisit all the steps to ensure that the policy statement is still valid, that the economic outlook has not changed, etc.

THE NEED FOR A POLICY STATEMENT

As noted in the previous section, a policy statement is a road map that guides the investment process. Constructing a policy statement is an invaluable planning tool that will help the investor understand his or her needs better as well as assist an advisor or portfolio manager in managing a client's funds. While it does not guarantee investment success, a policy statement will provide discipline for the investment process and reduce the possibility of making hasty, inappropriate decisions. There are two important reasons for constructing a policy statement: First, it helps the investor decide on realistic investment goals after learning about the financial markets and the risks of investing. Second, it creates a standard by which to judge the performance of the portfolio manager.

Understand and Articulate Realistic Investor Goals

When asked about their investment goal, people often say, "to make a lot of money," or some similar response. Such a goal has two drawbacks: First, it may not be appropriate for the investor, and second, it is too open-ended to provide guidance for specific investments and time frames. Such an objective is well suited for someone going to the racetrack or buying lottery tickets, but it is inappropriate for someone investing funds in financial and real assets for the long term.

An important purpose of writing a policy statement is to help investors understand their own needs, objectives, and investment constraints. As part of this, investors need to learn about financial markets and the risks of investing. This background will help prevent them from making inappropriate investment decisions in the future and will increase the possibility that they will satisfy their specific, measurable financial goals.

Thus, the policy statement helps the investor to specify realistic goals and become more informed about the risks and costs of investing. Market values of assets, whether they be stocks, bonds, or real estate, can fluctuate dramatically. For example, during the October 1987 crash, the Dow Jones Industrial Average (DJIA) fell more than 20 percent in one day; in October 1997, the Dow fell "only" 7 percent. A review of market history shows that it is not unusual for asset prices to decline by 10 percent to 20 percent over several months—for example, the months following the market peak in March 2000, and the major decline when the market reopened after September 11, 2001. Investors will typically focus on a single statistic, such as an 11 percent average annual rate of return on stocks, and expect the market to rise 11 percent every year. Such thinking ignores the risk of stock investing. Part of the process of developing a policy statement is for the investor to become familiar with the risks of investing, because we know that a strong positive relationship exists between risk and return.

One expert in the field recommends that investors should think about the following set of questions and explain their answers as part of the process of constructing a policy statement:

1. What are the real risks of an adverse financial outcome, especially in the short run?
2. What probable emotional reactions will I have to an adverse financial outcome?
3. How knowledgeable am I about investments and markets?
4. What other capital or income sources do I have? How important is this particular portfolio to my overall financial position?
5. What, if any, legal restrictions may affect my investment needs?
6. What, if any, unanticipated consequences of interim fluctuations in portfolio value might affect my investment policy?

Adapted from Charles D. Ellis, *Investment Policy: How to Win the Loser's Game* (Homewood, IL: Dow Jones–Irwin, 1985), 25–26. Reproduced with permission of the McGraw-Hill Companies.

In summary, constructing a policy statement is mainly the investor's responsibility. It is a process whereby investors articulate their realistic needs and goals and become familiar with financial markets and investing risks. Without this information, investors cannot adequately communicate their needs to the portfolio manager. Without this input from investors, the portfolio manager cannot construct a portfolio that will satisfy clients' needs; the result of bypassing this step will most likely be future aggravation, dissatisfaction, and disappointment.

Standards for Evaluating Portfolio Performance

The policy statement also assists in judging the performance of the portfolio manager. Performance cannot be judged without an objective standard; the policy statement provides that objective standard. The portfolio's performance should be compared to guidelines specified in the policy statement, not on the portfolio's overall return. For example, if an investor has a low tolerance for risky investments, the portfolio manager should not be fired simply because the portfolio does not perform as well as the risky S&P 500 stock index. Because risk drives returns, the investor's lower-risk investments, as specified in the investor's policy statement, will probably earn lower returns than if all the investor's funds were placed in the stock market.

The policy statement will typically include a **benchmark portfolio,** or comparison standard. The risk of the benchmark, and the assets included in the benchmark, should agree with the client's risk preferences and investment needs. Notably, both the client and the portfolio manager must agree that the benchmark portfolio reflects the risk preferences and appropriate return requirements of the client. In turn, the investment performance of the portfolio manager should be compared to this benchmark portfolio. For example, an investor who specifies low-risk investments in the policy statement should compare the portfolio manager's performance against a low-risk benchmark portfolio. Likewise, an investor seeking high-risk, high-return investments should compare the portfolio's performance against a high-risk benchmark portfolio.

Because it sets an objective performance standard, the policy statement acts as a starting point for periodic portfolio review and client communication with managers. Questions concerning portfolio performance or the manager's faithfulness to the policy can be addressed in the context of the written policy guidelines. Managers should mainly be judged by whether they consistently followed the client's policy guidelines. The portfolio manager who makes unilateral deviations from policy is not working in the best interests of the client. Therefore, even significant deviations that result in higher portfolio returns can and should be grounds for the manager's dismissal.

Thus, we see the importance of the client constructing the policy statement: The client must first understand his or her own needs before communicating them to the portfolio manager. In turn, the portfolio manager must implement the client's desires by following the investment guidelines. As long as policy is followed, shortfalls in performance should not be a major concern. Remember that the policy statement is designed to impose an investment discipline on the client and portfolio manager. The less knowledgeable they are, the more likely clients are to inappropriately judge the performance of the portfolio manager.

Other Benefits

A sound policy statement helps to protect the client against a portfolio manager's inappropriate investments or unethical behavior. Without clear, written guidance, some managers may consider investing in high-risk investments, hoping to earn a quick return. Such actions are probably counter to the investor's specified needs and risk preferences. Though legal recourse is a possibility against such action, writing a clear and unambiguous policy statement should reduce the possibility of such inappropriate manager behavior.

Just because one specific manager currently manages your account does not mean that person will always manage your funds. As with other positions, your portfolio manager may be promoted or dismissed or take a better job. Therefore, after a while, your funds may come under the management of an individual you do not know and who does not know you. To prevent costly delays during this transition, you can ensure that the new manager "hits the ground running" with a clearly written policy statement. A policy statement should prevent delays in monitoring and rebalancing your portfolio and will help create a seamless transition from one money manager to another.

To sum up, a clearly written policy statement helps avoid future potential problems. When the client clearly specifies his or her needs and desires, the portfolio manager can more effectively construct an appropriate portfolio. The policy statement provides an objective measure for evaluating portfolio performance, helps guard against ethical lapses by the portfolio manager, and aids in the transition between money managers. Therefore, the first step before beginning any investment program, whether it is for an individual or a multibillion-dollar pension fund, is to construct a policy statement.

An appropriate policy statement should satisfactorily answer the following questions:

1. Is the policy carefully designed to meet the specific needs and objectives of this particular investor? (Cookie-cutter or one-size-fits-all policy statements are generally inappropriate.)
2. Is the policy written so clearly and explicitly that a competent stranger could use it to manage the portfolio in conformance with the client's needs? In case of a manager transition, could the new manager use this policy statement to handle your portfolio in accordance with your needs?
3. Would the client have been able to remain committed to the policies during the capital market experiences of the past 60 to 70 years? That is, does the client fully understand investment risks and the need for a disciplined approach to the investment process?
4. Would the portfolio manager have been able to maintain the policies specified over the same period? (Discipline is a two-way street; we do not want the portfolio manager to change strategies because of a disappointing market.)
5. Would the policy, if implemented, have achieved the client's objectives? (Bottom line: Would the policy have worked to meet the client's needs?)

Adapted from Charles D. Ellis, *Investment Policy: How to Win the Loser's Game* (Homewood, IL: Dow Jones–Irwin, 1985), 62. Reproduced with permission of the McGraw-Hill Companies.

INPUT TO THE POLICY STATEMENT

Before an investor and advisor can construct a policy statement, they need to have an open and frank exchange of information, ideas, fears, and goals. To build a framework for this information-gathering process, the client and advisor need to discuss the client's investment objectives and constraints. To illustrate this framework, we discuss the investment objectives and constraints that may confront "typical" 25-year-old and 65-year-old investors.

Investment Objectives

The investor's **objectives** are his or her investment goals expressed in terms of both risk and returns. The relationship between risk and returns requires that goals not be expressed only in terms of returns. Expressing goals only in terms of returns can lead to inappropriate investment practices by the portfolio manager, such as the use of high-risk investment strategies or account "churning," which involves moving quickly in and out of investments in an attempt to buy low and sell high.

For example, a person may have a stated return goal such as "double my investment in five years." Before such a statement becomes part of the policy statement, the client must become fully informed of investment risks associated with such a goal, including the possibility of loss. *A careful analysis of the client's risk tolerance should precede any discussion of return objectives.* It makes little sense for a person who is risk averse to invest funds in high-risk assets. Investment firms survey clients to gauge their risk tolerance. Sometimes investment magazines or books contain tests that individuals can take to help them evaluate their risk tolerance (see Exhibit 2.4). Subsequently, an advisor will use the results of this evaluation to categorize a client's risk tolerance and suggest an initial asset allocation such as those contained in Exhibit 2.5.

Risk tolerance is more than a function of an individual's psychological makeup; it is affected by other factors, including a person's current insurance coverage and cash reserves. Risk tolerance is also affected by an individual's family situation (for example, marital status and the number and ages of children) and by his or her age. We know that older persons generally have shorter investment time frames within which to make up any losses; they also have years of experience, including living through various market gyrations and "corrections" (a euphemism for downtrends or crashes) that younger people have not experienced or whose effect they do not fully appreciate. Risk tolerance is also influenced by one's current net worth and income expectations. All else being equal, individuals with higher incomes have a greater propensity to undertake risk because their incomes can help cover any shortfall. Likewise, individuals with larger net worths can afford to place some assets in risky investments while the remaining assets provide a cushion against losses.

A person's return objective may be stated in terms of an absolute or a relative percentage return, but it may also be stated in terms of a general goal, such as capital preservation, current income, capital appreciation, or total return.

Capital preservation means that investors want to minimize their risk of loss, usually in real terms: They seek to maintain the purchasing power of their investment. In other words, the return needs to be no less than the rate of inflation. Generally, this is a strategy for strongly risk-averse investors or for funds needed in the short-run, such as for next year's tuition payment or a down payment on a house.

Capital appreciation is an appropriate objective when the investors want the portfolio to grow in real terms over time to meet some future need. Under this strategy, growth mainly occurs through capital gains. This is an aggressive strategy for investors willing to take on risk to meet their objective. Generally, longer-term investors seeking to build a retirement or college education fund may have this goal.

When **current income** is the return objective, the investors want the portfolio to concentrate on generating income rather than capital gains. This strategy sometimes suits investors who want to supplement their earnings with income generated by their portfolio to meet their living expenses. Retirees may favor this objective for part of their portfolio to help generate spendable funds.

The objective for the **total return** strategy is similar to that of capital appreciation; namely, the investors want the portfolio to grow over time to meet a future need. Whereas the capital appreciation strategy seeks to do this primarily through capital gains, the total

Exhibit 2.4	How Much Risk Is Right for You?

You've heard the expression "no pain, no gain"? In the investment world, the comparable phrase would be "no risk, no reward."

How you feel about risking your money will drive many of your investment decisions. The risk-comfort scale extends from very conservative (you don't want to risk losing a penny regardless of how little your money earns) to very aggressive (you're willing to risk much of your money for the possibility that it will grow tremendously). As you might guess, most investors' tolerance for risk falls somewhere in between.

If you're unsure of what your level of risk tolerance is, this quiz should help.

1. You win $300 in an office football pool. You: (a) spend it on groceries, (b) purchase lottery tickets, (c) put it in a money market account, (d) buy some stock.

2. Two weeks after buying 100 shares of a $20 stock, the price jumps to over $30. You decide to: (a) buy more stock; it's obviously a winner, (b) sell it and take your profits, (c) sell half to recoup some costs and hold the rest, (d) sit tight and wait for it to advance even more.

3. On days when the stock market jumps way up, you: (a) wish you had invested more, (b) call your financial advisor and ask for recommendations, (c) feel glad you're not in the market because it fluctuates too much, (d) pay little attention.

4. You're planning a vacation trip and can either lock in a fixed room-and-meals rate of $150 per day or book standby and pay anywhere from $100 to $300 per day. You: (a) take the fixed-rate deal, (b) talk to people who have been there about the availability of last-minute accommodations, (c) book standby and also arrange vacation insurance because you're leery of the tour operator, (d) take your chances with standby.

5. The owner of your apartment building is converting the units to condominiums. You can buy your unit for $75,000 or an option on a unit for $15,000. (Units have recently sold for close to $100,000, and prices seem to be going up.) For financing, you'll have to borrow the down payment and pay mortgage and condo fees higher than your present rent. You: (a) buy your unit, (b) buy your unit and look for another to buy, (c) sell the option and arrange to rent the unit yourself, (d) sell the option and move out because you think the conversion will attract couples with small children.

6. You have been working three years for a rapidly growing company. As an executive, you are offered the option of buying up to 2% of company stock: 2,000 shares at $10 a share. Although the company is privately owned (its stock does not trade on the open market), its majority owner has made handsome profits selling three other businesses and intends to sell this one eventually. You: (a) purchase all the shares you can and tell the owner you would invest more if allowed, (b) purchase all the shares, (c) purchase half the shares, (d) purchase a small amount of shares.

7. You go to a casino for the first time. You choose to play: (a) quarter slot machines, (b) $5 minimum-bet roulette, (c) dollar slot machines, (d) $25 minimum-bet blackjack.

8. You want to take someone out for a special dinner in a city that's new to you. How do you pick a place? (a) read restaurant reviews in the local newspaper, (b) ask coworkers if they know of a suitable place, (c) call the only other person you know in this city, who eats out a lot but only recently moved there, (d) visit the city sometime before your dinner to check out the restaurants yourself.

9. The expression that best describes your lifestyle is: (a) no guts, no glory, (b) just do it!, (c) look before you leap, (d) all good things come to those who wait.

10. Your attitude toward money is best described as: (a) a dollar saved is a dollar earned, (b) you've got to spend money to make money, (c) cash and carry only, (d) whenever possible, use other people's money.

SCORING SYSTEM: Score your answers this way: (1) a-1, b-4, c-2, d-3 (2) a-4, b-1, c-3, d-2 (3) a-3, b-4, c-2, d-1 (4) a-2, b-3, c-1, d-4 (5) a-3, b-4, c-2, d-1 (6) a-4, b-3, c-2, d-1 (7) a-1, b-3, c-2, d-4 (8) a-2, b-3, c-4, d-1 (9) a-4, b-3, c-2, d-1 (10) a-2, b-3, c-1, d-4.

What your total score indicates:

- 10–17: You're not willing to take chances with your money, even though it means you can't make big gains.
- 18–25: You're semi-conservative, willing to take a small chance with enough information.

- 26–32: You're semi-aggressive, willing to take chances if you think the odds of earning more are in your favor.
- 33–40: You're aggressive, looking for every opportunity to make your money grow, even though in some cases the odds may be quite long. You view money as a tool to make more money.

Exhibit 2.5	Initial Risk and Investment Goal Categories and Asset Allocations Suggested by Investment Firms

FIDELITY INVESTMENTS SUGGESTED ASSET ALLOCATIONS:

	Cash/ Short-Term	Bonds	Domestic Equities	Foreign Equities
Short-term	100%	0%	0%	0%
Conservative	30	50	20	0
Balanced	10	40	45	5
Growth	5	25	60	10
Aggressive growth	0	15	70	15
Most aggressive	0	0	80	20

VANGUARD INVESTMENTS SUGGESTED ASSET ALLOCATIONS:

	Cash/Short-Term	Bonds	Stocks
Income-oriented	0%	100%	0%
	0	80%	20%
	0	70%	30%
Balanced	0%	60%	40%
	0	50%	50%
	0	40%	60%
Growth	0%	30%	70%
	0	20%	80%
	0	0%	100%

T. ROWE PRICE MATRIX

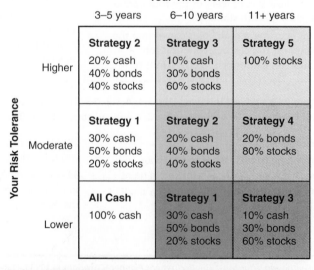

Non-retirement-goals Matrix

return strategy seeks to increase portfolio value by both capital gains and reinvesting current income. Because the total return strategy has both income and capital gains components, its risk exposure lies between that of the current income and capital appreciation strategies.

Investment Objective: 25-Year-Old What is an appropriate investment objective for our typical 25-year-old investor? Assume he holds a steady job, is a valued employee, has adequate insurance coverage, and has enough money in the bank to provide a cash reserve. Let's also assume that his current long-term, high-priority investment goal is to build a retirement fund. Depending on his risk preferences, he can select a strategy carrying moderate to high amounts of risk because the income stream from his job will probably grow over time. Further, given his young age and income growth potential, a low-risk strategy, such as capital preservation or current income, is inappropriate for his retirement fund goal; a total return or capital appreciation objective would be most appropriate. Here's a possible objective statement:

> Invest funds in a variety of moderate- to higher-risk investments. The average risk of the equity portfolio should exceed that of a broad stock market index, such as the NYSE stock index. Foreign and domestic equity exposure should range from 80 percent to 95 percent of the total portfolio. Remaining funds should be invested in short- and intermediate-term notes and bonds.

Investment Objective: 65-Year-Old Assume our typical 65-year-old investor likewise has adequate insurance coverage and a cash reserve. Let's also assume she is retiring this year. This individual will want less risk exposure than the 25-year-old investor, because her earning power from employment will soon be ending; she will not be able to recover any investment losses by saving more out of her paycheck. Depending on her income from social security and a pension plan, she may need some current income from her retirement portfolio to meet living expenses. Given that she can be expected to live an average of another 20 years, she will need protection against inflation. A risk-averse investor will choose a combination of current income and capital preservation strategy; a more risk-tolerant investor will choose a combination of current income and total return in an attempt to have principal growth outpace inflation. Here's an example of such an objective statement:

> Invest in stock and bond investments to meet income needs (from bond income and stock dividends) and to provide for real growth (from equities). Fixed-income securities should comprise 55–65 percent of the total portfolio; of this, 5–15 percent should be invested in short-term securities for extra liquidity and safety. The remaining 35–45 percent of the portfolio should be invested in high-quality stocks whose risk is similar to the S&P 500 index.

More detailed analyses for our 25-year-old and our 65-year-old would make more specific assumptions about the risk tolerance of each, as well as clearly enumerate their investment goals, return objectives, the funds they have to invest at the present, the funds they expect to invest over time, and the benchmark portfolio that will be used to evaluate performance.

Investment Constraints

In addition to the investment objective that sets limits on risk and return, certain other constraints also affect the investment plan. Investment constraints include liquidity needs, an investment time horizon, tax factors, legal and regulatory constraints, and unique needs and preferences.

Liquidity Needs An asset is **liquid** if it can be quickly converted to cash at a price close to fair market value. Generally, assets are more liquid if many traders are interested in a fairly standardized product. Treasury bills are a highly liquid security; real estate and venture capital are not.

Investors may have liquidity needs that the investment plan must consider. For example, although an investor may have a primary long-term goal, several near-term goals may require available funds. Wealthy individuals with sizable tax obligations need adequate liquidity to pay their taxes without upsetting their investment plan. Some retirement plans may need funds for shorter-term purposes, such as buying a car or a house or making college tuition payments.

Our typical 25-year-old investor probably has little need for liquidity as he focuses on his long-term retirement fund goal. This constraint may change, however, should he face a period of unemployment or should near-term goals, such as honeymoon expenses or a house down payment, enter the picture. Should any changes occur, the investor needs to revise his policy statement and financial plans accordingly.

Our soon-to-be-retired 65-year-old investor has a greater need for liquidity. Although she may receive regular checks from her pension plan and social security, it is not likely that they will equal her working paycheck. She will want some of her portfolio in liquid securities to meet unexpected expenses or bills.

Time Horizon   Time horizon as an investment constraint briefly entered our earlier discussion of near-term and long-term high-priority goals. A close (but not perfect) relationship exists between an investor's time horizon, liquidity needs, and ability to handle risk. Investors with long investment horizons generally require less liquidity and can tolerate greater portfolio risk: less liquidity because the funds are not usually needed for many years; greater risk tolerance because any shortfalls or losses can be overcome by returns earned in subsequent years.

Investors with shorter time horizons generally favor more liquid and less risky investments because losses are harder to overcome during a short time frame.

Because of life expectancies, our 25-year-old investor has a longer investment time horizon than our 65-year-old investor. But, as discussed earlier, this does not mean the 65-year-old should place all her money in short-term CDs; she needs the inflation protection that long-term investments such as common stock can provide. Still, because of the time horizon constraint, the 25-year-old will probably have a greater proportion of his portfolio in equities—including stocks in small firms and international firms—than the 65-year-old.

Tax Concerns   Investment planning is complicated by the tax code; taxes complicate the situation even more if international investments are part of the portfolio. Taxable income from interest, dividends, or rents is taxable at the investor's marginal tax rate. The marginal tax rate is the proportion of the next one dollar in income paid as taxes. Exhibit 2.6 shows the marginal tax rates for different levels of taxable income. As of 2004, the top federal marginal tax rate was 35 percent.

Capital gains or losses arise from asset price changes. They are taxed differently than income. Income is taxed when it is received; capital gains or losses are taxed only when an asset is sold and the gain or loss, relative to its initial cost or **basis**, is realized. **Unrealized capital gains** (or *losses*) reflect the price change in currently held assets that have *not* been sold; the tax liability on unrealized capital gains can be deferred indefinitely. If appreciated assets are passed on to an heir upon the investor's death, the basis of the assets is considered to be their value on the date of the holder's death. The heirs can then sell the assets and pay lower capital gains taxes if they wish. **Realized capital gains** occur when an appreciated asset has been sold; taxes are due on the realized capital gains only. As of 2004, the maximum tax rate on stock dividends and long-term capital gains is 15 percent.

Some find the difference between average and marginal income tax rates confusing. The **marginal tax rate** is the part of each additional dollar in income that is paid as tax. Thus,

Exhibit 2.6	Individual Marginal Tax Rates, 2004

For updates, go to the IRS Web site, *http://www.irs.gov.*

| | IF TAXABLE INCOME | | THE TAX IS | | |
| | | THEN | | | |
	Is Over	But Not Over	This Amount	Plus This %	Of the Excess Over
Single	$0	$7,150	$0.00	10%	$0.00
	$7,150	$29,050	$715.00	15%	$7,150
	$29,050	$70,350	$4,000.00	25%	$29,050
	$70,350	$146,750	$14,325.00	28%	$70,350
	$146,750	$319,100	$35,717.00	33%	$146,750
	$319,100	—	$92,592.50	35%	$319,100
Married Filing Jointly	$0	$14,300	$0.00	10%	$0.00
	$14,300	$58,100	$1,430	15%	$14,300
	$58,100	$117,250	$8,000	25%	$58,600
	$117,250	$178,650	$22,787	28%	$117,250
	$178,650	$319,100	$39,979	33%	$178,650
	$319,100	—	$86,328	35%	$319,100

a married person, filing jointly, with an income of $50,000 will have a marginal tax rate of 15 percent. The 15 percent marginal tax rate should be used to determine after-tax returns on investments.

The **average tax rate** is simply a person's total tax payment divided by their total income. It represents the average tax paid on each dollar the person earned. From Exhibit 2.6, a married person, filing jointly, will pay $6,785 in tax on a $50,000 income [$1,430 + 0.15($50,000 − $14,300)]. This average tax rate is $6,785/$50,000 or 13.6 percent. Note that the average tax rate is a weighted average of the person's marginal tax rates paid on each dollar of income. The first $14,000 of income has a 10 percent marginal tax rate; the next $36,000 has a 15 percent marginal tax rate:

$$\frac{\$14,000}{\$50,000} \times 0.10 + \frac{\$36,000}{\$50,000} \times 0.15 = 0.136, \text{ or the average tax rate of 13.6 percent}$$

Another tax factor is that some sources of investment income are exempt from federal and state taxes. For example, interest on federal securities, such as Treasury bills, notes, and bonds, is exempt from state taxes. Interest on municipal bonds (bonds issued by a state or other local governing body) is exempt from federal taxes. Further, if investors purchase municipal bonds issued by a local governing body of the state in which they live, the interest is exempt from both state and federal income tax. Thus, high-income individuals have an incentive to purchase municipal bonds to reduce their tax liabilities.

The after-tax return on taxable investment income is

After-Tax Income Return = Pre-Tax Income Return × (1 − Marginal Tax Rate)

Thus, the after-tax return on a taxable bond investment should be compared to that of municipals before deciding which a tax-paying investor should purchase.[1] Alternatively, we could compute a municipal's equivalent taxable yield, which is what a taxable bond investment would have to offer to produce the same after-tax return as the municipal. It is given by

$$\text{Equivalent Taxable Yield} = \frac{\text{Municipal Yield}}{(1 - \text{Marginal Tax Rate})}$$

To illustrate, if an investor is in the 28 percent marginal tax bracket, a taxable investment yield of 8 percent has an after-tax yield of 8 percent $\times$ (1 − 0.28) or 5.76 percent; an equivalent-risk municipal security offering a yield greater than 5.76 percent offers the investor greater after-tax returns. On the other hand, a municipal bond yielding 6 percent has an equivalent taxable yield of 6 percent/(1 − 0.28) = 8.33 percent; to earn more money after taxes, an equivalent-risk taxable investment has to offer a return greater than 8.33 percent.

There are other means of reducing investment tax liabilities. Contributions to an IRA (individual retirement account) may qualify as a tax deduction if certain income limits are met. Even without that deduction, taxes on any investment returns of an IRA, including any income, are deferred until the funds are withdrawn from the account. Any funds withdrawn from an IRA are taxable as current income, regardless of whether growth in the IRA occurs as a result of capital gains, income, or both. For this reason, to minimize taxes advisors recommend investing in stocks in taxable accounts and bonds in tax-deferred accounts such as IRAs. When funds are withdrawn from a tax-deferred account such as a regular IRA, assets are taxed (at most) at a 35 percent income tax rate (Exhibit 2.6)—even if the source of the stock return is primarily capital gains. In a taxable account, capital gains are taxed at the maximum 15 percent capital gains rate.

The benefits of deferring taxes can dramatically compound over time, as we saw in Chapter 1. For example, $1000 invested in an IRA at a tax-deferred rate of 8 percent grows to $10,062.66 over thirty years; in a taxable account (assuming a 28 percent marginal (federal + state) tax rate), the funds would grow to only $5,365.91. After thirty years, the value of the tax-deferred investment has grown to be nearly twice as large as the taxable investment.

With various stipulations, as of 2005, tax-deductible contributions of up to $4,000 (to be raised to $5,000 by 2008) can be made to a traditional IRA. A Roth IRA contribution is *not* tax deductible and contribution limits mirror those of the traditional IRA. The returns in a Roth IRA will grow on a tax-deferred basis and can be withdrawn, tax-free, if the funds are invested for at least five years and are withdrawn after the investor reaches age $59\frac{1}{2}$.[2]

For money you intend to invest in some type of IRA, the advantage of the Roth IRA's tax-free withdrawals will outweigh the tax-deduction benefit from the regular IRA—unless you expect your tax rate when the funds are withdrawn to be substantially less than when you initially invest the funds. Let's illustrate this with a hypothetical example.

Suppose you are considering investing $2,000 in either a regular or Roth IRA. Let's assume for simplicity that your combined federal and state marginal tax rate is 28 percent and that, over your 20-year time horizon, your $2,000 investment will grow to $20,000, tax-deferred in either account; this represents an average annual return of 12.2 percent.

In a Roth IRA, no tax is deducted when the $2,000 is invested; in a regular IRA, the $2,000 investment is tax-deductible and will lower your tax bill by $560 (0.28 $\times$ $2,000).

---

[1] Realized capital gains on municipal securities are taxed, as are all other capital gains; similarly for capital losses. Only the income from municipals is exempt from federal income tax.

[2] Earlier tax-free withdrawals are possible if the funds are to be used for educational purposes or first-time home purchases.

Exhibit 2.7	Comparing the Regular versus Roth IRA Returns	
	Regular IRA	**Roth IRA**
Invested funds:	$2,000 + $560 tax savings on the tax-deductible IRA investment	$2,000 (no tax deduction)
Time horizon:	20 years	20 years
Rate of return assumption:	12.2 percent tax-deferred on the IRA investment; 8.8 percent on invested tax savings (represents the after-tax return on 12.2 percent)	12.2 percent tax-deferred on the IRA investment
Funds available after 20 years (taxes ignored)	$20,000 (pre-tax) from IRA investment; $3,025 (after-tax) from invested tax savings	$20,000 from IRA investment
Funds available after 20 years, 15 percent marginal tax rate at retirement	$20,000 less tax (0.15 × $20,000) plus $3,025 from invested tax savings equals **$20,025**	**$20,000**
Funds available after 20 years, 28 percent marginal tax rate at retirement	$20,000 less tax (0.28 × $20,000) plus $3,025 from invested tax savings equals **$17,425**	**$20,000**
Funds available after 20 years, 40 percent marginal tax rate at retirement	$20,000 less tax (0.40 × $20,000) plus $3,025 from invested tax savings equals **$15,025**	**$20,000**

Thus, in a Roth IRA, only $2,000 is assumed to be invested; for a regular IRA, both the $2,000 and the $560 tax savings are assumed to be invested. We will assume the $560 is invested at an after-tax rate of $12.2\% \times (1 - 0.28) = 8.8$ percent. After 20 years, this amount will grow to $3,025. The calculations in Exhibit 2.7 show that at the end of the 20-year time horizon the Roth IRA will give you more after-tax dollars unless you believe your tax bracket will be lower then *and you invest the regular IRA tax savings.*

Another tax-deferred investment is the cash value of life insurance contracts; these accumulate tax-free until the funds are withdrawn. Also, employers may offer 401(k) or 403(b) plans, which allow the employee to reduce taxable income by making tax-deferred investments. Many times employee contributions are matched by employer donations (up to a specified limit), thus allowing the employees to double their investment with little risk.

At times investors face a trade-off between taxes and diversification needs. If entrepreneurs concentrate much of their wealth in equity holdings of their firm, or if employees purchase substantial amounts of their employer's stock through payroll deduction plans during their working life, their portfolios may contain a large amount of unrealized capital gains. In addition, the risk position of such a portfolio may be quite high because it is concentrated in a single company. The decision to sell some of the company stock in order to diversify the portfolio's risk by reinvesting the proceeds in other assets must be balanced against the resulting tax liability.

Our typical 25-year-old investor probably is in a fairly low tax bracket, so detailed tax planning and tax-exempt income, such as that available from municipals, will not be major concerns. Nonetheless, he should still invest as much as possible into such tax-deferred plans as IRAs or 401(k)s for the retirement portion of his portfolio. If other funds are available for investment, they should be allocated based on his shorter- and longer-term investment goals.

Our 65-year-old investor may face a different situation. If she had been in a high tax bracket prior to retiring—and therefore has sought tax-exempt income and tax-deferred invest-ments—her situation may change shortly after retirement. After her retirement, without large regular paychecks, the need for tax-deferred investments or tax-exempt income becomes less. Taxable income may then offer higher after-tax yields than tax-exempt municipals if her tax bracket is lower. If her employer's stock is a large component of her retirement account, she must make careful decisions regarding the need to diversify versus the cost of realizing large capital gains (in her lower tax bracket).

Legal and Regulatory Factors   Both the investment process and the financial markets are highly regulated and subject to numerous laws. At times, these legal and regulatory factors constrain the investment strategies of individuals and institutions.

For example, funds removed from a regular IRA, Roth IRA, or 401(k) plan before age $59\frac{1}{2}$ are taxable and subject to an additional 10 percent withdrawal penalty. You may also be famil-iar with the tag line in many bank CD advertisements—"substantial interest penalty upon early withdrawal." Regulations and rules such as these may make such investments unattractive for investors with substantial liquidity needs in their portfolios.

Regulations can also constrain the investment choices available to someone in a fiduciary role. A *fiduciary,* or trustee, supervises an investment portfolio of a third party, such as a trust account or discretionary account.[3] The fiduciary must make investment decisions in accor-dance with the owner's wishes; a properly written policy statement assists this process. In addition, trustees of a trust account must meet the prudent-man standard, which means that they must invest and manage the funds as a prudent person would manage his or her own affairs. Notably, the prudent-man standard is based on the composition of the entire portfolio, not each individual asset.[4]

All investors must respect certain laws, such as insider trading prohibitions against the purchase and sale of securities on the basis of important information that is not publicly known. Typically, the people possessing such private, or insider, information are the firm's managers, who have a fiduciary duty to their shareholders. Security transactions based on access to insider information violates the fiduciary trust the shareholders have placed with management because the managers seek personal financial gain from their privileged position as agents for the shareholders.

For our typical 25-year-old investor, legal and regulatory matters will be of little concern, with the possible exception of insider trading laws and the penalties associated with early with-drawal of funds from tax-deferred retirement accounts. Should he seek a financial advisor to assist him in constructing a financial plan, that advisor would have to obey the regulations per-tinent to a client–advisor relationship. Similar concerns confront our 65-year-old investor. In addition, as a retiree, if she wants to do estate planning and set up trust accounts, she should seek legal and tax advice to ensure her plans are properly implemented.

Unique Needs and Preferences   This category covers the individual and sometimes idio-syncratic concerns of each investor. Some investors may want to exclude certain investments from their portfolio solely on the basis of personal preference or for social consciousness rea-sons. For example, they may request that no firms that manufacture or sell tobacco, alcohol,

---

[3]A discretionary account is one in which the fiduciary, many times a financial planner or stockbroker, has the authority to purchase and sell assets in the owner's portfolio without first receiving the owner's approval.
[4]As we will discuss in Chapter 7, it is sometimes wise to hold assets that are individually risky in the context of a well-diversified portfolio, even if the investor is strongly risk averse.

pornography, or environmentally harmful products be included in their portfolio. Some mutual funds screen according to this type of social responsibility criterion.

Another example of a personal constraint is the time and expertise a person has for managing his or her portfolio. Busy executives may prefer to relax during nonworking hours and let a trusted advisor manage their investments. Retirees, on the other hand, may have the time but believe they lack the expertise to choose and monitor investments, so they also may seek professional advice.

In addition, a business owner with a large portion of her wealth—and emotion—tied up in her firm's stock may be reluctant to sell even when it may be financially prudent to do so and then reinvest the proceeds for diversification purposes. Further, if the stock holdings are in a private company, it may be difficult to find a buyer unless shares are sold at a discount from their fair market value. Because each investor is unique, the implications of this final constraint differ for each person; there is no "typical" 25-year-old or 65-year-old investor. Each individual will have to decide—and then communicate specific goals in a well-constructed policy statement.

CONSTRUCTING THE POLICY STATEMENT

As we have seen, the policy statement allows the investor to communicate his or her objectives (risk and return) and constraints (liquidity, time horizon, tax, legal and regulatory, and unique needs and preferences). This communication gives the advisor a better chance of implementing an investment strategy that will satisfy the investor. Even if an advisor is not used, each investor needs to take this first important step of the investment process and develop a financial plan to guide the investment strategy. To do without a plan or to plan poorly is to place the success of the financial plan in jeopardy.

General Guidelines

Constructing a policy statement is the investor's responsibility, but investment advisors often assist in the process. The following lists of recommendations for both the investor and the advisor provide guidelines for good policy statement construction.

In the process of constructing a policy statement, investors should think about the following set of questions and be able to explain their answers:

1. What are the real risks of an adverse financial outcome, especially in the short run?
2. What probable emotional reactions will I have to an adverse financial outcome?
3. How knowledgeable am I about investments and markets?
4. What other capital or income sources do I have? How important is this particular portfolio to my overall financial position?
5. What, if any, legal restrictions may affect my investment needs?
6. What, if any, unanticipated consequences of interim fluctuations in portfolio value might affect my investment policy?

Adapted from Charles D. Ellis, *Investment Policy: How to Win the Loser's Game,* Homewood IL: Dow Jones–Irwin, 1985, pp. 25–26.

In assisting an investor in the policy statement process, an advisor should ensure that the policy statement satisfactorily answers the following questions:

1. Is the policy carefully designed to meet the specific needs and objectives of this particular investor? (Cookie-cutter or one-size-fits-all policy statements are generally inappropriate.)
2. Is the policy written so clearly and explicitly that a competent stranger could manage the portfolio in conformance with the client's needs? In case of a manager transition, could the new manager use this policy to handle the portfolio in accordance with the client's needs?
3. Would the client have been able to remain committed to the policies during the capital market experiences of the past 60 to 70 years? That is, does the client fully understand investment risks and the need for a disciplined approach to the investment process?
4. Would the portfolio manager have been able to maintain fidelity to the policy over the same period? (Discipline is a two-way street; we do not want the portfolio manager to change strategies because of a disappointing market.)
5. Would the policy, if implemented, achieve the client's objectives? (Bottom line: would the policy have worked to meet the client's needs?)

Adapted from Charles D. Ellis, *Investment Policy: How to Win the Loser's Game,* Homewood, IL: Dow Jones–Irwin, 1985, p. 62.

Some Common Mistakes

When constructing their policy statements, participants in employer-sponsored retirement plans need to realize that through such plans 30–40 percent of their retirement funds may be invested in their employer's stock. Having so much money invested in one asset violates diversification principles and could be costly. To put this in context, most mutual funds are limited by law to having no more than 5 percent of their assets in any one company's stock; a firm's pension plan can invest no more than 10 percent of their funds in its own stock. As noted by Schulz (1996), individuals are unfortunately doing what government regulations prevent many institutional investors from doing. In addition, some studies point out that the average stock allocation in retirement plans is lower than it should be to allow for growth of principal over time.

Another consideration is the issue of stock trading. A number of studies by Barber and Odean (1999, 2000, 2001) and Odean (1998, 1999) have shown that many individual investors trade stocks too often (driving up commissions), sell stocks with gains too early (prior to further price increases), and hold onto losers too long (as the price continues to fall). These results are especially true for men and online traders.

Investors, in general, seem to neglect that important first step to achieve financial success: they do not plan for the future. Studies of retirement plans discussed by Ruffenach (2001) and Clements (1997a, b, c) show that Americans are not saving enough to finance their retirement years and they are not planning sufficiently for what will happen to their savings after they retire. Around 25 percent of workers have saved less than $50,000 for their retirement and 60 percent of workers surveyed confessed they were "behind schedule" in planning and saving for retirement.

THE IMPORTANCE OF ASSET ALLOCATION

A major reason why investors develop policy statements is to determine an overall investment strategy. Though a policy statement does not indicate which specific securities to purchase and when they should be sold, it should provide guidelines as to the asset classes to include and the relative proportions of the investor's funds to invest in each class. How the investor divides funds into different asset classes is the process of asset allocation. Rather than present strict percentages, asset allocation is usually expressed in ranges. This allows the investment manager some freedom, based on his or her reading of capital market trends, to invest toward the upper or lower end of the ranges. For example, suppose a policy statement requires that common stocks be 60 percent to 80 percent of the value of the portfolio and that bonds should be 20 percent to 40 percent of the portfolio's value. If a manager is particularly bullish about stocks, she will increase the allocation of stocks toward the 80 percent upper end of the equity range and decrease bonds toward the 20 percent lower end of the bond range. Should she be more optimistic about bonds, that manager may shift the allocation closer to 40 percent of the funds invested in bonds with the remainder in equities.

A review of historical data and empirical studies provides strong support for the contention that the asset allocation decision is a critical component of the portfolio management process. In general, there are four decisions involved in constructing an investment strategy:

- What asset classes should be considered for investment?
- What policy weights should be assigned to each eligible asset class?
- What are the allowable allocation ranges based on policy weights?
- What specific securities or funds should be purchased for the portfolio?

The asset allocation decision comprises the first two points. How important is the asset allocation decision to an investor? In a word, *very.* Several studies by Ibbotson and Kaplan (2000); Brinson, Hood, and Beebower (1986); and Brinson, Singer, and Beebower (1991) have examined the effect of the normal policy weights on investment performance, using data from both pension funds and mutual funds, from periods of time extending from the early 1970s to the late 1990s. The studies all found similar results: About 90 percent of a fund's returns over time can be explained by its target asset allocation policy. Exhibit 2.8 shows the relationship between returns on the target or policy portfolio allocation and actual returns on a sample mutual fund.

Rather than looking at just one fund and how the target asset allocation determines its returns, some studies have looked at how much the asset allocation policy affects returns on a variety of funds with different target weights. For example, Ibbotson and Kaplan (2000) found that, across a sample of funds, about 40 percent of the difference in fund returns is explained by differences in asset allocation policy. And what does asset allocation tell us about the *level* of a particular fund's returns? The studies by Brinson and colleagues (1986, 1991) and Ibbotson and Kaplan (2000) answered that question as well. They divided the policy return (what the fund return would have been had it been invested in indexes at the policy weights) by the actual fund return (which includes the effects of varying from the policy weights and security selection). Thus, a fund that was passively invested at the target weights would have a ratio value of 1.0, or 100 percent. A fund managed by someone with skill in market timing (for moving in and out of asset classes) and security selection would have a ratio less than 1.0 (or less than 100 percent); the manager's skill would result in a policy return less than the actual fund return. The studies showed the opposite: The policy return/ actual return ratio averaged over 1.0, showing that asset allocation explains slightly more than 100 percent of the level of a fund's returns. Because of market efficiency, fund managers practicing market timing and security selection, on average, have difficulty surpassing passively invested index returns, after taking into account the expenses and fees of investing.

Thus, asset allocation is a very important decision. Across all funds, the asset allocation decision explains an average of 40 percent of the variation in fund returns. For a single fund, asset allocation explains 90 percent of the fund's variation in returns over time and slightly more than 100 percent of the average fund's level of return.

Good investment managers may add some value to portfolio performance, but the major source of investment return—and risk—over time is the asset allocation decision (Brown, 2000).

Exhibit 2.8	**Time-Series Regression of Monthly Fund Return versus Fund Policy Return: One Mutual Fund, April 1988–March 1998**

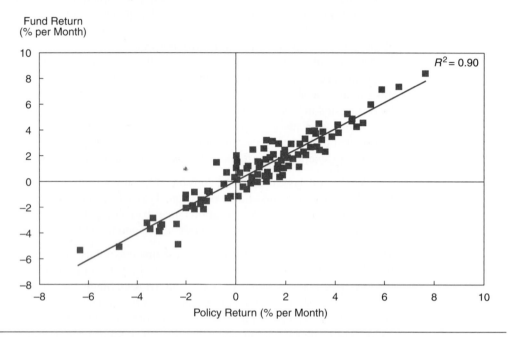

Note: The sample fund's policy allocations among the general asset classes were 52.4 percent U.S. large-cap stocks, 9.8 percent U.S. small-cap stocks, 3.2 percent non-U.S. stocks, 20.9 percent U.S. bonds, and 13.7 percent cash.

Source: Copyright 2000, Association for Investment Management and Research. Reproduced and republished from "Does Asset Allocation Policy Explain 40, 90 or 100 Percent of Performance?" in the *Financial Analysts Journal*, January/February 2000, with permission from the CFA Institute. All Rights Reserved.

Real Investment Returns after Taxes and Costs

Exhibit 2.9 provides additional historical perspectives on returns. It indicates how an investment of $1 would have grown over the 1981–2004 period and, using fairly conservative assumptions, examines how investment returns are affected by taxes and inflation.

Focusing first on stocks, funds invested in 1981 in the Dow Jones Wilshire 5000 stocks would have averaged a 12.36 percent annual return by the end of 2004. Unfortunately, this return is unrealistic because if the funds were invested over time, taxes would have to be paid and inflation would erode the real purchasing power of the invested funds.

Except for tax-exempt investors and tax-deferred accounts, annual tax payments reduce investment returns. Incorporating taxes into the analysis lowers the after-tax average annual return of a stock investment to 9.83 percent.

But the major reduction in the value of our investment is caused by inflation. The real after-tax average annual return on a stock over this time frame was only 6.52 percent, which is quite a bit less than our initial unadjusted 12.36 percent return!

This example shows the long-run impact of taxes and inflation on the real value of a stock portfolio. For bonds and bills, however, the results in Exhibit 2.9 show something even more surprising. After adjusting for taxes, long-term bonds maintained their purchasing power; T-bills barely provided value in real terms. One dollar invested in long-term government bonds

Exhibit 2.9	The Effect of Taxes and Inflation on Investment Returns: 1981–2004

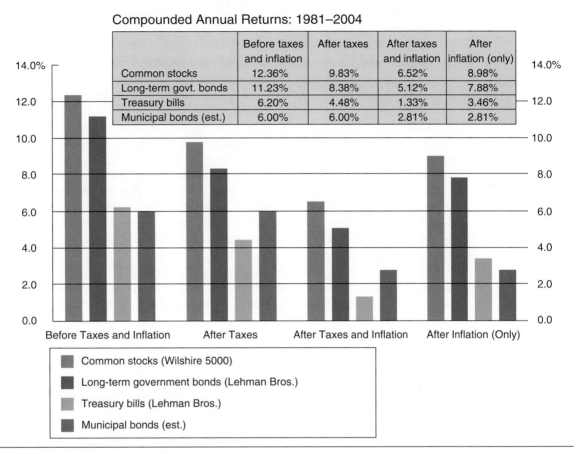

Compounded Annual Returns: 1981–2004

	Before taxes and inflation	After taxes	After taxes and inflation	After inflation (only)
Common stocks	12.36%	9.83%	6.52%	8.98%
Long-term govt. bonds	11.23%	8.38%	5.12%	7.88%
Treasury bills	6.20%	4.48%	1.33%	3.46%
Municipal bonds (est.)	6.00%	6.00%	2.81%	2.81%

■ Common stocks (Wilshire 5000)

■ Long-term government bonds (Lehman Bros.)

■ Treasury bills (Lehman Bros.)

■ Municipal bonds (est.)

Assumptions: 28 percent tax rate on income; 20 percent on price change.
Compound inflation rate was 3.1 percent for full period.

Source: Computations by authors, using data indicated.

in 1981 gave the investor an annual average after-tax real return of 5.12 percent. An investment in Treasury bills earned an average rate of only 1.33 percent after taxes and inflation. Municipal bonds, because of the protection they offer from taxes, earned an average annual real return of almost 3.00 percent during this time.

This historical analysis demonstrates that, for taxable investments, a reasonable way to maintain purchasing power over time when investing in financial assets is to invest in common stocks. Put another way, an asset allocation decision for a taxable portfolio that does not include a substantial commitment to common stocks makes it difficult for the portfolio to maintain real value over time.[5]

Notably, the fourth column, labeled "After inflation (only)," is more encouraging since it refers to results for a tax-free retirement account that is only impacted by inflation. These results should encourage investors to take advantage of such opportunities.

---

[5]Of course other equity-oriented investments, such as venture capital or real estate, may also provide inflation protection after adjusting for portfolio costs and taxes. Future studies of the performance of Treasury inflation-protected securities (TIPs) will likely show their usefulness in protecting investors from inflation as well.

Returns and Risks of Different Asset Classes

By focusing on returns, we have ignored its partner—risk. Assets with higher long-term returns have these returns to compensate for their risk. Exhibit 2.10 illustrates returns (unadjusted for costs and taxes) for several asset classes over time. As expected, the higher returns available from equities (both large cap and small cap) come at the cost of higher risk. This is precisely why investors need a policy statement and why the investor and manager must understand the capital markets and have a disciplined approach to investing. Safe Treasury bills will sometimes outperform equities, and, because of their higher risk, common stocks sometimes lose significant value. These are times when undisciplined and uneducated investors become frustrated, sell their stocks at a loss, and vow never to invest in equities again. In contrast, these are times when disciplined investors stick to their investment plan and position their portfolios for the next bull market.[6] By holding on to their stocks and perhaps purchasing more at depressed prices, the equity portion of the portfolio will experience a substantial increase in the future.

The asset allocation decision determines to a great extent both the returns and the volatility of the portfolio. Exhibit 2.10 indicates that stocks are riskier than bonds or T-bills. Exhibit 2.11 shows that stocks have sometimes earned returns lower than those of T-bills for extended periods of time. Sticking with an investment policy and riding out the difficult times can earn attractive long-term rates of return.[7]

One popular way to measure risk is to examine the variability of returns over time by computing a standard deviation or variance of annual rates of return for an asset class. This measure, which is contained in Exhibit 2.10, indicates that stocks are risky and T-bills are relatively safe. Another intriguing measure of risk is the probability of *not* meeting your

Exhibit 2.10	Summary Statistics of Annual Returns, 1984–2003, U.S. Securities

	Geometric Mean (%)	Arithmetic Mean (%)	Standard Deviation (%)
Large company stocks (S&P 500)	13.33	14.74	17.92
Small company stocks (S&P SmallCap 600)	10.82	12.86	21.21
Government bonds (Lehman Brothers)	9.07	9.20	5.33
Corporate bonds (Lehman Brothers)	10.07	10.24	5.99
Intermediate-term corporate bonds (Lehman Brothers)	9.25	9.34	4.37
Intermediate-term government bonds (Lehman Brothers)	8.43	8.50	3.84
30-day Treasury bill	5.23	5.23	0.64
U.S. inflation	3.01	3.01	0.81

Source: Calculations by authors, using data noted.

---

[6]Newton's law of gravity seems to work two ways in financial markets. What goes up must come down; it also appears over time that what goes down may come back up. Contrarian investors and some "value" investors use this concept of reversion to the mean to try to outperform the indexes over time.

[7]The added benefits of diversification—combining different asset classes in the portfolio—may reduce overall portfolio risk without harming potential return. The topic of diversification is discussed in Chapter 7.

Exhibit 2.11	**Higher Returns Offered by Equities over Long Time Periods** **Time Frame: 1934–2003**

Length of Holding Period (calendar years)	Percentage of Periods That Stock Returns Trailed T-Bill Returns*
1	35.7%
5	18.2
10	11.5
20	0.0
30	0.0

*Price change plus reinvested income
Source: Author calculations.

investment return objective. From this perspective, the results in Exhibit 2.11 show that if the investor has a long time horizon (i.e., approaching 20 years), the risk of equities is small and that of T-bills is large because of their differences in long-term expected returns.

Asset Allocation Summary

A carefully constructed policy statement determines the types of assets that should be included in a portfolio. The asset allocation decision, not the selection of specific stocks and bonds, determines most of the portfolio's returns over time. Although seemingly risky, investors seeking capital appreciation, income, or even capital preservation over long time periods will do well to include a sizable allocation to the equity portion in their portfolio. As noted in this section, a strategy's risk may depend on the investor's goals and time horizon. As demonstrated, investing in T-bills may be a riskier strategy than investing in common stocks due to reinvestment risks and the risk of not meeting long-term investment return goals after considering inflation and taxes.

Asset Allocation and Cultural Differences   Thus far, our analysis has focused on U.S. investors. Non-U.S. investors make their asset allocation decisions in much the same manner; but because they face different social, economic, political, and tax environments, their allocation decisions differ from those of U.S. investors. Exhibit 2.12 shows the equity allocations of pension funds in several countries. As shown, the equity allocations vary dramatically from 79 percent in Hong Kong to 37 percent in Japan and only 8 percent in Germany.

National differences can explain much of the divergent portfolio strategies. Of these six nations, the average age of the population is highest in Germany and Japan and lowest in the United States and the United Kingdom, which helps explain the greater use of equities in the latter countries. Government privatization programs during the 1980s in the United Kingdom encouraged equity ownership among individual and institutional investors. In Germany, regulations prevent insurance firms from having more than 20 percent of their assets in equities. Both Germany and Japan have banking sectors that invest privately in firms and whose officers sit on corporate boards. Since 1980, the cost of living in the United Kingdom has increased at a rate about two times that of Germany; this inflationary bias in the U.K. economy favors equities in U.K. asset allocations. Exhibit 2.13 shows the positive relationship between the level of inflation in a country and its pension fund allocation to equity. These results indicate that the

Exhibit 2.12	Equity Allocations in Pension Fund Portfolios

Country	Percentage in Equities
Hong Kong	79
United Kingdom	78
Ireland	68
United States	58
Japan	37
Germany	8

Exhibit 2.13	Asset Allocation and Inflation for Different Countries' Equity Allocation as of December 1997; Average Inflation Measured Over 1980–1997

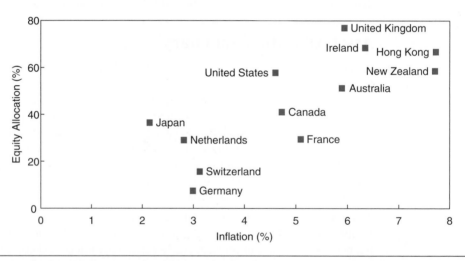

general economic environment, as well as demographics, has an effect on the asset allocation in a country.

The need to invest in equities for portfolio growth is less in Germany, where workers receive generous state pensions. Germans tend to show a cultural aversion to the stock market: Many Germans are risk averse and consider stock investing a form of gambling. Although this attitude is changing, the German stock market is rather illiquid, and Gumbel (1995) noted that only a handful of stocks account for 50 percent of total stock trading volume. New legislation that encourages 401(k)-like plans in Germany may encourage citizens to invest more in equities.

Other Organization for Economic Cooperation and Development (OECD) countries place regulatory restrictions on institutional investors. As noted by Witschi (1998) and Chernoff (1996), pension funds in Austria must have at least 50 percent of their assets in bank deposits or schilling-denominated bonds. Belgium limits pension funds to a minimum 15 percent investment in government bonds. Finland places a 5 percent limit on investments outside its borders by pension funds, and French pension funds must invest a minimum of 34 percent in public debt instruments.

Asset allocation policy and strategy are determined in the context of an investor's objectives and constraints. Among the factors that explain differences in investor behavior across countries, however, are their political and economic environments.

The Internet Investments Online

Many inputs go into an investment policy statement as an investor maps out his or her objectives and constraints. Some inputs and helpful information are available in the following Web sites. Many of the sites mentioned in Chapter 1 contain important information and insights about asset allocation decisions, as well.

http://www.ssa.gov Information on a person's expected retirement funds from Social Security can be obtained by using the Social Security Administration's Web site.

http://www.ibbotson.com Ibbotson is the source of much data and analysis that is helpful to the investor education and asset allocation process. Many professional financial planners make use of Ibbotson's data and education resources.

http://www.mfea.com/InvestmentStrategies/ Calculators/default.asp contains links to calculators on Web sites of mutual fund families.

Sites with information and sample Monte Carlo simulations for spending plans in retirement include: **http://www.financialengines.com, http://www.troweprice.com** (after getting to the individual investor page, click on investment planning and tools, then tools, and calculators, investment planning tools, then investment strategy planner); **http://www3.troweprice.com/ric/RIC/** (for a retirement income calculator), and **http://www.decisioneering.com.**

Many professional organizations have Web sites for use by their members, those interested in seeking professional finance designations, and those interested in seeking advice from a professional financial adviser.

These sites include:

http://www.cfainstitute.org CFA Institute awards the CFA (Chartered Financial Analyst) designation. This site provides information about the CFA designation, CFA Institute publications, investor education, and various Internet resources.

http://www.theamericancollege.edu This is the Web site for The American College, which is the training arm of the insurance industry. The American College offers the CLU and ChFC designations, which are typically earned by insurance professionals.

http://www.cfp.net The Certified Financial Planner Board of Standards home page. Contains links to find a CFP™ mark holder and other information about the financial planning profession.

http://www.napfa.org This is the home page for the National Association of Personal Financial Advisors. This is the trade group for fee-only financial planners. Fee-only planners do not sell products on commission, or, should they recommend a commission-generating product, they pass the commission on to the investor. This site features press releases, finding a fee-only planner in your area, a list of financial resources on the Web, and position openings in the financial planning field.

http://www.fpanet.org The Financial Planning Association's Web site. The site offers features and topics of interest to financial planners including information on earning the CFP designation and receiving the *Journal of Financial Planning*.

http://www.asec.org The home page of the American Saving Education Council.

SUMMARY

- In this chapter, we saw that investors need to prudently manage risk within the context of their investment goals and preferences. Income, spending, and investing behavior will change over a person's lifetime.
- We reviewed the importance of developing an investment policy statement before implementing a serious investment plan. By forcing investors to examine their needs, risk tolerance, and familiarity with the capital markets, policy statements help investors correctly identify appropriate

objectives and constraints. In addition, the policy statement becomes a standard by which to judge the performance of the portfolio manager.
- We also reviewed the importance of the asset allocation decision in determining long-run portfolio investment returns and risks. Because the asset allocation decision follows setting the objectives and constraints, it is clear that the success of the investment program depends on the first step, the construction of the policy statement.

SUGGESTED READINGS

Bhatia, Sanjiv, ed. *Managing Assets for Individual Investors.* Charlottesville, VA: AIMR, 1995.

Burns, Terence E., ed. *Investment Counseling for Private Clients.* Charlottesville, VA: AIMR, 1999.

Ellis, Charles D., *Investment Policy: How to Win the Loser's Game.* Homewood, IL: Dow Jones–Irwin, 1985.

Miller, Janet T., ed. *Investment Counseling for Private Clients, III.* Charlottesville, VA: AIMR, 2001.

Mitchell, Roger S., ed. *Investment Counseling for Private Clients, II.* Charlottesville, VA: AIMR, 2000.

QUESTIONS

1. "Young people with little wealth should not invest money in risky assets such as the stock market, because they can't afford to lose what little money they have." Do you agree or disagree with this statement? Why?
2. Your healthy 63-year-old neighbor is about to retire and comes to you for advice. From talking with her, you find out she was planning on taking all the money out of her company's retirement plan and investing it in bond mutual funds and money market funds. What advice should you give her?
3. Discuss how an individual's investment strategy may change as he or she goes through the accumulation, consolidation, spending, and gifting phases of life.
4. Why is a policy statement important?
5. Use the questionnaire "How much risk is right for you?" (Exhibit 2.4) to determine your risk tolerance. Use this information to help write a policy statement for yourself.
6. Your 45-year-old uncle is 20 years away from retirement; your 35-year-old older sister is about 30 years away from retirement. How might their investment policy statements differ?
7. What information is necessary before a financial planner can assist a person in constructing an investment policy statement?
8. Use the Internet to find the home pages for some financial-planning firms. What strategies do they emphasize? What do they say about their asset allocation strategy? What are their firms' emphases—for example, value investing, international diversification, principal preservation, retirement and estate planning?

9. *CFA Examination Level III*

    Mr. Franklin is 70 years of age, is in excellent health, pursues a simple but active lifestyle, and has no children. He has interest in a private company for $90 million and has decided that a medical research foundation will receive half the proceeds now; it will also be the primary beneficiary of his estate upon his death. Mr. Franklin is committed to the foundation's well-being because he believes strongly that, through it, a cure will be found for the disease that killed his wife. He now realizes that an appropriate investment policy and asset allocations are required if his goals are to be met through investment of his considerable assets. Currently, the following assets are available for use in building an appropriate portfolio:

> $45.0 million cash (from sale of the private company interest, net of pending
> $45 million gift to the foundation)
> 10.0 million stocks and bonds ($5 million each)
> 9.0 million warehouse property (now fully leased)
> 1.0 million Franklin residence
> _____
> $65.0 million total available assets

  a. Formulate and justify an investment policy statement setting forth the appropriate guidelines within which future investment actions should take place. Your policy statement must encompass all relevant objective and constraint considerations.

  b. Recommend and justify a long-term asset allocation that is consistent with the investment policy statement you created in Part a. Briefly explain the key assumptions you made in generating your allocation.

PROBLEMS

1. Suppose your first job pays you $28,000 annually. What percentage should your cash reserve contain? How much life insurance should you carry if you are unmarried? How much if you are married with two young children?

2. What is the marginal tax rate for a couple, filing jointly, if their taxable income is $20,000? $40,000? $60,000? What is their tax bill for each of these income levels? What is the average tax rate for each of these income levels?

3. What is the marginal tax rate for a single individual if her taxable income is $20,000? $40,000? $60,000? What is her tax bill for each of these income levels? What is her average tax rate for each of these income levels?

4. a. Someone in the 36 percent tax bracket can earn 9 percent annually on her investments in a tax-exempt IRA account. What will be the value of a one-time $10,000 investment in five years? Ten years? Twenty years?

   b. Suppose the preceding 9 percent return is taxable rather than tax-deferred and the taxes are paid annually. What will be the after-tax value of her $10,000 investment after 5, 10, and 20 years?

5. a. Someone in the 15 percent tax bracket can earn 10 percent on his investments in a tax-exempt IRA account. What will be the value of a $10,000 investment in 5 years? 10 years? 20 years?

   b. Suppose the preceding 10 percent return is taxable rather than tax-deferred. What will be the after-tax value of his $10,000 investment after 5, 10, and 20 years?

APPENDIX
Chapter 2   Objectives and Constraints of Institutional Investors

Institutional investors manage large amounts of funds in the course of their business. They include mutual funds, pension funds, insurance firms, endowments, and banks. In this appendix, we review the characteristics of various institutional investors and discuss their typical investment objectives and constraints.

Mutual Funds

A mutual fund pools sums of money from investors, which are then invested in financial assets. Each mutual fund has its own investment objective, such as capital appreciation, high current income, or money market income. A mutual fund will state its investment objective, and investors choose the funds in which to invest. Two basic constraints face mutual funds: those created by law to protect mutual fund investors and those that represent choices made by the mutual fund's managers. Some of these constraints will be discussed in the mutual fund's prospectus, which must be given to all prospective investors before they purchase shares in a mutual fund. Mutual funds are discussed in more detail in Chapter 24.

Pension Funds

Pension funds are a major component of retirement planning for individuals. As of 2004, U.S. pension assets were nearly $13 trillion. Basically, a firm's pension fund receives contributions from the firm, its employees, or both. The funds are invested with the purpose of giving workers either a lump-sum payment or the promise of an income stream after their retirement. **Defined benefit pension plans** promise to pay retirees a specific income stream after retirement. The size of the benefit is usually based on factors that include the worker's salary, or time of service, or both. The company contributes a certain amount each year to the pension plan; the size of the contribution depends on assumptions concerning future salary increases and the rate of return to be earned on the plan's assets. Under a defined benefit plan, the company carries the risk of paying the future pension benefit to retirees; should investment performance be poor, or should the company be unable to make adequate contributions to the plan, the shortfall must be made up in future years. "Poor" investment performance means the actual return on the plan's assets fell below the assumed **actuarial rate of return.** The actuarial rate is the discount rate used to find the present value of the plan's future obligations and thus determines the size of the firm's annual contribution to the pension plan.

Defined contribution pension plans do not promise set benefits; rather, employees' benefits depend on the size of the contributions made to the pension fund and the returns earned on the fund's investments. Thus, the plan's risk is borne by the employees. Unlike a defined benefit plan, employees' retirement income is not an obligation of the firm.

A pension plan's objectives and constraints depend on whether the plan is a *defined benefit plan* or a *defined contribution plan.* We review each separately below.

Defined Benefit   The plan's risk tolerance depends on the plan's funding status and its actuarial rate. For **underfunded plans** (where the present value of the fund's liabilities to employees exceeds the value of the fund's assets), a more conservative approach toward risk is taken to ensure that the funding gap is closed over time. This may entail a strategy whereby the firm makes larger plan contributions and assumes a lower actuarial rate. **Overfunded plans** (where the present value of the pension liabilities is less than the plan's assets) allow a more aggressive investment strategy in which the firm reduces its contributions and increases the risk exposure of the plan. The return objective is to meet the plan's actuarial rate of return, which is set by actuaries who estimate future pension obligations based on assumptions about future salary increases, current salaries, retirement patterns, worker life expectancies, and the firm's benefit formula. The actuarial rate also helps determine the size of the firm's plan contributions over time.

The liquidity constraint on defined benefit funds is mainly a function of the average age of employees. A younger employee base means less liquidity is needed; an older employee base generally means more liquidity is needed to pay current pension obligations to retirees. The time horizon constraint is also affected by the average age of employees, although some experts recommend using a 5- to 10-year horizon for planning purposes. Taxes are not a major concern to the plan, because pension plans are exempt from paying tax on investment returns. The major legal constraint is that the plan must be run in accordance with the Employee Retirement and Income Security Act (ERISA), and investments must satisfy the "prudent-expert" standard when evaluated in the context of the overall pension plan's portfolio.

Defined Contribution   As the individual worker decides how his contributions to the plan are to be invested, the objectives and constraints for defined contribution plans depend on the individual. Because the worker carries the risk of inadequate retirement funding rather than the firm, defined contribution plans are generally more conservatively invested (some suggest that employees tend to be too conservative). If, however, the plan is considered more of an estate planning tool for a wealthy founder or officer of the firm, a higher risk tolerance and return objective are appropriate because most of the plan's assets will ultimately be owned by the individual's heirs.

The liquidity and time horizon needs for the plan differ depending on the average age of the employees and the degree of employee turnover within the firm. Similar to defined benefit plans, defined contribution plans are tax-exempt and are governed by the provisions of ERISA.

Endowment Funds

Endowment funds arise from contributions made to charitable or educational institutions. Rather than immediately spending the funds, the organization invests the money for the purpose of providing a future stream of income to the organization. The investment policy of an endowment fund is the result of a "tension" between the organization's need for current income and the desire for a growing stream of income in the future to protect against inflation.

To meet the institution's operating budget needs, the fund's return objective is often set by adding the spending rate (the amount taken out of the funds each year) and the expected inflation rate. Funds that have more risk-tolerant trustees may have a higher spending rate than those overseen by more risk-averse trustees. Because a total return approach usually serves to meet the return objective over time, the organization is generally withdrawing both income and capital gain returns to meet budgeted needs. The risk tolerance of an endowment fund is largely affected by the collective risk tolerance of the organization's trustees.

Due to the fund's long-term time horizon, liquidity requirements are minor except for the need to spend part of the endowment each year and maintain a cash reserve for emergencies. Many endowments are tax-exempt, although income from some private foundations can be taxed at either a 1 percent or 2 percent rate. Short-term capital gains are taxable, but long-term capital gains are not. Regulatory and legal constraints arise on the state level, where most endowments are regulated. Unique needs and preferences may affect investment strategies, especially among college or religious endowments, which sometimes have strong preferences about social investing issues.

Insurance Companies

The investment objectives and constraints for an insurance company depend on whether it is a life insurance company or a nonlife (such as a property and casualty) insurance firm.

Life Insurance Companies   Except for firms dealing only in term life insurance, life insurance firms collect premiums during a person's lifetime that must be invested until a death benefit is paid to the insurance contract's beneficiaries. At any time, the insured can turn in her policy and receive its cash surrender value. Discussing investment policy for an insurance firm is also complicated by the insurance industry's proliferation of insurance and quasi-investment products.

Basically, an insurance company wants to earn a positive "spread," which is the difference between the rate of return on investment minus the rate of return it credits its various policyholders. This concept is similar to a defined benefit pension fund that tries to earn a rate of return in excess of its actuarial rate. If the spread is positive, the insurance firm's surplus reserve account rises; if not, the surplus account declines by an amount reflecting the negative spread. A growing surplus is an important competitive tool for life insurance companies. Attractive investment returns allow the company to advertise better policy returns than those of its competitors. A growing surplus also allows the firm to offer new products and expand insurance volume.

Because life insurance companies are quasi-trust funds for savings, fiduciary principles limit the risk tolerance of the invested funds. The National Association of Insurance Commissioners (NAIC) establishes risk categories for bonds and stocks; companies with excessive investments in higher-risk categories must set aside extra funds in a mandatory securities valuation reserve (MSVR) to protect policyholders against losses.

Insurance companies' liquidity needs have increased over the years due to increases in policy surrenders and product-mix changes. A company's time horizon depends upon its specific product mix. Life insurance policies require longer-term investments, whereas guaranteed insurance contracts (GICs) and shorter-term annuities require shorter investment time horizons.

Tax rules changed considerably for insurance firms in the 1980s. For tax purposes, investment returns are divided into two components: first, the policyholder's share, which is the return portion covering the actuarially assumed rate of return needed to fund reserves; and second, the balance that is transferred to reserves. Unlike pensions and endowments, life insurance firms pay income and capital gains taxes at the corporate tax rates on this second component of return.

Except for the NAIC, most insurance regulation is on the state level. Regulators oversee the eligible asset classes and the reserves (MSVR) necessary for each asset class and enforce the "prudent-expert" investment standard. Audits ensure that various accounting rules and investment regulations are followed.

Nonlife Insurance Companies   Cash outflows are somewhat predictable for life insurance firms, based on their mortality tables. In contrast, the cash flows required by major accidents, disasters, and lawsuit settlements are not as predictable for nonlife insurance firms.

Due to their fiduciary responsibility to claimants, risk exposures are low to moderate. Depending on the specific company and competitive pressures, premiums may be affected by both the probability of a claim and the investment returns earned by the firm. Typically, casualty insurance firms invest their insurance reserves in relatively safe bonds to provide needed income to pay claims; capital and surplus funds are invested in equities for their growth potential. As with life insurers, property and casualty firms have a stronger competitive position when their surplus accounts are larger than those of their competitors. Many insurers now focus on a total return objective as a means to increase their surplus accounts over time.

Because of uncertain claim patterns, liquidity is a concern for property and casualty insurers who also want liquidity so they can switch between taxable and tax-exempt investments as their underwriting activities generate losses and profits. The time horizon for investments is typically shorter than that of life insurers, although many invest in long-term bonds to earn the higher yields available on these instruments. Investing strategy for the firm's surplus account focuses on long-term growth.

Regulation of property and casualty firms is more permissive than for life insurers. Similar to life companies, states regulate classes and quality of investments for a certain percentage of the firm's assets. Beyond this restriction, insurers can invest in many different types and qualities of instruments, although some states limit the proportion that can be invested in real estate assets.

Banks

Pension funds, endowments, and insurance firms obtain virtually free funds for investment purposes. Not so with banks. To have funds to lend, they must attract investors in a competitive interest rate environment. They compete against other banks and also against companies that offer other investment vehicles, from bonds to common stocks. A bank's success relies primarily on its ability to generate returns in excess of its funding costs.

A bank tries to maintain a positive difference between its cost of funds and its returns on assets. If banks anticipate falling interest rates, they will try to invest in longer-term assets to lock in the returns while seeking short-term deposits, whose interest cost is expected to fall over time. When banks expect rising rates, they will try to lock in longer-term deposits with fixed-interest costs, while investing funds short term to capture rising interest rates. The risk of such strategies is that losses may occur should a bank incorrectly forecast the direction of interest rates. The aggressiveness of a bank's strategy will be related to the size of its capital ratio and the oversight of regulators.

Banks need substantial liquidity to meet withdrawals and loan demand. A bank has two forms of liquidity. *Internal liquidity* is provided by a bank's investment portfolio that includes highly liquid assets. A bank has *external liquidity* if it can borrow funds in the federal funds markets (where banks lend reserves to other banks), from the Federal Reserve Bank's discount window, or if it can sell certificates of deposit at attractive rates.

Banks have a short time horizon for several reasons. First, they have a strong need for liquidity. Second, because they want to maintain an adequate interest revenue–interest expense spread, they generally focus on shorter-term investments to avoid interest rate risk and to avoid getting "locked in" to a long-term revenue source. Third, because banks typically offer short-term deposit accounts (demand deposits, NOW accounts, and such), they need to match the maturity of their assets and liabilities to avoid taking undue risks.[8]

Banks are heavily regulated by numerous state and federal agencies. The Federal Reserve Board, the Comptroller of the Currency, and the Federal Deposit Insurance Corporation all oversee various components of bank operations. The Glass-Steagall Act restricts the equity investments that banks can make. Unique situations that affect each bank's investment policy depend on their size, market, and management skills in matching asset and liability sensitivity to interest rates. For example, a bank in a small community may have many customers who deposit their money with it for the sake of convenience. A bank in a more populated area will find its deposit flows are more sensitive to interest rates and competition from nearby banks.

Institutional Investment Summary

Among the great variety of institutions, each institution has its "typical" investment objectives and constraints. This discussion has indicated the differences that exist among types of institutions and some of the major issues confronting them. Notably, just as with individual investors, "cookie-cutter" policy statements are inappropriate for institutional investors. The specific objectives, constraints, and investment strategies must be determined on a case-by-case basis.

---

[8]An asset/liability mismatch caused the ultimate downfall of savings and loan associations. They attracted short-term liabilities (deposit accounts) and invested in long-term assets (mortgages). When interest rates became more volatile in the early 1980s and short-term rates increased dramatically, S&Ls suffered significant losses.

Chapter 3

Selecting Investments in a Global Market*

After you read this chapter, you should be able to answer the following questions:

- Why should investors have a global perspective regarding their investments?
- What has happened to the relative size of U.S. and foreign stock and bond markets?
- What are the differences in the rates of return on U.S. and foreign securities markets?
- How can changes in currency exchange rates affect the returns that U.S. investors experience on foreign securities?
- Is there additional advantage to diversifying in international markets beyond the benefits of domestic diversification?
- What alternative securities are available? What are their cash flow and risk properties?
- What are the historical return and risk characteristics of the major investment instruments?
- What is the relationship among the returns for foreign and domestic investment instruments? What is the implication of these relationships for portfolio diversification?

Individuals are willing to defer current consumption for many reasons. Some save for their children's college tuition or their own; others wish to accumulate down payments for a home, car, or boat; others want to amass adequate retirement funds for the future. Whatever the reason for an investment program, the techniques we used in Chapter 1 to measure risk and return will help you evaluate alternative investments.

But what are those alternatives? Thus far, we have said little about the investment opportunities available in financial markets. In this chapter, we address this issue by surveying investment alternatives. This is essential background for making the asset allocation decision discussed in Chapter 2 and for later chapters where we analyze several individual investments, such as bonds, common stock, and other securities. It is also important when we consider how to construct and evaluate portfolios of investments.

As an investor in the 21st century, you have an array of investment choices unavailable a few decades ago. As discussed by Miller (1991), a combination of dynamic financial markets,

*The authors acknowledge data collection help on this chapter from Edgar Norton of Illinois State University and David J. Wright from the University of Wisconsin–Parkside.

technological advances, and new regulations have resulted in numerous new investment instruments and expanded trading opportunities. Improvements in communications and relaxation of international regulations have made it easier for investors to trade in both domestic and global markets. Telecommunications networks enable U.S. brokers to reach security exchanges in London, Tokyo, and other European and Asian cities as easily as those in New York, Chicago, and other U.S. cities. The competitive environment in the brokerage industry and the deregulation of the banking sector have made it possible for more financial institutions to compete for investor dollars. This has spawned investment vehicles with a variety of maturities, risk–return characteristics, and cash flow patterns. In this chapter, we examine some of these choices.

As an investor, you need to understand the differences among investments so you can build a properly diversified **portfolio** that conforms to your objectives. That is, you should seek to acquire a group of investments with different patterns of returns over time. If chosen carefully, such portfolios minimize risk for a given level of return because low or negative rates of return on some investments during a period of time are offset by above-average returns on others. The goal is to build a balanced portfolio of investments with relatively stable overall rates of return. A major goal of this text is to help you understand and evaluate the risk–return characteristics of investment portfolios. An appreciation of alternative security types is the starting point for this analysis.

This chapter is divided into three main sections. Because investors can choose securities from around the world, we initially look at a combination of reasons why investors *should* include foreign as well as domestic securities in their portfolios. Taken together, these reasons provide a compelling case for global investing.

In the second section of this chapter, we discuss securities in domestic and global markets, describing their main features and cash flow patterns. You will see that the varying risk–return characteristics of alternative investments suit the preferences of different investors.

The third and final section contains the historical risk and return performance of several investment instruments from around the world and examines the relationship among the returns for many of these securities. These results provide strong empirical support for global investing.

THE CASE FOR GLOBAL INVESTMENTS

Twenty years ago, the bulk of investments available to individual investors consisted of U.S. stocks and bonds. Now, however, a call to your broker gives you access to a wide range of securities sold throughout the world. Currently, you can purchase stock in General Motors or Toyota, U.S. Treasury bonds or Japanese government bonds, a mutual fund that invests in U.S. biotechnology companies, a global growth stock fund or a German stock fund, or options on a U.S. stock index.

Several changes have caused this explosion of investment opportunities. For one, the growth and development of numerous foreign financial markets, such as those in Japan, the United Kingdom, and Germany, as well as in emerging markets, such as China, have made these markets accessible and viable for investors around the world. U.S. investment firms have recognized this opportunity and established facilities in these countries aided by advances in telecommunications technology that allowed constant contact with offices and financial markets around the world. In addition to the efforts by U.S. firms, foreign firms and investors undertook counterbalancing initiatives, including significant mergers of firms and security exchanges. As a result, as described by Pardee (1987), investors and investment firms can trade securities in markets around the world.

Three interrelated reasons U.S. investors should think of constructing global investment portfolios can be summarized as follows:

1. When investors compare the absolute and relative sizes of U.S. and foreign markets for stocks and bonds, they see that ignoring foreign markets reduces their choices to less than 50 percent of available investment opportunities. Because more opportunities broaden your range of risk–return choices, it makes sense to evaluate foreign securities when selecting investments and building a portfolio.
2. The rates of return available on non-U.S. securities often have substantially exceeded those for U.S.-only securities. The higher returns on non-U.S. *equities* can be justified by the higher growth rates for the countries where they are issued.
3. A major tenet of investment theory is that investors should diversify their portfolios. Because the relevant factor when diversifying a portfolio is low correlation between asset returns, diversification with foreign securities that have very low correlation with U.S. securities can help to substantially reduce portfolio risk.

In this section, we analyze these reasons to demonstrate the advantages to a growing role of foreign financial markets for U.S. investors and to assess the benefits and risks of trading in these markets. Notably, the reasons that global investing is appropriate for U.S. investors are generally even more compelling for non-U.S. investors.

Relative Size of U.S. Financial Markets

Prior to 1970, the securities traded in the U.S. stock and bond markets comprised about 65 percent of all the securities available in world capital markets. Therefore, a U.S. investor selecting securities strictly from U.S. markets had a fairly complete set of investments available. Under these conditions, most U.S. investors probably believed that it was not worth the time and effort to expand their investment universe to include the limited investments available in foreign markets. That situation has changed dramatically over the past 36 years. Currently, investors who ignore foreign stock and bond markets limit their investment choices substantially.

Exhibit 3.1 shows the breakdown of securities available in world capital markets in 1969 and 2003. Not only has the overall value of all securities increased dramatically (from $2.3 trillion to $70.9 trillion), but the composition has also changed. Concentrating on proportions of bond and equity investments, the exhibit shows that U.S. dollar bonds and U.S. equity securities made up 53 percent of the total value of all securities in 1969 versus 28.4 percent for the total of nondollar bonds and equity. By 2003, U.S. bonds and equities accounted for 45.4 percent of the total securities market versus 44.1 percent for nondollar bonds and stocks. These data indicate that if you consider only the stock and bond market, the U.S. proportion of this combined market has declined from 65 percent of the total in 1969 to about 51 percent in 2003.

The point is, the U.S. security markets now include a smaller proportion of the total world capital market, and it is likely that this trend will continue. The faster economic growth of many other countries compared to the United States will require foreign governments and individual companies to issue debt and equity securities to finance this growth. Therefore, U.S. investors should consider investing in foreign securities because of the growing importance of these foreign securities in world capital markets. Put another way, not investing in foreign stocks and bonds means you are ignoring about 49 percent of the securities that are available to you. This approximate 50-50 breakdown is about the same for stocks or bonds alone.

| Exhibit 3.1 | Total Investable Assets in the Global Capital Market |

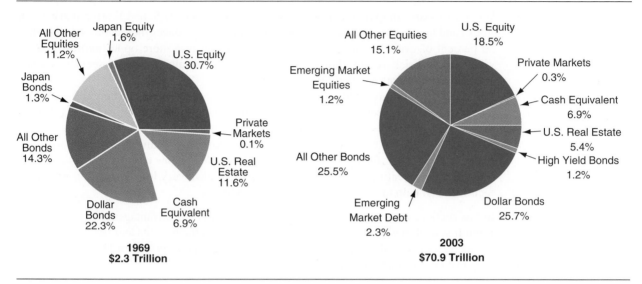

Source: UBS Global Asset Management.

Rates of Return on U.S. and Foreign Securities

An examination of the rates of return on U.S. and foreign securities not only demonstrates that many non-U.S. securities provide superior rates of return but also shows the impact of the exchange rate risk discussed in Chapter 1.

Global Bond-Market Returns Exhibit 3.2 reports annual compound rates of return for several major international bond markets for 1985–2003. The returns have been converted to U.S. dollar returns, so the exhibit shows mean annual returns and standard deviations that a U.S.-based investor would receive. An analysis of the returns in Exhibit 3.2 indicates that the performance of the U.S. bond market ranked fourth out of the six countries. Part of the reason for the better performance in dollar terms of the non-U.S. markets is that the dollar generally weakened during this time frame, giving U.S. investors a boost to their foreign returns. Put another way, U.S. investors who invested in these foreign bonds received the return on the bonds equal to local investors but also received a return for holding the currency that appreciated relative to the U.S. dollar.

Global Equity-Market Returns Exhibit 3.3 shows the annual returns in U.S. dollars for 34 major equity markets from 1997 through 2003. In spite of the U.S. market's stellar performance in the latter half of the 1990s, its average rank in U.S. dollar returns in 1997–2003 was 17.5 out of 34 countries (and it was in the top 10 only one year). Its performance was well behind the returns of numerous stock markets in these years.

These results for equity and bond markets around the world indicate that investors who limit themselves to the U.S. market may well experience rates of return below those in many other countries.

Risk of Combined Country Investments

Thus far, we have discussed the risk and return results for individual countries. In Chapter 1, we considered the idea of combining a number of assets into a portfolio and noted that

Exhibit 3.2	**Long-Term Government Bond Compound Annual Rates of Return in U.S. Dollars: 1985–2003**

	Arithmetic Mean (%)	Geometric Mean (%)	Standard Deviation (%)
Canada	12.42	11.75	12.37
France	15.62	14.61	15.49
Germany	9.70	8.86	13.79
Japan	10.84	9.58	17.06
United Kingdom	14.52	13.33	16.71
United States	11.33	10.83	10.54

Source: Citigroup.

investors should create diversified portfolios to reduce the variability of the returns over time. We discussed how proper diversification reduces the variability (our measure of risk) of the portfolio because alternative investments have different patterns of returns over time. Specifically, when the rates of return on some investments are negative or below average, other investments in the portfolio will be experiencing above-average rates of return. Therefore, if a portfolio is properly diversified, it should provide a more stable rate of return for the total portfolio (that is, it will have a lower standard deviation and therefore less risk). Although we will discuss and demonstrate portfolio theory in detail in Chapter 7, we need to consider the concept at this point to fully understand the benefits of global investing.

The way to measure whether two investments will contribute to diversifying a portfolio is to compute the correlation coefficient between their rates of return over time. Correlation coefficients can range from +1.00 to −1.00. A correlation of +1.00 means that the rates of return for these two investments move exactly together. Combining investments that move together in a portfolio would not help diversify the portfolio because they have identical rate-of-return patterns over time. In contrast, a correlation coefficient of −1.00 means that the rates of return for two investments move exactly opposite to each other. When one investment is experiencing above-average rates of return, the other is suffering through similar below-average rates of return. Combining two investments with large negative correlation in a portfolio would be ideal for diversification because it would stabilize the rates of return over time, reducing the standard deviation of the portfolio rates of return and hence the risk of the portfolio. Therefore, if you want to diversify your portfolio and reduce your risk, you want an investment that has either *low positive* correlation, *zero* correlation, or, ideally, *negative correlation* with the other investments in your portfolio. With this in mind, the following discussion considers the correlations of returns among U.S. bonds and stocks with the returns on foreign bonds and stocks.

Global Bond Portfolio Risk   Exhibit 3.4 lists the correlation coefficients between rates of return for bonds in the United States and bonds in major foreign markets in U.S. dollar terms from 1985 to 2003. For a U.S. investor, the important correlations are between the rates of return in U.S. dollars, and these correlations averaged less than 0.50.

These low positive correlations among returns in U.S. dollars mean that U.S. investors have substantial opportunities for risk reduction through global diversification of bond portfolios. A U.S. investor who bought bonds in these markets would substantially reduce the standard deviation of a well-diversified U.S. portfolio.

Exhibit 3.3 | Annual Returns in U.S.-Dollar Terms

PERFORMANCE OF DOW JONES GLOBAL INDEXES

Country	Year 2003 Returns U.S.-Dollar Returns	Rank	Year 2002 Returns U.S.-Dollar Returns	Rank	Year 2001 Returns U.S.-Dollar Returns	Rank	Year 2000 Returns U.S.-Dollar Returns	Rank	Year 1999 Returns U.S.-Dollar Returns	Rank	Year 1998 Returns U.S.-Dollar Returns	Rank	Year 1997 Returns U.S.-Dollar Returns	Rank
U.S.	28.44%	31	-23.32%	28	-13.09%	12	-10.15%	11	18.90%	21	26.78%	13	31.69%	7
Australia	45.95%	15	-3.06%	7	-1.30%	8	-10.03%	10	20.53%	20	5.40%	19	-10.31%	21
Austria	58.26%	9	21.16%	3	0.05%	7	-15.40%	17	-6.97%	30	-3.00%	22	-1.72%	19
Belgium	40.78%	18	-9.48%	10	-13.30%	13	-13.95%	13	-17.29%	34	62.73%	4	11.85%	14
Brazil	131.40%	2	-36.16%	34	-23.85%	23	-10.25%	12	50.99%	10	-46.19%	33		
Canada	51.54%	11	-12.56%	15	-20.09%	18	0.85%	6	42.98%	11	-5.10%	24	13.44%	13
Chile	83.53%	4	-14.32%	16	-4.08%	10	-17.61%	20	32.91%	17	-28.50%	28		
Denmark	49.35%	14	-14.54%	17	-23.21%	20	22.23%	1	5.38%	26	3.26%	20	34.05%	6
Finland	17.33%	34	-29.68%	31	-37.83%	33	-15.23%	16	153.14%	1	94.63%	2	11.53%	16
France	39.11%	20	-20.47%	24	-23.44%	22	-7.89%	8	32.18%	18	40.26%	7	22.67%	10
Germany	61.33%	7	-32.36%	33	-24.25%	24	-15.96%	18	20.87%	19	28.38%	12	21.20%	11
Greece	65.08%	6	-27.79%	29			-42.09%	29	39.30%	15	86.24%	3	39.27%	3
Hong Kong	38.69%	21	-19.90%	23	-20.52%	19	-14.96%	15	73.20%	5	-10.34%	25	-25.06%	24
Indonesia	65.95%	5	30.27%	2	-18.57%	16	-56.44%	33	77.31%	4	-41.94%	32	-63.25%	28
Ireland	44.26%	16	-21.38%	25	-3.50%	9	7.38%	4	-13.24%	33	38.05%	8	24.05%	9
Italy	38.35%	23	-10.33%	12	-28.23%	29	-5.46%	7	6.45%	25	50.57%	5	36.95%	5
Japan	37.61%	24	-9.36%	9	-29.47%	31	-31.15%	27	67.26%	7	5.42%	18	-26.39%	25
Malaysia	26.19%	32	-6.05%	8	3.52%	6	-20.81%	23	42.30%	12	-2.19%	21	-70.03%	30

Mexico	31.46%	28	−15.17%	19	19.06%	2	−22.25%	24	91.01%	3	−38.16%	31	54.21%	1
Netherlands	25.27%	33	−22.46%	27	−23.29%	21	−8.03%	9	7.24%	24	29.95%	11	24.19%	8
New Zealand	50.85%	12	16.63%	5	6.28%	4	−31.62%	28	9.27%	23	−23.57%	27	−17.98%	23
Norway	40.62%	19	−11.37%	13	−25.36%	27	2.43%	5	33.29%	16	−31.87%	30	6.55%	18
Philippines	49.62%	13	−19.04%	22	−27.33%	28	−43.70%	30	2.59%	28	14.47%	15	−62.36%	27
Portugal	38.53%	22	−15.79%	20	−24.47%	25	−20.45%	22	−7.17%	31	30.91%	10	51.04%	2
Singapore	36.27%	26	−9.82%	11	−19.91%	17	−23.75%	25	56.18%	9	−4.82%	23	−37.83%	26
South Africa	41.78%	17	43.60%	1	−24.81%	26	−19.20%	21	64.35%	8	−31.43%	29	−11.52%	22
South Korea	31.45%	29	4.88%	6	45.29%	1	−58.77%	34	110.63%	2	117.12%	1	−68.68%	29
Spain	55.59%	10	−14.77%	18	−13.44%	14	−25.29%	26	4.58%	27	48.09%	6	10.46%	17
Sweden	60.06%	8	−30.83%	32	−30.34%	32	−17.15%	19	70.72%	6	6.23%	17	11.56%	15
Switzerland	33.14%	27	−11.86%	14	−29.26%	30	16.21%	2	−6.70%	29	21.13%	14	38.36%	4
Taiwan	36.63%	25	−22.44%	26	11.51%	3	−45.43%	31	42.30%	13	−19.45%	26	−4.73%	20
Thailand	138.70%	1	17.75%	4	4.62%	5	−50.96%	32	39.46%	14	31.89%	9	−75.83%	31
U.K.	28.54%	30	−17.26%	21	−16.58%	15	−14.60%	14	14.26%	22	13.40%	16	17.79%	12
Venezuela	119.88%	3	−28.27%	30	−11.67%	11	11.93%	3	−12.57%	32	−55.46%	34		

Source: *The Wall Street Journal* (various issues) and author calculations.

Exhibit 3.4	Correlation Coefficients between U.S. Dollar Rates of Return on Bonds in the United States and Major Foreign Markets: 1985–2003 (Monthly Data)

	Correlation Coefficient
Canada	0.65
France	0.48
Germany	0.57
Japan	0.20
United Kingdom	0.39
Average	0.46

Source: Data from MSCI.

Why do these correlation coefficients for returns between U.S. bonds and those of various foreign countries differ? That is, why is the U.S.–Canada correlation 0.65 whereas the U.S.–Japan correlation is only 0.20? The answer is because the international trade patterns, economic growth, fiscal policies, and monetary policies of the countries differ. We do not have an integrated world economy but, rather, a collection of economies that are related to one another in different ways. As an example, the U.S. and Canadian economies are closely related because of these countries' geographic proximity, similar domestic economic policies, and the extensive trade between them. Each is the other's largest trading partner. In contrast, the United States has less trade with Japan and the fiscal and monetary policies of the two countries differ dramatically. For example, the U.S. economy was growing during much of the 1990s while the Japanese economy was in a recession.

The point is, macroeconomic differences cause the correlation of bond returns between the United States and each country to likewise differ. These differing correlations make it worthwhile to diversify with foreign bonds, and the different correlations indicate which countries will provide the greatest reduction in the standard deviation (risk) of bond portfolio returns for a U.S. investor.

Also, *the correlation of returns between a single pair of countries changes over time* because the factors influencing the correlations, such as international trade, economic growth, fiscal policy, and monetary policy, change over time. A change in any of these variables will produce a change in how the economies are related and in the relationship between returns on bonds. For example, the correlation in U.S. dollar returns between U.S. and Japanese bonds was 0.07 in the late 1960s and 1970s; it was 0.25 in the 1980s and 0.15 in the early 1990s but only about 0.05 in the 1995–2003 time frame.

Exhibit 3.5 shows what happens to the risk–return trade-off when we combine U.S. and foreign bonds. A comparison of a completely non-U.S. portfolio (100 percent foreign) and a 100 percent U.S. portfolio indicates that the non-U.S. portfolio has both a higher rate of return and a higher standard deviation of returns than the U.S. portfolio. Combining the two portfolios in different proportions provides an interesting set of points.

As we will discuss in Chapter 7, the expected rate of return is a weighted average of the two portfolios. In contrast, the risk (standard deviation) of the combination is *not* a weighted average but also depends on the correlation between the two portfolios. In this example, the risk levels of the combined portfolios decline below those of the individual portfolios. Therefore, by adding foreign bonds that have low correlation with a portfolio of U.S. bonds, a U.S.

| **Exhibit 3.5** | **Risk–Return Trade-Off for International Bond Portfolios** |

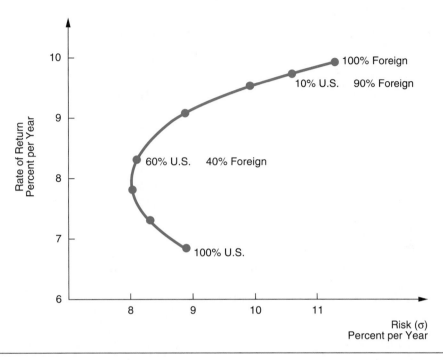

Source: Kenneth Cholerton, Pierre Piergerits, and Bruno Solnik, "Why Invest in Foreign Currency Bonds?" *Journal of Portfolio Management* 12, no. 4 (Summer 1986): 4–8. This copyrighted material is reprinted with permission from *Journal of Portfolio Management,* a publication of Institutional Investor, Inc.

investor is able to not only increase the expected rate of return but also reduce the risk compared to a total U.S. bond portfolio.

Global Equity Portfolio Risk   The correlation of world equity markets resembles that for bonds. Exhibit 3.6 lists the correlation coefficients between monthly equity returns in U.S. dollars of each country and the U.S. market for the period from 1985 to 2003. Only 2 of the 11 correlations between U.S. dollar returns were over 0.60, and the average correlation was only 0.55.

These relatively small positive correlations between U.S. stocks and foreign stocks have similar implications to those derived for bonds. Investors can reduce the overall risk of their stock portfolios by including foreign stocks.

Exhibit 3.7 demonstrates the impact of international equity diversification. These curves demonstrate that, as you increase the number of randomly selected securities in a portfolio, the standard deviation will decline due to the benefits of diversification *within your own country.* This is referred to as *domestic diversification.* After a certain number of securities (30 to 40), the curve will flatten out at a risk level that reflects the basic market risk for the domestic economy. The lower curve illustrates the benefits of international diversification. This curve demonstrates that adding foreign securities to a U.S. portfolio to create a global portfolio enables an investor to experience lower overall risk because the non-U.S. securities are not correlated with our economy or our stock market, allowing the investor to eliminate some of the basic market risks of the U.S. economy.

Exhibit 3.6	Correlation Coefficients between U.S. Dollar Rates of Return on Common Stocks in the United States and Major Foreign Stock Markets: 1985–2003

	Correlation Coefficient
Australia	0.48
Canada	0.77
France	0.58
Germany	0.54
Italy	0.37
Japan	0.31
Netherlands	0.66
Spain	0.55
Sweden	0.57
Switzerland	0.53
United Kingdom	0.64
Average	0.55

Source: Correlation table computed by the authors using monthly data from MSCI.

Exhibit 3.7	Risk Reduction through National and International Diversification

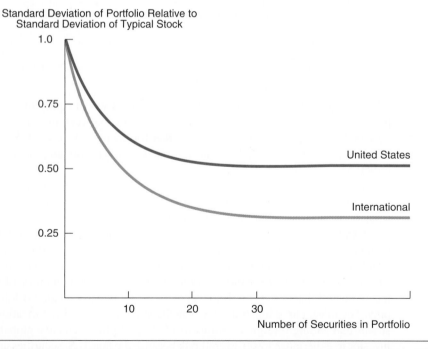

Source: Copyright 1974, Association for Investment Management and Research. Reproduced and republished from "Why Not Diversify Internationally Rather Than Domestically?" in the *Financial Analysts Journal,* July/August 1974, with permission from the Association for Investment Management and Research. All Rights Reserved.

To see how this works, consider, for example, the effect of inflation and interest rates on all U.S. securities. As discussed in Chapter 1, all U.S. securities will be affected by these variables. In contrast, a Japanese stock is mainly affected by what happens in the Japanese economy and will typically not be affected by changes in U.S. variables. Thus, adding Japanese, German, and Italian stocks to a U.S. stock portfolio reduces the portfolio risk of the global portfolio to a level that reflects only worldwide systematic factors.

Summary on Global Investing   At this point, we have considered the relative size of the market for non-U.S. bonds and stocks and found that it has grown in size and importance, becoming too big to ignore. We have also examined the rates of return for foreign bond and stock investments and determined that, when considering results, their rates of return were often superior to those in the U.S. market. Finally, we discussed constructing a portfolio of investments and the importance of diversification in reducing the variability of returns over time, which reduces the risk of the portfolio. As noted, to have successful diversification, an investor should combine investments with low positive or negative correlations between rates of return. An analysis of the correlation between rates of return on U.S. and foreign bonds and stocks indicated a consistent pattern of relatively low positive correlations. Therefore, the existence of similar rates of return on foreign securities combined with low correlation coefficients indicates that adding foreign stocks and bonds to a U.S. portfolio *will almost certainly reduce the risk of the portfolio and can possibly increase its average return.*

As promised, several rather compelling reasons exist for adding foreign securities to a U.S. portfolio. Therefore, developing a global investment perspective is important because such an approach has been shown to be justified, and this current trend in the investment world is expected to continue. Implementing this new global investment perspective will not be easy because it requires an understanding of new terms, instruments (such as Eurobonds), and institutions (such as non-U.S. stock and bond markets). Still, the effort is justified because you are developing a set of skills and a way of thinking that will enhance your investing results.

The next section presents an overview of investment alternatives from around the world, beginning with fixed-income investments and progressing through numerous alternatives.

GLOBAL INVESTMENT CHOICES

This section provides an important foundation for subsequent chapters in which we describe techniques to value individual investments and combine alternative investments into properly diversified portfolios that conform to your risk–return objectives. In this section, we briefly describe the numerous investment alternatives available. The purpose of this survey is to introduce each of these investment alternatives so you can appreciate the full spectrum of opportunities.

The investments are divided by asset classes. First, we describe fixed-income investments, including bonds and preferred stocks. In the second subsection, we discuss equity investments, and the third subsection contains a discussion of special equity instruments, such as warrants and options, which have characteristics of both fixed-income and equity instruments. In subsection four, we consider futures contracts that allow for a wide range of return–risk profiles. The fifth subsection considers investment companies.

All these investments are called *financial assets* because their payoffs are in money. In contrast, *real assets,* such as real estate, are discussed in the sixth subsection. We conclude with assets that are considered *low liquidity investments* because of the relative difficulty in buying and selling them. This includes art, antiques, coins, stamps, and precious gems.

The final section of the chapter describes the historical return and risk patterns for many individual investment alternatives and the correlations among the returns for these investments. This additional background and perspective will help you evaluate individual investments in order to build a properly diversified portfolio of global investments.

Fixed-Income Investments

Fixed-income investments have a contractually mandated payment schedule. Their investment contracts promise specific payments at predetermined times, although the legal force behind the promise varies and this affects their risks and required returns. At one extreme, if the issuing firm does not make its payment at the appointed time, creditors can declare the issuing firm bankrupt. In other cases (for example, income bonds), the issuing firm must make payments only if it earns profits. In yet other instances (for example, preferred stock), the issuing firm does not have to make payments unless its board of directors votes to do so.

Investors who acquire fixed-income securities (except preferred stock) are really lenders to the issuers. Specifically, you lend some amount of money, the *principal,* to the borrower. In return, the borrower promises to make periodic interest payments and to pay back the principal at the maturity of the loan.

Savings Accounts   You might not think of savings accounts as fixed-income investments, yet an individual who deposits funds in a savings account at a financial institution is really lending money to the institution and, as a result, earning a fixed payment. These investments are considered to be convenient, liquid, and low risk because almost all are insured. Consequently, their rates of return are generally low compared with other alternatives. Several versions of these accounts have been developed to appeal to investors with differing objectives.

Passbook savings accounts have no minimum balance, and funds may be withdrawn at any time with little loss of interest. Due to their flexibility, the promised interest on passbook accounts is relatively low.

For investors with larger amounts of funds who are willing to give up liquidity, financial institutions developed **certificates of deposit (CDs)**, which require minimum deposits (typically $500) and have fixed durations (usually three months, six months, one year, two years). The promised rates on CDs are higher than those for passbook savings accounts, and the rate increases with the size and the duration of the deposit. An investor who wants to cash in a CD prior to its stated expiration date must pay a heavy penalty in the form of a much lower interest rate.

Investors with large sums of money ($10,000 or more) can invest in Treasury bills (T-bills)—short-term obligations (maturing in 3 to 12 months) of the U.S. government. To compete against T-bills, banks issue money market certificates, which require minimum investments of $10,000 and have minimum maturities of six months. The promised rate on these certificates fluctuates at some premium over the weekly rate on six-month T-bills. Investors can redeem these certificates only at the bank of issue, and they incur penalties if they withdraw their funds before maturity.

Capital Market Instruments   **Capital market instruments** are fixed-income obligations that trade in the secondary market, which means you can buy and sell them to other individuals or institutions. Capital market instruments fall into four categories: (1) U.S. Treasury securities, (2) U.S. government agency securities, (3) municipal bonds, and (4) corporate bonds.

U.S. Treasury Securities   All government securities issued by the U.S. Treasury are fixed-income instruments. They may be bills, notes, or bonds depending on their times to maturity. Specifically, bills mature in one year or less, notes in over one to 10 years, and bonds in more than 10 years from time of issue. U.S. government obligations are essentially free of credit risk because there is little chance of default and they are highly liquid.

U.S. Government Agency Securities   Agency securities are sold by various agencies of the government to support specific programs, but they are not direct obligations of the Treasury. Examples of agencies that issue these bonds include the Federal National Mortgage Association (FNMA or Fannie Mae), which sells bonds and uses the proceeds to purchase mortgages from insurance companies or savings and loans; and the Federal Home Loan Bank (FHLB), which sells bonds and loans the money to its 12 banks, which in turn provide credit to savings and loans and other mortgage-granting institutions. Other agencies are the Government National Mortgage Association (GNMA or Ginnie Mae), Banks for Cooperatives, Federal Land Banks (FLBs), and the Federal Housing Administration (FHA).

Although the securities issued by federal agencies are not direct obligations of the government, they are virtually default-free because it is inconceivable that the government would allow them to default. Also, they are fairly liquid. Because they are not officially guaranteed by the Treasury, they are not considered riskless. Also, because they are not as liquid as Treasury bonds, they typically provide slightly higher returns than Treasury issues.

Municipal Bonds   Municipal bonds are issued by local government entities as either general obligation or revenue bonds. General obligation bonds (GOs) are backed by the full taxing power of the municipality, whereas revenue bonds pay the interest from revenue generated by specific projects (e.g., the revenue to pay the interest on sewer bonds comes from water taxes).

Municipal bonds differ from other fixed-income securities because they are tax-exempt. The interest earned from them is exempt from taxation by the federal government and by the state that issued the bond, provided the investor is a resident of that state. For this reason, municipal bonds are popular with investors in high tax brackets. For an investor having a marginal tax rate of 35 percent, a regular bond with an interest rate of 8 percent yields a net return after taxes of only 5.20 percent [$0.08 \times (1 - 0.35)$]. Such an investor would prefer a tax-free bond of equal risk with a 6 percent yield. This allows municipal bonds to offer yields that are generally 20 to 30 percent lower than yields on comparable taxable bonds.

Corporate Bonds   Corporate bonds are fixed-income securities issued by industrial corporations, public utility corporations, or railroads to raise funds to invest in plant, equipment, or working capital. They can be broken down by issuer, in terms of credit quality (measured by the ratings assigned by an agency on the basis of probability of default), in terms of maturity (short term, intermediate term, or long term), or based on some component of the indenture (sinking fund or call feature).

All bonds include an **indenture**, which is the legal agreement that lists the obligations of the issuer to the bondholder, including the payment schedule and features such as call provisions and sinking funds. **Call provisions** specify when a firm can issue a call for the bonds prior to their maturity, at which time current bondholders must submit the bonds to the issuing firm, which redeems them (that is, pays back the principal and a small premium). A **sinking fund** provision specifies payments the issuer must make to redeem a given percentage of the outstanding issue prior to maturity.

Corporate bonds fall into various categories based on their contractual promises to investors. They will be discussed in order of their seniority.

Secured bonds are the most senior bonds in a firm's capital structure and have the lowest risk of distress or default. They include various secured issues that differ based on the assets that are pledged. **Mortgage bonds** are backed by liens on specific assets, such as land and buildings. In the case of bankruptcy, the proceeds from the sale of these assets are used to pay off the mortgage bondholders. **Collateral trust bonds** are a form of mortgage bond except that the assets backing the bonds are financial assets, such as stocks, notes, and other high-quality bonds. Finally, **equipment trust certificates** are mortgage bonds that are secured by specific pieces of transportation equipment, such as locomotives and boxcars for a railroad and air-planes for an airline.

Debentures are promises to pay interest and principal, but they pledge no specific assets (referred to as *collateral*) in case the firm does not fulfill its promise. This means that the bond-holder depends on the success of the borrower to make the promised payment. Debenture own-ers usually have first call on the firm's earnings and any assets that are not already pledged by the firm as backing for senior secured bonds. If the issuer does not make an interest payment, the debenture owners can declare the firm bankrupt and claim any unpledged assets to pay off the bonds.

Subordinated bonds are similar to debentures, but, in the case of default, subordinated bondholders have claim to the assets of the firm only after the firm has satisfied the claims of all senior secured and debenture bondholders. That is, the claims of subordinated bondholders are secondary to those of other bondholders. Within this general category of subordinated issues, you can find senior subordinated, subordinated, and junior subordinated bonds. Junior subordinated bonds have the weakest claim of all bondholders.

Income bonds stipulate interest payment schedules, but the interest is due and payable only if the issuers earn the income to make the payment by stipulated dates. If the company does not earn the required amount, it does not have to make the interest payment and it cannot be declared bankrupt. Instead, the interest payment is considered in arrears and, if subse-quently earned, it must be paid off. Because the issuing firm is not legally bound to make its interest payments except when the firm earns it, an income bond is not considered as safe as a debenture or a mortgage bond, so income bonds offer higher returns to compensate investors for the added risk. There are a limited number of corporate income bonds. In contrast, income bonds are fairly popular with municipalities because municipal revenue bonds are basically income bonds.

Convertible bonds have the interest and principal characteristics of other bonds, with the added feature that the bondholder has the option to turn them back to the firm in exchange for its common stock. For example, a firm could issue a $1,000 face-value bond and stipulate that owners of the bond could turn the bond in to the issuing corporation and convert it into 40 shares of the firm's common stock. These bonds appeal to investors because they combine the features of a fixed-income security with the option of conversion into the common stock of the firm, should the firm prosper.

Because of their desirable conversion option, convertible bonds generally pay lower inter-est rates than nonconvertible debentures of comparable risk. The difference in the required interest rate increases with the growth potential of the company because this increases the value of the option to convert the bonds into common stock. These bonds are almost always subordinated to the nonconvertible debt of the firm, so they are considered to have higher credit risk and receive a lower credit rating from the bond rating firms.

An alternative to convertible bonds is a debenture with warrants attached. The **warrant** is likewise an option that allows the bondholder to purchase the firm's common stock from the firm at a specified price for a given time period. The specified purchase price for the stock set in the warrant is typically above the price of the stock at the time the firm issues the bond but below the expected future stock price. The warrant makes the debenture more desirable, which lowers its required yield. The warrant also provides the firm with future common stock capital when the holder exercises the warrant and buys the stock from the firm.

Unlike the typical bond that pays interest every six months and its face value at maturity, a **zero coupon bond** promises no interest payments during the life of the bond but only the pay-ment of the principal at maturity. Therefore, the purchase price of the bond is the present value of the principal payment at the required rate of return. For example, the price of a zero coupon bond that promises to pay $10,000 in five years with a required rate of return of 8 percent is $6,756. To find this, assuming semiannual compounding (which is the norm), use the present value factor for 10 periods at 4 percent, which is 0.6756.

Preferred Stock   **Preferred stock** is classified as a fixed-income security because its yearly payment is stipulated as either a coupon (for example, 5 percent of the face value) or a stated dollar amount (for example, $5 preferred). Preferred stock differs from bonds because its payment is a dividend and therefore not legally binding. For each period, the firm's board of directors must vote to pay it, similar to a common stock dividend. Even if the firm earned enough money to pay the preferred stock dividend, the board of directors could theoretically vote to withhold it. Because most preferred stock is cumulative, the unpaid dividends would accumulate to be paid in full at a later time.

Although preferred dividends are not legally binding, as are the interest payments on a bond, they are considered *practically* binding because of the credit implications of a missed dividend. Because corporations can exclude 80 percent of intercompany dividends from taxable income, preferred stocks have become attractive investments for financial corporations. For example, a corporation that owns preferred stock of another firm and receives $100 in dividends can exclude 80 percent of this amount and pay taxes on only 20 percent of it ($20). Assuming a 40 percent tax rate, the tax would only be $8 or 8 percent versus 40 percent on other investment income. Due to this tax benefit, the yield on high-grade preferred stock is typically lower than that on high-grade bonds.

International Bond Investing

As noted earlier, more than half of all fixed-income securities available to U.S. investors are issued by firms in countries outside the United States. Investors identify these securities in different ways: by the country or city of the issuer (for example, United States, United Kingdom, Japan); by the location of the primary trading market (for example, United States, London); by the home country of the major buyers; and by the currency in which the securities are denominated (for example, dollars, yen, euros). We identify foreign bonds by their country of origin and include these other differences in each description.

A **Eurobond** is an international bond denominated in a currency not native to the country where it is issued. Specific kinds of Eurobonds include Eurodollar bonds, Euroyen bonds, and Eurosterling bonds. A Eurodollar bond is denominated in U.S. dollars and sold outside the United States to non-U.S. investors. A specific example would be a U.S. dollar bond issued by General Electric and sold in London. Eurobonds are typically issued in Europe, with the major concentration in London.

Eurobonds can also be denominated in yen. For example, Nippon Steel can issue Euroyen bonds for sale in London. Also, if it appears that investors are looking for foreign currency bonds, a U.S. corporation can issue a Euroyen bond in London.

Yankee bonds are sold in the United States, denominated in U.S. dollars, but issued by foreign corporations or governments. This allows a U.S. citizen to buy the bond of a foreign firm or government but receive all payments in U.S. dollars, eliminating exchange rate risk.

An example would be a U.S. dollar–denominated bond issued by British Airways. Similar bonds are issued in other countries, including the Bulldog Market, which involves British sterling–denominated bonds issued in the United Kingdom by non-British firms, or the Samurai Market, which involves yen-denominated bonds issued in Japan by non-Japanese firms.

International domestic bonds are sold by an issuer within its own country in that country's currency. An example would be a bond sold by Nippon Steel in Japan denominated in yen. A U.S. investor acquiring such a bond would receive maximum diversification but would incur exchange rate risk.

Equity Instruments

This section describes several equity instruments, which differ from fixed-income securities because their returns are not contractual. As a result, you can receive returns that are much better or much worse than what you would receive on a bond. We begin with common stock, the most popular equity instrument and probably the most popular investment instrument.

Common stock represents *ownership* of a firm. Owners of the common stock of a firm share in the company's successes and problems. If—like Wal-Mart, Home Depot, Microsoft, or Intel—the company prospers, the investor receives high rates of return and can become wealthy. In contrast, the investor can lose money if the firm does not do well or even goes bankrupt, as the once formidable K-Mart, Enron, W. T. Grant, and several U.S. airlines all did. In these instances, the firm may be forced to liquidate its assets and pay off all its creditors. Notably, the firm's preferred stockholders and common stock owners receive what is left, which is usually little or nothing. Investing in common stock entails all the advantages and disadvantages of ownership and is a relatively risky investment compared with fixed-income securities.

Common Stock Classifications   When considering an investment in common stock, people tend to divide the vast universe of stocks into categories based on general business lines and by industry within these business lines. The division includes broad classifications for industrial firms, utilities, transportation firms, and financial institutions. Within each of these broad classes are industries. The industrial group, which is very diverse, includes such industries as automobiles, industrial machinery, chemicals, and beverages. Utilities include electrical power companies, gas suppliers, and the water industry. Transportation includes airlines, trucking firms, and railroads. Financial institutions include banks, savings and loans, insurance companies, and investment firms.

An alternative classification scheme might separate domestic (U.S.) and foreign common stocks. We avoid this division because the business line–industry breakdown is more appropriate and useful when constructing a diversified portfolio of global common stock investments. With a global capital market, the focus of analysis should include all the companies in an industry viewed in a global setting. The point is, it is not relevant whether a major chemical firm is located in the United States or Germany, just as it is not relevent whether a computer firm is located in Michigan or California. Therefore, when considering the automobile industry, it is necessary to go beyond pure U.S. auto firms like General Motors and Ford and consider auto firms from throughout the world, such as Honda Motors, Porsche, Daimler-Chrysler, Nissan, and Fiat.

Acquiring Foreign Equities   We begin our discussion on foreign equities regarding how you buy and sell these securities because this procedural information has often been a major impediment. Many investors may recognize the desirability of investing in foreign common stock because of the risk and return characteristics, but they may be intimidated by the logistics of the transaction. The purpose of this section is to alleviate this concern by explaining the alternatives available. Currently, there are several ways to acquire foreign common stock:

1. Purchase or sale of American Depository Receipts (ADRs)
2. Purchase or sale of American shares
3. Direct purchase or sale of foreign shares listed on a U.S. or foreign stock exchange
4. Purchase or sale of international or global mutual funds or exchange-traded funds (ETFs)

Purchase or Sale of American Depository Receipts   The easiest way to acquire foreign shares directly is through **American Depository Receipts (ADRs)**. These are certificates of ownership issued by a U.S. bank that represent indirect ownership of a certain number of shares of a specific foreign firm on deposit in a bank in the firm's home country. ADRs are a convenient way to own foreign shares because the investor buys and sells them in U.S. dollars and receives all dividends in U.S. dollars. Therefore, the price and returns reflect both the domestic returns for the stock and the exchange rate effect. Also, the price of an ADR can reflect the fact that it represents multiple shares—for example, an ADR can be for 5 or 10 shares of the foreign stock. ADRs can be issued at the discretion of a bank based on the demand for the stock. The shareholder absorbs the additional handling costs of an ADR through higher transfer expenses, which are deducted from dividend payments.

ADRs are quite popular in the United States because of their diversification benefits, as documented by Wahab and Khandwala (1993). By the end of 2004, 434 foreign companies had stocks listed on the New York Stock Exchange (NYSE) and 345 of these were available through ADRs, including all the stock listed from Japan, the United Kingdom, Australia, Mexico, and the Netherlands.

Purchase or Sale of American Shares   American shares are securities issued in the United States by a transfer agent acting on behalf of a foreign firm. Because of the added effort and expense incurred by the foreign firm, a limited number of American shares are available.

Direct Purchase or Sale of Foreign Shares   The most difficult and complicated foreign equity transaction takes place in the country where the firm is located because it must be carried out in the foreign currency and the shares must then be transferred to the United States. This routine can be cumbersome. A second alternative is a transaction on a foreign stock exchange outside the country where the securities originated. For example, if you acquired shares of a French auto company listed on the London Stock Exchange (LSE), the shares would be denominated in pounds and the transfer would be swift, assuming your broker has a membership on the LSE.

Finally, you could purchase foreign stocks listed on the NYSE or AMEX. This is similar to buying a U.S. stock, but only a limited number of foreign firms qualify for—and are willing to accept—the cost of listing. Still, this number is growing. At the end of 2003, more than 96 foreign firms (mostly Canadian) were directly listed on the NYSE, in addition to the firms that were available through ADRs. Also, many foreign firms are traded on the National Association of Securities Dealers Automatic Quotations (Nasdaq) system.

Purchase or Sale of Global Mutual Funds or ETFs   Numerous mutual funds or exchange-traded funds (ETFs) make it possible for investors to indirectly acquire the stocks of firms from outside the United States. The alternatives range from *global funds,* which invest in both U.S. stocks and foreign stocks, to *international funds,* which invest almost wholly outside the United States. In turn, international funds can (1) diversify across many countries, (2) concentrate in a segment of the world (for example, Europe, South America, the Pacific basin), (3) concentrate in a specific country (for example, the Japan Fund, the Germany Fund, the Italy Fund, or the Korea Fund), or (4) concentrate in types of markets (for example, emerging markets, which would include stocks from countries such as Thailand, Indonesia, India, and China). A mutual fund is a convenient path to global investing, particularly for a small investor, because the purchase or sale of one of these funds is similar to a transaction for a comparable U.S. mutual fund.

A recent innovation in the world of index products are exchange-traded funds (ETFs) that are depository receipts for a portfolio of securities deposited at a financial institution in a unit trust that issues a certificate of ownership for the portfolio of stocks (similar to ADRs discussed earlier). The stocks in a portfolio are those in an index like the S&P 500, and dozens of country or industry indexes. A significant advantage is that ETFs can be bought and sold (including short sales) continuously on an exchange like common stock. Another advantage is that they do not have management fees, but there is the typical transaction cost for the purchase or sale of ETF shares.[1]

Special Equity Instruments: Options

In addition to common stock investments, it is also possible to invest in equity-derivative securities, which are securities that have a claim on the common stock of a firm. This would include **options**—rights to buy or sell common stock at a specified price for a stated period of time. The two kinds of option instruments are (1) warrants and (2) puts and calls.

Warrants   As mentioned earlier, a warrant is an option issued by a corporation that gives the holder the right to acquire a firm's common stock from the company at a specified price within a designated time period. The warrant does not constitute ownership of the stock, only the option to buy the stock.

Puts and Calls   A **call option** is similar to a warrant because it is an option to buy the common stock of a company within a certain period at a specified price called the *striking price*. A call option differs from a warrant because it is not issued by the company but by another investor who is willing to assume the other side of the transaction. Options also are typically valid for a shorter time period than warrants. Call options are generally valid for less than a year, whereas warrants often extend more than five years. The holder of a **put option** has the right to sell a given stock at a specified price during a designated time period. Puts are useful to investors who expect a stock price to decline during the specified period or to investors who own the stock and want protection from a price decline.

Futures Contracts

Another instrument that provides an alternative to the purchase of an investment is a **futures contract**. This agreement provides for the future exchange of a particular asset at a specified delivery date (usually within nine months) in exchange for a specified payment at the time of delivery. Although the full payment is not made until the delivery date, a good-faith deposit, the **margin**, is made to protect the seller. This is typically about 10 percent of the value of the contract.

The bulk of trading on the commodity exchanges is in futures contracts. The current price of the futures contract is determined by the participants' beliefs about the future for the commodity. For example, in July of a given year, a trader could speculate on the Chicago Board of Trade for wheat in September, December, March, and May of the next year. If the investor expected the price of a commodity to rise, he or she could buy a futures contract on one of the commodity exchanges for later sale. If the investor expected the price to fall, he or she could sell a futures contract on an exchange with the expectation of buying similar contracts later when the price had declined to cover the sale.

Several differences exist between investing in an asset through a futures contract and investing in the asset itself. One is the use of a small good-faith deposit, which increases the volatility of returns. Because an investor puts up only a small portion of the total value of the futures contract (10 to 15 percent), when the price of the commodity changes, the change in the total value of the contract is large compared to the amount invested. Another unique aspect

---

[1]Mutual funds and ETFs are discussed further in the next section and in Chapters 16 and 25.

is the term of the investment: Although stocks can have infinite maturities, futures contracts typically expire in less than a year.

Financial Futures In addition to futures contracts on commodities, there also has been the development of futures contracts on financial instruments, such as T-bills, Treasury bonds, and Eurobonds. For example, it is possible to buy or sell a futures contract that promises future delivery of $100,000 of Treasury bonds at a set price and yield. The major exchanges for financial futures are the Chicago Mercantile Exchange (CME) and the Chicago Board of Trade (CBOT). These futures contracts allow individual investors, bond portfolio managers, and corporate financial managers to protect themselves against volatile interest rates. Certain currency futures allow individual investors or portfolio managers to speculate on or to protect against changes in currency exchange rates. Finally, futures contracts pertain to stock market series, such as the S&P (Standard & Poor's) 500, the *Value Line* Index, and the Nikkei Average on the Tokyo Stock Exchange.

Investment Companies

The investment alternatives described so far are individual securities that can be acquired from a government entity, a corporation, or another individual. However, rather than directly buying an individual stock or bond issued by one of these sources, you may choose to acquire these investments indirectly by buying shares in an investment company, also called a **mutual fund**, that owns a portfolio of individual stocks, bonds, or a combination of the two. Specifically, an **investment company** sells shares in itself and uses the proceeds of this sale to acquire bonds, stocks, or other investment instruments. As a result, an investor who acquires shares in an investment company is a partial owner of the investment company's portfolio of stocks or bonds. We will distinguish between investment companies by the types of investment instruments they acquire.

Money Market Funds **Money market funds** are investment companies that acquire high-quality, short-term investments (referred to as *money market* instruments), such as T-bills, high-grade commercial paper (public short-term loans) from various corporations, and large CDs from the major money center banks. The yields on the money market portfolios always surpass those on normal bank CDs because the investment by the money market fund is larger and the fund can commit to longer maturities than the typical individual. In addition, the returns on commercial paper are above the prime rate. The typical minimum initial investment in a money market fund is $1,000, it charges no sales commission, and minimum additions are $250 to $500. You can always withdraw funds from your money market fund without penalty (typically by writing a check on the account), and you receive interest to the day of withdrawal.

Individuals tend to use money market funds as alternatives to bank savings accounts because they are generally quite safe (although they are not insured, they typically limit their investments to high-quality, short-term investments), they provide yields above what is available on most savings accounts, and the funds are readily available. Therefore, you might use one of these funds to accumulate funds to pay tuition or for a down payment on a car. Because of relatively high yields and extreme flexibility and liquidity, the total value of these funds reached more than $2.0 trillion in 2004.

Bond Funds Bond funds generally invest in various long-term government, corporate, or municipal bonds. They differ by the type and quality of the bonds included in the portfolio as assessed by various rating services. Specifically, the bond funds range from those that invest only in risk-free government bonds and high-grade corporate bonds to those that concentrate in lower-rated corporate or municipal bonds, called **high-yield bonds** or *junk bonds*. The expected rate of return from various bond funds will differ, with the low-risk government bond funds paying the lowest returns and the high-yield bond funds expected to pay the highest returns.

Common Stock Funds   Numerous common stock funds invest to achieve stated investment objectives, which can include aggressive growth, income, precious metal investments, and international stocks. Such funds offer smaller investors the benefits of diversification and professional management. They include different investment styles, such as growth or value, and concentrate in alternative-sized firms, including small-cap, mid-cap, and large-capitalization stocks. To meet the diverse needs of investors, numerous funds have been created that concentrate in one industry or sector of the economy, such as chemicals, electric utilities, health, housing, and technology. These funds are diversified within a sector or an industry, but are not diversified across the total market. Investors who participate in a sector or an industry fund bear more risk than investors in a total market fund because the sector funds will tend to fluctuate more than an aggregate market fund that is diversified across all sectors. Also, international funds that invest outside the United States and global funds that invest in the United States and in other countries offer opportunities for global diversification by individual investors, as documented by Bailey and Lim (1992).

Balanced Funds   Balanced funds invest in a combination of bonds and stocks of various sorts depending on their stated objectives.

Index Funds   Index funds are mutual funds created to equal the performance of a market index like the S&P 500. Such funds appeal to *passive* investors who want to simply experience returns equal to some market index either because they do not want to try to "beat the market" or they believe in efficient markets and do not think it is possible to do better than the market in the long run. Given the popularity of these funds, they have been created to emulate numerous stock indexes including very broad indexes like the Dow Jones Wilshire 5000, broad foreign indexes like the EAFE index, as well as nonstock indexes including various bond indexes for those who want passive bond investing.

Exchange-Traded Funds (ETFs)   A problem with mutual funds in general and index funds in particular is that they are only priced daily at the close of the market and all transactions take place at that price. As a result, if you are aware of changes taking place for the aggregate market due to some economic event during the day and want to buy or sell to take advantage of this, you can put in an order for a mutual fund, but it will not be executed until the end of the day at closing prices. In response to this problem, the AMEX in 1993 created an indexed fund tied to the S&P 500—that is, an exchange-traded fund, ETF—that could be traded continuously because the prices for the 500 stocks are updated continuously so it is possible to buy and sell this ETF like a share of stock, as noted previously. This concept of an ETF has been applied to other foreign and domestic indexes including the Morgan Stanley Capital International (MSCI) indexes. Barclay's Global Investors (BGI) have created "i shares," using the MSCI indexes for numerous individual countries, that have been analyzed by Khorana, Nelling, and Trester (1998).

Real Estate

Like commodities, most investors view real estate as an interesting and profitable investment alternative but believe that it is only available to a small group of experts with a lot of capital to invest. In reality, some feasible real estate investments require no detailed expertise or large capital commitments. We will begin by considering low-capital alternatives.

Real Estate Investment Trusts (REITS)   A **real estate investment trust** is an investment fund designed to invest in various real estate properties. It is similar to a stock or bond mutual fund, except that the money provided by the investors is invested in property and buildings rather than in stocks and bonds. There are several types of REITs.

Construction and development trusts lend the money required by builders during the initial construction of a building. *Mortgage trusts* provide the long-term financing for properties. Specifically, they acquire long-term mortgages on properties once construction is completed. *Equity trusts* own various income-producing properties, such as office buildings, shopping centers, or apartment houses. Therefore, an investor who buys shares in an equity real estate investment trust is buying part of a portfolio of income-producing properties.

REITs have experienced periods of great popularity and significant depression in line with changes in the aggregate economy and the money market. Although they are subject to cyclical risks depending on the economic environment, they offer small investors a way to participate in real estate investments, as described by Hardy (1995), Kuhn (1996), and Myer and Webb (1993).

Direct Real Estate Investment   The most common type of direct real estate investment is the purchase of a home, which is the largest investment most people ever make. Today, according to the Federal Home Loan Bank, the average cost of a single family house exceeds $125,000. The purchase of a home is considered an investment because the buyer pays a sum of money either all at once or over a number of years through a mortgage. For most people, those unable to pay cash for a house, the financial commitment includes a down payment (typically 10 to 20 percent of the purchase price) and specific mortgage payments over a 20- to 30-year period that include reducing the loan's principal and paying interest on the outstanding balance. Subsequently, a homeowner hopes to sell the house for its cost plus a gain.

Raw Land   Another direct real estate investment is the purchase of raw land with the intention of selling it in the future at a profit. During the time you own the land, you have negative cash flows caused by mortgage payments, property maintenance, and taxes. An obvious risk is the possible difficulty of selling it for an uncertain price. Raw land generally has low liquidity compared to most stocks and bonds. An alternative to buying and selling the raw land is the development of the land.

Land Development   Land development can involve buying raw land, dividing it into individual lots, and building houses on it. Alternatively, buying land and building a shopping mall would also be considered land development. This is a feasible form of investment but requires a substantial commitment of capital, time, and expertise. Although the risks can be high because of the commitment of time and capital, the rates of return from a successful housing or commercial development can be significant, as shown in studies by Goetzmann and Ibbotson (1990) and Ross and Zisler (1991). Diversification benefits are documented in Hudson-Wilson and Elbaum (1995).

Rental Property   Many investors with an interest in real estate investing acquire apartment buildings or houses with low down payments, with the intention of deriving enough income from the rents to pay the expenses of the structure, including the mortgage payments. For the first few years following the purchase, the investor generally has no reported income from the building because of tax-deductible expenses, including the interest component of the mortgage payment and depreciation on the structure. Subsequently, rental property provides a cash flow and an opportunity to profit from the sale of the property, as discussed by Harris (1984).

Low-Liquidity Investments

Most of the investment alternatives we have described thus far are traded on securities markets and except for real estate, have good liquidity. In contrast, the investments we discuss in this section have very poor liquidity and financial institutions do not typically acquire them because of the illiquidity and high transaction costs compared to stocks and bonds. Many of these assets are sold at auctions, causing expected prices to vary substantially. In addition, transaction costs are high because there is generally no national market for these investments, so local dealers must be compensated for the added carrying costs and the cost of searching for buyers or sellers. Therefore, many financial theorists view the following low-liquidity investments more as hobbies than investments, even though studies have indicated that some of these assets have experienced substantial rates of return.

Antiques　　The greatest returns from antiques are earned by dealers who acquire them at estate sales or auctions to refurbish and sell at a profit. If we gauge the value of antiques based on prices established at large public auctions, it appears that many serious collectors enjoy substantial rates of return. In contrast, the average investor who owns a few pieces to decorate his or her home finds such returns elusive. The high transaction costs and illiquidity of antiques may erode any profit that the individual may expect to earn when selling these pieces.

Art　　The entertainment sections of newspapers or the personal finance sections of magazines often carry stories of the results of major art auctions, such as when Van Gogh's *Irises* and *Sunflowers* sold for $59 million and $36 million, respectively.

Obviously, these examples and others indicate that some paintings have increased significantly in value and thereby generated large rates of return for their owners. However, investing in art typically requires substantial knowledge of art and the art world, a large amount of capital to acquire the work of well-known artists, patience, and an ability to absorb high transaction costs. For investors who enjoy fine art and have the resources, these can be satisfying investments; but, for most small investors, it is difficult to get returns that compensate for the uncertainty and illiquidity.

Coins and Stamps　　Many individuals enjoy collecting coins or stamps as a hobby and as an investment. The market for coins and stamps is fragmented compared to the stock market, but it is more liquid than the market for art and antiques as indicated by the publication of weekly and monthly price lists.[2] An investor can get a widely recognized grading specification on a coin or stamp, and, once graded, a coin or stamp can usually be sold quickly through a dealer, as described by Henriques (1989) and Bradford (1989). It is important to recognize that the percentage difference between the bid price the dealer will pay to buy the stamp or coin and the asking or selling price the investor must pay the dealer is going to be substantially larger than the bid-ask spread on stocks and bonds.

Diamonds　　Diamonds can be and have been good investments during many periods. Still, investors who purchase diamonds must realize that (1) diamonds can be highly illiquid, (2) the grading process that determines their quality is quite subjective, (3) most investment-grade gems require substantial capital, and (4) they generate no positive cash flow during the holding period until the stone is sold. In fact, during the holding period, the investor must cover costs of insurance and storage and there are appraisal costs before selling.

---

[2]A weekly publication for coins is *Coin World,* published by Amos Press, Inc., 911 Vandermark Rd., Sidney, OH 45367. There are several monthly coin magazines, including *Coinage,* published by Miller Magazines, Ventura, CA. Amos Press also publishes several stamp magazines, including *Linn's Stamp News* and *Scott Stamp Monthly.* These magazines provide current prices for coins and stamps.

In this section, we have briefly described the most common investment alternatives. We will discuss many of these in more detail when we consider how you evaluate them for investment purposes.

In our final section, we will present data on historical rates of return and risk measures, as well as correlations among several of these investments. This should give you some insights into future expected returns and risk characteristics for these investment alternatives.

HISTORICAL RISK–RETURNS ON ALTERNATIVE INVESTMENTS

How do investors weigh the costs and benefits of owning investments and make decisions to build portfolios that will provide the best risk–return combinations? To help individual or institutional investors answer this question, financial theorists have examined extensive data to provide information on the return and risk characteristics of various investments.

There have been numerous studies of the historical rates of return on common stocks (both large-capitalization stocks in terms of aggregate market value and small-capitalization stocks).[3] In addition, there has been a growing interest in bonds. Because inflation has been so pervasive, many studies include both nominal and real rates of return on investments. Still other investigators have examined the performance of such assets as real estate, foreign stocks, art, antiques, and commodities. The subsequent review of these results should help you to make decisions on building your investment portfolio and on the allocation to the various asset classes.

World Portfolio Performance

A study by Reilly and Wright (2004) examined the performance of numerous assets, not only in the United States, but around the world. Specifically, for the period from 1980 to 2001, they examined the performance of stocks, bonds, cash (the equivalent of U.S. T-bills), real estate, and commodities from the United States, Canada, Europe, Japan, and the emerging markets. They computed annual returns, risk measures, and correlations among the returns for alternative assets. Exhibit 3.8 shows the geometric and arithmetic average annual rates of return, the standard deviations of returns, and the systematic risk (beta) for the 22-year period.

Asset Return and Total Risk   The results in Exhibit 3.8 generally confirm the expected relationship between annual rates of return and the total risk (standard deviation) of these securities. The riskier assets—those that had higher standard deviations—experienced higher returns. For example, the U.S. stock indexes had relatively high returns (10 to 15 percent) and large standard deviations (13 to 21 percent). It is not a surprise that the highest-risk asset class (without commodities) was emerging market stock with a standard deviation of 29.72 percent, whereas risk-free U.S. cash equivalents (30-day T-bills) had low returns (6.70 percent) and the smallest standard deviation (2.90 percent).

---

[3]Small-capitalization stocks were broken out as a separate class of asset because several studies have shown that firms with relatively small capitalization (stock with low market value) have experienced rates of return and risk significantly different from those of stocks in general. Therefore, they were considered a unique asset class. We will discuss these studies in Chapter 6, which deals with the efficient markets hypothesis. The large-company stock returns are based upon the S&P Composite Index of 500 stocks—the S&P 500 (described in Chapter 5).

Exhibit 3.8	Summary Risk–Return Results for Alternative Capital Market Assets: 1980–2001

Index	Arithmetic Mean Return	Geometric Mean Return	Standard Deviation Annual Return	Beta With SP500	Beta With Brinson
S&P 500	15.94	14.96	15.12	1.00	1.35
Wilshire 5000	14.96	13.89	15.66	1.01	1.41
Russell 1000	15.38	14.37	15.32	1.01	1.37
Russell 1000 Value	15.71	14.94	13.45	0.82	1.10
Russell 1000 Growth	15.23	13.51	19.71	1.15	1.58
Russell 2000	13.58	12.33	17.06	1.01	1.52
Russell 2000 Value	16.16	14.93	16.68	0.77	1.12
Russell 2000 Growth	11.69	9.78	21.31	1.07	1.61
Russell 3000	15.15	14.16	15.12	1.01	1.38
Russell 3000 Value	15.68	14.92	13.32	0.82	1.10
Russell 3000 Growth	14.95	13.29	19.37	1.00	1.39
IFC Emerging Markets	9.81	6.09	29.72	0.56	0.86
MSCI EAFE	13.50	11.38	22.74	0.61	1.23
Toronto Stock Exchange 300	7.64	6.69	14.65	0.85	1.29
Financial Times All-Share	12.39	11.51	13.83	0.71	1.07
Frankfurt (FAZ) Index	11.75	9.27	24.43	0.68	1.01
Nikkei Index	4.66	2.17	22.67	0.55	1.03
Tokyo Stock Exchange Index	6.41	3.71	24.20	0.43	0.84
M-S World Index	13.52	11.62	21.45	0.67	1.28
Brinson GSMI	12.67	12.13	11.04	0.62	1.00
LB Government Bond	9.98	9.76	7.24	0.09	0.20
LB Corporate Bond	10.86	10.47	9.69	0.16	0.31
LB Aggregate Bond	10.25	9.98	7.96	0.11	0.24
LB High Yield Bond	11.88	11.23	12.64	0.24	0.43
ML World Government Bond	8.59	8.31	8.12	0.03	0.18
ML World Government Bond without U.S.	9.64	8.96	12.81	0.00	0.23
Wilshire Real Estate	11.62	10.31	16.25	0.56	0.87
GS Commodities Index	9.20	6.64	23.29	0.06	0.11
GS Energy Commodities Sub-Index	17.55	9.84	43.25	−0.09	−0.13
GS Non-Energy Commodities Sub-Index	4.71	3.83	13.65	0.15	0.25
GS Industrial Metals Commodities Sub-Index	10.57	5.15	42.06	0.24	0.45
GS Precious Metals Commodities Sub-Index	−2.39	−3.38	13.88	0.11	0.29
GS Agriculture Commodities Sub-Index	1.33	−0.25	18.09	0.16	0.23
GS Livestock Commodities Sub-Index	10.00	8.45	18.81	0.10	0.18
Treasury Bill—30 Day	6.74	6.70	2.90	0.00	0.00
Treasury Bill—6 Month	7.38	7.33	3.37	0.00	0.01
Treasury Note—2 Year	8.43	8.35	4.36	0.04	0.08
Inflation	3.89	3.86	2.54	−0.01	−0.02

Statistics for Treasury Bill—6 month and Treasury Note—2 year are based on 1981–2001 data only.

Statistics for ML World Government Bond indexes are based on 1986–2001 data only.

Statistics for GS Commodities Sub-Index are based on 1983–2001 data only.

Source: Frank K. Reilly and David J. Wright, "An Analysis of Risk-Adjusted Performance for Global Market Assets," *Journal of Portfolio Management* 30, no. 3 (Spring 2004): 63–77. This copyrighted material is reprinted with permission from *Journal of Portfolio Management*, a publication of Institutional Investor, Inc.

Exhibit 3.9	Geometric Mean Return versus Brinson Beta for Alternative Capital Market Assets: 1980–2001

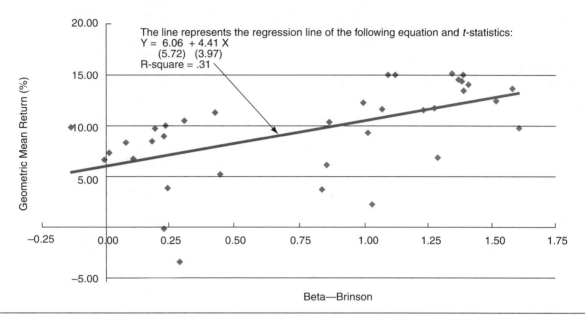

The line represents the regression line of the following equation and *t*-statistics:
Y = 6.06 + 4.41 X
(5.72)   (3.97)
R-square = .31

Beta—Brinson

Source: Frank K. Reilly and David J. Wright, "An Analysis of Risk-Adjusted Performance for Global Market Assets," *Journal of Portfolio Management* 30, no. 3 (Spring 2004): 63–77. This copyrighted material is reprinted with permission from *Journal of Portfolio Management*, a publication of Institutional Investor, Inc.

Return and Systematic Risk   As shown in Exhibit 3.8, in addition to total risk (standard deviation), the authors also considered systematic risk, which is the volatility of an asset relative to a market portfolio of risky assets (this was discussed briefly in Chapter 1). One of the conclusions of Reilly and Wright's (2004) study was that the systematic risk measure (beta) did a better job of explaining the returns during the period than the total risk measure. In addition, the beta risk measure that used the Brinson index as a market proxy was somewhat better than the beta that used the S&P 500 Index. Thus, Exhibit 3.9 contains the scatter plot of geometric mean rate of return and systematic risk and indicates the expected positive risk–return relationship.

Correlations between Asset Returns   Exhibit 3.10 is a correlation matrix of selected U.S. and world assets. The first column shows that U.S. equities (as represented by the broad Wilshire 5000 Index) have a reasonably high correlation with Canadian and U.K. stocks (0.793 and 0.672) but low correlation with emerging market stocks and Japanese stocks (0.441 and 0.335). Also, U.S. equities show almost zero correlation with world government bonds, except U.S. bonds (−0.013). Recall from our earlier discussion that you can use this information to build a diversified portfolio by combining those assets with low positive or negative correlations.

The correlation of returns with inflation has implications regarding the ability of an asset class to be an inflation hedge—a good hedge should have a strong positive correlation with inflation. As shown, most assets (including common stocks) have negative correlations, which implies that they are poor inflation hedges. The exceptions appear to be some commodities and short-term government bonds.

Exhibit 3.10	Correlations Among Global Capital Market Asset Monthly Returns: 1980–2001

Index	Dow-Jones Wilshire 5000	IFC Emerging Market Stock	MSCI EAFE	M-S World Stock	Brinson GSMI	Inflation
S&P 500	0.983	0.392	0.538	0.604	0.915	−0.115
Wilshire 5000	1.000	0.414	0.545	0.607	0.926	−0.116
Russell 1000	0.991	0.396	0.536	0.602	0.922	−0.121
Russell 1000 Value	0.851	0.339	0.458	0.518	0.801	−0.108
Russell 1000 Growth	0.968	0.378	0.524	0.586	0.897	−0.116
Russell 2000	0.877	0.401	0.470	0.513	0.811	−0.132
Russell 2000 Value	0.778	0.329	0.409	0.452	0.729	−0.138
Russell 2000 Growth	0.750	0.305	0.399	0.432	0.700	−0.113
Russell 3000	0.995	0.402	0.538	0.603	0.925	−0.123
Russell 3000 Value	0.858	0.344	0.462	0.521	0.807	−0.112
Russell 3000 Growth	0.828	0.283	0.449	0.489	0.781	−0.126
IFC Emerging Market	0.414	1.000	0.386	0.395	0.411	−0.002
MSCI EAFE	0.545	0.386	1.000	0.982	0.744	−0.155
Toronto Stock Exchange 300	0.793	0.451	0.547	0.604	0.780	−0.105
Financial Times All Share	0.672	0.443	0.581	0.597	0.685	−0.090
Frankfurt (FAZ) Index	0.537	0.433	0.486	0.499	0.545	−0.127
Nikkei Index	0.431	0.388	0.722	0.712	0.531	−0.057
Tokyo Stock Exchange Index	0.335	0.321	0.681	0.667	0.439	−0.061
M-S World Index	0.607	0.395	0.982	1.000	0.785	−0.157
Brinson GSMI	0.926	0.411	0.744	0.785	1.000	−0.161
LB Government Bond	0.209	−0.136	0.167	0.164	0.352	−0.097
LB Corporate Bond	0.298	−0.051	0.203	0.210	0.426	−0.139
LB Aggregate Bond	0.250	−0.092	0.188	0.188	0.389	−0.113
LB High Yield Bond	0.488	0.213	0.357	0.370	0.551	−0.151
ML World Government Bond	0.046	−0.187	0.423	0.400	0.280	−0.065
ML World Government Bond except U.S.	−0.013	−0.157	0.474	0.448	0.232	−0.049
Wilshire Real Estate	0.624	0.278	0.370	0.410	0.617	−0.167
Goldman Commodities Index	0.077	0.033	0.106	0.113	0.071	0.043
Goldman Energy Commodities Sub-Index	−0.032	−0.002	0.014	0.016	−0.042	0.161
Goldman Non-Energy Commodities Sub-Index	0.232	0.124	0.262	0.271	0.241	−0.054
Goldman Industrial Metals Commodities Sub-Index	0.173	−0.022	0.165	0.181	0.196	−0.076
Goldman Precious Metals Commodities Sub-Index	0.121	0.032	0.191	0.223	0.163	−0.011
Goldman Agriculture Commodities Sub-Index	0.178	0.087	0.158	0.171	0.160	−0.049
Goldman Livestock Commodities Sub-Index	0.106	0.055	0.152	0.148	0.130	−0.016
Treasury Bill—30 day	−0.064	−0.086	−0.035	−0.054	−0.037	0.529
Treasury Bill—6 Month	0.054	−0.116	0.014	0.008	0.125	0.277
Treasury Note—2 Year	0.178	−0.118	0.122	0.123	0.299	−0.028
Inflation	−0.116	−0.002	−0.155	−0.157	−0.161	1.000

ML World Government Bond indexes based on 1986–2001 data only.
GS Commodities Sub-Index based on 1983–2001 data only.
Treasury Bill—6 Month and Treasury Note—2 year based on 1981–2001 data only.

Source: Frank K. Reilly and David J. Wright, "An Analysis of Risk-Adjusted Performance for Global Market Assets," *Journal of Portfolio Management* 30, no. 3 (Spring 2004): 63–77. This copyrighted material is reprinted with permission from *Journal of Portfolio Management*, a publication of Institutional Investor, Inc.

Art and Antiques

Unlike financial securities, where the results of transactions are reported daily, art and antique markets are fragmented and lack any formal transaction reporting system. This makes it difficult to gather data. The best-known series that attempted to provide information about the changing value of art and antiques were developed by Sotheby's, a major art auction firm. These value indexes covered 13 areas of art and antiques and a weighted aggregate series that combined the 13 areas.

Reilly (1992) examined these series for the period from 1976 to 1991 and computed rates of return, measures of risk, and the correlations among the various art and antique series and compared them to stocks, bonds, and the rate of inflation.

Although there was a wide range of mean returns and risk, a risk–return plot indicated a fairly consistent relationship between risk and return during this 16-year period. Comparing the art and antique results to bond and stock indexes indicated that stocks and bonds experienced results that were very consistent with the art and antique series.

Analysis of the correlations among these assets using annual rates of return revealed several important relationships. First, the correlations among alternative antique and art categories vary substantially from above 0.90 to negative correlations. Second, the correlations between art/antiques and bonds were generally negative. Third, the correlations of art/antiques with stocks were typically small positive values. Finally, the correlation of art and antiques with the rate of inflation indicates that several of the categories were fairly good inflation hedges since they were positively correlated with inflation. Notably, they were clearly superior inflation hedges compared to long bonds and common stocks as documented in Fama (1991) and Jaffe and Mandelker (1976). The reader should recall our earlier observation that most art and antiques are quite illiquid and the transaction costs are fairly high compared to financial assets.

Real Estate

Somewhat similar to art and antiques, returns on real estate are difficult to derive because of the limited number of transactions and the lack of a national source of data for the transactions that allows one to accurately compute rates of return. In the study by Goetzmann and Ibbotson (1990), the authors gathered data on commercial real estate through REITs and Commingled Real Estate Funds (CREFs) and estimated returns on residential real estate from a series created by Case and Shiller (1987). The summary of the real estate returns compared to various stock, bond, and an inflation series is contained in Exhibit 3.11. As shown, the two commercial real estate series reflected strikingly different results. The CREFs had lower returns and low volatility, while the REIT index had higher returns and risk. Notably, the REIT returns were higher than those of common stocks, but the risk measure for real estate was lower (there was a small difference in the time period). The residential real estate series reflected lower returns and low risk. The longer-term results indicate that all the real estate series experienced lower returns and lower risk than common stock.

The correlations in Exhibit 3.12 among annual returns for the various asset groups indicate a relatively low positive correlation between commercial real estate and stocks. In contrast, there was negative correlation between stocks and residential and farm real estate. This negative relationship with real estate was also true for 20-year government bonds. Studies by Eichholtz (1996), Mull and Socnen (1997), and Quan and Titman (1997) that considered international commercial real estate and REITs indicated that the returns were correlated with stock prices but they still provided significant diversification benefits.

These results imply that returns on real estate are equal to or slightly lower than returns on common stocks, but real estate possesses favorable risk results. Specifically, real estate had much lower standard deviations as unique assets and either low positive or negative correlations with other asset classes in a portfolio context.

Exhibit 3.11 | **Summary Statistics of Commercial and Residential Real Estate Series Compared to Stocks, Bonds, T-bills, and Inflation**

Series	Date	Geometric Mean	Arithmetic Mean	Standard Deviation
Annual Returns 1969–1987				
CREF (Comm.)	1969–87	10.8%	10.9%	2.6%
REIT (Comm.)	1972–87	14.2	15.7	15.4
C&S (Res.)	1970–86	8.5	8.6	3.0
S&P (Stocks)	1969–87	9.2	10.5	18.2
LTG (Bonds)	1969–87	7.7	8.4	13.2
TBILL (Bills)	1969–87	7.6	7.6	1.4
CPI (Infl.)	1969–87	6.4	6.4	1.8
Annual Returns over the Long Term				
I&S (Comm.)	1960–87	8.9%	9.1%	5.0%
CPIHOME (Res.)	1947–86	8.1	8.2	5.2
USDA (Farm)	1947–87	9.6	9.9	8.2
S&P (Stocks)	1947–87	11.4	12.6	16.3
LTG (Bonds)	1947–87	4.2	4.6	9.8
TBILL (Bills)	1947–87	4.9	4.7	3.3
CPI (Infl.)	1947–87	4.5	4.6	3.9

Source: William N. Goetzmann and Roger G. Ibbotson, "The Performance of Real Estate as an Asset Class," *Journal of Applied Corporate Finance* 3, no. 1 (Spring 1990): 65–76. Reprinted with permission.

Exhibit 3.12 | **Correlations of Annual Real Estate Returns with the Returns on Other Asset Classes**

	I&S	CREF	CPI Home	C&S	Farm	S&P	20-Yr. Gvt.	1-Yr. Gvt.	Infl.
I&S	1								
CREF	0.79	1							
CPI Home	0.52	0.12	1						
C&S	0.26	0.16	0.82	1					
Farm	0.06	−0.06	0.51	0.49	1				
S&P	0.16	0.25	−0.13	−0.20	−0.10	1			
20-Yr. Gvt.	−0.04	0.01	−0.22	−0.54	−0.44	0.11	1		
1-Yr. Gvt.	0.53	0.42	0.13	−0.56	−0.32	−0.07	0.48	1	
Infl.	0.70	0.35	0.77	0.56	0.49	−0.02	−0.17	0.26	1

Note: Correlation coefficient for each pair of asset classes uses the maximum number of observations, that is, the minimum length of the two series in the pair.

Source: William N. Goetzmann and Roger G. Ibbotson, "The Performance of Real Estate as an Asset Class," *Journal of Applied Corporate Finance* 3, no. 1 (Spring 1990): 65–76. Reprinted with permission.

The Internet Investments Online

As this chapter describes, the variety of financial products is huge and potentially confusing to the novice (not to mention the experienced professional). Two good rules of investing are (1) stick to your risk tolerance; many people will try to sell instruments which may not be appropriate for the typical individual investor and (2) don't invest in something if you don't understand it. Web sites mentioned in Chapters 1 and 2 provide useful information on a variety of investments. Below we list a few others that may be of interest.

http://www.site-by-site.com This site features global financial news including market information and economic reports for a variety of countries with developed, developing, and emerging markets. Some company research is available on this site as is information on derivatives markets world-wide.

http://www.moneycafe.com MoneyCafe offers information on personal and commercial financial products and services, in addition to news, interest rate updates, and stock price quotes.

http://www.emgmkts.com The Emerging Markets Companion home page contains information on emerging markets in Asia, Latin America, Africa, and Eastern Europe. Available information and links includes news, prices, market information, and research.

http://www.law.duke.edu/globalmark Duke University's Global Capital Markets Center includes information and studies on a variety of financial market topics, most written from a legal perspective.

http://www.lebenthal.com Lebenthal is a firm specializing on municipal bond sales to individual investors. Their site contains a variety of research and information about municipal bonds.

http://www.sothebys.com Home page of Sotheby's Inc., the auction house. This site contains auction updates and information on collectibles, Internet resources, and featured upcoming sales.

SUMMARY

- Investors who want the broadest range of choices in investments must consider foreign stocks and bonds in addition to domestic financial assets. Many foreign securities offer investors higher risk-adjusted returns than do domestic securities. In addition, the low positive or negative correlations between foreign and U.S. securities make them ideal for building a diversified portfolio.

- Exhibit 3.13 summarizes the risk and return characteristics of the investment alternatives described in this chapter. Some of the differences are due to unique factors that we discussed. Foreign bonds are considered riskier than domestic bonds because of the unavoidable uncertainty due to exchange rate risk and country risk. The same is true for foreign and domestic common stocks. Such investments as art, antiques, coins, and stamps require heavy liquidity risk premiums. You should divide consideration of real estate investments between your personal home, on which you do not expect as high a return because of nonmonetary factors, and commercial real estate, which requires a much higher rate of return due to cash flow uncertainty and illiquidity.

- Studies on the historical rates of return for investment alternatives such as the excellent book by Ibbotson and Brinson (1993) (including bonds, commodities, real estate, foreign securities, and art and antiques) point toward two generalizations:

1. A positive relationship typically holds between the rate of return earned on an asset and the variability of its historical rate of return or its systematic risk (beta). This is expected in a world of risk-averse investors who require higher rates of return to compensate for more uncertainty.

2. The correlation among rates of return for selected alternative investments is typically quite low, especially for U.S. and foreign stocks and bonds and between these financial assets and real assets, as represented by art, antiques, and real estate. This confirms the advantage of diversification among investments from different asset classes and from around the world.

Exhibit 3.13 | Alternative Investment Risk and Return Characteristics

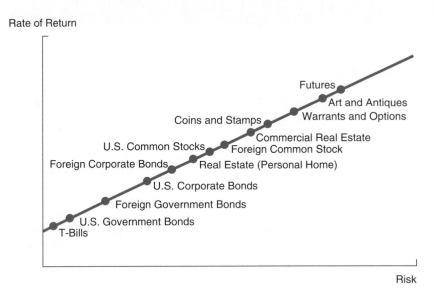

- In addition to describing many direct investments, such as stocks and bonds, we also discussed investment companies that allow investors to buy investments indirectly. These can be important to investors who want to take advantage of professional management but also want instant diversification with a limited amount of funds. With $10,000, you may not be able to buy many individual stocks or bonds, but you could acquire shares in a mutual fund or an ETF, which would give you a share of a diversified portfolio that might contain 100 to 150 different U.S. and international stocks or bonds.

- Now that we know the range of domestic and foreign investment alternatives, our next task is to learn about the markets in which they are bought and sold. That is the objective of the following chapter.

SUGGESTED READINGS

Grabbe, J. Orlin. *International Financial Markets.* New York: Elsevier Science Publishing, 1986.

Hamao, Yasushi. "Japanese Stocks, Bonds, Inflation, 1973–1987." *Journal of Portfolio Management* 16, no. 2 (Winter 1989).

Lessard, Donald R. "International Diversification." In *The Financial Analyst's Handbook,* 2d ed., ed. Sumner N. Levine. Homewood, IL: Dow Jones–Irwin, 1988.

Malvey, Jack. "Global Corporate Bond Portfolio Management." In *The Handbook of Fixed-Income Securities,* 7th ed., ed. Frank J. Fabozzi. New York: McGraw-Hill, 2005.

Rosenberg, Michael R. "International Fixed-Income Invest-

ing: Theory and Practice." In *The Handbook of Fixed-Income Securities,* 7th ed., ed. Frank J. Fabozzi. New York: McGraw-Hill, 2005.

Siegel, Laurence B., and Paul D. Kaplan. "Stocks, Bonds, Bills, and Inflation Around the World." In *Managing Institutional Assets,* ed. Frank J. Fabozzi. New York: Harper & Row, 1990.

Solnik, Bruno, and Dennis McLeavey. *International Investments,* 5th ed. Reading, Mass.: Addison-Wesley, 2004.

Steward, Christopher. "International Bond Markets and Instruments." In *The Handbook of Fixed-Income Securities,* 7th ed., ed. Frank J. Fabozzi. New York: McGraw-Hill, 2005.

QUESTIONS

1. What are the advantages of investing in the common stock rather than the corporate bonds of a company? Compare the certainty of returns for a bond with those for a common stock. Draw a line graph to demonstrate the pattern of returns you would envision for each of these assets over time.

2. Discuss three factors that cause U.S. investors to consider including global securities in their portfolios.

3. Discuss why international diversification reduces portfolio risk. Specifically, why would you expect low correlation in the rates of return for domestic and foreign securities?

4. Discuss why you would expect a *difference* in the correlation of returns between securities from the United States and from alternative countries (for example, Japan, Canada, South Africa).

5. Discuss whether you would expect any *change* in the correlations between U.S. stocks and the stocks for different countries. For example, discuss whether you would expect the correlation between U.S. and Japanese stock returns to change over time. If so, why?

6. When you invest in Japanese or German bonds, what major additional risks must you consider besides yield changes within the country?

7. Some investors believe that international investing introduces additional risks. Discuss these risks and how they can affect your return. Give an example.

8. What alternatives to direct investment in foreign stocks are available to investors?

9. You are a wealthy individual in a high tax bracket. Why might you consider investing in a municipal bond rather than a straight corporate bond, even though the promised yield on the municipal bond is lower?

10. You can acquire convertible bonds from a rapidly growing company or from a utility. Speculate on which convertible bond would have the lower yield and discuss the reason for this difference.

11. Compare the liquidity of an investment in raw land with that of an investment in common stock. Be specific as to why and how the liquidity differs. (Hint: Begin by defining *liquidity*.)

12. What are stock warrants and call options? How do they differ?

13. Discuss why financial analysts consider antiques and art to be illiquid investments. Why do they consider coins and stamps to be more liquid than antiques and art? What must an investor typically do to sell a collection of art and antiques? Briefly contrast this procedure to the sale of a portfolio of stocks listed on the New York Stock Exchange.

14. You have a fairly large portfolio of U.S. stocks and bonds. You meet a financial planner at a social gathering who suggests that you diversify your portfolio by investing in emerging market stocks. Discuss whether the correlation results in Exhibit 3.10 support this suggestion.

15. *CFA Examination Level 1*

    Chris Smith of XYZ Pension Plan has historically invested in the stocks of only U.S.-domiciled companies. Recently, he has decided to add international exposure to the plan portfolio.

    a. Identify and briefly discuss *three* potential problems that Smith may confront in selecting international stocks that he did not face in choosing U.S. stocks.

16. *CFA Examination Level III*

    TMP has been experiencing increasing demand from its institutional clients for information and assistance related to international investment management. Recognizing that this is an area of growing importance, the firm has hired an experienced analyst/portfolio manager specializing in international equities and market strategy. His first assignment is to represent TMP before a client company's investment committee to discuss the possibility of changing their present "U.S. securities only" investment approach to one including international investments. He is told that the committee wants a presentation that fully and objectively examines the basic, substantive considerations on which the committee should focus its attention, including both theory and evidence. The company's pension plan has no legal or other barriers to adoption of an international approach; no non-U.S. pension liabilities currently exist.

    a. Identify and briefly discuss *three* reasons for adding international securities to the pension portfolio and *three* problems associated with such an approach.

    b. Assume that the committee has adopted a policy to include international securities in its pension portfolio. Identify and briefly discuss *three* additional *policy-level* investment decisions the committee must make *before* management selection and actual implementation can begin.

PROBLEMS

1. Using a source of international statistics, compare the percentage change in the following economic data for Japan, Germany, Canada, and the United States for a recent year. What were the differences, and which country or countries differed most from the United States?
   a. Aggregate output (GDP)
   b. Inflation
   c. Money supply growth

2. Using a recent edition of *Barron's,* examine the weekly percentage change in the stock price indexes for Japan, Germany, United Kingdom, and the United States. For each of three weeks, which foreign series moved most closely with the U.S. series? Which series diverged most from the U.S. series? Discuss these results as they relate to international diversification.

3. Using published sources (for example, the *Wall Street Journal, Barron's, Federal Reserve Bulletin*), look up the exchange rate for U.S. dollars with Japanese yen for each of the past 10 years (you can use an average for the year or a specific time period each year). Based on these exchange rates, compute and discuss the yearly exchange rate effect on an investment in Japanese stocks by a U.S. investor. Discuss the impact of this exchange rate effect on the risk of Japanese stocks for a U.S. investor.

 4. *CFA Examination Level I* (Adapted)
   The following information is available concerning the historical risk and return relationships in the U.S. capital markets:

U.S. CAPITAL MARKETS TOTAL ANNUAL RETURNS, 1960–1984

Investment Category	Arithmetic Mean	Geometric Mean	Standard Deviation of Return[a]
Common stocks	10.28%	8.81%	16.9%
Treasury bills	6.54	6.49	3.2
Long-term government bonds	6.10	5.91	6.4
Long-term corporate bonds	5.75	5.35	9.6
Real estate	9.49	9.44	3.5

[a]Based on arithmetic mean.
Source: Adapted from R. G. Ibbotson, Laurence B. Siegel, and Kathryn S. Love, "World Wealth: Market Values and Returns," *Journal of Portfolio Management* 12, no. 1 (Fall 1985): 4–23. Copyright *Journal of Portfolio Management,* a publication of Institutional Investor, Inc. Used with permission.

   a. Explain why the geometric and arithmetic mean returns are not equal and whether one or the other may be more useful for investment decision making. [5 minutes]
   b. For the time period indicated, rank these investments on a risk-adjusted basis from most to least desirable. Explain your rationale. [6 minutes]
   c. Assume the returns in these series are normally distributed.
      (1) Calculate the range of returns that an investor would have expected to achieve 95 percent of the time from holding common stocks. [4 minutes]
      (2) Suppose an investor holds real estate for this time period. Determine the probability of at least breaking even on this investment. [5 minutes]
   d. Assume you are holding a portfolio composed entirely of real estate. Discuss the justification, if any, for adopting a mixed asset portfolio by adding long-term government bonds. [5 minutes]

5. You are given the following long-run annual rates of return for alternative investment instruments:

   U.S. Government T-bills   3.50%

Large-cap common stock	11.75
Long-term corporate bonds	5.50
Long-term government bonds	4.90
Small-capitalization common stock	13.10

The annual rate of inflation during this period was 3 percent. Compute the real rate of return on these investment alternatives.

THOMSON ONE | Business School Edition

1. Compare the performance of several country markets. Using the "index" tab, do a search on FTSE. You will obtain a list of many FTSE indexes. Select at least three from different countries or regions (such as Eurobloc, Americas, and Japan). How have their stock markets been performing of late?
2. Some indexes are presented in both U.S. dollar terms and in terms of other currencies. Compare the performance of the DJ Euro STOXX index in terms of euros and the U.S. dollar. Find one other index that will allow a comparison between two different currencies and discuss their relative performance.
3. Using daily stock prices for indexes from the United States, Japan, Canada, and a composite of emerging markets (or China, India, and Indonesia), compute daily percent changes for 25 trading days. Compute the correlations among these indexes. Rank the correlations from high to low.

APPENDIX
Chapter 3   Covariance and Correlation

Covariance

Because most students have been exposed to the concepts of covariance and correlation, the following discussion is set forth in intuitive terms with examples. A detailed, rigorous treatment is contained in DeFusco, McLeavey, Pinto, and Runkle (2004).

Covariance is an absolute measure of the extent to which two sets of numbers move together over time, that is, how often they move up or down together. In this regard, *move together* means they are generally above their means or below their means at the same time. Covariance between i and j is defined as

$$\text{COV}_{ij} = \frac{\sum (i - \bar{i})(j - \bar{j})}{n}$$

If we define $(i - \bar{i})$ as i' and $(j - \bar{j})$ as j', then

$$\text{COV}_{ij} = \frac{\sum i'j'}{n}$$

Obviously, if both numbers are consistently above or below their individual means at the same time, their products will be positive, and the average will be a large positive value. In contrast, if the i value is below its mean when the j value is above its mean or vice versa, their products will be large negative values, giving negative covariance.

Exhibit 3A.1 should make this clear. In this example, the two series generally moved together, so they showed positive covariance. As noted, this is an *absolute* measure of their relationship and, therefore, can range from $+\infty$ to $-\infty$. Note that the covariance of a variable with itself is its *variance*.

Exhibit 3A.1	Calculation of Covariance

Observation	i	j	$i - \bar{i}$	$j - \bar{j}$	$i'j'$
1	3	8	−4	−4	16
2	6	10	−1	−2	2
3	8	14	+1	+2	2
4	5	12	−2	0	0
5	9	13	+2	+1	2
6	11	15	+4	+3	12
Σ	42	72			34
Mean	7	12			

$$\text{COV}_{ij} = \frac{34}{6} = +5.67$$

Correlation

To obtain a relative measure of a given relationship, we use the **correlation coefficient** (r_{ij}), which is a measure of the relationship:

$$r_{ij} = \frac{\text{COV}_{ij}}{\sigma_i \sigma_j}$$

You will recall from your introductory statistics course that

$$\sigma_i = \sqrt{\frac{\sum (i - \bar{i})^2}{N}}$$

If the two series move completely together, then the covariance would equal $\sigma_i \sigma_j$ and

$$\frac{\text{COV}_{ij}}{\sigma_i \sigma_j} = 1.0$$

The correlation coefficient would equal unity in this case, and we would say the two series are perfectly correlated. Because we know that

$$r_{ij} = \frac{\text{COV}_{ij}}{\sigma_i \sigma_j}$$

we also know that $\text{COV}_{ij} = r_{ij} \sigma_i \sigma_j$. This relationship may be useful when computing the standard deviation of a portfolio, because in many instances the relationship between two securities is stated in terms of the correlation coefficient rather than the covariance.

Continuing the example given in Exhibit 3A.1, the standard deviations are computed in Exhibit 3A.2, as is the correlation between i and j. As shown, the two standard deviations are rather large and similar but not exactly the same. Finally, when the positive covariance is normalized by the product of the two standard deviations, the results indicate a correlation coefficient of 0.898, which is obviously quite large and close to 1.00. This implies that these two series are highly related.

Exhibit 3A.2	Calculation of Correlation Coefficient

Observation	$I - \bar{I}^a$	$(I - \bar{I})^2$	$J - \bar{J}^a$	$(J - \bar{J})^2$
1	−4	16	−4	16
2	−1	1	−2	4
3	+1	1	+2	4
4	−2	4	0	0
5	+2	4	+1	1
6	+4	16	+3	9
		42		34

$$\sigma_j^2 = 42/6 = 7.00 \qquad\qquad \sigma_j^2 = 34/6 = 5.67$$

$$\sigma_j = \sqrt{7.00} = 2.65 \qquad\qquad \sigma_j = \sqrt{5.67} = 2.38$$

$$r_{ij} = COV_{ij}/\sigma_i\sigma_j = \frac{5.67}{(2.65)(2.38)} = \frac{5.67}{6.31} = 0.898$$

Problems

1. As a new analyst, you have calculated the following annual rates of return for the stocks of both Lauren Corporation and Kayleigh Industries.

Year	Lauren's Rate of Return	Kayleigh's Rate of Return
2001	5	5
2002	12	15
2003	−11	5
2004	10	7
2005	12	−10

   Your manager suggests that because these companies produce similar products, you should continue your analysis by computing their covariance. Show all calculations.

2. You decide to go an extra step by calculating the coefficient of correlation using the data provided in Problem 1. Prepare a table showing your calculations and explain how to interpret the results. Would the combination of the common stock of Lauren and Kayleigh be good for diversification?

Chapter 4

Organization and Functioning of Securities Markets*

After you read this chapter, you should be able to answer the following questions:

- What is the purpose and function of a market?
- What are the characteristics that determine the quality of a market?
- What is the difference between a primary and secondary capital market and how do these two markets support each other?
- What are Rules 415 and 144A and how do they affect corporate security underwriting?
- For secondary equity markets, what are the two basic trading systems?
- What are call markets and when are they typically used in U.S. markets?
- How are national exchanges around the world linked and what is meant by "passing the book"?
- What is the third market?
- What are Electronic Communication Networks (ECNs) and alternative trading systems (ATSs) and how do they differ from the primary listing markets?
- What are the major types of orders available to investors and market makers?
- What new trading systems on the NYSE and on Nasdaq have made it possible to handle the growth in U.S. trading volume?
- What are the three recent innovations that contribute to competition within the U.S. equity market?
- What are Rule 390 and the trade-through rule and what is their effect regarding competition on the U.S. equity market?

The stock market, the Dow Jones Industrials, and the bond market are part of our everyday experience. Each evening on television news broadcasts we find out how stocks and bonds fared; each morning we read in our daily newspapers about expectations for a market rally or decline. Yet most people have an imperfect understanding of how domestic and world capital markets actually function. To be a successful investor in a global environment, you must know what financial markets are available around the world and how they operate.

*The authors acknowledge helpful comments on this chapter from Robert Battalio and Paul Schultz of the University of Notre Dame.

In this chapter we take a broad view of securities markets and provide a detailed discussion of how major stock markets function. We conclude with a consideration of how global securities markets have changed during recent years and probably will change in the near future.

We begin with a discussion of securities markets and the characteristics of a good market. We describe two components of the capital markets: primary and secondary. Our main emphasis is on the secondary stock market. We consider the national stock exchanges around the world and how these markets, separated by geography and by time zones, are becoming linked into a 24-hour market. We also consider regional stock markets and the Nasdaq market and provide a detailed analysis of how alternative exchange markets operate, including the Electronic Communication Networks (ECNs). In the final section we consider numerous historical changes in financial markets, additional current changes, and significant future changes expected. These numerous changes in our securities markets will have a profound effect on what investments are available from around the world and how we buy and sell them.

WHAT IS A MARKET?

A **market** is the means through which buyers and sellers are brought together to aid in the transfer of goods and/or services. Several aspects of this general definition seem worthy of emphasis. First, a market need not have a physical location. It is only necessary that the buyers and sellers can communicate regarding the relevant aspects of the transaction.

Second, the market does not necessarily own the goods or services involved. For a good market, ownership is not involved; the important criterion is the smooth, cheap transfer of goods and services. In most financial markets, those who establish and administer the market do not own the assets but simply provide a physical location or an electronic system that allows potential buyers and sellers to interact. They help the market function by providing information and facilities to aid in the transfer of ownership.

Finally, a market can deal in any variety of goods and services. For any commodity or service with a diverse clientele, a market should evolve to aid in the transfer of that commodity or service. Both buyers and sellers benefit from the existence of a market.

Characteristics of a Good Market

Throughout this book, we will discuss markets for different investments such as stocks, bonds, options, and futures in the United States and throughout the world. We will refer to these markets using various terms of quality such as *strong, active, liquid*, or *illiquid*. There are many financial markets, but they are not all equal—some are active and liquid, others are relatively illiquid and inefficient in their operations. To appreciate these discussions, you should be aware of the following characteristics that investors look for when evaluating the quality of a market.

One enters a market to buy or sell a good or service quickly at a price justified by the prevailing supply and demand. To determine the appropriate price, participants must have timely and accurate information on the volume and prices of past transactions and all currently outstanding bids and offers. Therefore, one attribute of a good market is **timely and accurate information**.

Another prime requirement is **liquidity**, the ability to buy or sell an asset quickly and at a known price—that is, a price not substantially different from the prices for prior transactions, assuming no new information is available. An asset's likelihood of being sold quickly, sometimes referred to as its *marketability*, is a necessary, but not a sufficient, condition for liquidity. The expected price should also be fairly certain, based on the recent history of transaction prices and current bid–ask quotes. For a formal discussion of liquidity, see Handa and Schwartz (1996) and AIMR's articles on *Best Execution and Portfolio Performance* (Jost, 2001).

A component of liquidity is **price continuity**, which means that prices do not change much from one transaction to the next unless substantial new information becomes available. Suppose no new information is forthcoming, and the last transaction was at a price of $20; if the next trade were at $20.10, the market would be considered reasonably continuous.[1] A continuous market without large price changes between trades is a characteristic of a liquid market.

A market with price continuity requires *depth,* which means that there are numerous potential buyers and sellers willing to trade at prices above and below the current market price. These buyers and sellers enter the market in response to changes in supply, demand, or both and thereby prevent drastic price changes. In summary, liquidity requires marketability and price continuity, which, in turn, requires depth.

Another factor contributing to a good market is the **transaction cost**. Lower costs (as a percent of the value of the trade) make for a more efficient market. An individual comparing the cost of a transaction between markets would choose a market that charges 2 percent of the value of the trade compared with one that charges 5 percent. Most microeconomic textbooks define an efficient market as one in which the cost of the transaction is minimal. This attribute is referred to as *internal efficiency*.

Finally, a buyer or seller wants the prevailing market price to adequately reflect all the information available regarding supply and demand factors in the market. If such conditions change as a result of new information, the price should change accordingly. Therefore, participants want prices to adjust quickly to new information regarding supply or demand, which means that prevailing market prices reflect all available information about the asset. This attribute is referred to as **external**, or **informational**, **efficiency**. We discuss this attribute extensively in Chapter 6.

In summary, a good market for goods and services has the following characteristics:

1. Timely and accurate information on the price and volume of past transactions.
2. Liquidity, meaning an asset can be bought or sold quickly at a price close to the prices for previous transactions (has price continuity), assuming no new information has been received. In turn, price continuity requires depth.
3. Low transaction costs, including the cost of reaching the market, the actual brokerage costs, and the cost of transferring the asset.
4. Prices that rapidly adjust to new information, so the prevailing price is fair since it reflects all available information regarding the asset.

Decimal Pricing

Prior to the initiation of changes in late 2000 that were completed in early 2001, common stocks in the United States were always quoted in fractions. Specifically, prior to 1997 they were quoted in eighths (e.g., $\frac{1}{8}, \frac{2}{8}, \ldots, \frac{7}{8}$), with each eighth equal to $0.125. This was modified in 1997 when the fractions for most stocks went to sixteenths (e.g., $\frac{1}{16}, \frac{2}{16}, \cdots, \frac{15}{16}$), equal to $0.0625. Now U.S. equities are priced in decimals (cents), so the minimum spread can be in cents (e.g., $30.10–$30.12).

The espoused reasons for the change to decimal pricing are threefold. First is the ease with which investors can understand the prices and compare them. Second, decimal pricing should save investors money since it reduces the size of the bid–ask spread from a minimum of 6.25 cents (when prices are quoted in sixteenths) to 1 cent (when prices are in decimals). (Of

---

[1] You should be aware that common stocks are currently sold in decimals (dollars and cents), which is a significant change from the pre-2000 period when they were priced in eighths and sixteenths. This change to decimals is discussed at the end of this subsection.

course, this is also why many brokers and investment firms were against the change—the spread is the price of liquidity for the investor and the compensation to the dealer.) Third, the change should make U.S. markets more competitive on a global basis since other countries price on a comparable basis. Thus, transaction costs should be lower.

The effect of decimalization has been substantial. Because it reduced spread size, there has been a decline in transaction costs. This has led to a decline in transaction size and a corresponding increase in the number of transactions—for example, the number of transactions on the NYSE went from a daily average of 877,000 in 2000 to 3,702,000 in 2004, while the average trade size went from 1,187 shares in 2000 to 393 shares in 2004.

Organization of the Securities Market

Before we discuss the specific operation of the securities market, we need to understand its overall organization. The principal distinction is between **primary markets**, where new securities are sold, and **secondary markets**, where outstanding securities are bought and sold. Each of these markets is further divided based on the economic unit that issued the security. We will consider each of these major segments of the securities market, with an emphasis on the individuals involved and the functions they perform.

PRIMARY CAPITAL MARKETS

The primary market is where new issues of bonds, preferred stock, or common stock are sold by government units, municipalities, or companies to acquire new capital. For a review of studies on the primary market, see Jensen and Smith (1986).

Government Bond Issues

All U.S. government bond issues are subdivided into three segments based on their original maturities. **Treasury bills** are negotiable, non-interest-bearing securities with original maturities of one year or less. **Treasury notes** have original maturities of 2 to 10 years. Finally, **Treasury bonds** have original maturities of more than 10 years.

To sell bills, notes, and bonds, the Treasury relies on Federal Reserve System auctions. (The bidding process and pricing are discussed in Chapter 17.)

Municipal Bond Issues

New municipal bond issues are sold by one of three methods: competitive bid, negotiation, or private placement. **Competitive bid** sales typically involve sealed bids. The bond issue is sold to the bidding syndicate of underwriters that submits the bid with the lowest interest cost in accordance with the stipulations set forth by the issuer. **Negotiated sales** involve contractual arrangements between underwriters and issuers wherein the underwriter helps the issuer prepare the bond issue and set the price and has the exclusive right to sell the issue. **Private placements** involve the sale of a bond issue by the issuer directly to an investor or a small group of investors (usually institutions).

Note that two of the three methods require an *underwriting* function. Specifically, in a competitive bid or a negotiated transaction, the investment banker typically underwrites the issue, which means the investment firm purchases the entire issue at a specified price, relieving the issuer from the risk and responsibility of selling and distributing the bonds. Subsequently, the underwriter sells the issue to the investing public. For municipal bonds, this underwriting function is performed by both investment banking firms and commercial banks.

The underwriting function can involve three services: origination, risk-bearing, and distribution. Origination involves the design of the bond issue and initial planning. To fulfill the risk-bearing function, the underwriter acquires the total issue at a price dictated by the competitive bid or through negotiation and accepts the responsibility and risk of reselling it for more than the purchase price. Distribution means selling it to investors, typically with the help of a selling syndicate that includes other investment banking firms and/or commercial banks.

In a negotiated bid, the underwriter will carry out all three services. In a competitive bid, the issuer specifies the amount, maturities, coupons, and call features of the issue and the competing syndicates submit a bid for the entire issue that reflects the yields they estimate for the bonds. The issuer may have received advice from an investment firm on the desirable characteristics for a forthcoming issue, but this advice would have been on a fee basis and would not necessarily involve the ultimate underwriter who is responsible for risk-bearing and distribution. Finally, a private placement involves no risk-bearing, but an investment banker would typically assist in locating potential buyers and negotiating the characteristics of the issue.

Corporate Bond Issues

Corporate bond issues are almost always sold through a negotiated arrangement with an investment banking firm that maintains a relationship with the issuing firm. In a global capital market that involves an explosion of new instruments, the origination function, which involves the design of the security in terms of characteristics and currency, is becoming more important because the corporate chief financial officer (CFO) will probably not be completely familiar with the availability and issuing requirements of many new instruments and the alternative capital markets around the world. Investment banking firms compete for underwriting business by creating new instruments that appeal to existing investors and by advising issuers regarding desirable countries and currencies. As a result, the expertise of the investment banker can help reduce the issuer's cost of new capital.

Once a stock or bond issue is specified, the underwriter will put together an underwriting syndicate of other major underwriters and a selling group of smaller firms for its distribution, as shown in Exhibit 4.1.

Corporate Stock Issues

In addition to the ability to issue fixed-income securities to get new capital, corporations can also issue equity securities—generally common stock. For corporations, new stock issues are typically divided into two groups: (1) seasoned equity issues and (2) initial public offerings (IPOs).

Seasoned equity issues are new shares offered by firms that already have stock outstanding. An example would be General Electric, which is a large, well-regarded firm that has had public stock trading on the NYSE for over 50 years. If General Electric needed additional capital, it could sell additional shares of its common stock to the public at a price very close to the current price of the firm's stock.

Initial public offerings (IPOs) involve a firm selling its common stock to the public for the first time. At the time of an IPO offering, there is no existing public market for the stock; that is, the company has been closely held. An example was an IPO by Polo Ralph Lauren at $26 per share. At the time, the company was a leading manufacturer and distributor of men's clothing. The purpose of the offering was to get additional capital to expand its operations.

New issues (seasoned or IPOs) are typically underwritten by investment bankers, who acquire the total issue from the company and sell the securities to interested investors. The underwriter

| Exhibit 4.1 | The Underwriting Organization Structure |

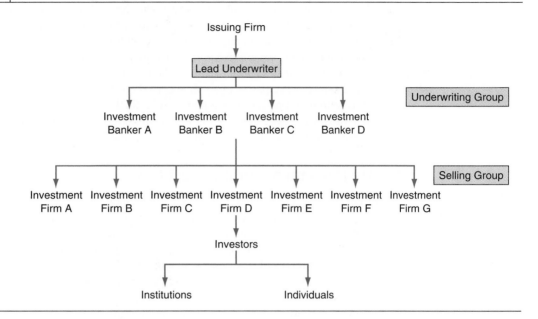

gives advice to the corporation on the general characteristics of the issue, its pricing, and the timing of the offering. The underwriter also accepts the risk of selling the new issue after acquiring it from the corporation. For further discussion, see Brealey and Myers (2004, Chapter 15).

Relationships with Investment Bankers   The underwriting of corporate issues typically takes one of three forms: negotiated, competitive bids, or best-efforts arrangements. As noted, negotiated underwritings are the most common, and the procedure is the same as for municipal issues.

A corporation may also specify the type of securities to be offered (common stock, preferred stock, or bonds) and then solicit competitive bids from investment banking firms. This is rare for industrial firms but is typical for utilities, which may be required by law to sell the issue via a competitive bid. Although a competitive bid typically reduces the cost of an issue, it also means that the investment banker gives less advice but still accepts the risk-bearing function by underwriting the issue and fulfills the distribution function.

Alternatively, an investment banker can agree to sell an issue on a *best-efforts basis*. This is usually done with speculative new issues. In this arrangement, the investment banker does not underwrite the issue because it does not buy any securities. The stock is owned by the company, and the investment banker acts as a *broker* to sell whatever it can at a stipulated price. Because it bears no risk, the investment banker earns a lower commission on such an issue than on an underwritten issue.

Introduction of Rule 415   The typical practice of negotiated arrangements involving numerous investment banking firms in syndicates and selling groups has changed with the introduction of Rule 415, which allows large firms to register security issues and sell them piecemeal during the following two years. These issues are referred to as *shelf registrations* because, after they are registered, the issues lie on the shelf and can be taken down and sold on short notice whenever it suits the issuing firm. As an example, General Electric could register an issue of 5 million shares of common stock during 2006 and sell a million shares in early 2006, another million shares late in 2006, 2 million shares in early 2007, and the rest in late 2007.

Each offering can be made with little notice or paperwork by one underwriter or several. In fact, because relatively few shares may be involved, the lead underwriter often handles the whole deal without a syndicate or uses only one or two other firms. This arrangement has benefited large corporations because it provides great flexibility, reduces registration fees and expenses, and allows firms issuing securities to request competitive bids from several investment banking firms.

On the other hand, some observers fear that shelf registrations do not allow investors enough time to examine the current status of the firm issuing the securities. Also, the follow-up offerings reduce the participation of small underwriters because the underwriting syndicates are smaller and selling groups are almost nonexistent. Shelf registrations have typically been used for the sale of straight debentures rather than common stock or convertible issues. For further discussion of Rule 415, see Rogowski and Sorensen (1985).

Private Placements and Rule 144A

Rather than a public sale using one of these arrangements, primary offerings can be sold privately. In such an arrangement, referred to as a *private placement,* the firm designs an issue with the assistance of an investment banker and sells it to a small group of institutions. The firm enjoys lower issuing costs because it does not need to prepare the extensive registration statement required for a public offering. The institution that buys the issue typically benefits because the issuing firm passes some of these cost savings on to the investor as a higher return. In fact, the institution should require a higher return because of the absence of any secondary market for these securities, which implies higher liquidity risk.

The private placement market changed dramatically when Rule 144A was introduced by the SEC. This rule allows corporations—including non-U.S. firms—to place securities privately with large, sophisticated institutional investors without extensive registration documents. It also allows these securities to be subsequently traded among these large sophisticated investors (those with assets in excess of $100 million). The SEC intends to provide more financing alternatives for U.S. and non-U.S. firms and possibly increase the number, size, and liquidity of private placements, as discussed by Milligan (1990) and Hanks (1990). Presently, over 80 percent of high-yield bonds are issued as 144A issues.

SECONDARY FINANCIAL MARKETS

In this section we first consider the purpose and importance of secondary markets and provide an overview of the secondary markets for bonds, financial futures, and stocks. Next, we consider national stock markets around the world. Finally, we discuss other primary listing markets, regional exchanges, third markets, and the rapidly growing electronic communication networks (ECNs) and provide a detailed presentation on the functioning of stock exchanges.

Secondary markets permit trading in outstanding issues; that is, stocks or bonds already sold to the public are traded between current and potential owners. The proceeds from a sale in the secondary market do not go to the issuing unit (the government, municipality, or company), but rather to the current owner of the security.

Why Secondary Markets Are Important

Before discussing the various segments of the secondary market, we must consider its overall importance. Because the secondary market involves the trading of securities initially sold in the primary market, *it provides liquidity to the individuals who acquired these securities.* After acquiring securities in the primary market, investors may want to sell them again to acquire other securities, buy a house, or go on a vacation. The primary market benefits greatly from the liquidity provided by the secondary market because investors would hesitate to acquire securities in the primary market if they thought they could not subsequently sell them in the secondary market. That is, without an active secondary market, potential issuers of stocks or bonds in the primary market would have to provide a much higher rate of return to compensate investors for the substantial liquidity risk.

Secondary markets are also important to those selling seasoned securities because the prevailing market price of the securities (*price discovery*) is determined by transactions in the secondary market. New issues of outstanding stocks or bonds to be sold in the primary market are based on prices and yields in the secondary market. Notably, the secondary market also has an effect on market efficiency and price volatility, as discussed by Foster and Viswanathan (1993) and Jones, Kaul, and Lipson (1994). Even forthcoming IPOs are priced based on the prices and values of comparable stocks or bonds in the public secondary market.

Secondary Bond Markets

The secondary market for bonds distinguishes among those issued by the federal government, municipalities, or corporations.

Secondary Markets for U.S. Government and Municipal Bonds   U.S. government bonds are traded by bond dealers that specialize in either Treasury bonds or agency bonds. Treasury issues are bought or sold through a set of 35 primary dealers, including large banks in New York and Chicago and some of the large investment banking firms (for example, Merrill Lynch, Goldman Sachs, Morgan Stanley). These institutions and other firms also make markets for government agency issues, but there is no formal set of dealers for agency securities.

The major market makers in the secondary municipal bond market are banks and investment firms. Banks are active in municipal bond trading and underwriting of general obligation issues since they invest heavily in these securities. Also, many large investment firms have municipal bond departments that underwrite and trade these issues.

Secondary Corporate Bond Markets   Currently, all corporate bonds are traded over the counter by dealers who buy and sell for their own accounts. The major bond dealers are the large investment banking firms that underwrite the issues: firms such as Merrill Lynch, Goldman Sachs, Salomon Brothers, Lehman Brothers, and Morgan Stanley. Because of the limited trading in corporate bonds compared to the fairly active trading in government bonds, corporate bond dealers do not carry extensive inventories of specific issues. Instead, they hold a limited number of bonds desired by their clients, and when someone wants to do a trade, they work more like brokers than dealers.

Notably, there is a movement toward a widespread transaction-reporting service as with stocks, especially for some large, actively traded bond issues. For example, *The Wall Street Journal* publishes a table entitled "Corporate Bonds" that contains daily trading information on forty active bonds. Also, as discussed further in Chapter 17, as of July 2005, dealers are required to report trades within 15 minutes of the transaction on 17,000 corporate bonds.

Financial Futures

In addition to the market for the bonds, a market has developed for futures contracts related to these bonds. These contracts allow the holder to buy or sell a specified amount of a given bond issue at a stipulated price. The two major futures exchanges are the Chicago Board of Trade (CBOT) and the Chicago Mercantile Exchange (CME). We discuss these futures contracts and the futures market in Chapter 19.

Secondary Equity Markets

Before 2000, the secondary equity markets in the United States and around the world were divided into three segments: national stock exchanges, regional stock exchanges, and over-the-counter (OTC) markets for stocks not on an exchange. Because of numerous changes over the past decade, a better classification has been suggested by Harris (2003), as presented in Exhibit 4.2. Following our background discussions on alternative trading systems and call versus continuous markets, we will describe the market types listed in Exhibit 4.2 and discuss how they complement and compete against each other to provide price discovery and liquidity to individual and institutional investors.

Basic Trading Systems   Although stock exchanges are similar in that only qualified stocks can be traded by individuals who are members of the exchange, they can differ in their *trading systems*. There are two major trading systems, and an exchange can use one or a combination of them. One is a *pure auction market* (also referred to as an *order-driven market*), in which interested buyers and sellers submit bid-and-ask prices for a given stock to a central location where the orders are matched by a broker who does not own the stock but acts as a facilitating

| Exhibit 4.2 | **U.S. Secondary Equity Markets: Classification and Examples** |

Market Type	Examples
Primary listing markets	New York Stock Exchange
	American Stock Exchange
	Nasdaq National Market System (NMS)
	Nasdaq Small-Cap Market (SCM)
	Nasdaq OTC Electronic Bulletin Board
	National Quotation Bureau (NQB) Pink Sheets
Regional markets	Boston Stock Exchange
	Chicago Stock Exchange
	Cincinnati Stock Exchange
	Pacific Exchange
	Philadelphia Stock Exchange
Third-market dealers/brokers	Madoff Investment Securities
	Knight Trading Group
	Jefferies Group
	ITG
	Nasdaq InterMarket
Alternative Trading Systems (ATSs)	
Electronic Communications	
Networks (ECNs)	Archipelago
	BRUT
	Instinet
	Island
	REDIBook
Electronic Crossing Systems (ECSs)	POSIT
	Global Instinet Crossing
	Arizona Stock Exchange

Source: Adapted from Larry Harris, *Trading and Exchanges* (Oxford University Press, 2003), p. 49.

agent. Participants also refer to this system as *price-driven* because shares of stock are sold to the investor with the highest bid price and bought from the seller with the lowest offering price. Advocates of an auction market argue for a very centralized market that ideally will include all the buyers and sellers of the stock.

The other major trading system is a *dealer market* (also referred to as a *quote-driven* market) where individual dealers provide liquidity for investors by buying and selling the shares of stock for themselves. Ideally, with this system there will be numerous dealers who will compete against each other to provide the highest bid prices when you are selling and the lowest asking price when you are buying stock. Clearly, this is a very decentralized system that derives its benefit from the competition among the dealers to provide the best price for the buyer and seller. When we discuss the various equity markets, we will indicate the trading system used.

Call versus Continuous Markets   Beyond the different trading systems for equities, the operation of exchanges can differ in terms of when and how the stocks are traded.

In **call markets**, the intent is to gather all the bids and asks for the stock at a point in time and attempt to arrive at a single price where the quantity demanded is as close as possible to the quantity supplied. Call markets are generally used during the early stages of development of an exchange when there are few stocks listed or a small number of active investors–traders. For an exchange that is strictly a call market with a few listed stocks and traders, a designated market maker would call the roll of stocks and ask for interest in one stock at a time. After determining the available buy and sell orders, exchange officials specify a single price that will satisfy *most* of the orders, and all orders are transacted at this price.

Notably, call markets also are used at the opening for stocks on a large exchange if there is an overnight buildup of buy and/or sell orders, in which case the opening price can differ from the prior day's closing price. Also, this concept is used if trading is suspended during the day because of some significant new information. In either case, the specialist or market maker would attempt to derive a new equilibrium price using a call-market approach that would reflect the imbalance and take care of most of the orders. For example, assume a stock has been trading at about $42 per share and some significant, new, positive information was released overnight or during the day. If it happened overnight it would affect the opening price; if it happened during the day, trading would be temporarily suspended and a call-market process would be used to determine a new equilibrium price that reflects the supply and demand due to the new information. If the buy orders were three or four times as numerous as the sell orders, the price based on the call market might be $44. For an analysis of price movements surrounding trading halts, see Hopewell and Schwartz (1978) and Fabozzi and Ma (1988). Several studies have shown that using the call-market mechanism contributes to a more orderly market and less volatility in such instances.

In a **continuous market**, trades occur at any time the market is open wherein stocks are priced either by auction or by dealers. In a dealer market, dealers make a market in the stock, which means that they are willing to buy or sell for their own account at a specified bid-and-ask price. In an auction market, enough buyers and sellers are trading to allow the market to be continuous; that is, when one investor comes to buy stock, there is another investor available and willing to sell stock. A compromise between a pure dealer market and a pure auction market is a combination structure wherein the market is basically an auction market, but there exists an intermediary who is willing to act as a dealer if the pure auction market does not have enough activity. These intermediaries who act as both brokers and dealers provide temporary liquidity to ensure the market will be liquid and continuous.

The two tables in the chapter appendix list the characteristics of stock exchanges around the world and indicate whether the exchange provides a continuous market, a call-market mechanism, or a mixture of the two. Notably, many continuous auction market exchanges employ a call-market mechanism on specific occasions at the open and during trading suspensions. The NYSE is such a market.

CLASSIFICATION OF U.S. SECONDARY EQUITY MARKETS

Now let's delve into the different secondary equity markets that currently exist in the United States, as listed in Exhibit 4.2.

Primary Listing Markets

Primary listing markets are formal exchanges or markets where a corporate stock is primarily or formally listed. This category includes the two traditional national exchanges (New York Stock Exchange and American Stock Exchange) and the Nasdaq markets that previously were considered over-the-counter markets but are now recognized as equity markets that simply differ in how they trade securities (as will be discussed).

New York Stock Exchange (NYSE)   The New York Stock Exchange (NYSE), the largest organized securities market in the United States, was established in 1817 as the New York Stock and Exchange Board. The Exchange dates its founding to when the famous Buttonwood Agreement was signed in May 1792 by 24 brokers.[2] The name was changed to the New York Stock Exchange in 1863.

At the end of 2004, approximately 2,747 companies had their stock listed on the NYSE, for a total of about 3,000 stock issues (common and preferred) with a total market value of more than $12.5 trillion. The specific listing requirements for the NYSE appear in Exhibit 4.3.

The average number of shares traded daily on the NYSE has increased steadily and substantially, as shown in Exhibit 4.4. Prior to the 1960s, the daily share trading volume averaged less than 3 million shares, compared with the 2004 average daily volume of about 1.46 billion shares.

Exhibit 4.3	**Listing Requirements for Stocks on the NYSE**

Pretax income last year	$2,500,000
Pretax income last two years	2,000,000
Shares publicly held	1,100,000
Market value of publicly held shares[a]	100,000,000
Minimum number of holders of round lots (100 shares or more)	2,000

[a]This minimum required market value is $60 million for spin-offs, carve-outs, or IPOs and it varies over time, depending on the value of the NYSE Common Stock Index. For specifics, see the *2004 NYSE Fact Book,* 37.

Source: *NYSE Fact Book* (New York: NYSE, 2004): 37.

---

[2]The NYSE considers the signing of this agreement the birth of the Exchange and celebrated its 200th birthday during 1992.

Exhibit 4.4	Average Daily Reported Share Volume Traded on Selected Stock Markets (× 1,000)

Year	NYSE	Nasdaq	Year	NYSE	Nasdaq
1955	2,578	N.A.	1996	411,953	543,700
1960	3,042	N.A.	1997	526,925	650,324
1965	6,176	N.A.	1998	673,590	801,747
1970	11,564	N.A.	1999	809,183	1,077,500
1975	18,551	5,500	2000	1,041,578	1,759,900
1980	44,871	26,500	2001	1,239,957	1,900,068
1985	109,169	82,100	2002	1,441,015	1,752,643
1990	156,777	131,900	2003	1,398,400	1,449,000
1995	346,101	401,400	2004	1,457,000	1,259,000

N.A. = not available.

Sources: *NYSE Fact Book* (various issues); Nasdaq Research Department.

Exhibit 4.5	Membership Prices on the NYSE ($000)

Year	High	Low	Year	High	Low
1925	$150	$99	1995	$1,050	$785
1935	140	65	1996	1,450	1,225
1945	95	49	1997	1,750	1,175
1955	90	49	1998	2,000	1,225
1960	162	135	1999	2,650	2,000
1965	250	190	2000	2,000	1,650
1970	320	130	2001	2,300	2,000
1975	138	55	2002	2,550	2,000
1980	275	175	2003	2,000	1,500
1985	480	310	2004	1,515	975
1990	430	250			

Source: *NYSE Fact Book* (New York: NYSE, 2005): 110. Reprinted by permission of the New York Stock Exchange.

The NYSE has dominated the other exchanges in the United States in trading volume. Given its stringent listing requirements and its prestige, most of the largest and best known U.S. companies are listed on the NYSE. Historically, about 80 percent of the trading volume for these stocks takes place on the NYSE.

The volume of trading and relative stature of the NYSE is reflected in the price of a membership on the exchange (referred to as a *seat*). As shown in Exhibit 4.5, the price of membership has fluctuated in line with trading volume and other factors that influence the profitability of membership, as discussed by Ip (1998a).

American Stock Exchange (AMEX) The American Stock Exchange (AMEX) was begun by a group who traded unlisted shares at the corner of Wall and Hanover Streets in New York. It was originally called the Outdoor Curb Market. In 1910, it established formal trading rules and changed its name to the New York Curb Market Association. The members moved inside a building in 1921 and continued to trade mainly in unlisted stocks (stocks not listed on one of the registered exchanges) until 1946, when its volume in listed stocks finally outnumbered that in unlisted stocks. The current name was adopted in 1953.

The AMEX is a national exchange, distinct from the NYSE because, except for a short period in the late 1970s, no stocks have been listed on both the NYSE and AMEX at the same time. Historically, the AMEX emphasized foreign securities and warrants.

The AMEX became a major stock options exchange in January 1975 and subsequently has added options on interest rates and stock indexes. In addition, exchange-traded funds (ETFs) that have grown in number and popularity (as discussed in Chapter 3) are almost all listed on the AMEX.

The AMEX and the Nasdaq merged in 1998, although they continued to operate as separate markets. In 2005 Nasdaq sold the AMEX back to its members (see Horowirtz and Kelly, 2005).

An Aside on Global Stock Exchanges   The equity-market environment outside the United States is similar in that each country typically will have one relatively large exchange that dominates the market. Examples include the Tokyo Stock Exchange, the London Stock Exchange, the Frankfurt Stock Exchange, and the Paris Bourse. Exhibit 4A.1 in the chapter appendix lists the exchanges in developed economies, along with some descriptive characteristics of these exchanges.

In a few instances there may also be regional exchanges, but these are rare. Notably, even in small or emerging economies, stock exchanges have been created because of the liquidity that secondary equity markets provide, as discussed earlier. Exhibit 4A.2 lists and describes many of the emerging-market exchanges.

Three points about these international exchanges: first, there has been a trend toward consolidations or affiliations that will provide more liquidity and greater economies of scale to support the technology required by investors. Second, many of the larger companies in these countries that can qualify for listing on a U.S. exchange become dual-listed. As a result, about 20 percent of the stocks listed on the NYSE are non-U.S. firms. Third, the existence of these strong international exchanges has made possible a global equity market wherein stocks that have a global constituency can be traded around the world continuously, as discussed in the following section. There is intense competition between the various exchanges, as discussed by Ewing and Ascarelli (2000) and Cherney and Beal (2000).

The Global 24-Hour Market   Our discussion of the global securities market will emphasize the markets in New York, London, and Tokyo because of their relative size and importance, and because they represent the major segments of a worldwide 24-hour stock market. You will often hear about a continuous market where investment firms "pass the book" around the world. This means the major active market in securities moves around the globe as trading hours for these three markets begin and end.

Consider the individual trading hours for each of the three exchanges, translated into a 24-hour eastern standard time (EST) clock:

	Local Time (24-hr. notations)	24-Hour EST
New York Stock Exchange (NYSE)	0930–1600	0930–1600
Tokyo Stock Exchange (TSE)	0900–1100	2300–0100
	1300–1500	0300–0500
London Stock Exchange (LSE)	0815–1615	0215–1015

Imagine trading starting in New York at 0930 and going until 1600 in the afternoon, being picked up by Tokyo late in the evening and going until 0500 in the morning, and continuing in London (with some overlap) until it begins in New York again (with some overlap) at 0930. Alternatively, it is possible to envision trading as beginning in Tokyo at 2300 hours and continuing until 0500, when it moves to London, then ends the day in New York. This latter model seems the most relevant, because the first question a London trader asks in the morning is, "What happened in Tokyo?" The U.S. trader asks, "What happened in Tokyo and what *is* happening in London?" The point is, the markets operate almost continuously and are related in their response to economic events. Therefore, investors are not dealing with three separate and distinct exchanges, but with one interrelated world market. Clearly, this interrelationship is growing daily because of numerous multiple listings where stocks are listed on several exchanges around the world (such as the NYSE and TSE) and the availability of sophisticated telecommunications. Examples of stocks that are part of this global market are General Electric, Pfizer, Johnson and Johnson, and McDonald's.

Nasdaq National Market System (NMS)[3]   This system has historically been known as the over-the-counter (OTC) market, which included stocks not formally listed on the two major exchanges (NYSE and AMEX). This description has changed since it has been recognized that this is an equity market similar to the major exchanges with several differences that are not relevant to the purpose of this market. The first difference is that it is a *dealer market,* in contrast to a broker/dealer (specialists) market as is the NYSE. Second, exchange trading takes place electronically rather than on a trading floor as in the other exchanges. What Nasdaq has in common with the other exchanges is a set of requirements for a stock to be traded on the Nasdaq NMS. Also, while Nasdaq dealers do not have to pay for a seat (membership) on the exchange, they are required to be members of the National Association of Security Dealers (NASD) and abide by its rules.

Size of the Nasdaq NMS   The Nasdaq NMS market is the largest segment of the U.S. secondary market in terms of the number of issues traded. As noted earlier, there are about 3,000 issues traded on the NYSE and about 600 issues on the AMEX. In contrast, more than 2,800 issues are actively traded on the Nasdaq NMS and almost 700 on the Nasdaq Small-Cap Market (SCM). The Nasdaq market is also the most diverse secondary market component in terms of quality because it has multiple minimum requirements. Stocks that trade on the total Nasdaq market (NMS and SCM) range from those of small, unprofitable companies to large, extremely profitable firms such as Microsoft and Intel.

Nasdaq's growth in average daily trading is shown in Exhibit 4.4 relative to that of the NYSE. At the end of 2004 almost 650 issues of Nasdaq were either foreign stocks or American Depository Receipts (ADRs), representing over 8 percent of total Nasdaq share volume. About 300 of these issues trade on both Nasdaq and a foreign exchange such as Toronto. Nasdaq has developed a link with the Singapore Stock Exchange that allows 24-hour trading from Nasdaq in New York to Singapore to a Nasdaq/London link and back to New York.

Although the Nasdaq market has the greatest number of issues, the NYSE has a larger total value of trading. In 2004 the approximate value of average daily equity trading on the NYSE was about $46 billion and on Nasdaq was about $27 billion.

Operation of the Nasdaq Market   As noted, stocks can be traded on the Nasdaq market as long as there are dealers who indicate a willingness to make a market by buying or selling for their own account.[4]

---

[3]Nasdaq is an acronym for National Association of Securities Dealers Automated Quotations. The system is discussed in detail in a later section. To be traded on the NMS, a firm must have a certain size and trading activity and at least four market makers. A specification of requirements for various components of the Nasdaq system is contained in Exhibit 4.6.

[4]*Dealer* and *market maker* are synonymous.

The Nasdaq System   The *National Association of Securities Dealers Automated Quotation (Nasdaq) system* is an automated, electronic quotation system. Any number of dealers can elect to make markets in a Nasdaq stock. The actual number depends on the activity in the stock. In 2004, the average number of market makers for all stocks on the Nasdaq NMS was about eight.

Nasdaq makes all dealer quotes available immediately. The broker can check the quotation machine and call the dealer with the best market, verify that the quote has not changed, and make the sale or purchase. The Nasdaq quotation system has three levels to serve firms with different needs and interests.

Level 1 provides a single median representative quote for the stocks on Nasdaq. This quotation system is for firms that want current quotes on Nasdaq stocks but do not consistently buy or sell these stocks for their customers and are not market makers. This representative quote changes constantly to adjust for any changes by individual market makers.

Level 2 provides instantaneous current quotations on Nasdaq stocks by all market makers in a stock. This quotation system is for firms that consistently trade Nasdaq stocks. Given an order to buy or sell, brokers check the quotation machine, call the market maker with the best market for their purposes (highest bid if they are selling, lowest offer if buying), and consummate the deal.

Level 3 is for Nasdaq market makers. Such firms want Level 2, but they also need the capability to change their own quotations, which Level 3 provides.

Listing Requirements for Nasdaq   Quotes and trading volume for the Nasdaq market are reported in two lists: a National Market System (NMS) list and a regular Nasdaq list. Exhibit 4.6 contains the alternative standards for initial listing and continued listing on the Nasdaq NMS as of late 2004. A company must meet all of the requirements under at least one of the three listing standards for initial listing and then meet at least one continued listing standard to maintain its listing on the NMS. For stocks on this system, reports include up-to-the-minute volume and last-sale information for the competing market makers as well as end-of-the-day information on total volume and high, low, and closing prices.

A Sample Trade   Assume you are considering the purchase of 100 shares of Intel. Although Intel is large enough and profitable enough to be listed on the NYSE, the company has never applied for listing because it enjoys an active market on Nasdaq. (It is one of the volume leaders, with daily volume typically above 25 million shares and often in excess of 50 million shares.) When you contact your broker, she will consult the Nasdaq electronic quotation machine to determine the current dealer quotations for INTC, the trading symbol for Intel.[5] The quote machine will show that about 35 dealers are making a market in INTC. An example of differing quotations might be as follows:

Dealer	Bid	Ask
1	30.60	30.75
2	30.55	30.65
3	30.50	30.65
4	30.55	30.70

---

[5]Trading symbols are one- to four-letter codes used to designate stocks. Whenever a trade is reported on a stock ticker, the trading symbol appears with the figures. Many symbols are obvious, such as GM (General Motors), F (Ford Motors), GE (General Electric), GS (Goldman Sachs), HD (Home Depot), AMGN (Amgen), and DELL (Dell).

Exhibit 4.6	**Nasdaq National Market Listing Requirements**

A company must meet all of the requirements under at least one of three listing standards for initial listing on The Nasdaq National Market®. A company must continue to meet at least one continued listing standard to maintain its listing.

	INITIAL LISTING			CONTINUED LISTING	
Requirements	**Standard 1 Marketplace Rule 4420(a)**	**Standard 2 Marketplace Rule 4420(b)**	**Standard 3 Marketplace Rule 4420(c)**	**Standard 1 Marketplace Rule 4450(a)**	**Standard 2 Marketplace Rule 4450(b)**
Stockholders' equity	$15 million	$30 million	N/A	$10 million	N/A
Market value of listed securities	N/A	N/A	$75 million[1,2]	N/A	$50 million
or			or		or
Total assets			$75 million		$50 million
and			and		and
Total revenue			$75 million		$50 million
Income from continuing operations before income taxes (in latest fiscal year or 2 of last 3 fiscal years)	$1 million	N/A	N/A	N/A	N/A
Publicly held shares[3]	1.1 million	1.1 million	1.1 million	750,000	1.1 million
Market value of publicly held shares	$8 million	$18 million	$20 million	$5 million	$15 million
Minimum bid price	$5	$5	$5[2]	$1	$1
Shareholders (round lot holders)[4]	400	400	400	400	400
Market makers[5]	3	3	4	2	4
Operating history	N/A	2 years	N/A	N/A	N/A
Corporate governance[6]	Yes	Yes	Yes	Yes	Yes

[1]For initial listing under Standard 3, a company must satisfy one of the following: the market value of listed securities requirement or the total assets and the total revenue requirement. Under Marketplace Rule 4200(a)(20), listed securities is defined as "securities quoted on Nasdaq or listed on a national securities exchange."
[2]Seasoned companies (those companies already listed or quoted on another market place) qualifying only under the market value of listed securities requirement of Standard 3 must meet the market value of listed securities and the bid price requirements for 90 consecutive trading days prior to applying for listing.
[3]Publicly held shares is defined as total shares outstanding less any shares held by officers, directors, or beneficial owners of 10 percent or more.
[4]Round lot holders are shareholders of 100 shares or more.
[5]An Electronic Communications Network (ECN) is not considered a market maker for the purpose of these rules.
[6]Marketplace Rules 4350 and 4351.
Source: http://www.Nasdaq.com (accessed September 2004).

Assuming these are the best markets available from the total group, your broker would call either dealer 2 or dealer 3 because they have the lowest offering prices. After verifying the quote, your broker would give one of these dealers an order to buy 100 shares of INTC at $30.65 a share. Because your firm was not a market maker in the stock, the firm would act as a broker and charge you $3,065 plus a commission for the trade. If your firm had been a market maker in INTC, with an asking price of $30.65 the firm would have sold the stock to you at \$30.65 net (without commission). If you had been interested in selling 100 shares of Intel instead of buying, the broker would have contacted dealer 1, who made the highest bid (\$30.60).

Changing Dealer Inventory   Let's consider the price quotations by a Nasdaq dealer who wants to change his inventory on a given stock. For example, assume dealer 4, with a current quote of 30.55 bid–30.70 ask, decides to increase his holdings of INTC. The Nasdaq quotes indicate that the highest bid is currently 30.60. Increasing the bid to 30.60 would bring some of the business currently going to dealer 1. Taking a more aggressive action, dealer 4 might raise the bid to 30.63 and buy all the stock offered, because he has the highest bid. In this example, the dealer raises the bid price but does not change the ask price, which was above those of dealers 2 and 3. This dealer will buy stock but probably will not sell any. A dealer who had excess stock would keep the bid below the market (lower than 30.60) and reduce the ask price to 30.65 or less. Dealers constantly change their bid-and-ask prices, depending on their current inventories or changes in the outlook based on new information for the stock.

Other Nasdaq Market Segments   Now that we are familiar with the Nasdaq system and its operation, we can easily describe the other segments of this market since the major differences relate to the size and liquidity of the stocks involved.

- **The Nasdaq Small-Cap Market (SCM)** has initial listing requirements that consider the same factors as the NMS but are generally about one-half to one-third of the values required for the NMS. As of May 31, 2004, there were 683 stocks listed in the Nasdaq small-cap segment. This compares to about 600 stocks listed in the section entitled "Nasdaq NM Issues Under \$100 Million Market Cap" and about 2,200 in the section entitled "Nasdaq National Market Issues." In total, the Nasdaq NMS contained 2,819 issues as of May 31, 2004. Therefore, the total Nasdaq market includes 3,502 issues (2,819 NMS and 683 issues on the SCM).
- **The Nasdaq** *OTC Electronic Bulletin Board (OTCBB)* reports indications for smaller stocks sponsored by NASD dealers. As of May 31, 2004, there were 3,305 stocks included on the OTCBB.
- **The National Quotation Bureau (NQB) Pink Sheets** report order indications for the smallest publicly traded stocks in the United States. Pre-1970, these pink sheets (actually printed on pink sheets of paper) were the primary daily source of OTC stock quotes. With the creation of the Nasdaq electronic quotation system, the sheets were superseded. Currently, the NQB publishes a weekly edition on paper and distributes a daily edition electronically with these small-stock quotes.

Regional Stock Exchanges

The second category in Harris's classfication of U.S. secondary markets (Exhibit 4.2) is the regional market. Regional exchanges typically have the same operating procedures as national exchanges in the same countries, but they differ in their listing requirements and the geographic distributions of the listed firms. Regional stock exchanges exist for two main reasons: First, they provide trading facilities for local companies not large enough to qualify for listing on one of the national exchanges. Their listing requirements are typically less stringent than those of the national exchanges.

Second, regional exchanges in some countries list firms that also list on one of the national exchanges to give local brokers who are not members of a national exchange access to these securities. As an example, Wal-Mart and General Motors are listed on both the NYSE and several regional exchanges. This dual listing allows a local brokerage firm that is not large enough to purchase a membership on the NYSE to buy and sell shares of the dual-listed stock without going through the NYSE and giving up part of the commission. In addition, regional exchanges can trade some stocks on the Nasdaq market under *unlisted trading privileges (UTP)* granted by the SEC. The majority of trading on regional exchanges is due to dual-listed and UTP stocks.

The regional exchanges in the United States are shown in Exhibit 4.2. The Chicago, Pacific, and PBW exchanges account for about 90 percent of all regional exchange volume. In turn, total regional exchange volume is 9 to 10 percent of total exchange volume in the United States.

The Third Market

Harris's third category is called the third market. The term **third market** involves dealers and brokers who trade shares that are listed on an exchange away from the exchange. Although most transactions in listed stocks do take place on an exchange, an investment firm that is not a member of an exchange can make a market in a listed stock away from the exchange. Most of the trading on the third market is in well-known stocks such as General Electric, IBM, and Ford. The success or failure of the third market depends on whether the non–exchange market in these stocks is as good as the exchange market and whether the relative cost of the transaction compares favorably with the cost on the exchange. This market is critical during the relatively few periods when trading is not available on the NYSE either because trading is suspended or the exchange is closed. This market has also grown because of the quality and cost factors mentioned. Third market dealers typically display their quotes on the *Nasdaq InterMarket* system. For articles that discuss the impact of regional exchanges and the practice of purchasing order flow, see Battalio (1997); Battalio, Greene, and Jennings (1997); and Easley, Kiefer, and O'Hara (1996).

Alternative Trading Systems (ATSs)

The final category in Exhibit 4.2 is alternative trading systems. This is the facet of the equity market where the biggest changes have occurred during the last decade. *Alternative trading systems (ATSs)* are nontraditional, computerized trading systems that compete with or supplement dealer markets and traditional exchanges. These trading systems facilitate the exchange of millions of shares every day through electronic means. Notably, they do not provide listing services. The most well-known ATSs are the Electronic Communication Networks (ECNs) and the Electronic Crossing Systems (ECSs).

- *Electronic Communication Networks (ECNs)* are electronic facilities that match buy and sell orders directly via computer, mainly for retail and small institutional trading. ECNs do *not* buy or sell from their own account but act as very cheap, efficient electronic brokers. As shown in Exhibit 4.2, the major ECNs are Archipelago, BRUT, Instinet, Island, and REDIBook.
- *Electronic Crossing Systems (ECSs)* are electronic facilities that act as brokers to match *large* buy and sell orders. The most well-known ECSs are POSIT, Global Instinet Crossing, and Arizona Stock Exchange.

The trading of exchange-listed stocks using one of these ATSs has become the *fourth market.*

DETAILED ANALYSIS OF EXCHANGE MARKETS

The importance of listed exchange markets requires that we discuss them at some length. In this section, we discuss alternative members on the exchanges, the major types of orders, and exchange market makers—a critical component of a good exchange market.

Exchange Membership

Stock exchanges typically have four major categories of membership: (1) specialist, (2) commission broker, (3) floor broker, and (4) registered trader. We will discuss specialists (or exchange market makers), who constitute about 25 percent of the total membership on exchanges, after our description of types of orders.

Commission brokers are employees of a member firm who buy or sell for the customers of the firm. When an investment firm receives an order to buy or sell a stock, it transmits it to a commission broker, who takes it to the appropriate trading post on the floor and completes the transaction.

Floor brokers are independent members of an exchange who act as brokers for other members. As an example, when commission brokers for Merrill Lynch become too busy to handle all of their orders, they will ask one of the floor brokers to help them. For a discussion of unwanted notoriety for these brokers, read Starkman and McGeehan (1998) and McGee (1998).

Registered traders use their memberships to buy and sell for their own accounts. While they save commissions on their trading, observers believe they provide the market with added liquidity, even though regulations limit how they trade and how many registered traders can be in a trading crowd around a specialist's booth at any time. Today they often are called **registered competitive market makers (RCMMs)** and have specific trading obligations set by the exchange. Their activity is reported as part of the specialist group.[6]

Types of Orders

It is important to understand the different types of orders available to investors and the specialist as a dealer.

Market Orders   The most frequent type of order is a **market order**, an order to buy or sell a stock at the best current price. An investor who enters a market sell order indicates a willingness to sell immediately at the highest bid available at the time the order reaches a specialist on an exchange, a Nasdaq dealer, or an ECN. A market buy order indicates the investor is willing to pay the lowest offering price available at the time on the exchange, Nasdaq, or an ECN. Market orders provide immediate liquidity for an investor willing to accept the prevailing market price.

Assume you are interested in General Electric (GE) and you call your broker to find out the current "market" on the stock. The quotation machine indicates that the prevailing market is 35 bid–35.10 ask. This means that the highest current bid on the books of the specialist is 35; that is, $35 is the most that anyone has offered to pay for GE. The lowest offer is 35.10; that is, this is the lowest price anyone is willing to accept to sell the stock. If you placed a market buy order for 100 shares, you would buy 100 shares at $35.10 a share (the lowest ask price) for a total cost of $3,510 plus commission. If you submitted a market sell order for 100 shares, you would sell the shares at $35 each and receive $3,500 less commission.

---

[6]Prior to the 1980s, there also were odd-lot dealers who bought and sold to individuals with orders for less than round lots (usually 100 shares). Currently, this function is handled by either the specialist or some large brokerage firm.

Limit Orders   The individual placing a **limit order** specifies the buy or sell price. You might submit a limit-order bid to purchase 100 shares of Coca-Cola (KO) stock at $50 a share when the current market is 60 bid–60.10 ask, with the expectation that the stock will decline to $50 in the near future.

You must also indicate how long the limit order will be outstanding. Alternative time specifications are basically boundless. A limit order can be instantaneous ("fill or kill," meaning fill the order instantly or cancel it). It can also be good for part of a day, a full day, several days, a week, or a month. It can also be open-ended, or good until canceled (GTC).

Rather than wait for a given price on a stock, because KO is listed on the NYSE your broker will give the limit order to the specialist, who will put it in a limit-order book and act as the broker's representative. When and if the market price for KO reaches the limit-order price, the specialist will execute the order and inform your broker. The specialist receives a small part of the commission for rendering this service.

Short Sales   Most investors purchase stock ("go long") expecting to derive their return from an increase in value. If you believe that a stock is overpriced, however, and want to take advantage of an expected decline in the price, you can sell the stock short. A **short sale** is the sale of stock that you do not own with the intent of purchasing it back later at a lower price. Specifically, you would *borrow* the stock from another investor through your broker, sell it in the market, and subsequently replace it at (you hope) a price lower than the price at which you sold it. The investor who lent the stock has the proceeds of the sale as collateral and can invest these funds in short-term, risk-free securities. Although a short sale has no time limit, the lender of the shares can decide to sell the shares, in which case your broker must find another investor willing to lend the shares. For discussions of both good and bad experiences with short-selling, see Power (1993), Loomis (1996), Weiss (1996), Beard (2001), and McKay (2005).

Three technical points affect short sales. First, a short sale can be made only on an *uptick trade,* meaning the price of the short sale must be higher than the last trade price. This is because the exchanges do not want traders to force a profit on a short sale by pushing the price down through continually selling short. Therefore, the transaction price for a short sale must be an uptick or, without any change in price, the previous price must have been higher than its previous price (a zero uptick). For an example of a zero uptick, consider the following set of transaction prices: 42, 42.25, 42.25. You could sell short at 42.25 even though it is no change from the previous trade at 42.25 because that previous trade was an uptick trade.

The second technical point concerns dividends. The short seller must pay any dividends due to the investor who lent the stock. The purchaser of the short-sale stock receives the dividend from the corporation, so the short seller must pay a similar dividend to the lender.

Finally, short sellers must post the same margin as an investor who had acquired stock. This margin can be in any unrestricted securities owned by the short seller.

Special Orders   In addition to these general orders, there are several special types of orders. A *stop loss order* is a conditional market order whereby the investor directs the sale of a stock if it drops to a given price. Assume you buy a stock at 50 and expect it to go up. If you are wrong, you want to limit your losses. To protect yourself, you could put in a stop loss order at 45. In this case, if the stock dropped to 45, your stop loss order would become a market sell order, and the stock would be sold at the prevailing market price. The stop loss order does not guarantee that you will get the $45; you can get a little bit more or a little bit less. Because of the possibility of market disruption caused by a large number of stop loss orders, exchanges have, on occasion, canceled all such orders on certain stocks and not allowed brokers to accept further stop loss orders on those issues.

A related stop loss tactic for an investor who has entered into a short sale is a *stop buy order.* Such an investor who wants to minimize loss if the stock begins to increase in value would enter

Exhibit 4.7 | **NYSE Member Firm Customers' Margin Debt in Dollars and as a Percentage of U.S. Market Capitalization: 1993–2004**

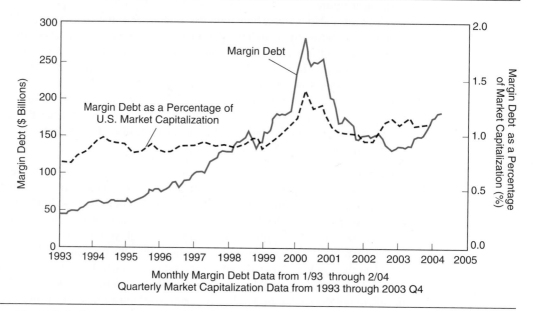

Monthly Margin Debt Data from 1/93 through 2/04
Quarterly Market Capitalization Data from 1993 through 2003 Q4

Sources: Federal Reserve Board; New York Stock Exchange; Goldman Sachs Portfolio Strategy.

this conditional buy order at a price above the short-sale price. Assume you sold a stock short at 50, expecting it to decline to 40. To protect yourself from an increase, you could put in a stop buy order to purchase the stock using a market buy order if it reached a price of 55. This conditional buy order would hopefully limit any loss on the short sale to approximately $5 a share.

Margin Transactions   When investors buy stock, they can pay for the stock with cash or borrow part of the cost, leveraging the transaction. Leverage is accomplished by buying on **margin**, which means the investor pays for the stock with some cash and borrows the rest through the broker, putting up the stock for collateral.

As shown in Exhibit 4.7, the dollar amount of margin credit extended by NYSE members increased consistently since 1993, hitting a peak in early 2000 followed by a decline into 2003 and a subsequent increase in dollar terms but not as a percent of market capitalization. The interest rate charged on these loans by the investment firms is typically 1.50 percent above the rate charged by the bank making the loan. The bank rate, referred to as the *call money rate,* is generally about 1 percent below the prime rate. For example, in May 2005 the prime rate was 6.00 percent, and the call money rate was 4.75 percent.

Federal Reserve Board Regulations T and U determine the maximum proportion of any transaction that can be borrowed. This *margin requirement* (the proportion of total transaction value that must be paid in cash) has varied over time from 40 percent (allowing loans of 60 percent of the value) to 100 percent (allowing no borrowing). As of May 2005, the initial margin requirement specified by the Federal Reserve was 50 percent, although individual investment firms can require higher percents.

After the initial purchase, changes in the market price of the stock will cause changes in the *investor's equity,* which is equal to the market value of the collateral stock minus the amount borrowed. Obviously, if the stock price increases, the investor's equity as a proportion of the total market value of the stock increases, that is, the investor's margin will exceed the initial margin requirement.

Assume you acquired 200 shares of a $50 stock for a total cost of $10,000. A 50 percent initial margin requirement allowed you to borrow $5,000, making your initial equity $5,000. If the stock price increases by 20 percent to $60 a share, the total market value of your position is $12,000, and your equity is now $7,000, or 58 percent ($7,000/$12,000). In contrast, if the stock price declines by 20 percent to $40 a share, the total market value would be $8,000, and your investor's equity would be $3,000, or 37.5 percent ($3,000/$8,000).

This example demonstrates that buying on margin provides all the advantages and the disadvantages of leverage. Lower margin requirements allow you to borrow more, increasing the percentage of gain or loss on your investment when the stock price increases or decreases. The leverage factor equals 1/percent margin. Thus, as in the example, if the margin is 50 percent, the leverage factor is 2, that is, 1/0.50. Therefore, when the rate of return on the stock is plus or minus 10 percent, the return on your equity is plus or minus 20 percent. If the margin requirement declines to 33 percent, you can borrow more (67 percent), and the leverage factor is 3(1/0.33). As discussed by Ip (2000), when you acquire stock or other investments on margin, you are increasing the financial risk of the investment beyond the risk inherent in the security itself. You should increase your required rate of return accordingly.

The following example shows how borrowing by using margin affects the distribution of your returns before commissions and interest on the loan. If the stock increased by 20 percent, your return on the investment would be as follows:

1. The market value of the stock is $12,000, which leaves you with $7,000 after you pay off the loan.
2. The return on your $5,000 investment is

$$\frac{7,000}{5,000} - 1 = 1.40 - 1$$

$$= 0.40 = 40\%$$

In contrast, if the stock declined by 20 percent to $40 a share, your return would be as follows:

1. The market value of the stock is $8,000, which leaves you with $3,000 after you pay off the loan.
2. The negative return on your $5,000 investment is

$$\frac{3,000}{5,000} - 1 = 0.60 - 1$$

$$= -0.40 = -40\%$$

Notably, this symmetrical increase in gains and losses is only true prior to commissions and interest. Obviously, if we assume a 6 percent interest on the borrowed funds (which would be $5,000 \times 0.06 = \$300$) and a $100 commission on the transaction, the results would indicate a lower increase and a larger negative return as follows:

$$20\% \text{ increase:} \quad \frac{\$12,000 - \$5,000 - \$300 - \$100}{5,000} - 1 = \frac{6,600}{5,000} - 1 = 0.32 = 32\%$$

$$20\% \text{ decline:} \quad \frac{\$8,000 - \$5,000 - \$300 - \$100}{5,000} - 1 = \frac{2,600}{5,000} - 1 = -0.48 = -48\%$$

In addition to the initial margin requirement, another important concept is the **maintenance margin**, which is the required proportion of your equity to the total value of the stock; the maintenance margin protects the broker if the stock price declines. At present, the minimum maintenance margin specified by the Federal Reserve is 25 percent, but, again, individual brokerage firms can dictate higher margins for their customers. If the stock price declines to the point where your investor's equity drops below 25 percent of the total value of the position, the account is considered undermargined, and you will receive a **margin call** to provide more equity. If you do not respond with the required funds in time, the stock will be sold to pay off the loan. The time allowed to meet a margin call varies between investment firms and is affected by market conditions. Under volatile conditions, the time allowed to respond to a margin call can be shortened drastically.

Given a maintenance margin of 25 percent, when you buy on margin you must consider how far the stock price can fall before you receive a margin call. The computation for our example is as follows: If the price of the stock is P and you own 200 shares, the value of the position is 200P and the equity in the account is 200P − $5,000. The percentage margin is (200P − 5,000)/200P. To determine the price, P, that is equal to 25 percent (0.25), we use the following equation:

$$\frac{200P - \$5,000}{200P} = 0.25$$

$$200P - \$5,000 = 50P$$

$$150P = \$5,000$$

$$P = \$33.33$$

Therefore, when the stock is at $33.33, the equity value is exactly 25 percent; so if the stock declines from $50 to below $33.33, you will receive a margin call.

To continue the previous example, if the stock declines to $30 a share, its total market value would be $6,000 and your equity would be $1,000, which is only about 17 percent of the total value ($1,000/$6,000). You would receive a margin call for approximately $667, which would give you equity of $1,667, or 25 percent of the total value of the account ($1,667/$6,667). If the stock declined further, you would receive additional margin calls.

Exchange Market Makers

Now that we have discussed the overall structure of the exchange markets and the orders that are used to buy and sell stocks, we can discuss the role and function of the market makers on the exchange. These people and the role they play differ among exchanges. For example, on U.S. exchanges these people are called **specialists**. Most exchanges do not have a single market maker but have competing dealers. On exchanges that have central market makers, these individuals are critical to the smooth and efficient functioning of these markets.

As noted, a major requirement for a good market is liquidity, which depends on how the market makers do their job. Our initial discussion centers on the specialist's role in U.S. markets, followed by a consideration of comparable roles on exchanges in other countries.

U.S. Markets   The specialist is a member of the exchange who applies to the exchange to be assigned stocks to handle. The typical specialist will handle 10 to 15 stocks. The minimum capital requirement for specialists is currently $1 million or the value of 15,000 shares of each stock assigned, whichever is greater.

Functions of the Specialist   Specialists have two major functions. First, they serve as *brokers* to match buy and sell orders and to handle special limit orders placed with member brokers. As noted earlier, an individual broker who receives a limit order (or stop loss or stop buy order) leaves it with the specialist, who executes it when the specified price occurs.

The second major function of a specialist is to act as a *dealer* to maintain a fair and orderly market by providing liquidity when the normal flow of orders is not adequate. As a dealer, the specialist must buy and sell for his or her own account (like a Nasdaq dealer) when public supply or demand is insufficient to provide a continuous, liquid market.

Consider the following example. If a stock is currently selling for about $40 per share, assume that the current bid and ask in an auction market (without the intervention of the specialist) was 40 bid–41 ask. Under such conditions, random market buy and sell orders might cause the stock price to fluctuate between 40 and 41 constantly—a movement of 2.5 percent between trades. Most investors would probably consider such a price pattern too volatile; the market would not be considered liquid. Under such conditions, the specialist is expected to provide "bridge liquidity" by entering alternative bids and asks or both to narrow the spread and improve the stock's price continuity. In this example, the specialist could enter a bid of 40.25 or 40.50 or an ask of 40.50 or 40.75 to narrow the spread to one-half or one-quarter point.

Specialists can enter either side of the market, depending on several factors, including the trend of the market. Notably, they are expected to buy or sell against the market when prices are clearly moving in one direction. Specifically, they are required to buy stock for their own inventories when there is a clear excess of sell orders and the market is definitely declining. Alternatively, they must sell stock from their inventories or sell it short (i.e., borrow shares) to accommodate an excess of buy orders when the market is rising. Specialists are not expected to prevent prices from rising or declining, but only to ensure that *prices change in an orderly fashion* (that is, to maintain price continuity). Evidence that they have fulfilled this requirement is that during recent years NYSE stocks traded unchanged from, or within 10 cents of, the price of the previous trade about 95 percent of the time.

Assuming that there is not a clear trend in the market, several factors will affect how specialists close the bid–ask spread. One factor is their current inventory position in the stock. For example, if they have large inventories of a given stock, all other factors being equal, they would probably enter on the ask (sell) side to reduce these heavy inventories. In contrast, specialists who have little or no inventory of shares because they had been selling from their inventories, or selling short, would tend toward the bid (buy) side of the market to rebuild their inventories or close out their short positions.

Second, the position of the limit-order book will influence how they narrow the spread. Numerous limit buy orders (bids) close to the current market and few limit sell orders (asks) might indicate a tendency toward higher prices because demand is apparently heavy and supply is limited. Under such conditions, a specialist who is not bound by one of the other factors would probably opt to accumulate stock in anticipation of a price increase. The specialists on the NYSE have historically participated as dealers in about 15 percent of the trades, but this percent has been increasing in recent years—from about 18 percent in 1996 to about 27 percent in 2000, as discussed by Ip (2001a).

Specialist Income   The specialist derives income from the broker and dealer functions. The actual breakdown between the two sources depends on the specific stock. In an actively traded stock such as IBM or GE, a specialist has little need to act as a dealer because the substantial public interest in the stock creates a tight market (that is, a narrow bid–ask spread). In such a case, the main source of income would come from maintaining the limit orders for the stock. The broker income derived from a high-volume stock such as IBM is substantial and without risk.

In contrast, a stock with low trading volume and substantial price volatility would probably have a fairly wide bid–ask spread, and the specialist would have to be an active dealer. The specialist's income from such a stock would depend on his or her ability to trade it profitably. Specialists have a major advantage when trading because of their limit-order books. Officially, only specialists are supposed to see the limit-order book, which means that they would have a monopoly on very important information regarding the current supply and demand for a stock. The fact is, most specialists routinely share the limit-order book with other brokers, so it is not a competitive advantage.

Most specialists attempt to balance their portfolios between strong broker stocks that provide steady, riskless income and stocks that require active dealer roles. It has been noted that the increase in dealer activity has been matched with an increase in return on capital for specialists. For further analysis of specialists, see Madhaven and Sofianos (1998) and Benveniste, Marcus, and Wilhelm (1992).

New Trading Systems

As daily trading volume has gone from about 5 million shares to more than a billion shares on both the NYSE and Nasdaq, it has become necessary to introduce new technology into the trading process. Following are some technological innovations that assist in the trading process.

On the NYSE:

- **Super Dot.** Super Dot is an electronic order-routing system through which member firms transmit market and limit orders in NYSE-listed securities directly to the posts where securities are traded or to the member firm's booth. After the order has been executed, a report of execution is returned directly to the member firm office over the same electronic circuit, and the execution is submitted directly to the comparison systems. Member firms can enter market orders up to 2,099 shares and limit orders in round or odd lots up to 30,099 shares. An estimated 85 percent of all market orders enter the NYSE through the Super Dot system.
- **The Display Book.** The Display Book is an electronic workstation that keeps track of all limit orders and incoming market orders. This includes incoming Super Dot limit orders.
- **Opening Automated Report Service (OARS).** OARS, the opening feature of the Super Dot system, accepts member firms' preopening market orders up to 30,099 shares. OARS automatically and continuously pairs buy and sell orders and presents the imbalance to the specialist prior to the opening of a stock. This system helps the specialist determine the opening price and the potential need for a preopening call market, as discussed earlier.
- **Market-Order Processing.** Super Dot's postopening market-order system is designed to accept member firms' postopening market orders up to 30,099 shares. The system provides rapid execution and reporting of market orders. During 2004, 94.5 percent of market orders were executed and reported in less than thirty seconds.
- **Limit-Order Processing.** The limit-order processing system electronically files orders to be executed when and if a specific price is reached. The system accepts limit orders up to 99,999 shares and electronically updates the Specialists' Display Book. Good-until-canceled orders that are not executed on the day of submission are automatically stored until executed or canceled.

On Nasdaq:

- *Small-Order Execution System (SOES).* SOES was introduced in 1984. Market makers receiving SOES orders must honor their bids for automatic executions up to 1,000 shares. SOES became compulsory following the October 1987 crash, when many small investors could not trade and suffered significant losses.
- *SelectNet.* Introduced in 1990, SelectNet is an order-routing and execution service for institutional investors that allows brokers and dealers to communicate through Nasdaq terminals instead of the phone. Once two parties agree to a trade on SelectNet, the execution is automatic.

Innovations for Competition

By this time you should realize that the U.S. secondary equity market is being served by two competing models. As mentioned early in this chapter, the first is the *order-driven* stock exchange market where buy and sell orders interact directly with the specialist market maker acting as both a broker and a dealer when necessary. This model is ideal for a secondary market when there is a concentration of participants and all orders come to one central location (either physically or electronically).

The second model is a *quote-driven* market, also referred to as a dealer market, where numerous dealers compete against each other by providing bid–ask quotations and commit to buy and sell given securities at these quoted prices. Generally, in this model buy and sell orders never interact directly, but the best prices are derived due to the competition among dealers who are independent and separated—it is a fragmented market.

Given these two models, the Securities and Exchange Commission has encouraged competition between the two market models by encouraging three innovations: the CQS, the ITS, and the CAES.

The *Consolidated Quotation System (CQS)* is an electronic service that provides quotations on issues listed on the NYSE, the AMEX, and regional exchanges, and issues traded by market makers in the Nasdaq InterMarket (the third market). Provided to subscribers by the Composite Quotation Service, the CQS makes it possible for subscribers to see all competing dealer and exchange quotes for a stock listed on any exchange. The volume of trading for stocks on the consolidated tape has grown dramatically and is now over 400 billion shares annually.

The *Intermarket Trading System (ITS)* is a centralized quotation and routing system developed by the American, Boston, Chicago, New York, Pacific, and Philadelphia Stock Exchanges and the NASD. ITS consists of a central computer facility with interconnected terminals in the participating market centers. As shown in Exhibit 4.8, the number of issues included, the volume of trading, and the size of trades have all grown substantially. There were over 5,000 issues included on the system in 2004.

With ITS, brokers and market makers in each market center indicate specific buying and selling commitments through a composite quotation display that shows the current quotes for each stock in every market center. A broker is expected to go to the best market to execute a customer's order by sending a message committing to a buy or sell at the price quoted. When this commitment is accepted, a message reports the transaction. The following example illustrates how ITS works.

A broker on the NYSE has a market order to sell 100 shares of GE stock. Assuming the quotation display at the NYSE shows that the best current bid for GE is on the Pacific Stock Exchange (PSE), the broker will enter an order to sell 100 shares at the bid on the PSE. Within seconds, the commitment flashes on the computer screen and is printed out at the PSE specialist's post, where it is executed against the PSE bid. The transaction is reported back to New York and on the consolidated tape. Both brokers receive immediate confirmation and the results are transmitted at the end of each day. Thereafter, each broker completes his or her own clearance and settlement procedure.

The ITS system currently provides centralized quotations for stocks listed on the NYSE and specifies whether a bid or ask *away* from the NYSE market is superior to that *on* the NYSE. Note, however, that the system lacks several characteristics. It does not automatically execute at the best market. Instead, an investor must contact the market maker and indicate that he wants to buy or sell, at which time the bid or ask may be withdrawn. Also, it is not mandatory that a broker go to the best market. Although the best price may be at another market center, a broker might consider it inconvenient to trade on that exchange if the price difference is not substantial. Still, even with these shortcomings, substantial technical and operational progress has occurred through this central quotation and routing system.

| Exhibit 4.8 | Intermarket Trading System (ITS) Activity |

	DAILY AVERAGE			
Year	Issues Eligible	Share Volume	Executed Trades	Average Size of Trade
1980	884	1,565,900	2,868	546
1985	1,288	5,669,400	5,867	966
1990	2,126	9,387,114	8,744	1,075
1995	3,542	12,185,064	10,911	1,117
1996	4,001	12,721,968	11,426	1,113
1997	4,535	15,429,377	14,057	1,098
1998	4,844	18,136,472	17,056	1,063
1999	5,056	21,617,723	19,315	1,119
2000	4,664	28,176,178	23,972	1,175
2001	4,575	34,029,513	29,728	1,145
2002	4,718	50,036,437	37,694	1,327
2003	4,808	64,077,468	46,582	1,376
2004	5,041	70,924,190	53,331	1,330

Source: *NYSE Fact Book* (New York: NYSE, 2005): 28. Reprinted by permission of the New York Stock Exchange.

The *Computer-Assisted Execution System (CAES)* is a service created by Nasdaq that automates order routing and transaction execution for securities listed on domestic exchanges that are part of the ITS. This system makes it possible for market makers who are involved with ITS to execute trades with specialists on the exchanges using CAES.

Where Do We Go from Here?

One cannot help but be struck by the significant changes that have taken place in both the U.S. and global equity markets during the new millennium. The technological advances and the decimalization of prices have contributed to significant reductions in trading costs for institutional and retail investors. Although we have two different trading models (order-driven and quote-driven), it appears that they can survive together. But both are challenged by the ECNs that can match orders electronically and provide faster, cheaper transactions. Based on the percent of Nasdaq transactions completed on the ECNs (about 25 to 30 percent), it appears that the ECNs are very good at finding, matching, and executing trades for dealer stocks (as brokers) and when they cannot broker the trade they send the orders to the Nasdaq market. The unknown factor with ECNs is "best price."

In response to challenge from the ECNs, the order-driven exchanges (mainly the NYSE) have attempted regulations to protect the exchange from competition. The first was Rule 390, which was motivated by the concept that the best auction market is one where *all* participants are *centralized* in one location so that the market benefits from having all bids and offers available to interact and provide the very best prices. To help create and protect this centralized auction market, the NYSE introduced Rule 390, which required members to obtain the exchange's permission to carry out a transaction in a listed stock off the exchange. The NYSE argued that without such a rule, the market would become fragmented and many orders would be internalized (members would match orders between customers) rather than exposed to the public.

After several years of debate, in late 1999 the SEC ruled that this regulation was clearly anti-competitive and Rule 390 was rescinded (the final order was dated May 5, 2000).

The second regulation that constrains the ECNs from competing with the NYSE is the *trade-through rule.* Specifically, this rule dictates that markets *not* ignore superior prices that are available in competing markets. Put another way, traders are not allowed to "trade through" superior prices—for example, if the best bid is at $30, a dealer cannot fill the order at $29.95. Notably, this rule almost always works to the advantage of the NYSE for stocks listed on the exchange because the bulk of trading in these listed stocks (about 70 to 80 percent) is done on the exchange, so one would expect it to have the best price. The problem is that the search for the best price and the ensuing order transfer can slow the trade by about 30 seconds, which is a long time on the exchange, and prices can change in the interim. Thus the debate is over *speed of execution* versus *best price.* The discussion between the SEC, the NYSE, and the several advocates of electronic trading heated up during 2004 and 2005. Some earlier discussions on the controversy included Solomon and Kelly (2003), Kelly (2004a, b), Craig and Kelly (2004), and Kelly and Solomon (2004). As the votes approached, the NYSE actively lobbied the SEC as discussed by Lucchetti (2005a).

The speed-of-execution contingent (ECNs and other ATSs) want some flexibility on the price: either allow the customer to specify a price range of one to three cents a share from the best price or have a general band whereby the order can be consummated if the electronic price is within one or two cents of the best price. The NYSE is considering such price bands but contend that block traders need to have the benefit of specialists who can ensure the best price for the total block. There is also a greater need for specialists for very small illiquid shares. The point is, relatively small transactions (e.g., under 5,000 shares) for large, liquid stocks (e.g., GE, IBM, 3M, and Johnson and Johnson) can be handled quickly and at very low cost via electronic trading and will typically be at the best price. But very large block trades for liquid stocks and most trades for very small illiquid stocks usually need human intervention.

So, where *do* we go from here? Most likely, further technological advances and the Internet will greatly influence the answer. But it is also likely that human financial experts will always be needed to exercise judgment in the investment process. Coincident with the debate on how stocks should be traded is a related question on the basic future of the NYSE as a public entity, as discussed in Der Hovanesian (2004), Anderson (2005), and Ascarelli and McKay (2005). This question was answered in late April 2005 when the NYSE announced plans to acquire Archipelago (a public firm) and thereby enter the electronic trading business and become public as discussed by Lucchetti (2005b). Shortly thereafter, the NASDAQ market announced plans to acquire Instinet.

The Internet Investments Online

Many Internet sites deal with different aspects of investing. Earlier site suggestions led you to information and prices of securities traded both in the U.S. and around the globe. Here are some additional sites of interest:

http://finance.yahoo.com One of the best sites for a variety of investment information including market quotes, commentary, and research, both domestic and international.

http://finance.lycos.com This site offers substantial market information, including price quotes on stocks, selected bonds, and options. Price charts are available.

http://www.sec.gov The Web site of the SEC (Securities and Exchange Commission) offers news and information, investor assistance and complaint handling, SEC rules, enforcement, and data.

http://www.nyse.com, http://www.amex.com, http://www.nasdaq.com The Web sites of the New York Stock Exchange, the American Stock Exchange, and the Nasdaq Exchange system offer information about the relevant market, price quotes, listings of firms, and investor services. The AMEX site includes price quotes for SPDRs (S&P Depository Receipts, which represent ownership in the S&P 500 index or the S&P Midcap 400 index) and iShares MSCI Index Funds, which track the Morgan Stanley Capital International (MSCI) indexes of over 20 countries and regions.

http://www.etrade.com, http://www.schwab.com, http://www.ml.com Many brokerage houses have Web pages. These are three examples of such sites. E*Trade Securities is an example of an on-line brokerage firm that allows investors to trade securities over the Internet. Schwab is a discount broker, whereas Merrill Lynch is a full-service broker with a reputation for good research.

http://www.fibv.com The Web site of the World Federation of Exchanges contains links and data on virtually every public exchange (including stock, bond, and derivatives exchanges) on the globe.

Links to country stock and other financial markets are available at **http://www.internationalist.com/business/stocks/, http://biz.yahoo.com/ifc/,** and **http://www.wall-street.com/foreign.html.**

SUMMARY

- The securities market is divided into primary and secondary markets. While primary markets are important sources of new capital for the issuers of securities, the secondary markets provide the liquidity that is critical to the primary markets.

- The composition of the secondary bond market has experienced small changes over the past 20 years. In sharp contrast, the secondary equity market has experienced significant change and is continuing to evolve due to new technology and consolidation. In addition to several primary listing markets that include exchanges and several Nasdaq components, the secondary market includes several robust regional exchanges, a viable third market, and most recently, the creation, growth, and consolidation of numerous alternative trading systems that provide automatic electronic transactions for stocks on both exchanges and dealer markets.

- The components of a good exchange market include several types of membership as well as various types of orders. In addition, market makers play a critical role in maintaining the liquidity of the market.

- It appears that changes, especially those due to these technological innovations, have only just begun. Therefore, it is important for investors who will be involved in this market to understand how this market has evolved, what is its current structure, and how it can develop in the future. As an investor, you will need to understand how to analyze securities to find the best securities for your portfolio, but also you need to know the best way to buy/sell the security, that is, how and where to complete the transaction. Our discussion in this chapter should provide the background you need to make that trading decision.

SUGGESTED READINGS

Barclay, Michael, Terrence Hendershott, and D. Timothy McCormick. "Competition among Trading Venues: Information and Trading on Electronic Communications Networks." *Journal of Finance* 58, no. 6 (December 2003).

Christie, William, and Paul Schultz. "Why Do NASDAQ Market-Makers Avoid Odd-Eighth Quotes?" *Journal of Finance* 49, no. 5 (December 1994).

Huang, Roger. "The Quality of ECN and Nasdaq Market-Maker Quotes." *Journal of Finance* 57, no. 3 (June, 2002).

Huang, Roger, and Hans Stoll. "Dealer versus Auction Markets: A Paired Comparison of Execution Costs on NASDAQ and the NYSE." *Journal of Financial Economics* 41, no. 3 (July 1996).

Sherrerd, Katrina F., ed. *Execution Techniques, True Trading Costs, and the Microstructure of Markets.* Charlottesville, VA: AIMR, 1993.

Stoll, Hans. *The Stock Exchange Specialist System: An Economic Analysis.* Monograph Series in Financial Economics. New York University, 1985.

QUESTIONS

1. Define *market* and briefly discuss the characteristics of a good market.
2. You own 100 shares of General Electric stock and you want to sell it because you need the money to make a down payment on a car. Assume there is absolutely no secondary market system in common stocks. How would you go about selling the stock? Discuss what you would have to do to find a buyer, how long it might take, and the price you might receive.
3. Define *liquidity* and discuss the factors that contribute to it. Give examples of a liquid asset and an illiquid asset, and discuss why they are considered liquid and illiquid.
4. Define a primary and secondary market for securities and discuss how they differ. Discuss how the primary market is dependent on the secondary market.
5. Give an example of an initial public offering (IPO) in the primary market. Give an example of a seasoned equity issue in the primary market. Discuss which would involve greater risk to the buyer.
6. Find an advertisement for a recent primary offering in *The Wall Street Journal.* Based on the information in the ad, indicate the characteristics of the security sold and the major underwriters. How much new capital did the firm derive from the offering before paying commissions?
7. Briefly explain the difference between a competitive-bid underwriting and a negotiated underwriting.
8. The figures in Exhibit 4.5 reveal a major change over time in the price paid for a membership (seat) on the NYSE. What has caused this change over time?
9. What are the major reasons for the existence of regional stock exchanges? Discuss how they differ from the national exchanges.
10. Which segment of the secondary stock market (listed exchanges or Nasdaq) is larger in terms of the number of issues? Which is larger in terms of the value of the issues traded?
11. Discuss the three levels of Nasdaq in terms of what each provides and who would subscribe to each.
12. a. Define the third market. Give an example of a third-market stock.
    b. Define the fourth market. Discuss why a financial institution would use the fourth market.
13. Briefly define each of the following terms and give an example.
    a. *Market order*
    b. *Limit order*
    c. *Short sale*
    d. *Stop loss order*
14. Briefly discuss the two major functions and sources of income for the NYSE specialist.

PROBLEMS

1. You have $40,000 to invest in Sophie Shoes, a stock selling for $80 a share. The initial margin requirement is 60 percent. Ignoring taxes and commissions, show in detail the impact on your rate of return if the stock rises to $100 a share and if it declines to $40 a share assuming: (a) you pay cash for the stock, and (b) you buy it using maximum leverage.
2. Lauren has a margin account and deposits $50,000. Assuming the prevailing margin requirement is 40 percent, commissions are ignored, and the Gentry Shoe Corporation is selling at $35 per share.
    a. How many shares can Lauren purchase using the maximum allowable margin?
    b. What is Lauren's profit (loss) if the price of Gentry's stock
       i. rises to $45?
       ii. falls to $25?
    c. If the maintenance margin is 30 percent, to what price can Gentry Shoe fall before Lauren will receive a margin call?

3. Suppose you buy a round lot of Maginn Industries stock on 55 percent margin when the stock is selling at $20 a share. The broker charges a 10 percent annual interest rate, and commissions are 3 percent of the total stock value on both the purchase and sale. A year later you receive a $0.50 per share dividend and sell the stock for 27. What is your rate of return on the investment?

4. You decide to sell short 100 shares of Charlotte Horse Farms when it is selling at its yearly high of 56. Your broker tells you that your margin requirement is 45 percent and that the commission on the purchase is $155. While you are short the stock, Charlotte pays a $2.50 per share dividend. At the end of one year, you buy 100 shares of Charlotte at 45 to close out your position and are charged a commission of $145 and 8 percent interest on the money borrowed. What is your rate of return on the investment?

5. You own 200 shares of Shamrock Enterprises that you bought at $25 a share. The stock is now selling for $45 a share.
   a. You put in a stop loss order at $40. Discuss your reasoning for this action.
   b. If the stock eventually declines in price to $30 a share, what would be your rate of return with and without the stop loss order?

6. Two years ago, you bought 300 shares of Kayleigh Milk Co. for $30 a share with a margin of 60 percent. Currently, the Kayleigh stock is selling for $45 a share. Assuming no dividends and ignoring commissions, compute (a) the annualized rate of return on this investment if you had paid cash, and (b) your rate of return with the margin purchase.

7. The stock of the Madison Travel Co. is selling for $28 a share. You put in a limit buy order at $24 for one month. During the month, the stock price declines to $20, then jumps to $36. Ignoring commissions, what would have been your rate of return on this investment? What would be your rate of return if you had put in a market order? What if your limit order was at $18?

THOMSON ONE | Business School Edition

1. On which stock markets are the following firms traded: Abbott Labs, Apple Computer, ExxonMobil, Intel, Johnson and Johnson, Microsoft?

2. Suppose you purchased Microsoft stock on January 15, 2005 and sold it two months later on March 15, 2005. What would your percentage price return be? What would the percentage return be if you had used 75 percent margin? 50 percent margin?

3. Redo exercise 2 but this time assume you purchased Microsoft on March 15, 2005 and sold it two months later on May 15, 2005. What would the annualized returns be if you bought the stock with cash? If you used 75 percent margin? 50 percent margin?

APPENDIX
Chapter 4

Characteristics of Developed and Developing Markets around the World

(Exhibits 4A.1 and 4A.2 on the following pages)

Exhibit 4A.1 | Developed Markets around the World

Country	Principal Exchange	Other Exchanges	Total Market Capitalization ($ billions)	Available Market Capitalization ($ billions)	Trading Volume ($ billions)	Domestic Issues Listed	Total Issues Listed	Auction Mechanism	Official Specialists	Options/Futures Trading	Price Limits	Principal Market Indexes
Australia	Sydney	5	82.3	53.5	39.3	N.A.	1,496	Continuous	No	Yes	None	All Ordinaries—324 issues
Austria	Vienna	—	18.7	8.3	37.2	125	176	Call	Yes	No	5%	GZ Aktienindex—25 issues
Belgium	Brussels	3	48.5	26.2	6.8	186	337	Mixed	No	Few	10%	Brussels Stock Exchange Index—186 issues
Canada	Toronto	4	186.8	124.5	71.3	N.A.	1,208	Continuous	Yes	Yes	None	TSE 300 Composite Index
Denmark	Copenhagen	—	29.7	22.2	11.1	N.A.	284	Mixed	No	No	None	Copenhagen Stock Exchange Index—38 issues
Finland	Helsinki	—	9.9	1.7	5.2	N.A.	125	Mixed	N.A.	N.A.	N.A.	KOP (Kansallis-Osake-Pannki) Price Index
France	Paris	6	256.5	137.2	129.0	463	663	Mixed	Yes	Yes	4%	CAC General Index—240 issues
Germany	Frankfurt	7	297.7	197.9	1,003.7	N.A.	355	Continuous	Yes	Options	None	DAX; FAZ (Frankfurter Allgemeine Zeitung)
Hong Kong	Hong Kong	—	67.7	37.1	34.6	N.A.	479	Continuous	No	Futures	None	Hang Seng Index—33 issues

(continued)

Exhibit 4A.1 | Developed Markets around the World (continued)

Country	Principal Exchange	Other Exchanges	Total Market Capitalization ($ billions)	Available Market Capitalization ($ billions)	Trading Volume ($ billions)	Domestic Issues Listed	Total Issues Listed	Auction Mechanism	Official Specialists	Options/Futures Trading	Price Limits	Principal Market Indexes
Ireland	Dublin	—	8.4	6.4	5.5	N.A.	N.A.	Continuous	No	No	None	J&E Davy Total Market Index
Italy	Milan	9	137.0	73.2	42.6	N.A.	317	Mixed	No	No	10–20%	Banca Commerziale—209 issues
Japan	Tokyo	7	2,754.6	1,483.5	1,602.4	N.A.	1,576	Continuous	Yes	No	10% down	TOPIX—1,097 issues; TSE II—423 issues; Nikkei 225
Luxembourg	Luxembourg	—	1.5	0.9	0.1	61	247	Continuous	N.A.	N.A.	N.A.	Domestic Share Price Index—9 issues
Malaysia	Kuala Lumpur	—	199.3	95.0	126.4	430	478	Continuous	No	No	None	Kuala Lumpur Composite Index—83 issues
The Netherlands	Amsterdam	—	112.1	92.4	80.4	279	569	Continuous	Yes	Options	Variable	ANP—CBS General Index—51 issues
New Zealand	Wellington	—	6.7	5.3	2.0	295	451	Continuous	No	Futures	None	Barclay's International Price Index—40 issues
Norway	Oslo	9	18.4	7.9	14.1	N.A.	128	Call	No	No	None	Oslo Bors Stock Index—50 issues
Singapore	Singapore	—	28.6	15.6	8.2	N.A.	324	Continuous	No	No	None	Straits Times Index—30 issues; SES—32 issues

Country	City	No. of Exchanges	Market Cap (Total)	Market Cap (Available)	Trading Value	No. Listed (Available)	No. Listed (Total)	Trading Method	Continuous	Options	Foreign Restriction	Market Index
South Africa	Johannesburg	—	72.7	N.A.	8.2	N.A.	N.A.	Continuous	No	None	None	JSE Actuaries Index—141 issues
Spain	Madrid	3	86.6	46.8	41.0	N.A.	368	Mixed	No	No	10%	Madrid Stock Exchange Index—72 issues
Sweden	Stockholm	—	59.0	24.6	15.8	N.A.	151	Mixed	No	Yes	None	Jacobson & Ponsbach—30 issues
Switzerland	Zurich	6	128.5	75.4	376.6	161	380	Mixed	No	Yes	5%	Société de Banque Suisse—90 issues
United Kingdom	London	5	756.2	671.1	280.7	1,911	2,577	Continuous	No	Yes	None	Financial Times—(FT) Ordinaries—750 issues; FTSE 100; FT 33
United States	New York	6	9,431.1	8,950.3	5,778.7	N.A.	3,358	Continuous	Yes	Yes	None	S&P 500; Dow Jones Industrial Average; Wilshire 5000; Russell 3000

Notes: Market capitalizations (both total and available) are as of December 31, 1990, except for South African market capitalization, which is from 1988. Available differs from total market capitalization by subtracting cross holdings, closely held and government-owned shares, and takes into account restrictions on foreign ownership. Number of issues listed are from 1988 except for Malaysia, which is from 1994. Trading volume data are from 1990 except for Switzerland, which are from 1988. Trading institutions data are from 1987. Market capitalizations (both total and available) for all countries except the United States and South Africa are from the Salomon-Russell Global Equity Indices. U.S. market capitalization (both total and available) is from the Frank Russell Company. All trading volume information (except for Switzerland) and Malaysian total issues listed are from the *Emerging Stock Markets Factbook: 1991*, International Finance Corp., 1991. Trading institutions information is from Richard Roll, "The International Crash of 1987," *Financial Analysts Journal*, September/October 1988. South African market capitalization, number of issues listed for all countries (except Malaysia), and Swiss trading volume are reproduced courtesy of Euromoney Books, extracted from *The G.T. Guide to World Equity Markets: 1989, 1988.*

Source: From *Global Investing: The Professional Guide to the World Capital Markets* by Roger G. Ibbotson and Gary P. Brinson, pp. 109–111. Copyright © 1993. Reprinted by permission of The McGraw-Hill Companies, Inc.

Exhibit 4A.2 | **Emerging Markets around the World**

Country	Principal Exchange	Other Exchanges	Market Capitalization ($ billions)	Trading Volume ($ billions)	Total Issues Listed	Auction Mechanism	Principal Market Indexes
Argentina	Buenos Aires	4	36.9	11.4	156	N.A.	Buenos Aires Stock Exchange Index
Brazil	São Paulo	9	189.2	109.5	544	Continuous	BOVESPA Share Price Index—83 issues
Chile	Santiago	—	68.2	5.3	279	Mixed	IGPA Index—180 issues
China	Shanghai	1	43.5	97.5	291	Continuous	Shanghai Composite Index
Colombia	Bogotá	1	14.0	2.2	90	N.A.	Bogotá General Composite Index
Greece	Athens	—	14.9	5.1	216	Continuous	Athens Stock Exchange Industrial Price Index
India	Bombay	14	127.5	27.3	4,413	Continuous	Economic Times Index—72 issues
Indonesia	Jakarta	—	47.2	11.8	216	Mixed	Jakarta Stock Exchange Index
Israel	Tel Aviv	—	10.6	5.5	267	Call	General Share Index—all listed issues
Jordan	Amman	—	4.6	0.6	95	N.A.	Amman Financial Market Index
Mexico	Mexico City	—	130.2	83.0	206	Continuous	Bolsa de Valores Index—49 issues
Nigeria	Lagos	—	2.7	N.A.	177	Call	Nigerian Stock Exchange General Index
Pakistan	Karachi	—	12.2	3.2	724	Continuous	State Bank of Pakistan Index
Philippines	Makati	1	55.5	13.9	189	N.A.	Manila Commercial & Industrial Index—25 issues
Portugal	Lisbon	1	16.2	5.2	195	Call	Banco Totta e Acores Share Index—50 issues

South Korea	Seoul	—	191.8	286.0	699	Continuous	Korea Composite Stock Price Index
Taiwan	Taipei	—	247.3	711.0	313	Continuous	Taiwan Stock Exchange Index
Thailand	Bangkok	—	131.4	80.2	389	Continuous	Securities Exchange of Thailand Price Index
Turkey	Istanbul	—	21.6	21.7	176	Continuous	Istanbul Stock Exchange Index—50 issues
Venezuela	Caracas	1	4.1	0.9	90	Continuous	Indice de Capitalization de la BVC
Zimbabwe	N.A.	—	1.8	0.2	64	N.A.	Zimbabwe S.E. Industrial Index

Notes: Market capitalizations, trading volume, and total issues listed are as of 1994. Market capitalization, trading volume, and total issues listed for Brazil and São Paulo only. Trading volume for the Philippines is for both Manila and Makati. Total issues listed for India is Bombay only. Trading institutions information is from 1987 and 1988. Market capitalizations, trading volume, and total issues listed are from the *Emerging Stock Markets Factbook: 1995*, International Finance Corp., 1995. Trading institutions information is from Richard Roll, "The International Crash of 1987," *Financial Analysts Journal*, September/October 1988.

Source: From *Global Investing: The Professional Guide to the World Capital Markets* by Roger G. Ibbotson and Gary P. Brinson, pp. 125–126. Copyright © 1993. Reprinted by permission of The McGraw-Hill Companies, Inc.

Chapter 5

Security-Market Indexes

After you read this chapter, you should be able to answer the following questions:

- What are some major uses of security-market indexes?
- What are the major characteristics that cause various indexes to differ?
- What are the major stock-market indexes in the United States and globally, and what are their characteristics?
- What are the major bond-market indexes for the United States and the world?
- Why are bond indexes more difficult to create and maintain than stock indexes?
- What are some of the composite stock–bond market indexes?
- Where can you get historical and current data for all these indexes?
- What is the relationship among many of these indexes in the short run (monthly)?

A fair statement regarding **security-market indexes**—especially those outside the United States—is that everybody talks about them but few people understand them. Even those investors familiar with widely publicized stock-market series, such as the Dow Jones Industrial Average (DJIA), usually know little about indexes for the U.S. bond market or for non-U.S. stock markets such as Tokyo or London.

Although portfolios are obviously composed of many different individual stocks, investors typically ask, "What happened to the market today?" The reason for this question is that if an investor owns more than a few stocks or bonds, it is cumbersome to follow each stock or bond individually to determine the composite performance of the portfolio. Also, there is an intuitive notion that most individual stocks or bonds move with the aggregate market. Therefore, if the overall market rose, an individual's portfolio probably also increased in value. To supply investors with a composite report on market performance, some financial publications or investment firms have developed stock-market and bond-market indexes.

In the initial section of this chapter we discuss several ways that investors use market indexes. An awareness of these significant functions should provide an incentive for becoming familiar with these series and indicates why we present a full chapter on this topic. In the second section we consider what characteristics cause various indexes to differ. Investors need to understand these differences and why one index is preferable for a given task because of its characteristics. In the third section we present the most well-known U.S. and global stock-market indexes, separated into groups based on the weighting scheme used. Then, in the fourth section, we consider bond-market indexes—a relatively new topic because the creation and maintenance of total return bond indexes are new. Again, we consider international bond indexes following the domestic indexes. In the fifth section we consider composite stock market–bond market series. In our final section we examine how alternative indexes relate to each other over monthly intervals. This comparison demonstrates the important factors that cause high or low correlation among series. With this background, you should be able to make an intelligent choice of the index that is best for you based on how you want to use it.

USES OF SECURITY-MARKET INDEXES

Security-market indexes have at least five specific uses. A primary application is to use the index values to compute total returns and risk for an aggregate market or some component of a market over a specified time period and use the computed return as a *benchmark* to judge the performance of individual portfolios. A basic assumption when evaluating portfolio performance is that any investor should be able to experience a risk-adjusted rate of return comparable to the market by randomly selecting a large number of stocks or bonds from the total market; hence, a superior portfolio manager should consistently do better than the market. Therefore, *an aggregate stock- or bond-market index can be used as a benchmark to judge the performance of professional money managers.*

An obvious use of indexes is to develop an index portfolio. As we have discussed, it is difficult for most money managers to consistently outperform specified market indexes on a risk-adjusted basis over time.[1] If this is true, an obvious alternative is to invest in a portfolio that will emulate this market portfolio. This notion led to the creation of *index funds* and *exchange-traded funds* (ETFs), whose purpose is to track the performance of the specified market series (index) over time. The original index funds were common-stock funds as discussed in Malkiel (2004), Chapter 14, and Mossavar-Rahmani (2005). The development of comprehensive, well-specified bond-market indexes and bond-portfolio managers' inability to outperform these indexes has led to a similar phenomenon in the fixed-income area (bond-index funds), as noted by Hawthorne (1986) and Dialynas (2001).

Securities analysts, portfolio managers, and academicians doing research use security-market indexes to examine the factors that influence aggregate security price movements (that is, the indexes are used to measure aggregate market movements) and to compare the risk-adjusted performance of alternative asset classes (e.g., stocks versus bonds versus real estate).

Another group interested in an aggregate market index is composed of "technicians," who believe past price changes can be used to predict future price movements. For example, to project future stock price movements, technicians would plot and analyze price and volume changes for a stock-market series like the Dow Jones Industrial Average.

Finally, work in portfolio and capital market theory has implied that the relevant risk for an individual risky asset is its *systematic risk,* which is the relationship between the rates of return for a risky asset and the rates of return for a market portfolio of risky assets.[2] Therefore, in this case an aggregate market index is used as a proxy for the market portfolio of risky assets.

---

[1]Throughout this chapter and the book, we will use *indicator series* and *indexes* interchangeably, although *indicator series* is the more correct specification because it refers to a broad class of series; one popular type of series is an index, but there can be other types and many different indexes.

[2]This concept and its justification are discussed in Chapter 7 and Chapter 8. Subsequently, in Chapter 25, we consider the difficulty of finding an index that is an appropriate proxy for the market portfolio of risky assets.

DIFFERENTIATING FACTORS IN CONSTRUCTING MARKET INDEXES

Because the indexes are intended to reflect the overall movements of a group of securities, we need to consider three factors that are important when constructing an index intended to represent a total population.

The Sample

The first factor is the sample used to construct an index. The size, the breadth, and the source of the sample are all important.

A small percentage of the total population will provide valid indications of the behavior of the total population *if* the sample is properly selected. In some cases, because of the economics of computers, virtually all the stocks on an exchange or market are included, with a few deletions of unusual securities. The sample should be *representative* of the total population; otherwise, its size will be meaningless. A large biased sample is no better than a small biased sample. The sample can be generated by completely random selection or by a nonrandom selection technique designed to incorporate the important characteristics of the desired population. Finally, the *source* of the sample is important if there are any differences between segments of the population, in which case samples from each segment are required.

Weighting Sample Members

The second factor is the weight given to each member in the sample. Three principal weighting schemes are used for security-market indexes: (1) a price-weighted index, (2) a market-value-weighted index, and (3) an unweighted index, or what would be described as an equal-weighted index. We will discuss each of these in detail shortly.

Computational Procedure

The final consideration is the computational procedure used. One alternative is to take a simple arithmetic mean of the various members in the index. Another is to compute an index and have all changes, whether in price or value, reported in terms of the basic index. Finally, some prefer using a geometric mean of the components rather than an arithmetic mean.

STOCK-MARKET INDEXES

As mentioned previously, we hear a lot about what happens to the Dow Jones Industrial Average (DJIA) each day. You might also hear about other stock indexes, such as the S&P 500 index, the Nasdaq composite, or even the Nikkei Average. If you listen carefully, you will realize that these indexes experience different percentage changes (which is the way that the changes should be reported). Reasons for some differences are obvious, such as the DJIA versus the Nikkei Average, but others are not. In this section we briefly review how the major series differ in terms of the characteristics discussed in the prior section, which will help you understand why the percent changes over time for alternative indexes *should* differ.

We have organized the discussion of the indexes by the weighting of the sample of stocks. We begin with the price-weighted index because some of the most popular indexes are in this

Exhibit 5.1	Example of Change in DJIA Divisor When a Sample Stock Splits

Stock	Before Split	After Three-for-One Split by Stock A	
	Prices	Prices	
A	30	10	
B	20	20	
C	10	10	
	$60 \div 3 = 20$	$40 \div X = 20$	X = 2 (New Divisor)

category. The next group is the value-weighted index, which is the technique currently used for most indexes. Finally, we will examine the unweighted indexes.

Price-Weighted Index

A **price-weighted index** is an arithmetic mean of current prices, which means that index movements are influenced by the differential prices of the components.

Dow Jones Industrial Average   The best-known price-weighted index is also the oldest and certainly the most popular stock-market index, the Dow Jones Industrial Average (DJIA). The DJIA is a price-weighted average of thirty large, well-known industrial stocks that are generally the leaders in their industry (blue chips). The DJIA is computed by totaling the current prices of the 30 stocks and dividing the sum by a divisor that has been adjusted to take account of stock splits and changes in the sample over time.[3] The divisor is adjusted so the index value will be the same before and after the split. An adjustment of the divisor is demonstrated in Exhibit 5.1. The equation is

$$\text{DJIA}_t = \sum_{i=1}^{30} \frac{P_{it}}{D_{adj}}$$

where:

DJIA_t = the value of the DJIA on day t
P_{it} = the closing price of stock i on day t
D_{adj} = the adjusted divisor on day t

In Exhibit 5.1, we employ three stocks to demonstrate the procedure used to derive a new divisor for the DJIA when a stock splits. When stocks split, the divisor becomes smaller, as shown. The cumulative effect of splits can be derived from the fact that the divisor was originally 30.0, but as of May 2005, it was 0.13532775.

The adjusted divisor ensures that the new value for the index is the same as it would have been without the split. In this case, the presplit index value was 20. Therefore, after the split, given the new sum of prices, the divisor is adjusted downward to maintain this value of 20. The divisor is also changed when there is a change in the sample makeup of the index.

---

[3]A complete list of all events that have caused a change in the divisor since the DJIA went to 30 stocks on October 1, 1928, is contained in Phyllis S. Pierce, ed., *The Business One Irwin Investor's Handbook* (Burr Ridge, IL: Dow Jones Books, annual).

| Exhibit 5.2 | Demonstration of the Impact of Differently Priced Shares on a Price-Weighted Index |

		PERIOD T + 1	
Stock	Period T	Case A	Case B
A	100	110	100
B	50	50	50
C	30	30	33
Sum	180	190	183
Divisor	3	3	3
Average	60	63.3	61
Percentage change		5.5	1.7

Because the index is price weighted, a high-priced stock carries more weight than a low-priced stock. As shown in Exhibit 5.2, a 10 percent change in a $100 stock ($10) will cause a larger change in the index than a 10 percent change in a $30 stock ($3). For Case A, when the $100 stock increases by 10 percent, the average rises by 5.5 percent; for Case B, when the $30 stock increases by 10 percent, the average rises by only 1.7 percent.

The DJIA has been criticized on several counts. First, the sample used for the index is limited to 30 nonrandomly selected blue-chip stocks that cannot be representative of the thousands of U.S. stocks. Further, the stocks included are large, mature, blue-chip firms rather than typical companies. Several studies have shown that the DJIA has not been as volatile as other market indexes, and its long-run returns are not comparable to other NYSE stock indexes.

In addition, because the DJIA is price weighted, when companies have a stock split, their prices decline and therefore their weight in the DJIA is reduced—even though they may be large and important. Therefore, the weighting scheme causes a downward bias in the DJIA; because high-growth stocks will have higher prices and because such stocks tend to split, they will consistently lose weight within the index. For a discussion of specific differences between indexes, see Ip (1998b). Dow Jones also publishes a price-weighted index of 20 stocks in the transportation industry and 15 utility stocks. Detailed reports of the averages are contained daily in *The Wall Street Journal* and weekly in *Barron's,* including hourly figures.

Nikkei–Dow Jones Average   Also referred to as the Nikkei Stock Average Index, the Nikkei–Dow Jones Average is an arithmetic mean of prices for 225 stocks on the First Section of the Tokyo Stock Exchange (TSE). This best-known series in Japan shows stock price trends since the reopening of the TSE. Notably, it was formulated by Dow Jones and Company, and, similar to the DJIA, it is a price-weighted index. It is also criticized because the 225 stocks only comprise about 15 percent of all stocks on the First Section. It is reported daily in *The Wall Street Journal* and the *Financial Times* and weekly in *Barron's.*

Value-Weighted Index

A **value-weighted index** is generated by deriving the initial total market value of all stocks used in the index (Market Value = Number of Shares Outstanding (or freely floating shares) × Current Market Price). Prior to 2004, the tradition was to consider all outstanding shares. In mid-2004,

Exhibit 5.3	**Example of a Computation of a Value-Weighted Index**

Stock	Share Price	Number of Shares	Market Value
December 31, 2005			
A	$10.00	1,000,000	$ 10,000,000
B	15.00	6,000,000	90,000,000
C	20.00	5,000,000	100,000,000
Total			$200,000,000
			Base Value Equal to an Index of 100
December 31, 2006			
A	$12.00	1,000,000	$ 12,000,000
B	10.00	12,000,000[a]	120,000,000
C	20.00	5,500,000[b]	110,000,000
Total			$242,000,000

$$\text{New Index Value} = \frac{\text{Current Market Value}}{\text{Base Value}} \times \text{Beginning Index Value}$$

$$= \frac{\$242,000,000}{\$200,000,000} \times 100$$

$$= 1.21 \times 100$$

$$= 121$$

[a]Stock split two-for-one during the year.
[b]Company paid a 10 percent stock dividend during the year.

Standard & Poor's began only considering "freely floating shares" that exclude shares held by insiders. This initial figure is typically established as the base and assigned an index value (the most popular beginning index value is 100, but it can vary—say, 10, 50). Subsequently, a new market value is computed for all securities in the index, and the current market value is compared to the initial "base" market value to determine the percentage of change, which in turn is applied to the beginning index value.

$$\text{Index}_t = \frac{\sum P_t Q_t}{\sum P_b Q_b} \times \text{Beginning Index Value}$$

where:

Index_t = index value on day t
P_t = ending prices for stocks on day t
Q_t = number of outstanding or freely floating shares on day t
P_b = ending price for stocks on base day
Q_b = number of outstanding or freely floating shares on base day

A simple example for a three-stock index in Exhibit 5.3 indicates that there is an *automatic adjustment* for stock splits and other capital changes with a value-weighted index because the decrease in the stock price is offset by an increase in the number of shares

Exhibit 5.4	Demonstration of the Impact of Different Values on a Market-Value-Weighted Stock Index

| | DECEMBER 31, 2005 | | | DECEMBER 31, 2006 | | | |
| | | | | Case A | | Case B | |
Stock	Number of Shares	Price	Value	Price	Value	Price	Value
A	1,000,000	$10.00	$ 10,000,000	$12.00	$ 12,000,000	$10.00	$ 10,000,000
B	6,000,000	15.00	90,000,000	15.00	90,000,000	15.00	90,000,000
C	5,000,000	20.00	100,000,000	20.00	100,000,000	24.00	120,000,000
			$200,000,000		$202,000,000		$220,000,000
Index Value			100.00		101.00		110.00

outstanding. In a value-weighted index, the importance of individual stocks in the sample depends on the market value of the stocks. Therefore, a specified percentage change in the value of a large company has a greater impact than a comparable percentage change for a small company. As shown in Exhibit 5.4, if we assume that the only change is a 20 percent increase in the value of stock A, which has a beginning value of $10 million, the ending index value would be $202 million, or an index of 101. In contrast, if only stock C increases by 20 percent from $100 million, the ending value will be $220 million or an index value of 110. The point is, price changes for the large market value stocks in a value-weighted index will dominate changes in the index value over time. Therefore, it is important to be aware of the large-value stocks in the index.

Unweighted Index

In an **unweighted index**, all stocks carry equal weight regardless of their price or market value. A $20 stock is as important as a $40 stock, and the total market value of the company is unimportant. Such an index can be used by individuals who randomly select stock for their portfolio and invest the same dollar amount in each stock. One way to visualize an unweighted index is to assume that equal dollar amounts are invested in each stock in the portfolio (for example, an equal $1,000 investment in each stock would work out to 50 shares of a $20 stock, 100 shares of a $10 stock, and 10 shares of a $100 stock). In fact, the actual movements in the index are typically based on *the arithmetic mean of the percent changes in price or value for the stocks in the index.* The use of percentage price changes means that the price level or the market value of the stock does not make a difference—each percentage change has equal weight. This arithmetic mean of percent changes procedure is used in academic studies when the authors specify equal weighting.

In contrast to computing an arithmetic mean of percentage changes, both Value Line and the *Financial Times* Ordinary Share Index compute a *geometric* mean of the holding period returns and derive the holding period yield from this calculation. Exhibit 5.5, which contains an example of an arithmetic and a geometric mean, demonstrates the downward bias of the geometric calculation. Specifically, the geometric mean of holding period yields (HPY) shows an average change of only 5.3 percent versus the actual change in wealth of 6 percent.

Exhibit 5.5	Example of an Arithmetic and Geometric Mean of Percentage Changes

	SHARE PRICE			
Stock	T	T + 1	HPR	HPY
X	10	12	1.20	0.20
Y	22	20	.91	−0.09
Z	44	47	1.07	0.07

$$\Pi = 1.20 \times .91 \times 1.07 \qquad\qquad \Sigma = 0.18$$

$$= 1.168 \qquad\qquad 0.18/3 = 0.06$$

$$1.168^{1/3} = 1.0531 \qquad\qquad = 6\%$$

$$\text{Index Value (T)} \times 1.0531 = \text{Index Value (T + 1)}$$

$$\text{Index Value (T)} \times 1.06 = \text{Index Value (T + 1)}$$

Style Indexes

Financial service firms such as Dow Jones, Moody's, Standard & Poor's, Russell, and Wilshire Associates are generally very fast in responding to changes in investment practices. One example is the growth in popularity of small-cap stocks following academic research in the 1980s that suggested that over long-term periods, small-cap stocks outperformed large-cap stocks on a risk-adjusted basis. In response to this, Ibbotson Associates created the first small-cap stock index, and this was followed by small-cap indexes by Frank Russell Associates (the Russell 2000 index), the Standard & Poor's 600, the Wilshire 1750, and the Dow Jones Small-Cap Index. For a comparative analysis of these indexes, see Reilly and Wright (2002). This led to sets of size indexes, including large-cap, midcap, small-cap, and micro-cap. These new size indexes were used to evaluate the performance of money managers who concentrated in those size sectors.

The next innovation was for money managers to concentrate in *types* of stocks—that is, *growth* stocks or *value* stocks. We included a designation of these stocks in Chapter 2 in terms of what they are and how they are identified. As this money management innovation evolved, the financial services firms again responded by creating indexes of growth stocks and value stocks based on relative P/E, price–book value, price–cash flow ratios, and other metrics such as return on equity (ROE) and revenue growth rates.

Eventually, these two styles (size and type) were combined into six categories:

Small-cap growth	Small-cap value
Midcap growth	Midcap value
Large-cap growth	Large-cap value

Currently, most money managers identify their investment style as one of these, and consultants generally use these categories to identify money managers.

The most recent addition to style indexes are those created to track ethical funds referred to as *socially responsible investment* (SRI) funds. These SRI indexes are further broken down by country and include a global ethical stock index.

The best source for style stock indexes (both size and type of stock) is *Barron's.*

Exhibit 5.6 shows the "Stock-Market Data Bank" from *The Wall Street Journal* of February 2, 2005, which contains values for many of the U.S. stock indexes we have

Exhibit 5.6 | Stock-Market Data Bank

Major Stock Indexes

Dow Jones Averages	HIGH	LOW	CLOSE	NET CHG	% CHG	HIGH	LOW	% CHG	YTD % CHG
			DAILY				52-WEEK		
30 Industrials	10570.26	10489.64	10551.94	+62.00	+0.59	10854.54	9749.99	+ 0.45	−2.14
20 Transportations	3614.84	3597.14	3605.73	+ 7.25	+0.20	3811.62	2750.80	+26.46	−5.06
15 Utilities	345.84	342.88	345.40	+ 1.94	+0.56	345.40	261.89	+26.64	+3.12
65 Composite	3331.17	3310.86	3326.83	+15.65	+0.47	3412.44	2852.12	+11.66	−2.03
Dow Jones Indexes									
Wilshire 5000	11729.47	11639.56	11721.58	+79.01	+0.68	11987.82	10293.52	+ 5.98	−2.08
US Total Market	283.77	281.56	283.55	+ 1.91	+0.68	289.74	250.37	+ 5.52	−2.01
US Large-Cap	255.24	253.22	255.00	+ 1.71	+0.68	260.21	229.69	+ 3.49	−1.82
US Mid-Cap	362.10	359.27	361.86	+ 2.31	+0.64	370.71	301.79	+12.47	−2.37
US Small-Cap	402.01	398.63	401.79	+ 3.01	+0.75	415.01	335.75	+ 8.92	−3.03
US Growth	1066.78	1058.83	1065.66	+ 5.80	+0.55	1092.49	944.85	+ 1.61	−2.30
US Value	1494.46	1481.78	1493.51	+11.61	+0.78	1523.39	1308.11	+ 8.49	−1.85
Global Titans 50	192.19	190.56	191.94	+ 1.24	+0.65	195.41	176.36	+ 2.01	−1.57
Asian Titans 50	117.59	116.76	116.77	− 0.51	−0.43	120.26	98.30	+ 7.56	−2.90
DJ STOXX 50	2844.20	2815.80	2844.20	+25.01	+0.89	2844.20	2541.84	+ 5.53	+2.50
Nasdaq Stock Market									
Nasdaq Comp	2071.52	2058.66	2068.70	+ 6.29	+0.30	2178.34	1752.49	+ 0.12	−4.91
Nasdaq 100	1527.91	1517.30	1523.66	+ 4.03	+0.27	1627.46	1304.43	+ 2.13	−6.01
Biotech	731.22	723.96	729.59	+ 4.32	+0.60	845.11	622.19	− 7.73	−5.07
Computer	930.18	923.04	928.44	+ 3.09	+0.33	973.84	768.60	− 3.01	−3.82
Standard & Poor's Indexes									
500 Index	1190.39	1180.95	1189.41	+ 8.14	+0.69	1213.55	1063.23	+ 4.70	−1.86
MidCap 400	651.15	645.66	650.82	+ 4.85	+0.75	664.50	549.51	+10.80	−1.88
SmallCap 600	323.85	321.11	323.82	+ 2.71	+0.84	329.58	263.47	+16.52	−1.51
SuperComp 1500	267.13	265.02	266.93	+ 1.85	+0.70	272.32	236.65	+ 5.63	−1.85
New York Stock Exchange and Others									
NYSE Comp	7149.52	7089.83	7146.21	+56.38	+0.80	7253.56	6217.06	+ 8.69	−1.43
NYSE Financial	7354.18	7275.66	7343.47	+67.80	+0.93	7493.92	6322.00	+ 6.74	−2.01
Russell 2000	628.61	623.43	628.14	+ 4.12	+0.66	654.57	517.10	+ 8.46	−3.60
Value Line	391.34	388.47	391.34	+ 2.56	+0.66	404.84	332.98	+ 5.00	−3.24
Amex Comp	1435.58	1424.45	1433.16	+ 4.77	+0.33	1434.34	1160.18	+18.10	−0.08

Source: Reuters

Source: From *The Wall Street Journal,* February 2, 2005, p. C2. Copyright © 2005 Dow Jones. Reprinted by permission of Copyright Clearance Center.

discussed. Exhibit 5.7 shows a table for numerous international stock indexes contained in *The Wall Street Journal.*

Global Equity Indexes

As shown in Exhibit 5.7 and 5A.2 (the latter is in this chapter's appendix), there are stock-market indexes available for most individual foreign markets. While these local indexes are closely followed within each country, a problem arises in comparing the results implied by these indexes to one another because of a lack of consistency among them in sample selection, weighting, or computational procedure. To solve these comparability problems, several investment data firms have computed a set of consistent country stock indexes. As a result, these indexes can be directly compared and combined to create various regional indexes (for example, Pacific Basin). We will describe the three major sets of global equity indexes.

FT/S&P-Actuaries World Indexes   The FT/S&P-Actuaries World Indexes are jointly compiled by the Financial Times Limited, Goldman Sachs & Company, and Standard &

Exhibit 5.7 | International Stock-Market Indexes

International Stock Market Indexes

COUNTRY	INDEX	2/1/05 CLOSE	NET CHG	% CHG	YTD NET CHG	YTD % CHG	P/E
World	DJ World Index	210.33	+0.91	+0.43	−3.67	−1.71	17
Argentina	Merval	1373.41	−0.38	−0.03	−1.96	−0.14	...
Australia	S&P/ASX 200	4127.70	+20.40	+0.50	+77.10	+1.90	17
Belgium	Bel-20	3010.57	+12.97	+0.43	+77.95	+2.66	12
Brazil	Sao Paulo Bovespa	24149.46	−201.16	−0.83	−2046.79	−7.81	11
Canada	S&P/TSX Composite	9270.13	+66.08	+0.72	+23.48	+0.25	17
Chile	Santiago IPSA	1803.58	−6.30	−0.35	+2.34	+0.13	17
China	Dow Jones CBN China 600	9605.95	−20.56	−0.21	−566.94	−5.57	19
China	Dow Jones China 88	107.36	+0.34	+0.32	−3.52	−3.17	18
Europe	DJ STOXX 600	258.86	+2.01	+0.78	+7.84	+3.12	21
Europe	DJ STOXX 50	2844.20	+25.01	+0.89	+69.43	+2.50	20
Euro Zone	DJ Euro STOXX	274.52	+1.96	+0.72	+7.14	+2.67	21
Euro Zone	DJ Euro STOXX 50	3008.85	+24.26	+0.81	+57.61	+1.95	18
France	Paris CAC 40	3939.18	+25.49	+0.65	+118.02	+3.09	16
Germany	Frankfurt Xetra DAX	4279.97	+25.12	+0.59	+23.89	+0.56	14
Hong Kong	Hang Seng	13578.26	−143.43	−1.05	−651.88	−4.58	16
India	Bombay Sensex	6552.47	−3.47	−0.05	−50.22	−0.76	16
Israel	Tel Aviv 25	635.32	+0.02	...	+17.38	+2.81	...
Italy	S&P/MIB	31515	+181	+0.58	+612	+1.98	19
Japan	Tokyo Nikkei Stock Average	11384.40	−3.19	−0.03	−104.36	−0.91	...
Japan	Tokyo Nikkei 300	219.16	+0.09	+0.04	−2.91	−1.31	...
Japan	Tokyo Topix Index	1146.49	+0.35	+0.03	−3.14	−0.27	115
Mexico	I.P.C. All-Share	13340.52	+243.40	+1.86	+422.64	+3.27	16
Netherlands	Amsterdam AEX	364.41	+3.99	+1.11	+16.33	+4.69	11
Russia	DJ Russia Titans 10	2058.30	+12.38	+0.61	+83.02	+4.20	32
Singapore	Straits Times	2094.65	−1.67	−0.08	+28.51	+1.38	14
South Africa	Johannesburg All Share	12957.44	+158.89	+1.24	+300.58	+2.37	15
South Korea	KOSPI	923.69	−9.01	−0.97	+27.77	+3.10	16
Spain	IBEX 35	9257.00	+33.10	+0.36	+176.20	+1.94	17
Sweden	SX All Share	232.25	+2.29	+1.00	+3.84	+1.68	22
Switzerland	Zurich Swiss Market	5797.90	+26.50	+0.46	+104.70	+1.84	16
Taiwan	Weighted	5981.54	−12.69	−0.21	−158.15	−2.58	12
Turkey	Istanbul National 100	27849.79	+519.44	+1.90	+2878.11	+11.53	26
U.K.	London FTSE 100-share	4906.20	+53.90	+1.11	+91.90	+1.91	16
U.K.	London FTSE 250-share	7225.40	+59.20	+0.83	+288.60	+4.16	18

Source: From *The Wall Street Journal*, February 2, 2005, p. C18. Copyright 2005 by DOW JONES & CO INC. Reproduced with permission of DOW JONES & CO INC in the format Other Book via Copyright Clearance Center.

Poor's (the "compilers") in conjunction with the Institute of Actuaries and the Faculty of Actuaries. Approximately 2,500 equity securities in 30 countries are measured, covering at least 70 percent of the total value of all listed companies in each country. All securities included must allow direct holdings of shares by foreign nationals.

The indexes are market value weighted and have a base date of December 31, 1986 = 100. The index results are typically reported in U.S. dollars, but, on occasion, have been reported in U.K. pound sterling, Japanese yen, euros, and the local currency of the country. In addition to the individual countries and the world index, there are several geographic subgroups, as shown in Exhibit 5.8.

Morgan Stanley Capital International (MSCI) Indexes   The Morgan Stanley Capital International Indexes consist of three international, 19 national, and 38 international industry indexes. The indexes consider some 1,673 companies listed on stock exchanges in 19 countries, with a combined market capitalization that represents approximately 60 percent of the aggregate market value of the stock exchanges of these countries. All the indexes are market value weighted. Exhibit 5.9 contains the countries included, the number of stocks, and market values for stocks in the various countries and groups.

In addition to reporting the indexes in U.S. dollars and the country's local currency, the following valuation information is available: (1) price-to-book value (P/BV) ratio, (2) price-to-cash

| Exhibit 5.8 | Financial Times Global Equity Index Series |

FTSE GLOBAL EQUITY INDEX SERIES

Feb 04

Countries & regions	No of stocks	US $ index	Day %	Mth %	YTD %	Total retn	YTD %	Gross Div Yield	FTSE All-World Industry Sectors	No of stocks	US $ index	Day %	Mth %	YTD %	Total retn	YTD %	Gross Div Yield
FTSE Global All-Cap	7581	303.67	0.9	1.2	-0.7	317.09	-0.6	2.0	Resources	157	288.50	0.8	8.4	4.7	325.98	4.8	2.5
FTSE Global Large Cap	1085	286.10	0.9	0.6	-1.1	299.51	-0.9	2.1	Mining	48	484.36	-0.1	7.2	2.4	544.80	2.4	2.0
FTSE Global Mid Cap	1907	346.13	1.0	2.4	0.1	359.56	0.2	1.7	Oil & Gas	109	271.14	0.9	8.6	5.1	306.68	5.3	2.5
FTSE Global Small Cap	4589	360.75	0.9	3.0	0.3	373.68	0.4	1.5	Basic Industries	340	309.13	1.2	3.0	0.9	345.16	1.0	2.0
FTSE All-World (Large/Mid Cap)	2992	181.58	0.9	1.0	-0.8	198.19	-0.7	2.0	Chemicals	117	280.65	1.0	1.9	-0.3	313.26	-0.2	2.0
FTSE World (Large/Mid Cap)	2564	323.46	0.9	1.0	-0.9	473.65	-0.8	2.0	Construction & Building Materials	119	338.94	1.7	6.6	5.2	377.71	5.3	1.8
FTSE Global All-Cap ex UK	7082	303.40	0.9	1.1	-0.9	315.88	-0.8	1.8	Forestry & Paper	32	274.28	1.8	-3.3	-5.7	311.95	-5.5	2.9
FTSE Global All-Cap ex USA	5129	330.80	0.7	0.9	-0.6	348.90	-0.5	2.3	Steel & Other Metals	72	363.72	0.6	3.5	0.4	400.91	0.8	1.9
FTSE Global All-Cap ex Japan	6246	303.13	0.9	1.3	-0.6	317.14	-0.5	2.1	General Industrials	287	186.13	0.8	1.0	-0.9	202.03	-0.7	1.7
FTSE Global All-Cap ex Eurobloc	6829	298.91	0.9	1.3	-0.7	311.36	-0.5	1.9	Aerospace & Defence	24	210.85	0.7	4.6	1.3	230.07	1.4	1.8
FTSE All-World Developed	2107	293.45	0.9	0.9	-0.9	306.50	-0.8	2.0	Diversified Industrials	62	178.73	0.6	0.3	-0.7	196.29	-0.6	2.1
FTSE Developed All-Cap	6076	300.35	0.9	1.1	-0.8	313.39	-0.7	1.9	Electronic & Electrical Equipment	106	168.33	0.9	-0.4	-2.5	179.41	-2.2	1.3
FTSE Developed Large Cap	769	281.89	0.9	0.5	-1.2	294.90	-1.1	2.1	Engineering & Machinery	95	291.11	0.9	1.6	-0.5	317.71	-0.4	1.5
									Cyclical Consumer Goods	173	202.82	0.6	-1.4	-2.5	220.91	-2.4	1.8
FTSE Developed Europe Large Cap	189	305.63	0.8	0.1	-1.3	325.27	-1.1	2.8	Automobiles & Parts	80	211.60	0.8	-1.4	-2.1	231.91	-2.1	2.0
FTSE Developed Europe Mid Cap	325	355.96	0.8	1.9	0.8	377.21	1.0	2.3	Household Goods & Textiles	93	185.04	0.4	-1.4	-3.2	198.89	-3.1	1.4
FTSE Developed Europe Small Cap	1026	409.65	0.6	4.3	3.1	433.16	3.2	2.2	Non-Cyclical Consumer Goods	354	202.85	0.8	0.7	-0.8	220.22	-0.7	1.9
FTSE All-World Developed Europe	514	195.60	0.8	0.4	-0.9	220.53	-0.7	2.7	Beverages	50	221.11	1.3	1.8	0.7	241.46	0.8	2.2
									Food Producers & Processors	92	275.43	0.2	1.6	0.2	305.30	0.3	2.3
FTSE North America Large Cap	281	265.12	1.0	1.0	-0.9	275.42	-0.7	1.8	Health	77	263.24	0.8	5.6	3.5	273.20	3.6	0.4
FTSE North America Mid Cap	539	328.79	1.3	2.7	-0.4	338.61	-0.3	1.3	Personal Care & Household Products	27	256.73	-0.3	2.0	0.6	278.47	0.9	1.8
FTSE North America Small Cap	1875	338.61	1.2	2.0	-1.6	347.93	-1.5	1.3	Pharmaceuticals	93	153.31	0.8	-2.6	-4.2	165.20	-4.1	2.0
FTSE All-World North America	820	170.75	1.1	1.4	-0.8	183.64	-0.6	1.7	Tobacco	15	402.61	3.3	6.4	5.6	497.83	5.9	4.0
FTSE All-World Dev ex North Am	1287	190.11	0.8	0.2	-1.1	211.34	-1.0	2.4	Cyclical Services	491	198.07	0.7	-0.2	-1.8	208.91	-1.8	1.2
									General Retailers	114	260.15	0.6	-1.0	-2.4	272.67	-2.3	1.1
FTSE Japan Large Cap	177	288.83	0.6	-2.0	-3.5	294.96	-3.5	1.0	Leisure & Hotels	62	197.06	1.0	-0.2	-1.6	208.09	-1.6	1.5
FTSE Japan Mid Cap	303	358.77	0.6	2.8	1.5	366.51	1.5	0.9	Media & Entertainment	128	149.60	0.7	-0.1	-1.6	157.62	-1.6	0.9
FTSE Japan Small Cap	855	393.52	0.5	5.4	4.1	404.30	4.1	1.1	Support Services	67	167.82	0.8	-1.0	-3.0	178.14	-2.9	1.3
FTSE Japan (Large/Mid Cap)	480	115.40	0.6	-1.0	-2.5	133.33	-2.5	1.0	Transport	120	271.21	0.9	2.4	0.4	292.67	0.5	1.6
FTSE Asia Pacific Large Cap ex Japan	302	343.43	0.4	2.3	1.0	366.75	1.2	2.9	Non-Cyclical Services	150	129.19	0.9	-0.9	-2.2	141.62	-2.0	2.4
FTSE Asia Pacific Mid Cap ex Japan	563	361.67	0.2	0.9	-0.4	382.98	-0.1	2.5	Food & Drug Retailers	38	177.40	0.3	3.9	2.9	190.05	3.0	1.4
FTSE Asia Pacific Small Cap ex Japan	714	345.91	0.3	3.1	2.6	365.61	2.7	2.6	Telecommunication Services	112	121.93	1.0	-1.8	-3.2	134.30	-2.9	2.6
FTSE All-World Asia Pacific ex Japan	865	260.43	0.3	2.0	0.7	296.84	0.9	2.8	Utilities	145	214.26	1.0	4.1	2.2	252.98	2.4	3.4
									Electricity	94	232.83	0.9	4.1	2.2	276.69	2.5	3.5
FTSE All Emerging All-Cap	1505	374.09	0.5	2.9	1.0	396.17	1.3	2.6	Utilities Other	51	228.32	1.3	4.2	2.1	268.92	2.3	3.1
FTSE All Emerging Large Cap	316	370.06	0.5	3.1	1.1	392.02	1.5	2.7	Financials	638	222.03	0.8	-0.1	-1.5	248.53	-1.3	2.6
FTSE All Emerging Mid Cap	569	371.74	0.5	1.4	-0.5	391.41	-0.2	2.4	Banks	259	253.62	0.7	-0.2	-1.3	290.92	-1.1	3.1
FTSE All Emerging Small Cap	620	356.43	0.5	3.8	3.0	375.60	3.2	2.3	Insurance	74	169.21	1.2	0.2	-0.6	180.55	-0.6	1.6
FTSE All-World All Emerging Europe	57	343.43	0.8	5.0	4.2	374.50	4.2	1.6	Life Assurance	35	174.80	0.7	0.7	-0.7	196.01	-0.7	2.3
FTSE Latin Americas All-Cap	175	481.90	1.8	7.0	2.5	517.30	2.7	3.5	Investment Companies	21	227.31	0.3	2.0	0.6	252.88	0.8	2.4
FTSE Middle East Africa All-Cap	173	399.85	0.4	-2.9	-5.5	427.62	-5.2	2.6	Real Estate	102	267.63	1.1	-1.1	-3.2	312.95	-3.1	3.3
									Speciality & Other Finance	147	195.70	1.0	-0.5	-2.3	209.40	-2.2	1.4
FTSE UK All-Cap	499	306.35	0.9	2.5	1.2	328.55	1.3	3.0	Information Technology	257	83.96	1.6	-1.2	-3.6	86.11	-3.6	0.7
FTSE USA All-Cap	2452	281.58	1.1	1.5	-0.8	291.61	-0.6	1.6	Information Technology Hardware	174	72.28	1.9	-0.8	-3.7	74.28	-3.6	0.7
FTSE Europe All-Cap	1624	305.65	0.8	0.9	-0.4	346.04	-0.3	2.6	Software & Computer Services	83	119.45	1.1	-1.8	-3.6	121.99	-3.6	0.7
FTSE Eurobloc All-Cap	752	336.59	0.8	0.3	-1.0	357.35	-0.8	2.6									

www.ftse.com. On September 22 2003, FTSE launched the FTSE Global Equity Index Series. The family contains the new FTSE Global Small Cap Indices and broader FTSE Global All Cap Indices (large/mid/small cap) as well as the enhanced FTSE All-World Index Series (large/mid cap). This table has been updated to reflect the additional indices. The FTSE Industry Sectors table relates to the FTSE All-World Index Series Sectors (large/mid cap). To learn more about the enhancement and new indices, please visit www.ftse.com/geis. © FTSE International Limited 2005. All rights reserved. 'FTSE', 'FT-SE' and 'Footsie' are trade marks of the London Stock Exchange and The Financial Times and are used by FTSE International under license. Latest prices were unavailable for this edition.

Source: *Financial Times,* February 8, 2005, p. 27. Reprinted by permission of The Financial Times Limited.

earnings (earnings plus depreciation) (P/CE) ratio, (3) price-to-earnings (P/E) ratio, and (4) dividend yield (YLD). These ratios help in analyzing different valuation levels among countries and over time for specific countries.

Notably, the Morgan Stanley group index for Europe, Australia, and the Far East (EAFE) is the basis for futures and options contracts on the Chicago Mercantile Exchange and the Chicago Board Options Exchange. Several of the MSCI country indexes, the EAFE index, and a world index are reported daily in *The Wall Street Journal,* as shown in Exhibit 5.10.

Dow Jones World Stock Index   In January 1993, Dow Jones introduced its World Stock Index. Composed of more than 2,200 companies worldwide and organized into 120 industry groups, the index includes 28 countries representing more than 80 percent of the combined capitalization of these countries. In addition to the 34 individual countries shown in Exhibit 5.11, the countries are grouped into three regions: Asia/Pacific, Europe/Africa, and the Americas. Finally, each country's index is calculated in its own currency as well as in U.S. dollars, British

| Exhibit 5.9 | Market Coverage of Morgan Stanley Capital International Indexes as of November 30, 2004 |

| | GDP WEIGHTS[a] | | | WEIGHT AS PERCENT OF INDEX | |
	Percent EAFE	Companies in Index	Market Cap. U.S. $ Billion	EAFE	World
Austria	1.8	13	69.6	0.3	0.1
Belgium	2.3	20	239.5	1.3	0.5
Denmark	3.4	20	137.8	0.8	0.3
Finland	2.0	19	198.2	1.8	0.6
France	10.7	57	1,412.7	9.4	3.9
Germany	14.8	47	1,056.1	6.8	2.8
Greece	1.1	20	109.9	0.5	0.2
Ireland	1.0	15	93.9	0.8	0.3
Italy	9.6	41	606.7	4.0	1.6
The Netherlands	3.2	26	508.9	4.8	1.9
Norway	1.6	14	133.0	0.6	0.2
Portugal	0.9	10	67.2	0.4	0.1
Spain	5.3	31	774.7	3.8	1.5
Sweden	1.9	44	353.6	2.5	1.0
Switzerland	1.8	35	707.0	6.9	2.8
United Kingdom	10.8	121	2,560.0	25.2	10.3
Europe	69.1	563	9,118.0	69.5	28.5
Australia	3.5	72	675.0	5.4	2.2
Hong Kong	1.0	37	402.5	1.7	0.7
Japan	25.4	344	3,492.2	22.3	9.1
New Zealand	0.5	16	25.8	0.2	0.1
Singapore	0.6	35	169.0	0.6	0.3
Pacific	30.9	504	4,764.4	30.5	12.5
Pacific ex Japan	5.6	160	1,272.2	6.2	3.4
EAFE	100.0	1,067	13,002.4	100.0	40.9
Canada	—	90	1,083.7	—	2.9
United States	—	51.6	14,816.4	—	51.3
The World Index	—	1,673	29,782.5	—	100.0
EMU	51.5	299	5,217.8	—	13.6
Europe ex UK	58.2	412	6,549.2	—	18.1
Far East	27.0	416	4,062.7	24.8	10.2
North America	—	606	15,900.1	—	54.1
Kokusai Index (World ex Japan)	—	1,329	29,453.7	—	90.9

[a]GDP weight figures represent the initial weights applicable for the first month. They are used exclusively in the MSCI "GDP weighted" indexes.

Source: MSCI. Reprinted with permission.

Exhibit 5.10	Listing of Morgan Stanley Capital International Stock Index Values

MSCI Indexes

	JAN 31	JAN 28	% CHG FROM 12/03
U.S.	1108.2	1099.1	+6.0
Britain	1467.7	1461.8	+8.8
Canada	1132.2	1123.8	+11.0
Japan	689.4	686.8	+8.2
France	1290.1	1276.5	+10.6
Germany	522.0	515.5	+6.1
Hong Kong	7375.7	7338.0	+16.3
Switzerland	756.7	754.1	+5.9
Australia	813.0	811.1	+24.0
World Index	1142.3	1133.4	+10.2
MSCI EAFE	1487.0	1476.2	+15.4

As calculated by Morgan Stanley Capital International Perspective, Geneva. Each index, calculated in local currencies, is based on the close of 1969 equaling 100.

Source: From *The Wall Street Journal,* February 2, 2005, p. C14. Copyright 2005 by DOW JONES & CO INC. Reproduced with permission of DOW JONES & CO INC in the format Other Book via Copyright Clearance Center.

Exhibit 5.11	Dow Jones Country Indexes

Dow Jones Country Indexes

Feb. 1, 2005 5:15 p.m. ET

In U.S. dollar terms

COUNTRY	INDEX	CHG	% CHG	YTD % CHG	COUNTRY	INDEX	CHG	% CHG	YTD % CHG
Australia	282.84	+0.40	+0.14	+0.78	Mexico	265.33	+5.47	+2.10	+3.14
Austria	272.71	+1.82	+0.67	−1.72	Netherlands	281.22	+3.18	+1.14	+0.64
Belgium	307.19	+1.57	+0.51	−1.19	New Zealand	232.64	+0.96	+0.41	−1.04
Brazil	494.46	+1.83	+0.37	−2.70	Norway	223.53	+2.28	+1.03	−2.04
Canada	281.74	+1.66	+0.59	−3.24	Philippines	92.05	−1.32	−1.41	+9.35
Chile	253.14	−2.09	−0.82	−6.80	Portugal	200.14	+1.16	+0.58	+1.68
Denmark	301.92	+2.13	+0.71	−1.90	Singapore	161.05	−1.01	−0.62	+1.53
Finland	813.07	+6.79	+0.84	−2.51	South Africa	204.01	−2.74	−1.33	−6.73
France	248.12	+1.01	+0.41	−0.94	South Korea	139.17	−1.54	−1.09	+5.45
Germany	199.36	+0.66	+0.33	−3.58	Spain	273.56	+0.37	+0.14	−2.19
Greece	193.15	−1.28	−0.66	−0.51	Sweden	335.42	+3.54	+1.07	−3.86
Hong Kong	242.98	−2.58	−1.05	−5.01	Switzerland	382.19	−0.34	−0.09	−2.95
Indonesia	77.95	−0.17	−0.22	+7.50	Taiwan	121.06	−0.05	−0.04	−2.91
Ireland	469.28	+5.79	+1.25	−0.33	Thailand	78.01	+0.76	+0.98	+6.93
Italy	213.50	+0.78	+0.37	−2.12	U.K.	207.44	+1.53	+0.74	+0.08
Japan	88.81	−0.49	−0.55	−1.98	U.S.	283.55	+1.91	+0.68	−2.02
Malaysia	122.13	Closed	...	+1.19	Venezuela	41.04	+2.17	+5.58	−7.15

Source: From *The Wall Street Journal,* February 2, 2005, p. C18. Copyright 2005 by DOW JONES & CO INC. Reproduced with permission of DOW JONES & CO INC in the format Other Book via Copyright Clearance Center.

pounds, euros, and Japanese yen. The index for the individual countries is reported daily in *The Wall Street Journal* (domestic), in *The Wall Street Journal Europe,* and in *The Asian Wall Street Journal.* It is published weekly in *Barron's.*

Comparison of World Stock Indexes   As shown in Exhibit 5.12, the correlations between the three series since December 31, 1991, when the DJ series became available, indicate that the results with the various world stock indexes are quite comparable.

A summary of the characteristics of the major price-weighted, market-value-weighted, and equal-weighted stock price indexes for the United States and major foreign countries is contained in Exhibit 5A.1 in the chapter appendix. As shown, the major differences are

| Exhibit 5.12 | Correlations of Percentage Price Changes of Alternative World Stock Indexes 12/31/91–12/31/03 |

	U.S. Dollars
FT–MS:	.997
FT–DJ:	.996
MS–DJ:	.994

the number of stocks in alternative indexes, but more important is the *source* of the sample (e.g., stocks from the NYSE, Nasdaq, all U.S. stocks, or stocks from a foreign country such as the United Kingdom or Japan).

BOND-MARKET INDEXES[4]

Investors know little about the several bond-market indexes because these indexes are relatively new and not widely published. Knowledge regarding these indexes is becoming more important because of the growth of fixed-income mutual funds and the consequent need to have a reliable set of benchmarks to use in evaluating their performance. Also, because the performance of many fixed-income money managers has been unable to match that of the aggregate bond market, interest has been growing in bond-index funds, which requires the development of an index to emulate as discussed by Dialynas (2001) and Volpert (2005).

Notably, it is more difficult to create and compute a bond-market index than a stock-market index for several reasons. First, the universe of bonds is much broader than that of stocks, ranging from U.S. Treasury securities to bonds in default. Second, the universe of bonds is changing constantly because of new issues, bond maturities, calls, and bond sinking funds. Third, the volatility of prices for individual bonds and bond portfolios changes because bond price volatility is affected by duration, which is likewise changing constantly because of changes in maturity, coupon, and market yield (see Chapter 17). Finally, significant problems can arise in correctly pricing the individual bond issues in an index (especially corporate and mortgage bonds) compared to the current and continuous transactions prices available for most stocks used in stock indexes.

Our subsequent discussion will be divided into the following three subsections: (1) U.S. investment-grade bond indexes, including Treasuries; (2) U.S. high-yield bond indexes; and (3) global government bond indexes. All of these indexes indicate total rates of return for the portfolio of bonds and the indexes are market value weighted. Exhibit 5.13 is a summary of the characteristics for the indexes available for these three segments of the bond market.

U.S. Investment-Grade Bond Indexes

As shown in Exhibit 5.13, four investment firms have created and maintain indexes for Treasury bonds and other bonds considered investment grade, that is, the bonds are rated Bbb or higher. As demonstrated in a subsequent section, the relationship among the returns for

---

[4]The discussion in this section draws heavily from Reilly and Wright (2005).

Exhibit 5.13 | Summary of Bond-Market Indexes

Name of Index	Number of Issues	Maturity	Size of Issues	Weighting	Pricing	Reinvestment Assumption	Subindexes Available
U.S. Investment-Grade Bond Indexes							
Lehman Brothers	5,000+	Over 1 year	Over $100 million	Market value	Trader priced and model priced	No	Government, gov./corp., corporate mortgage-backed, asset-backed
Merrill Lynch	5,000+	Over 1 year	Over $50 million	Market value	Trader priced and model priced	In specific bonds	Government, gov./corp., corporate, mortgage
Ryan Treasury	300+	Over 1 year	All Treasury	Market value and equal	Market priced	In specific bonds	Treasury
Smith Barney	5,000+	Over 1 year	Over $50 million	Market value	Trader priced	In one-month T-bill	Broad inv. grade, Treas.-agency, corporate, mortgage
U.S. High-Yield Bond Indexes							
C. S. First Boston	423	All maturities	Over $75 million	Market value	Trader priced	Yes	Composite and by rating
Lehman Brothers	624	Over 1 year	Over $100 million	Market value	Trader priced	No	Composite and by rating
Merrill Lynch	735	Over 1 year	Over $25 million	Market value	Trader priced	Yes	Composite and by rating
Smith Barney	299	Over 7 years	Over $50 million	Market value	Trader priced	Yes	Composite and by rating

(continued)

Exhibit 5.13 | Summary of Bond-Market Indexes (continued)

Name of Index	Number of Issues	Maturity	Size of Issues	Weighting	Pricing	Reinvestment Assumption	Subindexes Available
Global Government Bond Indexes							
Lehman Brothers	800	Over 1 year	Over $200 million	Market value	Trader priced	Yes	Composite and 13 countries, local and U.S. dollars
Merrill Lynch	9,736	Over 1 year	Over $50 million	Market value	Trader priced	Yes	Composite and 9 countries, local and U.S. dollars
J. P. Morgan	445	Over 1 year	Over $100 million	Market value	Trader priced	Yes in index	Composite and 11 countries, local and U.S. dollars
Smith Barney	400	Over 1 year	Over $250 million	Market value	Trader priced	Yes at local short-term rate	Composite and 14 countries, local and U.S. dollars

Source: Frank K. Reilly, Wenchi Kao, and David J. Wright, "Alternative Bond Market Indexes," *Financial Analysts Journal* 48, no. 3 (May–June, 1992): 14–58; Frank K. Reilly and David J. Wright, "An Analysis of High-Yield Bond Benchmarks," *Journal of Fixed Income* 3, no. 4 (March 1994): 6–24; and Frank K. Reilly and David J. Wright, "Global Bond Markets: Alternative Benchmarks and Risk–Return Performance," presented at Midwest Finance Association Meeting, Chicago, IL, March 2000.

these investment-grade bonds is strong (that is, correlations average about 0.95), regardless of the segment of the market.

High-Yield Bond Indexes

One of the fastest-growing segments of the U.S. bond market during the past 20 years has been the high-yield bond market, which includes bonds that are not investment grade—that is, they are rated Bb, B, Ccc, Cc, and C. Because of this growth, four investment firms created indexes related to this market. A summary of the characteristics for these indexes is included in Exhibit 5.13. For an analysis of the alternative high-yield bond benchmarks, see Reilly and Wright (1994); for an analysis of this whole market, see Reilly and Wright (2001).

Global Government Bond Indexes

The global bond market has experienced significant growth in size and importance during the past fifteen years. Unlike the high-yield bond market, the global segment is completely dominated by government bonds because few non-U.S. countries have a corporate bond market. Once again, several major investment firms have created indexes that reflect the performance for the global bond market. As shown in Exhibit 5.13, the various indexes have similar characteristics. At the same time, the total sample sizes and the numbers of countries included differ.

COMPOSITE STOCK-BOND INDEXES

Beyond separate stock indexes and bond indexes for individual countries, a natural step is the development of a composite index that measures the performance of all securities in a given country. With a composite index investors can examine the benefits of diversifying with a combination of asset classes such as stocks and bonds in addition to diversifying within the asset classes of stocks or bonds. There are two such indexes available.

First, a market-value-weighted index called Merrill Lynch–Wilshire Capital Markets Index (ML–WCMI) measures the total return performance of the combined U.S. taxable fixed-income and equity markets. It is basically a combination of the Merrill Lynch fixed-income indexes and the Dow Jones Wilshire 5000 common-stock index. As such, it tracks more than 10,000 U.S. stocks and bonds and, as of March 2005, the relative weights are about 33 percent bonds and 67 percent stocks.

The second composite index is the Brinson Partner Global Security Market Index (GSMI), which contains U.S. stocks and bonds as well as non-U.S. equities and nondollar bonds along with an allocation to cash. The specific breakdown as of February 2005 was U.S. equities, 40 percent; non-U.S. equities, 25 percent; U.S. bonds, 24 percent; and non-U.S. bonds, 11 percent.

Although related to the relative market values of these asset classes, the weights specified were derived using optimization techniques to identify the portfolio mix of available global asset classes that matches the risk level of a typical U.S. pension plan. The index is balanced to the policy weights monthly.

Because the GSMI contains both U.S. and international stocks and bonds, it is clearly the most diversified benchmark available with a weighting scheme that approaches market values. As such, it is closest to the theoretically specified "market portfolio of risky assets" referred to in the CAPM literature. It is used in Reilly and Akhtar (1995) to demonstrate the impact of alternative benchmarks when evaluating portfolio performance.

COMPARISON OF INDEXES OVER TIME

We now look at price movements in the different indexes for monthly intervals.

Correlations between Monthly Equity Price Changes

Exhibit 5.14 contains a listing of the correlation coefficients of the monthly percentage of price changes for a set of U.S. and non-U.S. equity-market indexes with the S&P 500 index during the 22-year period from 1980 to 2001. Most of the correlation differences are attributable to the different sample of firms listed on the different stock exchanges. Most of the major indexes—except the Nikkei Stock Average—are market-value-weighted indexes that include a large number of stocks. Therefore, the computational procedure is generally similar and the sample sizes are large or all-encompassing. Thus, the major difference between the indexes is that the sample of stocks are from different segments of the U.S. stock market or from different countries.

There is a high positive correlation (0.98–0.99) between the S&P 500 and the several comprehensive U.S. equity indexes, Wilshire, NYSE, and Russell 3000. In contrast, there are lower correlations between these comprehensive indexes and various style indexes such as the Russell Large-Cap 1000 (0.886) or the Russell 2000 Small-Cap index (0.783).

The correlations between the S&P 500 and indexes from Canada, the United Kingdom, Germany, and Japan support the case for global investing. Specifically, the U.S.–Toronto correlation was about 0.75, the U.S.–*Financial Times* correlation was about 0.67, and the U.S.–Japan correlations (the Nikkei and the Tokyo S.E.) averaged about 0.38. These diversification results were confirmed with the composite international series—with the MSCI EAFE and the IFC Emerging Market the correlations were about 0.54 and 0.39, respectively. These results confirm the benefits of global diversification because such low correlations would reduce the variance of a pure U.S. stock portfolio.

Correlations between Monthly Bond Indexes

The correlations with the monthly Lehman Bros. Govt. bond return index in Exhibit 5.14 consider a variety of bond indexes. The correlations between the longer-term U.S. investment-grade bond indexes ranged from about 0.94 to 0.98, confirming that although the *level* of interest rates differs due to the risk premium, the overriding factors that determine the rates of return for investment-grade bonds over time are *systematic* interest rate variables.

The correlations among investment-grade bonds and high-yield bonds indicate significantly lower correlations (about 0.49) caused by definite equity characteristics of high-yield bonds as shown in Reilly and Wright (2001). Finally, the low and diverse relationships among U.S. investment-grade bonds and world government bonds without the United States (about 0.35) reflect different interest rate movements and exchange rate effects (these non-U.S. government results are presented as U.S. dollar returns). Again, these results support global diversification of bond portfolios.

Mean Annual Security Returns and Risk

The use of security indexes to measure returns and risk was demonstrated in Exhibit 3.14, which showed the average annual price change, or rate of return, and risk measure for a large set of asset indexes. As one would expect, there were clear differences between the indexes due to the different asset classes (e.g., stocks versus bonds) and the different samples within asset classes (e.g., the results for NYSE stocks versus Nasdaq stocks). Equally important, the results

Exhibit 5.14	Correlation Coefficients between Monthly Percentage Price Changes in Various Stock and Bond Indexes, 1980–2001

Stock Indexes	S&P 500	Bond Indexes	Lehman Brothers Govt. Bonds
Wilshire 5000	0.983	LB Aggregate Bonds	0.981
NYSE Composite	0.993	LB Corporate Bonds	0.945
Russell 3000	0.992	LB High-Yield Bonds	0.489
Russell 1000	0.886	ML World Govt Bonds[a]	0.596
Russell 2000	0.783	ML World Govt Bonds	0.345
MSCI EAFE	0.538	w/o U.S.[a]	
Toronto S.E. 300	0.753	Treasury Bill—30-day	0.186
Financial Times	0.667	Treasury Bill—6-month[b]	0.561
All-Share		Treasury Bill—2-year[b]	0.917
Frankfurt (FAZ) Index	0.536		
Nikkei Index	0.418		
Tokyo S.E. Index	0.328		
IFC Emerging Mkt.	0.392		
M.S. World Index	0.604		
Brinson GSMI	0.915		

[a]Based on 1986–2001 data only
[b]Based on 1981–2001 data only

Source: Frank K. Reilly and David J. Wright, "An Analysis of Risk-Adjusted Performance for Global Market Assets," *Journal of Portfolio Management* 30, no. 3 (Spring, 2004), pp. 63–77. This copyrighted material is reprinted with permission from *Journal of Portfolio Management,* a publication of Institutional Investor, Inc.

were generally consistent with what one should expect in a risk-averse world—that is, there was a positive relationship between the average rate of return for an asset and its measure of risk (e.g., the return-risk results for T-Bills versus the results for the S&P 500 stocks).

The Internet   *Investments Online*

We've seen several previous Web sites which offer online users a look at current market conditions in the form of a time-delayed market index (some sites offer real-time stock and index prices, but only at a cost to their customers). Here are a few others:

http://www.bloomberg.com The site is somewhat of an Internet version of the "Bloomberg machine," which is prevalent in many brokerage house offices. It offers both news and current data on a wide variety of global market securities and indexes, including historical charts. The site contains information on interest rates, commodities, and currencies.

http://www.barra.com Barra offers downloadable historical data on several S&P/Barra equity indexes, including S&P 500, midcap, and small cap indexes as well as Canadian equity indexes. Also included is information about the characteristics of the indexes.

http://www.msci.com Morgan Stanley Capital International contains links to sites which offer downloadable data on several of its international equity indexes. Information and graphics on several fixed income indexes are available, too.

https://ecommerce.barcap.com/indices/ and the home page of Barclays Capital, **http://www.barcap.com**, offer information on European bond market indexes.

Additional global bond index performance information can be found on this page of the Thomson Financial Web site: **http://www.thomson.com/financial/financial_products_az.jsp**

Information on Japanese bond indexes is available at a Daiwa Institute of Research site, **http://www.dir.co.jp/InfoManage/dbi/menu.html**

SUMMARY

- Given the several uses of security-market indexes, it is important to know how they are constructed and the differences between them. To use one of the many indexes to learn how the market is doing, you need to be aware of what market you are dealing with so you can select the appropriate index. As an example, are you only interested in the NYSE or do you also want to consider Nasdaq? Beyond the U.S. market, are you interested in Japanese or U.K. stocks, or do you want to examine the total world market? This choice is discussed in Merjos (1990).

- Indexes are also used as benchmarks to evaluate portfolio performance.[5] In this case, you must be sure the index (benchmark) is consistent with your investing universe.

If you are investing worldwide, you should not judge your performance relative to the DJIA, which is limited to 30 U.S. blue-chip stocks. For a bond portfolio, the index should match your investment philosophy. Finally, if your portfolio contains both stocks and bonds, you must evaluate your performance against an appropriate combination of indexes.

- Investors need to examine numerous market indexes to evaluate the performance of their investments. The selection of the appropriate indexes for information or evaluation will depend on how knowledgeable you are regarding the various indexes. The background from this chapter should help you understand what to look for and how to make the right decision in this area.

SUGGESTED READINGS

Fisher, Lawrence, and James H. Lorie. *A Half Century of Returns on Stocks and Bonds.* Chicago: University of Chicago Graduate School of Business, 1977.

Ibbotson Associates. *Stocks, Bonds, Bills, and Inflation.* Chicago: Ibbotson Associates, annual.

QUESTIONS

1. Discuss briefly several uses of security-market indexes.
2. What major factors must be considered when constructing a market index? Put another way, what characteristics differentiate indexes?

---

[5]Chapter 25 includes an extensive discussion of the purpose and construction of benchmarks and considers the use of benchmarks in the evaluation of portfolio performance.

3. Explain how a market index is price weighted. In such a case, would you expect a $100 stock to be more important than a $25 stock? Give an example.
4. Explain how to compute a value-weighted index.
5. Explain how a price-weighted index and a value-weighted index adjust for stock splits.
6. Describe an unweighted price index and describe how you would construct such an index. Assume a 20 percent price change in GM ($40/share; 50 million shares outstanding) and Coors Brewing ($25/share and 15 million shares outstanding). Explain which stock's change will have the greater impact on this index.
7. If you correlated percentage changes in the Wilshire 5000 equity index with percentage changes in the NYSE composite and the Nasdaq composite index, would you expect a difference in the correlations? Why or why not?
8. There are high correlations between the monthly percentage price changes for the alternative NYSE indexes. Discuss the reason for this similarity: is it size of sample, source of sample, or method of computation?
9. Discuss the correlation of 0.82 between the two stock price indexes for the Tokyo Stock Exchange (TSE). Examine the correlations among the TSE and S&P 500 indexes. Explain why these relationships differ.
10. You learn that the Wilshire 5000 market-value-weighted index increased by 16 percent during a specified period, whereas a Wilshire 5000 equal-weighted index increased by 23 percent during the same period. Discuss what this difference in results implies.
11. Why is it contended that bond-market indexes are more difficult to construct and maintain than stock-market indexes?
12. Suppose the Wilshire 5000 market-value-weighted index increased by 5 percent, whereas the Merrill Lynch–Wilshire Capital Markets Index increased by 15 percent during the same period. What does this difference in results imply?
13. Suppose the Russell 1000 increased by 8 percent during the past year, whereas the Russell 2000 increased by 15 percent. Discuss the implication of these results.
14. Based on what you know about the *Financial Times* (FT) World Index, the Morgan Stanley Capital International World Index, and the Dow Jones World Stock Index, what level of correlation would you expect between monthly rates of return? Discuss the reasons for your answer based on the factors that affect indexes.
15. How would you explain that the ML High-Yield Bond Index was more highly correlated with the NYSE composite stock index than the ML Aggregate Bond Index?
16. Assuming that the mandate to a portfolio manager was to invest in a broadly diversified portfolio of U.S. stocks, which two or three indexes should be considered as an appropriate benchmark? Why?

PROBLEMS

1. You are given the following information regarding prices for a sample of stocks.

Stock	Number of Shares	PRICE	
		T	T + 1
A	1,000,000	60	80
B	10,000,000	20	35
C	30,000,000	18	25

a. Construct a *price-weighted* index for these three stocks, and compute the percentage change in the index for the period from T to T + 1.
b. Construct a *value-weighted* index for these three stocks, and compute the percentage change in the index for the period from T to T + 1.
c. Briefly discuss the difference in the results for the two indexes.

2. a. Given the data in Problem 1, construct an equal-weighted index by assuming $1,000 is invested in each stock. What is the percentage change in wealth for this portfolio?
    b. Compute the percentage of price change for each of the stocks in Problem 1. Compute the arithmetic mean of these percentage changes. Discuss how this answer compares to the answer in Part a.
    c. Compute the geometric mean of the percentage changes in Part b. Discuss how this result compares to the answer in Part b.
3. For the past five trading days, on the basis of figures in *The Wall Street Journal,* compute the daily percentage price changes for the following stock indexes.
    a. DJIA
    b. S&P 500
    c. Nasdaq Composite Index
    d. FT-100 Share Index
    e. Nikkei 225 Stock Price Average
    Discuss the difference in results for Parts a and b, a and c, a and d, a and e, and d and e. What do these differences imply regarding diversifying within the United States versus diversifying between countries?
4.

	PRICE			SHARES		
Company	A	B	C	A	B	C
Day 1	12	23	52	500	350	250
Day 2	10	22	55	500	350	250
Day 3	14	46	52	500	175[a]	250
Day 4	13	47	25	500	175	500[b]
Day 5	12	45	26	500	175	500

[a]Split at close of Day 2.
[b]Split at close of Day 3.

a. Calculate a Dow Jones Industrial Average for days 1 through 5.
b. What effects have the splits had in determining the next day's index? (Hint: think of the relative weighting of each stock.)
c. From a copy of *The Wall Street Journal,* find the divisor that is currently being used in calculating the DJIA. (Normally this value can be found on pages C2 and C3.)
5. Utilizing the price and volume data in Problem 4,
    a. Calculate a Standard & Poor's Index for days 1 through 5 using a beginning index value of 10.
    b. Identify what effects the splits had in determining the next day's index. (Hint: think of the relative weighting of each stock.)
6. Based on the following stock price and shares outstanding information, compute the beginning and ending values for a price-weighted index and a market-value-weighted index.

	DECEMBER 31, 2005		DECEMBER 31, 2006	
	Price	Shares Outstanding	Price	Shares Outstanding
Stock K	20	100,000,000	32	100,000,000
Stock M	80	2,000,000	45	4,000,000[a]
Stock R	40	25,000,000	42	25,000,000

[a]Stock split two-for-one during the year.

a. Compute the percentage change in the value of each index.
b. Explain the difference in results between the two indexes.
c. Compute the percentage change for an unweighted index and discuss why these results differ from those of the other indexes.

THOMSON ONE | Business School Edition

1. Collect price and number of outstanding share data from the past ten days on the following firms: Amazon (AMZN), Family Dollar (FDO), J.C. Penney (JCP), Target (TGT), and Wal-mart (WMT). Using this data, create a "retail sales stock index" by computing a value-weighted index. What is the overall percent change on the index over the ten days?
2. Using the market values for each stock on day 1, compute the relative weight for each of the five stocks. Which stock has the largest weight and which stock has the smallest weight?
3. Using the data from above, compute a price-weighted and unweighted stock index. What is the overall percent change on each index? How do the behaviors of the value-weighted, price-weighted, and unweighted indexes compare over the ten days?
4. Compare the performance during the ten-day time frame of a) the price-weighted retail sales stock index with the Dow Jones Industrial Average and b) the value-weighted retail sales stock index with the S&P 500.

APPENDIX
Chapter 5   **Stock-Market Indexes**

Exhibit 5A.1 | **Summary of Stock-Market Indexes**

Name of Index	Weighting	Number of Stocks	Source of Stocks
Dow Jones Industrial Average	Price	30	NYSE, OTC
Nikkei–Dow Jones Average	Price	225	TSE
S&P 400 Industrial	Market value	400	NYSE, OTC
S&P Transportation	Market value	20	NYSE, OTC
S&P Utilities	Market value	40	NYSE, OTC
S&P Financials	Market value	40	NYSE, OTC
S&P 500 Composite	Market value	500	NYSE, OTC
NYSE			
Industrial	Market value	1,601	NYSE
Utility	Market value	253	NYSE
Transportation	Market value	55	NYSE
Financial	Market value	909	NYSE
Composite	Market value	2,818	NYSE
Nasdaq			
Composite	Market value	5,575	OTC
Industrial	Market value	3,394	OTC
Banks	Market value	375	OTC
Insurance	Market value	103	OTC
Other finance	Market value	610	OTC
Transportation	Market value	104	OTC
Telecommunications	Market value	183	OTC
Computer	Market value	685	OTC
Biotech	Market value	121	OTC

(continued)

Exhibit 5A.1	Summary of Stock-Market Indexes (continued)

Name of Index	Weighting	Number of Stocks	Source of Stocks
AMEX Market Value	Market value	900	AMEX
Dow Jones Equity Market Index	Market value	2,300	NYSE, AMEX, OTC
Wilshire 5000 Equity Value	Market value	5,000	NYSE, AMEX, OTC
Russell Indexes			
3000	Market value	3,000	NYSE, AMEX, OTC
1000	Market value	1,000 largest	NYSE, AMEX, OTC
2000	Market value	2,000 smallest	NYSE, AMEX, OTC
Financial Times Actuaries Index			
All Share	Market value	700	LSE
FT100	Market value	100 largest	LSE
Small-Cap	Market value	250	LSE
Midcap	Market value	250	LSE
Combined	Market value	350	LSE
Tokyo Stock Exchange Price Index (TOPIX)	Market value	1,800	TSE
Value Line Averages			
Industrials	Equal (geometric mean)	1,499	NYSE, AMEX, OTC
Utilities	Equal	177	NYSE, AMEX, OTC
Rails	Equal	19	NYSE, AMEX, OTC
Composite	Equal	1,695	NYSE, AMEX, OTC
Financial Times Ordinary Share Index	Equal (geometric mean)	30	LSE
FT-Actuaries World Indexes	Market value	2,275	24 countries, 3 regions (returns in $, £, ¥, DM, and local currency)
Morgan Stanley Capital International (MSCI) Indexes	Market value	1,375	19 countries, 3 international, 38 international industries (returns in $ and local currency)
Dow Jones World Stock Index	Market value	2,200	13 countries, 3 regions, 120 industry groups (returns in $, £, ¥, DM, and local currency)

(continued)

Exhibit 5A.1 | Summary of Stock-Market Indexes (continued)

Name of Index	Weighting	Number of Stocks	Source of Stocks
Euromoney—First Boston Global Stock Index	Market value	—	17 countries (returns in $ and local currency)
Salomon-Russell World Equity Index	Market value	Russell 1000 and S-R PMI of 600 non-U.S. stocks	22 countries (returns in $ and local currency)

Source: Compiled by authors.

Exhibit 5A.2 | Foreign Stock-Market Indexes

Name of Index	Weighting	Number of Stocks	History of Index
ATX-index (Vienna)	Market value	All listed stocks	Base year 1967, 1991 began including all stocks (Value = 100)
Swiss Market Index	Market value	18	Base year 1988, stocks selected from the Basle, Geneva, and Zurich Exchanges (Value = 1500)
Stockholm General Index	Market value	All listed stocks	Base year 1979, continuously updated (Value = 100)
Copenhagen Stock Exchange Share Price Index	Market value	All traded stocks	Share price is based on average price of the day
Oslo SE Composite Index (Sweden)	Market value	25	Base year 1972 (Value = 100)
Johannesburg Stock Exchange Actuaries Index	Market value	146	Base year 1959 (Value = 100)
Mexican Market Index	Market value	Variable number, based on capitalization and liquidity	Base year 1978, high dollar returns in recent years
Milan Stock Exchange MIB	Market value	Variable number, based on capitalization and liquidity	Change base at beginning of each year (Value = 1000)
Belgium BEL-20 Stock Index	Market value	20	Base year 1991 (Value = 1000)

(continued)

Exhibit 5A.2 | Foreign Stock-Market Indexes (continued)

Name of Index	Weighting	Number of Stocks	History of Index
Madrid General Stock Index	Market value	92	Change base at beginning of each year
Hang Seng Index (Hong Kong)	Market value	33	Started in 1969, accounts for 75 percent of total market
FT-Actuaries World Indexes	Market value	2,212	Base year 1986
FT-SE 100 Index (London)	Market value	100	Base year 1983 (Value = 1000)
CAC General Share Index (French)	Market value	212	Base year 1981 (Value =100)
Morgan Stanley World Index	Market value	1,482	Base year 1970 (Value = 100)
Singapore Straits Times Industrial Index	Unweighted	30	
German Stock Market Index (DAX)	Market value	30	Base year 1987 (Value =1000)
Frankfurter Allgemeine Zeitung Index (FAZ) (German)	Market value	100	Base year 1958 (Value = 100)
Australian Stock Exchange Share Price Indexes	Market value	250	Introduced in 1979
Dublin ISEQ Index	Market value	All stocks traded	Base year 1988 (Value = 1000)
HEX Index (Helsinki)	Market value	Varies with different indexes	Base changes every day
Jakarta Stock Exchange	Market value	All listed shares	Base year 1982 (Value = 100)
Taiwan Stock Exchange Index	Market value	All listed stocks	Base year 1966 (Value = 100)
TSE 300 Composite Index (Toronto)	Market value	300	Base year 1975 (Value = 1000)
KOSPI (Korean Composite Stock Price Index)	Market value (adjusted for cross-holdings)	All listed stocks	Base year 1980 (Value = 100)

Source: Compiled by authors.

Part 2

Developments in Investment Theory

The chapters in Part 1 provided background on why individuals invest their funds and what they expect to derive from this activity. We also argued very strongly for a global investment program, described the major instruments and capital markets in a global investment environment, and showed the relationship among these instruments and markets.

We now are ready to discuss how to analyze and value the various investment instruments available. In turn, valuation requires the estimation of expected returns (cash flows) and a determination of the risk involved in the securities. Before we can begin the analysis, we need to understand several major developments in investment theory that have influenced how we specify and measure risk in the valuation process. The purpose of the four chapters in Part 2 is to provide this background on risk and asset valuation.

Chapter 6 describes the concept of efficient capital markets, which hypothesizes that security prices reflect the effect of all information. This chapter considers why markets should be efficient, discusses how one goes about testing this hypothesis, describes the results of numerous tests that both support the hypotheses and indicate the existence of anomalies that are inconsistent with the hypotheses. There is also a consideration of behavioral finance, which provides a rationale for some of the results. We conclude the chapter with a discussion of the implications of the results for those engaged in technical and fundamental analysis as well as portfolio management.

Chapter 7 provides an introduction to portfolio theory, which was developed by Harry Markowitz. This theory provided the first rigorous measure of risk for investors and showed how one selects alternative assets to diversify and reduce the risk of a portfolio. Markowitz also derived a risk measure for individual securities within the context of an efficient portfolio.

Following the development of the Markowitz portfolio model, William Sharpe and several other academicians extended the Markowitz model into a general equilibrium asset pricing model that included an alternative risk measure for all risky assets. Chapter 8 contains a detailed description of these developments and an explanation of the relevant risk measure implied by this valuation model, referred to as the *capital asset pricing model* (CAPM). We introduce the CAPM at this early point in the book because the risk measure implied by this model has been used extensively in various valuation models. Although the CAPM has long been the preeminent theoretical explanation in finance for the connection

between risk and expected return, the past several decades have seen the rise of several competing models.

Chapter 9 is devoted to exploring several alternative asset pricing models, which differ from the CAPM primarily by specifying multiple risk factors in lieu of a single market portfolio-based variable. The chapter begins with an examination of the *arbitrage pricing theory* (APT), which is the conceptual foundation for virtually all of the subsequent multi-factor asset pricing models. The APT, which was developed by Steve Ross in response to criticisms of the CAPM, suggests a linear relationship between a stock's expected return and many systematic risk factors.

One severe challenge for investors attempting to use the APT in practice is that it offers no theoretical guidance as to either the number or the identity of the risk factors. To overcome this problem, researchers have developed several *multi-factor models,* which attempt to link a stock's realized returns to market data on a collection of pre-specified variables that are believed to proxy for the APT risk factors. In specifying these variables, both macroeconomic and microeconomic approaches and risk factors have been adopted. After explaining these various approaches, we demonstrate how they are used by investors to both evaluate individual companies and assess the investment styles of money managers and mutual funds.

Chapter 6

Efficient Capital Markets

After you read this chapter, you should be able to answer the following questions:

- What does it mean to say that capital markets are efficient?
- Why *should* capital markets be efficient?
- What factors contribute to an efficient market?
- Given the overall efficient market hypothesis (EMH), what are the three subhypotheses and what are the implications of each of them?
- How do you test the three efficient market subhypotheses and what are the results of the tests?
- For each set of tests, which results support the EMH and which results indicate an anomaly related to the hypothesis?
- What is behavioral finance and how does it relate to the EMH?
- What are some of the major findings of behavioral finance and what are the implications of these findings for the EMH?
- What are the implications of the efficient market hypothesis test results for the following?
  - Technical analysis
  - Fundamental analysis
  - Portfolio managers with superior analysts
  - Portfolio managers with inferior analysts

An **efficient capital market** is one in which security prices adjust rapidly to the arrival of new information and, therefore, the current prices of securities reflect all information about the security. Some of the most interesting and important academic research during the past 20 years has analyzed whether our capital markets are efficient. This extensive research is important because its results have significant real-world implications for investors and portfolio managers. In addition, the question of whether capital markets are efficient is one of the most controversial areas in investment research. Recently, a new dimension has been added to the controversy because of the rapidly expanding research in behavioral finance that likewise has major implications regarding the concept of efficient capital markets.

Because of its importance and controversy, you need to understand the meaning of the terms *efficient capital markets* and the *efficient market hypothesis (EMH)*. You should understand the analysis performed to test the EMH and the results of studies that either support or contradict the hypothesis. Finally, you should be aware of the implications of these results when you analyze alternative investments and work to construct a portfolio.

We are considering the topic of efficient capital markets at this point for two reasons. First, the prior discussion indicated how the capital markets function, so now it seems natural to consider the efficiency of the market in terms of how security prices react to new information. Second, the overall evidence on capital market efficiency is best described as mixed; some studies support the hypothesis, and others do not. The implications of these diverse results are important for you as an investor involved in analyzing securities and building a portfolio.

This chapter contains five major sections. The first discusses why we would expect capital markets to be efficient and the factors that contribute to an efficient market where the prices of securities reflect available information.

The efficient market hypothesis has been divided into three subhypotheses to facilitate testing. The second section describes these three subhypotheses and the implications of each of them.

The third section is the largest section because it contains a discussion of the results of numerous studies. This review of the research reveals that a large body of evidence supports the EMH, but a growing number of other studies do not support the hypotheses.

In the fourth section, we discuss the concept of behavioral finance, the studies that have been done in this area related to efficient markets, and the conclusions as they relate to the EMH.

The final section discusses what these results imply for an investor who uses either technical analysis or fundamental analysis or what they mean for a portfolio manager who has access to superior or inferior analysts. We conclude with a brief discussion of the evidence for markets in foreign countries.

WHY SHOULD CAPITAL MARKETS BE EFFICIENT?

As noted earlier, in an efficient capital market, security prices adjust rapidly to the infusion of new information, and, therefore, current security prices fully reflect all available information. To be absolutely correct, this is referred to as an **informationally efficient market**. Although the idea of an efficient capital market is relatively straightforward, we often fail to consider *why* capital markets *should* be efficient. What set of assumptions imply an efficient capital market?

An initial and important premise of an efficient market requires that *a large number of profit-maximizing participants analyze and value securities,* each independently of the others.

A second assumption is that *new information regarding securities comes to the market in a random fashion,* and the timing of one announcement is generally independent of others.[1]

The third assumption is especially crucial: *profit-maximizing investors adjust security prices rapidly to reflect the effect of new information.* Although the price adjustment may be imperfect, it is unbiased. This means that sometimes the market will overadjust and other times it will underadjust, but you cannot predict which will occur at any given time. Security prices adjust rapidly because of the many profit-maximizing investors competing against one another.

The combined effect of (1) information coming in a random, independent, unpredictable fashion and (2) numerous competing investors adjusting stock prices rapidly to reflect this new information means that one would expect price changes to be independent and random.

---

[1]New information, by definition, must be information that was not known before, and it is not predictable. If it were predictable, it would have been impounded in the security price.

You can see that the adjustment process requires a large number of investors following the movements of the security, analyzing the impact of new information on its value, and buying or selling the security until its price adjusts to reflect the new information. This scenario implies that informationally efficient markets require some minimum amount of trading and that more trading by numerous competing investors should cause a faster price adjustment, making the market more efficient. We will return to this need for trading and investor attention when we discuss some anomalies of the EMH.

Finally, because security prices adjust to all new information, these security prices should reflect all information that is publicly available at any point in time. Therefore, the security prices that prevail at any time should be an unbiased reflection of all currently available information, including the risk involved in owning the security. Therefore, in an efficient market, *the expected returns implicit in the current price of the security should reflect its risk,* which means that investors who buy at these informationally efficient prices should receive a rate of return that is consistent with the perceived risk of the stock. Put another way, in terms of the CAPM, all stocks should lie on the SML such that their expected rates of return are consistent with their perceived risk.

ALTERNATIVE EFFICIENT MARKET HYPOTHESES

Most of the early work related to efficient capital markets was based on the *random walk hypothesis,* which contended that changes in stock prices occurred randomly. This early academic work contained extensive empirical analysis without much theory behind it. An article by Fama (1970) attempted to formalize the theory and organize the growing empirical evidence. Fama presented the efficient market theory in terms of a *fair game model,* contending that investors can be confident that a current market price fully reflects all available information about a security and the expected return based upon this price is consistent with its risk.

In his original article, Fama divided the overall efficient market hypothesis (EMH) and the empirical tests of the hypothesis into three subhypotheses depending on the information set involved: (1) weak-form EMH, (2) semistrong-form EMH, and (3) strong-form EMH.

In a subsequent review article, Fama (1991a) again divided the empirical results into three groups but shifted empirical results between the prior categories. Therefore, the following discussion uses the original categories but organizes the presentation of results using the new categories.

In the remainder of this section, we describe the three subhypotheses and the implications of each of them. As will be noted, the three subhypotheses are based on alternative information sets. In the following section, we briefly describe how researchers have tested these hypotheses and summarize the results of these tests.

Weak-Form Efficient Market Hypothesis

The **weak-form EMH** assumes that current stock prices fully reflect *all security market information,* including the historical sequence of prices, rates of return, trading volume data, and other market-generated information, such as odd-lot transactions, block trades, and transactions by exchange specialists. Because it assumes that current market prices already reflect all past returns and any other security market information, this hypothesis implies that past rates of return and other historical market data should have no relationship with future rates of return (that is, rates of return should be independent). Therefore, this hypothesis contends that you should gain little from using any trading rule that decides whether to buy or sell a security based on past rates of return or any other past security market data.

Semistrong-Form Efficient Market Hypothesis

The **semistrong-form EMH** asserts that security prices adjust rapidly to the release of *all public information;* that is, current security prices fully reflect all public information. The semistrong hypothesis encompasses the weak-form hypothesis, because all the market information considered by the weak-form hypothesis, such as stock prices, rates of return, and trading volume, is public. Public information also includes all nonmarket information, such as earnings and dividend announcements, price-to-earnings (P/E) ratios, dividend-yield (D/P) ratios, price-book value (P/BV) ratios, stock splits, news about the economy, and political news. This hypothesis implies that investors who base their decisions on any important new information *after it is public* should not derive above-average risk-adjusted profits from their transactions, considering the cost of trading because the security price already reflects all such new public information.

Strong-Form Efficient Market Hypothesis

The **strong-form EMH** contends that stock prices fully reflect *all information from public and private sources.* This means that no group of investors has monopolistic access to information relevant to the formation of prices. Therefore, this hypothesis contends that no group of investors should be able to consistently derive above-average risk-adjusted rates of return. The strong-form EMH encompasses both the weak-form and the semistrong-form EMH. Further, the strong-form EMH extends the assumption of efficient markets, in which prices adjust rapidly to the release of new public information, to assume perfect markets, in which all information is cost-free and available to everyone at the same time.

TESTS AND RESULTS OF EFFICIENT MARKET HYPOTHESES

Now that you understand the three components of the EMH and what each of them implies regarding the effect on security prices of different sets of information, we can consider the tests used to see whether the data support the hypotheses. Therefore, in this section we discuss the specific tests and summarize the results of these tests.

Like most hypotheses in finance and economics, the evidence on the EMH is mixed. Some studies have supported the hypotheses and indicate that capital markets are efficient. Results of other studies have revealed some **anomalies** related to these hypotheses, indicating results that do not support the hypotheses.

Weak-Form Hypothesis: Tests and Results

Researchers have formulated two groups of tests of the weak-form EMH. The first category involves statistical tests of independence between rates of return. The second set of tests entails a comparison of risk–return results for trading rules that make investment decisions based on past market information relative to the results from a simple buy-and-hold policy, which assumes that you buy stock at the beginning of a test period and hold it to the end.

Statistical Tests of Independence As discussed earlier, the EMH contends that security returns over time should be independent of one another because new information comes to the market in a random, independent fashion and security prices adjust rapidly to this new information. Two major statistical tests have been employed to verify this independence.

First, **autocorrelation tests** of independence measure the significance of positive or negative correlation in returns over time. Does the rate of return on day t correlate with the rate of return on day $t - 1$, $t - 2$, or $t - 3$?[2] Those who believe that capital markets are efficient would expect insignificant correlations for all such combinations.

Several researchers have examined the serial correlations among stock returns for several relatively short time horizons including 1 day, 4 days, 9 days, and 16 days. The results typically indicated insignificant correlation in stock returns over time. Some recent studies that considered portfolios of stocks of different market size have indicated that the autocorrelation is stronger for portfolios of small market size stocks. Therefore, although the older results tend to support the hypothesis, the more recent studies cast doubt on it for portfolios of small firms, although these results could be affected by transaction costs of small-cap stocks and non-synchronous trading for small-cap stocks.

The second statistical test of independence as discussed by DeFusco et al. (2004), is the **runs test**. Given a series of price changes, each price change is either designated a plus (+) if it is an increase in price or a minus (–) if it is a decrease in price. The result is a set of pluses and minuses as follows: +++−+−−++−−++. A run occurs when two consecutive changes are the same; two or more consecutive positive or negative price changes constitute one run. When the price changes in a different direction, such as when a negative price change is followed by a positive price change, the run ends and a new run may begin. To test for independence, you would compare the number of runs for a given series to the number in a table of expected values for the number of runs that should occur in a random series.

Studies that have examined stock price runs have confirmed the independence of stock price changes over time. The actual number of runs for stock price series consistently fell into the range expected for a random series. Therefore, these statistical tests of stocks on the NYSE and on the Nasdaq market have likewise confirmed the independence of stock price changes over time.

Although short-horizon stock returns have generally supported the weak-form EMH, several studies that examined price changes for individual *transactions* on the NYSE found significant serial correlations. Notably, none of these studies attempted to show that the dependence of transaction price movements could be used to earn above-average risk-adjusted returns after considering the trading rule's substantial transaction costs.

Tests of Trading Rules The second group of tests of the weak-form EMH were developed in response to the assertion that the prior statistical tests of independence were too rigid to identify the intricate price patterns examined by technical analysts. As we will discuss in Chapter 15, technical analysts do not expect a set number of positive or negative price changes as a signal of a move to a new equilibrium in the market. They typically look for a general consistency in the price trends over time. Such a trend might include both positive and negative changes. For this reason, technical analysts believed that their trading rules were too sophisticated and complicated to be properly tested by rigid statistical tests.

In response to this objection, investigators attempted to examine alternative technical trading rules through simulation. Advocates of an efficient market hypothesized that investors could not derive abnormal profits above a buy-and-hold policy using any trading rule that depended solely on past market information.

---

[2]For a discussion of tests of time series independence, see DeFusco, McLeavey, Pinto, and Runkle (2004), Chapter 10.

The trading rule studies compared the risk–return results derived from trading-rule simulations, including transaction costs, to the results from a simple buy-and-hold policy. Three major pitfalls can negate the results of a trading-rule study:

1. The investigator should *use only publicly available data* when implementing the trading rule. As an example, the trading activities of specialists as of December 31 may not be publicly available until February 1, so you should not factor in information about specialist trading activity until the information is public.
2. When computing the returns from a trading rule, you should *include all transaction costs* involved in implementing the trading strategy because most trading rules involve many more transactions than a simple buy-and-hold policy.
3. You must *adjust the results for risk* because a trading rule might simply select a portfolio of high-risk securities that should experience higher returns.

Researchers have encountered two operational problems in carrying out these tests of specific trading rules. First, some trading rules require too much subjective interpretation of data to simulate mechanically. Second, the almost infinite number of potential trading rules makes it impossible to test all of them. As a result, only the better-known technical trading rules have been examined.

Another factor that should be recognized is that the simulation studies have typically been restricted to relatively simple trading rules, which many technicians contend are rather naïve. In addition, many of these studies employed readily available data from the NYSE, which is biased toward well-known, heavily traded stocks that certainly should trade in efficient markets. Recall that markets should be more efficient when there are numerous aggressive, profit-maximizing investors attempting to adjust stock prices to reflect new information, so market efficiency will be related to trading volume. Specifically, *more trading in a security should promote market efficiency.* Alternatively, for securities with relatively few stockholders and little trading activity, the market could be inefficient simply because fewer investors would be analyzing the effect of new information, and this limited interest would result in insufficient trading activity to move the price of the security quickly to a new equilibrium value that reflects the new information. Therefore, using only active, heavily traded stocks when testing a trading rule could bias the results toward finding efficiency.

Results of Simulations of Specific Trading Rules   In the most popular trading technique, **filter rule**, an investor trades a stock when the price change exceeds a filter value set for it. As an example, an investor using a 5 percent filter would envision a positive breakout if the stock were to rise 5 percent from some base, suggesting that the stock price would continue to rise. A technician would acquire the stock to take advantage of the expected continued rise. In contrast, a 5 percent decline from some peak price would be considered a breakout on the downside, and the technician would expect a further price decline and would sell any holdings of the stock and possibly even sell the stock short.

Studies of this trading rule have used a range of filters from 0.5 percent to 50 percent. The results indicated that small filters would yield above-average profits *before* taking account of trading commissions. However, small filters generate numerous trades and, therefore, substantial trading costs. When these trading costs were considered, all the trading profits turned to losses. Alternatively, trading using larger filters did not yield returns above those of a simple buy-and-hold policy.

Researchers have simulated other trading rules that used past market data other than stock prices. Trading rules have been devised that consider advanced-decline ratios, short sales, short positions, and specialist activities.[3] These simulation tests have generated mixed results.

---

[3]Many of these trading rules are discussed in Chapter 15, which deals with technical analysis.

Most of the early studies suggested that these trading rules generally would not outperform a buy-and-hold policy on a risk-adjusted basis after commissions, although several recent studies have indicated support for specific trading rules. Therefore, most evidence from simulations of specific trading rules indicates that most trading rules tested have not been able to beat a buy-and-hold policy. Therefore, these test results generally support the weak-form EMH, but the results are not unanimous.

Semistrong-Form Hypothesis: Tests and Results

Recall that the semistrong-form EMH asserts that security prices adjust rapidly to the release of all public information; that is, security prices fully reflect all public information. Studies that have tested the semistrong-form EMH can be divided into the following sets of studies:

1. *Studies to predict future rates of return using available public information beyond pure market information such as prices and trading volume considered in the weak-form tests.* These studies can involve either *time-series analysis* of returns or the *cross-section distribution* of returns for individual stocks. Advocates of the EMH contend that it would not be possible to predict *future* returns using past returns or to predict the distribution of future returns (e.g., the top quartile or decile of returns) using public information.
2. *Event studies that examine how fast stock prices adjust to specific significant economic events.* A corollary approach would be to test whether it is possible to invest in a security after the public announcement of a significant event and experience significant abnormal rates of return. Again, advocates of the EMH would expect security prices to adjust rapidly, such that it would not be possible for investors to experience superior risk-adjusted returns by investing after the public announcement and paying normal transaction costs.

Adjustment for Market Effects   For any of these tests, you need to adjust the security's rates of return for the rates of return of the overall market during the period considered. The point is, a 5 percent return in a stock during the period surrounding an announcement is meaningless until you know what the aggregate stock market did during the same period and how this stock normally acts under such conditions. If the market had experienced a 10 percent return during this announcement period, the 5 percent return for the stock may be lower than expected.

Authors of pre-1970 studies generally recognized the need to make such adjustments for market movements. They typically assumed that the individual stocks should experience returns equal to the aggregate stock market. This assumption meant that the market-adjustment process simply entailed subtracting the market return from the return for the individual security to derive its **abnormal rate of return**, as follows:

6.1
$$AR_{it} = R_{it} - R_{mt}$$

where:

AR_{it} = abnormal rate of return on security i during period t
R_{it} = rate of return on security i during period t
R_{mt} = rate of return on a market index during period t

In the example where the stock experienced a 5 percent increase while the market increased 10 percent, the stock's abnormal return would be minus 5 percent.

Since the 1970s, many authors have adjusted the rates of return for securities by an amount different from the market rate of return because they recognize that, based on work with the CAPM, all stocks do not change by the same amount as the market. That is, as will be discussed in Chapter 8, some stocks are more volatile than the market, and some are less volatile. These possibilities mean that you must determine an **expected rate of return** for the stock based on the market rate of return *and* the stock's relationship with the market (its beta). As an example, suppose a stock is generally 20 percent more volatile than the market (that is, it has a beta of 1.20). In such a case, if the market experiences a 10 percent rate of return, you would expect this stock to experience a 12 percent rate of return. Therefore, you would determine the abnormal rate of return by computing the difference between the stock's actual rate of return and its *expected rate of return* as follows:

6.2
$$AR_{it} = R_{it} - E(R_{it})$$

where:

$E(R_{it})$ = the expected rate of return for stock i during period t based on the market rate of return and the stock's normal relationship with the market (its beta)

Continuing with the example, if the stock that was expected to have a 12 percent return (based on a market return of 10 percent and a stock beta of 1.20) had only a 5 percent return, its abnormal rate of return during the period would be minus 7 percent. Over the normal long-run period, you would expect the abnormal returns for a stock to sum to zero. Specifically, during one period the returns may exceed expectations and the next period they may fall short of expectations.

To summarize, there are two sets of tests of the semistrong-form EMH. The first set of studies are referred to as **return prediction studies**. For this set of studies, investigators attempt to predict the time series of future rates of return for individual stocks or the aggregate market using public information. For example, is it possible to predict abnormal returns over time for the market based on public information such as specified values or changes in the aggregate dividend yield or the risk premium spread for bonds? Another example would be **event studies** that examine abnormal rates of return for a period immediately after an announcement of a significant economic event, such as a stock split, a proposed merger, or a stock or bond issue, to determine whether an investor can derive above-average risk-adjusted rates of return by investing after the release of public information.

The second set of studies are those that predict cross-sectional returns. In these studies, investigators look for public information regarding individual stocks that will allow them to predict the cross-sectional distribution of future risk-adjusted rates of return. For example, they test whether it is possible to use variables such as the price-earnings ratio, market value size, the price/book-value ratio, the P/E/growth rate (PEG) ratio, or the dividend yield to predict which stocks will experience above-average (e.g., top quartile) or below-average risk-adjusted rates of return in the future.

In both sets of tests, the emphasis is on the analysis of abnormal rates of return that deviate from long-term expectations or returns that are adjusted for a stock's specific risk characteristics and overall market rates of return during the period.

Results of Return Prediction Studies   The **time-series analysis** assumes that in an efficient market the best estimate of *future* rates of return will be the long-run *historical* rates of return. The point of the tests is to determine whether any public information will provide superior estimates of returns for a short-run horizon (one to six months) or a long-run horizon (one to five years).

The results of these studies have indicated limited success in predicting short-horizon returns, but the analysis of long-horizon returns has been quite successful. A prime example is dividend yield studies. After postulating that the aggregate dividend yield (D/P) was a proxy for the risk premium on stocks, they found a positive relationship between the D/P and future long-run stock market returns.

In addition, several studies have considered two variables related to the term structure of interest rates: (1) a *default spread,* which is the difference between the yields on lower-grade and Aaa-rated long-term corporate bonds (this spread has been used in earlier chapters of this book as a proxy for a market risk premium), and (2) the *term structure spread,* which is the difference between the long-term Treasury bond yield and the yield on one-month Treasury bills. These variables have been used to predict stock returns and bond returns. Similar variables in foreign countries have also been useful for predicting returns for foreign common stocks.

The reasoning for these empirical results is as follows: When the two most significant variables—the dividend yield (D/P) and the bond default spread—are high, it implies that investors are expecting or requiring a high return on stocks and bonds. Notably, this occurs during poor economic environments, as reflected in the growth rate of output. A poor economic environment also implies a low-wealth environment wherein investors perceive higher risk for investments. As a result, for investors to invest and shift consumption from the present to the future, they will require a high rate of return. It is suggested that, if you invest during this risk-averse period, your subsequent returns will be above normal. In contrast, when these values are small, it implies that investors have reduced their risk premium and required rates of return and, therefore, your future returns will be below normal.

Quarterly Earnings Reports   Studies that address quarterly reports are considered part of the times-series analysis. Specifically, these studies question whether it is possible to predict future returns for a stock based on publicly available quarterly earnings reports. The typical test examined firms that experienced changes in quarterly earnings that differed from expectations. The results generally indicated abnormal returns during the 13 or 26 weeks *following* the announcement of a large *unanticipated* earnings change—referred to as an **earnings surprise**. These results suggest that an earnings surprise is *not* instantaneously reflected in security prices.

An extensive analysis by Rendleman, Jones, and Latané (1982) and a follow-up by Jones, Rendleman, and Latané (1985) using a large sample and daily data from 20 days before a quarterly earnings announcement to 90 days after the announcement indicated that 31 percent of the total response in stock returns came before the earnings announcement, 18 percent on the day of the announcement, and 51 percent *afterward.*

Several studies examined reasons for the earnings drift following earnings announcements and found that unexpected earnings explained more than 80 percent of the subsequent stock price drift for the total time period. Authors who reviewed the prior studies such as Benesh and Peterson (1986), Bernard and Thomas (1989), and Baruch (1989), contended that the reason for the stock price drift was the *earnings revisions* that followed the earnings surprises and contributed to the positive correlations of prices.

In summary, these results indicate that the market has not adjusted stock prices to reflect the release of quarterly earnings surprises as fast as expected by the semistrong EMH, which implies that earnings surprises and earnings revisions can be used to predict returns for individual stocks. These results are evidence against the EMH.[4]

The final set of calendar studies questioned whether some regularities in the rates of return during the calendar year would allow investors to predict returns on stocks. These studies include numerous studies on "the January anomaly" and studies that consider a variety of other daily and weekly regularities.

---

[4]Academic studies such as these, which have indicated the importance of earnings surprises, have led *The Wall Street Journal* to publish a section on earnings surprises in connection with regular quarterly earnings reports.

The January Anomaly   Several years ago, Branch (1977) and Branch and Chang (1985) proposed a unique trading rule for those interested in taking advantage of tax selling. Investors (including institutions) tend to engage in tax selling toward the end of the year to establish losses on stocks that have declined. After the new year, the tendency is to reacquire these stocks or to buy other stocks that look attractive. This scenario would produce downward pressure on stock prices in late November and December and positive pressure in early January. Such a seasonal pattern is inconsistent with the EMH since it should be eliminated by arbitrageurs who would buy in December and sell in early January.

A supporter of the hypothesis found that December trading volume was abnormally high for stocks that had declined during the previous year and that significant abnormal returns occurred during January for stocks that had experienced losses during the prior year. It was concluded that, because of transaction costs, arbitrageurs must not be eliminating the January tax-selling anomaly. Subsequent analysis showed that most of the January effect was concentrated in the first week of trading, particularly on the first day of the year.

Several studies provided support for a January effect inconsistent with the tax-selling hypothesis by examining what happened in foreign countries that did not have our tax laws or a December year-end. They found abnormal returns in January, but the results could not be explained by tax laws. It has also been shown that the classic relationship between risk and return is strongest during January and there is a year-end trading volume bulge in late December–early January.

As pointed out by Keim (1986), despite numerous studies, the January anomaly poses as many questions as it answers.

Other Calendar Effects   Several other "calendar" effects have been examined, including a monthly effect, a weekend/day-of-the-week effect, and an intraday effect. One study found a significant monthly effect wherein all the market's cumulative advance occurred during the first half of trading months.

An analysis of the weekend effect found that the mean return for Monday was significantly negative during five-year subperiods and a total period. In contrast, the average return for the other four days was positive.

A study decomposed the Monday effect that is typically measured from Friday close to Monday close into a *weekend effect* (from Friday close to Monday open), and a *Monday trading effect* (from Monday open to the Monday close). It was shown that the negative Monday effect found in prior studies actually occurs from the Friday close to the Monday open (it is really a weekend effect). After adjusting for the weekend effect, the Monday trading effect was positive. Subsequently, it was shown that the Monday effect was on average positive in January and negative for all other months.

Finally, for *large firms,* the negative Monday effect occurred before the market opened (it was a weekend effect), whereas for *smaller firms* most of the negative Monday effect occurred during the day on Monday (it was a Monday trading effect).

Predicting Cross-Sectional Returns   Assuming an efficient market, *all securities should have equal risk-adjusted returns* because security prices should reflect all public information that would influence the security's risk. Therefore, studies in this category attempt to determine if you can use public information to predict what stocks will enjoy above-average or below-average risk-adjusted returns.

These studies typically examine the usefulness of alternative measures of size or quality to rank stocks in terms of risk-adjusted returns. Notably, all of these tests involve *a joint hypothesis* because they not only consider the efficiency of the market but also are dependent on the asset pricing model that provides the measure of risk used in the test. Specifically, if a test determines that it is possible to predict risk-adjusted returns, these results could occur because the market is not efficient, *or* they could be because the measure of risk is faulty and, therefore, the measures of risk-adjusted returns are wrong.

Price-Earnings Ratios   Several studies beginning with Basu (1977) have examined the relationship between the historical **price-earnings (P/E) ratios** for stocks and the returns on the stocks. Some have suggested that low P/E stocks will outperform high P/E stocks because growth companies enjoy high P/E ratios, but the market tends to overestimate the growth potential and thus overvalues these growth companies, while undervaluing low-growth firms with low P/E ratios. A relationship between the historical P/E ratios and subsequent risk-adjusted market performance would constitute evidence against the semistrong EMH, because it would imply that investors could use publicly available information regarding P/E ratios to predict future abnormal returns.

Performance measures that consider both return and risk indicated that low P/E ratio stocks experienced superior risk-adjusted results relative to the market, whereas high P/E ratio stocks had significantly inferior risk-adjusted results.[5] Subsequent analysis concluded that publicly available P/E ratios possess valuable information regarding future returns, which is inconsistent with semistrong efficiency.

Peavy and Goodman (1983) examined P/E ratios with adjustments for firm size, industry effects, and infrequent trading and likewise found that the risk-adjusted returns for stocks in the lowest P/E ratio quintile were superior to those in the highest P/E ratio quintile.

Price-Earnings/Growth Rate (PEG) Ratios   During the past decade, there has been a significant increase in the use of the ratio of a stock's price-earnings ratio divided by the firm's expected growth rate of earnings (referred to as the PEG ratio) as a relative valuation tool, especially for stocks of growth companies that have P/E ratios substantially above average. Advocates of the PEG ratio hypothesize an inverse relationship between the PEG ratio and subsequent rates of return—that is, they expect that stocks with relatively low PEG ratios (i.e., less than one) will experience above-average rates of return while stocks with relatively high PEG ratios (i.e., in excess of three or four) will have below-average rates of return. A study by Peters (1991) using quarterly rebalancing supported the hypothesis of an inverse relationship. These results would constitute an anomaly and would not support the EMH. A subsequent study by Reilly and Marshall (1999) assumed annual rebalancing and divided the sample on the basis of a risk measure (beta), market value size, and by expected growth rate. Except for stocks with low betas and very low expected growth rates, the results were not consistent with the hypothesis of an inverse relationship between the PEG ratio and subsequent rates of return.

In summary, the results related to using the PEG ratio to select stocks are mixed—several studies that assume either monthly or quarterly rebalancing indicate an anomaly because the authors use public information and derive above-average rates of return. In contrast, a study with more realistic annual rebalancing indicated that no consistent relationship exists between the PEG ratio and subsequent rates of return.

The Size Effect   Banz (1981) examined the impact of size (measured by total market value) on the risk-adjusted rates of return. The risk-adjusted returns for extended periods (20 to 35 years) indicated that the small firms consistently experienced significantly larger risk-adjusted returns than the larger firms. Reinganum (1981) contended that it was the size, not the P/E ratio, that caused the results discussed in the prior subsection, but this contention was disputed by Basu (1983).

---

[5]Composite performance measures are discussed in Chapter 25.

Recall that abnormal returns may occur because the markets are inefficient or because the market model provides incorrect estimates of risk and expected returns.

It was suggested that the riskiness of the small firms was improperly measured because small firms are traded less frequently. An alternative risk measure technique confirmed that the small firms had much higher risk, but the difference in beta did not account for the large difference in rates of return.

A study by Stoll and Whaley (1983) that examined the impact of transaction costs confirmed the size effect but also found that firms with small market value have low stock prices. Because transaction costs vary inversely with price per share, these costs must be considered when examining the small-firm effect. It was shown that there was a significant difference in the percentage total transaction cost for large firms (2.71 percent) versus small firms (6.77 percent). This differential in transaction costs, with frequent trading, can have a significant impact on the results. Assuming daily transactions, the original small-firm effects are reversed. The point is, size-effect studies must consider realistic transaction costs and specify holding period assumptions. A study by Reinganum (1983) that considered both factors over long periods demonstrated that infrequent rebalancing (about once a year) is almost ideal—the results are better than long-run buy-and-hold and avoids frequent rebalancing that experiences excess costs. In summary, the small firms outperformed the large firms after considering risk and transaction costs, assuming annual rebalancing.

Most studies on the size effect employed large databases and long time periods (over 50 years) to show that this phenomenon has existed for many years. In contrast, a study that examined the performance over various intervals of time concluded that *the small-firm effect is not stable.* During most periods they found the negative relationship between size and return; but, during others (such as 1967 to 1975), they found that large firms outperformed the small firms. Notably, this positive relationship held during the following recent periods: 1984–87; 1989–90; and 1995–99. A study by Reinganum (1992) acknowledges this instability but contends that the small-firm effect is still a long-run phenomenon.

In summary, firm size is a major efficient market anomaly. Numerous attempts to explain the size anomaly indicate that the two strongest explanations are the risk measurements and the higher transaction costs. Depending on the frequency of trading, these two factors may account for much of the differential. Keim (1983) also related it to seasonality. These results indicate that the size effect must be considered in any event study that considers long time periods and contains a sample of firms with significantly different market values.

Neglected Firms and Trading Activity   Arbel and Strebel (1983) considered an additional influence beyond size—attention or neglect. They measured attention in terms of the number of analysts who regularly follow a stock and divided the stocks into three groups: (1) highly followed, (2) moderately followed, and (3) neglected. They confirmed the small-firm effect but also found a neglected-firm effect caused by the lack of information and limited institutional interest. The neglected-firm concept applied across size classes. Contrary results are reported by Beard and Sias (1997) who found no evidence of a neglected firm premium after controlling for capitalization.

James and Edmister (1983) examined the impact of trading volume by considering the relationship between returns, market value, and trading activity. The results confirmed the relationship between size and rates of return, but the results indicated no significant difference between the mean returns of the highest and lowest trading activity portfolios. A subsequent study hypothesized that firms with less information require higher returns. Using the period of listing as a proxy for information, they found a negative relationship between returns and the period of listing after adjusting for firm size and the January effect.

Book Value–Market Value Ratio   This ratio relates the book value (BV) of a firm's equity to the market value (MV) of its equity. Rosenberg, Reid, and Lanstein (1985) found a significant positive relationship between current values for this ratio and future stock returns and contended that such a relationship between available public information on the BV/MV ratio and future returns was evidence against the EMH.[6]

Strong support for this ratio was provided by Fama and French (1992) who evaluated the joint effects of market beta, size, E/P ratio, leverage, and the BV/MV ratio (referred to as BE/ME) on a cross section of average returns. They analyzed the hypothesized positive relationship between beta and expected returns and found that this positive relationship held pre-1969 but disappeared during the period 1963 to 1990. In contrast, the negative relationship between size and average return was significant by itself and significant after inclusion of other variables.

In addition, they found a significant positive relationship between the BV/MV ratio and average return that persisted even when other variables are included. Most importantly, *both* size and the BV/MV ratio are significant when included together and they dominate other ratios. Specifically, although leverage and the E/P ratio were significant by themselves or with size, they become insignificant when *both* size and the BV/MV ratio are considered.

The results in Exhibit 6.1 show the separate and combined effect of the two variables. As shown, going across the Small-ME (small size) row, BV/MV captures strong variation in average returns (0.70 to 1.92 percent). Alternatively, controlling for the BV/MV ratio leaves a size effect in average returns (the high BV/MV results decline from 1.92 to 1.18 percent when going from small to large). These positive results for the BV/MV ratio were replicated for returns on Japanese stocks.

In summary, studies that have used publicly available ratios to predict the cross section of expected returns for stocks have provided substantial evidence in conflict with the semistrong-form EMH. Significant results were found for P/E ratios, market value size, neglected firms, and BV/MV ratios. Although the research by Fama and French indicated that the optimal combination appears to be size and the BV/MV ratio, a study by Jensen, Johnson, and Mercer (1997) indicates that this combination only works during periods of expansive monetary policy.

Results of Event Studies   Recall that the intent of event studies is to examine abnormal rates of return surrounding significant economic information. Those who advocate the EMH would expect returns to adjust quickly to announcements of new information such that investors cannot experience positive abnormal rates of return by acting after the announcement. Because of space constraints, we can only summarize the results for some of the more popular events considered.

The discussion of results is organized by event or item of public information. Specifically, we will examine the price movements and profit potential surrounding stock splits, the sale of initial public offerings, exchange listings, unexpected world or economic events, and the announcements of significant accounting changes. Notably, the results for most of these studies have supported the semistrong-form EMH.

Stock Split Studies   Many investors believe that the prices of stocks that split will increase in value because the shares are priced lower, which increases demand for them. In contrast, advocates of efficient markets would not expect a change in value because the firm has simply issued additional stock and nothing fundamentally affecting the value of the firm has occurred.

The classic study by Fama, Fisher, Jensen, and Roll (1969), referred to hereafter as FFJR, hypothesized no significant price change following a stock split, because any relevant information (such as earnings growth) that caused the split would have already been discounted.

---

[6]Many studies define this ratio as "book-to-market value" (BV/MV) because it implies a positive relationship, but most practitioners refer to it as the "price-to-book value" (P/B) ratio. Obviously the concept is the same, but the sign changes.

Exhibit 6.1	**Average Monthly Returns on Portfolios Formed on Size and Book-to-Market Equity; Stocks Sorted by ME (Down) and Then BE/ME (Across); July 1963 to December 1990**

In June of each year *t*, the NYSE, AMEX, and Nasdaq stocks that meet the CRSP-COMPUSTAT data requirements are allocated to 10 size portfolios using the NYSE size (ME) breakpoints. The NYSE, AMEX, and Nasdaq stocks in each size decile are then sorted into 10 BE/ME portfolios using the book-to-market ratios for year *t* – 1. BE/ME is the book value of common equity plus balance-sheet deferred taxes for fiscal year *t* – 1, over market equity for December of year *t* – 1. The equal-weighted monthly portfolio returns are then calculated for July of year *t* to June of year *t* + 1.

Average monthly return is the time-series average of the monthly equal-weighted portfolio returns (in percent). The All column shows average returns for equal-weighted size decile portfolios. The All row shows average returns for equal-weighted portfolios of the stocks in each BE/ME group.

BOOK-TO-MARKET PORTFOLIOS

	All	Low	2	3	4	5	6	7	8	9	High
All	1.23	0.64	0.98	1.06	1.17	1.24	1.26	1.39	1.40	1.50	1.63
Small-ME	1.47	0.70	1.14	1.20	1.43	1.56	1.51	1.70	1.71	1.82	1.92
ME-2	1.22	0.43	1.05	0.96	1.19	1.33	1.19	1.58	1.28	1.43	1.79
ME-3	1.22	0.56	0.88	1.23	0.95	1.36	1.30	1.30	1.40	1.54	1.60
ME-4	1.19	0.39	0.72	1.06	1.36	1.13	1.21	1.34	1.59	1.51	1.47
ME-5	1.24	0.88	0.65	1.08	1.47	1.13	1.43	1.44	1.26	1.52	1.49
ME-6	1.15	0.70	0.98	1.14	1.23	0.94	1.27	1.19	1.19	1.24	1.50
ME-7	1.07	0.95	1.00	0.99	0.83	0.99	1.13	0.99	1.16	1.10	1.47
ME-8	1.08	0.66	1.13	0.91	0.95	0.99	1.01	1.15	1.05	1.29	1.55
ME-9	0.95	0.44	0.89	0.92	1.00	1.05	0.93	0.82	1.11	1.04	1.22
Large-ME	0.89	0.93	0.88	0.84	0.71	0.79	0.83	0.81	0.96	0.97	1.18

Source: Eugene F. Fama and Kenneth French, "The Cross Section of Expected Stock Returns," *Journal of Finance* 47, no. 2 (June 1992): 446. Reprinted with permission of Blackwell Publishing.

The FFJR study analyzed abnormal price movements surrounding the time of the split and divided the stock split sample into those stocks that did or did not raise their dividends. Both groups experienced positive abnormal price changes prior to the split. Stocks that split but did *not* increase their dividend experienced abnormal price *declines* following the split and within 12 months lost all their accumulated abnormal gains. In contrast, stocks that split and increased their dividend experienced no abnormal returns after the split.

These results support the semistrong EMH because they indicate that investors cannot gain from the information on a stock split after the public announcement. These results were confirmed by most (but not all) subsequent studies. In summary, most studies found no short-run or long-run positive impact on security returns because of a stock split, although the results are not unanimous.

Initial Public Offerings (IPOs)   During the past 20 years, a number of closely held companies have gone public by selling some of their common stock. Because of uncertainty about the appropriate offering price and the risk involved in underwriting such issues, it has been hypothesized that the underwriters would tend to underprice these new issues.

Given this general expectation of underpricing, the studies in this area have generally considered three sets of questions: (1) How great is the underpricing on average? Does the underpricing vary over time? If so, why? (2) What factors cause different amounts of underpricing for alternative issues? (3) How fast does the market adjust the price for the underpricing?

The answer to the first question is an average underpricing of almost 18 percent, but it varies over time as shown by the results in Exhibit 6.2. The major variables that cause differential underpricing seem to be: various risk measures, the size of the firm, the prestige of the underwriter, and the status of the firm's accounting firms. On the question of direct interest to the EMH, results in Miller and Reilly (1987) and Ibbotson, Sindelar, and Ritter (1994) indicate that the price adjustment to the underpricing takes place within one day after the offering. Therefore, it appears that some underpricing occurs based on the original offering price, but the only ones who benefit from this underpricing are investors who receive allocations of the original issue. More specifically, institutional investors captured most (70 percent) of the short-term profits. This rapid adjustment of the initial underpricing would support the semistrong EMH. Finally, studies by Ritter (1991); Carter, Dark, and Singh (1998); and Loughran and Ritter (1995) that examined the long-run returns on IPOs indicate that investors who acquire the stock after the initial adjustment do *not* experience positive long-run abnormal returns.

Exchange Listing   A significant economic event for a firm is its stock's being listed on a national exchange, especially the NYSE. Such a listing is expected to increase the market liquidity of the stock and add to its prestige. An important question is, can an investor derive abnormal returns from investing in the stock when a new listing is announced or around the time of the actual listing? The results regarding abnormal returns from such investing were mixed. All the studies agreed that (1) the stocks' prices increased before any listing announcements, and (2) stock prices consistently declined after the actual listing. The crucial question is, what happens between the announcement of the application for listing and the actual listing (a period of four to six weeks)? A study by McConnell and Sanger (1989) points toward profit opportunities immediately after the announcement that a firm is applying for listing and there is the possibility of excess returns from price declines after the actual listing. Finally, studies that have examined the impact of listing on the risk of the securities found no significant change in systematic risk or the firm's cost of equity.

In summary, listing studies that provide some evidence of short-run profit opportunities for investors using public information would not support the semistrong-form EMH.

Unexpected World Events and Economic News   The results of several studies that examined the response of security prices to world or economic news have supported the semistrong-form EMH. An analysis of the reaction of stock prices to unexpected world events, such as the Eisenhower heart attack, the Kennedy assassination, and military events, found that prices adjusted to the news before the market opened or before it reopened after the announcement (generally, as with the World Trade Center attack, the Exchanges are closed immediately for various time periods—e.g., one to four days). A study by Pierce and Roley (1985) that examined the response to announcements about money supply, inflation, real economic activity, and the discount rate found an impact that did not persist beyond the announcement day. Finally, Jain (1988) did an analysis of hourly stock returns and trading volume response to surprise announcements and found that unexpected information about money supply impacted stock prices within one hour. For a review of studies that considered the impact of news on individual stocks, see Chan (2003).

Announcements of Accounting Changes   Numerous studies have analyzed the impact of announcements of accounting changes on stock prices. In efficient markets, security prices should react quickly and predictably to announcements of accounting changes. An announcement of

Exhibit 6.2	Numbers of Offerings, Average First-Day Returns, and Gross Proceeds of Initial Public Offerings in 1975–2000

Year	Number of Offerings[a]	Average First-Day Return, %[b]	Gross Proceeds, $ Millions[c]
1975	14	−1.9	264
1976	35	2.9	237
1977	35	21.0	151
1978	50	25.7	247
1979	81	24.6	429
1980	238	49.4	1,404
1981	438	16.8	3,200
1982	198	20.3	1,334
1983	848	20.8	13,168
1984	516	11.5	3,932
1985	507	12.4	10,450
1986	953	10.0	17,571
1987	630	10.4	13,841
1988	223	9.8	4,514
1989	210	12.6	5,721
1990	172	14.5	4,749
1991	365	14.7	16,202
1992	513	12.5	22,989
1993	665	15.2	30,587
1994	567	13.4	19,039
1995	571	20.5	29,422
1996	831	17.0	43,150
1997	603	13.2	34,010
1998	357	20.2	35,052
1999	543	66.7	65,653
2000	449	55.5	66,480
1975–79	215	14.5	1,328
1980–89	4,761	15.3	75,139
1990–99	5,187	20.6	300,853
2000	449	55.5	66,480
Total	14,698	18.6	443,800

[a]The number of offerings excludes IPOs with an offer price of less than $5.00, ADRs, best efforts offers, unit offers, Regulation A offerings (small issues, raising less than $1.5 million during the 1980s), real estate investment trusts (REITs), partnerships, and closed-end funds.
[b]First-day returns are computed as the percentage return from the offering price to the first closing market price.
[c]Gross proceeds data are from Securities Data Co. and exclude overallotment options but include the international tranche, if any. No adjustments for inflation have been made.

Source: Jay R. Ritter, "Summary Statistics on 1975–2000 Initial Public Offerings with an Offer Price of $5.00 or More" (University of Florida, January 29, 2001).

an accounting change that affects the economic value of the firm should cause a rapid change in stock prices. An accounting change that affects reported earnings but has no economic significance should not affect stock prices. For example, when a firm changes its depreciation accounting method for reporting purposes from accelerated to straight line, the firm should experience an increase in reported earnings, but there is no economic consequence. An analysis of stock price movements surrounding this accounting change supported the EMH because there were no positive price changes following the change, and there were some negative price changes because firms making such an accounting change are typically performing poorly.

During periods of high inflation, many firms will change their inventory method from first-in, first-out (FIFO) to last-in, first-out (LIFO), which causes a decline in reported earnings but benefits the firm because it reduces its taxable earnings and, therefore, tax expenses. Advocates of efficient markets would expect positive price changes because of the tax savings, and study results confirmed this expectation.

Therefore, studies such as those by Bernard and Thomas (1990) and Ou and Penman (1989) indicate that the securities markets react quite rapidly to accounting changes and adjust security prices as expected on the basis of changes in true value (that is, analysts pierce the accounting veil and value securities on the basis of economic events).

Corporate Events   Corporate finance events such as mergers and acquisitions, reorganization, and various security offerings (common stock, straight bonds, convertible bonds) have been examined, relative to two general questions: (1) What is the market impact of these alternative events? (2) How fast does the market adjust the security prices?

Regarding the reaction to corporate events, the answer is very consistent—stock prices react as one would expect based on the underlying economic impact of the action. For example, the reaction to mergers is that the stock of the firm being acquired increases in line with the premium offered by the acquiring firm, whereas the stock of the acquiring firm typically declines because of the concern that they overpaid for the firm. On the question of speed of reaction, the evidence indicates fairly rapid adjustment—that is, the adjustment period declines as shorter interval data is analyzed (using daily data, most studies find that the price adjustment is completed in about three days). Studies related to financing decisions are reviewed by Smith (1986). Studies on corporate control that consider mergers and reorganizations are reviewed by Jensen and Warner (1988). Numerous corporate spin-offs have generated interesting stock performance as shown by Desai and Jain (1999) and Chemmanur and Yan (2004).

Summary on the Semistrong-Form EMH   Clearly, the evidence from tests of the semistrong EMH is mixed. The hypothesis receives almost unanimous support from the numerous event studies on a range of events including stock splits, initial public offerings, world events and economic news, accounting changes, and a variety of corporate finance events. About the only mixed results come from exchange listing studies.

In sharp contrast, the numerous studies on predicting rates of return over time or for a cross section of stocks presented evidence counter to semistrong efficiency. This included time-series studies on risk premiums, calender patterns, and quarterly earnings surprises. Similarly, the results for cross-sectional predictors such as size, the BV/MV ratio (when there is expansive monetary policy), P/E ratios, and some neglected firm studies indicated nonefficiencies.

Strong-Form Hypothesis: Tests and Results

The strong-form EMH contends that stock prices fully reflect *all information,* public and private. This implies that no group of investors has access to *private information* that will allow them to consistently experience above-average profits. This extremely rigid hypothesis requires not only that stock prices must adjust rapidly to new public information but also that no group has access to private information.

Tests of the strong-form EMH have analyzed returns over time for different identifiable investment groups to determine whether any group consistently received above-average risk-adjusted returns. Such a group must have access to and act upon important private information or an ability to act on public information before other investors, which would indicate that security prices were not adjusting rapidly to *all* new information.

Investigators have tested this form of the EMH by analyzing the performance of the following four major groups of investors: (1) *corporate insiders,* (2) *stock exchange specialists,* (3) *security analysts* at Value Line and elsewhere, and (4) *professional money managers.*

Corporate Insider Trading   Corporate insiders are required to report monthly to the SEC on their transactions (purchases or sales) in the stock of the firm for which they are insiders. Insiders include major corporate officers, members of the board of directors, and owners of 10 percent or more of any equity class of securities. About six weeks after the reporting period, this insider trading information is made public by the SEC. These insider trading data have been used to identify how corporate insiders have traded and determine whether they bought on balance before abnormally good price movements and sold on balance before poor market periods for their stock. The results of studies including Chowdhury, Howe, and Lin (1993) and Pettit and Venkatesh (1995) have generally indicated that corporate insiders consistently enjoyed above-average profits, heavily dependent on selling prior to low returns and not selling before strong returns. This implies that many insiders had private information from which they derived above-average returns on their company stock.

In addition, an earlier study found that *public* investors who consistently traded with the insiders based on announced insider transactions would have enjoyed excess risk-adjusted returns (after commissions), although a subsequent study concluded that the market had eliminated this inefficiency after considering total transaction costs.

Overall, these results provide mixed support for the EMH because several studies indicate that insiders experience abnormal profits, while subsequent studies indicate it is no longer possible for noninsiders to use this information to generate excess returns. Notably, because of investor interest in these data as a result of academic research, the *Wall Street Journal* currently publishes a monthly column entitled "Inside Track" that discusses the largest insider transactions.

Stock Exchange Specialists   Several studies have determined that specialists have monopolistic access to certain important information about unfilled limit orders, and they should be able to derive above-average returns from this information. This expectation is generally supported by the data. First, specialists generally make money because they typically sell shares at higher prices than their purchased price. Also, they apparently make money when they buy or sell after unexpected announcements and when they trade in large blocks of stock. An article by Ip (2001b) supported this belief; it contended that specialists are doing more trading as dealers and the return on their capital during 2000 was 26 percent.

Security Analysts   Several tests have considered whether it is possible to identify a set of analysts who have the ability to select undervalued stocks. The analysis involves determining whether, after a stock selection by an analyst is made known, a significant abnormal return is available to those who follow these recommendations. These studies and those that discuss performance by money managers are more realistic and relevant than those that considered corporate insiders and stock exchange specialists because these analysts and money managers are full-time investment professionals with no obvious advantage except emphasis and training. If anyone should be able to select undervalued stocks, it should be these "pros." We initially examine Value Line rankings and then analyze the usefulness of recommendations by individual analysts.

The Value Line Enigma Value Line (VL) is a large well-known advisory service that publishes financial information on approximately 1,700 stocks. Included in its report is a timing rank, which indicates Value Line's expectation regarding a firm's common stock performance over the coming 12 months. A rank of 1 is the most favorable performance and 5 the worst. This ranking system, initiated in April 1965, assigns numbers based on four factors:

1. An earnings and price rank of each security relative to all others
2. A price momentum factor
3. Year-to-year relative changes in quarterly earnings
4. A quarterly earnings "surprise" factor (actual quarterly earnings compared with VL estimated earnings)

The firms are ranked based on a composite score for each firm. The top and bottom 100 are ranked 1 and 5, respectively; the next 300 from the top and bottom are ranked 2 and 4; and the rest (approximately 900) are ranked 3. Rankings are assigned every week based on the latest data. Notably, all the data used to derive the four factors are public information.

Several years after the ranking was started, Value Line contended that the stocks rated 1 substantially outperformed the market and the stocks rated 5 seriously underperformed the market (the performance figures did not include dividend income but also did not charge commissions).

Studies on the Value Line enigma indicate that there is information in the VL rankings (especially either rank 1 or 5) and in changes in the rankings (especially going from 2 to 1). Further, recent evidence indicates that the market is fairly efficient, because the abnormal adjustments appear to be complete by Day + 2. An analysis of study results over time indicates a faster adjustment to the rankings during recent years. Also, despite statistically significant price changes, mounting evidence indicates that it is not possible to derive abnormal returns from these announcements after considering realistic transaction costs. The strongest evidence regarding not being able to use this information is that Value Line's Centurion Fund, which concentrates on investing in rank-1 stocks, has consistently underperformed the market over the past decade.

Analysts' Recommendations There is evidence in favor of the existence of superior analysts who apparently possess private information. A study by Womack (1996) found that analysts appear to have both market timing and stock-picking ability, especially in connection with relatively rare sell recommendations. Jegadeesh et al. (2004) found that consensus recommendations do not contain incremental information for most stocks beyond other available signals (momentum and volume), but *changes* in consensus recommendations are useful. Alternatively, research by Ivkovic and Jegadeesh (2004) indicated that the most useful information consisted of upward earning revisions in the week prior to earnings announcements.

Performance of Professional Money Managers The studies of professional money managers are more realistic and widely applicable than the analysis of insiders and specialists because money managers typically do not have monopolistic access to important new information but are highly trained professionals who work full time at investment management. Therefore, if any "normal" set of investors should be able to derive above-average profits, it should be this group. Also, if any noninsider should be able to derive inside information, professional money managers should, because they conduct extensive management interviews.

Most studies on the performance of money managers have examined mutual funds because performance data is readily available for them. Recently, data have become available for bank trust departments, insurance companies, and investment advisers. The original mutual fund studies indicated that most funds did not match the performance of a buy-and-hold policy.[7] When risk-adjusted returns were examined *without* considering commission costs, slightly more than half of the money managers did better than the overall market. When commission costs, load fees, and management costs were considered, approximately two-thirds of the mutual funds did *not* match aggregate market performance. It was also found that successful funds during individual years were inconsistent in their performance.

Now that it is possible to get performance data for pension plans and endowment funds, several studies have documented that the performances of pension plans and endowments did not match that of the aggregate market.

The figures in Exhibit 6.3 provide a rough demonstration of these results for recent periods. These data are collected by Russell/Mellon Analytical Services as part of its performance

Exhibit 6.3	Annualized Rates of Return for Russell/Mellon U.S. Equity Universes and for Benchmark Indexes during Alternative Periods ending December 31, 2003

	1 Year	2 Years	3 Years	4 Years	5 Years	8 Years	10 Years
U.S. Equity Universe-Medians							
Equity accounts	30.0	1.0	−2.3	−2.2	2.2	10.6	11.8
Equity oriented accounts	30.3	1.0	−2.4	−2.5	2.7	10.7	11.8
Equity pooled	29.6	0.9	−2.3	−2.2	1.2	10.1	11.5
Special equity pooled	47.0	11.3	13.0	14.0	13.6	13.5	14.1
Value equity accounts	31.1	5.0	3.7	6.0	5.8	11.3	12.6
Market oriented accounts	29.3	0.7	−2.7	−3.0	1.2	10.5	11.7
Midcap equity accounts	38.6	6.5	4.6	7.4	9.4	13.1	13.8
Growth equity accounts	29.1	−2.8	−9.0	−9.9	−1.6	9.9	10.6
Small cap accounts	45.7	10.4	10.8	11.6	13.3	13.4	13.9
Mutual Fund Universe-Medians							
Balanced mutual funds	18.6	2.6	0.3	0.6	2.6	7.3	7.8
Equity mutual funds	−1.7	−8.4	−6.6	−3.3	−0.3	8.4	8.9
Benchmark Indexes							
Russell 1000 Growth Index	29.75	−3.27	−9.36	−12.82	−5.11	6.97	9.21
Russell 1000 Index	29.89	0.88	−3.78	−4.79	−0.13	9.41	11.00
Russell 1000 Value Index	30.03	4.81	1.22	2.64	3.56	10.76	11.88
Russell 2000 Growth Index	48.54	1.78	−2.03	−7.59	0.86	3.61	5.43
Russell 2000 Index	47.25	8.21	6.27	3.86	7.13	8.78	9.47
Russell 2000 Value Index	46.03	13.73	13.83	16.01	12.28	13.06	12.70
Russell 2500 Index	45.51	9.37	6.58	6.00	9.40	11.15	11.74
Russell 3000 Index	31.06	1.40	−3.08	−4.19	0.37	9.25	10.77
Russell Midcap Index	40.06	8.35	3.47	4.65	7.23	11.54	12.18

Source: Russell/Mellon Analytical Services, Tacoma, WA. Reprinted by permission.

---

[7]These studies and others on this topic are reviewed in Chapter 24.

evaluation service. Exhibit 6.3 contains the median rates of return for several investment groups compared to a set of Russell indexes, including the very broad Russell 3000 index.[8] These results show that all but one equity universe always beat the Russell 3000 universe in all periods. In contrast, the Russell 3000 index beat the mutual fund universes for periods of five years and longer, but not for periods of three years or less. Therefore, for these periods, the money manager results are mixed related to the strong-form EMH.

Conclusions Regarding the Strong-Form EMH   The tests of the strong-form EMH have generated mixed results. The result for two unique groups of investors (corporate insiders and stock exchange specialists) did not support the hypothesis because both groups apparently have monopolistic access to important information and use it to derive above-average returns.

Tests to determine whether there are any analysts with private information concentrated on the Value Line rankings and publications of analysts' recommendations. The results for Value Line rankings have changed over time and currently tend toward support for the EMH. Specifically, the adjustment to rankings and ranking changes is fairly rapid, and it appears that trading is not profitable after transaction costs. Alternatively, individual analysts' recommendations and overall consensus changes seem to contain significant information.

Finally, recent performance by professional money managers provided mixed support for the strong-form EMH. Most money manager performance studies before 2002 have indicated that these highly trained, full-time investors could not consistently outperform a simple buy-and-hold policy on a risk-adjusted basis. In contrast, the recent results shown in Exhibit 6.3 show that about half the non-mutual fund universe beat the broad Russell 3000 index, while the equity mutual fund results supported the EMH for long-term periods. Because money managers are similar to most investors who do not have access to inside information, these latter results are considered more relevant to the hypothesis. Therefore, it appears that there is mixed support for the strong-form EMH as applied to most investors.

BEHAVIORAL FINANCE

Our discussion up to this point has dealt with standard finance theory, how this theory assumes that capital markets function, and how to test within this theoretical context whether capital markets are informationally efficient. However, in the 1990s, a new branch of financial economics has been added to the mix. **Behavioral finance** considers how various psychological traits affect the ways that individuals or groups act as investors, analysts, and portfolio managers. As noted by Olsen (1998), behavioral finance advocates recognize that the standard finance model of rational behavior and profit maximization can be true within specific boundaries but assert that it is an *incomplete* model since it does not consider individual behavior. Specifically, according to Olsen (1998), behavioral finance

> seeks to understand and predict systematic financial market implications of psychological decisions processes . . . behavioral finance is focused on the implication of psychological and economic principles for the improvement of financial decision-making. (p. 11)

While it is acknowledged that currently there is no unified theory of behavioral finance, the emphasis has been on identifying portfolio anomalies that can be explained by various

---

[8]The results for these individual accounts have an upward bias because they consider only accounts retained (for example, if a firm or bank does a poor job on an account and the client leaves, those results would not be included).

psychological traits in individuals or groups or pinpointing instances when it is possible to experience above-normal rates of return by exploiting the biases of investors, analysts, or portfolio managers.

Explaining Biases

Over time it has been noted that investors have a number of biases that negatively affect their investment performance. Advocates of behavioral finance have been able to explain a number of these biases based on psychological characteristics. One major bias documented by Scott, Stumpp, and Xu (1999) is the propensity of investors to hold on to "losers" too long and sell "winners" too soon. Apparently, investors fear losses much more than they value gains. This is explained by *prospect theory,* which contends that utility depends on deviations from moving reference points rather than absolute wealth.

Another bias documented by Solt and Statman (1989) and Shefrin and Statman (1996) for growth companies is *overconfidence* in forecasts, which causes analysts to overestimate growth rates for growth companies and overemphasize good news and ignore negative news for these firms. Analysts and many investors generally believe that the stocks of growth companies will be "good" stocks. This bias is also referred to as *confirmation bias,* whereby investors look for information that supports their prior opinions and decisions. As a result, they will misvalue the stocks of these generally popular companies.

A study by Brown (1999) examined the effect of *noise traders* (nonprofessionals with no special information) on the volatility of closed-end mutual funds. When there is a shift in sentiment, these traders move together, which increases the prices and the volatility of these securities during trading hours. Also, Clark and Statman (1998) find that noise traders tend to follow newsletter writers, who in turn tend to "follow the herd." These writers and "the herd" are almost always wrong, which contributes to excess volatility.

Shefrin (2001) describes *escalation bias,* which causes investors to put more money into a failure that they feel responsible for rather than into a success. This leads to the relatively popular investor practice of "averaging down" on an investment that has declined in value since the initial purchase rather than consider selling the stock if it was a mistake. The thinking is that if it was a buy at $40, it is a screaming bargain at $30. Obviously, an alternative solution is to reevaluate the stock to see if some important bad news was missed in the initial valuation (therefore, sell it and accept the loss), or to confirm the initial valuation and acquire more of the "bargain." The difficult psychological factor noted by Shefrin (1999) is to seriously look for the bad news and consider the negative effects of that on the valuation.

Fusion Investing

According to Charles M. C. Lee (2003), *fusion investing* is the integration of two elements of investment valuation—fundamental value and investor sentiment. In Robert Shiller's (1984) formal model, the market price of securities is the expected dividends discounted to infinity (its fundamental value) plus a term that indicates the demand from noise traders who reflect investor sentiment. It is contended that when noise traders are bullish, stock prices will be higher than normal or higher than what is justified by fundamentals. Under this combination pricing model of fusion investing, investors will engage in fundamental analysis but also should consider investor sentiment in terms of fads and fashions. During some periods, investor sentiment is rather muted and noise traders are inactive, so that fundamental valuation dominates market returns. In other periods, when investor sentiment is strong, noise traders are very active and market returns are more heavily impacted by investor sentiments. Both investors and analysts should be cognizant of these dual effects on the aggregate market, various economic sectors, and individual stocks.

Beyond advocating awareness of the dual components of fusion investing, results from other studies have documented that fundamental valuation may be the dominant factor but takes much longer to assert itself—about three years. To derive some estimate of changing investor sentiment, Lee proposes several measures of investor sentiment, most notably analysts' recommendations, price momentum, and high trading turnover. Significant changes in these variables for a stock will indicate a movement from a glamour stock to a neglected stock or vice versa.

IMPLICATIONS OF EFFICIENT CAPITAL MARKETS

Having reviewed the results of numerous studies related to different facets of the EMH, the important question is, What does this mean to individual investors, financial analysts, portfolio managers, and institutions? Overall, the results of many studies indicate that the capital markets are efficient as related to numerous sets of information. At the same time, research has uncovered a substantial number of instances where the market fails to adjust prices rapidly to public information. Given these mixed results regarding the existence of efficient capital markets, it is important to consider the implications of this contrasting evidence of market efficiency.

The following discussion considers the implications of both sets of evidence. Specifically given results that support the EMH, we consider what techniques will not work and what you should do if you cannot beat the market. In contrast, because of the evidence that fails to support the EMH, we discuss what information and psychological biases should be considered when attempting to derive superior investment results through active security valuation and portfolio management.

Efficient Markets and Technical Analysis

The assumptions of technical analysis directly oppose the notion of efficient markets. A basic premise of technical analysis is that stock prices move in trends that persist.[9] Technicians believe that when new information comes to the market, it is not immediately available to everyone but is typically disseminated from the informed professional to the aggressive investing public and then to the great bulk of investors. Also, technicians contend that investors do not analyze information and act immediately. This process takes time. Therefore, they hypothesize that stock prices move to a new equilibrium after the release of new information in a gradual manner, which causes trends in stock price movements that persist.

Technical analysts believe that nimble traders can develop systems to detect the beginning of a movement to a new equilibrium (called a "breakout"). Hence, they hope to buy or sell the stock immediately after its breakout to take advantage of the subsequent, gradual price adjustment.

The belief in this pattern of price adjustment directly contradicts advocates of the EMH who believe that security prices adjust to new information very rapidly. These EMH advocates do not contend, however, that prices adjust perfectly, which implies a chance of overadjustment or underadjustment. Still, because it is uncertain whether the market will over- or underadjust at any time, you cannot derive abnormal profits from adjustment errors.

If the capital market is weak-form efficient as indicated by most of the results, then prices fully reflect all relevant market information so technical trading systems that depend only on past trading data *cannot* have any value. By the time the information is public, the price adjustment has taken place. Therefore, a purchase or sale using a technical trading rule should not generate abnormal returns after taking account of risk and transaction costs.

---

[9]Chapter 15 contains an extensive discussion of technical analysis.

Efficient Markets and Fundamental Analysis

As you know from our prior discussion, fundamental analysts believe that, at any time, there is a basic intrinsic value for the aggregrate stock market, various industries, or individual securities and that these values depend on underlying economic factors. Therefore, investors should determine the intrinsic value of an investment asset at a point in time by examining the variables that determine value such as current and future earnings or cash flows, interest rates, and risk variables. If the prevailing market price differs from the estimated intrinsic value by enough to cover transaction costs, you should take appropriate action: You buy if the market price is substantially below intrinsic value and do not buy, or you sell, if the market price is above the intrinsic value. Investors who are engaged in fundamental analysis believe that, occasionally, market price and intrinsic value differ but eventually investors recognize the discrepancy and correct it.

An investor who can do a superior job of *estimating* intrinsic value can consistently make superior market timing (asset allocation) decisions or acquire undervalued securities and generate above-average returns. Fundamental analysis involves aggregate market analysis, industry analysis, company analysis, and portfolio management. The divergent results from the EMH research have important implications for all of these components.

Aggregate Market Analysis with Efficient Capital Markets   Chapter 11 makes a strong case that intrinsic value analysis should begin with aggregate market analysis. Still, the EMH implies that if you examine only *past* economic events, it is unlikely that you will be able to outperform a buy-and-hold policy because the market rapidly adjusts to known economic events. Evidence suggests that the market experiences long-run price movements; but, to take advantage of these movements in an efficient market, you must do a superior job of *estimating* the relevant variables that cause these long-run movements. Put another way, if you only use *historical* data to estimate future values and invest on the basis of these estimates, you will *not* experience superior, risk-adjusted returns.

Industry and Company Analysis with Efficient Capital Markets   As we will discuss in Chapter 13, the wide distribution of returns from different industries and companies clearly justifies industry and company analysis. Again, the EMH does not contradict the potential value of such analysis but implies that you need to (1) understand the relevant variables that affect rates of return and (2) do a superior job of *estimating future* values for these relevant valuation variables. To demonstrate this, Malkiel and Cragg (1970) developed a model that did an excellent job of explaining past stock price movements using historical data. When this valuation model was employed to project *future* stock price changes using *past* company data, however, the results were consistently inferior to a buy-and-hold policy. This implies that, even with a good valuation model, you *cannot* select stocks that will provide superior future returns using only past data as inputs. The point is, most analysts are aware of the several well-specified valuation models, so the factor that differentiates superior from inferior analysts is the ability to *provide more accurate estimates* of the critical inputs to the valuation models.

A study by Benesh and Peterson (1986) showed that the crucial difference between the stocks that enjoyed the best and worst price performance during a given year was the relationship between expected earnings of professional analysts and actual earnings (that is, it was *earnings surprises*). Specifically, stock prices increased if actual earnings substantially exceeded expected earnings and stock prices fell if actual earnings did not reach expected levels. As suggested by Fogler (1993), if you can do a superior job of projecting earnings and your expectations *differ from the consensus* (i.e., you project earnings surprises)*, you will have a superior stock selection record. Put another way, there are two factors that are required to be superior: (1) you must be *correct* in your estimates, and (2) you must be *different* from the consensus. Remember, if you are only correct and not different, that assumes you were predicting the consensus and the consensus was correct, which implies no surprise and no abnormal price movement.

The quest to be a superior analyst holds some good news and some suggestions. The good news is related to the strong-form tests that indicated the likely existence of superior analysts. It was shown that the rankings by Value Line contained information value, even though it might not be possible to profit from the work of these analysts after transaction costs. Also, the price adjustments to the publication of analyst recommendations also point to the existence of superior analysts. The point is, there are some superior analysts, but only a limited number, and it is *not* an easy task to be among this select group. Most notably, to be a superior analyst you must do a superior job of *estimating* the relevant valuation variables and *predicting earnings surprises.*

The suggestions for those involved in fundamental analysis are based on the studies that considered the cross section of future returns. As noted, these studies indicated that P/E ratios, size, and the BV/MV ratios were able to differentiate future return patterns with size and the BV/MV ratio appearing to be the optimal combination. Therefore, these factors should be considered when selecting a universe or analyzing firms. In addition, the evidence suggests that neglected firms should be given extra consideration. Although these ratios and characteristics have been shown to be useful in isolating superior stocks from a large sample, it is our suggestion that they are best used to derive a viable sample to analyze from the total universe (e.g., select 200 stocks to analyze from a universe of 3,000). Then the 200 stocks should be rigorously valued using the techniques discussed in this text.

How to Evaluate Analysts or Investors   If you want to determine if an individual is a superior analyst or investor, you should examine the performance of numerous securities that this analyst or investor recommends over time in relation to the performance of a set of randomly selected stocks of the same risk class. The stock selections of a superior analyst or investor should *consistently* outperform the randomly selected stocks. The consistency requirement is crucial because you would expect a portfolio developed by random selection to outperform the market about half the time.

Conclusions about Fundamental Analysis   A text on investments can indicate the relevant variables that you should analyze and describe the important analysis techniques, but actually estimating the relevant variables is as much an art and a product of hard work as it is a science. If the estimates could be done on the basis of some mechanical formula, you could program a computer to do it, and there would be no need for analysts. Therefore, the superior analyst or successful investor must understand what variables are relevant to the valuation process and have the ability and work ethic to do a superior job of *estimating* these important valuation variables. Alternatively, one can be superior if he or she has the ability to interpret the impact or estimate the effect of some public information better than others.

Efficient Markets and Portfolio Management

As noted, studies have indicated that the majority of professional money managers cannot beat a buy-and-hold policy on a risk-adjusted basis. One explanation for this generally inferior performance is that there are no superior analysts and the cost of research and trading forces the results of merely adequate analysis into the inferior category. Another explanation, which is favored by the authors and has some empirical support from the Value Line and analyst recommendation results, is that money management firms employ both superior and inferior analysts and the gains from the recommendations by the few superior analysts are offset by the costs and the poor results derived from the recommendations of the inferior analysts.

This raises the question, Should a portfolio be managed actively or passively? The following discussion indicates that the decision of how to manage the portfolio (actively or passively) should depend on whether the manager has access to superior analysts. A portfolio manager with superior analysts or an investor who believes that he or she has the time and expertise to be a superior investor can manage a portfolio actively by looking for undervalued or overvalued securities and trading accordingly. In contrast, without access to superior analysts or the time and ability to be a superior investor, you should manage passively and assume that all securities are properly priced based on their levels of risk.

Portfolio Management with Superior Analysts A portfolio manager with access to superior analysts who have unique insights and analytical ability should follow their recommendations. The superior analysts should make investment recommendations for a certain proportion of the portfolio, and the portfolio manager should ensure that the risk preferences of the client are maintained.

Also, the superior analysts should be encouraged to concentrate their efforts in mid-cap and small-cap stocks that possess the liquidity required by institutional portfolio managers. But because these stocks typically do not receive the attention given the top-tier stocks, the markets for these neglected stocks may be less efficient than the market for large well-known stocks.

Recall that capital markets are expected to be efficient because many investors receive new information and analyze its effect on security values. If the number of analysts following a stock differ, one could conceive of differences in the efficiency of the markets. New information on top-tier stocks is well publicized and rigorously analyzed so the price of these securities should adjust rapidly to reflect the new information. In contrast, middle-tier firms receive less publicity and fewer analysts follow these firms, so prices might be expected to adjust less rapidly to new information. Therefore, the possibility of finding temporarily undervalued securities among these neglected stocks is greater. Again, in line with the cross-section study results, these superior analysts should pay particular attention to the BV/MV ratio, to the size of stocks being analyzed, and to the monetary policy environment.

Portfolio Management without Superior Analysts A portfolio manager who does not have access to superior analysts should proceed as follows. First, he or she should *measure the risk preferences* of his or her clients, then build a portfolio to match this risk level by investing a certain proportion of the portfolio in risky assets and the rest in a risk-free asset, as discussed in Chapter 8.

The risky asset portfolio must be *completely diversified* on a global basis so it moves consistently with the world market. In this context, proper diversification means eliminating all unsystematic (unique) variability. In our prior discussion, it was estimated that it required about 20 securities to gain most of the benefits (more than 90 percent) of a completely diversified portfolio. More than 100 stocks are required for complete diversification. To decide how many securities to actually include in your global portfolio, you must balance the added benefits of complete worldwide diversification against the costs of research for the additional stocks.

Finally, you should *minimize transaction costs*. Assuming that the portfolio is completely diversified and is structured for the desired risk level, excessive transaction costs that do not generate added returns will detract from your expected rate of return. Three factors are involved in minimizing total transaction costs:

1. *Minimize taxes.* Methods of accomplishing this objective vary, but it should receive prime consideration.

2. *Reduce trading turnover.* Trade only to liquidate part of the portfolio or to maintain a given risk level.
3. *When you trade, minimize liquidity costs by trading relatively liquid stocks.* To accomplish this, submit limit orders to buy or sell several stocks at prices that approximate the specialist's quote. That is, you would put in limit orders to buy stock at the bid price or sell at the ask price. The stock bought or sold first is the most liquid one; all other orders should be withdrawn.

In summary, if you lack access to superior analysts, you should do the following:

1. Determine and quantify your risk preferences.
2. Construct the appropriate risk portfolio by dividing the total portfolio between risk-free assets and a risky asset portfolio.
3. Diversify completely on a global basis to eliminate all unsystematic risk.
4. Maintain the specified risk level by rebalancing when necessary.
5. Minimize total transaction costs.

The Rationale and Use of Index Funds and Exchange-Traded Funds   As the preceding discussion indicates, efficient capital markets and a lack of superior analysts imply that many portfolios should be managed *passively* so that their performance matches that of the aggregate market, minimizing the costs of research and trading. In response to this demand, several institutions have introduced *market funds,* also referred to as *index funds,* which are security portfolios designed to duplicate the composition, and therefore the performance, of a selected market index series.

Notably, this concept of stock-market index funds has been extended to other areas of investments and, as discussed by Gastineau (2001) and Kostovetsky (2003), has been enhanced by the introduction of exchange-traded funds (ETFs). Index bond funds attempt to emulate the bond-market indexes discussed in Chapter 5. Also, some index funds focus on specific segments of the market such as international bond-index funds, international stock-index funds that target specific countries, and index funds that target small-cap stocks in the United States and Japan. When financial planners decide that they want a given asset class in their portfolios, they often look for index funds or to ETFs to fulfill this need. Index funds or ETFs are less costly in terms of research and commissions, and during almost all time periods they can provide the same or better performance than what is available from the majority of active portfolio managers.

Insights from Behavioral Finance   As noted earlier, the major contributions of behavioral finance researchers are explanations for some of the anomalies discovered by prior academic research and opportunities to derive abnormal rates of return by acting on some of the deeply ingrained biases of investors. Clearly, their findings support the notion that the stocks of growth companies typically will not actually be growth stocks because analysts become overconfident in their ability to predict future growth rates and eventually derive valuations that either fully value or overvalue future growth. Behavioral finance research also supports the notion of contrary investing, confirming the notion of the herd mentality of analysts in stock recommendations or quarterly earning estimates and the recommendations by newsletter writers. Also, it is important to recall the loss aversion and escalation bias that causes investors to ignore bad news and hold losers too long and in some cases acquire additional shares of losers to average down the cost. Before averaging down, be sure you reevaluate the stock and consider all the potential bad news we tend to ignore. Finally, recognize that valuation is a combination of fundamental value and investor sentiment.

The Internet   *Investments Online*

Capital market prices reflect current news items fairly quickly. On the other hand, a portfolio manager should not ignore news just because prices adjust quickly. News provides information he/she can use to structure portfolios and allows the managers to update potential future scenarios.

A number of news sources are available on the Internet. Some of them, such as **http://www. bloomberg.com, http://news.ft.com,** and **http://online.wsj.com,** were listed in previous chapters. Other sites include:

http://finance.yahoo.com contains links to a number of news, information, commentary, and finance-related sites.

http://money.cnn.com The financial network site for the Cable News Network and *Money* magazine. The CNN Web site is **http://www.cnn.com**.
http://www.foxnews.com,   http://www. abcnews.go.com,   http://www.cbsnews.com and **http://www.msnbc.msn.com** are the URLs for news from Fox, ABC, CBS, and NBC. Meir Statman (**http://lsb.scu.edu/finance/faculty/Statman**) and Richard Thaler (**http://gsbwww.uchicago. edu/fac/richard.thaler/research**) are two leading researchers in the area of behavioral finance. These pages contain links to their research.

SUMMARY

- The efficiency of capital markets has implications for the investment analysis and management of your portfolio. Capital markets should be efficient because numerous rational, profit-maximizing investors react quickly to the release of new information. Assuming prices reflect new information, they are unbiased estimates of the securities' true, intrinsic value, and there should be a consistent relationship between the return on an investment and its risk.
- The voluminous research on the EMH has been divided into three segments that have been tested separately. The weak-form EMH states that stock prices fully reflect all market information, so any trading rule that uses past market data to predict future returns should have no value. The results of most studies consistently supported this hypothesis.
- The semistrong-form EMH asserts that security prices adjust rapidly to the release of all public information. The tests of this hypothesis either examine the opportunities to predict future rates of return (either a time series or a cross section) or they involve event studies in which investigators analyzed whether investors could derive above-average returns from trading on the basis of public information. The test results for this hypothesis were clearly mixed. On the one hand, the results for almost all the event studies related to economic events such as stock splits, initial public offerings, and accounting changes

consistently supported the semistrong hypothesis. In contrast, several studies that examined the ability to predict rates of return on the basis of unexpected quarterly earnings, P/E ratios, size, neglected stocks, and the BV/MV ratio, as well as several calendar effects, generally did not support the hypothesis.
- The strong-form EMH states that security prices reflect all information. This implies that nobody has private information, so no group should be able to derive above-average returns consistently. Studies that examined the results for corporate insiders and stock exchange specialists do not support the strong-form hypothesis. An analysis of individual analysts as represented by Value Line or by recommendations published in *The Wall Street Journal* give mixed results. The results indicated that the Value Line rankings have significant information but it may not be possible to profit from it, whereas the recommendations by analysts indicated the existence of private information. In contrast, the performance by professional money managers supported the EMH because their risk-adjusted investment performance (whether mutual funds, pension funds, or endowment funds) was typically inferior to results achieved with buy-and-hold policies.
- During the past decade, there has been significant research in behavioral finance by investigators who contend

that the standard finance theory model is incomplete since it does not consider implications of psychological decisions made by individuals that both help explain many anomalies and the existence of several biases and provide opportunities for excess returns. It is important to be aware of a number of biases for two reasons: first, they can lead to inferior performance as an analyst and portfolio manager; second, it is possible to exploit them for excess returns.

- Given the mixed results, it is important to consider the implications of all of this for technical or fundamental analysts and for portfolio managers. The EMH indicates that technical analysis should be of no value. All forms of fundamental analysis are useful, but they are difficult to implement because they require the ability *to estimate future values* for relevant economic variables. Superior analysis is possible but difficult because it requires superior projections. Those who manage portfolios should constantly evaluate investment advice to determine whether it is superior.

- Without access to superior analytical advice, you should run your portfolio like an index fund or an ETF. In contrast, those with superior analytical ability should be allowed to make decisions, but they should concentrate their efforts on mid-cap firms and neglected firms where there is a higher probability of discovering misvalued stocks. The analysis should be particularly concerned with a firm's BV/MV ratio, its size, and the monetary environment.

- This chapter contains some good news and some bad news. The good news is that the practice of investment analysis and portfolio management is not an art that has been lost to the great computer in the sky. Viable professions still await those willing to extend the effort and able to accept the pressures. The bad news is that many bright, hardworking people with extensive resources make the game tough. In fact, those competitors have created a fairly efficient capital market in which it is extremely difficult for most analysts and portfolio managers to achieve superior results.

SUGGESTED READINGS

Ball, Ray. "The Theory of Stock Market Efficiency: Accomplishments and Limitations." *Journal of Applied Corporate Finance* 8, no. 1 (Spring 1995).

Berkowitz, Stephen A., Louis D. Finney, and Dennis Logue. *The Investment Performance of Corporate Pension Plans.* New York: Quorum Books, 1988.

Bernard, Victor. "Capital Markets Research in Accounting During the 1980s: A Critical Review," in *The State of Accounting Research as We Enter the 1990s,* ed. Thomas J. Frecka. Urbana: University of Illinois Press, 1989.

Keim, Donald B., and Robert F. Stambaugh. "Predicting Returns in Stock and Bond Markets." *Journal of Financial Economics* 17, no. 2 (December 1986).

Shefrin, Hersh, and Meir Statman. "Behavioral Capital Asset Pricing Theory." *Journal of Financial and Quantitative Analysis* 30, no. 3 (September 1995a).

Wood, Arnold S., ed. *Behavioral Finance and Decision Theory in Investment Management.* Charlottesville, VA: AIMR, April 1995.

QUESTIONS

1. Discuss the rationale for expecting an efficient capital market. What factor would you look for to differentiate the market efficiency for two alternative stocks?

2. Define and discuss the weak-form EMH. Describe the two sets of tests used to examine the weak-form EMH.

3. Define and discuss the semistrong-form EMH. Describe the two sets of tests used to examine the semistrong-form EMH.

4. What is meant by the term *abnormal rate of return?*

5. Describe how you would compute the abnormal rate of return for a stock for a period surrounding an economic event. Give a brief example for a stock with a beta of 1.40.

6. Assume you want to test the EMH by comparing alternative trading rules to a buy-and-hold policy. Discuss the three common mistakes that can bias the results against the EMH.

7. Describe the results of a study that supported the semistrong-form EMH. Discuss the nature of the test and specifically why the results support the hypothesis.

8. Describe the results of a study that did *not* support the semistrong-form EMH. Discuss the nature of the test and specifically why the results did not support the hypothesis.

9. For many of the EMH tests, it is really a test of a "joint hypothesis." Discuss what is meant by this concept. What are the joint hypotheses being tested?

10. Define and discuss the strong-form EMH. Why do some observers contend that the strong-form hypothesis really requires a perfect market in addition to an efficient market? Be specific.

11. Discuss how you would test the strong-form EMH. Why are these tests relevant? Give a brief example.

12. Describe the results of a study that did *not* support the strong-form EMH. Discuss the test involved and specifically why the results reported did not support the hypothesis.

13. Describe the results of a study that supported the strong-form EMH. Discuss the test involved and specifically why these results support the hypothesis.

14. Describe the general goal of behavioral finance.

15. Why do the advocates of behavioral finance contend that the standard finance theory is incomplete?

16. What does the EMH imply for the use of technical analysis?

17. What does the EMH imply for fundamental analysis? Discuss specifically what it does not imply.

18. In a world of efficient capital markets, what do you have to do to be a superior analyst? How would you test whether an analyst was superior?

19. What advice would you give to your superior analysts in terms of the set of firms to analyze and variables that should be considered in the analysis? Discuss your reasoning for this advice.

20. How should a portfolio manager without any superior analysts run his or her portfolio?

21. Describe the goals of an index fund. Discuss the contention that index funds are the ultimate answer in a world with efficient capital markets.

22. At a social gathering, you meet the portfolio manager for the trust department of a local bank. He confides to you that he has been following the recommendations of the department's six analysts for an extended period and has found that two are superior, two are average, and two are clearly inferior. What would you recommend that he do to run his portfolio?

23. *CFA Examination Level I*
    a. List and briefly define the *three* forms of the efficient market hypothesis. [6 minutes]
    b. Discuss the role of a portfolio manager in a perfectly efficient market. [9 minutes]

24. *CFA Examination Level II*
    Tom Max, TMP's quantitative analyst, has developed a portfolio construction model about which he is excited. To create the model, Max made a list of the stocks currently in the S&P 500 Stock Index and obtained annual operating cash flow, price, and total return data for each issue for the past five years. As of each year-end, this universe was divided into five equal-weighted portfolios of 100 issues each, with selection based solely on the price/cash flow rankings of the individual stocks. Each portfolio's average annual return was then calculated.

    During this five-year period, the linked returns from the portfolios with the lowest price/cash flow ratio generated an annualized total return of 19.0 percent, or 3.1 percentage points better than the 15.9 percent return on the S&P 500 Stock Index. Max also noted that the lowest price–cash-flow portfolio had a below-market beta of 0.91 over this same time span.

    a. Briefly comment on Max's use of the beta measure as an indicator of portfolio risk in light of recent academic tests of its explanatory power with respect to stock returns. [5 minutes]
    b. You are familiar with the literature on market anomalies and inefficiencies. Against this background, discuss Max's use of a single-factor model (price–cash flow) in his research. [8 minutes]
    c. Identify and briefly describe *four* specific concerns about Max's test procedures and model design. (The issues already discussed in your answers to Parts a and b may *not* be used in answering Part c.) [12 minutes]

25. *CFA Examination Level III*
    a. Briefly explain the concept of the *efficient market hypothesis* (EMH) and each of its three forms—*weak, semistrong, and strong*—and briefly discuss the degree to which existing empirical evidence supports each of the three forms of the EMH. [8 minutes]

b. Briefly discuss the implications of the efficient market hypothesis for investment policy as it applies to:
   (i) technical analysis in the form of charting, and
   (ii) fundamental analysis. [4 minutes]
c. Briefly explain *two* major roles or responsibilities of portfolio managers in an efficient market environment. [4 minutes]
d. Briefly discuss whether active asset allocation among countries could consistently outperform a world market index. Include a discussion of the implications of *integration versus segmentation* of international financial markets as it pertains to portfolio diversification, but ignore the issue of stock selection. [6 minutes]

PROBLEMS

1. Compute the abnormal rates of return for the following stocks during period t (ignore differential systematic risk):

Stock	R_{it}	R_{mt}
B	11.5%	4.0%
F	10.0	8.5
T	14.0	9.6
C	12.0	15.3
E	15.9	12.4

R_{it} = return for stock i during period t
R_{mt} = return for the aggregate market during period t

2. Compute the abnormal rates of return for the five stocks in Problem 1 assuming the following systematic risk measures (betas):

Stock	β_i
B	0.95
F	1.25
T	1.45
C	0.70
E	−0.30

3. Compare the abnormal returns in Problems 1 and 2 and discuss the reason for the difference in each case.
4. Look up the daily trading volume for the following stocks during a recent five-day period:
   - Merck
   - Anheuser Busch
   - Intel
   - McDonald's
   - General Electric

   Randomly select five stocks from the NYSE and examine their daily trading volume for the same five days.
   a. What are the average volumes for the two samples?
   b. Would you expect this difference to have an impact on the efficiency of the markets for the two samples? Why or why not?

Chapter 7

An Introduction to Portfolio Management

After you read this chapter, you should be able to answer the following questions:

- What do we mean by *risk aversion*, and what evidence indicates that investors are generally risk averse?
- What are the basic assumptions behind the Markowitz portfolio theory?
- What do we mean by *risk*, and what are some of the measures of risk used in investments?
- How do we compute the expected rate of return for an individual risky asset or a portfolio of assets?
- How do we compute the standard deviation of rates of return for an individual risky asset?
- What do we mean by the *covariance* between rates of return, and how is it computed?
- What is the relationship between covariance and correlation?
- What is the formula for the standard deviation for a *portfolio* of risky assets, and how does it differ from the standard deviation of an individual risky asset?
- Given the formula for the standard deviation of a portfolio, why and how do we diversify a portfolio?
- What happens to the standard deviation of a portfolio when we change the correlation between the assets in the portfolio?
- What is the risk–return efficient frontier of risky assets?
- Is it reasonable for different investors to select different portfolios from the set of portfolios on the efficient frontier?
- What determines which portfolio on the efficient frontier is selected by an individual investor?

One of the major advances in the investment field during the past few decades has been the recognition that the creation of an optimum investment portfolio is not simply a matter of combining numerous unique individual securities that have desirable risk–return characteristics. Specifically, it has been shown that an investor must consider the relationship *among* the investments to build an optimum portfolio that will meet investment objectives. The recognition of what is important in creating a portfolio was demonstrated in the derivation of portfolio theory.

In this chapter we explain portfolio theory step by step. We introduce the basic portfolio risk formula for combining different assets. Once you understand this formula and its implications, you will understand not only *why* you should diversify your portfolio but also *how* you should diversify.

SOME BACKGROUND ASSUMPTIONS

Before presenting portfolio theory, we need to clarify some general assumptions of the theory. This includes not only what we mean by an *optimum portfolio* but also what we mean by the terms *risk aversion* and *risk.*

One basic assumption of portfolio theory is that as an investor you want to maximize the returns from your total set of investments for a given level of risk. To adequately deal with such an assumption, certain ground rules must be laid. First, your portfolio should *include all of your assets and liabilities*, not only your stocks or even your marketable securities but also such items as your car, house, and less marketable investments such as coins, stamps, art, antiques, and furniture. The full spectrum of investments must be considered because the returns from all these investments interact, and *this relationship among the returns for assets in the portfolio is important.* Hence, a good portfolio is not simply a collection of individually good investments.

Risk Aversion

Portfolio theory also assumes that investors are basically **risk averse**, meaning that, given a choice between two assets with equal rates of return, they will select the asset with the lower level of risk. Evidence that most investors are risk averse is that they purchase various types of insurance, including life insurance, car insurance, and health insurance. Buying insurance basically involves an outlay of a given known amount to guard against an uncertain, possibly larger, outlay in the future. Further evidence of risk aversion is the difference in promised yield (the required rate of return) for different grades of bonds that supposedly have different degrees of credit risk. Specifically, the promised yield on corporate bonds increases from AAA (the lowest risk class) to AA to A, and so on, indicating that investors require a higher rate of return to accept higher risk.

This does not imply that everybody is risk averse, or that investors are completely risk averse regarding all financial commitments. The fact is, not everybody buys insurance for everything. Some people have no insurance against anything, either by choice or because they cannot afford it. In addition, some individuals buy insurance related to some risks such as auto accidents or illness, but they also buy lottery tickets and gamble at race tracks or in casinos, where it is known that the expected returns are negative (which means that participants are willing to pay for the excitement of the risk involved). This combination of risk preference and risk aversion can be explained by an attitude toward risk that depends on the amount of money involved. Researchers such as Friedman and Savage (1948) speculate that this is the case for people who like to gamble for small amounts (in lotteries or slot machines) but buy insurance to protect themselves against large losses such as fire or accidents.

While recognizing such attitudes, our basic assumption is that most investors committing large sums of money to developing an investment portfolio are risk averse. Therefore, we expect a positive relationship between expected return and expected risk. Notably, this is also what we generally find in terms of historical results—that is, most studies find a positive relationship between the rates of return on various assets and their measures of risk (as shown in Chapter 3).

Definition of Risk

Although there is a difference in the specific definitions of *risk* and *uncertainty*, for our purposes and in most financial literature the two terms are used interchangeably. For most investors, *risk* means *the uncertainty of future outcomes*. An alternative definition might be *the probability of an adverse outcome*. In our subsequent discussion of portfolio theory, we will consider several measures of risk that are used when developing and applying the theory.

MARKOWITZ PORTFOLIO THEORY

In the early 1960s, the investment community talked about risk, but there was no specific measure for the term. To build a portfolio model, however, investors had to quantify their risk variable. The basic portfolio model was developed by Harry Markowitz (1952, 1959), who derived the expected rate of return for a portfolio of assets and an expected risk measure. Markowitz showed that the variance of the rate of return was a meaningful measure of portfolio risk under a reasonable set of assumptions, and he derived the formula for computing the variance of a portfolio. This portfolio variance formula not only indicated the importance of diversifying investments to reduce the total risk of a portfolio but also showed *how* to effectively diversify. The Markowitz model is based on several assumptions regarding investor behavior:

1. Investors consider each investment alternative as being represented by a probability distribution of expected returns over some holding period.
2. Investors maximize one-period expected utility, and their utility curves demonstrate diminishing marginal utility of wealth.
3. Investors estimate the risk of the portfolio on the basis of the variability of expected returns.
4. Investors base decisions solely on expected return and risk, so their utility curves are a function of expected return and the expected variance (or standard deviation) of returns only.
5. For a given risk level, investors prefer higher returns to lower returns. Similarly, for a given level of expected return, investors prefer less risk to more risk.

Under these assumptions, *a single asset or portfolio of assets is considered to be efficient if no other asset or portfolio of assets offers higher expected return with the same (or lower) risk or lower risk with the same (or higher) expected return.*

Alternative Measures of Risk

One of the best-known measures of risk is the *variance*, or *standard deviation of expected returns*.[1] It is a statistical measure of the dispersion of returns around the expected value whereby a larger variance or standard deviation indicates greater dispersion. The idea is that the more disperse the expected returns, the greater the uncertainty of future returns.

Another measure of risk is the *range of returns*. It is assumed that a larger range of expected returns, from the lowest to the highest expected return, means greater uncertainty and risk regarding future expected returns.

Instead of using measures that analyze all deviations from expectations, some observers believe that investors should be concerned only with returns below expectations, which means only deviations below the mean value. A measure that only considers deviations below the

---

[1]We consider the variance and standard deviation as one measure of risk because the standard deviation is the square root of the variance.

mean is the *semivariance*. An extension of the semivariance measure only computes expected returns *below zero* (that is, negative returns), or returns below the returns of some specific asset such as T-bills, the rate of inflation, or a benchmark. These measures of risk implicitly assume that investors want to *minimize the damage* (regret) from returns less than some target rate. Assuming that investors would welcome returns above some target rate, the returns above such a target rate are not considered when measuring risk.

Although there are numerous potential measures of risk, we will use the variance or standard deviation of returns because (1) this measure is somewhat intuitive, (2) it is a correct and widely recognized risk measure, and (3) it has been used in most of the theoretical asset pricing models.

Expected Rates of Return

We compute the expected rate of return for an *individual investment* as shown in Exhibit 7.1. The expected return for an individual risky asset with the set of potential returns and an assumption of the different probabilities used in the example would be 10.3 percent.

The expected rate of return for a *portfolio* of investments is simply the weighted average of the expected rates of return for the individual investments in the portfolio. The weights are the proportion of total value for the individual investment.

The expected rate of return for a hypothetical portfolio with four risky assets is shown in Exhibit 7.2. The expected return for this portfolio of investments would be 11.5 percent. The effect of adding or dropping any investment from the portfolio would be easy to

Exhibit 7.1	**Computation of the Expected Return for an Individual Asset**

Probability	Possible Rate of Return (percent)	Expected Return (percent)
0.35	0.08	0.0280
0.30	0.10	0.0300
0.20	0.12	0.0240
0.15	0.14	0.0210
		$E(R) = 0.1030$

Exhibit 7.2	**Computation of the Expected Return for a Portfolio of Risky Assets**

Weight (w_i) (percent of portfolio)	Expected Security Return (R_i)	Expected Portfolio Return ($w_i \times R_i$)
0.20	0.10	0.0200
0.30	0.11	0.0330
0.30	0.12	0.0360
0.20	0.13	0.0260
		$E(R_{port}) = 0.1150$

determine; we would use the new weights based on value and the expected returns for each of the investments. We can generalize this computation of the expected return for the portfolio $E(R_{port})$ as follows:

7.1
$$E(R_{port}) = \sum_{i=1}^{n} w_i R_i$$

where:

w_i = the weight of an individual asset in the portfolio, or the percent of the portfolio in Asset i

R_i = the expected rate of return for Asset i

Variance (Standard Deviation) of Returns for an Individual Investment

As noted, we will be using the variance or the standard deviation of returns as the measure of risk. Therefore, at this point we demonstrate how to compute the standard deviation of returns for an individual investment. Subsequently, after discussing some other statistical concepts, we will consider the determination of the standard deviation for a *portfolio* of investments.

The variance, or standard deviation, is a measure of the variation of possible rates of return R_i from the expected rate of return $E(R_i)$ as follows:

7.2
$$\text{Variance} = \sigma^2 = \sum_{i=1}^{n} [R_i - E(R_i)]^2 P_i$$

where:

P_i = probability of the possible rate of return R_i

7.3
$$\text{Standard Deviation} = \sigma = \sqrt{\sum_{i=1}^{n} [R_i - E(R_i)]^2 P_i}$$

The computation of the variance and standard deviation of returns for the individual risky asset in Exhibit 7.1 is set forth in Exhibit 7.3.

Exhibit 7.3	Computation of the Variance for an Individual Risky Asset

Possible Rate of Return (R_i)	Expected Return $E(R_i)$	$R_i - E(R_i)$	$[R_i - E(R_i)]^2$	P_i	$[R_i - E(R_i)]^2 P_i$
0.08	0.103	−0.023	0.0005	0.35	0.000185
0.10	0.103	−0.003	0.0000	0.30	0.000003
0.12	0.103	0.017	0.0003	0.20	0.000058
0.14	0.103	0.037	0.0014	0.15	0.000205
					0.000451

Variance = σ^2 = 0.000451
Standard Deviation = σ = 0.021237

Variance (Standard Deviation) of Returns for a Portfolio

Two basic concepts in statistics, covariance and correlation, must be understood before we discuss the formula for the variance of the rate of return for a portfolio.

Covariance of Returns   In this subsection we discuss what the covariance of returns is intended to measure, give the formula for computing it, and present an example of its computation. **Covariance** is a measure of the degree to which two variables move together relative to their individual mean values over time. In portfolio analysis, we usually are concerned with the covariance of *rates of return* rather than prices or some other variable.[2] A positive covariance means that the rates of return for two investments tend to move in the same direction relative to their individual means during the same time period. In contrast, a negative covariance indicates that the rates of return for two investments tend to move in different directions relative to their means during specified time intervals over time. The *magnitude* of the covariance depends on the variances of the individual return series, as well as on the relationship between the series.

Exhibit 7.4 contains the monthly closing index values for U.S. stocks (measured by the Wilshire 5000 index) and bonds (measured by the Lehman Brothers Treasury Bond Index). Both indexes are total return indexes—that is, the stock index includes dividends paid and the bond index includes accrued interest, as discussed in Chapter 5. We can use these data to compute monthly rates of return for these two assets during 2004. Exhibits 7.5 and 7.6 contain a time-series plot of the monthly rates of return for the two assets during 2004. Although the rates of return for the two assets moved together during some months, in other months they

Exhibit 7.4	**Computation of Monthly Rates of Return for U.S. Stocks and Bonds**

Date	WILSHIRE 5000 INDEX Monthly Rate of Return (%)	LEHMAN BROTHERS TREASURY BONDS Monthly Rate of Return (%)
Jan-04	2.23	1.77
Feb-04	1.46	2.00
Mar-04	−1.07	1.50
Apr-04	−2.13	−5.59
May-04	1.38	−0.54
Jun-04	2.08	0.95
Jul-04	−3.82	1.73
Aug-04	0.33	3.74
Sep-04	1.78	0.84
Oct-04	1.71	1.51
Nov-04	4.68	−2.19
Dec-04	3.63	2.31
	Mean = 1.02	Mean = 0.67

Sources: Wilshire Associates and Lehman Brothers.

[2]Returns, of course, can be measured in a variety of ways, depending on the type of asset. You will recall that we defined returns (R_i) in Chapter 1 as:

$$R_i = \frac{EV - BV + CF}{BV}$$

where EV is ending value, BV is beginning value, and CF is the cash flow during the period.

| Exhibit 7.5 | Time-Series Plot of Monthly Returns for Wilshire 5000 Index, 2004 |

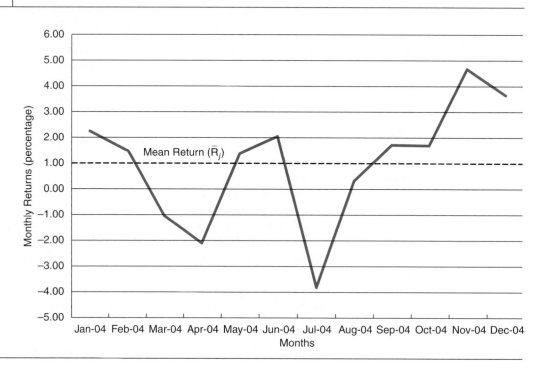

| Exhibit 7.6 | Time-Series Plot of Monthly Returns for Lehman Brothers Treasury Bond Index, 2004 |

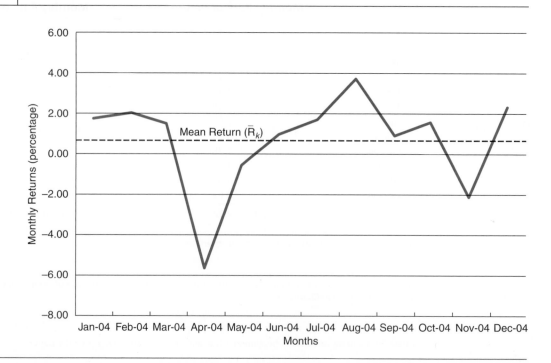

moved in opposite directions. The covariance statistic provides an *absolute* measure of how they moved together over time.

For two assets, i and j, we define the covariance of rates of return as

7.4
$$\text{Cov}_{ij} = E\{[R_i - E(R_i)][R_j - E(R_j)]\}$$

When we apply this formula to the monthly rates of return for the Wilshire 5000 and the Treasury bond indexes during 2004, it becomes

$$\frac{1}{11}\sum_{i=1}^{12}[R_i - \overline{R}_i][R_j - \overline{R}_j]$$

Note that when we apply formula 7.4 to actual sample data, we use the sample mean $(\overline{R})$ as an estimate of the expected return and divide the values by $(n-1)$ rather than by n to avoid statistical bias.

As can be seen, if the rates of return for one asset are above (below) its mean rate of return $(\overline{R})$ during a given period and the returns for the other asset are likewise above (below) its mean rate of return during this same period, then the *product* of these deviations from the mean is positive. If this happens consistently, the covariance of returns between these two assets will be some large positive value. If, however, the rate of return for one of the securities is above its mean return while the return on the other security is below its mean return, the product will be negative. If this contrary movement happens consistently, the covariance between the rates of return for the two assets will be a large negative value.

Exhibit 7.7 contains the monthly rates of return during 2004 for the Wilshire 5000 index and the Lehman Brothers Treasury Bond Index as computed in Exhibit 7.4. One might expect the returns for the two asset indexes to have reasonably low covariance because of the differences in the nature of these assets. The arithmetic mean of the monthly returns were

$$(\overline{R}_i) = \frac{1}{11}\sum_{i=1}^{12}R_{it} = 1.02$$

and

$$(\overline{R}_j) = \frac{1}{11}\sum_{j=1}^{12}R_{jt} = 0.67$$

We rounded all figures to the nearest hundredth of 1 percent, so there may be small rounding errors. The average monthly return was 1.02 percent for the Wilshire 5000 and 0.67 percent for the Treasury bonds. The results in Exhibit 7.7 show that the covariance between the rates of return for these two assets was

$$\text{Cov}_{ij} = \frac{1}{11} \times 7.00$$

$$= 0.637$$

Interpretation of a number such as 0.637 is difficult; is it high or low for covariance? We know the relationship between the two assets is generally positive, but it is not possible to be more specific. Exhibit 7.8 contains a scatterplot with paired values of R_{it} and R_{jt} plotted against each other. This plot demonstrates the linear nature and strength of the relationship. It is not surprising that the relationship during 2004 was not very strong, since during five months the two assets moved counter to each other. As a result, the overall covariance was a small positive value.

Exhibit 7.7 | **Computation of Covariance of Returns for Wilshire 5000 Index and Lehman Brothers Treasury Bond Index, 2004**

Date	WILSHIRE 5000 (R_i)	LEHMAN TREASURY BOND INDEX (R_j)	WILSHIRE 5000 $R_i - \bar{R}_i$	LEHMAN TREASURY BOND INDEX $R_j - \bar{R}_j$	WILSHIRE 5000 $R_i - \bar{R}_i$ $\times$ LEHMAN TREASURY BOND INDEX $R_j - \bar{R}_j$
Jan-04	2.23	1.77	1.21	1.10	1.33
Feb-04	1.46	2.00	0.44	1.34	0.59
Mar-04	−1.07	1.50	−2.09	0.83	−1.74
Apr-04	−2.13	−5.59	−3.15	−6.26	19.73
May-04	1.38	−0.54	0.36	−1.21	−0.43
Jun-04	2.08	0.95	1.06	0.28	0.30
Jul-04	−3.82	1.73	−4.84	1.06	−5.16
Aug-04	0.33	3.74	−0.69	3.07	−2.12
Sep-04	1.78	0.84	0.76	0.17	0.13
Oct-04	1.71	1.51	0.69	0.84	0.58
Nov-04	4.68	−2.19	3.66	−2.86	−10.46
Dec-04	3.63	2.31	2.61	1.64	4.28
Mean =	1.02	0.67			Sum = 7.00

$Cov_{ij} = 7.00/11 = 0.637$

| Exhibit 7.8 | **Scatterplot of Monthly Returns for Wilshire 5000 and Lehman Brothers Treasury Bond Index, 2004** |

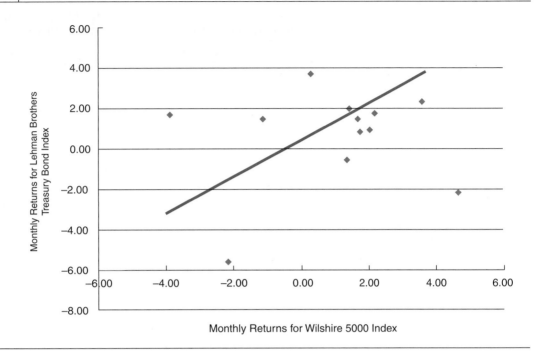

Covariance and Correlation Covariance is affected by the variability of the two individual return indexes. Therefore, a number such as the 0.637 in our example might indicate a weak positive relationship if the two individual indexes were volatile, but would reflect a strong positive relationship if the two indexes were stable. Obviously, we want to standardize this covariance measure. We do so by taking into consideration the variability of the two individual return indexes, as follows:

7.5
$$r_{ij} = \frac{\text{Cov}_{ij}}{\sigma_i \sigma_j}$$

where:

r_{ij} = the correlation coefficient of returns
σ_i = the standard deviation of R_{it}
σ_j = the standard deviation of R_{jt}

Standardizing the covariance by the product of the individual standard deviations yields the **correlation coefficient** r_{ij}, which can vary only in the range −1 to +1. A value of +1 indicates a perfect positive linear relationship between R_i and R_j, meaning the returns for the two assets move together in a completely linear manner. A value of −1 indicates a perfect negative relationship between the two return indexes, so that when one asset's rate of return is above its mean, the other asset's rate of return will be below its mean by a comparable amount.

To calculate this standardized measure of the relationship, we need to compute the standard deviation for the two individual return indexes. We already have the values for $(R_{it} - \overline{R}_i)$ and $(R_{jt} - \overline{R}_j)$ in Exhibit 7.7. We can square each of these values and sum

Exhibit 7.9	Computation of Standard Deviation of Returns for the Wilshire 5000 Index and Lehman Brothers Treasury Bond Index, 2004

| Date | WILSHIRE 5000 INDEX | | LEHMAN BROTHERS TREASURY BONDS | |
	$R_i - \bar{R}_i$	$(R_i - \bar{R}_i)^2$	$R_j - \bar{R}_j$	$(R_j - \bar{R}_j)^2$
Jan-04	1.21	1.46	1.10	1.21
Feb-04	0.44	0.19	1.34	1.79
Mar-04	−2.09	4.38	0.83	0.69
Apr-04	−3.15	9.93	−6.26	39.17
May-04	0.36	0.13	−1.21	1.47
Jun-04	1.06	1.12	0.28	0.08
Jul-04	−4.84	23.44	1.06	1.13
Aug-04	−0.69	0.48	3.07	9.42
Sep-04	0.76	0.58	0.17	0.03
Oct-04	0.69	0.47	0.84	0.70
Nov-04	3.66	13.38	−2.86	8.18
Dec-04	2.61	6.80	1.64	2.69
		Sum = 62.36		Sum = 66.56

Variance$_i$ = 62.36/11 = 5.67   Variance$_j$ = 66.56/11 = 6.05

Standard Deviation$_i$ = $(5.67)^{1/2}$ = 2.38   Standard Deviation$_j$ = $(6.05)^{1/2}$ = 2.46

them as shown in Exhibit 7.9 to calculate the variance of each return series; again, we divide by $(n - 1)$ to avoid statistical bias.

$$\sigma_i^2 = \frac{1}{11} 62.36 = 5.67$$

and

$$\sigma_j^2 = \frac{1}{11} 66.56 = 6.05$$

The standard deviation for each index is the square root of the variance for each, as follows:

$$\sigma_i = \sqrt{5.67} = 2.38$$

$$\sigma_j = \sqrt{6.05} = 2.46$$

Thus, based on the covariance between the two indexes and the individual standard deviations, we can calculate the correlation coefficient between returns for common stocks and Treasury bonds during 2004:

$$r_{ij} = \frac{Cov_{ij}}{\sigma_i \sigma_j} = \frac{0.637}{(2.38)(2.46)} = \frac{0.637}{5.8548} = 0.109$$

Obviously, this formula also implies that

$$Cov_{ij} = r_{ij}\sigma_i\sigma_j = (0.109)(2.38)(2.46) = 0.638$$

Standard Deviation of a Portfolio

As noted, a correlation of $+1.0$ indicates perfect positive correlation, and a value of -1.0 means that the returns moved in completely opposite directions. A value of zero means that the returns had no linear relationship, that is, they were uncorrelated statistically. That does *not* mean that they are independent. The value of $r_{ij} = 0.109$ is not significantly different from zero. This insignificant positive correlation is not unusual for stocks versus bonds during short time intervals such as one year.

Portfolio Standard Deviation Formula   Now that we have discussed the concepts of covariance and correlation, we can consider the formula for computing the standard deviation of returns for a *portfolio* of assets, our measure of risk for a portfolio. In Exhibit 7.2, we showed that the expected rate of return of the portfolio was the weighted average of the expected returns for the individual assets in the portfolio; the weights were the percentage of value of the portfolio. One might assume it is possible to derive the standard deviation of the portfolio in the same manner, that is, by computing the weighted average of the standard deviations for the individual assets. This would be a mistake. Markowitz (1959) derived the general formula for the standard deviation of a portfolio as follows:

7.6
$$\sigma_{\text{port}} = \sqrt{\sum_{i=1}^{n} w_i^2 \sigma_i^2 + \sum_{i=1}^{n}\sum_{\substack{j=1 \\ i \neq j}}^{n} w_i w_j \text{Cov}_{ij}}$$

where

σ_{port} = the standard deviation of the portfolio

w_i = the weights of an individual asset in the portfolio, where weights are determined by the proportion of value in the portfolio

σ_i^2 = the variance of rates of return for asset i

Cov_{ij} = the covariance between the rates of return for assets i and j, where $\text{Cov}_{ij} = r_{ij}\sigma_i\sigma_j$

This formula indicates that the standard deviation for a portfolio of assets is a function of the weighted average of the individual variances (where the weights are squared), *plus* the weighted covariances between all the assets in the portfolio. The very important point is that the standard deviation for a portfolio of assets encompasses not only the variances of the individual assets but *also* includes the covariances between all the pairs of individual assets in the portfolio. Further, it can be shown that, in a portfolio with a large number of securities, this formula reduces to the sum of the weighted covariances.

Impact of a New Security in a Portfolio   Although in most of the following discussion we will consider portfolios with only two assets (because it is possible to show the effect in two dimensions), we will also demonstrate the computations for a three-asset portfolio. Still, it is important at this point to consider what happens in a large portfolio with many assets. Specifically, what happens to the portfolio's standard deviation when we add a new security to such a portfolio? As shown by the formula, we see two effects. The first is the asset's own variance of returns, and the second is the covariance between the returns of this new asset and the returns of *every other asset that is already in the portfolio*. The relative weight of these numerous covariances is substantially greater than the asset's unique variance; the more assets in the portfolio, the more this is true. This means that the important factor to consider when adding an investment to a portfolio that contains a number of other investments is *not* the new security's own variance but *its average covariance with all the other investments in the portfolio*.

Portfolio Standard Deviation Calculation   Because of the assumptions used in developing the Markowitz portfolio model, any asset or portfolio of assets can be described by two characteristics: the expected rate of return and the expected standard deviation of returns. Therefore, the following demonstrations can be applied to two *individual* assets, two *portfolios* of assets, or two *asset classes* with the indicated return–standard deviation characteristics and correlation coefficients.

Equal Risk and Return—Changing Correlations   Consider first the case in which both assets have the same expected return and expected standard deviation of return. As an example, let's assume

$$E(R_1) = 0.20, \quad E(\sigma_1) = 0.10$$
$$E(R_2) = 0.20, \quad E(\sigma_2) = 0.10$$

To show the effect of different covariances, we assume different levels of correlation between the two assets. We also assume that the two assets have equal weights in the portfolio ($w_1 = 0.50$; $w_2 = 0.50$). Therefore, the only value that changes in each example is the correlation between the returns for the two assets.

Now consider the following five correlation coefficients and the covariances they yield. Since $Cov_{ij} = r_{ij}\sigma_i\sigma_j$, the covariance will be equal to $r_{1,2}(0.10)(0.10)$ because the standard deviation of both assets is 0.10.

a. For $r_{1,2} = 1.00$, $Cov_{1,2} = (1.00)(0.10)(0.10) = 0.01$
b. For $r_{1,2} = 0.50$, $Cov_{1,2} = (0.50)(0.10)(0.10) = 0.005$
c. For $r_{1,2} = 0.00$, $Cov_{1,2} = (0.00)(0.10)(0.10) = 0.000$
d. For $r_{1,2} = -0.50$, $Cov_{1,2} = (-0.50)(0.10)(0.10) = -0.005$
e. For $r_{1,2} = -1.00$, $Cov_{1,2} = (-1.00)(0.10)(0.10) = -0.01$

Now let's see what happens to the standard deviation of the portfolio under these five conditions.

When we apply the general portfolio formula from equation 7.6 to a two-asset portfolio, it is

7.7 $$\sigma_{port} = \sqrt{w_1^2\sigma_1^2 + w_2^2\sigma_2^2 + 2w_1w_2r_{1,2}\sigma_1\sigma_2}$$

or

$$\sigma_{port} = \sqrt{w_1^2\sigma_1^2 + w_2^2\sigma_2^2 + 2w_1w_2Cov_{1,2}}$$

Thus, in Case a:

$$\sigma_{port(a)} = \sqrt{(0.5)^2(0.10)^2 + (0.5)^2(0.10)^2 + 2(0.5)(0.5)(0.01)}$$
$$= \sqrt{(0.25)(0.01) + (0.25)(0.01) + 2(0.25)(0.01)}$$
$$= \sqrt{0.01}$$
$$= 0.10$$

In this case, where the returns for the two assets are perfectly positively correlated, the standard deviation for the portfolio is, in fact, the weighted average of the individual standard deviations. The important point is that we get no real benefit from combining two assets that are perfectly correlated; they are like one asset already because their returns move together.

Now consider Case b, where $r_{1,2}$ equals 0.50.

$$\sigma_{port(b)} = \sqrt{(0.5)^2(0.10)^2 + (0.5)^2(0.10)^2 + 2(0.5)(0.5)(0.005)}$$
$$= \sqrt{(0.0025) + (0.0025) + 2(0.25)(0.005)}$$
$$= \sqrt{0.0075}$$
$$= 0.0866$$

Exhibit 7.10	Time Patterns of Returns for Two Assets with Perfect Negative Correlation

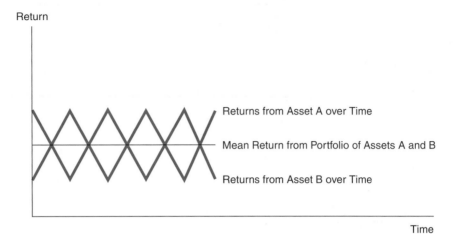

The only term that changed from Case a is the last term, $Cov_{1,2}$, which changed from 0.01 to 0.005. As a result, the standard deviation of the portfolio declined by about 13 percent, from 0.10 to 0.0866. Note that *the expected return of the portfolio did not change* because it is simply the weighted average of the individual expected returns; it is equal to 0.20 in both cases.

You should be able to confirm through your own calculations that the standard deviations for Portfolios c and d are as follows:

c. 0.0707
d. 0.05

The final case, where the correlation between the two assets is -1.00, indicates the ultimate benefits of diversification.

$$\sigma_{port(e)} = \sqrt{(0.5)^2(0.10)^2 + (0.5)^2(0.10)^2 + 2(0.5)(0.5)(-0.01)}$$

$$= \sqrt{(0.0050) + (-0.0050)}$$

$$= \sqrt{0}$$

$$= 0$$

Here, the negative covariance term exactly offsets the individual variance terms, leaving an overall standard deviation of the portfolio of zero. *This would be a risk-free portfolio.*

Exhibit 7.10 illustrates a graph of such a pattern. Perfect negative correlation gives a mean combined return for the two securities over time equal to the mean for each of them, so the returns for the portfolio show no variability. Any returns above and below the mean for each of the assets are *completely offset* by the return for the other asset, so there is *no variability* in total returns—that is, *no risk*—for the portfolio. Thus, a pair of completely negatively correlated assets provides the maximum benefits of diversification by completely eliminating risk.

The graph in Exhibit 7.11 shows the difference in the risk–return posture for our five cases. As noted, the only effect of the change in correlation is the change in the standard deviation of

Exhibit 7.11 | **Risk–Return Plot for Portfolios with Equal Returns and Standard Deviations but Different Correlations**

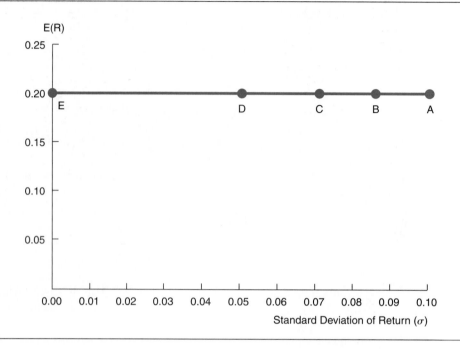

this two-asset portfolio. Combining assets that are not perfectly correlated does *not* affect the expected return of the portfolio, but it *does* reduce the risk of the portfolio (as measured by its standard deviation). When we eventually reach the ultimate combination of perfect negative correlation, risk is eliminated.

Combining Stocks with Different Returns and Risk   We have seen what happens when only the correlation coefficient (covariance) differs between the assets. We now consider two assets (or portfolios) with different expected rates of return and individual standard deviations.[3] We will show what happens when we vary the correlations between them. We will assume two assets with the following characteristics.

Asset	$E(R_i)$	w_i	σ_i^2	σ_i
1	0.10	0.50	0.0049	0.07
2	0.20	0.50	0.0100	0.10

We will use the previous set of correlation coefficients, but we must recalculate the covariances because this time the standard deviations of the assets are different. The results are shown in the following table.

---

[3]As noted, these could be two asset classes. For example, Asset 1 could be low risk–low return bonds and Asset 2 could be higher return–higher risk stocks.

Case	Correlation Coefficient ($r_{1,2}$)	Covariance ($r_{1,2}\sigma_1\sigma_2$)
a	+1.00	0.0070
b	+0.50	0.0035
c	0.00	0.0000
d	−0.50	−0.0035
e	−1.00	−0.0070

Because we are assuming the same weights in all cases (0.50 − 0.50), the expected return in every instance will be

$$E(R_{port}) = 0.50\,(0.10) + 0.50\,(0.20)$$
$$= 0.15$$

The portfolio standard deviation for Case a will be

$$\sigma_{port(a)} = \sqrt{(0.5)^2(0.07)^2 + (0.5)^2(0.10)^2 + 2(0.5)(0.5)(0.0070)}$$

$$= \sqrt{0.007225}$$

$$= 0.085$$

Again, with perfect positive correlation, the portfolio standard deviation is the weighted average of the standard deviations of the individual assets:

$$(0.5)\,(0.07) + (0.5)\,(0.10) = 0.085$$

As you might envision, changing the weights with perfect positive correlation causes the portfolio standard deviation to change in a linear fashion. This will be an important point to remember when we discuss the capital asset pricing model (CAPM) in the next chapter.

For Cases b, c, d, and e, the portfolio standard deviations are as follows:[4]

$$\sigma_{port(b)} = \sqrt{(0.001225) + (0.0025) + (0.5)(0.0035)}$$

$$= \sqrt{0.005475}$$

$$= 0.07399$$

$$\sigma_{port(c)} = \sqrt{(0.001225) + (0.0025) + (0.5)(0.00)}$$

$$= 0.0610$$

$$\sigma_{port(d)} = \sqrt{(0.001225) + (0.0025) + (0.5)(-0.0035)}$$

$$= 0.0444$$

$$\sigma_{port(e)} = \sqrt{(0.003725) + (0.5)(-0.0070)}$$

$$= 0.015$$

---

[4]In all the following examples, we will skip some steps because you are now aware that only the last term changes. You are encouraged to work out the individual steps to ensure that you understand the computational procedure.

Exhibit 7.12	Risk–Return Plot for Portfolios with Different Returns, Standard Deviations, and Correlations

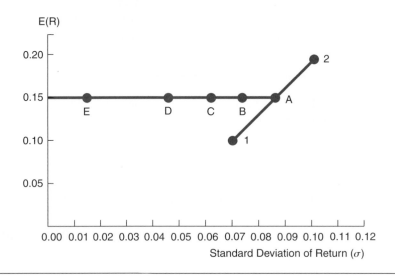

Note that, in this example, with perfect negative correlation the portfolio standard deviation is not zero. This is because the different examples have equal weights, but the asset standard deviations are not equal.[5]

Exhibit 7.12 shows the results for the two individual assets and the portfolio of the two assets assuming the correlation coefficients vary as set forth in Cases a through e. As before, the expected return does not change because the proportions are always set at 0.50–0.50, so all the portfolios lie along the horizontal line at the return, R = 0.15.

Constant Correlation with Changing Weights   If we changed the weights of the two assets while holding the correlation coefficient constant, we would derive a set of combinations that trace an ellipse starting at Asset 2, going through the 0.50–0.50 point, and ending at Asset 1. We can demonstrate this with Case c, in which the correlation coefficient of zero eases the computations. We begin with 100 percent in Asset 2 (Case f) and change the weights as follows, ending with 100 percent in Asset 1 (Case l):

Case	w_1	w_2	$E(R_i)$
f	0.00	1.00	0.20
g	0.20	0.80	0.18
h	0.40	0.60	0.16
i	0.50	0.50	0.15
j	0.60	0.40	0.14
k	0.80	0.20	0.12
l	1.00	0.00	0.10

---

[5]The two appendixes to this chapter show proofs for equal weights with equal variances and solve for the appropriate weights to get zero standard deviation when standard deviations are not equal.

We already know the standard deviation (σ) for portfolio (i). In Cases f, g, h, j, k, and l, the standard deviations are[6]

$$\sigma_{\text{port(g)}} = \sqrt{(0.20)^2 (0.07)^2 + (0.80)^2 (0.10)^2 + 2 (0.20) (0.80) (0.00)}$$

$$= \sqrt{(0.04) (0.0049) + (0.64) (0.01) + (0)}$$

$$= \sqrt{0.006596}$$

$$= 0.0812$$

$$\sigma_{\text{port(h)}} = \sqrt{(0.40)^2 (0.07)^2 + (0.60)^2 (0.10)^2 + 2 (0.40) (0.60) (0.00)}$$

$$= \sqrt{0.004384}$$

$$= 0.0662$$

$$\sigma_{\text{port(j)}} = \sqrt{(0.60)^2 (0.07)^2 + (0.40)^2 (0.10)^2 + 2 (0.60) (0.40) (0.00)}$$

$$= \sqrt{0.003364}$$

$$= 0.0580$$

$$\sigma_{\text{port(k)}} = \sqrt{(0.80)^2 (0.07)^2 + (0.20)^2 (0.10)^2 + 2 (0.80) (0.20) (0.00)}$$

$$= \sqrt{0.003536}$$

$$= 0.0595$$

The various weights with a constant correlation yield the following risk–return combinations.

Case	w_1	w_2	$E(R_i)$	$E(\sigma_{\text{port}})$
f	0.00	1.00	0.20	0.1000
g	0.20	0.80	0.18	0.0812
h	0.40	0.60	0.16	0.0662
i	0.50	0.50	0.15	0.0610
j	0.60	0.40	0.14	0.0580
k	0.80	0.20	0.12	0.0595
l	1.00	0.00	0.10	0.0700

A graph of these combinations appears in Exhibit 7.13. We could derive a complete curve by simply varying the weighting by smaller increments.

A notable result is that with low, zero, or negative correlations, it is possible to derive portfolios that have *lower risk than either single asset.* In our set of examples where $r_{ij} = 0.00$, this occurs in Cases h, i, j, and k. This ability to reduce risk is the essence of diversification.

---

[6]Again, you are encouraged to fill in the steps we skipped in the computations.

Exhibit 7.13 | **Portfolio Risk–Return Plots for Different Weights When $r_{i,j} = +1.00; +0.50; 0.00; -0.50; -1.00$**

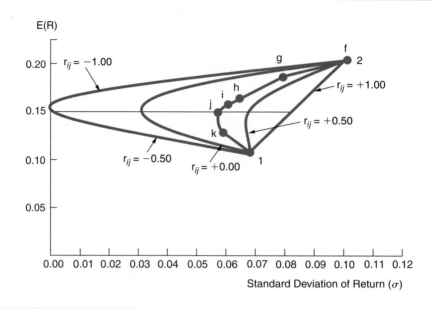

As shown in Exhibit 7.13, assuming the normal risk–return relationship where assets with higher risk (larger standard deviation of returns) provide high rates of return, it is possible for a conservative investor to experience *both* lower risk *and* higher return by diversifying into a higher risk–higher return asset, assuming that the correlation between the two assets is fairly low. Exhibit 7.13 shows that, in the case where we used the correlation of zero (0.00), the low-risk investor at Point 1—who would receive a return of 10 percent and risk of 7 percent—could *increase* the return to 14 percent *and* experience a *decline* in risk to 5.8 percent by investing (diversifying) 40 percent of the portfolio in riskier Asset 2. As noted, the benefits of diversification are critically dependent on the correlation between assets. The exhibit shows that there is even some benefit when the correlation is 0.50 rather than zero.

Exhibit 7.13 also shows that the curvature in the graph depends on the correlation between the two assets or portfolios. With $r_{ij} = +1.00$, the combinations lie along a straight line between the two assets. When $r_{ij} = 0.50$, the curve is to the right of the $r_{ij} = 0.00$ curve; when $r_{ij} = -0.50$, it is to the left. Finally, when $r_{ij} = -1.00$, the graph would be two straight lines that would touch at the vertical line (zero risk) with some combination. It is possible to solve for the specified set of weights that would give a portfolio with zero risk. In this case, it is $w_1 = 0.412$ and $w_2 = 0.588$.

A Three-Asset Portfolio

A demonstration of what occurs with a three-asset portfolio is useful because it shows the dynamics of the portfolio process when assets are added. It also shows the rapid growth in the computations required, which is why we will stop at three!

In this example, we will combine three asset classes we have been discussing: stocks, bonds, and cash equivalents.[7] We will assume the following characteristics:

Asset Classes	$E(R_i)$	$E(\sigma_i)$	w_i
Stocks (S)	0.12	0.20	0.60
Bonds (B)	0.08	0.10	0.30
Cash equivalent (C)	0.04	0.03	0.10

The correlations are

$$r_{S,B} = 0.25; \; r_{S,C} = -0.08; \; r_{B,C} = 0.15$$

Given the weights specified, the $E(R_{port})$ is

$$E(R_{port}) = (0.60)(0.12) + (0.30)(0.08) + (0.10)(0.04)$$

$$= (0.072 + 0.024 + 0.004) = 0.100 = 10.00\%$$

When we apply the generalized formula from equation 7.6 to the expected standard deviation of a three-asset portfolio, it is

7.8
$$\sigma_{port}^2 = (w_S^2\sigma_S^2 + w_B^2\sigma_B^2 + w_C^2\sigma_C^2)$$
$$+ (2w_Sw_B\sigma_S\sigma_Br_{S,B} + 2w_Sw_C\sigma_S\sigma_Cr_{S,C} + 2w_Bw_C\sigma_B\sigma_Cr_{B,C})$$

From the characteristics specified, the standard deviation of this three-asset-class portfolio (σ_{port}) would be

$$\sigma_{port}^2 = [(0.6)^2(0.20)^2 + (0.3)^2(0.10)^2 + (0.1)^2(0.03)^2]$$
$$+ \{[2(0.6)(0.3)(0.20)(0.10)(0.25)] + [2(0.6)(0.1)(0.20)(0.03)(-0.08)]$$
$$+ [2(0.3)(0.1)(0.10)(0.03)(0.15)]\}$$
$$= [0.015309 + (0.0018) + (-0.0000576) + (0.000027)]$$
$$= 0.0170784$$

$$\sigma_{port} = (0.0170784)^{1/2} = 0.1306 = 13.06\%$$

Estimation Issues

It is important to keep in mind that the results of this portfolio asset allocation depend on the accuracy of the statistical inputs. In the current instance, this means that for every asset (or asset class) being considered for inclusion in the portfolio, we must estimate its expected returns and standard deviation. We must also estimate the correlation coefficient among the entire set of assets. The number of correlation estimates can be significant—for example, for a portfolio of 100 securities, the number is 4,950 (that is, 99 + 98 + 97 +...). The potential source of error that arises from these approximations is referred to as *estimation risk.*

---

[7]The asset allocation articles regularly contained in the *Wall Street Journal* generally refer to these three asset classes.

We can reduce the number of correlation coefficients that must be estimated by assuming that stock returns can be described by the relationship of each stock to a market index—that is, a single index market model, as follows:

7.9 $R_i = a_i + b_iR_m + \varepsilon_i$

where:

b_i = the slope coefficient that relates the returns for Security i to the returns for the aggregate stock market

R_m = the returns for the aggregate stock market

If all the securities are similarly related to the market and a slope coefficient b_i is derived for each one, it can be shown that the correlation coefficient between two Securities i and j is

7.10 $r_{ij} = b_ib_j\dfrac{\sigma_m^2}{\sigma_i\sigma_j}$

where:

σ_m^2 = the variance of returns for the aggregate stock market

This reduces the number of estimates from 4,950 to 100—that is, once we have derived a slope estimate b_i for each security, we can compute the correlation estimates. Keep in mind that this assumes that the single index market model provides a good estimate of security returns.

The Efficient Frontier

If we examined different two-asset combinations and derived the curves assuming all the possible weights, we would have a graph like that in Exhibit 7.14. The envelope curve that contains the best of all these possible combinations is referred to as the **efficient frontier**. Specifically, the efficient frontier represents that set of portfolios that has the maximum rate of return for every given level of risk or the minimum risk for every level of return. An example of such a frontier is

Exhibit 7.14	**Numerous Portfolio Combinations of Available Assets**

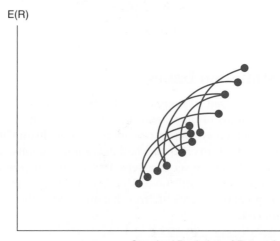

Standard Deviation of Return (σ)

Exhibit 7.15	**Efficient Frontier for Alternative Portfolios**

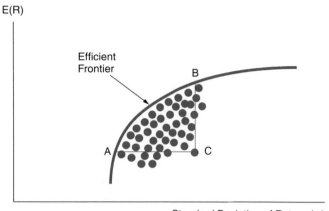

shown in Exhibit 7.15. Every portfolio that lies on the efficient frontier has either a higher rate of return for equal risk or lower risk for an equal rate of return than some portfolio beneath the frontier. Thus, we would say that Portfolio A in Exhibit 7.15 *dominates* Portfolio C because it has an equal rate of return but substantially less risk. Similarly, Portfolio B dominates Portfolio C because it has equal risk but a higher expected rate of return. Because of the benefits of diversification among imperfectly correlated assets, we would expect the efficient frontier to be made up of *portfolios* of investments rather than individual securities. Two possible exceptions arise at the end points, which represent the asset with the highest return and the asset with the lowest risk.

As an investor, you will target a point along the efficient frontier based on your *utility function,* which reflects your attitude toward risk. No portfolio on the efficient frontier can dominate any other portfolio on the efficient frontier. All of these portfolios have different return and risk measures, with expected rates of return that increase with higher risk.

The Efficient Frontier and Investor Utility

The curve in Exhibit 7.15 shows that the slope of the efficient frontier curve decreases steadily as we move upward. This implies that adding equal increments of risk as we move up the efficient frontier gives diminishing increments of expected return. To evaluate this situation, we calculate the slope of the efficient frontier as follows:

7.11
$$\frac{\Delta E(R_{port})}{\Delta E(\sigma_{port})}$$

An individual investor's utility curves specify the trade-offs he or she is willing to make between expected return and risk. In conjunction with the efficient frontier, these utility curves determine which *particular* portfolio on the efficient frontier best suits an individual investor. Two investors will choose the same portfolio from the efficient set only if their utility curves are identical.

Exhibit 7.16 shows two sets of utility curves along with an efficient frontier of investments. The curves labeled U_1, U_2, and U_3 are for a strongly risk-averse investor. These utility curves are quite steep, indicating that the investor will not tolerate much additional risk to obtain additional returns. The investor is equally disposed toward any E(R), E(σ) combinations along the specific utility curve U_1.

Exhibit 7.16 | **Selecting an Optimal Risky Portfolio**

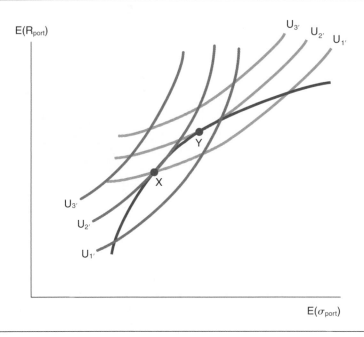

The curves labeled ($U_{3'}$, $U_{2'}$, $U_{1'}$) characterize a less risk-averse investor. Such an investor is willing to tolerate a bit more risk to get a higher expected return.

The **optimal portfolio** is the efficient portfolio that has the highest utility for a given investor. It lies at the point of tangency between the efficient frontier and the U_1 curve with the highest possible utility. A conservative investor's highest utility is at Point X in Exhibit 7.16, where the U_2 curve just touches the efficient frontier. A less risk-averse investor's highest utility occurs at Point Y, which represents a portfolio on the efficient frontier with higher expected returns and higher risk than the portfolio at X.

money managers. Items on the home page include links to news of interest to managers, and ePIPER performance data on a number of equity, fixed income, real estate, and global portfolios from money manager and pension funds. Contains many links to organizations such as central banks, consultants, and sellers of investment-related products.

http://www.investmentnews.com *Investment News* is a sister publication to *Pensions and Investments*, with a focus toward the financial advisor. This site includes information on financial planning, the mutual fund industry, regulation, equity performance, and industry trends.

Software for creating efficient frontiers is available from firms such as Ibbotson Associates (**http://www.ibbotson.com**), Zephyr Associates (**http://www.styleadvisor.com**), Wagner Associates (**http://www.wagner.com**), and Efficient Solutions, Inc. (**http://www.effisols.com**).

William J. Bernstein's Web site, **http://www.efficientfrontier.com**, offers articles from his web-zine, *Efficient Frontier*, an online journal of practical asset allocation.

SUMMARY

- The basic Markowitz portfolio model derives the expected rate of return for a portfolio of assets and a measure of expected risk, which is the standard deviation of expected rate of return. Markowitz showed that the expected rate of return of a portfolio is the weighted average of the expected return for the individual investments in the portfolio. The standard deviation of a portfolio is a function not only of the standard deviations for the individual investments but *also* of the covariance between the rates of return for all the pairs of assets in the portfolio. In a large portfolio, these covariances are the important factors.

- Different weights or amounts of a portfolio held in various assets yield a curve of potential combinations. Correlation coefficients among assets are the critical factor to consider when selecting investments. Investors can maintain their rate of return while reducing the risk level of their portfolio by combining assets or portfolios that have low-positive or negative correlation.

- Assuming numerous assets and a multitude of combination curves, the efficient frontier is the envelope curve that encompasses all of the best combinations. It defines the set

of portfolios that has the highest expected return for each given level of risk or the minimum risk for each given level of return. From this set of dominant portfolios, investors select the one that lies at the point of tangency between the efficient frontier and their highest utility curve. Because risk–return utility functions differ, the point of tangency and, therefore, the portfolio choice will differ among investors.

At this point, you understand that an optimum portfolio is a combination of investments, each having desirable individual risk–return characteristics that also fit together based on their correlations. This deeper understanding of portfolio theory should lead you to reflect back on our earlier discussion of global investing. Because many foreign stock and bond investments provide superior rates of return compared with U.S. securities *and* have low correlations with portfolios of U.S. stocks and bonds (as shown in Chapter 3), including these foreign securities in your portfolio will help you to reduce the overall risk of your portfolio while possibly increasing your rate of return.

SUGGESTED READINGS

CFA Institute, *Managing Investment Portfolios: A Dynamic Process*, 3rd ed. Charlottesville, VA: CFA Institute, 2005.

Elton, Edwin J., Martin J. Gruber, Stephen J. Brown, and William N. Goetzmann. *Modern Portfolio Theory and Investment Analysis*, 6th ed. New York: Wiley, 2003.

Farrell, James L., Jr. *Portfolio Management: Theory and Application*, 2nd ed. New York: McGraw-Hill, 1997.

QUESTIONS

1. Why do most investors hold diversified portfolios?
2. What is covariance, and why is it important in portfolio theory?
3. Why do most assets of the same type show positive covariances of returns with each other? Would you expect positive covariances of returns between *different* types of assets such as returns on Treasury bills, General Electric common stock, and commercial real estate? Why or why not?
4. What is the relationship between covariance and the correlation coefficient?
5. Explain the shape of the efficient frontier.
6. Draw a properly labeled graph of the Markowitz efficient frontier. Describe the efficient frontier in exact terms. Discuss the concept of dominant portfolios, and show an example of one on your graph.
7. Assume you want to run a computer program to derive the efficient frontier for your feasible set of stocks. What information must you input to the program?
8. Why are investors' utility curves important in portfolio theory?
9. Explain how a given investor chooses an optimal portfolio. Will this choice always be a diversified portfolio, or could it be a single asset? Explain your answer.
10. Assume that you and a business associate develop an efficient frontier for a set of investments. Why might the two of you select different portfolios on the frontier?
11. Draw a hypothetical graph of an efficient frontier of U.S. common stocks. On the same graph, draw an efficient frontier assuming the inclusion of U.S. bonds as well. Finally, on the same graph, draw an efficient frontier that includes U.S. common stocks, U.S. bonds, and stocks and bonds from around the world. Discuss the differences in these frontiers.
12. Stocks K, L, and M each have the same expected return and standard deviation. The correlation coefficients between each pair of these stocks are:

$$K \text{ and } L \text{ correlation coefficient} = +0.8$$
$$K \text{ and } M \text{ correlation coefficient} = +0.2$$
$$L \text{ and } M \text{ correlation coefficient} = -0.4$$

Given these correlations, a portfolio constructed of which pair of stocks will have the lowest standard deviation? Explain.

 13. *CFA Examination Level II*
A three-asset portfolio has the following characteristics.

Asset	Expected Return	Expected Standard Deviation	Weight
X	0.15	0.22	0.50
Y	0.10	0.08	0.40
Z	0.06	0.03	0.10

The expected return on this three-asset portfolio is
a. 10.3%.
b. 11.0%.
c. 12.1%.
d. 14.8%. (2 minutes)

14. *CFA Examination Level II*
An investor is considering adding another investment to a portfolio. To achieve the maximum diversification benefits, the investor should add, if possible, an investment that has which of the following correlation coefficients with the other investments in the portfolio?
a. −1.0
b. −0.5
c. 0.0
d. +1.0 (1 minute)

PROBLEMS

1. Considering the world economic outlook for the coming year and estimates of sales and earning for the pharmaceutical industry, you expect the rate of return for Lauren Labs common stock to range between −20 percent and +40 percent with the following probabilities.

Probability	Possible Returns
0.10	−0.20
0.15	−0.05
0.20	0.10
0.25	0.15
0.20	0.20
0.10	0.40

   Compute the expected rate of return $E(R_i)$ for Lauren Labs.

2. Given the following market values of stocks in your portfolio and their expected rates of return, what is the expected rate of return for your common stock portfolio?

Stock	Market Value ($ Mil.)	$E(R_i)$
Phillips Petroleum	$15,000	0.14
Starbucks	17,000	−0.04
International Paper	32,000	0.18
Intel	23,000	0.16
Walgreens	7,000	0.12

3. The following are the monthly rates of return for Madison Corp. and for Sophie Electric during a six-month period.

Month	Madison Corp.	Sophie Electric
1	−0.04	0.07
2	0.06	−0.02
3	−0.07	−0.10
4	0.12	0.15
5	−0.02	−0.06
6	0.05	0.02

   Compute the following.
   a. Average monthly rate of return $\overline{R}_i$ for each stock
   b. Standard deviation of returns for each stock
   c. Covariance between the rates of return
   d. The correlation coefficient between the rates of return
   What level of correlation did you expect? How did your expectations compare with the computed correlation? Would these two stocks offer a good chance for diversification? Why or why not?

4. You are considering two assets with the following characteristics.
   $E(R_1) = 0.15 \quad E(\sigma_1) = 0.10 \quad w_1 = 0.5$
   $E(R_2) = 0.20 \quad E(\sigma_2) = 0.20 \quad w_2 = 0.5$

Compute the mean and standard deviation of two portfolios if $r_{1,2} = 0.40$ and -0.60, respectively. Plot the two portfolios on a risk–return graph and briefly explain the results.

5. Given:
$$E(R_1) = 0.10$$
$$E(R_2) = 0.15$$
$$E(\sigma_1) = 0.03$$
$$E(\sigma_2) = 0.05$$

Calculate the expected returns and expected standard deviations of a two-stock portfolio in which Stock 1 has a weight of 60 percent under the following conditions.

a. $r_{1,2} = 1.00$
b. $r_{1,2} = 0.75$
c. $r_{1,2} = 0.25$
d. $r_{1,2} = 0.00$
e. $r_{1,2} = -0.25$
f. $r_{1,2} = -0.75$
g. $r_{1,2} = -1.00$

6. Given:
$$E(R_1) = 0.12$$
$$E(R_2) = 0.16$$
$$E(\sigma_1) = 0.04$$
$$E(\sigma_2) = 0.06$$

Calculate the expected returns and expected standard deviations of a two-stock portfolio having a correlation coefficient of 0.70 under the following conditions.

a. $w_1 = 1.00$
b. $w_1 = 0.75$
c. $w_1 = 0.50$
d. $w_1 = 0.25$
e. $w_1 = 0.05$

Plot the results on a return–risk graph. Without calculations, draw in what the curve would look like first if the correlation coefficient had been 0.00 and then if it had been –0.70.

7. The following are monthly percentage price changes for four market indexes.

Month	DJIA	S&P 500	Russell 2000	Nikkei
1	0.03	0.02	0.04	0.04
2	0.07	0.06	0.10	-0.02
3	-0.02	-0.01	-0.04	0.07
4	0.01	0.03	0.03	0.02
5	0.05	0.04	0.11	0.02
6	-0.06	-0.04	-0.08	0.06

Compute the following.
a. Average monthly rate of return for each index
b. Standard deviation for each index
c. Covariance between the rates of return for the following indexes:
   DJIA–S&P 500
   S&P 500–Russell 2000
   S&P 500–Nikkei
   Russell 2000–Nikkei
d. The correlation coefficients for the same four combinations
e. Using the answers from parts (a), (b), and (d), calculate the expected return and standard deviation of a portfolio consisting of equal parts of (1) the S&P and the Russell 2000 and (2) the S&P and the Nikkei. Discuss the two portfolios.

8. The standard deviation of Shamrock Corp. stock is 19 percent. The standard deviation of Sophie Co. stock is 14 percent. The covariance between these two stocks is 100. What is the correlation between Shamrock and Sophie stock?

THOMSON ONE | Business School Edition

1. Collect daily price data for the past 30 trading days and compute the daily price returns for each: Avon Products, Inc. (AVP), Best Buy Inc. (BBY), and Cisco Systems (CSCO).
2. Compute the mean daily return for each stock and the standard deviation of daily returns.
3. Compute the covariance and correlations between the three possible pairs.
4. Assuming equal weight between each pair of stocks, compute the mean daily return and the standard deviation of each of the three portfolios.
5. Create a risk–return scatterplot and enter the average daily return (vertical axis) and standard deviation (horizontal axis) for the three individual stocks and the three portfolios. Briefly discuss the results based on the material in this chapter.

APPENDIX
Chapter 7

A. Proof That Minimum Portfolio Variance Occurs with Equal Weights When Securities Have Equal Variance

When $\sigma_1 = \sigma_2$, we have:

$$\sigma_{port}^2 = w_1^2(\sigma_1)^2 + (1 - w_1)^2(\sigma_1)^2 - 2w_1(1 - w_1)r_{1,2}(\sigma_1)^2$$

$$= (\sigma_1)^2[w_1^2 + 1 - 2w_1 + w_1^2 + 2w_1r_{1,2} - 2w_1^2r_{1,2}]$$

$$= (\sigma_1)^2[2w_1^2 + 1 - 2w_1 + 2w_1r_{1,2} - 2w_1^2r_{1,2}]$$

For this to be a minimum,

$$\frac{\partial(\sigma_{port}^2)}{\partial w_1} = 0 = (\sigma_1)^2[4w_1 \times 2 + 2r_{1,2} \times 4w_1r_{1,2}]$$

Assuming $(\sigma_1)^2 > 0$,

$$4w_1 - 2 + 2r_{1,2} - 4w_1r_{1,2} = 0$$

$$4w_1(1 - r_{1,2}) - 2(1 - r_{1,2}) = 0$$

from which

$$w_1\frac{2(1 - r_{1,2})}{4(1 - r_{1,2})} = \frac{1}{2}$$

regardless of $r_{1,2}$. Thus, if $\sigma_1 = \sigma_2$, σ_{port}^2 will *always* be minimized by choosing $w_1 = w_2 = 1/2$, regardless of the value of $r_{1,2}$, except when $r_{1,2} = +1$ (in which case $\sigma_{port} = \sigma_1 = \sigma_2$). This can be verified by checking the second-order condition

$$\frac{\partial(\sigma_{port}^2)}{\partial w_1^2} > 0$$

Problems

1. The following information applies to Questions 1a and 1b. The general equation for the weight of the first security to achieve minimum variance (in a two-stock portfolio) is given by

$$w_1 = \frac{(\sigma_2)^2 - r_{1,2}(\sigma_1)(\sigma_2)}{(\sigma_1)^2 + (\sigma_2)^2 - 2r_{1,2}(\sigma_1)(\sigma_2)}$$

1a. Show that $w_1 = 0.5$ when $\sigma_1 = \sigma_2$.

1b. What is the weight of Security 1 that gives minimum portfolio variance when $r_{1,2} = 0.5$, $\sigma_1 = 0.04$, and $\sigma_2 = 0.06$?

B. Derivation of Weights That Will Give Zero Variance When Correlation Equals –1.00

$$\sigma_{port}^2 = w_1^2(\sigma_1)^2 + (1 - w_1)^2(\sigma_2)^2 + 2w_1(1 - w_1)r_{1,2}(\sigma_1)(\sigma_2)$$

$$= w_1^2(\sigma_1)^2 + (\sigma_2)^2 - 2w_1(\sigma_2) - w_1^2(\sigma_2)^2 + 2w_1 r_{1,2}(\sigma_1)(\sigma_2) - 2w_1^2 r_{1,2}(\sigma_1)(\sigma_2)$$

If $r_{1,2} = 1$, this can be rearranged and expressed as

$$\sigma_{port}^2 = w_1^2[(\sigma_1)^2 + 2(\sigma_1)(\sigma_2) + (\sigma_2)^2] - 2w[(\sigma_2)^2 + (\sigma_1)(\sigma_2)] + (\sigma_2)^2$$

$$= w_1^2[(\sigma_1) + (\sigma_2)]^2 - 2w_1(\sigma_2)[(\sigma_1) - (\sigma_2)] + (\sigma_2)^2$$

$$= \{w_1[(\sigma_1) + (\sigma_2)] - (\sigma_2)^2\}$$

We want to find the weight, w_1, which will reduce (σ_{port}^2) to *zero;* therefore,

$$w_1[(\sigma_1) + (\sigma_2)] - (\sigma_2) = 0$$

which yields

$$w_1 = \frac{(\sigma_2)}{(\sigma_1) + (\sigma_2)}, \text{ and } w_2 = 1 - w_1 = \frac{(\sigma_1)}{(\sigma_1) + (\sigma_2)}$$

Problem

1. Given two assets with the following characteristics:

$$E(R_1) = .12 \qquad \sigma_1 = .04$$
$$E(R_2) = .16 \qquad \sigma_2 = .06$$

Assume that $r_{1,2} = -1.00$. What is the weight that would yield a zero variance for the portfolio?

Chapter 8

An Introduction to Asset Pricing Models

After you read this chapter, you should be able to answer the following questions:

- What are the assumptions of the capital asset pricing model?
- What is a risk-free asset and what are its risk–return characteristics?
- What is the covariance and correlation between the risk-free asset and a risky asset or port-folio of risky assets?
- What is the expected return when you combine the risk-free asset and a portfolio of risky assets?
- What is the standard deviation when you combine the risk-free asset and a portfolio of risky assets?
- When you combine the risk-free asset and a portfolio of risky assets on the Markowitz efficient frontier, what does the set of possible portfolios look like?
- Given the initial set of portfolio possibilities with a risk-free asset, what happens when you add financial leverage (that is, borrow)?
- What is the market portfolio, what assets are included in this portfolio, and what are the relative weights for the alternative assets included?
- What is the capital market line (CML)?
- What do we mean by complete diversification?
- How do we measure diversification for an individual portfolio?
- What are systematic and unsystematic risk?
- Given the CML, what is the separation theorem?
- Given the CML, what is the relevant risk measure for an individual risky asset?
- What is the security market line (SML), and how does it differ from the CML?
- What is *beta*, and why is it referred to as a standardized measure of systematic risk?
- How can you use the SML to determine the expected (required) rate of return for a risky asset?
- Using the SML, what do we mean by an undervalued and overvalued security, and how do we determine whether an asset is undervalued or overvalued?
- What is an asset's characteristic line, and how do you compute the characteristic line for an asset?

- What is the impact on the characteristic line when you compute it using different return intervals (such as weekly versus monthly) and when you employ different proxies (that is, benchmarks) for the market portfolio (for example, the S&P 500 versus a global stock index)?
- What happens to the capital market line (CML) when you assume there are differences in the risk-free borrowing and lending rates?
- What is a zero-beta asset and how does its use impact the CML?
- What happens to the security line (SML) when you assume transaction costs, heterogeneous expectations, different planning periods, and taxes?
- What are the major questions considered when empirically testing the CAPM?
- What are the empirical results from tests that examine the stability of beta?
- How do alternative published estimates of beta compare?
- What are the results of studies that examine the relationship between systematic risk and return?
- What other variables besides beta have had a significant impact on returns?
- What is the theory regarding the "market portfolio" and how does this differ from the market proxy used for the market portfolio?
- Assuming there is a benchmark problem, what variables are affected by it?

Following the development of portfolio theory by Markowitz, two major theories have been put forth that derive a model for the valuation of risky assets. In this chapter, we introduce one of these two models—that is, the capital asset pricing model (CAPM). The background on the CAPM is important at this point in the book because the risk measure implied by this model is a necessary input for our subsequent discussion on the valuation of risky assets. The presentation concerns capital market theory and the capital asset pricing model that was developed almost concurrently by three individuals. Subsequently, an alternative multifactor asset valuation model was proposed, the arbitrage pricing theory (APT). This has led to the development of numerous other multifactor models that are the subject of the following chapter.

CAPITAL MARKET THEORY: AN OVERVIEW

Because capital market theory builds on portfolio theory, this chapter begins where the discussion of the Markowitz efficient frontier ended. We assume that you have examined the set of risky assets and derived the aggregate efficient frontier. Further, we assume that you and all other investors want to maximize your utility in terms of risk and return, so you will choose portfolios of risky assets on the efficient frontier at points where your utility maps are tangent to the frontier as shown in Exhibit 7.16. When you make your investment decision in this manner, you are referred to as a *Markowitz efficient investor.*

Capital market theory extends portfolio theory and develops a model for pricing all risky assets. The final product, the **capital asset pricing model (CAPM)**, will allow you to determine the required rate of return for any risky asset.

We begin with a discussion of the underlying assumptions of the capital market theory and the factors that led to its development following the Markowitz portfolio theory. This includes an analysis of the effect of assuming the existence of a risk-free asset.

Notably, assuming the existence of a risk-free rate has significant implications for the potential return and risk and alternative risk–return combinations. This discussion implies the existence of a portfolio of risky assets on the efficient frontier, which we call the market portfolio. We discuss the market portfolio in the third section and what it implies regarding different types of risk.

The fourth section considers which types of risk are relevant to an investor who believes in capital market theory. Having defined a measure of risk, we consider how you determine your required rate of return on an investment. A final step in the investment process is when you compare this required rate of return to your estimate of the asset's expected rate of return during your investment horizon to determine whether the asset is undervalued or overvalued. The section ends with a demonstration of how to calculate the risk measure implied by capital market theory.

Background for Capital Market Theory

When dealing with any theory in science, economics, or finance, it is necessary to articulate a set of assumptions that specify how the world is expected to act. This allows the theoretician to concentrate on developing a theory that explains how some facet of the world will respond to changes in the environment. In this section, we consider the main assumptions that underlie the development of capital market theory.

Assumptions of Capital Market Theory   Because capital market theory builds on the Markowitz portfolio model, it requires the same assumptions, along with some additional ones:

1. All investors are Markowitz efficient investors who want to target points on the efficient frontier. The exact location on the efficient frontier and, therefore, the specific portfolio selected will depend on the individual investor's risk–return utility function.
2. Investors can borrow or lend any amount of money at the risk-free rate of return *(RFR)*. Clearly, it is always possible to lend money at the nominal risk-free rate by buying risk-free securities such as government T-bills. It is not always possible to borrow at this risk-free rate, but we will see that assuming a higher borrowing rate does not change the general results.
3. All investors have homogeneous expectations; that is, they estimate identical probability distributions for future rates of return. Again, this assumption can be relaxed. As long as the differences in expectations are not vast, their effects are minor.
4. All investors have the same one-period time horizon such as one month, six months, or one year. The model will be developed for a single hypothetical period, and its results could be affected by a different assumption. A difference in the time horizon would require investors to derive risk measures and risk-free assets that are consistent with their investment horizons.
5. All investments are infinitely divisible, which means that it is possible to buy or sell fractional shares of any asset or portfolio. This assumption allows us to discuss investment alternatives as continuous curves. Changing it would have little impact on the theory.
6. There are no taxes or transaction costs involved in buying or selling assets. This is a reasonable assumption in many instances. Neither pension funds nor religious groups have to pay taxes, and the transaction costs for most financial institutions are less than 1 percent on most financial instruments. Again, relaxing this assumption modifies the results, but it does not change the basic thrust.
7. There is no inflation or any change in interest rates, or inflation is fully anticipated. This is a reasonable initial assumption, and it can be modified.
8. Capital markets are in equilibrium. This means that we begin with all investments properly priced in line with their risk levels.

You may consider some of these assumptions unrealistic and wonder how useful a theory we can derive with these assumptions. In this regard, two points are important. First, as mentioned, relaxing many of these assumptions would have only a minor effect on the model and would not change its main implications or conclusions. Second, a theory should never be judged on the basis of its assumptions but rather on how well it explains and helps us predict behavior in the real world. If this theory and the model it implies help us explain the rates of return on a wide variety of risky assets, it is useful, even if some of its assumptions are unrealistic. Such success implies that the questionable assumptions must be unimportant to the ultimate objective of the model, which is to explain asset pricing and rates of return on assets.

Development of Capital Market Theory   The major factor that allowed portfolio theory to develop into capital market theory is the concept of a risk-free asset. Following the development of the Markowitz portfolio model, several authors considered the implications of assuming the existence of a **risk-free asset**, that is, an asset with *zero variance*. As we will show, such an asset would have zero correlation with all other risky assets and would provide the *risk-free rate of return (RFR)*. It would lie on the vertical axis of a portfolio graph.

This assumption of a risk-free asset allows us to derive a generalized theory of capital asset pricing under conditions of uncertainty from the Markowitz portfolio theory. This achievement is generally attributed to William Sharpe (1964), who received a Nobel Prize for it, but Lintner (1965) and Mossin (1966) derived similar theories independently. Consequently, you may see references to the Sharpe-Lintner-Mossin (SLM) capital asset pricing model.

Risk-Free Asset

As noted, the assumption of a risk-free asset in the economy is critical to asset pricing theory. Therefore, this section explains the meaning of a risk-free asset and shows the effect on the risk and return measures when this risk-free asset is combined with a portfolio on the Markowitz efficient frontier.

We have defined a **risky asset** as one from which future returns are uncertain, and we have measured this uncertainty by the variance, or standard deviation, of expected returns. Because the expected return on a risk-free asset is entirely certain, the standard deviation of its expected return is zero ($\sigma_{RF} = 0$). The rate of return earned on such an asset should be the risk-free rate of return *(RFR)*, which, as we discussed in Chapter 1, should equal the expected long-run growth rate of the economy with an adjustment for short-run liquidity. The next subsections show what happens when we introduce this risk-free asset into the risky world of the Markowitz portfolio model.

Covariance with a Risk-Free Asset   Recall that the covariance between two sets of returns is

8.1
$$\text{Cov}_{ij} = \sum_{i=1}^{n} [R_i - E(R_i)][R_j - E(R_j)]/n$$

Because the returns for the risk-free asset are certain, $\sigma_{RF} = 0$, which means that $R_i = E(R_i)$ during all periods. Thus, $R_i - E(R_i)$ will equal zero, and the product of this expression with any other expression will equal zero. Consequently, the covariance of the risk-free asset with any risky asset or portfolio of assets will always equal zero. Similarly, the correlation between any risky asset *i,* and the risk-free asset, RF, would be zero because it is equal to

$$r_{RF,i} = \text{Cov}_{RF,i}/\sigma_{RF}\sigma_j$$

Combining a Risk-Free Asset with a Risky Portfolio   What happens to the average rate of return and the standard deviation of returns when you combine a risk-free asset with a portfolio of risky assets such as those that exist on the Markowitz efficient frontier?

Expected Return   Like the expected return for a portfolio of two risky assets, the expected rate of return for a portfolio that includes a risk-free asset is the weighted average of the two returns:

$$E(R_{port}) = w_{RF}(RFR) + (1 - w_{RF})E(R_i)$$

where:

w_{RF} = the proportion of the portfolio invested in the risk-free asset
$E(R_i)$ = the expected rate of return on risky Portfolio i

Standard Deviation   Recall from Chapter 7 (Equation 7.7) that the expected variance for a two-asset portfolio is

$$\sigma_{port}^2 = w_1^2\sigma_1^2 + w_2^2\sigma_2^2 + 2w_1w_2r_{1,2}\sigma_1\sigma_2$$

Substituting the risk-free asset for Security 1, and the risky asset portfolio for Security 2, this formula would become

$$\sigma_{port}^2 = w_{RF}^2\sigma_{RF}^2 + (1 - w_{RF})^2\sigma_i^2 + 2w_{RF}(1 - w_{RF})r_{RFi}\sigma_{RF}\sigma_i$$

We know that the variance of the risk-free asset is zero, that is, $\sigma_{RF}^2 = 0$. Because the correlation between the risk-free asset and any risky asset, i, is also zero, the factor r_{RFi} in the preceding equation also equals zero. Therefore, any component of the variance formula that has either of these terms will equal zero. When you make these adjustments, the formula becomes

$$\sigma_{port}^2 = (1 - w_{RF})^2\sigma_i^2$$

The standard deviation is

$$\sigma_{port} = \sqrt{(1 - w_{RF})^2\sigma_i^2}$$
$$= (1 - w_{RF})\sigma_i$$

Therefore, the standard deviation of a portfolio that combines the risk-free asset with risky assets is *the linear proportion of the standard deviation of the risky asset portfolio.*

The Risk–Return Combination   Because both the expected return *and* the standard deviation of return for such a portfolio are linear combinations, a graph of possible portfolio returns and risks looks like a straight line between the two assets. Exhibit 8.1 shows a graph depicting portfolio possibilities when a risk-free asset is combined with alternative risky portfolios on the Markowitz efficient frontier.

You can attain any point along the straight line *RFR*-A by investing some portion of your portfolio in the risk-free asset w_{RF} and the remainder $(1 - w_{RF})$ in the risky asset portfolio at Point A on the efficient frontier. This set of portfolio possibilities dominates all the risky asset portfolios on the efficient frontier below Point A because some portfolio along Line *RFR*-A has equal variance with a higher rate of return than the portfolio on the original efficient frontier. Likewise, you can attain any point along the Line *RFR*-B by investing in some combination of the risk-free asset and the risky asset portfolio at Point B. Again, these potential combinations dominate all portfolio possibilities on the original efficient frontier below Point B (including Line *RFR*-A).

Exhibit 8.1	**Portfolio Possibilities Combining the Risk-Free Asset and Risky Portfolios on the Efficient Frontier**

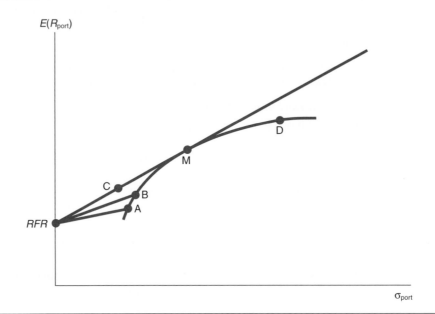

You can draw further lines from the *RFR* to the efficient frontier at higher and higher points until you reach the point where the line is tangent to the frontier, which occurs in Exhibit 8.1 at Point M. The set of portfolio possibilities along Line *RFR*-M dominates *all* portfolios below Point M. For example, you could attain a risk and return combination between the *RFR* and Point M (Point C) by investing one-half of your portfolio in the risk-free asset (that is, lending money at the *RFR*) and the other half in the risky portfolio at Point M.

Risk–Return Possibilities with Leverage   An investor may want to attain a higher expected return than is available at Point M in exchange for accepting higher risk. One alternative would be to invest in one of the risky asset portfolios on the efficient frontier beyond Point M such as the portfolio at Point D. A second alternative is to add *leverage* to the portfolio by *borrowing* money at the risk-free rate and investing the proceeds in the risky asset portfolio at Point M. What effect would this have on the return and risk for your portfolio?

If you borrow an amount equal to 50 percent of your original wealth at the risk-free rate, w_{RF} will not be a positive fraction but, rather, a negative 50 percent ($w_{RF} = -0.50$). The effect on the expected return for your portfolio is:

$$E(R_{port}) = w_{RF}(RFR) + (1 - w_{RF})E(R_M)$$
$$= -0.50(RFR) + [1 - (-0.50)]E(R_M)$$
$$= -0.50(RFR) + 1.50E(R_M)$$

The return will increase in a *linear* fashion along the Line *RFR*-M because the gross return increases by 50 percent, but you must pay interest at the *RFR* on the money borrowed. For

Exhibit 8.2	Derivation of Capital Market Line Assuming Lending or Borrowing at the Risk-Free Rate

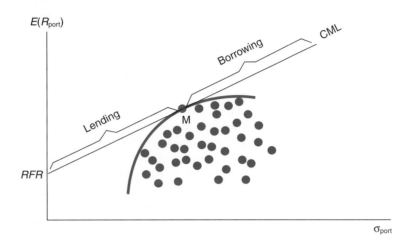

example, assume that $E(RFR) = .06$ and $E(R_M) = .12$. The return on your leveraged portfolio would be:

$$E(R_{port}) = -0.50(0.06) + 1.5(0.12)$$
$$= -0.03 + 0.18$$
$$= 0.15$$

The effect on the standard deviation of the leveraged portfolio is similar.

$$\sigma_{port} = (1 - w_{RF})\, \sigma_M$$
$$= [1 - (-0.50)]\, \sigma_M = 1.50\sigma_M$$

where:

σ_M = the standard deviation of the M portfolio

Therefore, *both return and risk increase in a linear fashion along the original Line RFR-M,* and this extension dominates everything below the line on the original efficient frontier. Thus, you have a new efficient frontier: the straight line from the *RFR* tangent to Point M. This line is referred to as the **capital market line (CML)** and is shown in Exhibit 8.2.

Our discussion of portfolio theory stated that, when two assets are perfectly correlated, the set of portfolio possibilities falls along a straight line. Therefore, because the CML is a straight line, it implies that all the portfolios on the CML are perfectly positively correlated. This positive correlation appeals to our intuition because all these portfolios on the CML combine the risky asset Portfolio M and the risk-free asset. You either invest part of your portfolio in the risk-free asset (i.e., you *lend* at the *RFR*) and the rest in the risky asset Portfolio M, or you *borrow* at the risk-free rate and invest these funds in the risky asset portfolio. In either case, all the variability comes from the risky asset M portfolio. The only difference between the alternative portfolios on the CML is the magnitude of the variability, which is caused by the proportion of the risky asset portfolio in the total portfolio.

The Market Portfolio

Because Portfolio M lies at the point of tangency, it has the highest portfolio possibility line, and everybody will want to invest in Portfolio M and borrow or lend to be somewhere on the CML. This portfolio must, therefore, include *all risky assets*. If a risky asset were not in this portfolio in which everyone wants to invest, there would be no demand for it and therefore it would have no value.

Because the market is in equilibrium, it is also necessary that all assets are included in this portfolio *in proportion to their market value*. If, for example, an asset accounts for a higher proportion of the M portfolio than its market value justifies, excess demand for this asset will increase its price until its relative market value becomes consistent with its proportion in the M portfolio.

This portfolio that includes all risky assets is referred to as the **market portfolio**. It includes not only U.S. common stocks but *all* risky assets, such as non-U.S. stocks, U.S. and non-U.S. bonds, options, real estate, coins, stamps, art, or antiques. Because the market portfolio contains all risky assets, it is a **completely diversified portfolio**, which means that all the risk unique to individual assets in the portfolio is diversified away. Specifically, the unique risk of any single asset is offset by the unique variability of all the other assets in the portfolio.

This unique (diversifiable) risk is also referred to as **unsystematic risk**. This implies that only **systematic risk**, which is defined as the variability in all risky assets caused by macro-economic variables, remains in the market portfolio. This systematic risk, measured by the standard deviation of returns of the market portfolio, can change over time if and when there are changes in the macroeconomic variables that affect the valuation of all risky assets.[1] Examples of such macroeconomic variables would be variability of growth in the money supply, interest rate volatility, and variability in such factors as industrial production, corporate earnings, and corporate cash flow.

How to Measure Diversification   As noted earlier, all portfolios on the CML are perfectly positively correlated, which means that all portfolios on the CML are perfectly correlated with the completely diversified market Portfolio M. As noted by Lorie (1975), this implies a measure of complete diversification. Specifically, a completely diversified portfolio would have a correlation with the market portfolio of +1.00. This is logical because complete diversification means the elimination of all the unsystematic or unique risk. Once you have eliminated all unsystematic risk, only systematic risk is left, which cannot be diversified away. Therefore, completely diversified portfolios would correlate perfectly with the market portfolio because it has only systematic risk.

Diversification and the Elimination of Unsystematic Risk   As discussed in Chapter 7, the purpose of diversification is to reduce the standard deviation of the total portfolio. This assumes imperfect correlations among securities.[2] Ideally, as you add securities, the average covariance for the portfolio declines. An important question is, about how many securities must be included to arrive at a completely diversified portfolio? To discover the answer, you must observe what happens as you increase the sample size of the portfolio by adding securities that have some positive correlation. The typical correlation between U.S. securities is about 0.5 to 0.6.

One set of studies examined the average standard deviation for numerous portfolios of randomly selected stocks of different sample sizes. Specifically, Evans and Archer (1968) and Tole (1982) computed the standard deviation for portfolios of increasing numbers up to 20 stocks. The results indicated a large initial impact wherein the major benefits of diversification were

---

[1]For an analysis of changes in the standard deviation (volatility) of returns for stocks and bonds in the United States, see Schwert (1989); Spiro (1990); Officer (1973); and Reilly, Wright, and Chan (2000).
[2]The discussion in Chapter 7 leads one to conclude that securities with negative correlation would be ideal. Although this is true in theory, it is difficult to find such assets in the real world.

Exhibit 8.3	**Number of Stocks in a Portfolio and the Standard Deviation of Portfolio Return**

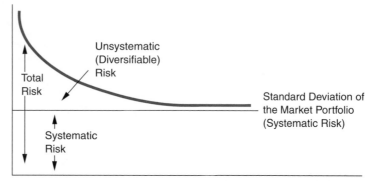

achieved rather quickly. Specifically, about 90 percent of the maximum benefit of diversification was derived from portfolios of 12 to 18 stocks. Exhibit 8.3 shows a graph of the effect.

A subsequent study by Statman (1987) compared the benefits of lower risk from diversification to the added transaction costs with more securities. It concluded that a well-diversified stock portfolio must include at least 30 stocks for a borrowing investor and 40 stocks for a lending investor.

An important point to remember is that, by adding stocks to the portfolio that are not perfectly correlated with stocks in the portfolio, you can reduce the overall standard deviation of the portfolio but you *cannot eliminate variability*. The standard deviation of your portfolio will eventually reach the level of the market portfolio, where you will have diversified away all unsystematic risk, but you still have market or systematic risk. You cannot eliminate the variability and uncertainty of macroeconomic factors that affect all risky assets. At the same time, you will recall from the discussion in Chapter 3 that you can attain a lower level of systematic risk by diversifying globally versus only diversifying within the United States because some of the systematic risk factors in the U.S. market (such as U.S. monetary policy) are not correlated with systematic risk variables in other countries such as Germany and Japan. As a result, if you diversify globally, you eventually get down to a world systematic risk level.

The CML and the Separation Theorem   The CML leads all investors to invest in the same risky asset portfolio, the M portfolio. Individual investors should only differ regarding their position on the CML, which depends on their risk preferences.

In turn, how they get to a point on the CML is based on their *financing decisions*. If you are relatively risk averse, you will lend some part of your portfolio at the *RFR* by buying some risk-free securities and investing the remainder in the market portfolio of risky assets. For example, you might invest in the portfolio combination at Point A in Exhibit 8.4. In contrast, if you prefer more risk, you might borrow funds at the *RFR* and invest everything (all of your capital plus what you borrowed) in the market portfolio, building the portfolio at Point B. This financing decision provides more risk but greater returns than the market portfolio. As discussed earlier, because portfolios on the CML dominate other portfolio possibilities, the CML becomes the efficient frontier of portfolios, and investors decide where they want to be along this efficient frontier. Tobin (1958) called this division of the investment decision from the financing decision the **separation theorem**. Specifically, to be somewhere on the CML

| Exhibit 8.4 | **Choice of Optimal Portfolio Combinations on the CML** |

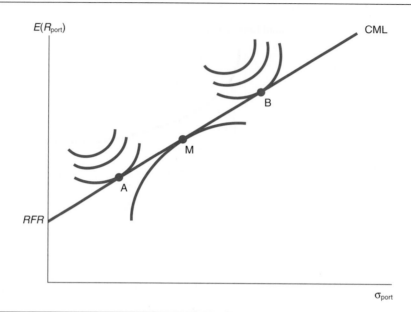

efficient frontier, you initially decide to invest in the market Portfolio M, which means that you will be on the CML. This is your *investment* decision. Subsequently, based on your risk preferences, you make a separate *financing* decision either to borrow or to lend to attain your preferred risk position on the CML.

A Risk Measure for the CML   In this section, we show that the relevant risk measure for risky assets is *their covariance with the M portfolio,* which is referred to as their systematic risk. The importance of this covariance is apparent from two points of view.

First, in discussing the Markowitz portfolio model, we noted that the relevant risk to consider when adding a security to a portfolio is *its average covariance with all other assets in the portfolio.* In this chapter, we have shown that *the only relevant portfolio is the M portfolio.* Together, these two findings mean that the only important consideration for any individual risky asset is its average covariance with all the risky assets in the M portfolio or, simply, *the asset's covariance with the market portfolio.* This covariance, then, is the relevant risk measure for an individual risky asset.

Second, because all individual risky assets are a part of the M portfolio, one can describe their rates of return in relation to the returns for the M portfolio using the following linear model:

8.2
$$R_{it} = a_i + b_i R_{Mt} + \varepsilon$$

where:

$R_{i,t}$ = return for asset i during period t
a_i = constant term for asset i
b_i = slope coefficient for asset i
R_{Mt} = return for the M portfolio during period t
ε = random error term

The variance of returns for a risky asset could be described as

8.3
$$
\begin{aligned}
\text{Var}(R_{it}) &= \text{Var}(a_i + b_i R_{Mt} + \varepsilon) \\
&= \text{Var}(a_i) + \text{Var}(b_i R_{Mt}) + \text{Var}(\varepsilon) \\
&= 0 + \text{Var}(b_i R_{Mt}) + \text{Var}(\varepsilon)
\end{aligned}
$$

Note that $\text{Var}(b_i R_{Mt})$ is the variance of return for an asset related to the variance of the market return, or the *systematic variance or risk.* Also, $\text{Var}(\varepsilon)$ is the residual variance of return for the individual asset that is not related to the market portfolio. This residual variance is the variability that we have referred to as the unsystematic or *unique risk* or unsystematic or unique *variance* because it arises from the unique features of the asset. Therefore:

8.4
$$
\text{Var}(R_{i,t}) = \text{Systematic Variance} + \text{Unsystematic Variance}
$$

We know that a completely diversified portfolio such as the market portfolio has had all the unsystematic variance eliminated. Therefore, the unsystematic variance of an asset is not relevant to investors, because they can and do eliminate it when making an asset part of the market portfolio. Therefore, investors should not expect to receive added returns for assuming this unsystematic (unique) risk. Only the systematic variance is relevant because it *cannot* be diversified away, because it is caused by macroeconomic factors that affect all risky assets.

THE CAPITAL ASSET PRICING MODEL: EXPECTED RETURN AND RISK

Up to this point, we have considered how investors make their portfolio decisions, including the significant effects of a risk-free asset. The existence of this risk-free asset resulted in the derivation of a capital market line (CML) that became the relevant efficient frontier. Because all investors want to be on the CML, an asset's covariance with the market portfolio of risky assets emerged as the relevant risk measure.

Now that we understand this relevant measure of risk, we can proceed to use it to determine an appropriate expected rate of return on a risky asset. This step takes us into the **capital asset pricing model (CAPM),** which is a model that indicates what should be the expected or required rates of return on risky assets. This transition is important because it helps you to value an asset by providing an appropriate discount rate to use in any valuation model. Alternatively, if you have already estimated the rate of return that you think you will earn on an investment, you can compare this *estimated* rate of return to the *required* rate of return implied by the CAPM and determine whether the asset is undervalued, overvalued, or properly valued.

To accomplish the foregoing, we demonstrate the creation of a security market line (SML) that visually represents the relationship between risk and the expected or the required rate of return on an asset. The equation of this SML, together with estimates for the return on a risk-free asset and on the market portfolio, can generate expected or required rates of return for any asset based on its systematic risk. You compare this required rate of return to the rate of return that you estimate that you will earn on the investment to determine if the investment is undervalued or overvalued. After demonstrating this procedure, we finish the section with a demonstration of how to calculate the systematic risk variable for a risky asset.

The Security Market Line (SML)

We know that the relevant risk measure for an individual risky asset is its covariance with the market portfolio ($Cov_{i,M}$). Therefore, we can draw the risk–return relationship as shown in Exhibit 8.5 with the systematic covariance variable ($Cov_{i,M}$) as the risk measure.

The return for the market portfolio (R_M) should be consistent with its own risk, which is the covariance of the market with itself. If you recall the formula for covariance, you will see that the covariance of any asset with itself is its variance, $Cov_{i,i} = \sigma_i^2$. In turn, the covariance of the market with itself is the variance of the market rate of return $Cov_{M,M} = \sigma_M^2$. Therefore, the equation for the risk–return line in Exhibit 8.5 is:

8.5
$$E(R_i) = RFR + \frac{R_M - RFR}{\sigma_M^2}(Cov_{i,M})$$

$$= RFR + \frac{Cov_{i,M}}{\sigma_M^2}(R_M - RFR)$$

Defining $Cov_{i,M}/\sigma_M^2$ as beta, (β_i), this equation can be stated:

8.6
$$E(R_i) = RFR + \beta_i(R_M - RFR)$$

Beta can be viewed as a *standardized* measure of systematic risk. Specifically, we already know that the covariance of any asset i with the market portfolio (Cov_{iM}) is the relevant risk measure. Beta is a standardized measure of risk because it relates this covariance to the variance of the market portfolio. As a result, the market portfolio has a beta of 1. Therefore, if the β_i for an asset is above 1.0, the asset has higher normalized systematic risk than the market, which means that it is more volatile than the overall market portfolio.

Given this standardized measure of systematic risk, the SML graph can be expressed as shown in Exhibit 8.6. This is the same graph as in Exhibit 8.5, except there is a different

Exhibit 8.5	**Graph of Security Market Line**

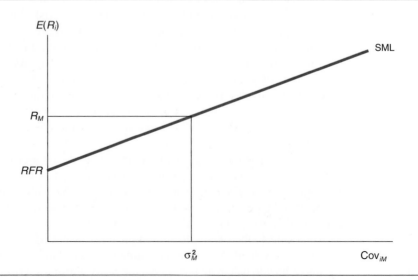

Exhibit 8.6 | **Graph of SML with Normalized Systematic Risk**

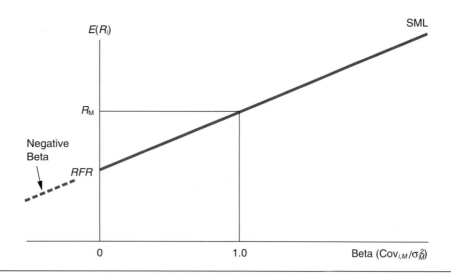

measure of risk. Specifically, the graph in Exhibit 8.6 replaces the covariance of an asset's returns with the market portfolio as the risk measure with the standardized measure of systematic risk (beta), which is the covariance of an asset with the market portfolio divided by the variance of the market portfolio.

Determining the Expected Rate of Return for a Risky Asset   Equation 8.6 and the graph in Exhibit 8.6 tell us that the expected (required) rate of return for a risky asset is determined by the *RFR* plus a risk premium for the individual asset. In turn, the risk premium is determined by the systematic risk of the asset (β_i), and the prevailing **market risk premium** $(R_M - RFR)$. To demonstrate how you would compute the expected or required rates of return, consider the following example stocks assuming you have already computed betas:

Stock	Beta
A	0.70
B	1.00
C	1.15
D	1.40
E	−0.30

Assume that we expect the economy's *RFR* to be 5 percent (0.05) and the return on the market portfolio (R_M) to be 9 percent (0.09). This implies a market risk premium of 4 percent (0.04). With these inputs, the SML equation would yield the following expected (required) rates of return for these five stocks:

$$E(R_i) = RFR + \beta_i (R_M - RFR)$$
$$E(R_A) = 0.05 + 0.70 (0.09 - 0.05)$$
$$= 0.078 = 7.80\%$$

$$E(R_B) = 0.05 + 1.00\,(0.09 - 0.05)$$
$$= 0.09 = 9.00\%$$
$$E(R_C) = 0.05 + 1.15\,(0.09 - 0.05)$$
$$= 0.096 = 9.60\%$$
$$E(R_D) = 0.05 + 1.40\,(0.09 - 0.05)$$
$$= 0.106 = 10.60\%$$
$$E(R_E) = 0.05 + (-0.30)\,(0.09 - 0.05)$$
$$= 0.05 - 0.012$$
$$= 0.038 = 3.8\%$$

As stated, these are the expected (required) rates of return that these stocks should provide based on their systematic risks and the prevailing SML.

Stock A has lower risk than the aggregate market, so you should not expect (require) its return to be as high as the return on the market portfolio of risky assets. You should expect (require) Stock A to return 7.80 percent. Stock B has systematic risk equal to the market's (beta = 1.00), so its required rate of return should likewise be equal to the expected market return (9 percent). Stocks C and D have systematic risk greater than the market's, so they should provide returns consistent with their risk. Finally, Stock E has a *negative* beta (which is quite rare in practice), so its required rate of return, if such a stock could be found, would be below the *RFR* of 5 percent.

In equilibrium, *all* assets and *all* portfolios of assets should plot on the SML. That is, all assets should be priced so that their **estimated rates of return**, which are the actual holding period rates of return that you anticipate, are consistent with their levels of systematic risk. Any security with an estimated rate of return that plots above the SML would be considered under-priced because it implies that you *estimated* you would receive a rate of return on the security that is above its *required* rate of return based on its systematic risk. In contrast, assets with estimated rates of return that plot below the SML would be considered overpriced. This position relative to the SML implies that your estimated rate of return is below what you should require based on the asset's systematic risk.

In a completely efficient market in equilibrium, you would not expect any assets to plot off the SML because, in equilibrium, all stocks should provide holding period returns that are equal to their required rates of return. Alternatively, a market that is fairly efficient but not completely efficient may misprice certain assets because not everyone will be aware of all the relevant information for an asset.

As we discussed in Chapter 6 on the topic of efficient markets, a superior investor has the ability to derive value estimates for assets that are consistently superior to the consensus market evaluation. As a result, such an investor will earn better rates of return than the average investor on a risk-adjusted basis.

Identifying Undervalued and Overvalued Assets   Now that we understand how to compute the rate of return one should expect or require for a specific risky asset using the SML, we can compare this *required* rate of return to the asset's *estimated* rate of return over a specific investment horizon to determine whether it would be an appropriate investment. To make this comparison, you need an independent estimate of the return outlook for the security based on either fundamental or technical analysis techniques, which will be discussed in subsequent chapters. Let us continue the example for the five assets discussed in the previous subsection.

Exhibit 8.7 | **Price, Dividend, and Rate of Return Estimates**

Stock	Current Price (P_t)	Expected Price (P_{t+1})	Expected Dividend (D_{t+1})	Estimated Future Rate of Return (Percent)
A	25	26	1.00	8.00%
B	40	42	0.50	6.20
C	33	37	1.00	15.15
D	64	66	1.10	5.16
E	50	53	—	6.00

Exhibit 8.8 | **Comparison of Required Rate of Return to Estimated Rate of Return**

Stock	Beta	Required Return $E(R_i)$	Estimated Return	Estimated Return Minus $E(R_i)$	Evaluation
A	0.70	7.80	8.00	0.20	Properly valued
B	1.00	9.00	6.20	−2.80	Overvalued
C	1.15	9.60	15.15	5.55	Undervalued
D	1.40	10.60	5.16	−5.44	Overvalued
E	−0.30	3.80	6.00	2.20	Undervalued

Assume that analysts in a major trust department have been following these five stocks. Based on extensive fundamental analysis, the analysts provide the expected price and dividend estimates contained in Exhibit 8.7. Given these projections, you can compute the estimated rates of return the analysts would anticipate during this holding period.

Exhibit 8.8 summarizes the relationship between the required rate of return for each stock based on its systematic risk as computed earlier, and its estimated rate of return (from Exhibit 8.7) based on the current and future prices, and its dividend outlook. This difference between estimated return and expected (required) return is sometimes referred to as a stock's *alpha* or its excess return. This alpha can be positive (the stock is undervalued) or negative (the stock is overvalued). If the alpha is zero, the stock is on the SML and is properly valued in line with its systematic risk.

Plotting these estimated rates of return and stock betas on the SML we specified earlier gives the graph shown in Exhibit 8.9. Stock A is almost exactly on the line, so it is considered properly valued because its estimated rate of return is almost equal to its required rate of return. Stocks B and D are considered overvalued because their estimated rates of return during the coming period are less than what an investor should expect (require) for the risk involved. As a result, they plot below the SML. In contrast, Stocks C and E are expected to provide rates of return greater than we would require based on their systematic risk. Therefore, both stocks plot above the SML, indicating that they are undervalued stocks.

Assuming that you trusted your analyst to forecast estimated returns, you would take no action regarding Stock A, but you would buy Stocks C and E and sell Stocks B and D. You might even sell Stocks B and D short if you favored such aggressive tactics.

Exhibit 8.9 | **Plot of Estimated Returns on SML Graph**

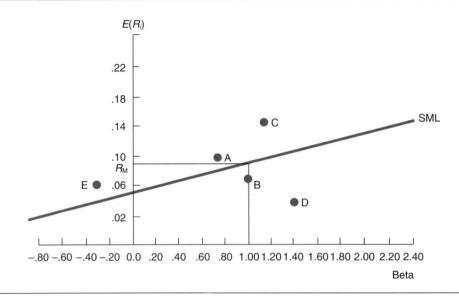

Calculating Systematic Risk: The Characteristic Line   The systematic risk input for an individual asset is derived from a regression model, referred to as the asset's **characteristic line** with the market portfolio:

8.7 $R_{i,t} = \alpha_i + \beta_i R_{M,t} + \varepsilon$

where:

$R_{i,t}$ = the rate of return for Asset i during Period t
$R_{M,t}$ = the rate of return for the market portfolio M during Period t
α_i = the constant term, or intercept, of the regression, which equals $\overline{R}_i - \beta_i \overline{R}_M$
β_i = the systematic risk (beta) of Asset i equal to $\text{Cov}_{i,M}/\sigma_M^2$
ε = the random error term

The characteristic line (Equation 8.7) is the regression line of best fit through a scatterplot of rates of return for the individual risky asset and for the market portfolio of risky assets over some designated past period, as shown in Exhibit 8.10.

The Impact of the Time Interval   In practice, the number of observations and the time interval used in the regression vary. Value Line Investment Services derives characteristic lines for common stocks using weekly rates of return for the most recent five years (260 weekly observations). Merrill Lynch, Pierce, Fenner & Smith uses monthly rates of return for the most recent five years (60 monthly observations). Because there is no theoretically correct time interval for analysis, we must make a trade-off between enough observations to eliminate the impact of random rates of return and an excessive length of time, such as 15 or 20 years, over which the subject company may have changed dramatically. Remember that what you really want is the *expected* systematic risk for the potential investment. In this analysis, you are analyzing historical data to help you derive a reasonable estimate of the asset's expected systematic risk.

Exhibit 8.10	Scatterplot of Rates of Return

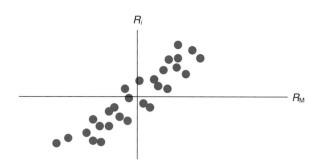

A couple of studies have considered the effect of the time interval used to compute betas (weekly versus monthly). Statman (1981) examined the relationship between Value Line (VL) betas and Merrill Lynch (ML) betas and found a relatively weak relationship. Reilly and Wright (1988) analyzed the differential effects of return computation, market index, and the time interval and showed that the major cause of the differences in beta was the use of monthly versus weekly return intervals. Also, the interval effect depended on the sizes of the firms. The shorter weekly interval caused a larger beta for large firms and a smaller beta for small firms. For example, the average beta for the smallest decile of firms using monthly data was 1.682, but the average beta for these small firms using weekly data was only 1.080. The authors concluded that the return time interval makes a difference, and its impact increases as the firm size declines.

The Effect of the Market Proxy   Another significant decision when computing an asset's characteristic line is which indicator series to use as a proxy for the market portfolio of all risky assets. Most investigators use the Standard & Poor's 500 Composite Index as a proxy for the market portfolio, because the stocks in this index encompass a large proportion of the total market value of U.S. stocks and it is a value-weighted series, which is consistent with the theoretical market series. Still, this series contains only large-cap U.S. stocks, most of them listed on the NYSE. Previously, it was noted that the market portfolio of all risky assets should include U.S. stocks and bonds, non-U.S. stocks and bonds, real estate, coins, stamps, art, antiques, and any other marketable risky asset from around the world.[3]

Example Computations of a Characteristic Line   The following examples show how you would compute characteristic lines for General Electric (GE) based on the monthly rates of return during 2004.[4] Twelve monthly rates are not enough observations for statistical purposes, but they provide a good example. We demonstrate the computations using two different proxies for the market portfolio. First, we use the standard S&P 500 as the market proxy. Second,

---

[3]Substantial discussion surrounds the market index used and its impact on the empirical results and usefulness of the CAPM. This concern is discussed further and demonstrated in the subsequent section on computing an asset's characteristic line. The effect of the market proxy is also considered when we discuss the arbitrage pricing theory (APT) in Chapter 9 and in Chapter 25 when we discuss the evaluation of portfolio performance.

[4]These betas are computed using only monthly price changes for GE, the S&P 500, and the M-S World Index (dividends are not included). This is done for simplicity but it is also based on a study by Sharpe and Cooper (1972a) that indicated that betas derived with and without dividends have a correlation coefficient of 0.99.

we use the Morgan Stanley (M-S) World Equity Index as the market proxy. This analysis demonstrates the effect of using a global portfolio of stocks as the market proxy.

The monthly price changes are computed using the closing prices for the last day of each month. These data for GE, the S&P 500, and the M-S World Index are contained in Exhibit 8.11. Exhibit 8.12 contains the scatterplot of the percentage price changes for GE and the S&P 500. During this 12-month period, there were only 2 months when GE had returns that were not consistent with the S&P 500. As a result, the covariance between GE and the S&P 500 series was a reasonable positive value (3.57). The covariance divided by the variance of the S&P 500 market portfolio (4.38) indicates that GE's beta relative to the S&P 500 was equal to 0.82. This analysis indicates that, during this limited time period, GE was less risky than the aggregate market proxied by the S&P 500. When we draw the computed characteristic line on Exhibit 8.12, the scatterplots are reasonably close to the characteristic line except for two observations, which is consistent with the correlation coefficient of 0.43.

The computation of the characteristic line for GE using the M-S World Index as the proxy for the market is contained in Exhibit 8.11, and the scatterplots are in Exhibit 8.13. At this point, it is important to consider what one might expect to be the relationship between the beta relative to the S&P 500 versus the betas with the M-S World Index. This requires a consideration of the two components that go into the computation of beta: (1) the covariance between the stock and the benchmark and (2) the variance of returns for the benchmark series. Notably, there is no obvious answer regarding what will happen to the beta for either series because one would expect both components to change. Specifically, the covariance of GE with the S&P 500 will probably be higher than the covariance with the global series because you are matching a U.S. stock with a U.S. market index rather than a world index. Thus, one would expect the covariance with the global index to be smaller. At the same time, the variance of returns for the world stock index should also be smaller than the variance for the S&P 500 because the world index is a more diversified stock portfolio.

Therefore, the direction of change for the beta will depend on the relative change in the two components. Empirically, as demonstrated by Reilly and Akhtar (1995), the beta is typically smaller with the world stock index because the covariance is definitely lower, but the variance is only slightly smaller. The results of this example were consistent with these expectations. The beta of GE with the world stock index was definitely smaller (0.59 vs. 0.82) because the covariance of GE with the global index was smaller as expected (3.30 vs. 3.57), but the variance of the global market proxy was not smaller as hypothesized (it was 5.59 vs. 4.38). The fact that the betas with the alternative market proxies differed is significant and reflects the potential problem in a global investment environment. Specifically, it means that selecting the appropriate proxy for the market portfolio is an important decision when measuring risk.

RELAXING THE ASSUMPTIONS

Earlier in the chapter, several assumptions were set forth related to the CAPM. In this section, we discuss the impact on the capital market line (CML) and the security market line (SML) when we relax several of these assumptions.

Differential Borrowing and Lending Rates

One of the first assumptions of the CAPM was that investors could borrow and lend any amount of money at the risk-free rate. It is reasonable to assume that investors can *lend* unlimited amounts at the risk-free rate by buying government securities (e.g., T-bills). In contrast,

Exhibit 8.11 | Computation of Beta for General Electric with Selected Indexes

Date	INDEX S&P 500	INDEX MSCI World	INDEX GE	RETURN S&P 500	RETURN MSCI World	RETURN GE	S&P 500 $R(S\&P) - \bar{R}(S\&P)$ (1)	MSCI World $R(MSCI) - \bar{R}(MSCI)$ (2)	GE $R(GE) - \bar{R}(GE)$ (3)	(4)[a]	(5)[b]
Dec-03	1111.92	1,036.32	30.98	—	—	—					
Jan-04	1131.13	1,052.29	33.63	1.73	1.54	8.55	0.99	0.50	7.11	7.02	3.58
Feb-04	1144.94	1,068.65	32.52	1.22	1.55	(3.30)	0.48	0.52	(4.75)	(2.28)	(2.46)
Mar-04	1126.21	1,059.16	30.52	(1.64)	(0.89)	(6.15)	(2.38)	(1.93)	(7.60)	18.05	14.63
Apr-04	1107.3	1,035.66	29.95	(1.68)	(2.22)	(1.87)	(2.42)	(3.26)	(3.32)	8.02	10.79
May-04	1120.68	1,042.63	31.12	1.21	0.67	3.91	0.47	(0.36)	2.46	1.15	(0.90)
Jun-04	1140.84	1,062.51	32.40	1.80	1.91	4.11	1.06	0.87	2.67	2.82	2.32
Jul-04	1101.72	1,026.99	33.25	(3.43)	(3.34)	2.62	(4.17)	(4.38)	1.18	(4.90)	(5.15)
Aug-04	1104.24	1,029.63	32.79	0.23	0.26	(1.38)	(0.51)	(0.78)	(2.83)	1.45	2.21
Sep-04	1114.58	1,047.86	33.58	0.94	1.77	2.41	0.20	0.73	0.96	0.19	0.71
Oct-04	1130.2	1,072.70	34.12	1.40	2.37	1.61	0.66	1.33	0.16	0.11	0.21
Nov-04	1173.82	1,127.34	35.36	3.86	5.09	3.63	3.12	4.06	2.19	6.82	8.87
Dec-04	1211.92	1,169.34	36.50	3.25	3.73	3.22	2.51	2.69	1.78	4.45	4.78
Average (R)				0.74	1.04	1.45			Total =	42.89	39.59
Standard Deviation				2.09	2.36	3.97					

$Cov_{(GE, S\&P)} = 42.89/12 = 3.57$

$Cov_{(GE, MSCI)} = 39.59/12 = 3.30$

$Var_{(S\&P)} = St. Dev._{(S\&P)}^2 = 2.09^2 = 4.38$

$Var_{(MSCI)} = St. Dev._{(MSCI)}^2 = 2.36^2 = 5.59$

$Beta_{(GE, S\&P)} = 3.57/4.38 = 0.82$

$Beta_{(GE, MSCI)} = 3.30/5.59 = 0.59$

$Alpha_{(GE, S\&P)} = 1.45 - (0.82 \times 0.74) = 0.843$

$Alpha_{(GE, MSCI)} = 1.45 - (0.59 \times 1.04) = 0.836$

Correlation Coef._{(GE, S\&P)} = 3.57/(2.09 × 3.97) = 0.430

Correlation Coef._{(GE, MSCI)} = 3.30/(2.36 × 3.97) = 0.352

[a] Column 4 is equal to Column 1 multiplied by Column 3.

[b] Column 5 is equal to Column 2 multiplied by Column 3.

Exhibit 8.12 | **Scatterplot of General Electric (GE) and the S&P 500 with Characteristic Line for GE: 2004**

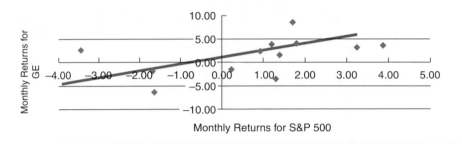

Monthly Returns for S&P 500

Exhibit 8.13 | **Scatterplot of General Electric (GE) and the MSCI World Index with Characteristic Line for GE: 2004**

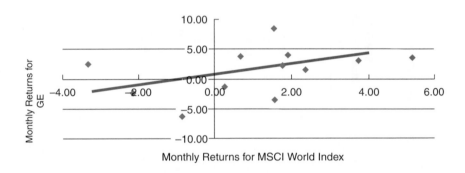

Monthly Returns for MSCI World Index

one may question the ability of investors to borrow unlimited amounts at the T-bill rate because most investors must pay a premium relative to the prime rate when borrowing money. For example, when T-bills are yielding 4 percent, the prime rate will probably be about 6 percent, and most individuals would have to pay about 7 percent to borrow at the bank.

Because of this differential, there will be two different lines going to the Markowitz efficient frontier, as shown in Exhibit 8.14. The segment *RFR–F* indicates the investment opportunities available when an investor combines risk-free assets (i.e., lending at the *RFR*) and Portfolio F on the Markowitz efficient frontier. It is not possible to extend this line any farther if it is assumed that you cannot borrow at this risk-free rate to acquire further units of Portfolio F. If it is assumed that you can borrow at R_b, the point of tangency from this rate would be on the curve at Point K. This indicates that you could borrow at R_b and use the proceeds to invest in Portfolio K to extend the CML along the line segment *K–G*. Therefore, the CML is made up of *RFR–F–K–G;* that is, a line segment (*RFR–F*), a curve segment (*F–K*), and another line segment (*K–G*). As noted by Brennan (1969), this implies that you can either lend or borrow, but the borrowing portfolios are not as profitable as when it was assumed that you could borrow at the *RFR*. In this instance, because you must pay a borrowing rate that is higher than the *RFR,* your net return is less—that is, the slope of the borrowing line (*K–G*) is below that for *RFR–F.*

Exhibit 8.14	Investment Alternatives When the Cost of Borrowing Is Higher Than the Cost of Lending

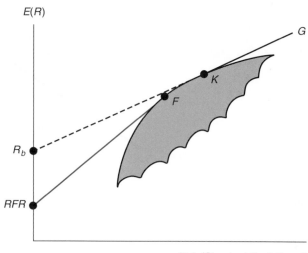

Zero-Beta Model

If the market portfolio (M) is mean-variance efficient (i.e., it has the lowest risk for a given level of return among the attainable set of portfolios), an alternative model, derived by Black (1972), does not require a risk-free asset. Specifically, within the set of feasible alternative portfolios, several portfolios exist where the returns are completely uncorrelated with the market portfolio; the beta of these portfolios with the market portfolio is zero. From among the several zero-beta portfolios, you would select the one with minimum variance. Although this portfolio does not have any systematic risk, it does have some unsystematic risk. The availability of this zero-beta portfolio will not affect the CML, but it will allow construction of a linear SML, as shown in Exhibit 8.15. In the model, the intercept is the expected return for the zero-beta portfolio. Similar to the earlier proof in this chapter, the combinations of this zero-beta portfolio and the market portfolio will be a linear relationship in return and risk because the covariance between the zero-beta portfolio (R_z) and the market portfolio is similar to what it was with the risk-free asset. Assuming the return for the zero-beta portfolio is greater than that for a risk-free asset, the slope of the line through the market portfolio would not be as steep; that is, the market risk premium would be smaller. The equation for this zero-beta CAPM line would be:

8.8
$$E(R_i) = E(R_z) + B_i[E(R_M) - E(R_z)]$$

Obviously, the risk premiums for individual assets would be a function of the beta for the individual security and the market risk premium:

$$[E(R_M) - E(R_z)]$$

Some of the empirical results discussed in the next section support this model with its higher intercept and flatter slope. Alternatively, several studies have specifically tested this model and

Exhibit 8.15 | **Security Market Line with a Zero-Beta Portfolio**

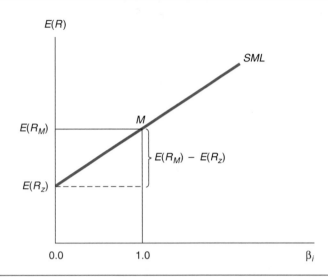

had conflicting results. Specifically, studies by Gibbons (1982) and Shanken (1985b) rejected the model, while a study by Stambaugh (1982) supported the zero-beta CAPM.

Transaction Costs

The basic assumption is that there are no transaction costs, so investors will buy or sell mispriced securities until they again plot on the SML. For example, if a stock plots above the SML, it is underpriced so investors should buy it and bid up its price until its estimated return is in line with its risk—that is, until it plots on the SML. Assuming there are transaction costs, investors will not correct all mispricing because in some instances the cost of buying and selling the mispriced security will offset any potential excess return. Therefore, securities will plot very close to the SML—but not exactly on it. Thus, the SML will be a band of securities, as shown in Exhibit 8.16, rather than a single line. Obviously, the width of the band is a function of the amount of the transaction costs. In a world with a large proportion of trading by institutions at pennies per share and with discount brokers available for individual investors, the band should be quite narrow.

Dimson (1979) considered the existence of transaction costs and how they affect the extent of diversification by investors. Earlier in the chapter, we discussed the relationship between the number of stocks in a portfolio and the variance of the portfolio (see Exhibit 8.3). Initially, the variance declined rapidly, approaching about 90 percent of complete diversification with about 15 to 18 securities. An important question is, How many securities must be added to derive the last 10 percent? Because of transaction costs, Brennan and Subramanyam (1996) show that at some point the additional cost of diversification would exceed its benefit, especially when considering the costs of monitoring and analyzing the added securities.

Heterogeneous Expectations and Planning Periods

If all investors had different expectations about risk and return, each would have a unique CML and/or SML, and the composite graph would be a set (band) of lines with a breadth determined by the divergence of expectations. If all investors had similar information and background, the band would be reasonably narrow.

Exhibit 8.16	**Security Market Line with Transaction Costs**

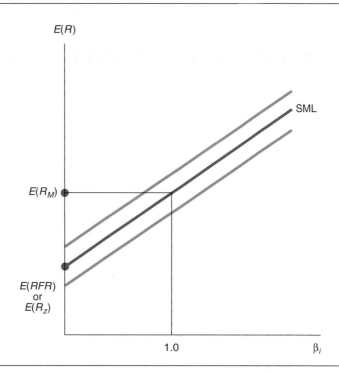

The impact of *planning periods* is similar. Recall that the CAPM is a one-period model, corresponding to the planning period for the individual investor. Thus, if you are using a one-year planning period, your CML and SML could differ from mine, if I assume a one-month planning period.

Taxes

The rates of return that we normally record and that were used throughout the model were pre-tax returns. In fact, the actual returns for most investors are affected as follows:

8.9
$$E(R_i)(AT) = \frac{(P_e - P_b) \times (1 - T_{cg}) + (Div) \times (1 - T_i)}{P_b}$$

where:

$R_i(AT)$ = after-tax rate of return
P_e = ending price
P_b = beginning price
T_{cg} = tax on capital gain or loss
Div = dividend paid during period
T_i = tax on ordinary income

Clearly, tax rates differ between individuals and institutions. For institutions that do not pay taxes, the original pretax model is correctly specified—that is, T_{cg} and T_i take on values of zero. As noted by Black and Scholes (1979) and Litzenberger and Ramaswamy (1979), because investors have heavy tax burdens, this could cause major differences in the CML and

SML among investors. Studies by Elton, Gruber, and Rentzler (1983); Miller and Scholes (1982); and Christie (1990) have examined the effect of the differential taxes on dividends versus capital gains but the evidence is not unanimous.

EMPIRICAL TESTS OF THE CAPM

When we discussed the assumptions of capital market theory, we pointed out that a theory should not be judged on the basis of its assumptions, but on *how well it explains the relationships that exist in the real world*. When testing the CAPM, there are two major questions. First, *How stable is the measure of systematic risk (beta)?* Because beta is our principal risk measure, it is important to know whether past betas can be used as estimates of future betas. Also, how do the alternative published estimates of beta compare? Second, *Is there a positive linear relationship as hypothesized between beta and the rate of return on risky assets?* More specifically, how well do returns conform to the following SML equation, discussed earlier as Equation 8.6.

$$E(R_i) = RFR + \beta_i(R_M - RFR)$$

Some specific questions might include:

- Does the intercept approximate the prevailing *RFR?*
- Was the slope of the line positive and was it consistent with the slope implied by the prevailing risk premium $(R_M - RFR)?$

We consider these two major questions in the following section.

Stability of Beta

Numerous studies have examined the stability of beta and generally concluded that the risk measure was *not* stable for individual stocks, but the stability of the beta for *portfolios* of stocks increased dramatically. Further, the larger the portfolio of stocks (e.g., over 50 stocks) and the longer the period (over 26 weeks), the more stable the beta of the portfolio. Also, the betas tended to regress toward the mean. Specifically, high-beta portfolios tended to decline over time toward unity (1.00), whereas low-beta portfolios tended to increase over time toward unity.

Carpenter and Upton (1981) considered the influence of the trading volume on beta stability and contended that the predictions of betas were slightly better using the volume-adjusted betas. A small-firm effect wherein the beta for low-volume securities was biased downward was documented by Ibbotson, Kaplan, and Peterson (1997).

Comparability of Published Estimates of Beta

In contrast to deriving your own estimate of beta for a stock, you may want to use a published source for speed or convenience, such as Merrill Lynch's *Security Risk Evaluation Report* (published monthly) and the weekly *Value Line Investment Survey*. Both services use the following market model equation:

$$(R_{i,t}) = RFR + \beta_i R_{M,t} + E_t$$

Notably, they differ in the data used. Specifically, Merrill Lynch uses *60 monthly observations* and the S&P 500 as the market proxy, whereas the *Value Line* estimates beta using *260 weekly observations* and the NYSE composite series as the market proxy. They both use an adjustment process because of the regression tendencies.

As noted earlier, Statman (1981) documented a difference between the betas for the two services. Subsequently, Reilly and Wright (1988) showed that the reason for the difference was due to the return interval used (weekly vs. monthly) by the two services and demonstrated that market value also made a difference. Handa, Kothari, and Wasley (1989) concurred with the differences in betas and showed that the specific reason the return interval was the cause was that an asset's covariance with the market and the market's variance did not change proportionally with the returns interval. They also confirmed that size impacted the effect.

RELATIONSHIP BETWEEN SYSTEMATIC RISK AND RETURN

The ultimate question regarding the CAPM is whether it is useful in explaining the return on risky assets. Specifically, is there a positive linear relationship between the systematic risk and the rates of return on these risky assets? Sharpe and Cooper (1972b) found a positive relationship between return and risk, although it was not completely linear.

Because of the statistical problems with individual stocks, Black, Jensen, and Scholes (1972) examined the risk and return for portfolios of stocks and found a positive linear relationship between monthly excess return and portfolio beta, although the intercept was higher than the zero value expected. Exhibit 8.17 contains charts from this study, which show that (1) most of the measured SMLs had a positive slope, (2) the slopes change between periods, (3) the intercepts are not zero, and (4) the intercepts likewise change between periods.

Effect of Skewness on the Relationship

Beyond the analysis of return and beta, several authors also have considered the impact of skewness on expected returns. You will recall from your statistics course that skewness reflects the presence of too many large positive or negative observations in a distribution. A normal distribution is symmetric, which means that balance exists between positive and negative observations. In contrast, positive skewness indicates an abnormal number of large positive price changes.

Investigators contended that skewness helped explain the prior results wherein the model appeared to underprice low-beta stocks (so investors received returns above expectations) and overprice high-beta stocks (so investors received returns lower than expected). Some early results confirmed these expectations, but also found that high-beta stocks had high-positive skewness, which implied that investors prefer stocks with high-positive skewness that provide an opportunity for very large returns.

Kraus and Litzenberger (1976) tested a CAPM with a skewness term and confirmed that investors are willing to pay for positive skewness. The importance of skewness was supported in studies by Sears and Wei (1988) and subsequently by Lim (1989).

Effect of Size, P/E, and Leverage

In the efficient markets hypothesis (EMH) chapter, we discussed the size effect (the small-firm anomaly) and the P/E effect and showed that these variables have an inverse impact on returns after considering the CAPM. These results imply that size and P/E are additional risk factors that need to be considered along with beta. Specifically, expected returns are a positive function

Exhibit 8.17	Average Excess Monthly Rates of Return Compared to Systematic Risk During Alternative Time Periods

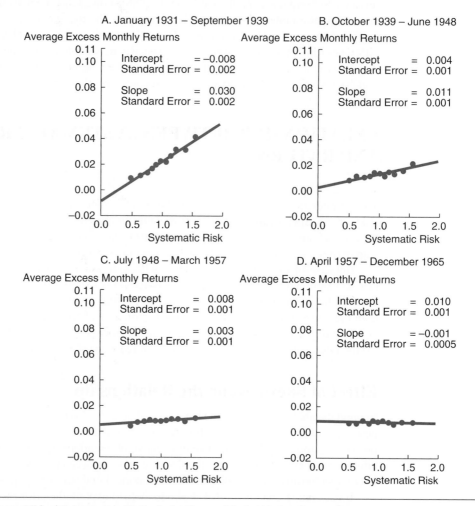

Source: Michael C. Jensen, ed., *Studies in the Theory of Capital Markets* (New York: Praeger Publishers, 1972): 96–97. Reprinted with permission.

of beta, but investors also require higher returns from relatively small firms and for stocks with relatively low P/E ratios.

Bhandari (1988) found that financial leverage also helps explain the cross section of average returns after both beta and size are considered. This implies a multivariate CAPM with three risk variables: beta, size, and financial leverage.

Effect of Book-to-Market Value: The Fama-French Study

A study by Fama and French (1992) attempted to evaluate the joint roles of market beta, size, E/P, financial leverage, and the book-to-market equity ratio in the cross section of average returns on the NYSE, AMEX, and Nasdaq stocks. While some earlier studies found a significant positive relationship between returns and beta, this study finds that the relationship between beta and the average rate of return disappears during the recent period 1963 to 1990, even when beta is used alone to explain average returns. In contrast, univariate tests between average returns and size, leverage, E/P, and book-to-market equity (BE/ME) indicate that all of these variables are significant and have the expected sign.

In the multivariate tests, the results contained in Exhibit 8.18 show that the negative relationship between size [In (ME)] and average returns is robust to the inclusion of other variables. Further, the positive relation between BE/ME and average returns also persists when the other variables are included. Interestingly, when both of these variables are included, the book-to-market value ratio (BE/ME) has the consistently stronger role in explaining average returns. The joint effect of size and BE/ME is shown in Exhibit 8.18. The seventh regression that includes both of these variables indicates that both coefficients are significant. Further, they are still significant when the two P/E ratio variables are included in the tenth regression.

Fama and French conclude that between 1963 and 1990, size and book-to-market equity capture the cross-sectional variation in average stock returns associated with size, E/P, book-to-market equity, and leverage. Moreover, of the two variables, the book-to-market equity ratio appears to subsume E/P and leverage. Following these results, Fama and French (1993) suggested the use of a three-factor CAPM model. This model was used by Fama and French (1996) to explain a number of the anomalies from prior studies.[5]

Summary of CAPM Risk–Return Empirical Results

Most of the early evidence regarding the relationship between rates of return and systematic risk of portfolios supported the CAPM; there was evidence that the intercepts were generally higher than implied by the *RFR* that prevailed, which is either consistent with a zero-beta model or the existence of higher borrowing rates. In a search for other variables that could explain these unusual returns, additional variables were considered including the third moment of the distribution (skewness). The results indicated that positive skewness and high betas were correlated.

The efficient markets literature provided extensive evidence that size, the P/E ratio, financial leverage, and the book-to-market value ratio have explanatory power regarding returns beyond beta.

The Fama-French study considered most of the variables suggested and concluded that the two dominant variables were size and the book value to market value ratio.

In contrast to Fama and French, who measure beta with monthly returns, Kothari, Shanken, and Sloan (1995) measured beta with annual returns to avoid trading problems and found substantial compensation for beta risk. They suggested that the results obtained by Fama and French may have been periodic to this time frame and might not be significant over a longer period. Pettengill, Dundaram, and Matthur (1995) noted that empirical studies typically use realized returns to test the CAPM model when theory specifies expected returns. When they adjusted for negative market excess returns, they found a consistent and significant relationship between beta and rates of return. When Jagannathan and Wang (1996) employed a conditional CAPM that allows for changes in betas and in the market risk premium, this model

---

[5]This three-factor model by Fama and French is discussed further and demonstrated in the following chapter, which deals with multifactor models of risk and return.

Exhibit 8.18 | **Average Slopes (*t*-Statistics) from Month-by-Month Regressions of Stock Returns on β, Size, Book-to-Market Equity, Leverage, and E/P: July 1963 to December 1990**

Stocks are assigned the post-ranking β of the size-β portfolio they are in at the end of June of year *t*. BE is the book value of common equity plus balance-sheet deferred taxes, A is total book assets, and E is earnings (income before extraordinary items, plus income-statement deferred taxes, minus preferred dividends). BE, A, and E are for each firm's latest fiscal year ending in calendar year *t* − 1. The accounting ratios are measured using market equity ME in December of year *t* − 1. Firm size ln(ME) is measured in June of year *t*. In the regressions, these values of the explanatory variables for individual stocks are matched with returns for the CRSP tapes from the University of Chicago for the months from July of year *t* to June of year *t* + 1. The gap between the accounting data and the returns ensures that the accounting data are available prior to the returns. If earnings are positive, E(+)/P is the ratio of total earnings to market equity and E/P dummy is 0. If earnings are negative, E(+)/P is 0 and E/P dummy is 1.

The average slope is the time-series average of the monthly regression slopes for July 1963 to December 1990, and the *t*-statistic is the average slope divided by its time-series standard error.

On average, there are 2,267 stocks in the monthly regressions. To avoid giving extreme observations heavy weight in the regressions, the smallest and largest 0.5% of the observations of E(+)/P, BE/ME, A/ME, and A/BE are set equal to the next largest or smallest values of the ratios (the 0.005 and 0.995 fractiles). This has no effect on inferences.

β	ln(ME)	ln(BE/ME)	ln(A/ME)	ln(A/BE)	E/P Dummy	E(+)/P
0.15						
(0.46)						
	−0.15					
	(−2.58)					
−0.37	−0.17					
(−1.21)	(−3.41)					
		0.50				
		(5.71)				
			0.50	−0.57		
			(5.69)	(−5.34)		
					0.57	4.72
					(2.28)	(4.57)
	−0.11	0.35				
	(−1.99)	(4.44)				
	−0.11		0.35	−0.50		
	(−2.06)		(4.32)	(−4.56)		
	−0.16				0.06	2.99
	(−3.06)				(0.38)	(3.04)
	−0.13	0.33			−0.14	0.87
	(−2.47)	(4.46)			(−0.90)	(1.23)
	−0.13		0.32	−0.46	−0.08	1.15
	(−2.47)		(4.28)	(−4.45)	(−0.56)	(1.57)

Source: Eugene F. Fama and Kenneth French, "The Cross Section of Expected Stock Returns," *Journal of Finance* 47, no. 2 (June 1992): 439. Reprinted with permission of Blackwell Publishing.

performed well in explaining the cross section of returns. Grundy and Malkiel (1996) also contend that beta is a very useful measure of risk during declining markets, which is when it is important. Finally, when Reilly and Wright (2004) examined the risk-adjusted performance for 31 different asset classes utilizing betas computed using a very broad proxy for the market portfolio, the risk–return relationship was significant and as expected in theory.

THE MARKET PORTFOLIO: THEORY VERSUS PRACTICE

Throughout our presentation of the CAPM, we noted that the market portfolio included *all* the risky assets in the economy. Further, in equilibrium, the various assets would be included in the portfolio in proportion to their market value. Therefore, this market portfolio should contain not only U.S. stocks and bonds but also real estate, options, art, stamps, coins, foreign stocks and bonds, and so on, with weights equal to their relative market value.

Although this concept of a market portfolio of all risky assets is reasonable in theory, it is difficult to implement when testing or using the CAPM. The easy part is getting a stock series for U.S. and foreign stocks. As noted in Chapter 5, there also are some well-regarded U.S. and global bond series available. Because of the difficulty in deriving series that are available monthly in a timely fashion for numerous other assets, most studies have been limited to using a stock or bond series alone. In fact, the vast majority of studies have chosen the S&P 500 series or some other broad stock series that is obviously limited to only U.S. stocks, which constitutes *less than 20 percent* of a truly global risky asset portfolio (see Exhibit 3.1). At best, it was assumed that the particular series used as a proxy for the market portfolio was highly correlated with the true market portfolio.

Most academicians recognize this potential problem but assume that the deficiency is not serious. Several articles by Roll (1977a, 1978, 1980, 1981), however, concluded that, on the contrary, the use of these indexes as a proxy for the market portfolio had very serious implications for tests of the model and especially for using the model when evaluating portfolio performance. Roll referred to this problem as a **benchmark error** because the practice is to compare the performance of a portfolio manager to the return of an unmanaged portfolio of equal risk—that is, the market portfolio adjusted for risk would be the benchmark. Roll's point is that, if the benchmark is mistakenly specified, you cannot measure the performance of a portfolio manager properly. A mistakenly specified market portfolio can have two effects. First, the beta computed for alternative portfolios would be wrong because the market portfolio used to compute the portfolio's systematic risk is inappropriate. Second, the SML derived would be wrong because it goes from the *RFR* through the improperly specified M portfolio. Exhibit 8.19 shows an example where the true portfolio risk (β_T) is underestimated (β_e), possibly because of the proxy market portfolio used in computing the estimated beta. As shown, the portfolio being evaluated may appear to be above the SML using β_e, which would imply superior management. If, in fact, the true risk (β_T) is greater, the portfolio being evaluated will shift to the right and be below the SML, which would indicate inferior performance.

Exhibit 8.20 indicates that the intercept and slope will differ if (1) there is an error in selecting a proper risk-free asset and (2) if the market portfolio selected is not the correct mean-variance efficient portfolio. Obviously, it is very possible that under these conditions, a portfolio judged to be superior relative to the first SML (i.e., the portfolio plotted above the measured SML) could be inferior relative to the true SML (i.e., the portfolio would plot below the true SML).

Exhibit 8.19 | **Differential Performance Based on an Error in Estimating Systematic Risk**

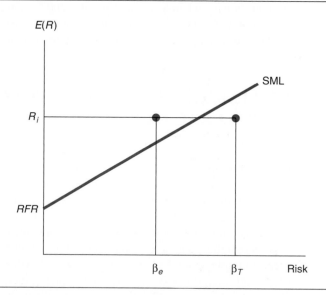

Exhibit 8.20 | **Differential SML Based on Measured Risk-Free Asset and Proxy Market Portfolio**

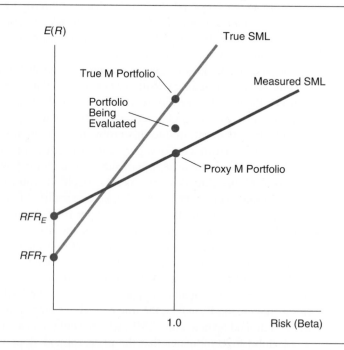

Roll contends that a test of the CAPM requires an analysis of whether the proxy used to represent the market portfolio is mean-variance efficient (on the Markowitz efficient frontier) and whether it is the true optimum market portfolio. Roll showed that if the proxy market portfolio (e.g., the S&P 500 index) is mean-variance efficient, it is mathematically possible to

Exhibit 8.21	**Differential SML Using Market Proxy that Is Mean-Variance Efficient**

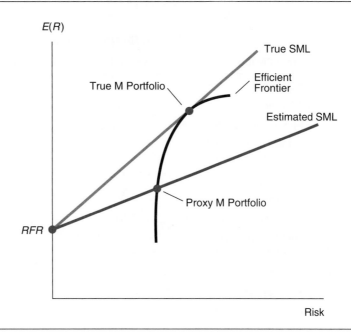

show a linear relationship between returns and betas derived with this portfolio. Unfortunately, this is not a true test of the CAPM because you are not working with the true SML (see Exhibit 8.21).

A demonstration of the impact of the benchmark problem is provided in a study by Reilly and Akhtar (1995). Exhibit 8.22 shows the substantial difference in average beta for the 30 stocks in the DJIA during three alternative periods using two different proxies for the market portfolio: (1) the S&P 500 Index, and (2) the Brinson Partners Global Security Market Index (GSMI). The GSMI includes not only U.S. and international stocks but also U.S. and international bonds. The results in Exhibit 8.22 are as one would expect because, as we know from earlier discussions in this chapter (Equations 8.5 and 8.6), beta is equal to:

$$\text{Beta} = \frac{\text{Cov}_{i,\text{M}}}{\sigma_{\text{M}}^2}$$

where:

$\text{Cov}_{i,\text{M}}$ = the covariance between asset i and the M portfolio
σ_{M}^2 = the variance of the M portfolio

As we change from an all–U.S. stock index to a world stock and bond index (GSMI), we would expect the covariance with U.S. stocks to decline. The other component of beta is the variance for the market portfolio. As shown in Exhibit 8.22, although the covariance between the U.S. stocks and the GSMI is lower, the variance of the GSMI market portfolio, which is highly diversified with stocks *and* bonds from around the world, is substantially lower (about 25 to 33 percent). As a result, the beta is substantially larger (about 27 to 48 percent larger) when the Brinson GSMI is used rather than the S&P 500 Index. Notably, the Brinson GSMI

Exhibit 8.22	The Average Beta for the 30 Stocks in the Dow Jones Industrial Average during Alternative Time Periods Using Different Proxies for the Market Portfolio

	ALTERNATIVE MARKET PROXIES	
Time Period	S&P 500	Brinson GSMI
2000–2004		
Average beta	0.961	1.305
Mean index return	−0.006	0.001
Standard deviation of index returns	0.048	0.031
1989–1994		
Average beta	0.991	1.264
Mean index return	0.010	0.008
Standard deviation of index returns	0.036	0.026
1983–1988		
Average beta	0.820	1.215
Mean index return	0.014	0.014
Standard deviation of index returns	0.049	0.031

Source: Adapted from Frank K. Reilly and Rashid A. Akhtar, "The Benchmark Error Problem with Global Capital Markets," *Journal of Portfolio Management* 22, no. 1 (Fall 1995): 33–52. The updated results were provided by Frank K. Reilly. This copyrighted material is reprinted with permission from *Journal of Portfolio Management,* a publication of Institutional Investor, Inc.

Exhibit 8.23	Components of Security Market Lines Using Alternative Market Proxies

	2000–2004			1989–1994			1983–1988		
	R_M	RFR	$(R_M - RFR)$	R_M	RFR	$(R_M - RFR)$	R_M	RFR	$(R_M - RFR)$
S&P 500	−2.01	3.05	−5.06	13.07	5.71	7.36	18.20	8.31	9.90
Brinson GSMI	3.02	3.05	−0.03	10.18	5.71	4.48	18.53	8.31	10.22

Source: Adapted from Frank K. Reilly and Rashid A. Akhtar, "The Benchmark Error Problem with Global Capital Markets," *Journal of Portfolio Management* 22, no. 1 (Fall 1995): 33–52. The updated results were provided by Frank K. Reilly. This copyrighted material is reprinted with permission from *Journal of Portfolio Management,* a publication of Institutional Investor, Inc.

has a composition of assets that is substantially closer to the true M portfolio than the S&P 500 proxy that contains only U.S. stocks. Notably, the results for the recent period were completely consistent with the original results from 1983–1994.

There also was a difference in the SMLs implied by each of the market proxies. Exhibit 8.23 contains the average *RFR,* the market returns, and the slope of the SML during three time periods for the two indexes. Clearly, the slopes differ dramatically among the alternative indexes and over time. Needless to say, the benchmark used does make a difference.

In summary, an incorrect market proxy will affect both the beta risk measures and the position and slope of the SML that is used to evaluate portfolio performance. In general, the errors will tend to overestimate the performance of portfolio managers because the proxy used for the market portfolio is probably not as efficient as the true market portfolio, so the slope of the SML will be underestimated. Also, the beta measure generally will be underestimated because the true market portfolio will have a lower variance than the typical market proxy because the true market portfolio is more diversified.

Roll's benchmark problems, however, do not invalidate the value of the CAPM as *a normative model of asset pricing;* they only indicate a problem in *measurement* when attempting to test the theory and when using this model for evaluating portfolio performance. Therefore, it is necessary to develop a better market portfolio proxy similar to the Brinson GSMI.

WHAT IS NEXT?

At this point, we have discussed the basic theory of the CAPM, the impact of changing some of its major assumptions, the empirical evidence that does and does not support the theory, and its dependence on a market portfolio of all risky assets. In addition, the model assumes that investors have quadratic utility functions and that the distribution of security prices is normal (symmetrically distributed), with a variance term that can be estimated.

The tests of the CAPM indicated that the beta coefficients for individual securities were not stable, but the portfolio betas generally were stable assuming long enough sample periods and adequate trading volume. There was mixed support for a positive linear relationship between rates of return and systematic risk for portfolios of stock, with some recent evidence indicating the need to consider additional risk variables. In addition, several papers have criticized the tests of the model and the usefulness of the model in portfolio evaluation because of its dependence on a market portfolio of risky assets that is not currently available.

Consequently, the academic community has considered alternative asset pricing models, which are considered in the following chapter.

The Internet Investments Online

Asset pricing models show how risk measures or underlying return-generating factors will affect asset returns. Estimates from such models are usually proprietary and are available from providers only by buying their research. Of course, users can always purchase their raw data elsewhere (see some of our earlier Internet discussions) and develop their own estimates of beta and factor sensitivities.

http://www.valueline.com The Value Line Investment Survey has been a long-time favorite of investors and many local and college/university libraries subscribe to it. It is a popular source of finding a stock's beta. Value Line Publishing, Inc.'s Web site contains useful information for the on-line researcher and student of investments. Its site features investment-related articles, sample pages from the Value Line Investment

Survey, and a product directory, which lists the venerable investment survey as well as Value Line's mutual fund, options, and convertibles survey, and others.

http://www.wsharpe.com William F. Sharpe, the 1990 winner of the Nobel prize in Economics because of his development of the Capital Asset Pricing Model, has a home page on the Internet. Among other items, Web surfers can read drafts of a sophisticated textbook in progress, some of his published papers, and case studies he has written. Sharpe's site offers monthly returns data on a number of mutual funds, stock indices, and bond indices, and links to other finance sites.

http://gsb.uchicago.edu/fac/eugene.fama/ The home page of Eugena Fama, whose empirical work first found support. . . and then lack of support . . . for beta as a risk measure.

http://www.moneychimp.com This is an informative education site on investments and includes CAPM calculators for estimating a stock's return and a "market simulator" to show the effect of randomness on a portfolio's return over time.

SUMMARY

- The assumptions of capital market theory expand on those of the Markowitz portfolio model and include consideration of the risk-free rate of return. The correlation and covariance of any asset with a risk-free asset are zero, so that any combination of an asset or portfolio with the risk-free asset generates a linear return and risk function. Therefore, when you combine the risk-free asset with any risky asset on the Markowitz efficient frontier, you derive a set of straight-line portfolio possibilities.

- The dominant line is the one that is tangent to the efficient frontier. This dominant line is referred to as the *capital market line (CML)*, and all investors should target points along this line depending on their risk preferences.

- Because all investors want to invest in the risky portfolio at the point of tangency, this portfolio—referred to as the market portfolio—must contain all risky assets in proportion to their relative market values. Moreover, the investment decision and the financing decision can be separated because, although everyone will want to invest in the market portfolio, investors will make different financing decisions about whether to lend or borrow based on their individual risk preferences.

- Given the CML and the dominance of the market portfolio, the relevant risk measure for an individual risky asset is its covariance with the market portfolio, that is, its *systematic risk*. When this covariance is standardized by the covariance for the market portfolio, we derive the well-known beta measure of systematic risk and a security market line (SML) that relates the expected or required rate of return for an asset to its beta. Because all individual securities and portfolios should plot on this SML, you can determine the expected (required) return on a security based on its systematic risk (its beta).

- Alternatively, assuming security markets are not always completely efficient, you can identify undervalued and overvalued securities by comparing your estimate of the rate of return to be earned on an investment to its expected (required) rate of return. The systematic risk variable (beta) for an individual risky asset is computed using a regression model that generates an equation referred to as the asset's *characteristic line*.

- When we relax several of the major assumptions of the CAPM, the required modifications are reasonably minor and do not change the overall concept of the model. Empirical studies have indicated stable portfolio betas, especially when enough observations were used to derive the betas and there was adequate volume. Although the early tests confirmed the expected relationship between returns and systematic risk (with allowance for the zero-beta model), several subsequent studies indicated that the univariate beta model needed to be supplemented with additional variables that considered skewness, size, P/E, leverage, and the book value/market value ratio. A study by Fama and French contended that during the period 1963 to 1990, beta was not relevant. In their study, the most significant variables were book-to-market value (BE/ME) and size. Subsequent studies both supported their findings and differed with them because some more recent authors have found a significant relationship between beta and rates of return on stocks.

- Another problem has been raised by Roll, who contends that it is not possible to empirically derive a true market portfolio, so it is not possible to test the CAPM model properly or to use the model to evaluate portfolio performance. A study by Reilly and Akhtar provided empirical support for this contention by demonstrating significant differences in betas, SMLs, and expected returns with alternative benchmarks.

SUGGESTED READINGS

Black, Fischer. "Capital Market Equilibrium with Restricted Borrowing." *Journal of Business* 45, no. 3 (July 1972).

Brinson, Gary P., Jeffrey J. Diermeier, and Gary Schlarbaum. "A Composite Portfolio Benchmark for Pension Plans." *Financial Analysts Journal* 42, no. 2 (March–April 1986).

Campbell, John Y., and John Ammer. "What Moves the Stock and Bond Markets? A Variance Decomposition for Long-Term Asset Returns." *Journal of Finance* 48, no. 1 (March 1993).

Elton, Edwin J., and Martin J. Gruber. *Modern Portfolio Theory and Investment Analysis,* 5th ed. New York: Wiley, 1995.

QUESTIONS

1. Explain why the set of points between the risk-free asset and a portfolio on the Markowitz efficient frontier is a straight line.
2. Draw a graph that shows what happens to the Markowitz efficient frontier when you combine a risk-free asset with alternative risky asset portfolios on the Markowitz efficient frontier. Explain this graph.
3. Draw and explain why the line from the *RFR* that is tangent to the efficient frontier defines the dominant set of portfolio possibilities.
4. Discuss what risky assets are in Portfolio M and why they are in it.
5. Discuss leverage and its effect on the CML.
6. Discuss and justify a measure of diversification for a portfolio in terms of capital market theory.
7. What changes would you expect in the standard deviation for a portfolio of between 4 and 10 stocks, between 10 and 20 stocks, and between 50 and 100 stocks?
8. Discuss why the investment and financing decisions are separate when you have a CML.
9. Given the CML, discuss and justify the relevant measure of risk for an individual security.
10. Capital market theory divides the variance of returns for a security into systematic variance and unsystematic or unique variance. Describe each of these terms.
11. The capital asset pricing model (CAPM) contends that there is systematic and unsystematic risk for an individual security. Which is the relevant risk variable and why is it relevant? Why is the other risk variable not relevant?
12. How does the SML differ from the CML?

13. *CFA Examination Level I*

    Identify and briefly discuss *three* criticisms of beta as used in the capital asset pricing model (CAPM). [6 minutes]

14. *CFA Examination Level I*

    Briefly explain whether investors should expect a higher return from holding Portfolio A versus Portfolio B under capital asset pricing theory (CAPM). Assume that both portfolios are fully diversified. [6 minutes]

	Portfolio A	Portfolio B
Systematic risk (beta)	1.0	1.0
Specific risk for each individual security	High	Low

15. *CFA Examination Level II*

    You have recently been appointed chief investment officer of a major charitable foundation. Its large endowment fund is currently invested in a broadly diversified portfolio of stocks (60 percent) and bonds (40 percent). The foundation's board of trustees is a group of prominent individuals whose knowledge of modern investment theory and practice is superficial. You decide a discussion of basic investment principles would be helpful.

    a. Explain the concepts of *specific risk, systematic risk, variance, covariance, standard deviation,* and *beta* as they relate to investment management [12 minutes].

You believe that the addition of other asset classes to the endowment portfolio would improve the portfolio by reducing risk and enhancing return. You are aware that depressed conditions in U.S. real estate markets are providing opportunities for property acquisition at levels of expected return that are unusually high by historical standards. You believe that an investment in U.S. real estate would be both appropriate and timely, and have decided to recommend a 20 percent position be established with funds taken equally from stocks and bonds.

Preliminary discussions revealed that several trustees believe real estate is too risky to include in the portfolio. The board chairman, however, has scheduled a special meeting for further discussion of the matter and has asked you to provide background information that will clarify the risk issue.

To assist you, the following expectational data have been developed:

Asset Class	Return	Standard Deviation	CORRELATION MATRIX			
			U.S. Stocks	U.S. Bonds	U.S. Real Estate	U.S. T-Bills
U.S. Stocks	12.0%	21.0%	1.00			
U.S. Bonds	8.0	10.5	0.14	1.00		
U.S. Real Estate	12.0	9.0	−0.04	−0.03	1.00	
U.S. Treasury Bills	4.0	0.0	−0.05	−0.03	0.25	1.00

b. Explain the effect on *both* portfolio risk *and* return that would result from the addition of U.S. real estate. Include in your answer *two* reasons for any change you expect in portfolio risk. (Note: It is *not* necessary to compute expected risk and return.) [8 minutes]

c. Your understanding of capital market theory causes you to doubt the validity of the expected return and risk for U.S. real estate. Justify your skepticism. [5 minutes]

16. In the empirical testing of the CAPM, what are two major concerns? Why are they important?

17. Briefly discuss why it is important for beta coefficients to be stationary over time.

18. Discuss the empirical results relative to beta stability for individual stocks and portfolios of stocks.

19. In the tests of the relationship between systematic risk (beta) and return, what are you looking for?

20. Draw an ideal SML. Based on the early empirical results, what did the actual risk–return relationship look like relative to the ideal relationship implied by the CAPM?

21. According to the CAPM, what assets are included in the market portfolio, and what are the relative weightings? In empirical studies of the CAPM, what are the typical proxies used for the market portfolio?

22. Assuming that the empirical proxy for the market portfolio is not a good proxy, what factors related to the CAPM will be affected?

23. Some studies related to the efficient market hypothesis generated results that implied additional factors beyond beta should be considered to estimate expected returns. What are these other variables and why should they be considered?

24. According to the Fama-French study, discuss what variables you should consider when selecting a cross section of stocks.

PROBLEMS

1. Assume that you expect the economy's rate of inflation to be 3 percent, giving an RFR of 6 percent and a market return (R_M) of 12 percent.
   a. Draw the SML under these assumptions.
   b. Subsequently, you expect the rate of inflation to increase from 3 percent to 6 percent. What effect would this have on the RFR and the R_M? Draw another SML on the graph from Part a.
   c. Draw an SML on the same graph to reflect an RFR of 9 percent and an R_M of 17 percent. How does this SML differ from that derived in Part b? Explain what has transpired.

2. You expect an RFR of 10 percent and the market return (R_M) of 14 percent. Compute the expected (required) return for the following stocks, and plot them on an SML graph.

Stock	Beta	$E(R_i)$
U	0.85	
N	1.25	
D	−0.20	

3. You ask a stockbroker what the firm's research department expects for the three stocks in Problem 2. The broker responds with the following information:

Stock	Current Price	Expected Price	Expected Dividend
U	22	24	0.75
N	48	51	2.00
D	37	40	1.25

Plot your estimated returns on the graph from Problem 2 and indicate what actions you would take with regard to these stocks. Discuss your decisions.

4. Select a stock from the NYSE and collect its month-end prices for the latest 13 months to compute 12 monthly percentage of price changes ignoring dividends. Do the same for the S&P 500 series. Prepare a scatterplot of these series on a graph and draw a visual characteristic line of best fit (the line that minimizes the deviations from the line). Compute the slope of this line from the graph.

5. Given the returns derived in Problem 4, compute the beta coefficient using the formula and techniques employed in Exhibit 8.11. How many negative products did you have for the covariance? How does this computed beta compare to the visual beta derived in Problem 4?

6. Look up the index values and compute the monthly rates of return for either the FT World Index or the Morgan Stanley World Index.
   a. Compute the beta for your NYSE stock from Problem 4 using one of these world stock indexes as the proxy for the market portfolio.
   b. How does this world stock index beta compare to your S&P beta? Discuss the difference.

7. Look up this stock in *Value Line* and record the beta derived by *VL*. How does this *VL* beta compare to the beta you computed using the S&P 500? Discuss reasons why the betas might differ.

8. Select a stock that is listed on Nasdaq and plot the returns during the past 12 months relative to the S&P 500. Compute the beta coefficient. Did you expect this stock to have a higher or lower beta than the NYSE stock? Explain your answer.

9. Given the returns for the Nasdaq stock in Problem 8, plot the stock returns relative to monthly rates of return for the Nasdaq composite index and compute the beta coefficient. Does this beta differ from that derived in Problem 8? If so, how can you explain this? (Hint: analyze the specific components of the formula for the beta coefficient. How did the components differ between Problems 8 and 9?)

10. Using the data from the prior questions, compute the beta coefficient for the Nasdaq composite index relative to the S&P 500 Index. A priori, would you expect a beta less than or greater than 1.00? Discuss your expectations and the actual results.

11. Based on five years of monthly data, you derive the following information for the companies listed:

Company	a_i (Intercept)	σ_i	r_{iM}
Intel	0.22	12.10%	0.72
Ford	0.10	14.60	0.33
Anheuser Busch	0.17	7.60	0.55
Merck	0.05	10.20	0.60
S&P 500	0.00	5.50	1.00

a. Compute the beta coefficient for each stock.

b. Assuming a risk-free rate of 8 percent and an expected return for the market portfolio of 15 percent, compute the expected (required) return for all the stocks and plot them on the SML.

c. Plot the following estimated returns for the next year on the SML and indicate which stocks are undervalued or overvalued.

- Intel—20 percent
- Ford—15 perent
- Anheuser Busch—19 percent
- Merck—10 percent

12. Calculate the expected (required) return for each of the following stocks when the risk-free rate is 0.08 and you expect the market return to be 0.14.

Stock	Beta
A	1.72
B	1.14
C	0.76
D	0.44
E	0.03
F	−0.79

13. The following are the historic returns for the Chelle Computer Company:

Year	Chelle Computer	General Index
1	37	15
2	9	13
3	−11	14
4	8	−9
5	11	12
6	4	9

Based on this information, compute the following:

a. The correlation coefficient between Chelle Computer and the General Index.

b. The standard deviation for the company and the index.

c. The beta for the Chelle Computer Company.

14. *CFA Examination Level II*

The following information describes the expected return and risk relationship for the stocks of two of WAH's competitors.

	Expected Return	Standard Deviation	Beta
Stock X	12.0%	20%	1.3
Stock Y	9.0	15	0.7
Market Index	10.0	12	1.0
Risk-free rate	5.0		

Using only the data shown in the preceding table:

a. Draw and label a graph showing the security market line and position Stocks X and Y relative to it. [5 minutes]

b. Compute the alphas *both* for Stock X *and* for Stock Y. Show your work. [4 minutes]

c. Assume that the risk-free rate increases to 7 percent with the other data in the preceding matrix remaining unchanged. Select the stock providing the higher expected risk-adjusted return and justify your selection. Show your calculations. [6 minutes]

15. *CFA Examination Level II*

An analyst expects a risk-free return of 4.5 percent, a market return of 14.5 percent, and the returns for Stocks A and B that are shown in the following table.

STOCK INFORMATION		
Stock	Beta	Analyst's Estimated Return
A	1.2	16%
B	0.8	14%

a. Show on the graph provided in the answer book:
  (1) Where Stocks A and B would plot on the security market line (SML) if they were fairly valued using the capital asset pricing model (CAPM)
  (2) Where Stocks A and B actually plot on the same graph according to the returns estimated by the analyst and shown in the table [6 minutes]
b. State whether Stocks A and B are undervalued or overvalued if the analyst uses the SML for strategic investment decisions. [4 minutes]

16. Given the following results, indicate what will happen to the beta for Sophie Fashion Co., relative to the market proxy, compared to the beta relative to the true market portfolio:

	YEARLY RATES OF RETURN		
Year	Sophie Fashion (Percent)	Market Proxy (Percent)	True Market (Percent)
1	10	8	6
2	20	14	11
3	−14	−10	−7
4	−20	−18	−12
5	15	12	10

Discuss the reason for the differences in the measured betas for Sophie Fashion Co. Does the suggested relationship appear reasonable? Why or why not?

17. Draw the implied SMLs for the following two sets of conditions:
  a. $RFR = 0.07$; R_M (S + P 500) = 0.16
  b. $R_z = 0.09$; R_M (True) = 0.18
  Under which set of conditions would it be more difficult for a portfolio manager to be superior?

18. Using the graph and equations from Problem 17, which of the following portfolios would be superior?
  a. $R_a = 11\%$; $\beta = 0.09$
  b. $R_b = 14\%$; $\beta = 1.00$
  c. $R_c = 12\%$; $\beta = -0.40$
  d. $R_d = 20\%$; $\beta = 1.10$
  Does it matter which SML you use?

19. Draw the security market line for each of the following conditions:
  a. (1) $RFR = 0.08$; R_M(proxy) = 0.12
    (2) $R_z = 0.06$; R_M(true) = 0.15

b. Rader Tire has the following results for the last six periods. Calculate and compare the betas using each index.

	RATES OF RETURN		
Period	Rader Tire (Percent)	Proxy Specific Index (Percent)	True General Index (Percent)
1	29	12	15
2	12	10	13
3	−12	−9	−8
4	17	14	18
5	20	25	28
6	−5	−10	0

c. If the current period return for the market is 12 percent and for Rader Tire it is 11 percent, are superior results being obtained for either index beta?

THOMSON ONE | Business School Edition

1. Collect daily price information for a year for Walgreens, ExxonMobil, and the S&P 500 index and compute daily returns for each.
   a. For each of the twelve months, compute the beta for Walgreens and ExxonMobil using the S&P 500 as the market index. (Excel's "slope" function will be helpful.) You will have twelve monthly estimates for beta for each stock. Are the monthly betas consistent over time?
   b. Using all the daily returns for the past year, compute beta for each stock. How do the monthly beta estimates compare to the annual beta calculation?
   c. For each of the twelve months, compute a monthly return for each stock and the S&P 500 index. Compute an annual beta estimate for Walgreens and for ExxonMobil using the twelve monthly returns. How does the beta computed using monthly data differ from the estimates using daily data?
2. Collect monthly price data for Walgreens, the S&P 500 index, and the MSCI World index for five years.
   a. Compute the beta for Walgreens relative to the S&P 500 index.
   b. Compute the beta for Walgreens relative to the MSCI World index.
   c. Compare the two betas and discuss what could have caused the difference.

Multifactor Models of Risk and Return

After you read this chapter, you should be able to answer the following questions:

- What are the deficiencies of the capital asset pricing model (CAPM) as an explanation of the relationship between risk and expected asset returns?
- What is the arbitrage pricing theory (APT) and what are its similarities and differences relative to the CAPM?
- What are the strengths and weaknesses of the APT as a theory of how risk and expected return are related?
- How can the APT be used in the security valuation process?
- How do you test the APT by examining anomalies found with the CAPM and why do some authors contend that the APT model is untestable?
- What are multifactor models and how are they related to the APT?
- What are the steps necessary in developing a usable multifactor model?
- What are the two primary approaches employed in defining common risk factors?
- What are the main macroeconomic variables used in practice as risk factors?
- What are the main security characteristic-oriented variables used in practice as risk factors?
- How can multifactor models be used to identify the investment "bets" that an active portfolio manager is making relative to a benchmark?
- How are multifactor models used to estimate the expected risk premium of a security or portfolio?

Chapter 7 and Chapter 8 introduced in detail the Markowitz portfolio theory and the capital asset pricing model (CAPM), which collectively represent the foundation for understanding the connection between risk and expected return in financial markets. This chapter considers several important extensions of this framework. Specifically, whereas the CAPM designated a single risk factor to account for the volatility inherent in an individual security or portfolio of securities, in this chapter we develop the intuition and application of *multifactor* explanations of risk and return. In particular, we begin with an explanation of the leading alternative to the CAPM—the arbitrage pricing theory (APT), which was developed by Stephen Ross. The chief difference between the CAPM and the APT is that the latter specifies several risk factors, thereby allowing for a more expansive definition of systematic investment risk than that implied by the CAPM's single market portfolio.

After developing the conceptual basis for the APT in the next section and contrasting its major assumptions with those of the CAPM, we also examine the empirical evidence supporting the theory. Despite several appealing features, one of the practical challenges that an investor faces when attempting to implement the APT is that the risk factors in the model are not defined in terms of their quantity (i.e., how many there are) or their identity (i.e., what they are). We conclude the chapter by discussing how investors use **multifactor models**, which can be viewed as attempts to convert the APT into a tractable working tool in the area of security analysis, thus turning theory into practice. A wide variety of factor models are currently in use. These models differ primarily in how they define the risk factors and can be grouped broadly into those models that use *macroeconomic* factor definitions and those that specify *microeconomic* factors. Several examples of the different approaches that have been taken in developing multifactor explanations of risk and return are given to illustrate the myriad forms these important models can assume.

ARBITRAGE PRICING THEORY

The last chapter highlighted many of the ways in which the CAPM has contributed to the investment management field. Indeed, in many respects, the CAPM has been one of the most useful—and frequently used—financial economic theories ever developed. However, many of the empirical studies cited also point out some of the deficiencies in the model as an explanation of the link between risk and return. For example, tests of the CAPM indicated that the beta coefficients for individual securities were not stable but that portfolio betas generally were stable assuming long enough sample periods and adequate trading volume. There was mixed support for a positive linear relationship between rates of return and systematic risk for portfolios of stock, with some recent evidence indicating the need to consider additional risk variables or a need for different risk proxies. In addition, several papers criticized the tests of the model and the usefulness of the model in portfolio evaluation because of its dependence on a market portfolio of risky assets that is not currently available.

One especially compelling challenge to the efficacy of the CAPM was the set of results suggesting that it is possible to use knowledge of certain firm or security characteristics to develop profitable trading strategies, even after adjusting for investment risk as measured by beta. Typical of this work were the findings of Banz (1981), who showed that portfolios of stocks with low market capitalizations (i.e., "small" stocks) outperformed "large" stock portfolios on a risk-adjusted basis, and Basu (1977), who documented that stocks with low price-earnings (P-E) ratios similarly outperformed high P-E stocks. More recent work by Fama and French (1992) also demonstrates that "value" stocks (i.e., those with high book value-to-market price ratios) tend to produce larger risk-adjusted returns than "growth" stocks (i.e., those with low book-to-market ratios). Of course, in an efficient market, these return differentials should not occur, which in turn leads to one of two conclusions: (1) markets are not particularly efficient for extended periods of time (i.e., investors have been ignoring profitable investment opportunities for decades), or (2) market prices are efficient but there is something wrong with the way the single-factor models such as the CAPM measure risk.

Given the implausibility of the first possibility, in the early 1970s, financial economists began to consider in earnest the implications of the second. In particular, the academic community searched for an alternative asset pricing theory to the CAPM that was reasonably intuitive, required only limited assumptions, and allowed for multiple dimensions of investment risk. The result was the **arbitrage pricing theory (APT)**, which was developed by Ross (1976, 1977) in the mid-1970s and has three major assumptions:

1. Capital markets are perfectly competitive.
2. Investors always prefer more wealth to less wealth with certainty.
3. The stochastic process generating asset returns can be expressed as a linear function of a set of K risk factors (or indexes).

Equally important, the following major assumptions—which were used in the development of the CAPM—are *not* required: (1) Investors possess quadratic utility functions, (2) normally distributed security returns, and (3) a market portfolio that contains all risky assets and is mean-variance efficient. Obviously, if such a model is simpler and can also explain differential security prices, it will be considered a superior theory to the CAPM.

Prior to discussing the empirical tests of the APT, we provide a brief review of the basics of the model. As noted, the theory assumes that the stochastic process generating asset returns can be represented as a K factor model of the form:

9.1
$$R_i = E(R_i) + b_{i1}\delta_1 + b_{i2}\delta_2 + \cdots + b_{ik}\delta_k + \varepsilon_i \text{ for } i = 1 \text{ to } n$$

where:

R_i = the actual return on asset i during a specified time period, $i = 1, 2, 3, \ldots n$
$E(R_i)$ = the expected return for asset i if all the risk factors have zero changes
b_{ij} = the reaction in asset i's returns to movements in a common risk factor j
δ_k = a set of common factors or indexes with a zero mean that influences the returns on all assets
ε_i = a unique effect on asset i's return (i.e., a random error term that, by assumption, is completely diversifiable in large portfolios and has a mean of zero)
n = number of assets

Two terms require elaboration: δ_j and b_{ij}. As indicated, δ terms are the multiple risk factors expected to have an impact on the returns of *all* assets. Examples of these factors might include inflation, growth in gross domestic product (GDP), major political upheavals, or changes in interest rates. The APT contends that there are many such factors that affect returns, in contrast to the CAPM, where the only relevant risk to measure is the covariance of the asset with the market portfolio (i.e., the asset's beta).

Given these common factors, the b_{ij} terms determine how each asset reacts to the jth particular common factor. To extend the earlier intuition, although all assets may be affected by growth in GDP, the impact (i.e., reaction) to a factor will differ. For example, stocks of cyclical firms will have larger b_{ij} terms for the "growth in GDP" factor than will noncyclical firms, such as grocery store chains. Likewise, you will hear discussions about interest-sensitive stocks. All stocks are affected by changes in interest rates; however, some experience larger impacts. For example, an interest-sensitive stock would have a b_j interest of 2.0 or more, whereas a stock that is relatively insensitive to interest rates would have a b_j of 0.5. Other examples of common factors include changes in unemployment rates, exchange rates, and yield curve shifts. It is important to note, however, that when we apply the theory, *the factors are not identified.* That is, when we discuss the empirical studies of the APT, the investigators will note that they found three, four, or five factors that affect security returns, but *they will give no indication of what these factors represent.*

Similar to the CAPM model, the APT assumes that the unique effects (ε_i) are independent and will be diversified away in a large portfolio. Specifically, the APT requires that in equilibrium the return on a zero-investment, zero-systematic-risk portfolio is zero when the unique

Exhibit 9.1	Comparing the Capital Asset Pricing Model (CAPM) and the Arbitrage Pricing Theory (APT)

	CAPM	APT
Form of Equation	Linear	Linear
Number of Risk Factors	1	$K\ (\geq 1)$
Factor Risk Premium	$[E(R_m) - RFR]$	$\{\lambda_j\}$
Factor Risk Sensitivity	β_i	$\{b_{ij}\}$
"Zero-Beta" Return	RFR	λ_0

effects are diversified away. This assumption (and some theoretical manipulation using linear algebra) implies that the expected return on any asset i (i.e., $E(R_i)$), can be expressed as:

$$E(R_i) = \lambda_0 + \lambda_1 b_{i1} + \lambda_2 b_{i2} + \ldots + \lambda_k b_{ik} \qquad \text{(APT)}$$

where:

λ_0 = the expected return on an asset with zero systematic risk
λ_j = the risk premium related to the jth common risk factor
b_{ij} = the pricing relationship between the risk premium and the asset; that is, how responsive asset i is to the jth common factor. (These are called factor betas or factor loadings.)

This equation represents the fundamental result of the APT. It is useful to compare the form of the APT's specification of the expected return-risk relationship with that of the CAPM. Recall from Chapter 8 that the comparable result for the CAPM is:

$$E(R_i) = RFR + \beta_i[E(R_m) - RFR] \qquad \text{(CAPM)}$$

Exhibit 9.1 compares the relevant features of the two models. From this summary, it should be clear that the ultimate difference between these two theories lies in the way systematic investment risk is defined: a single, market-wide risk factor for the CAPM versus a few (or several) factors in the APT that capture the salient nuances of that market-wide risk. It is important to recognize, though, that both theories specify linear models based on the common belief that investors are compensated for performing two functions: committing capital and bearing risk. Finally, notice that the equation for the APT suggests a relationship that is analogous to the security market line associated with the CAPM. However, instead of a line connecting risk and expected return, the APT implies a *security market plane* with $(K + 1)$ dimensions—K risk factors and one additional dimension for the security's expected return. Exhibit 9.2 illustrates this relationship for two risk factors (i.e., $K = 2$).

Using the APT

As noted earlier, the primary challenge in using the APT in security valuation involves the identification of the risk factors. The complexities of this issue are addressed later, so in order to illustrate how the model works we will assume that there are two common factors: one related to unexpected changes in the level of inflation and another related to unanticipated

Exhibit 9.2	**The Relationship between Expected Return and Two Common Risk Factors ($\lambda_0 = 4\%$, $\lambda_1 = 2\%$, $\lambda_2 = 3\%$)**

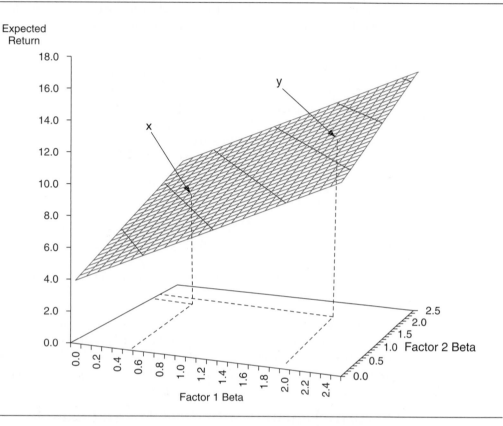

changes in the real level of GDP. If we further assume that the risk premium related to GDP sensitivity is 0.03 and a stock that is sensitive to GDP has a b_j (where j represents the GDP factor) of 1.5, this means that this factor would cause the stock's expected return to increase by 4.5 percent ($= 1.5 \times 0.03$).

To develop this notion further, consider the following example of two stocks and a two-factor model. First, consider these risk factor definitions and sensitivities:

δ_1 = unanticipated changes in the rate of inflation. The risk premium related to this factor is 2 percent for every 1 percent change in the rate ($\lambda_1 = 0.02$)

δ_2 = unexpected changes in the growth rate of real GDP. The average risk premium related to this factor is 3 percent for every 1 percent change in the rate of growth ($\lambda_2 = 0.03$)

λ_0 = the rate of return on a zero-systematic risk asset (i.e., zero beta) is 4 percent ($\lambda_0 = 0.04$)

Assume also that there are two assets (x and y) that have the following response coefficients to these common risk factors:

b_{x1} = the response of asset x to changes in the inflation factor is 0.50 ($b_{x1} = 0.50$)

b_{x2} = the response of asset x to changes in the GDP factor is 1.50 ($b_{x2} = 1.50$)

b_{y1} = the response of asset y to changes in the inflation factor is 2.00 ($b_{y1} = 2.00$)

b_{y2} = the response of asset y to changes in the GDP factor is 1.75 ($b_{y2} = 1.75$)

These factor sensitivities can be interpreted in much the same way as beta in the CAPM; that is, the higher the level of b_{ij}, the greater the sensitivity of asset i to changes in the jth risk factor. Thus, the response coefficients listed indicate that if these are the major factors influencing asset returns, asset y is a higher risk asset than asset x, and, therefore, its expected return should be greater. The overall expected return equation will be:

$$E(R_i) = \lambda_0 + \lambda_1 b_{i1} + \lambda_2 b_{i2}$$
$$= 0.04 + (0.02)b_{i1} + (0.03)b_{i2}$$

Therefore, for assets x and y:

$$E(R_x) = 0.04 + (0.02)(0.50) + (0.03)(1.50)$$
$$= 0.0950 = 9.50\%$$

and

$$E(R_y) = 0.04 + (0.02)(2.00) + (0.03)(1.75)$$
$$= 0.1325 = 13.25\%$$

The positions of the factor loadings and expected returns for these two assets are illustrated in Exhibit 9.2. If the prices of the two assets do not reflect these expected returns, we would expect investors to enter into arbitrage arrangements whereby they would sell overpriced assets short and use the proceeds to purchase the underpriced assets until the relevant prices were corrected. Given these linear relationships, it should be possible to find an asset or a combination of assets with equal risk to the mispriced asset, yet providing a higher expected return. A detailed example of how the APT can be used in the security valuation process follows.

Security Valuation with the APT: An Example

Suppose that three stocks (A, B, and C) and two common systematic risk factors (1 and 2) have the following relationship (for simplicity, it is assumed that the zero-beta return (λ_0) equals zero):

$$E(R_A) = (0.80)\,\lambda_1 + (0.90)\,\lambda_2$$
$$E(R_B) = (-0.20)\,\lambda_1 + (1.30)\,\lambda_2$$
$$E(R_C) = (1.80)\,\lambda_1 + (0.50)\,\lambda_2$$

If $\lambda_1 = 4\%$ and $\lambda_2 = 5\%$, then the returns expected by the market over the next year can be expressed:

$$E(R_A) = (0.80)\,(4\%) + (0.90)\,(5\%) = 7.7\%$$
$$E(R_B) = (-0.20)\,(4\%) + (1.30)\,(5\%) = 5.7\%$$
$$E(R_C) = (1.80)\,(4\%) + (0.50)\,(5\%) = 9.7\%$$

which, assuming that all three stocks are currently priced at \$35 and will not pay a dividend over the next year, implies the following expected prices a year from now:

$$E(P_A) = \$35\,(1.077) = \$37.70$$
$$E(P_B) = \$35\,(1.057) = \$37.00$$
$$E(P_C) = \$35\,(1.097) = \$38.40$$

Now, suppose you "know" that in one year the actual prices of stocks A, B, and C will be $37.20, $37.80, and $38.50. How can you best take advantage of what you consider to be a market mispricing?

The first thing to note is that, according to your forecasts of future prices, Stock A will not achieve a price level in one year consistent with investor return expectations. Accordingly, you conclude that at a current price of $35 a share, Stock A is *overvalued*. Similarly, Stock B is *undervalued* and Stock C is (slightly) *undervalued*. Consequently, any investment strategy designed to take advantage of these discrepancies will, at the very least, need to consider purchasing Stocks B and C while short selling Stock A.

The idea of *riskless arbitrage* is to assemble a portfolio that: (1) requires no net wealth invested initially and (2) will bear no systematic or unsystematic risk but (3) still earns a profit. Letting w_i represent the percentage investment in security i, the conditions that must be satisfied can be written formally as follows:

1. $\Sigma_i\, w_i = 0$ [i.e., no net wealth invested]
2. $\Sigma_i\, w_i\, b_{ij} = 0$ for all K factors [i.e., no systematic risk] and w_i is "small" for all i [i.e., unsystematic risk is fully diversified]
3. $\Sigma_i\, w_i\, R_i > 0$ [i.e., the actual portfolio return is positive]

In this example, since Stock A is the only one that is overvalued, assume that it is the only one that actually is short sold. The proceeds from the short sale of Stock A can then be used to purchase the two undervalued securities, Stocks B and C. To illustrate this process, consider the following investment proportions:

$$w_A = -1.0$$
$$w_B = +0.5$$
$$w_C = +0.5$$

These investment weights imply the creation of a portfolio that is *short two shares of Stock A for each one share of Stock B and one share of Stock C held long*. Notice that this portfolio meets the net investment and risk mandates of an arbitrage-based trade:

Net Initial Investment:

Short 2 shares of A:	+70
Purchase 1 share of B:	−35
Purchase 1 share of C:	−35
Net investment:	0

Net Exposure to Risk Factors:

	Factor 1	Factor 2
Weighted exposure from Stock A:	(−1.0)(0.8)	(−1.0)(0.9)
Weighted exposure from Stock B:	(0.5)(−0.2)	(0.5)(1.3)
Weighted exposure from Stock C:	(0.5)(1.8)	(0.5)(0.5)
Net risk exposure:	0	0

Assuming prices in one year actually rise to the levels that you initially "knew" they would, your net profit from covering the short position and liquidating the two long holdings will be:

Net Profit:

$$[2(35) - 2(37.20)] + [37.80 - 35] + [38.50 - 35] = \$1.90$$

Thus, from a portfolio in which you invested no net wealth and assumed no net risk, you have realized a positive profit. This is the essence of arbitrage investing and is an example of the "long-short" trading strategies often employed by hedge funds.

Finally, if everyone else in the market today begins to believe the way you do about the future price levels of A, B, and C—but do not revise their forecasts about the expected factor returns or factor betas for the individual stocks—then the current prices for the three stocks will be adjusted by the resulting volume of arbitrage trading to:

$$P_A = (\$37.20) \div (1.077) = \$34.54$$
$$P_B = (\$37.80) \div (1.057) = \$35.76$$
$$P_C = (\$38.50) \div (1.097) = \$35.10$$

Thus, the price of Stock A will be bid down while the prices of Stocks B and C will be bid up until arbitrage trading in the current market is no longer profitable.

Empirical Tests of the APT

Although the APT is considerably newer than the CAPM, it has undergone numerous empirical studies. A brief overview of this literature is provided below. Before we begin discussing the empirical tests, remember the crucial earlier caveat that when applying the theory, we do not know what the factors generated by the formal model actually represent. This becomes a major point in some discussions of test results.

Roll and Ross Study   Roll and Ross (1980) produced one of the first large-scale empirical tests of the APT. Their methodology followed a two-step procedure:

1. Estimate the expected returns and the factor coefficients from time-series data on individual asset returns.
2. Use these estimates to test the basic cross-sectional pricing conclusion implied by the APT. Specifically, are the expected returns for these assets consistent with the common factors derived in Step 1?

In particular, the authors tested the following pricing relationship:

H_0: There exist nonzero constants $(\lambda_0, \lambda_i, \ldots \lambda_k)$ such that for any asset i:
$$[E(R_i) - \lambda_0] = \lambda_1 b_{i1} + \lambda_2 b_{i2} + \cdots + \lambda_k b_{ik}$$

The specific b_i coefficients were estimated using the statistical technique of factor analysis. Their database consisted of daily returns for the period from 1962 through 1972. Stocks were put into 42 portfolios of 30 stocks each (1,260 stocks) by alphabetical order. The initial estimation of the factor model indicated that the maximum reasonable number of factors was five. The factors derived were applied to all 42 portfolios, with the understanding that the importance of the various factors might differ among portfolios (e.g., the first factor in Portfolio A might not be first in Portfolio B). Assuming a risk-free rate of 6 percent ($\lambda_0 = 0.06$), the subsequent analysis revealed the existence of at least three meaningful factors but probably not more than four. However, when they allowed the model to estimate the risk-free rate (λ_0), only two factors were consistently significant.

Roll and Ross also tested whether the three or four factors that affect Group A were the same as the factors that affect Group B. The analysis involved testing for cross-sectional consistency by examining whether the λ_0 terms for the 42 groups are similar. The results yielded no evidence that the intercept terms were different, although the test was admittedly weak. The authors concluded that the evidence generally supported the APT but acknowledged that their tests were not conclusive.

Extensions of the Roll-Ross Tests   Cho, Elton, and Gruber (1984) tested the APT by examining the number of factors in the return-generating process that were priced. Because the APT model contends that more factors affect stock returns than are implied by the CAPM, they examined different sets of data to determine what happened to the number of factors priced in the model compared to prior studies that found between three and five significant factors. The authors concluded that even when returns were generated by a two-factor model, two or three factors are required to explain the returns. These results support the APT model because it allows for the consideration of these additional factors, which is not possible with the classical CAPM.

Dhrymes, Friend, and Gultekin (1984) reexamined the methodology used in prior studies and contended that these techniques have several major limitations. They found *no* relationship between the factor loadings for groups of 30 stocks and for a group of 240 stocks. Also, they could not identify the actual number of factors that characterize the return-generating process. When they applied the model to portfolios of different sizes, the number of factors changed. For example, for 15 securities, it is a two-factor model; for 30 securities, a three-factor model; for 45, a four-factor model; for 60, a six-factor model; and for 90, a nine-factor model.

Roll and Ross (1984) acknowledged that the number of risk factors differ with 30 stocks versus 240 but contended that the important consideration is whether the resulting estimates are *consistent* because it is not feasible to consider all of the stocks together. When they tested for consistency, the APT was generally supported. They point out that the number of factors is a secondary issue compared to how well the model explains expected security returns compared to alternative models. The relevant question is: How many of these factors are significant in a diversified portfolio?

Dhrymes, Friend, Gultekin, and Gultekin (1985) repeated the prior tests for larger groups of securities. When they increased the number of securities in each group (30, 60, and 90 securities), both the number of factors that entered the model and the number of statistically significant (i.e., "priced") factors increased, although most factors are not priced. These results confirmed their earlier findings. In addition, they found that the unique or total standard deviation for a period was as good at predicting subsequent returns as the factor loadings. These results are not favorable to the empirical relevance of APT because they indicate extreme instability in the relationships and suggest that the risk-free rate implied by the model depends on group size and the number of observations.

Finally, Connor and Korajczyk (1993) argued that most tests for the number of priced risk factors are valid only for strict factor models in which diversifiable returns are uncorrelated across the set of stocks in the sample. They developed a test that identifies the number of factors in a less-restrictive model that does allow the unsystematic components of risk to be correlated across assets. Using this framework, they showed that between one and six priced factors exist in their sample of stock returns for NYSE- and ASE-listed stocks.

The APT and Stock Market Anomalies   An alternative set of tests of the APT considers how well the theory explains pricing anomalies that are not explained by a competing model (i.e., the CAPM). Two anomalies considered are the **small-firm effect** and the **January effect**.

APT Tests of the Small-Firm Effect   Reinganum (1981) addressed the APT's ability to account for the differences in average returns between small firms and large firms. He contended that this anomaly, which could not be explained by the CAPM, should be explained by the APT if the latter was to be considered a superior theory. The critical element of Reinganum's test procedure involved sorting stocks into 10 separate portfolios based on market capitalization. According to the APT, these size-based portfolios should possess identical average excess returns, which should be insignificantly different from zero. If the 10 portfolios do not have identical average excess returns, this evidence would be inconsistent with the APT.

The test results were clearly inconsistent with the APT. Specifically, the average excess returns of the 10 portfolios were not equal to zero for either a three-, four-, or five-factor model. The small-firm portfolio experienced a positive and statistically significant average excess return, whereas the large-firm portfolio had a statistically significant negative average excess return. The mean difference in excess returns between the small and large firms was about 25 percent a year. Also, the mean excess returns of smallest through largest portfolios were perfectly inversely ordered with firm size.

In contrast to Reinganum's work, Chen (1983) compared the APT model to the CAPM and provided contrary evidence related to the small-firm effect. The analysis employed 180 stocks and 5 factors. The cross-sectional results indicated that the first factor was highly correlated with the CAPM beta. Chen's test of the two models for performance measurement was based on the contention that if the CAPM does not capture all the information related to returns, this remaining information will be in the residual series. In turn, if the APT can provide factors to explain these residual returns, it will be superior. He concluded that the CAPM was misspecified and that the missing price information was picked up by the APT.

APT Tests of the January Effect   Given the so-called *January effect,* where returns in January are significantly larger than in any other month, Gultekin and Gultekin (1987) tested the ability of the APT model to adjust for this anomaly. The APT model was estimated separately for each month, and risk premia were *always* significant in January but rarely priced in other months. It was concluded that the APT model, like the CAPM, can explain the risk–return relation only in January, which indicates that the APT model does not explain this anomaly any better than the CAPM.

Burmeister and McElroy (1988) estimated a linear factor model (LFM), the APT, and a CAPM. They found a significant January effect that was not captured by any of the models. When they moved beyond the January effect, however, they rejected the CAPM in favor of the APT. Kramer (1994) shows that an empirical form of the APT accounts for the January seasonal effect in average stock returns while the CAPM cannot.

Is the APT Even Testable?   Similar to Roll's critique of the CAPM, Shanken (1982) challenged whether it is possible for the APT to be empirically verified at all. He questioned whether the APT is more susceptible to testing than the CAPM based on the usual empirical test that determines whether asset returns conform to a *K* factor model. One problem is that if stock returns are not explained by such a model, it is not considered a rejection of the model; however, if the factors do explain returns, it is considered support. Also, equivalent sets of securities may conform to different factor structures, meaning that the APT may yield different empirical implications regarding the expected returns for a given set of securities. Unfortunately, this implies that the theory cannot explain differential returns between securities because it cannot identify the relevant factor structure that explains the differential returns. This need to identify the relevant factor structure that affects asset returns is similar to the CAPM benchmark problem. In summary, each of the models has a problem with testing. Specifically, before you can test the CAPM, you must identify and use the true market portfolio; whereas, before you can test the APT, you must identify the relevant factor structure that affects security returns.

Dybvig and Ross (1985) replied by suggesting that the APT is testable as an equality rather than the "empirical APT" proposed by Shanken. Shanken (1985a) responded that what has developed is a set of equilibrium APT pricing models that are testable but that arbitrage-based models are not testable as originally specified.

Alternative Techniques for Testing the APT   In addition to the test procedures just described, several other articles have proposed alternative statistical techniques for testing the APT model. Jobson (1982) proposes that the APT be tested using a multivariate linear regression model. Brown and Weinstein (1983) propose an approach to estimating and testing asset pricing models using a bilinear paradigm. Geweke and Zhou (1996) produce an exact Bayesian framework for testing the APT and conclude that there is little reduction in pricing error from including additional factors beyond the first one. A number of subsequent papers have proposed new methodologies for testing the APT.[1]

MULTIFACTOR MODELS AND RISK ESTIMATION

When it comes to putting theory into practice, one advantage of the CAPM framework is that the identity of the single risk factor (i.e., the excess return to the market portfolio) is well specified. As noted earlier, the empirical challenge in implementing the CAPM successfully is to accurately estimate the market portfolio, a process that first requires identifying the relevant investment universe. As we saw in the last chapter, however, this is not a trivial problem as an improperly chosen proxy for the market portfolio (e.g., using the S&P 500 index to represent the market when evaluating a fixed-income portfolio) can lead to erroneous judgments. However, we also saw that once the returns to an acceptable surrogate for the market portfolio are identified (i.e., R_m), the process for estimating the parameters of the CAPM is straightforward and can be accomplished by either of the following regression equations:

1. A security or portfolio's *characteristic line* can be estimated via regression techniques using the *single-index market model:*

$$R_{it} = a_i + b_i R_{mt} + e_t$$

2. Alternatively, this equation can also be estimated in *excess return form* by netting the risk-free rate from the period t returns to security i and the market portfolio:

$$(R_{it} - RFR_t) = \alpha_i + b_i(R_{mt} - RFR_t) + e_{it}$$

In contrast to the CAPM, we have seen that the primary practical problem associated with implementing the APT is that neither the identity nor the exact number of the underlying risk factors are developed by theory and therefore must be specified in an ad hoc manner. Said differently, before the APT can be used to value securities or measure investment performance, the investor must fill in a considerable amount of missing information about the fundamental relationship between risk and expected return.

As discussed earlier, the first attempts to implement a usable form of the APT relied on multivariate statistical techniques, wherein many periods of realized returns for a large number of securities are analyzed simultaneously in order to detect recognizable patterns of behavior. A consistent finding of these studies is that there appear to be as many as three or four "priced" (i.e., statistically significant) factors, although researchers were not able to

---

[1]Among these papers are works by Cho (1984), McCulloch and Rossi (1990), and Shakla and Trzcinka (1990).

establish that the same set of factors was generated by different subsets of their sample. Indeed, we also saw that the inability to identify the risk factors is a major limitation to the usefulness of the APT.

A different approach to developing an empirical model that captures the essence of the APT relies on the direct specification of the form of the relationship to be estimated. That is, in a *multifactor model,* the investor chooses the exact number and identity of risk factors in the following equation:

9.2 $$R_{it} = a_i + [b_{i1}F_{1t} + b_{i2}F_{2t} + \cdots + b_{iK}F_{Kt}] + e_{it}$$

where F_{jt} is the period t return to the jth designated risk factor and R_{it} can be measured as either a nominal or excess return to security i. The advantage of this approach is that the investor knows precisely how many and what things need to be estimated to fit the regression equation. On the other hand, the major disadvantage of a multifactor model is that it is developed with little theoretical guidance as to the true nature of the risk–return relationship. In this sense, developing a useful factor model is as much an art form as it is a theoretical exercise.

Multifactor Models in Practice

A wide variety of empirical factor specifications have been employed in practice. A hallmark of each alternative model that has been developed is that it attempts to identify a set of economic influences that is simultaneously broad enough to capture the major nuances of investment risk but small enough to provide a workable solution to the analyst or investor. Two general approaches have been employed in this factor identification process. First, risk factors can be *macroeconomic* in nature; that is, they can attempt to capture variations in the underlying reasons an asset's cash flows and investment returns might change over time (e.g., changes in inflation or real GDP growth in the example discussed earlier). On the other hand, risk factors can also be identified at a *microeconomic* level by focusing on relevant characteristics of the securities themselves, such as the size of the firm in question or some of its financial ratios. A few examples representative of both of these approaches to the problem are discussed in the following sections.

Macroeconomic-Based Risk Factor Models   One particularly influential model was developed by Chen, Roll, and Ross (1986), who hypothesized that security returns are governed by a set of broad economic influences in the following fashion:

9.3 $$R_{it} = a_i + [b_{i1}R_{mt} + b_{i2}MP_t + b_{i3}DEI_t + b_{i4}UI_t + b_{i5}UPR_t + b_{i6}UTS_t] + e_{it}$$

where:

R_m = the return on a value-weighted index of NYSE-listed stocks
MP = the monthly growth rate in U.S. industrial production
DEI = the change in inflation, measured by the U.S. consumer price index
UI = the difference between actual and expected levels of inflation
UPR = the unanticipated change in the bond credit spread (Baa yield $- RFR$)
UTS = the unanticipated term structure shift (long-term less short-term RFR)

In estimating this model, the authors used a series of monthly returns for a large collection of securities from the Center for Research in Security Prices (CRSP) database over the period 1958–1984. Exhibit 9.3 shows the factor sensitivities (along with the associated t-statistics in parentheses) that they established. Notice two things about these findings. First, the economic

| Exhibit 9.3 | **Estimating a Multifactor Model with Macroeconomic Risk Factors** |

Period	Constant	R_M	MP	DEI	UI	UPR	UTS
1958–84	10.71	−2.40	11.76	−0.12	−0.80	8.27	−5.91
	(2.76)	(−0.63)	(3.05)	(−1.60)	(−2.38)	(2.97)	(−1.88)
1958–67	9.53	1.36	12.39	0.01	−0.21	5.20	−0.09
	(1.98)	(0.28)	(1.79)	(0.06)	(−0.42)	(1.82)	(−0.04)
1968–77	8.58	−5.27	13.47	−0.26	−1.42	12.90	−11.71
	(1.17)	(−0.72)	(2.04)	(−3.24)	(−3.11)	(2.96)	(−2.30)
1978–84	15.45	−3.68	8.40	−0.12	−0.74	6.06	−5.93
	(1.87)	(−0.49)	(1.43)	(−0.46)	(−0.87)	(0.78)	(−0.64)

Source: Nai-fu Chen, Richard Roll, and Stephen A. Ross, "Economic Forces and the Stock Market," *Journal of Business* 59, no. 3 (April 1986).

significance of the designated risk factors changed dramatically over time. For instance, the inflation factors (*DEI* and *UI*) appear to only be relevant during the 1968–1977 period. Second, the parameter on the stock market proxy is never significant, suggesting that it contributes little to the explanation beyond the information contained in the other macroeconomic risk factors.

Burmeister, Roll, and Ross (1994) analyzed the predictive ability of a model based on a different set of macroeconomic factors. Specifically, they define the following five risk exposures: (1) *confidence risk,* based on unanticipated changes in the willingness of investors to take on investment risk; (2) *time horizon risk,* which is the unanticipated changes in investors' desired time to receive payouts; (3) *inflation risk,* based on a combination of the unexpected components of short-term and long-term inflation rates; (4) *business cycle risk,* which represents unanticipated changes in the level of overall business activity; and (5) *market-timing risk,* defined as the part of the Standard & Poor's 500 total return that is not explained by the other four macroeconomic factors. Using monthly data through the first quarter of 1992, the authors estimated risk premia (i.e., the market "price" of risk) for these factors:

Risk Factor	Risk Premium
Confidence	2.59%
Time horizon	−0.66
Inflation	−4.32
Business cycle	1.49
Market timing	3.61

They also compared the factor sensitivities for several different individual stocks and stock portfolios. Panel A and Panel B of Exhibit 9.4 show these factor beta estimates for a particular stock (Reebok International Ltd.) versus the S&P 500 index and for a portfolio of small-cap firms versus a portfolio of large-cap firms. Also included in these graphs is the security's or portfolio's exposure to the BIRR composite risk index, which is designed to indicate which position has the most overall systematic risk. These comparisons highlight how a multifactor model can help investors distinguish the nature of the risk they are assuming when they hold with a particular position. For instance, notice that Reebok has greater exposures to all sources

Exhibit 9.4 | Macroeconomic Risk Exposure Profiles

A. Reebok International LTD. versus S&P 500 Index

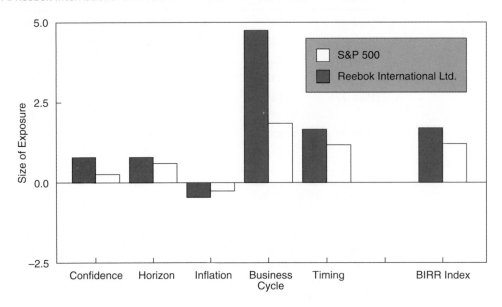

B. Large-Cap versus Small-Cap Firms

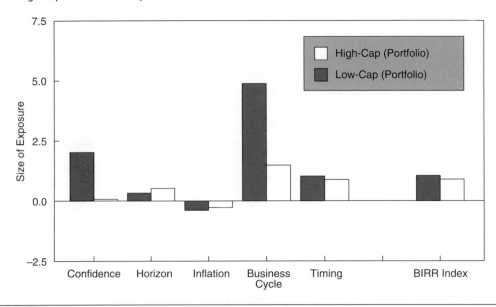

of risk than the S&P 500, with the incremental difference in the business cycle exposure being particularly dramatic. Additionally, smaller firms are more exposed to business cycle and confidence risk than larger firms but less exposed to horizon risk.

Microeconomic-Based Risk Factor Models   In contrast to macroeconomic-based explanations of the connection between risk and expected return, it is also possible to specify risk in microeconomic terms using certain characteristics of the underlying sample of securities. Typical of this *characteristic-based approach* to forming a multifactor model is the work of Fama and French (1993), who use the following functional form:

9.4 $$(R_{it} - RFR_t) = \alpha_i + b_{i1}(R_{mt} - RFR_t) + b_{i2}SMB_t + b_{i3}HML_t + e_{it}$$

where, in addition to the excess return on a stock market portfolio, two other risk factors are defined:

> *SMB* (i.e., small minus big) is the return to a portfolio of small capitalization stocks less the return to a portfolio of large capitalization stocks
>
> *HML* (i.e., high minus low) is the return to a portfolio of stocks with high ratios of book-to-market values less the return to a portfolio of low book-to-market value stocks

In this specification, *SMB* is designed to capture elements of risk associated with firm size while *HML* is intended to distinguish risk differentials associated with "growth" (i.e., low book-to-market ratio) and "value" (i.e., high book-to-market) firms. As we saw earlier, these are two dimensions of a security—or portfolio of securities—that have consistently been shown to matter when evaluating investment performance. Also, notice that without the *SMB* and *HML* factors this model simply reduces to the excess returns form of the single-index market model.

Fama and French examined the behavior of a broad sample of stocks grouped into quintile portfolios by their price-earnings (P-E) ratios on a yearly basis over the period from July 1963 to December 1991. The results for both the single-index and multifactor versions of the model for the two extreme quintiles are shown in Exhibit 9.5 (*t*-statistics for the

Exhibit 9.5	**Estimating a Multifactor Model with Characteristic-Based Risk Factors**

Portfolio	Constant	Market	SMB	HML	R²
		(1) Single-Index Model			
Lowest P-E	0.46	0.94	—	—	0.78
	(3.69)	(34.73)			
Highest P-E	−0.20	1.10	—	—	0.91
	(−2.35)	(57.42)			
		(2) Multifactor Model			
Lowest P-E	0.08	1.03	0.24	0.67	0.91
	(1.01)	(51.56)	(8.34)	(19.62)	
Highest P-E	0.04	0.99	−0.01	−0.50	0.96
	(0.70)	(66.78)	(−0.55)	(−19.73)	

Source: Reprinted from Eugene F. Fama and Kenneth R. French, "Common Risk Factors in the Returns on Stocks and Bonds," *Journal of Financial Economics* 33, no. 1 (January 1993), with permission from Elsevier Science.

estimated coefficients are listed parenthetically). There are several important things to note about these findings. First, while the estimated beta from the single-factor model indicates that there are substantial differences between low and high P-E stocks (i.e., 0.94 vs. 1.10), this gap is dramatically reduced in the multifactor specification (i.e., 1.03 vs. 0.99). This suggests that the market portfolio in a one-factor model serves as a proxy for some, but not all, of the additional risk dimensions provided by *SMB* and *HML*. Second, it is apparent that low P-E stocks tend to be positively correlated with the small-firm premium, but the reverse is not reliably true for high P-E stocks. Finally, low P-E stocks also tend to have high book-to-market ratios while high P-E stocks tend to have low book-to-market ratios (i.e., estimated *HML* parameters of 0.67 and −0.50, respectively). Not surprisingly, relative levels of P-E and book-to-market ratios are both commonly employed in practice to classify growth and value stocks.

Extensions of Characteristic-Based Risk Factor Models   There have been other interesting characteristic-based approaches to estimating a multifactor model of risk and return. Three of those approaches are described here. First, Carhart (1997) directly extends the Fama-French three-factor model by including a fourth common risk factor that accounts for the tendency for firms with positive (negative) past returns to produce positive (negative) future returns. He calls this additional risk dimension a *momentum factor* and estimates it by taking the average return to a set of stocks with the best performance over the prior year minus the average return to stocks with the worst returns. In this fashion, Carhart defines the momentum factor—which he labels *PR1YR*—in a fashion similar to *SMB* and *HML*. Formally, the model he proposes is:

9.5 $(R_{it} - RFR_t) = \alpha_i + b_{i1}(R_{mt} - RFR_t) + b_{i2}SMB_t + b_{i3}HML_t + b_{i4}PR1YR_t + e_{it}$

He demonstrates that the typical factor sensitivity (i.e., factor beta) for the momentum variable is positive and its inclusion into the Fama-French model increases explanatory power by as much as 15 percent.

A second type of security characteristic-based method for defining systematic risk exposures involves the use of index portfolios (e.g., S&P 500, Wilshire 5000) as common factors. The intuition behind this approach is that, if the indexes themselves are designed to emphasize certain investment characteristics, they can act as proxies for the underlying exposure that determines returns to that characteristic. Examples of this include the Russell 1000 Growth index, which emphasizes large-cap stocks with low book-to-market ratios, or the EAFE (Europe, Australia, and the Far East) index that selects a variety of companies that are domiciled outside the United States. Typical of these index-based factor models is the work of Elton, Gruber, and Blake (1996), who rely on four indexes: the S&P 500, the Lehman Brothers aggregate bond index, the Prudential Bache index of the difference between large- and small-cap stocks, and the Prudential Bache index of the difference between value and growth stocks. Ferson and Schadt (1996) have developed an interesting variation on this approach, which, in addition to using stock and bond indexes as risk factors, also includes other "public information" variables, such as the shape of the yield curve and dividend payouts.

BARRA, a leading risk forecasting and investment consulting firm, provides a final example of the microeconomic approach to building a multifactor model. The model they employ for analyzing U.S. equities includes as risk factors several characteristic-based variables and more than 50 industry indexes.[2] Exhibit 9.6 provides a brief description of the

---

[2]A more complete description of the BARRA approach to analyzing investment risk can be found in Richard Grinold and Ronald N. Kahn (1994).

Exhibit 9.6	Description of BARRA Characteristic-Based Risk Factors

- **Volatility (VOL)** Captures both long-term and short-term dimensions of relative return variability

- **Momentum (MOM)** Differentiates between stocks with positive and negative excess returns in the recent past

- **Size (SIZ)** Based on a firm 's relative market capitalization

- **Size Nonlinearity (SNL)** Captures deviations from linearity in the relationship between returns and firm size

- **Trading Activity (TRA)** Measures the relative trading in a stock, based on the premise that more actively traded stocks are more likely to be those with greater interest from institutional investors

- **Growth (GRO)** Uses historical growth and profitability measures to predict future earnings growth

- **Earnings Yield (EYL)** Combines current and historical earnings-to-price ratios with analyst forecasts under the assumption that stocks with similar earnings yields produce similar returns

- **Value (VAL)** Based on relative book-to-market ratios

- **Earnings Variability (EVR)** Measures the variability in earnings and cash flows using both historical values and analyst forecasts

- **Leverage (LEV)** Measures the relative financial leverage of a company

- **Currency Sensitivity (CUR)** Based on the relative sensitivity of a company's stock return to movements in a basket of foreign currencies

- **Dividend Yield (YLD)** Computes a measure of the predicted dividend yield using a firm's past dividend and stock price history

- **Nonestimation Indicator (NEU)** Uses returns to firms outside the equity universe to account for risk dimensions not captured by the other risk factors

Source: Adapted from BARRA U.S Equity Model Version 3 (E3) Handbook.

characteristic-based factors representative of the BARRA approach to decomposing investment risk. One useful application for this model is to understand where the investment "bets" in an actively managed portfolio are being placed relative to a performance benchmark. Exhibit 9.7 illustrates this sort of comparison for a small-cap-oriented mutual fund (POOL2) versus the S&P 500 index (SAP500). As you would expect, there are dramatic differences between the fund and the benchmark in terms of the firm-size risk factors (i.e., size, SIZ, and size nonlinearity, SNL). However, it also appears that POOL2 contains more highly leveraged companies (LEV) with more emphasis on earnings momentum (MOM).

Connor (1995) has analyzed the ability of the BARRA model to explain the returns generated by a sample of U.S. stocks over the period from 1985 to 1993. Interestingly, he found that the industry indexes, taken collectively, provided about four times the explanatory power as any single characteristic-based factor, followed in importance by volatility, growth, dividend yield, and momentum. Overall, the BARRA model was able to explain slightly more return variability than the other models to which it was compared, in part because of the large number of factors it employs.

Exhibit 9.7	BARRA Risk Decomposition for a Small-Cap Fund versus S&P 500

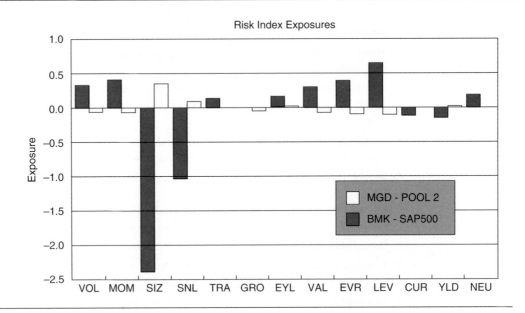

Estimating Risk in a Multifactor Setting: Examples

Estimating Expected Returns for Individual Stocks   One direct way in which to employ a multifactor risk model is to use it to estimate the expected return for an individual stock position. In order to accomplish this task, the following steps must be taken: (1) a specific set of K common risk factors must be identified, (2) the risk premia (F_j) for the factors must be estimated, (3) the sensitivities (b_{ij}) of the ith stock to each of those K factors must be estimated, and (4) the expected returns can be calculated by combining the results of the previous steps in the appropriate way.

As an example of this process, we will use the Fama-French model discussed earlier. This immediately solves the first step by designating the following three common risk factors: the excess return on the market portfolio (R_m), the return differential between small and large capitalization stocks *(SMB),* and the return differential between high and low book-to-market stocks *(HML).* The second step is often addressed in practice by using historical return data to calculate the average values for each of the risk factors. However, it is important to recognize that these averages can vary tremendously depending on the time period the investor selects. For example, for the three-factor model, the top panel of Exhibit 9.8 lists the average annual risk premia over three different time frames: a 10-year period ending in December 2004, a 20-year period ending in December 2004, and a 78-year period ending in December 2004.[3] Notice that these data confirm that small stocks earn higher returns than large stocks and value stocks outperform growth stocks (i.e., positive risk premia for the *SMB* and *HML* factors).

To illustrate the final steps involved in estimating expected stock returns, risk factor sensitivities were estimated by regression analysis for three different stocks using monthly return

---

[3]The data in these calculations are available from Professor Kenneth French's Web site at http://mba.tuck.dartmouth.edu/pages/faculty/ken.french.

Exhibit 9.8	**Estimates for Risk Factor Premia and Factor Sensitivities**

A. Risk Factor Premia Estimates Using Historical Data

	RISK PREMIUM ESTIMATE		
Risk Factor	1995–2004	1985–2004	1927–2004
Market	10.00%	9.48%	8.51%
SMB	3.73	1.42	3.94
HML	3.42	3.26	4.53

B. Regression Estimates of Risk Factor Sensitivities

Stock	Market	SMB	HML
GE	1.073	−0.709	−0.249
BHI	0.651	0.032	0.673
ADM	0.414	−0.185	0.573

data over the period from January 1999 to December 2004. The three stocks were General Electric (GE), a multinational conglomerate, Baker Hughes (BHI), a mid-sized oil field services firm, and Archer Daniels Midland (ADM), a food processing company. The estimated factor betas are listed in Panel B of Exhibit 9.8. These factor betas provide some interesting comparisons between the three stocks. First, the positive coefficients on the market factor indicate that all of these stocks are positively correlated with general movement in the stock market. The coefficients on the SMB factor confirm that GE and ADM produce returns consistent with large-cap stocks (i.e, negative SMB exposures), while BHI acts like a small- or mid-cap stock. Finally, BHI and ADM are more likely to be considered value stocks (i.e., positive HML exposures) while the multinational company GE can be considered a growth-oriented stock.

Whichever specific factor risk estimates are used, the expected return for any stock in excess of the risk-free rate (i.e., the expected risk premium) can be calculated with the formula:

9.6
$$[E(R_i) - RFR] = b_{im}\lambda_m + b_{iSMB}\lambda_{SMB} + b_{iHML}\lambda_{HML.}$$

Using the data for the most recent ten-year period reported in Exhibit 9.8, the expected excess returns for the three stocks are as follows:

$$\text{GE: } [E(R) - RFR] = (1.073)(10.00) + (-0.709)(3.73) + (-0.249)(3.42)$$
$$= 7.23\%$$
$$\text{BHI: } [E(R) - RFR] = (0.651)(10.00) + (0.032)(3.73) + (0.673)(3.42)$$
$$= 8.93\%$$
$$\text{ADM: } [E(R) - RFR] = (0.414)(10.00) + (-0.185)(3.73) + (0.573)(3.42)$$
$$= 5.41\%$$

Notice that while these values differ from the longer-term historical norms—especially the market factor premium—they reflect the conditions that prevailed in the capital markets at the time.

Comparing Mutual Fund Risk Exposures   To get a better sense of how risk factor sensitivity is estimated at the portfolio level, consider the returns produced by two popular mutual funds: Fidelity's Disciplined Equity Fund (FDEQX) and Gabelli's Asset Fund (GABAX). Morningstar Inc., an independent stock and mutual fund advisory service, classifies FDEQX's investment style into the "Large-Cap Blend" category. This means that the typical equity holding of FDEQX is characterized as a large market capitalization firm whose P-E and book-to-market ratios place it somewhere in the spectrum between a value and a growth company. Exhibit 9.9 shows a sample page for FDEQX from Morningstar's public-access Web site and shows graphically where the fund fit into the investment "style box" as of its last reporting date in 2004. Conversely, as shown in Exhibit 9.10, Morningstar puts GABAX into the "Mid-Cap Blend" category, meaning that the fund generally emphasizes smaller companies than does FDEQX. This implies that, assuming Morningstar's classification system makes a meaningful distinction, there should be measurable differences in the relative sensitivities on the *SMB* factor.

Using monthly returns over the period July 1999 to June 2004, the risk parameters for both funds were estimated relative to three different specifications: (1) a single-factor model using the Standard & Poor's 500 index as proxy for the market portfolio, (2) a single-factor model using a broader composite index of the U.S. stock market as a market proxy, and (3) the Fama-French three-factor model using the U.S. market composite. The results of these estimations are summarized in Exhibit 9.11.

Looking first at the findings for the two versions of the one-factor market model, it is apparent that FDEQX and GABAX are reasonably similar in their systematic risk. In particular, the beta coefficients for both funds indicate lower than average market risk (i.e., less than 1.00), regardless of how the market portfolio is proxied. Additionally, notice that during the July 1999 to June 2004 sample period, the beta estimates for the two funds are lower when the market portfolio is defined by the S&P 500 rather than the U.S. Composite index (e.g., 0.81 vs. 0.77 for GABAX). This suggests that S&P 500 was the less volatile of the two market indicators over this time period.

The multifactor model gives a much better sense of how the risk exposures of the FDEQX and GABAX portfolios actually differ from one another. First, notice that the inclusion of the *SMB* and *HML* factors do not affect the systematic market exposures of the two funds. For instance, the beta relative to the S&P 500 index for FDEQX is 0.85 in the single-index model, but changes only slightly to 0.84 when estimated as part of the broader three-factor model.

A second implication of the multifactor equation involves the differential sensitivities to the *SML* variable. As suggested by the Morningstar style categories, FDEQX is more oriented toward large capitalization stocks; its *SMB* sensitivity of −0.13 is statistically significant and shows that FDEQX's returns move inversely to a risk factor that, by its construction, is implicitly long in small-cap stocks and short in large-cap stocks. Conversely, the *SMB* coefficient is positive (i.e., 0.08) but of marginal statistical reliability, which is as expected for a fund that tends to hold stocks that are neither overly small nor overly large.

Finally, although not implied by the Morningstar classification system that places them both in the "Blend" category, FDEQX and GABAX also differ in their sensitivity to the *HML* risk factor. Specifically, while not significant at conventional levels, the negative parameter for FDEQX (i.e., −0.03) indicates that the portfolio is slightly tilted toward stocks that have lower book-to-market ratio. Recall that a low book-to-market ratio, like a high P-E ratio, is a characteristic of a growth-oriented stock. GABAX's sensitivity to the *HML* risk factor shows the opposite tendency in that its estimated parameter is positive (i.e., 0.22) and significant. This suggests that, on balance, the GABAX portfolio is tilted toward value-oriented stocks that have higher book-to-market—and lower P-E—ratios.

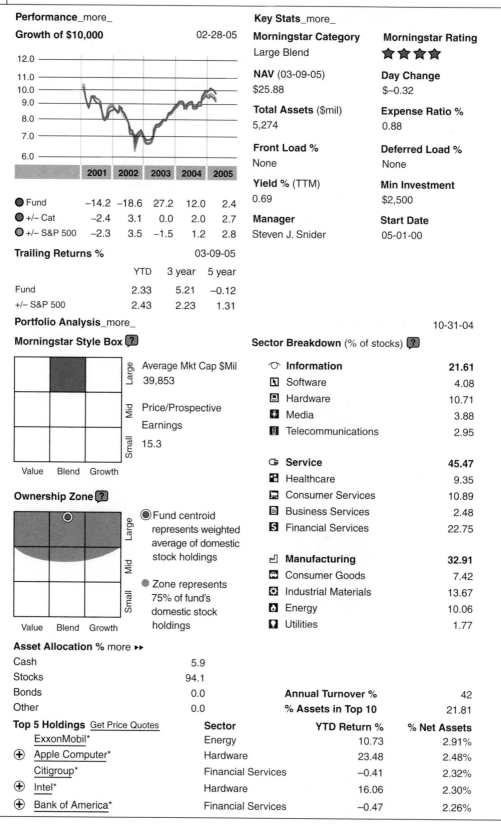

Performance _more_

Growth of $10,000   02-28-05

	2001	2002	2003	2004	2005
● Fund	−14.2	−18.6	27.2	12.0	2.4
● +/− Cat	−2.4	3.1	0.0	2.0	2.7
○ +/− S&P 500	−2.3	3.5	−1.5	1.2	2.8

Trailing Returns %   03-09-05

	YTD	3 year	5 year
Fund	2.33	5.21	−0.12
+/− S&P 500	2.43	2.23	1.31

Portfolio Analysis _more_   10-31-04

Morningstar Style Box ?

Average Mkt Cap $Mil
39,853

Price/Prospective
Earnings
15.3

Value   Blend   Growth
Large / Mid / Small

Ownership Zone ?

● Fund centroid represents weighted average of domestic stock holdings

● Zone represents 75% of fund's domestic stock holdings

Value   Blend   Growth
Large / Mid / Small

Asset Allocation % more ▶▶

Cash	5.9
Stocks	94.1
Bonds	0.0
Other	0.0

Key Stats _more_

Morningstar Category Large Blend	**Morningstar Rating** ★★★★
NAV (03-09-05) $25.88	**Day Change** $−0.32
Total Assets ($mil) 5,274	**Expense Ratio %** 0.88
Front Load % None	**Deferred Load %** None
Yield % (TTM) 0.69	**Min Investment** $2,500
Manager Steven J. Snider	**Start Date** 05-01-00

Sector Breakdown (% of stocks) ?

☁ **Information**	**21.61**
▣ Software	4.08
▣ Hardware	10.71
▣ Media	3.88
▣ Telecommunications	2.95
☞ **Service**	**45.47**
▣ Healthcare	9.35
▣ Consumer Services	10.89
▣ Business Services	2.48
▣ Financial Services	22.75
⊿ **Manufacturing**	**32.91**
▣ Consumer Goods	7.42
▣ Industrial Materials	13.67
◔ Energy	10.06
▣ Utilities	1.77

Annual Turnover %	42
% Assets in Top 10	21.81

Top 5 Holdings _Get Price Quotes_

	Sector	YTD Return %	% Net Assets
ExxonMobil*	Energy	10.73	2.91%
⊕ Apple Computer*	Hardware	23.48	2.48%
Citigroup*	Financial Services	−0.41	2.32%
⊕ Intel*	Hardware	16.06	2.30%
⊕ Bank of America*	Financial Services	−0.47	2.26%

Exhibit 9.10 | **Morningstar Report for Gabelli Asset (GABAX) Fund**

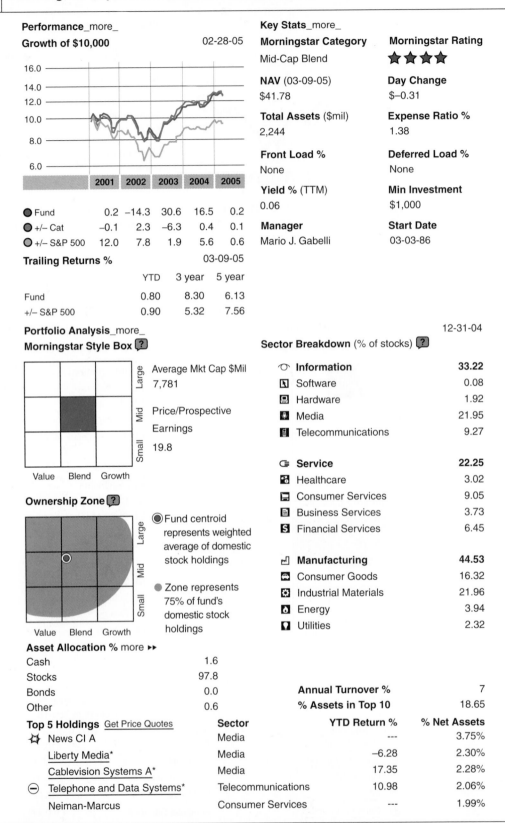

Performance _more_
Growth of $10,000   02-28-05

	2001	2002	2003	2004	2005
● Fund	0.2	−14.3	30.6	16.5	0.2
◗ +/− Cat	−0.1	2.3	−6.3	0.4	0.1
◗ +/− S&P 500	12.0	7.8	1.9	5.6	0.6

Trailing Returns %   03-09-05

	YTD	3 year	5 year
Fund	0.80	8.30	6.13
+/− S&P 500	0.90	5.32	7.56

Portfolio Analysis _more_
Morningstar Style Box ?

Average Mkt Cap $Mil
7,781

Price/Prospective
Earnings
19.8

Value Blend Growth
Large / Mid / Small

Ownership Zone ?

◉ Fund centroid
represents weighted
average of domestic
stock holdings

● Zone represents
75% of fund's
domestic stock
holdings

Value Blend Growth
Large / Mid / Small

Asset Allocation % more ▶▶

Cash	1.6
Stocks	97.8
Bonds	0.0
Other	0.6

Top 5 Holdings Get Price Quotes

	Sector	YTD Return %	% Net Assets
✡ News Cl A	Media	---	3.75%
Liberty Media*	Media	−6.28	2.30%
Cablevision Systems A*	Media	17.35	2.28%
⊖ Telephone and Data Systems*	Telecommunications	10.98	2.06%
Neiman-Marcus	Consumer Services	---	1.99%

Key Stats _more_

Morningstar Category	**Morningstar Rating**
Mid-Cap Blend	★★★★
NAV (03-09-05)	**Day Change**
$41.78	$−0.31
Total Assets ($mil)	**Expense Ratio %**
2,244	1.38
Front Load %	**Deferred Load %**
None	None
Yield % (TTM)	**Min Investment**
0.06	$1,000
Manager	**Start Date**
Mario J. Gabelli	03-03-86

Sector Breakdown (% of stocks) ?   12-31-04

↻ **Information**	**33.22**
▣ Software	0.08
▦ Hardware	1.92
🎙 Media	21.95
▤ Telecommunications	9.27
☞ **Service**	**22.25**
▤ Healthcare	3.02
▢ Consumer Services	9.05
▤ Business Services	3.73
S Financial Services	6.45
▱ **Manufacturing**	**44.53**
▤ Consumer Goods	16.32
✿ Industrial Materials	21.96
◔ Energy	3.94
▯ Utilities	2.32

Annual Turnover %	7
% Assets in Top 10	18.65

Exhibit 9.11	Risk Factor Estimates for FDEQX and GABAX

Mutual Fund	Constant	Market	*SMB*	*HML*	R^2
(1) Single-Index Model (Market = S&P 500)					
FDEQX	0.00	0.85	—	—	0.94
	(0.41)	(28.96)			
GABAX	0.00	0.81	—	—	0.83
	(2.02)	(16.74)			
(2) Single-Index Model (Market = U.S. Composite)					
FDEQX	0.00	0.82	—	—	0.94
	(−0.19)	(30.13)			
GABAX	0.00	0.77	—	—	0.82
	(1.63)	(16.16)			
(3) Multifactor Model (Market = U.S. Composite)					
FDEQX	0.00	0.84	−0.13	−0.03	0.95
	(1.06)	(33.71)	(−4.21)	(−1.30)	
GABAX	0.00	0.80	0.08	0.22	0.89
	(0.98)	(20.92)	(1.68)	(6.31)	

The Internet — Investments Online

Multifactor models are the focus of much research in the academic and practitioner literature. Using "multifactor model" in a Web search engine results in thousands of references, many of which are research papers. Academics have realized that the empirical CAPM does not explain variation in asset returns as much as theory indicates that it should. Thus, a search for models to explain the returns of stocks and other assets continues.

http://www.kellogg.northwestern.edu/faculty/korajczy/htm/aptlist.htm is a list of research papers on multifactor and APT models. The list is maintained by Professor Robert A. Korajczyk of Northwestern University.

http://www.barra.com For subscribers, Barra's Web site offers a gold mine of data and analytical analysis. Links offer information on portfolio management, investment data, market indices, and research. Barra offers its clients data, software, consulting, as well as money management services for equity, fixed income, currency, and other global financial instruments. Barra estimates multiple factor models and their global and single country equity models provide risk analysis on over 25,000 globally traded securities, including predicted and historical beta values. Explore this data to discover its data resources, charts, and graphs.

http://www.dfaus.com Dimensional Fund Advisors uses the tools of academic research to help guide portfolio decisions. The Web site provides information on Dimension's investment strategies, its academic consultants, and its various funds.

http://www.mba.tuck.dartmouth.edu/pages/faculty/ken.french Maintained by Professor Kenneth French, this Web site gives users access to monthly, quarterly, and annual data series on the three Fama and French risk factors: the excess market return, the *SMB* factor return, and the *HML* factor return. The site also provides excellent documentation as to how the risk factor portfolios are constructed and maintained. The data are offered in a download-able format, making it easy for the user to customize the three-factor characteristic-based risk model to his or her own purposes.

SUMMARY

- Although the CAPM is an elegant and appealing explana-tion for the way in which investment risk and expected return are related, a number of empirical anomalies—such as the small-firm effect—have caused financial econo-mists to seek other answers. Ross subsequently devised an alternative asset pricing model—the APT—that makes fewer assumptions than the CAPM and does not specifi-cally require the designation of a market portfolio. Instead, the APT posits that expected security returns are related in a linear fashion to multiple common risk factors. Unfortu-nately, the theory does not offer guidance as to how many factors exist or what their identities might be. The results from the empirical tests of the APT have thus far been mixed.

- Given that the common risk factors are not identified, the APT is difficult to put into practice in a theoretically rigor-ous fashion. Multifactor models of risk and return attempt to bridge this gap between theory and practice by specify-ing a set of variables that are thought to capture the essence of the systematic risk exposures that exist in the capital mar-ket. Over the past two decades, there have been a number of alternative risk factors suggested and tested by financial re-searchers. One general approach that has been adopted suc-cessfully has been to use macroeconomic variables—such as unexpected inflation, changes in consumer confidence, unanticipated shifts in the yield curve, or unexpected changes in real GDP—as surrogates for the types of expo-sures that will have an impact on all securities. Once se-lected, historical data are often employed to determine the risk premium (i.e., market "price") for each common factor.

- An equally successful second approach to identifying the risk exposures in a multifactor model has focused on the characteristics of the securities themselves. Typical of this sort of microeconomic approach is the work of Fama and French, who posit that three risk factors should be employed: the excess returns to a broad market index, the return difference between portfolios of small- and large-cap stocks, and the return difference between portfolios of value- and growth-oriented stocks. One immediate advan-tage of this specification is that it accounts directly for some of the anomalies that plagued the CAPM (i.e., the small-firm effect). Another advantage of the characteristic-based approach to forming factor models is the flexibility to modify the equation to changing market conditions. For instance, the Fama-French model has been expanded to include a factor accounting for stock return momentum.

- In conclusion, it is probably safe to assume that both the CAPM and APT will continue to be used to price capital assets. Coincident with their use will be further empirical tests of both theories, the ultimate goal being to determine which theory does the best job of explaining current returns and predicting future ones. Notably, although the APT model requires fewer assumptions and considers multiple factors to explain the risk of an asset, the CAPM has an advantage in that its single risk factor is well defined. Future work in this area will continue to seek to identify the set of factors that best captures the relevant dimension of investment risk as well as explore the intertemporal dynamics of the models (e.g., factor betas and risk premia that change over time).

SUGGESTED READINGS

Elton, Edwin J., Martin J. Gruber, Stephen J. Brown, and William N. Goetzmann. *Modern Portfolio Theory and Investment Analysis,* 6th ed. New York: John Wiley & Sons, 2003.

Grinold, Richard C., and Ronald N. Kahn. *Active Portfolio Management,* 2nd ed. New York: McGraw-Hill, 2000.

Lehmann, B. N., and D. M. Modest. "The Empirical Foundations of the Arbitrage Pricing Theory." *Journal of Financial Economics* 21, no. 3 (September 1988).

Peavy, John, ed. *A Practitioner's Guide to Factor Models.* Charlottesville, VA: Research Foundation of the CFA Institute, 1994.

Sharpe, William F. "Factor Models, CAPMs, and the APT." *Journal of Portfolio Management* 11, no. 1 (Fall 1984).

QUESTIONS

1. Both the capital asset pricing model and the arbitrage pricing theory rely on the proposition that a no-risk, no-wealth investment should earn, on average, no return. Explain why this should be the case, being sure to describe briefly the similarities and differences between the CAPM and the APT. Also, using either of these theories, explain how superior investment performance can be established.

2. *CFA Examination Level III*
   You are an investment officer at Pegasus Securities and are preparing for the next meeting of the investment committee. Several committee members are interested in reviewing two asset pricing models—the capital asset pricing model (CAPM) and the arbitrage pricing theory (APT)—and their use in portfolio management and stock selection.
   a. Describe both the CAPM and the APT, and identify the factor(s) that determines returns in each.
   b. "The APT model is more general than the CAPM." Explain how this observation has meaning in the stock selection process.

3. The *small-firm effect* refers to the observed tendency for stock prices to behave in a manner that is contrary to normal expectations. Describe this effect and discuss whether it represents sufficient information to conclude that the stock market does not operate efficiently. In formulating your response, consider: (a) what it means for the stock market to be inefficient, and (b) what role the measurement of risk plays in your conclusions about each effect.

4. Some studies related to the efficient market hypothesis generated results that implied additional factors beyond beta should be considered to estimate expected returns. What are these other variables and why should they be considered?

5. Suppose you are considering the purchase of shares in the XYZ mutual fund. As part of your investment analysis, you regress XYZ's monthly returns for the past five years against the three factors specified in the Fama and French models. This procedure generates the following coefficient estimates: market factor = 1.2, *SMB* factor = –0.3, *HML* factor = 1.4. Explain what each of these coefficient values means. What types of stocks is XYZ likely to be holding?

6. *CFA Examination Level III*
   As the manager of a large, broadly diversified portfolio of stocks and bonds, you realize that changes in certain macroeconomic variables may directly affect the performance of your portfolio. You are considering using an arbitrage pricing theory (APT) approach to strategic portfolio planning and want to analyze the possible impacts of the following four factors:
   • Industrial production
   • Inflation
   • Risk premia or quality spreads
   • Yield curve shifts
   Indicate how each of these four factors influences the cash flows and/or the discount rates in the traditional discounted cash flow model. Explain how unanticipated changes in each of these four factors could affect portfolio returns.

7. Describe the intuition underlying: (a) the macroeconomic approach to identifying risk factors, and (b) the microeconomic (i.e., characteristic-based) approach to identifying risk factors. Is it conceptually and practically possible for these two approaches to lead to the same estimate of expected return for any given security?

8. How can multifactor models be used to help investors understand the relative risk exposures in their portfolios relative to a benchmark portfolio? Support your answer with examples using both macroeconomic and microeconomic approaches to factor identification.

9. Consider the following questions related to empirical tests of the APT:
   a. Briefly discuss one study that does not support the APT. Briefly discuss a study that does support the APT. Which position seems more plausible?
   b. Briefly discuss why Shanken contends that the APT is not testable. What is the contrary view to Shanken's position?

10. *CFA Examination Level II*

Jeffrey Bruner, CFA, uses the capital asset pricing model (CAPM) to help identify mispriced securities. A consultant suggests Bruner use the arbitrage pricing theory (APT) instead. In comparing the CAPM and the APT, the consultant made the following arguments:

a. Both the CAPM and the APT require a mean-variance efficient market portfolio.

b. Neither the CAPM nor the APT assumes normally distributed security returns.

c. The CAPM assumes that one specific factor explains security returns, but the APT does not.

State whether *each* of the consultant's arguments is correct or incorrect. Indicate, for each incorrect argument, why the argument is incorrect.

PROBLEMS

1. Consider the following data for two risk factors (1 and 2) and two securities (J and L):

$\lambda_0 = 0.05$ $b_{J1} = 0.80$
$\lambda_1 = 0.02$ $b_{J2} = 1.40$
$\lambda_2 = 0.04$ $b_{L1} = 1.60$
 $b_{L2} = 2.25$

a. Compute the expected returns for both securities.

b. Suppose that Security J is currently priced at $22.50 while the price of Security L is $15.00. Further, it is expected that both securities will pay a dividend of $0.75 during the coming year. What is the expected price of each security one year from now?

2. Earlier in the text, it was demonstrated how the Fama and French three-factor model could be used to estimate the expected risk compensation for a set of equities (GE, BHI, and ADM). Specifically, using return data from the 1995–2004 period, the following equations were estimated:

$$\text{GE: } [E(R) - RFR] = (1.073)(\lambda_m) + (-0.709)(\lambda_{SMB}) + (-0.249)(\lambda_{HML})$$
$$\text{BHI: } [E(R) - RFR] = (0.651)(\lambda_m) + (0.032)(\lambda_{SMB}) + (0.673)(\lambda_{HML})$$
$$\text{ADM: } [E(R) - RFR] = (0.414)(\lambda_m) + (-0.185)(\lambda_{SMB}) + (0.573)(\lambda_{HML})$$

Using the estimated factor risk premia of $\lambda_m = 10.00\%$, $\lambda_{SMB} = 3.73\%$, and $\lambda_{HML} = 3.42\%$, it was then shown that the expected excess returns for the three stocks were 7.23%, 8.93%, and 5.41%, respectively.

a. Exhibit 9.8 lists factor risk prices calculated over two different time frames: (1) 1985–2004 ($\lambda_m = 9.48\%$, $\lambda_{SMB} = 1.42\%$, and $\lambda_{HML} = 3.26\%$), and (2) 1927–2004 ($\lambda_m = 8.51\%$, $\lambda_{SMB} = 3.94\%$, and $\lambda_{HML} = 4.53\%$). Calculate the expected excess returns for GE, BHI, and ADM using both of these alternative sets of factor risk premia.

b. Do all of the expected excess returns you calculated in Part a make sense? If not, identify which ones seem inconsistent with asset pricing theory and discuss why.

c. Would you expect the factor betas to remain constant over time? Discuss how and why these co-efficients might change in response to changing market conditions.

3. You have been assigned the task of estimating the expected returns for three different stocks: QRS, TUV, and WXY. Your preliminary analysis has established the historical risk premiums associated with three risk factors that could potentially be included in your calculations: the excess return on a proxy for the market portfolio (MKT), and two variables capturing general macroeconomic exposures (MACRO1 and MACRO2). These values are: $\lambda_{MKT} = 7.5\%$, $\lambda_{MACRO1} = -0.3\%$, and $\lambda_{MACRO2} = 0.6\%$. You have also estimated the following factor betas (i.e., loadings) for all three stocks with respect to each of these potential risk factors:

	FACTOR LOADING		
Stock	MKT	MACRO1	MACRO2
QRS	1.24	−0.42	0.00
TUV	0.91	0.54	0.23
WXY	1.03	−0.09	0.00

a. Calculate expected returns for the three stocks using just the MKT risk factor. Assume a risk-free rate of 4.5%.

b. Calculate the expected returns for the three stocks using all three risk factors and the same 4.5% risk-free rate.

c. Discuss the differences between the expected return estimates from the single-factor model and those from the multifactor model. Which estimates are most likely to be more useful in practice?

d. What sort of exposure might MACRO2 represent? Given the estimated factor betas, is it really reasonable to consider it a common (i.e., systematic) risk factor?

4. Consider the following information about two stocks (D and E) and two common risk factors (1 and 2):

Stock	b_{i1}	b_{i2}	$E(R_i)$
D	1.2	3.4	13.1%
E	2.6	2.6	15.4%

a. Assuming that the risk-free rate is 5.0%, calculate the levels of the factor risk premia that are consistent with the reported values for the factor betas and the expected returns for the two stocks.

b. You expect that in one year the prices for Stocks D and E will be $55 and $36, respectively. Also, neither stock is expected to pay a dividend over the next year. What should the price of each stock be today to be consistent with the expected return levels listed at the beginning of the problem?

c. Suppose now that the risk premium for Factor 1 that you calculated in Part a suddenly increases by 0.25% (i.e., from x% to $(x +0.25)$%, where x is the value established in Part a). What are the new expected returns for Stocks D and E?

d. If the increase in the Factor 1 risk premium in Part c does not cause you to change your opinion about what the stock prices will be in one year, what adjustment will be necessary in the current (i.e., today's) prices?

5. Suppose that three stocks (A, B, and C) and two common risk factors (1 and 2) have the following relationship:

$$E(R_A) = (1.1)\,\lambda_1 + (0.8)\,\lambda_2$$
$$E(R_B) = (0.7)\,\lambda_1 + (0.6)\,\lambda_2$$
$$E(R_C) = (0.3)\,\lambda_1 + (0.4)\,\lambda_2$$

a. If λ_1 = 4% and λ_2 = 2%, what are the prices expected next year for each of the stocks? Assume that all three stocks currently sell for $30 and will not pay a dividend in the next year.

b. Suppose that you know that next year the prices for Stocks A, B, and C will actually be $31.50, $35.00, and $30.50. Create and demonstrate a riskless, arbitrage investment to take advantage of these mispriced securities. What is the profit from your investment? You may assume that you can use the proceeds from any necessary short sale.

Problems 6–7 refer to the data contained in Exhibit 9.12, which lists 30 monthly excess returns to two different actively managed stock portfolios (A and B) and three different common risk factors (1, 2, and 3). (Note: You may find it useful to use a computer spreadsheet program such as Microsoft Excel to calculate your answers.)

6. a. Compute the average monthly return and monthly standard return deviation for each portfolio and all three risk factors. Also state these values on an annualized basis. (Hint: Monthly returns can be annualized by multiplying them by 12, while monthly standard deviations can be annualized by multiplying them by the square root of 12.)

   b. Based on the return and standard deviation calculations for the two portfolios from Part a, is it clear whether one portfolio outperformed the other over this time period?

   c. Calculate the correlation coefficients between each pair of the common risk factors (i.e., 1 & 2, 1 & 3, and 2 & 3).

   d. In theory, what should be the value of the correlation coefficient between the common risk factors? Explain why.

   e. How close do the estimates from Part b come to satisfying this theoretical condition? What conceptual problem(s) is created by a deviation of the estimated factor correlation coefficients from their theoretical levels?

7. a. Using regression analysis, calculate the factor betas of each stock associated with each of the common risk factors. Which of these coefficients are statistically significant?

   b. How well does the factor model explain the variation in portfolio returns? On what basis can you make an evaluation of this nature?

   c. Suppose you are now told that the three factors in Exhibit 9.12 represent the risk exposures in the Fama-French characteristic-based model (i.e., excess market, *SMB,* and *HML*). Based on your regression results, which one of these factors is the most likely to be the market factor? Explain why.

   d. Suppose it is further revealed that Factor 3 is the *HML* factor. Which of the two portfolios is most likely to be a growth-oriented fund and which is a value-oriented fund? Explain why.

| Exhibit 9.12 | Monthly Excess Return Data for Two Portfolios and Three Risk Factors |

Period	Portfolio A	Portfolio B	Factor 1	Factor 2	Factor 3
1	1.08%	0.00%	0.01%	−1.01%	−1.67%
2	7.58	6.62	6.89	0.29	−1.23
3	5.03	6.01	4.75	−1.45	1.92
4	1.16	0.36	0.66	0.41	0.22
5	−1.98	−1.58	−2.95	−3.62	4.29
6	4.26	2.39	2.86	−3.40	−1.54
7	−0.75	−2.47	−2.72	−4.51	−1.79
8	−15.49	−15.46	−16.11	−5.92	5.69
9	6.05	4.06	5.95	0.02	−3.76
10	7.70	6.75	7.11	−3.36	−2.85
11	7.76	5.52	5.86	1.36	−3.68
12	9.62	4.89	5.94	−0.31	−4.95
13	5.25	2.73	3.47	1.15	−6.16
14	−3.19	−0.55	−4.15	−5.59	1.66
15	5.40	2.59	3.32	−3.82	−3.04
16	2.39	7.26	4.47	2.89	2.80
17	−2.87	0.10	−2.39	3.46	3.08
18	6.52	3.66	4.72	3.42	−4.33
19	−3.37	−0.60	−3.45	2.01	0.70
20	−1.24	−4.06	−1.35	−1.16	−1.26
21	−1.48	0.15	−2.68	3.23	−3.18
22	6.01	5.29	5.80	−6.53	−3.19
23	2.05	2.28	3.20	7.71	−8.09
24	7.20	7.09	7.83	6.98	−9.05
25	−4.81	−2.79	−4.43	4.08	−0.16
26	1.00	−2.04	2.55	21.49	−12.03
27	9.05	5.25	5.13	−16.69	7.81
28	−4.31	−2.96	−6.24	−7.53	8.59
29	−3.36	−0.63	−4.27	−5.86	5.38
30	3.86	1.80	4.67	13.31	−8.78

Part 3

Valuation Principles and Practices

In Parts 1 and 2 you learned the purpose of investing and the importance of an appropriate asset allocation decision. You also learned about the numerous investment instruments available on a global basis and the background regarding the institutional characteristics of the capital markets. In addition, you are now aware of the major developments in investment theory as they relate to efficient capital markets, portfolio theory, capital asset pricing, and multifactor valuation models. Therefore, at this point you are in a position to consider the theory and practice of estimating the value of various securities, which is the heart of investing and leads to the construction of a portfolio that is consistent with your risk–return objectives. You will recall that the investment decision is based on a comparison of an asset's intrinsic value and its market price.

The major source of information regarding a stock or bond is the corporation's financial statements. Chapter 10 considers what financial statements are available and what information they provide, followed by a discussion of the financial ratios used to answer several important questions about a firm's liquidity, its operating performance, its risk profile, and its growth potential.

Chapter 11 considers the basic principles of valuation and applies those principles to the valuation of bonds, preferred stock, and common stock. Because it is recognized that the valuation of common stock is the most challenging task, we present two general approaches to equity valuation (discounted cash flow models and relative valuation ratios) and several techniques for each of these approaches. We conclude this chapter by reviewing the basic factors that influence the two critical variables that determine the intrinsic value of an asset irrespective of the valuation model: (1) the required rate of return for an investment, and (2) the estimated growth rate of earnings, dividends, and cash flows for the investment.

When you master these two chapters you will have the tools and the theoretical understanding to apply the valuation models to the range of entities included in the top-down approach—the aggregate market, alternative industries, and individual companies and stocks. These specific valuations are the topics considered in Part 4.

Chapter 10

Analysis of Financial Statements

Chapter 11

An Introduction to Security Valuation

Chapter 10

Analysis of Financial Statements

After you read this chapter, you should be able to answer the following questions:

- What are the major financial statements provided by firms and what specific information does each of them contain?
- Why do we use financial ratios to examine the performance of a firm, and why is it important to examine performance relative to the economy and to a firm's industry?
- What are the major categories for financial ratios and what questions are answered by the ratios in these categories?
- What specific ratios help determine a firm's internal liquidity, operating performance, risk profile, and growth potential?
- How can DuPont analysis help evaluate a firm's past and future return on equity?
- What is a quality balance sheet or income statement?
- Why is financial statement analysis done if markets are efficient and forward-looking?
- What major financial ratios are used by analysts in the following areas: stock valuation, estimating and evaluating systematic risk, predicting the credit ratings on bonds, and predicting bankruptcy?

You have probably already noted that this is a fairly long chapter with several financial statements and numerous financial ratios. The reason for this extensive discussion of how to analyze financial statements is that our ultimate goal (as noted earlier) is to construct a portfolio of investments that will provide rates of return that are consistent with the risk of the portfolio. In turn, to determine the expected rates of return on different assets we must *estimate the future value* of each asset since a major component of the rate of return is the change in value for the asset over time. Therefore, the crux of investments is *valuation*. Although we will consider various valuation models for common stocks in the next chapter, you are already aware that the value of any earning asset is the present value of the expected cash flows generated by the asset. Therefore, as noted in previous chapters, to estimate the value of an asset we must derive an estimate of the discount rate for the asset (the required rate of return) and its expected cash flows. The main source of the information needed to make these two estimates is the financial statements. To derive an estimate of the required rate of return, we need to understand the business and financial risk of the firm. To estimate future cash flows, we must understand the composition of cash flows and what will contribute to the short-run and long-run growth of these cash flows. Financial statements, business and financial risk, and analysis of the composition and growth of cash flow are all topics of this chapter. In other words, a primary purpose of this chapter is to help you understand how to estimate the variables in valuation models.

Financial statements are also the main source of information when deciding whether to lend money to a firm (invest in its bonds) or to buy warrants or options on a firm's stock. In this chapter, we first introduce a corporation's major financial statements and discuss why and how financial ratios are useful. We also provide example computations of ratios that reflect internal liquidity, operating performance, risk analysis, and growth analysis. In addition, we address four major areas in investments where financial ratios have been effectively employed.

Our example company in this chapter is Walgreens Co., the largest retail drugstore chain in the United States. It operates 4,582 drugstores in 44 states and Puerto Rico. Pharmacy prescription sales generate over 63 percent of total sales. The firm leads its industry (retail drugstores) in sales, profit, and store growth. The firm's goal is to be America's most convenient and technologically advanced health-care retailer. It takes great pride in its steady sales and earnings growth that have been reflected in outstanding stock performance—e.g., dividends have increased in each of the past 29 years and since 1980 the stock has been split two-for-one seven times.

MAJOR FINANCIAL STATEMENTS

Financial statements are intended to provide information on the resources available to management, how these resources were financed, and what the firm accomplished with them. Corporate shareholder annual and quarterly reports include three required financial statements: the balance sheet, the income statement, and the statement of cash flows. In addition, reports that must be filed with the Securities and Exchange Commission (SEC) (for example, the 10-K and 10-Q reports) carry detailed information about the firm, such as information on loan agreements and data on product line and subsidiary performance. Information from the basic financial statements can be used to calculate financial ratios and to analyze the operations of the firm to determine what factors influence a firm's earnings, cash flows, and risk characteristics.

Generally Accepted Accounting Principles

Among the input used to construct the financial statements are **generally accepted accounting principles (GAAP)**, which are formulated by the Financial Accounting Standards Board (FASB). The FASB recognizes that it would be improper for all companies to use identical and restrictive accounting principles. Some flexibility and choice are needed because industries and firms within industries differ in their operating environments. Therefore, the FASB allows companies some flexibility to choose among appropriate GAAP. This flexibility allows the firm's managers to choose accounting standards that best reflect company practice. On the negative side, this flexibility can allow firms to appear healthier than they really are.[1] Given this possibility, the financial analyst must rigorously analyze the available financial information to separate those firms that *appear* attractive from those that actually are in good financial shape.

Fortunately, the FASB requires that financial statements include footnotes that indicate which accounting principles were used by the firm. Because accounting principles frequently differ among firms, the footnote information assists the financial analyst in adjusting the financial statements of companies so the analyst can better compare "apples with apples."

---

[1]The recent Enron fiasco clearly makes this point. For a general discussion on this topic, see Byrnes and Henry (2001), Henry (2001), and McNamee (2002).

Balance Sheet

The **balance sheet** shows what resources (assets) the firm controls and how it has financed these assets. Specifically, it indicates the current and fixed assets available to the firm *at a point in time* (the end of the fiscal year or the end of a quarter). In most cases, the firm owns these assets, but some firms lease assets on a long-term basis. How the firm has financed the acquisition of these assets is indicated by its mixture of current liabilities (accounts payable or short-term borrowing), long-term liabilities (fixed debt and leases), and owners' equity (preferred stock, common stock, and retained earnings).

The balance sheet for Walgreens in Exhibit 10.1 represents the *stock* of assets and its financing mix as of the end of Walgreen Co.'s fiscal year, August 31, 2002, 2003, and 2004.

Income Statement

The **income statement** contains information on the operating performance of the firm during some *period of time* (a quarter or a year). In contrast to the balance sheet, which is at a fixed point in time, the income statement indicates the *flow* of sales, expenses, and earnings during a period of time. The income statement for Walgreens for the years 2002, 2003, and 2004 appears in Exhibit 10.2. We concentrate on earnings from operations after tax as the relevant net earnings figure. For Walgreens, this is typically the same as net income because the firm generally has no nonrecurring or unusual income or expense items.

Statement of Cash Flows

Our earlier discussion on valuation indicates that cash flows are a critical input. Therefore accountants now require firms to provide such information. The **statement of cash flows** integrates the information on the balance sheet and income statement to show the effects on the firm's cash flow of income flows (based on the most recent year's income statement) and changes on the balance sheet (based on the two most recent annual balance sheets) that imply an effect on cash flows. Analysts use these cash flow values to estimate the value of a firm and to evaluate the risk and return of the firm's bonds and stock.

The statement of cash flows has three sections: cash flows from operating activities, cash flows from investing activities, and cash flows from financing activities. The total cash flows from the three sections is the net change in the cash position of the firm that should equal the difference in the cash balance between the ending and beginning balance sheets. The statements of cash flow for Walgreens for 2002, 2003, and 2004 appear in Exhibit 10.3.

Cash Flows from Operating Activities   This section of the statement lists the sources and uses of cash that arise from the normal operations of a firm. In general, the net cash flow from operations is computed as the net income reported on the income statement including changes in net working capital items (i.e., receivables, inventories, and so on) plus adjustments for non-cash revenues and expenses (such as depreciation), or:

10.1   Cash Flow from Operating Activities = Net Income + Noncash Revenue and Expenses
+ Changes in Net Working Capital Items

Consistent with our previous discussion, the cash account is not included in the calculations of cash flow from operations. Notably, Walgreens has been able to generate consistently large and growing cash flows from operations even after accounting for consistent substantial increases in receivables and inventory required by the firm's growth.

| Exhibit 10.1 | Walgreen Co. and Subsidiaries Consolidated Balance Sheet ($ Millions), Years Ended August 31, 2002, 2003, and 2004 |

	2004	2003	2002
Assets			
Current assets			
Cash and cash equivalents	$ 1,696	$ 1,268	$ 450
Accounts receivable, net of allowances	1,169	1,018	955
Inventories	4,739	4,203	3,645
Other current assets	161	121	117
Total current assets	7,765	6,610	5,167
Property, plant, and equipment, gross	7,094	6,362	5,918
Less accumulated depreciation and amortization	1,648	1,422	1,327
Property, plant, and equipment, net	5,446	4,940	4,591
Other noncurrent assets	131	108	121
Total assets	$ 13,342	$ 11,658	$ 9,879
Liabilities and shareholders' equity			
Current liabilities			
Short-term borrowings	$ 0	$ 0	$ 0
Current maturities of long-term debt	0	0	0
Trade accounts payable	2,642	2,408	1,836
Total accrued expenses and other liabilities	1,370	1,158	1,018
Accrued expenses and other liabilities	0	0	0
Income taxes payable	66	106	101
Total current liabilities	4,078	3,672	2,955
Deferred income taxes	328	228	177
Long-term debt, net of current maturities	0	0	0
Other noncurrent liabilities	709	562	517
Preferred stock, $0.0625 par value;			
authorized 32 million shares; none issued	0	0	0
Common shareholders' equity			
Common stock, $0.078125 par value; authorized 3.2 billion shares; issued and outstanding 1,205,400,000 in 2004 1,204,908,276 in 2003, 2002	80	80	80
Paid-in capital	632	698	748
Retained earnings	7,591	6,418	5,402
Treasury stock at cost, 2,107,263 shares in 2004	(76)	0	0
Total shareholders' equity	8,227	7,196	6,230
Total liabilities and common shareholders' equity	$ 13,342	$ 11,658	$ 9,879

Source: Reprinted with permission from Walgreen Co., Deerfield, IL.

Exhibit 10.2	**Walgreen Co. and Subsidiaries Consolidated Statement of Earnings and Shareholders' Equity ($ Millions, Except per Share Data), Years Ended August 31, 2002, 2003, and 2004**

	2004	2003	2002
Net sales	$ 37,508	$ 32,505	$ 28,681
Cost of sales	27,310	23,706	21,076
Gross profit	10,198	8,799	7,605
Selling, occupancy, and administrative expense	8,055	6,951	5,981
Operating profit (EBIT)	2,143	1,848	1,624
Interest income	17	11	7
Interest expense	0	0	0
Other income	16	30	6
Operating income before income taxes	2,176	1,889	1,637
Provision for income taxes	816	713	618
Reported net income	1,360	1,176	1,019
Reported net income available for common	1,360	1,176	1,019
Net earnings (loss) per share	$ 1.33	$ 1.14	$ 0.99
Dividends per common share	$ 0.18	$ 0.16	$ 0.15
Average number of common shares outstanding (millions)	1,032	1,032	1,032

Source: Reprinted with permission from Walgreen Co., Deerfield, IL.

Cash Flows from Investing Activities A firm makes investments in both its own noncurrent and fixed assets and the equity of other firms (which may be subsidiaries or joint ventures of the parent firm. They are listed in the "investment" account of the balance sheet). Increases and decreases in these noncurrent accounts are considered investment activities. The cash flow from investing activities is the change in gross plant and equipment plus the change in the investment account. The changes are positive if they represent a source of funds (e.g., sale of some plant and/or equipment); otherwise they are negative. The dollar changes in these accounts are computed using the firm's two most recent balance sheets. Most firms (including Walgreens) experience negative cash flows from investments due to significant capital expenditures.

Cash Flows from Financing Activities Cash inflows are created by increasing notes payable and long-term liability and equity accounts, such as bond and stock issues. Financing uses (outflows) include decreases in such accounts (that is, paying down liability accounts or the repurchase of common shares). Dividend payments are a significant financing cash outflow. For Walgreens and for many firms, the repurchase of shares has also been a major outflow in recent years.

The total cash flows from operating, investing, and financing activities are the net increase or decrease in the firm's cash. The statement of cash flows provides cash flow detail that is lacking in the balance sheet and income statement.

Measures of Cash Flow

There are several cash flow measures an analyst can use to determine the underlying health of the corporation.

Exhibit 10.3 | **Walgreen Co. and Subsidiaries Consolidated Statement of Cash Flows for Fiscal Years Ended August 31, 2002, 2003, and 2004 ($ Millions)**

	2004	2003	2002
Cash flow from operating activities			
Net income	$ 1,360	$ 1,176	$ 1,019
Adjustments to reconcile net income to net cash provided by operating activities:			
Cumulative effect of accounting changes	0	0	0
Depreciation and amortization	403	346	307
Deferred income taxes	72	59	23
Income tax savings from employee stock plans	50	24	57
Other net income adjustments	31	29	(9)
Changes in operating assets and liabilities (used in) provided from continuing operations:			
(Increase) decrease in inventories	(536)	(558)	(163)
(Increase) decrease in accounts receivable	(172)	(57)	(171)
Increase (decrease) in trade accounts payable	234	295	254
Increase (decrease) in accrued expenses and other liabilities	208	136	141
Income taxes	(40)	5	14
Other operating assets and liabilities	42	48	31
Net cash flows from operating activities	$ 1,653	$ 1,504	$ 1,504
Cash flows from investing activities:			
Additions to property and equipment	(940)	(795)	(934)
Disposition of property and equipment	6	85	368
Net proceeds from corporate-owned life insurance	10	8	14
Net (purchase) sales of marketable security	0	0	0
Net cash flows from investing activities	$ (923)	$ (702)	$ (552)
Cash flows from financing activities:			
(Payments of) proceeds from short-term borrowing	0	0	(441)
Cash dividends paid	(177)	(152)	(147)
Stock purchases	(299)	(149)	(25)
Proceeds from employee stock plans	145	82	137
Other	29	(3)	(12)
Net cash flows from financing activities	$ (302)	$ (222)	$ (488)
Net increase (decrease) in cash and cash equivalents	428	580	463
Cash and cash equivalents at beginning of year	1268	688	225
Cash and cash equivalents at end of year	$1,696	$ 1,268	$ 688

Source: Reprinted with permission from Walgreen Co., Deerfield, IL.

Traditional Cash Flow The traditional measure of cash flow equals net income plus depreciation expense and deferred taxes. But as we have just seen, it is also necessary to adjust for changes in operating (current) assets and liabilities that either use or provide cash. These changes can add to or subtract from the cash flow estimated from the traditional measure of cash flow: net income plus noncash expenses.

The table below compares the cash flow from operations figures (Exhibit 10.3) to the traditional cash flow figures for Walgreens from 2002 to 2004.

	Traditional Cash Flow Equals Net Income + Depreciation + Change in Deferred Taxes	Cash Flow from Operations from Statement of Cash Flows
2004	1,863	1,653
2003	1,581	1,504
2002	1,349	1,504

In two of the three years the cash flow from operations was less than the traditional cash flow estimate because of the several adjustments needed to arrive at cash flow from operations. Therefore, using this more exact measure of cash flow for these two years, the Walgreens ratios would not have been as strong. For many firms, this is fairly typical because the effect of working capital changes is often a large negative cash flow due to necessary increases in receivables or inventory to support sales growth (especially for high-growth companies).

Free Cash Flow   **Free cash flow** modifies cash flow from operations to recognize that some investing and financing activities are critical to the firm. It is assumed that these expenditures must be made before a firm can use its cash flow for other purposes such as reducing debt outstanding or repurchasing common stock. Two additional items are considered: (1) capital expenditures (an investing expenditure) and (2) the disposition of property and equipment (a divestment source of cash). These two items are used to modify Walgreen Co.'s cash flow from operations as follows (most analysts only subtract net capital expenditures, but conservative analysts also subtract dividends).

	Cash Flow from Operations	−	Capital Expenditures	+	Disposition of Property and Equipment	=	Free Cash Flow
2004	1,653	−	940	+	6	=	719
2003	1,504	−	795	+	85	=	794
2002	1,504	−	934	+	368	=	938

For firms involved in leveraged buyouts, this free cash flow number is critical because the new owners typically want to use the firm's free cash flow as funds available for retiring outstanding debt. It is not unusual for a firm's free cash flow to be a negative value. For Walgreens, the free cash flow value has been positive but has declined because of significant capital expenditures related to store growth. Notably, this free cash flow value or a variation of it will be used in the subsequent cash flow valuation models.[2]

---

[2]As we will show in the next chapter, small modifications of this free cash flow—called free cash flow to equity (FCFE), free cash flow to the firm (FCFF), and net operating profits less applicable taxes (NOPLAT)—are used in valuation models and also the economic value added (EVA) model.

EBITDA The EBITDA (earnings before interest, taxes, depreciation, and amortization) measure of cash flow is extremely liberal. This very generous measure of operating earnings does not consider any of the adjustments noted previously. Specifically, it adds back depreciation and amortization (as in the traditional measure) along with both interest expense and taxes, but does not consider the effect of changes in working capital items (such as additions to receivables and inventory) or the significant impact of capital expenditures. The following table, which compares this measure to the other three measures of cash flow for Walgreens, demonstrates the large differences among these measures.

Year	EBITDA	Traditional Cash Flow	Cash Flow from Operations	Free Cash Flow
2004	2,579	1,863	1,653	719
2003	2,235	1,581	1,504	794
2002	1,944	1,349	1,504	938

Some analysts have used EBITDA as a proxy for cash flow and a metric for valuation similar to earnings—that is, they refer to EBITDA multiples as other analysts would refer to price-earnings (P/E) multiples. Yet given what this measure does not consider, this is a very questionable practice and is *not* recommended by the authors.[3]

Purpose of Financial Statement Analysis

Financial statement analysis seeks to evaluate management performance in several important areas, including profitability, efficiency, and risk. Although we will necessarily analyze historical data, the ultimate goal of this analysis is to provide insights that will help us to project *future* management performance, including pro forma balance sheets, income statements, cash flows, and risk. It is the firm's *expected future* performance that determines whether we should lend money to a firm or invest in it.

ANALYSIS OF FINANCIAL RATIOS

Analysts use financial ratios because numbers in isolation typically convey little meaning. For example, knowing that a firm earned a net income of $100,000 is not very informative unless we also know the sales figure that generated this income ($1 million or $10 million) and the assets or capital committed to the enterprise. Thus, ratios are intended to provide meaningful *relationships* between individual values in the financial statements.

Because the major financial statements report numerous individual items, it is possible to produce a vast number of potential ratios, many of which will have little value. Therefore, we limit our examination to the most relevant ratios and group them into categories that will provide information on important economic characteristics of the firm.

---

[3]For a detailed discussion of the problems with using EBITDA, see Greenberg (2000).

Importance of Relative Financial Ratios

Just as a single number from a financial statement is of little use, an individual financial ratio has little value except in relation to comparable ratios for other entities. That is, *only relative financial ratios are relevant.* Therefore, it is important to compare a firm's performance relative to

- The aggregate economy
- Its industry or industries
- Its major competitors within the industry
- Its past performance (time-series analysis)

The comparison to the aggregate economy is important because almost all firms are influenced by economic fluctuations. For example, it is unreasonable to expect an increase in the profit margin for a firm during a recession; a stable margin might be encouraging under such conditions. In contrast, a small increase in a firm's profit margin during a major business expansion may be a sign of weakness. Thus, this analysis that considers the economic environment helps investors understand how a firm reacts to the business cycle and *estimate* the future performance of the firm during subsequent business cycles.

Probably the most significant comparison relates a firm's performance to that of its industry. Different industries affect the firms within them differently, but this relationship is always significant. The industry effect is strongest for industries with homogeneous products such as steel, rubber, glass, and wood products, because all firms within these industries experience coincidental shifts in demand. In addition, these firms employ fairly similar technology and production processes. For example, even the best-managed steel firm experiences a decline in sales and profit margins during a recession. In such a case, the relevant question is not whether sales and margins declined, but how bad was the decline relative to other steel firms? In addition, investors should examine an industry's performance relative to the economy to understand how the industry responds to the business cycle, as discussed in Chapter 13.

When comparing a firm's financial ratios to industry ratios, investors may not want to use the average (mean) industry value when there is wide variation among firms in the industry. Alternatively, if we believe that a firm has a unique component, a **cross-sectional analysis** in which we compare the firm to a subset of industry firms comparable in size or characteristics, may be appropriate. As an example, we would compare the performance of Kroger to that of other national food chains rather than regional food chains or specialty food chains.

Another practical problem with comparing a firm to its industry is that many large firms are multi-industry. Inappropriate comparisons can arise when a multi-industry firm is evaluated against the ratios from a single industry. To mitigate this problem, we can use a cross-sectional analysis that compares the firm against a rival that operates in many of the same industries. Alternatively, we can construct composite industry average ratios for the firm. To do this, we use the firm's annual report or 10-K filing to identify each industry in which the firm operates and the proportion of total firm sales derived from each industry. The composite industry ratios would be the weighted-average ratios based on the proportion of firm sales derived from each industry.

Finally, **time-series analysis,** in which we examine a firm's relative performance over time to determine whether it is progressing or declining, is helpful when estimating future performance. Calculating the five or ten year average of a ratio without considering the time-series trend can result in misleading conclusions. For example, an average rate of return of 10 percent can be the result of rates of return that have increased from 5 percent to 15 percent over time or the result of a series that declined from 15 percent to 5 percent. Obviously, the difference in the trend for these series would have a major impact on our estimate for the future. Ideally, we would examine a firm's time series of *relative* financial ratios compared to its industry and the economy.

COMPUTATION OF FINANCIAL RATIOS

In the following discussion, we divide the financial ratios into five major categories that underscore the important economic characteristics of a firm. The five categories are

1. Common size statements
2. Internal liquidity (solvency)
3. Operating performance
   a. Operating efficiency
   b. Operating profitability
4. Risk analysis
   a. Business risk
   b. Financial risk
   c. External liquidity risk
5. Growth analysis

Common Size Statements

Common size statements normalize balance sheet and income statement items to allow easier comparison of different sized firms. A common size *balance sheet* expresses all balance sheet accounts as a *percentage of total assets*. A common size *income statement* expresses all income statement items as a *percentage of sales*. Exhibit 10.4 is the common size balance sheet for Walgreens, and Exhibit 10.5 contains the common size income statement. Common size ratios are useful to quickly compare two different sized firms and to examine trends over time within a single firm. Common size statements also give insight into a firm's financial condition, for example, the proportion of liquid assets or the proportion of short-term liabilities, and the percentage of sales consumed by production costs or interest expense. In the case of Walgreens, the common size balance sheet shows a consistent increase in the percent of current assets (due to a cash increase), and an increase followed by a decline in the proportion of net property. Alternatively, the common size income statement shows that Walgreen Co.'s cost of goods sold and its selling and administrative expenses were quite stable from 2000 to 2004 in proportion to sales. As a result of this stability, the firm has experienced virtually a constant operating profit margin before and after taxes. The ability of Walgreens to experience strong growth in sales (over 14 percent a year) *and* a constant profit margin during a period that included a recession is very impressive.

EVALUATING INTERNAL LIQUIDITY

Internal liquidity (solvency) ratios are intended to indicate the ability of the firm to meet future short-term financial obligations. They compare near-term financial obligations, such as accounts payable or notes payable, to current assets or cash flows that will be available to meet these obligations.

Exhibit 10.4	Walgreen Co. and Subsidiaries Common Size Balance Sheet ($ Millions), Years Ended August 31, 2000, 2001, 2002, 2003, and 2004

	2004	2003	2002	2001	2000
Assets					
Current assets					
Cash and cash equivalents	12.71%	10.88%	4.56%	0.19%	0.18%
Accounts receivable, net of allowances	8.76	8.73	9.67	9.04	8.65
Inventories	35.52	36.05	36.90	39.42	39.85
Other current assets	1.21	1.04	1.18	1.09	1.30
Total current assets	58.20	56.70	52.30	49.74	49.98
Property, plant, and equipment, gross	53.17	54.57	59.90	62.30	62.22
Less accumulated depreciation and amortization	12.35	12.20	13.43	13.11	13.96
Property, plant, and equipment, net	40.82	42.37	46.47	49.19	48.26
Other noncurrent assets	0.98	0.93	1.22	1.07	1.77
Total assets	100.00%	100.00%	100.00%	100.00%	100.00%
Liabilities and shareholders' equity					
Current liabilities					
Short-term borrowings	0.00%	0.00%	0.00%	4.99%	0.00%
Current maturities of long-term debt	0	0	0	0	0
Trade accounts payable	19.80	20.66	18.58	17.51	19.20
Total accrued expenses and other liabilities	10.27	9.93	10.30	10.61	11.93
Income taxes payable	0.49	0.91	1.02	0.98	1.30
Total current liabilities	30.57	31.50	29.91	34.09	32.43
Deferred income taxes	2.46	1.96	1.79	1.55	1.43
Long-term debt, net of current maturities	0	0	0	0	0
Other noncurrent liabilities	5.31	4.82	5.23	5.41	6.54
Preferred stock, $0.0625 par value; authorized 32 million shares; none issued	0	0	0	0	0
Common shareholders' equity					
Common stock, $0.078125 par value; authorized 3.2 billion shares; issued and outstanding 1,205,400,000 in 2004 1,204,908,276 in 2003, 2002	0.60	0.69	0.81	0.90	1.11
Paid-in capital	4.74	5.99	7.57	6.75	5.17
Retained earnings	56.90	55.05	54.68	51.29	53.32
Treasury stock at cost, 2,107,263 shares in 2004	0.57	0	0	0	0
Total shareholders' equity	61.66	61.73	63.06	58.95	59.60
Total liabilities and common shareholders' equity	100.00%	100.00%	100.00%	100.00%	100.00%

Source: Information calculated using publicly available data of Walgreen Co. Reprinted with the permission of Walgreen Co.

| Exhibit 10.5 | Walgreen Co. and Subsidiaries Common Size Statement of Income ($ Millions, Except per Share Data), Years Ended August 31, 2000, 2001, 2002, 2003, and 2004 | | | | | | | | | |

	2004	%	2003	%	2002	%	2001	%	2000	%
Net sales	$ 37,508	100.00	$ 32,505	100.00	$ 28,681	100.00	$ 37,508	100.00	$ 32,505	100.00
Cost of sales	27,310	72.81	23,706	72.93	21,076	73.48	27,310	72.81	23,706	72.93
Gross profit	10,198	27.19	8,799	27.07	7,605	26.52	10,198	27.19	8,799	27.07
Selling, occupancy, and administrative expense	8,055	21.48	6,951	21.38	5,981	20.85	8,055	21.48	6,951	21.38
Operating profit (EBIT)	2,143	5.71	1,848	5.69	1,624	5.66	2,143	5.71	1,848	5.69
Interest income	17	0.05	11	0.03	7	0.02	17	0.05	11	0.03
Interest expense	0	0.00	0	0	0	0	0	0	0	0
Other income	16	0.04	30	0.09	6	0.02	16	0.04	30	0.09
Operating income before income taxes	2,176	5.80	1,889	5.81	1,637	5.71	2,176	5.80	1,889	5.81
Provision for income taxes	816	2.18	713	2.19	618	2.15	816	2.18	713	2.19
Reported net income	1,360	3.63	1,176	3.62	1,019	3.55	1,360	3.63	1,176	3.62

Source: Information calculated using publicly available data of Walgreen Co. Reprinted with the permission of Walgreen Co.

Internal Liquidity Ratios

Current Ratio   Clearly the best-known liquidity measure is the current ratio, which examines the relationship between current assets and current liabilities as follows:

$$
10.2 \qquad \text{Current Ratio} = \frac{\text{Current Assets}}{\text{Current Liabilities}}
$$

For Walgreens, the current ratios (in thousands of dollars) were:

$$
2004: \quad \frac{7{,}764}{4{,}078} = 1.90
$$

$$
2003: \quad \frac{6{,}609}{3{,}671} = 1.80
$$

$$
2002: \quad \frac{5{,}167}{2{,}955} = 1.75
$$

These current ratios experienced a consistent increase during the three years and are consistent with the typical current ratio. As always, it is important to compare these values with similar figures for the firm's industry and the aggregate market. If the ratios differ from the industry results, we need to determine what might explain it. (We will discuss comparative analysis in a later section.)

Quick Ratio   Some observers question using total current assets to gauge the ability of a firm to meet its current obligations because inventories and some other current assets might not be very liquid. They prefer the quick ratio, which relates current liabilities to only relatively liquid current assets (cash items and accounts receivable) as follows:

$$
10.3 \qquad \text{Quick Ratio} = \frac{\text{Cash} + \text{Marketable Securities} + \text{Receivables}}{\text{Current Liabilities}}
$$

Walgreen Co.'s quick ratios were

$$
2004: \quad \frac{2{,}865}{4{,}078} = 0.70
$$

$$
2003: \quad \frac{2{,}286}{3{,}672} = 0.62
$$

$$
2002: \quad \frac{1{,}405}{2{,}955} = 0.48
$$

These quick ratios were respectable and increased over the three years. As before, we should compare these values relative to other firms in the industry and to the aggregate economy.

Cash Ratio   The most conservative liquidity ratio is the cash ratio, which relates the firm's cash and short-term marketable securities to its current liabilities as follows:

$$
10.4 \qquad \text{Cash Ratio} = \frac{\text{Cash and Marketable Securities}}{\text{Current Liabilities}}
$$

Walgreens Co.'s cash ratios were

$$2004: \quad \frac{1{,}696}{4{,}078} = 0.42$$

$$2003: \quad \frac{1{,}268}{3{,}672} = 0.35$$

$$2002: \quad \frac{450}{2{,}955} = 0.15$$

The cash ratios grew substantially from 2002 to 2004, to a point that they were almost excessive for a fast-growing retailer with inventories being financed by accounts payable to its suppliers. In addition, the firm has strong lines of credit at various banks.

Receivables Turnover In addition to examining total liquid assets, it is useful to analyze the quality (liquidity) of the accounts receivable by calculating how often the firm's receivables turn over, which implies an average collection period. The faster these accounts are paid, the sooner the firm gets the funds to pay off its own current liabilities. Receivables turnover is computed as

10.5 $$\text{Receivable Turnover} = \frac{\text{Net Annual Sales}}{\text{Average Receivables}}$$

The average receivables figure is typically equal to the beginning receivables figure plus the ending value divided by two. Receivables turnover ratios for Walgreens were

$$2004: \quad \frac{37{,}508}{(1{,}169 + 1{,}018)/2} = 34.30 \text{ times}$$

$$2003: \quad \frac{32{,}505}{(1{,}018 + 955)/2} = 32.95 \text{ times}$$

We cannot compute a turnover value for 2002 because the tables used do not include a beginning receivables figure for 2002 (that is, we lack the ending receivables figure for 2001).

Given these annual receivables turnover figures, the average collection period is

10.6 $$\text{Average Receivable Collection Period} = \frac{365 \text{ Days}}{\text{Annual Receivables Turnover}}$$

For Walgreens,

$$2004: \quad \frac{365}{34.30} = 10.6 \text{ days}$$

$$2003: \quad \frac{365}{32.95} = 11.1 \text{ days}$$

These results indicate that Walgreens currently collects its accounts receivable in about 11 days, on average. To determine whether these account collection numbers are good or bad, it is essential that they be related to the firm's credit policy and to comparable numbers for other firms in the industry. The point is, the receivables collection period value varies dramatically for different firms (e.g., from 10 to over 60), and it is mainly due to the product and the industry. An industry comparison would indicate similar rapid collection periods for other drugstore chains, since most sales are for cash. The reason for a small increase in the collection period over several years (since 2000) is that a significant change has occurred in pharmacy sales: about 92 percent of pharmacy sales are now to a third party (i.e., they are reimbursed by a managed-care or insurance company), which has caused the increase in receivables.

The receivables turnover is one of the ratios in which a firm *does not want to deviate too much from the norm.* In an industry where the norm is 40 days, a collection period of 80 days would indicate slow-paying customers, which increases the capital tied up in receivables and the possibility of bad debts. Therefore, the firm wants to be somewhat below the norm (for example, 35 days vs. 40 days), but a figure *substantially below* the norm (e.g., 20 days) might indicate overly stringent credit terms relative to the competition, which could be detrimental to sales.

Inventory Turnover

We should also examine the liquidity of inventory based on the firm's inventory turnover (i.e., how many times it is sold during a year) and the implied processing time. Inventory turnover can be calculated relative to sales or cost of goods sold. The preferred turnover ratio is relative to cost of goods sold (CGS), which does not include the profit implied in sales.

10.7
$$\text{Inventory Turnover} = \frac{\text{CGS}}{\text{Average Inventory}}$$

For Walgreens, the inventory turnover ratios were

$$2004: \quad \frac{27,310}{(4,739 + 4,203)/2} = 6.11 \text{ times}$$

$$2003: \quad \frac{23,706}{(4,203 + 3,645)/2} = 6.04 \text{ times}$$

Given these turnover values, we can compute the average inventory processing time as follows:

10.8
$$\text{Average Inventory Processing Period} = \frac{365}{\text{Annual Inventory Turnover}}$$

For Walgreens,

$$2004: \quad \frac{365}{6.11} = 59.8 \text{ days}$$

$$2003: \quad \frac{365}{6.04} = 60.4 \text{ days}$$

Although this seems like a low turnover figure, it is encouraging that the inventory processing period is very stable and has declined over the longer run. Still, it is essential to examine this turnover ratio relative to an industry norm and/or the firm's prime competition. Notably, this ratio will also be affected by the products carried by the chain—for instance, if a drugstore chain adds high-profit margin items, such as cosmetics and liquor, these products may have a lower turnover.

As with receivables, a firm does not want an extremely low inventory turnover value and long processing time, because this implies that capital is being tied up in inventory and could signal obsolete inventory (especially for firms in the technology sector). Alternatively, an abnormally high inventory turnover and a short processing time could mean inadequate inventory that could lead to outages, backorders, and slow delivery to customers, which would eventually have an adverse effect on sales.

Cash Conversion Cycle   A very useful measure of overall internal liquidity is the cash conversion cycle, which combines information from the receivables turnover, the inventory turnover, and the accounts payable turnover. Cash is tied up in assets for a certain number of days. Specifically, cash is committed to receivables for the collection period and in inventory for a number of days—the inventory processing period. At the same time, the firm receives an offset to this capital commitment from its own suppliers who provide interest-free loans to the firm by carrying the firm's payables. Specifically, the payables' payment period is equal to 365 divided by the payables' turnover ratio. In turn, the payables turnover ratio is

10.9
$$\text{Payables Turnover Ratio} = \frac{\text{Cost of Goods Sold}}{\text{Average Trade Payables}}$$

For Walgreens, the payables turnover ratios were

$$2004: \quad \frac{27,310}{(2,642 + 2,408)/2} = 10.8 \text{ times}$$

$$2003: \quad \frac{23,706}{(2,408 + 1,836)/2} = 11.2 \text{ times}$$

10.10
$$\text{Payables Payment Period} = \frac{365 \text{ days}}{\text{Payable Turnover}}$$

$$2004: \quad \frac{365}{10.8} = 33.8 \text{ days}$$

$$2003: \quad \frac{365}{11.2} = 32.6 \text{ days}$$

Therefore, the cash conversion cycle for Walgreens (with components rounded) equals:

Year	Receivables Collection Days	+	Inventory Processing Days	−	Payables Payment Period	=	Cash Conversion Cycle
2004	11	+	60	−	34	=	37 days
2003	11	+	60	−	33	=	38 days

Walgreens has experienced stability in its receivables days and in its inventory processing days and is taking one day longer to pay its bills. The overall result is a very small decline in its cash conversion cycle. Although the overall cash conversion cycle appears to be quite good (about 37 days), as always we should examine the firm's long-term trend and compare it to other drugstore chains.

EVALUATING OPERATING PERFORMANCE

The operating performance ratios can be divided into two subcategories: (1) **operating efficiency ratios** and (2) **operating profitability ratios**. Efficiency ratios examine how the management uses its assets and capital, measured by dollars of sales generated by various asset or capital categories. Profitability ratios analyze the profits as a percentage of sales and as a percentage of the assets and capital employed.

Operating Efficiency Ratios

Total Asset Turnover   The total asset turnover ratio indicates the effectiveness of the firm's use of its total asset base (net assets equals gross assets minus depreciation on fixed assets). It is computed as

10.11 $$\text{Total Asset Turnover} = \frac{\text{Net Sales}}{\text{Average Total Net Assets}}$$

Walgreen Co.'s total asset turnover values were

$$2004: \quad \frac{37,508}{(13,342 + 11,658)/2} = 3.00 \text{ times}$$

$$2003: \quad \frac{32,505}{(11,658 + 9,879)/2} = 3.02 \text{ times}$$

This ratio must be compared to that of other firms *within* an industry because it varies substantially between industries. For example, total asset turnover ratios range from less than 1 for large, capital-intensive industries (steel, autos, and heavy manufacturing companies) to over 10 for some retailing or service operations. It also can be affected by the use of leased facilities.

Again, we must consider a *range* of turnover values consistent with the industry. It is poor management to have an exceedingly high asset turnover relative to the industry because this might imply too few assets for the potential business (sales), or it could be due to the use of outdated, fully depreciated assets. It is equally poor management to have an extremely low asset turnover because this implies that the firm is tying up capital in excess assets relative to the needs of the firm and its competitors.

Beyond the analysis of the firm's total asset base, it is insightful to examine the utilization of some specific assets, such as receivables, inventories, and fixed assets. This is especially important if the firm has experienced a major decline in its total asset turnover because we want to know the cause of the decline, that is, which of the component turnovers (receivables, inventory, fixed assets) contributed to the decline. We have already examined the receivables and inventory turnover as part of our liquidity analysis; we now examine the fixed asset turnover ratio.

Net Fixed Asset Turnover   The net fixed asset turnover ratio reflects the firm's utilization of fixed assets. It is computed as

10.12 $$\text{Fixed Asset Turnover} = \frac{\text{Net Sales}}{\text{Average Net Fixed Assets}}$$

Walgreen Co.'s fixed asset turnover ratios were

$$2004: \quad \frac{37,508}{(5,446 + 4,940)/2} = 7.22 \text{ times}$$

$$2003: \quad \frac{32,505}{(4,940 + 4,591)/2} = 6.82 \text{ times}$$

These turnover ratios, which indicate a small increase for Walgreens during the last few years, must be compared with industry competitors and should consider the impact of leased assets (this is especially significant for retail firms). Again, an abnormally low turnover implies capital tied up in excessive fixed assets. An abnormally high asset turnover ratio can indicate a lack of productive capacity to meet sales demand, or it might imply the use of old, fully depreciated plant and equipment that may be obsolete.[4]

Equity Turnover   In addition to specific asset turnover ratios, it is useful to examine the turnover for capital components. An important one, equity turnover, is computed as

10.13
$$\text{Equity Turnover} = \frac{\text{Net Sales}}{\text{Average Equity}}$$

Equity includes preferred and common stock, paid-in capital, and total retained earnings.[5] This ratio differs from total asset turnover in that it excludes current liabilities and long-term debt. Therefore, when examining this series, it is very important to consider the firm's capital structure ratios, because the firm can increase (or decrease) its equity turnover ratio by increasing (or decreasing) its proportion of debt capital.

Walgreen Co.'s equity turnover ratios were

$$2004: \quad \frac{37,508}{(8,227 + 7,196)/2} = 4.86 \text{ times}$$

$$2003: \quad \frac{32,505}{(7,196 + 6,230)/2} = 4.84 \text{ times}$$

This ratio has not changed during the past several years. In our later analysis of sustainable growth, we examine the variables that affect the equity turnover ratio to understand what variables might cause changes.

Following an analysis of the firm's operating efficiency, the next step is to examine its profitability in relation to its sales and capital.

Operating Profitability Ratios

There are two facets of profitability: (1) the rate of profit on sales (profit margin) and (2) the percentage return on capital employed. The analysis of profitability of sales actually entails several component profit margins that consider various expense categories. These component margins provide important information relative to the final net profit margin. Thus, if we determine that a firm has experienced a significant increase or decrease in its net profit margin, the analysis of the component profit margins will help us to determine the specific causes of the change. Therefore, we will briefly discuss each of the margins but will defer calculations and comments on the trends until we discuss the common size income statement.

Gross Profit Margin   Gross profit equals net sales minus the cost of goods sold. The gross profit margin is computed as

10.14
$$\text{Gross Profit Margin} = \frac{\text{Gross Profit}}{\text{Net Sales}}$$

This ratio indicates the basic cost structure of the firm. An analysis of this ratio over time relative to a comparable industry figure shows the firm's relative cost–price position. As always, we

---

[4]The "DuPont System" section of this chapter contains an analysis of this total asset turnover ratio over a longer term.
[5]Some investors prefer to consider only *owner's* equity, which would not include preferred stock.

must compare these margins to the industry and major competitors. Notably, this margin can also be impacted by a change in the firm's product mix toward higher or lower profit margin items.

Operating Profit Margin   Operating profit is gross profit minus sales, general, and administrative (SG&A) expenses. It is also referred to as EBIT—earnings before interest and taxes.

$$\text{10.15} \qquad \text{Operating Profit Margin} = \frac{\text{Operating Profit}}{\text{Net Sales}}$$

The variability of the operating profit margin over time is a prime indicator of the business risk for a firm. Again, this volatility should be compared to similar ratios for competitors and the industry.

There are two additional deductions from operating profit—interest expense and net foreign exchange loss. After these deductions, we have income before income taxes.

Some investors add back to the operating income value (EBIT) the firm's depreciation expense and compute a profit margin that consists of earnings before interest, taxes, depreciation, and amortization (EBITDA). This alternative operating profit margin has been used by some analysts as a proxy for pretax cash flow. As noted earlier, we do *not* recommend the use of this series because it is a biased cash flow estimate.

Net Profit Margin   This margin relates after-tax net income to sales. In the case of Walgreens, this is the same as operating income after taxes, because the firm does *not* have any significant nonoperating adjustments. This margin is equal to

$$\text{10.16} \qquad \text{Net Profit Margin} = \frac{\text{Net Income}}{\text{Net Sales}}$$

This ratio should be computed using sales and earnings from *continuing* operations, because our analysis seeks to derive insights about *future* expectations. Therefore, we do not consider earnings from discontinued operations, the gain or loss from the sale of these operations, or any nonrecurring income or expenses.

Common Size Income Statement   As noted earlier, these profit margin ratios are basically included in a common size income statement, which lists all expense and income items as a percentage of sales. This statement provides useful insights regarding the trends in cost figures and profit margins.

Exhibit 10.5 shows a common size statement for Walgreens for 2000–2004. As noted earlier in the chapter when Exhibit 10.5 was presented, the most striking characteristic of the various profit margins for Walgreens (gross, operating, and net) is the *significant stability* in those margins over time. This stability is notable for two reasons. First, the firm experienced significant sales growth during this period (about 14 percent a year), and it is generally a challenge to control costs when growing rapidly. Second, this time interval included the economic recession of 2001–2002 (the official recession was during 2001, but it carried over for most corporations into 2002), and the sales and profit margins of most corporations were negatively impacted by this environment. Therefore, the stability of profit margins for Walgreens is an impressive accomplishment by management.

Beyond the analysis of earnings on sales, the ultimate measure of management performance is the profits earned on the assets or the capital committed to the enterprise. Several ratios help us evaluate this important relationship.

Return on Total Invested Capital   The return on total invested capital ratio (referred to as ROIC) relates the firm's earnings to all the invested capital involved in the enterprise (debt, preferred stock, and common stock). Therefore, the earnings figure used is the net income from continuing operations (before any dividends) *plus* the interest paid on debt. While there might be a tendency to equate total capital with total assets, most analysts differentiate due to the term *invested capital*, which does *not* include non-interest-bearing liabilities such as trade accounts payable, accrued expenses, income taxes payable, and deferred income taxes. In contrast, short-term debt such as bank borrowings and principal payments due on long-term debt are interest bearing and would be included as invested capital. Therefore, the ratio would be:

$$10.17 \qquad \text{Return on Total Invested Capital} = \frac{\text{Net Income } + \text{ Interest Expense}}{\text{Average Total Invested Capital*}}$$

*Interest bearing debt plus shareholders' equity

Walgreens incurred interest expense for long- and short-term debt. The gross interest expense value used in this ratio differs from the net interest expense item in the income statement, which is measured as gross interest expense minus interest income.[6]

Walgreen Co.'s rates of return on total invested capital (ROIC) were

$$2004: \quad \frac{1,360 + 0.2}{(8,936.6 + 7,757.4)/2} = \frac{1,360.2}{8,347.0} = 16.29\%$$

$$2003: \quad \frac{1,176 + 0.2}{(7,757.4 + 6,747.1)/2} = \frac{1,176.2}{7,252.3} = 16.22\%$$

This ratio indicates the firm's return on all its invested capital. It should be compared with the ratio for other firms in the industry and the economy. For Walgreens, the results are stable, with an increase during the last several years.

Return on Owner's Equity   The return on owner's equity (ROE) ratio is extremely important to the owner of the enterprise (the common stockholder) because it indicates the rate of return that management has earned on the capital provided by stockholders after accounting for payments to all other capital suppliers. If we consider all equity (including preferred stock), this return would equal

$$10.18 \qquad \text{Return on Total Equity } = \frac{\text{Net Income}}{\text{Average Total Equity}}$$

If we are concerned only with owner's equity (the common stockholder's equity), the ratio would be[7]

$$10.19 \qquad \text{Return on Owner's Equity } = \frac{\text{Net Income } - \text{ Preferred Dividend}}{\text{Average Common Equity}}$$

---

[6]Subsequently, in connection with the analysis of financial risk, we discuss why and how to capitalize the operating lease payments that are reported in footnotes. When we do this, we will add this capitalized value to the balance sheet additional leased assets and also lease obligations along with the implied interest on the leases. At that point, we demonstrate the affect of this on the firm's ROIC and several other financial ratios—mainly financial risk ratios.

[7]In the case of Walgreens, return on total equity and return on owner's equity is the same, since there is no preferred stock outstanding (it is authorized but not issued).

Walgreens generated return on owner's equity of

$$2004: \quad \frac{1{,}360 - 0}{(8{,}227 + 7{,}196)/2} = 17.64\%$$

$$2003: \quad \frac{1{,}176 - 0}{(7{,}196 + 6{,}230)/2} = 17.52\%$$

This ratio reflects the rate of return on the stockholder's capital. It should be consistent with the firm's overall business risk, but it also should reflect the financial risk assumed by the common stockholder because of the prior claims of the firm's bondholders.

The DuPont System   The importance of ROE as an indicator of performance makes it desirable to divide the ratio into several component ratios that provide insights into the causes of a firm's ROE or any changes in it. This breakdown is generally referred to as the **DuPont System**. First, the return on equity (ROE) ratio can be broken down into two ratios that we have discussed—net profit margin and equity turnover.

10.20 $$ROE = \frac{\text{Net Income}}{\text{Common Equity}} = \frac{\text{Net Income}}{\text{Net Sales}} \times \frac{\text{Net Sales}}{\text{Common Equity}}$$

This breakdown is an identity because we have both multiplied and divided by net sales. To maintain the identity, the common equity value used is the year-end figure rather than the average of the beginning and ending value.[8] This identity reveals that ROE equals the net profit margin times the equity turnover, which implies that a firm can improve its return on equity by *either* using its equity more efficiently (increasing its equity turnover) *or* by becoming more profitable (increasing its net profit margin).

As noted previously, a firm's equity turnover is affected by its capital structure. Specifically, a firm can increase its equity turnover by employing a higher proportion of debt capital. We can see this effect by considering the following relationship:

10.21 $$\frac{\text{Net Sales}}{\text{Common Equity}} = \frac{\text{Net Sales}}{\text{Total Assets}} \times \frac{\text{Total Assets}}{\text{Common Equity}}$$

Similar to the prior breakdown, this is an identity because we have both multiplied and divided the equity turnover ratio by total assets. This equation indicates that the equity turnover ratio equals the firm's *total asset turnover* (a measure of efficiency) times the ratio of *total assets to equity* (a measure of financial leverage). Specifically, this leverage ratio indicates the proportion of total assets financed with debt. *All assets have to be financed by either equity or some form of debt* (either current liabilities or long-term debt). Therefore, the higher the ratio of assets to equity, the higher the proportion of debt to equity. A total asset–equity ratio of 2, for example, indicates that for every two dollars of assets there is a dollar of equity, which means the firm financed one-half of its assets with equity and the other half with debt. Likewise, a total asset–equity ratio of 3 indicates that only one-third of total assets was financed with equity and two-thirds must have been financed with debt. Thus a firm can increase its equity turnover either by increasing its total asset turnover (becoming more efficient) or by increasing its

---

[8]The effect of using the year-end equity rather than the average for the year will cause a lower ROE since the equity is generally increasing over time. Two points regarding this difference: First, the conservative bias is generally small—for Walgreens (which is growing fast), the average equity result above was 17.64% versus 16.53% using the year-end equity. Second, the important trend results will show, along with the component trends that are very important.

financial leverage ratio (financing assets with a higher proportion of debt capital). This financial leverage ratio is also referred to as the financial leverage multiplier, because the first two ratios (profit margin times total asset turnover) equal return on total assets (ROTA), and ROTA times the financial leverage multiplier equals ROE.

Combining these two breakdowns, we see that a firm's ROE is composed of three ratios, as follows:

$$10.22 \qquad \frac{\text{Net Income}}{\text{Common Equity}} = \frac{\text{Net Income}}{\text{Net Sales}} \times \frac{\text{Net Sales}}{\text{Total Assets}} \times \frac{\text{Total Assets}}{\text{Common Equity}}$$

$$= \frac{\text{Profit}}{\text{Margin}} \times \frac{\text{Total Asset}}{\text{Turnover}} \times \frac{\text{Financial}}{\text{Leverage}}$$

As an example of this important set of relationships, the figures in Exhibit 10.6 indicate what has happened to the ROE for Walgreens and the components of its ROE during the 23-year

| **Exhibit 10.6** | **Components of Return on Total Equity for Walgreen Co.[a]** |

Year	(1) Sales–Total Assets	(2) Net Profit Margin (%)	(3)[b] Return On Total Assets	(4) Total Assets–equity	(5)[c] Return On Equity (%)
1982	3.31	2.75	9.09	2.06	18.73
1983	3.29	2.96	9.72	2.04	19.84
1984	3.26	3.11	10.16	2.03	20.60
1985	3.29	2.98	9.79	2.00	19.58
1986	3.06	2.82	8.62	2.16	18.64
1987	3.14	2.42	7.60	2.19	16.63
1988	3.23	2.64	8.54	2.12	18.12
1989	3.20	2.87	9.18	2.04	18.74
1990	3.16	2.89	9.12	2.02	18.42
1991	3.21	2.90	9.31	1.94	18.04
1992	3.15	2.95	9.30	1.92	17.90
1993	3.27	2.67	8.74	1.84	16.07
1994	3.17	3.05	9.69	1.85	17.91
1995	3.20	3.09	9.86	1.81	17.85
1996	3.24	3.16	10.23	1.78	18.19
1997	3.18	3.26	10.37	1.77	18.35
1998	3.12	3.34	10.42	1.72	17.93
1999	3.02	3.50	10.57	1.70	17.91
2000	2.99	3.66	10.94	1.68	18.35
2001	2.79	3.60	10.03	1.70	17.01
2002	2.90	3.55	10.32	1.59	16.36
2003	2.85	3.62	10.31	1.59	16.34
2004	2.81	3.63	10.20	1.62	16.52

[a]Ratios use year-end data for total assets and common equity rather than averages of the year.
[b]Column (3) is equal to column (1) times column (2).
[c]Column (5) is equal to column (3) times column (4).

Note: When you multiply the three component ratios, this product may not be equal to the ROE based on year-end statements due to the rounding of the three ratios.

period from 1982 to 2004. As noted, these ratio values employ year-end balance sheet figures (assets and equity) rather than the average of beginning and ending data, so they will differ from our individual ratio computations.

The DuPont results in Exhibit 10.6 indicate several significant trends:

1. The total asset turnover ratio was relatively stable: a total range of 2.79 to 3.31, with a small decline in the ratio to its level in 2004 of 2.81.
2. The profit margin series experienced a stable increase from 2.75 to almost a peak value of 3.63 in 2004.
3. The product of the total asset turnover and the net profit margin is equal to return on total assets (ROTA), which experienced an overall increase from 9.09 percent to a peak of 10.94 percent in 2000, followed by a small decline to 10.20 percent in 2004.
4. The financial leverage multiplier (total assets/equity) experienced a steady decline from 2.06 to 1.62. Notably, most of this debt is trade credit, which is non-interest-bearing. The fact is, the firm has almost no interest-bearing debt, except for the long-term leases on drugstores that are not on the formal balance sheet but are discussed and analyzed in the subsequent financial risk section.
5. Finally, as a result of the overall increase in ROTA and a clear decline in financial leverage, the firm's ROE has experienced a small decline overall, beginning at 18.73 and ending at 16.52.

An Extended Dupont System   Beyond the original DuPont system, some analysts have suggested using an extended DuPont system,[9] which provides additional insights into the effect of financial leverage on the firm and also pinpoints the effect of income taxes on the firm's ROE. Because both financial leverage and tax rates have changed dramatically over the past decade, these additional insights are important. The concept and use of the model is the same as the basic DuPont system except for a further breakdown of components.

In the prior presentation, we started with the ROE and divided it into components. In contrast, we now begin with the operating profit margin (EBIT divided by sales) and introduce additional ratios to derive an ROE value. Combining the operating profit margin and the total asset turnover ratio yields the following:

$$\frac{\text{EBIT}}{\text{Net Sales}} \times \frac{\text{Net Sales}}{\text{Total Assets}} = \frac{\text{EBIT}}{\text{Total Assets}}$$

This ratio is the operating profit return on total assets. To consider the negative effects of financial leverage, we examine the effect of interest expense as a percentage of total assets:

$$\frac{\text{EBIT}}{\text{Total Assets}} - \frac{\text{Interest Expense}}{\text{Total Assets}} = \frac{\text{Net Before Tax (NBT)}}{\text{Total Assets}}$$

We consider the positive effect of financial leverage with the financial leverage multiplier as follows:

$$\frac{\text{Net Before Tax (NBT)}}{\text{Total Assets}} \times \frac{\text{Total Assets}}{\text{Common Equity}} = \frac{\text{Net Before Tax (NBT)}}{\text{Common Equity}}$$

---

[9]The original DuPont system was the three-component breakdown discussed in the prior section. Because this extended analysis also involves the components of ROE, some still refer to it as the DuPont system. In our presentation, we refer to it as the extended DuPont system to differentiate it from the original three-component analysis.

This indicates the pretax return on equity. Finally, to arrive at ROE, we must consider the tax-rate effect. We do this by multiplying the pre-tax ROE by a tax-retention rate as follows:

$$\frac{\text{Net Before Tax}}{\text{Common Equity}} \times \left(100\% - \frac{\text{Income Taxes}}{\text{Net Before Tax}}\right) = \frac{\text{Net Income}}{\text{Common Equity}}$$

In summary, we have the following five components:

1. $\dfrac{\text{EBIT}}{\text{Sales}}$ = Operating Profit Margin

2. $\dfrac{\text{Sales}}{\text{Total Assets}}$ = Total Asset Turnover

3. $\dfrac{\text{Interest Expense}}{\text{Total Assets}}$ = Interest Expense Rate

4. $\dfrac{\text{Total Assets}}{\text{Common Equity}}$ = Financial Leverage Multiplier

5. $\left(100\% - \dfrac{\text{Income Taxes}}{\text{Net Before Tax}}\right)$ = Tax Retention Rate

To demonstrate the use of this extended DuPont system, Exhibit 10.7 contains the calculations, using the five components for the years 1982 through 2004. The first column indicates that the firm's operating profit margin peaked in 1985, subsequently declined to a low point in 1990, followed by an increase to a new peak of 5.81 percent in 2003. We know from the prior discussion that the firm's total asset turnover (Column 2) experienced an overall decline to around 2.80 in 2003–2004. The resulting operating profit return on assets declined to a low point in 2001 followed by a partial recovery through 2004. As discussed, because of virtually no interest-bearing debt (except off-balance sheet leases), Column 4 shows zero negative impact on leverage.

Column 5 reflects the firm's operating performance before the positive impact of financing (the leverage multiplier) and the impact of taxes. These results are virtually identical to Column 3 due to no debt. Column 6 reflects the steady decline in non-lease financial leverage. As a result of the reduced leverage multiplier, the before-tax ROE in Column 7 has declined since 1984. Column 8 shows the strong positive effect of lower tax rates, which caused a higher tax-retention rate that increased from the mid-50 percent range to the recent 62 percent rate.

In summary, this breakdown helps you to understand *what* happened to a firm's ROE and *why* it happened. The intent is to determine what happened to the firm's internal operating results, what has been the effect of its financial leverage policy, and what was the effect of external government tax policy. Although the two breakdowns should provide the same ending value, they typically differ by small amounts because of the rounding of components.

RISK ANALYSIS

Risk analysis examines the uncertainty of income flows for the total firm and for the individual sources of capital (that is, debt, preferred stock, and common stock). The typical approach examines the major factors that cause a firm's income flows to vary. More volatile income flows mean greater risk (uncertainty) facing the investor.

Exhibit 10.7	Extended DuPont System Analysis for Walgreens: 1982–2004[a]

	1	2	3	4	5	6	7	8	9
Year	EBIT/ Sales (Percent)	Sales/ Total Assets (Times)	EBIT/ Total Assets (Percent)[b]	Interest Expense/ Total Assets (Percent)	Net before Tax/ Total Assets (Percent)[c]	Total Assets/ Common Equity (Times)	Net before Tax/ Common Equity (Percent)[d]	Tax Retention Rate	Return on Equity (Percent)[e]
1982	4.32	3.31	14.30	(0.85)	15.15	2.06	31.20	0.60	18.75
1983	5.16	3.29	17.00	0.25	16.75	2.04	34.20	0.56	19.30
1984	5.57	3.26	18.20	(0.24)	18.44	2.03	37.40	0.55	20.65
1985	5.63	3.29	18.50	0.43	18.07	2.00	36.10	0.54	19.57
1986	5.37	3.06	16.40	0.74	15.66	2.16	33.90	0.55	18.63
1987	4.92	3.14	15.50	1.22	14.28	2.19	31.30	0.53	16.69
1988	4.59	3.23	14.80	1.01	13.79	2.12	29.30	0.62	18.10
1989	4.71	3.20	15.10	0.57	14.53	2.04	29.70	0.63	18.79
1990	4.70	3.16	14.90	0.17	14.73	2.02	29.80	0.62	18.52
1991	4.77	3.21	15.30	0.44	14.86	1.94	28.80	0.63	18.00
1992	4.80	3.15	15.10	0.23	14.87	1.92	28.60	0.62	17.87
1993	4.90	3.31	16.20	0.26	15.94	1.82	29.00	0.61	17.80
1994	4.93	3.21	15.90	(0.10)	16.00	1.83	29.20	0.62	17.96
1995	5.00	3.20	15.99	0.04	15.95	1.81	28.90	0.61	17.70
1996	5.13	3.24	16.62	0.06	16.56	1.78	29.50	0.61	18.07
1997	5.30	3.18	16.85	0.05	16.80	1.77	29.74	0.61	18.14
1998	5.46	3.12	17.04	0.02	17.02	1.72	29.28	0.61	17.93
1999	5.69	3.02	17.19	0.00	17.19	1.70	29.22	0.61	17.83
2000	5.77	2.99	17.25	0.00	17.25	1.68	28.98	0.61	17.78
2001	5.08	2.79	15.84	0.00	16.11	1.70	27.33	0.62	17.07
2002	5.71	2.90	16.57	0.00	16.57	1.62	26.28	0.62	16.36
2003	5.81	2.79	16.20	0.00	16.20	1.62	26.25	0.62	16.34
2004	5.80	2.81	16.31	0.00	16.31	1.62	26.45	0.62	16.53

[a]The percents in this table may not be the same as in Exhibit 10.6 due to rounding.
[b]Column 3 is equal to Column 1 times Column 2.
[c]Column 5 is equal to Column 3 minus Column 4.
[d]Column 7 is equal to Column 5 times Column 6.
[e]Column 9 is equal to Column 7 times Column 8.

The total risk of the firm has two internal components: business risk and financial risk. We first discuss the concept of business risk: how to measure it, what causes it, and how to measure its individual causes. Then we consider financial risk and the several ratios by which we measure it. Following this analysis of a firm's internal risk factors, we discuss an important external risk factor, external liquidity risk—that is, the ability to buy or sell the firm's stock in the secondary equity market.

Business Risk

Recall that **business risk**[10] is the uncertainty of operating income caused by the firm's industry. In turn, this uncertainty is due to the firm's variability of sales caused by its products, customers, and the way it produces its products. Specifically, a firm's operating earnings vary over time and is measured by the volatility of the firm's operating income over time, which is due to two factors: (1) the volatility of the firm's sales over time, and (2) how the firm produces its products and its mix of fixed and variable costs—that is, its operating leverage. Specifically, a firm's operating earnings vary over time because its sales and production costs vary. As an example, the earnings for a steel firm will probably vary more than those of a grocery chain because (1) over the business cycle, steel sales are more volatile than grocery sales; and (2) the steel firm's large fixed production costs (operating leverage) make its earnings vary more than its sales.

Business risk is generally measured by the variability of the firm's operating income over time. In turn, the earnings variability is measured by the standard deviation of the historical operating earnings series. You will recall from Chapter 1 that the standard deviation is influenced by the size of the numbers, so investors standardize this measure of volatility by dividing it by the mean value for the series (i.e., the average operating earnings). The resulting ratio of the standard deviation of operating earnings divided by the average operating earnings is the coefficient of variation (CV) of operating earnings:

$$
\begin{aligned}
\text{Business Risk} \ &= \ f(\text{Coefficient of Variation of Operating Earnings}) \\
&= \ \frac{\text{Standard Deviation of Operating Earnings (OE)}}{\text{Mean Operating Earnings}} \\
&= \ \frac{\sqrt{\sum_{i=1}^{n} (OE_i - \overline{OE})^2 / n}}{\sum_{i=1}^{n} OE_i / n}
\end{aligned}
$$

The CV of operating earnings allows comparisons between standardized measures of business risk for firms of different sizes. To compute the CV of operating earnings, you need a minimum of 5 years up to about 10 years. Less than 5 years is not very meaningful, and data more than 10 years old are typically out of date. Besides measuring overall business risk, it is very insightful to examine the two factors that contribute to the variability of operating earnings: sales variability and operating leverage.

Sales Variability   Sales variability is the prime determinant of operating earnings variability. In turn, the variability of sales is mainly caused by a firm's industry and is largely outside the control of management. For example, sales for a firm in a cyclical industry, such as automobiles or steel, will be quite volatile over the business cycle compared to sales of a firm in a noncyclical industry, such as retail food or hospital supplies. Like operating earnings, the variability of a firm's sales is typically measured by the CV of sales during the most recent 5 to 10 years. The CV of sales equals the standard deviation of sales divided by the mean sales for the period.

$$
\begin{aligned}
\text{Sales Volatility} \ &= \ f(\text{Coefficient of Variation of Sales}) \\
&= \ \frac{\sqrt{\sum_{i=1}^{n} (S_i - \overline{S})^2 / n}}{\sum_{i=1}^{n} S_i / n}
\end{aligned}
$$

---

[10]For further discussion of this topic, see Brigham and Gapenski (2003), Chapters 6 and 10.

Adjusting Volatility Measure for Growth   Besides normalizing the standard deviation for size by computing the CV, it is also important to recognize that the standard deviation is measured relative to the mean value for the series—that is, it computes deviations from "expected value." The problem arises for firms that experience significant growth that will create very large deviations from the mean for the series even if it is *constant* growth. The way to avoid this bias is to measure deviations from the growth path of the series. For details, see Appendix C of this chapter, which demonstrates this adjustment using 10 years of data for Walgreens.

Operating Leverage   The variability of a firm's operating earnings also depends on its mixture of production costs. Total production costs of a firm with no *fixed* production costs would vary directly with sales, and operating profits would be a constant proportion of sales. In such an example, the firm's operating profit margin would be constant and its operating profits would have the same relative volatility as its sales. Realistically, firms always have some fixed production costs such as buildings, machinery, or relatively permanent personnel. Fixed production costs cause operating profits to vary more than sales over the business cycle. Specifically, during slow periods, operating profits will decline by a larger percentage than sales, while during an economic expansion, operating profits will increase by a larger percentage than sales.

The employment of fixed production costs is referred to as **operating leverage**. Clearly, greater operating leverage (caused by a higher proportion of fixed production costs) makes the operating earnings series more volatile relative to the sales series (see Lee, Finnerty, and Norton, 2003). This basic relationship between operating profit and sales leads us to measure operating leverage as the percentage change in operating earnings relative to the percentage change in sales during a specified period as follows:

$$\text{Operating Leverage} = \frac{\sum_{i=1}^{n} \left| \frac{\%\Delta OE}{\%\Delta S} \right|}{n}$$

We take the absolute value of the percentage changes because the two series can move in opposite directions. The direction of the change is not important, but the relative size of the change is relevant. By implication, the more volatile the operating earnings as compared to the volatility of sales, the greater the firm's operating leverage.

Financial Risk

Financial risk you will recall, is the additional uncertainty of returns to equity holders due to a firm's use of fixed financial obligation securities. This financial uncertainty is in addition to the firm's business risk. When a firm sells bonds to raise capital, the interest payments on this capital precede the computation of common stock earnings, and these interest payments are fixed contractual obligations. As with operating leverage, during an economic expansion, the net earnings available for common stock after the fixed interest payments will experience a larger percentage increase than operating earnings. In contrast, during a business decline, the earnings available to stockholders will decline by a larger percentage than operating earnings because of these fixed financial costs (i.e., interest payments). Notably, as a firm increases its relative debt financing with fixed contractual obligations, it increases its financial risk and the possibility of default and bankruptcy.

Relationship between Business Risk and Financial Risk   A very important point to remember is that *the acceptable level of financial risk for a firm depends on its business risk.* If the firm has low business risk (i.e., stable operating earnings), investors are willing to accept higher financial risk. For example, retail food companies typically have stable operating earnings over time, which implies *low* business risk, and means that investors and bond-rating firms will allow the firms to have *higher* financial risk. In contrast, if a firm is in an industry that is subject to high business risk (i.e., it experiences high sales volatility and it has high operating leverage), such as steel, auto, and airline companies, an investor would *not* want these firms to also have high financial risk. The two risks would compound and the probability of bankruptcy would be substantial.[11]

In our analysis, we employ three sets of financial ratios to measure financial risk, and *all three* sets should be considered. First, there are balance sheet ratios that indicate the proportion of capital derived from debt securities compared to equity capital. Second are ratios that consider the earnings or cash flows available to pay fixed financial charges. Third are ratios that consider the cash flows available and relate these cash flows to the book value of the outstanding debt. Before we discuss and demonstrate these financial risk ratios, it is necessary to consider the topic of operating lease obligations.

Consideration of Lease Obligations   Many firms lease facilities (buildings) and equipment rather than borrow the funds and purchase the assets—it is basically a lease or borrow decision since the lease contract is like a bond obligation. The accounting for the lease obligation depends on the type of lease. If it is a *capital* lease, the value of the asset and the lease obligation is included on the balance sheet as an asset and liability. If it is an *operating* lease, it is noted in the footnotes but is not specifically included on the balance sheet.[12] Because operating leases are a form of financing used extensively by retailers (such as Walgreens, Sears, and McDonald's) and airlines, it is necessary to recognize this obligation, capitalize estimated future lease payments, and include this capitalized lease value on the balance sheet as both an asset and a long-term liability. In the following subsection, we discuss how to do this, and we demonstrate the significant impact this adjustment can have on several financial risk ratios.

Capitalizing Operating Leases   Capitalizing leases basically involves an estimate of the present value of a firm's future required lease payments. Therefore, an analyst must estimate: (1) an appropriate discount rate (typically the firm's long-term debt rate) and (2) the firm's future lease payment obligations as specified in a footnote.

An estimate of the discounted value of the future lease payments can be done one of two ways: (1) a multiple of the forthcoming minimum lease payments or (2) the discounted value of the future lease payments provided in the annual report at the firm's cost of long-term debt. The traditional multiple technique multiplies the minimum lease payment in year $t + 1$ by 8. In the case of Walgreens, the future minimum lease payments in the annual report for the year 2004 are as follows:

Years Relating to Year-End	1	2	3	4	5	Later
Minimum Payments ($ millions)	1,309	1,346	1,309	1,242	1,215	15,455

Given these data, the estimate using the first technique would produce an estimate of $8 \times$ $1,309 million = $10.47 billion. To derive an estimate using the second technique, we need to estimate the firm's cost of long-term debt and consider how to handle the lump-sum later

[11]Support for this specific relationship is found in a set of tables (see Standard & Poor, 2002, p. 57) that suggest specific required financial risk ratios necessary for a firm to be considered for a specific bond rating. The required ratios differ on the basis of the perceived business risk of the firm.

[12]A discussion of the technical factors that will cause a lease to be capital versus operating is beyond the scope of this book, but it is covered in most intermediate accounting texts.

payments. Our debt rate estimate is 7.00 percent, which is consistent with the prevailing rate on 20-year, A-rated corporate bonds, which is conservative for Walgreens (it is probably between AA and A). For the later lump-sum payment, we need to derive a reasonable estimate regarding how many years to assume for this payout. A liberal assumption is that the lump-sum payment is spread evenly over 15 years, based on a typical building lease of 20 years ($15,455/15 = $1,030 million per year). An alternative estimate of the spread period is derived by dividing the lump-sum payment in period $t + 6$ by the $t + 5$ payment, which implies a time estimate ($15,455/1,215 = 12.72$). If we round this up to 13 years, we have an annual payment of $15,455/13 = $1,189 million per year for 13 years.

If we discount at 7.00 percent all the annual flows and the later flows over 15 years, we derive an estimate of the lease debt of $11.97 *billion*. A similar computation using the 13-year spread indicates an estimate of lease debt of $12.37 *billion*. Therefore, we have the following three estimates:[13]

8 times the $t + 1$ lease payment	$10.47 billion
Discounting the lease payments assuming a 15-year spread	$11.97 billion
Discounting the lease payments assuming a 13-year spread	$12.37 billion

We will use the $11.97 billion discounted lease payment estimate since this estimate is midway between the liberal multiple method and the conservative discounting method that assumes a 13-year spread. If we add this amount (or that estimated by the other methods) to both fixed assets and long-term debt we will have a better measure of the assets utilized by the firm and the complete funding of the assets (recognition of more debt).

Implied Interest for Leased Assets   When computing the return on total capital (ROTC) that considers these leased assets, we must also add the implied interest expense for the leases. The interest expense component of a lease is typically estimated by bond-rating agencies and many other analysts as equal to one-third of the lease payment in year $t + 1$ (in our example, $1,309 million/3 = $436 million).

An alternative to this rule of thumb would be to derive a specific estimate based on an estimate of the firm's cost of debt capital (7.00 percent) and the estimate of the present value (PV) of the lease obligation, as follows:

Estimating Technique	PV of Lease Obligation ($ Billion)	Interest Expense at 7.00 Percent ($ Million)
8 times estimate of $t + 1$ payment	10.47	733
PV with 15-year spread	11.97	838
PV with 13-year spread	12.37	866

Notably, all of these estimates of the implied interest expense are substantially higher than the one-third rule-of-thumb estimate of $436 million. Again, the rule of thumb underestimates the financial leverage related to these lease obligations.

To calculate the ROTC for 2003 and 2004, we need to compute the value of the lease obligations and the implied interest expense for the three years (2002, 2003, and 2004) as follows:

---

[13] Notably, the "8 times" estimate almost always provides the lowest estimate of debt value, which means that this rule of thumb will tend to underestimate the financial leverage for these firms and the resulting implied interest expense. As noted, we have opted to use the discounted value of future lease payments, assuming a 15-year spread of the later payments, as computed in Appendix A on page 354.

Year	Estimate of PV of Lease Obligation[a] ($ Billion)	Estimate of Interest Component of Lease[b] ($ Million)
2004	11.97	838
2003	10.63	744
2002	8.37	586

[a]See calculations in Appendix B on page 355.
[b]Equal to 0.07 of the PV of lease obligation.

Adding these values to the prior ratios results in the following lease-adjusted return on total invested capital (ROIC) values

$$2004: \quad \frac{1,360 + 0.2 + 838}{(20,908.7 + 18,390.7)/2} = \frac{2,198.2}{19,649.7} = 11.19\%$$

$$2003: \quad \frac{1,176 + 0.2 + 744}{(18,390.7 + 15,121.5)/2} = \frac{1,920.2}{16,756.1} = 11.46\%$$

As shown, the ROICs that include the leased assets and lease debt are lower (over 11 percent versus over 16 percent), but they are still quite reasonable.

Implied Depreciation on Leased Assets   Another factor is the implied depreciation expense that would be taken if these were not leased assets. One way to calculate this value is to simply use the typical term of the lease or weighted-average term. In the case of Walgreens, this is reasonably clear since almost all leases are 20-year leases on buildings. However, if the value were not clear, a second alternative would be the average percent of depreciation as a percent of beginning-of-year net fixed assets. In the case of Walgreens, for 2004 this would be

Depreciation (2004) $403 million; Net Fixed Assets at End of 2003: $4,940

This implies a percent of 0.0816 (403/4,940), which is clearly higher than the 5 percent on buildings. Obviously, Walgreens has many assets being depreciated over shorter lives. For these calculations related to leases on buildings, we assume the 20-year life as follows:

Year	Estimate of PV of Lease Obligation ($ Billion)	Estimate of Implied Depreciation Expense of Lease* ($ Million)
2004	11.97	599
2003	10.63	532
2002	8.37	419

*Assumes straight-line depreciation over a 20-year life.

These implied depreciation charges should be included in ratios that include depreciation expenses.

Proportion of Debt (Balance Sheet) Ratios

The proportion of debt ratios indicate what proportion of the firm's capital is derived from debt compared to other sources of capital, such as preferred stock, common stock, and retained earnings. A higher proportion of debt capital compared to equity capital makes earnings more volatile (i.e., more financial leverage) and increases the probability that a firm could default on the debt. Therefore, higher proportion of debt ratios indicate greater financial risk. The following are the major proportion of debt ratios used to measure financial risk.

Debt–Equity Ratio   The debt–equity ratio is

$$10.23 \qquad \text{Debt–Equity Ratio} = \frac{\text{Total Long-Term Debt}}{\text{Total Equity}}$$

The debt figure includes all long-term fixed obligations, including subordinated convertible bonds. The equity typically is the book value of equity and includes preferred stock, common stock, and retained earnings. Some analysts prefer to exclude preferred stock and consider only common equity. Total equity is preferable if some of the firms being analyzed have preferred stock.

Notably, debt ratios can be computed *with and without deferred taxes.* Most balance sheets include an accumulated deferred tax figure. There is some controversy regarding whether these deferred taxes should be treated as a liability or as part of permanent capital. Some argue that if the deferred tax has accumulated because of the difference in accelerated and straight-line depreciation, this liability may never be paid. That is, as long as the firm continues to grow and add new assets, this total deferred tax account continues to grow. Alternatively, if the deferred tax account is caused by differences in the recognition of income on long-term contracts, there will be a reversal and this liability must eventually be paid. As suggested by White, Sondhi, and Fried (2003), to resolve this question, the analyst must determine the reason for the deferred tax account and examine its long-term trend. Walgreen Co.'s deferred tax account is because of a depreciation difference and it has typically grown over time.

A second consideration when computing debt ratios is the existence of operating leases, as mentioned in a prior section. As noted, given a firm like Walgreens with extensive leased facilities, it is necessary to include an estimate of the present value of the lease payments as long-term debt.

To show the effect of these two significant items on the financial risk of Walgreens, we define the ratios to include both of these factors, but they will be broken out to identify the effect of each of the components of total debt. Thus, the debt–equity ratio is

$$10.24 \qquad \text{Debt–Equity Ratio} = \frac{\text{Total Long-Term Debt}}{\text{Total Equity}}$$

$$= \frac{\text{Noncurrent Liabilities} + \text{Deferred Taxes} + \text{PV of Lease Obligations}}{\text{Total Equity}}$$

For Walgreens, the debt–equity ratios were

$$2004: \quad \frac{709 + 328 + 11{,}972}{8{,}228} = \frac{13{,}009}{8{,}228} = 158.1\%$$

$$2003: \quad \frac{562 + 228 + 10{,}633}{7{,}196} = \frac{11{,}423}{7{,}196} = 158.7\%$$

$$2002: \quad \frac{517 + 177 + 8{,}374}{6{,}230} = \frac{9{,}068}{6{,}230} = 145.6\%$$

These ratios demonstrate the significant impact of including the present value of the lease payments as part of long-term debt—for example, the debt–equity percent for 2004 went from less than 13 percent without lease obligations to over 158 percent when capitalized leases are included.

Long-Term Debt–Total Capital Ratio The long-term debt–total capital ratio indicates the proportion of long-term capital derived from long-term debt capital. It is computed as

$$\text{10.25} \qquad \text{Long-Term Debt–Total Capital Ratio} = \frac{\text{Total Long-Term Debt}}{\text{Total Long-Term Capital}}$$

The total long-term debt values are the same as above. The total long-term capital would include all long-term debt, any preferred stock, and total equity. The long-term debt–total capital ratios for Walgreens were

Including Deferred Taxes and Lease Obligations as Long-Term Debt

$$2004: \quad \frac{13,009}{13,009 + 8,228} = 61.3\%$$

$$2003: \quad \frac{11,423}{11,423 + 7,196} = 61.4\%$$

$$2002: \quad \frac{9,068}{9,068 + 6,230} = 59.3\%$$

Again, this ratio, which includes the present value of lease obligations, shows that a significant percent of long-term capital is debt obligations, which differs substantially from a ratio without the lease obligations.

Total Debt–Total Capital Ratios In many cases, it is useful to compare *total* debt to *total* invested capital. Earlier when we computed return on invested capital, we did not consider non-interest-bearing capital such as accounts payable, accrued expenses, income taxes payable, or deferred taxes (caused by depreciation). In such a case, total debt would be long-term debt (without deferred taxes), which would be other noncurrent liabilities plus capitalized leases. Total capital would be this interest-bearing debt plus shareholders' equity, as follows:

$$\text{Total Debt–Total Capital Ratio} = \frac{\text{Total Interest-Bearing Debt}}{\text{Total Invested Capital}}$$

$$= \frac{\text{Capitalized Leases} + \text{Noncurrent Liabilities}}{\text{Total Interest-Bearing Debt} + \text{Shareholders' Equity}}$$

$$2004: \quad \frac{11,972 + 709}{11,972 + 709 + 8,228} = \frac{12,681}{20,909} = 60.6\%$$

$$2003: \quad \frac{10,633 + 562}{10,633 + 562 + 7,196} = \frac{11,195}{18,391} = 60.9\%$$

$$2002: \quad \frac{8,374 + 517}{8,374 + 517 + 6,230} = \frac{8,891}{15,121} = 58.8\%$$

While these adjustments cause the debt percents to be lower, they are still quite high, which confirms the importance of considering the impact of lease obligations on the financial risk of firms like Walgreens that employ this form of financing.

Earnings and Cash Flow Coverage Ratios

In addition to ratios that indicate the proportion of debt on the balance sheet, investors are very conscious of ratios that relate the *flow* of earnings or cash flows available to meet the required interest and lease payments. A higher ratio of available earnings or cash flow relative to fixed financial charges indicates lower financial risk.

Interest Coverage Ratio   The standard interest coverage ratio is computed as

10.26 $$\text{Interest Coverage} = \frac{\text{Income before Interest and Taxes (EBIT)}}{\text{Debt Interest Charges}}$$

$$= \frac{\text{Net Income} + \text{Income Taxes} + \text{Interest Expense}}{\text{Interest Expense}}$$

This ratio indicates how many times the fixed interest charges are earned, based on the earnings available to pay these expenses.[14] Alternatively, one minus the reciprocal of the interest coverage ratio indicates how far earnings could decline before it would be impossible to pay the interest charges from current earnings. For example, a coverage ratio of 5 means that earnings could decline by 80 percent (1 minus $\frac{1}{5}$), and the firm could still pay its fixed financial charges. Again, for firms like Walgreens that have heavy lease obligations, it is necessary to consider the impact of the lease obligations on this ratio because if we only consider Walgreen Co.'s public interest-bearing debt, the interest cost is about a half-million dollars and the coverage ratio exceeds 3,000 times. In contrast, if we recognize the lease obligations as debt and include the implied interest on the capitalized leases as computed earlier, the coverage ratio would be restated as follows:

10.27 $$\frac{\text{Fixed Financial}}{\text{Cost Coverage}} = \frac{\text{Earnings before Interest and Taxes} + \text{Implied Lease Interest}}{\text{Gross Interest Expense} + \text{Implied Lease Interest}}$$

Hence, the fixed financial cost coverage ratios for Walgreens were

$$2004: \quad \frac{1,360 + 816 + 838}{838} = \frac{3,014}{838} = 3.60 \text{ times}$$

$$2003: \quad \frac{1,176 + 713 + 744}{744} = \frac{2,633}{744} = 3.54 \text{ times}$$

$$2002: \quad \frac{1,019 + 618 + 586}{586} = \frac{2,233}{586} = 3.79 \text{ times}$$

These fixed financial cost coverage ratios show a substantially different picture than the coverage ratios that do not consider the impact of the lease obligations. Even so, these coverage ratios are not unreasonable for a firm with very low business risk.

The trend of Walgreen Co.'s coverage ratios has been consistent with the overall trend in the proportion of debt ratios. The point is, the proportion of debt ratios and the earnings flow ratios do not always give consistent results because the proportion of debt ratios are not sensitive to changes in earnings or to changes in the interest rates on the debt. For example, if interest rates increase or if the firm replaces old debt with new debt that has a higher interest rate, no change would occur in the proportion of debt ratios, but the interest coverage ratio would decline. Also, the interest coverage ratio is sensitive to an increase or decrease in earnings. Therefore, the results using balance sheet ratios and coverage ratios can differ. Given a difference between the two sets of ratios, we have a strong preference for the coverage ratios that reflect the ability of the firm to meet its financial obligations.

---

[14]The interest expense for Walgreens other than for leased assets is clearly insignificant (about $200,000), so it is not included in the computations although it is in the formulas to be considered for other firms.

Alternatives to these earnings coverage ratios are several ratios that relate the cash flow available from operations to either interest expense or total fixed charges.

Cash Flow Coverage Ratio The motivation for this ratio is that a firm's earnings and cash flow typically will differ substantially (these differences have been noted and will be considered in a subsequent section). The cash flow value used is the cash flow from operating activities figure contained in the cash flow statement. As such, it includes depreciation expense, deferred taxes, and the impact of all working capital changes. Again, it is appropriate to specify the ratio in terms of total fixed financial costs including leases, as follows:

10.28 Cash Flow Coverage of Fixed Financial Cost

$$= \frac{\text{Net Cash Flow from Operating Activities} + \text{Interest Expense} + \text{Implied Lease Interest}}{\text{Interest Expense} + \text{Implied Lease Interest}}$$

We use the values given in the cash flow statement, since we are specifically interested in the cash flow effect.

The cash flow coverage ratios for Walgreens were:

$$2004: \quad \frac{1,652 + 838}{838} = \frac{2,490}{838} = 2.97 \text{ times}$$

$$2003: \quad \frac{1,504 + 744}{744} = \frac{2,248}{744} = 3.02 \text{ times}$$

$$2002: \quad \frac{1,504 + 586}{586} = \frac{2,090}{586} = 3.57 \text{ times}$$

While these coverage ratios are not alarming for a firm with very low business risk, it is noteworthy that they have declined steadily over the past three years.

Cash Flow–Long-Term Debt Ratio Several studies have used a ratio that relates cash flow to a firm's outstanding debt. The cash flow–outstanding debt ratios are unique because they relate the *flow* of earnings plus noncash expenses to the *stock* of outstanding debt. These ratios have been significant variables in numerous studies concerned with predicting bankruptcies and bond ratings. (These studies are listed in the reference section.) The cash flow figure we use is the cash flow from operating activities. Obviously, the higher the percent of cash flow to long-term debt, the stronger the company—i.e., the lower its financial risk. This ratio would be computed as

10.29 $\dfrac{\text{Cash Flow}}{\text{Long-Term Debt}}$

$$= \frac{\text{Cash Flow from Operating Activities}}{\text{Book Value of Long-Term Debt} + \text{Present Value of Lease Obligations}}$$

For Walgreens, the ratios were as follows, assuming that deferred taxes are not included, since they are not interest-bearing. Thus, the long-term debt is noncurrent liabilities and the lease obligations:

$$2004: \quad \frac{1,653}{709 + 11,972} = \frac{1,653}{12,681} = 13.0\%$$

$$2003: \quad \frac{1,504}{562 + 10,633} = \frac{1,504}{11,195} = 13.4\%$$

$$2002: \quad \frac{1,504}{517 + 8,374} = \frac{1,504}{8,891} = 16.9\%$$

The large percent during 2002 was caused by the increase in cash flow due to a smaller increase in inventory during the year (see Exhibit 10.3).

Cash Flow–Total Debt Ratio   Investors also should consider the relationship of cash flow to *total* debt to check that a firm has not had a significant increase in its short-term borrowing.

$$10.30 \quad \frac{\text{Cash Flow}}{\text{Total Debt}} = \frac{\text{Cash Flow from Operating Activities}}{\text{Total Long-Term Debt} + \text{Interest-Bearing Current Liabilities}}$$

For Walgreens, these ratios are the same as with long-term debt because the firm does not have any interest-bearing short-term debt. When firms do have short-term debt, the percents for this ratio will be lower; how much lower will indicate the amount of short-term borrowing by the firm. As before, it is important to compare these flow ratios with similar ratios for other companies in the industry and with the overall economy to gauge the firm's relative performance.

Alternative Measures of Cash Flow[15]   As noted, many past studies that included a cash flow variable used the traditional measure of cash flow. The requirement that companies must prepare and report the statement of cash flows to stockholders has raised interest in other exact measures of cash flow. The first alternative measure is the *cash flow from operations,* which is taken directly from the statement of cash flows and is the one we have used. A second alternative measure is *free cash flow,* which is a modification of the cash flow from operations—that is, capital expenditures (minus the cash flow from the sale of assets) are also deducted and some analysts also subtract dividends. The following table summarizes the values for Walgreens derived earlier in the section entitled "Measures of Cash Flow."

Year	Traditional Cash Flow	Cash Flow from Operations	Net Cap Exp	FREE CASH FLOW Before Div.	Div.	After Div.
2004	1863	1653	933	719	177	542
2003	1581	1492	711	781	152	629
2002	1349	1474	566	908	147	761

As shown, Walgreens has strong and growing cash flow from operations even after considering significant working capital requirements, but the firm experiences positive but declining free cash flow because of substantial net capital expenditures necessitated by the firm's growth.

External Market Liquidity Risk

External Market Liquidity Defined   In Chapter 1 we discussed external market liquidity as the ability to buy or sell an asset quickly with little price change from a prior transaction assuming no new information. GE and Pfizer are examples of liquid common stocks because investors can sell them quickly with little price change from the prior trade. Investors might be able to sell an illiquid stock quickly, but the price would be significantly different from the prior price. Alternatively, the broker might be able to get a specified price, but could take several days doing so.

---

[15]A list of studies in which financial ratios or cash flow variables are used to predict bankruptcies or bond ratings is included in the reference section.

Determinants of External Market Liquidity   Investors should know the liquidity characteristics of the securities they currently own or may buy because liquidity can be important if they want to change the composition of their portfolios. Although the major determinants of market liquidity are reflected in market trading data, several internal corporate variables are good proxies for these market variables. The most important determinant of external market liquidity is the number of shares or the dollar value of shares traded (the dollar value adjusts for different price levels). More trading activity indicates a greater probability that one can find someone to take the other side of a desired transaction. A very good measure that is usually available is **trading turnover** (the percentage of outstanding shares traded during a period of time), which indicates relative trading activity. During calendar year 2004, about 700 million shares of Walgreens were traded, which indicates annual trading turnover of approximately 68 percent (700 million/1,032 million). This compares with the average turnover for the NYSE of about 90 percent. Another measure of market liquidity is the bid–ask spread, where a smaller spread indicates greater liquidity. In addition, certain corporate variables are correlated with these trading variables:

1. Total market value of outstanding securities (number of common shares outstanding times the market price per share)
2. Number of security owners

Numerous studies have shown that the main determinant of the bid–ask spread (besides price) is the dollar value of trading.[16] In turn, the value of trading correlates highly with the market value of the outstanding securities and the number of security holders because with more shares outstanding, there will be more stockholders to buy or sell at any time for a variety of purposes. Numerous buyers and sellers provide liquidity.

We can estimate the market value of Walgreen Co.'s outstanding stock as the average number of shares outstanding during the year (adjusted for stock splits) times the average market price for the year (equal to the high price plus the low price divided by 2) as follows:[17]

$$2004: \quad 1,032 \times \frac{39 + 32}{2} = \$36.64 \text{ billion}$$

$$2003: \quad 1,032 \times \frac{40 + 31}{2} = \$36.64 \text{ billion}$$

$$2002: \quad 1,032 \times \frac{45 + 31}{2} = \$39.22 \text{ billion}$$

These market values clearly would place Walgreens in the large-cap category, which usually begins at about $5 billion. Walgreens stockholders number 600,000, including more than 650 institutions that own approximately 56 percent of the outstanding stock. These large values for market value, the number of stockholders, institutional holders, and the high trading turnover indicate a highly liquid market in Walgreens stock, which implies extremely low external liquidity risk.

ANALYSIS OF GROWTH POTENTIAL

Importance of Growth Analysis

The analysis of **sustainable growth potential** examines ratios that indicate how fast a firm should grow. Analysis of a firm's growth potential is important for both lenders and owners.

---

[16]Studies on this topic were discussed in Chapter 4.
[17]These stock prices (which are for the calendar year) are rounded to the nearest whole dollar.

Owners know that the value of the firm depends on its future growth in earnings, cash flow, and dividends. In the following chapter, we discuss various valuation models that are based on alternative cash flows, the investor's required rate of return for the stock, and the firm's expected growth rate of earnings and cash flows.

Creditors also are interested in a firm's growth potential because the firm's future success is the major determinant of its ability to pay obligations, and the firm's future success is influenced by its growth. Some credit analysis ratios measure the book value of a firm's assets relative to its financial obligations, assuming that the firm can sell these assets to pay off the loan in case of default. Selling assets in a forced liquidation will typically yield only about 10 to 15 cents on the dollar. Currently, it is widely recognized that the more relevant analysis is the ability of the firm to pay off its obligations as an ongoing enterprise, which is impacted by its growth potential. This analysis of growth is also relevant to changes of bond ratings.

Determinants of Growth

The growth of business, like the growth on any economic entity, including the aggregate economy, depends on

1. The amount of resources retained and reinvested in the entity
2. The rate of return earned on the reinvested funds

The more a firm reinvests, the greater its potential for growth. Alternatively, for a given level of reinvestment, a firm will grow faster if it earns a higher rate of return on the funds reinvested. Therefore, the growth rate of equity earnings and cash flows is a function of two variables: (1) the percentage of net earnings retained (the firm's retention rate) and (2) the rate of return earned on the firm's equity capital (the firm's ROE), because when earnings are retained they become part of the firm's equity.

10.31 $$g = \text{Percentage of Earnings Retained} \times \text{Return on Equity}$$
$$= \text{RR} \times \text{ROE}$$

where:

g = potential (i.e., sustainable) growth rate
RR = the retention rate of earnings
ROE = the firm's return on equity

The retention rate is a decision by the board of directors based on the investment opportunities available to the firm. Theory suggests that the firm should retain earnings and reinvest them as long as the expected rate of return on the investment exceeds the firm's cost of capital.

As discussed earlier regarding the DuPont System, a firm's ROE is a function of three components:

- Net profit margin
- Total asset turnover
- Financial leverage (total assets/equity)

Therefore, a firm can increase its ROE by increasing its profit margin, by becoming more efficient (increasing its total asset turnover), or by increasing its financial leverage (and its financial risk). As discussed, investors should examine and estimate each of the components when estimating the ROE for a firm.

The sustainable growth potential analysis for Walgreens begins with the retention rate (RR):

10.32
$$\text{Retention Rate} = 1 - \frac{\text{Dividends Declared}}{\text{Operating Income after Taxes}}$$

Walgreens RR figures were

$$2004: \ 1 - \frac{0.18}{1.33} = 0.86$$

$$2003: \ 1 - \frac{0.16}{1.14} = 0.86$$

$$2002: \ 1 - \frac{0.15}{0.99} = 0.85$$

The historical results in Exhibit 10.7 indicate that the retention rate for Walgreens has been relatively stable during the 22-year period in excess of 70 percent, including recent increases to about 85 percent.

Exhibit 10.6 contains the three components of ROE for the period 1982–2004. Exhibit 10.7 contains the two factors that determine a firm's growth potential and the implied growth rate during the past 23 years. Overall, Walgreens experienced a slight decline in its growth potential during the early 1990s, but since 1995 the firm has experienced a potential growth rate in excess of 14 percent, which is very consistent with its actual performance.

Exhibit 10.8 reinforces our understanding of the importance of the firm's ROE. Walgreen Co.'s retention rate was quite stable throughout the period with an increase during the last five years. Even with this, it has been the firm's ROE that has mainly determined its sustainable growth rate. This analysis indicates that the important consideration is *the long-run outlook for the components of sustainable growth.* Investors need to *project* changes in each of the components of ROE and employ these projections to estimate an ROE to use in the growth model along with an estimate of the firm's long-run retention rate. We will come back to these concepts on numerous occasions when discussing stock valuation. This detailed analysis of ROE is extremely important for growth companies where the ROEs are notably above average for the economy and, therefore, vulnerable to competition.

COMPARATIVE ANALYSIS OF RATIOS

We have discussed the importance of comparative analysis, but so far we have concentrated on the selection and computation of specific ratios. Exhibit 10.9 contains most of the ratios discussed for Walgreens, the retail drug store industry (as derived from the *S&P Analysts Handbook*), and the S&P Industrials Index. The three-year comparison should provide some insights, although we typically would want to examine data for a 5- to 10-year period. It was necessary to do the comparison for the period 2001–2003 because industry and market data from Standard and Poor's were not available for 2004 at the time of this writing.

Internal Liquidity

The three basic ratios (current ratio, quick ratio, and cash ratio) provided mixed results regarding liquidity for Walgreens relative to the industry and market. The current ratio is about equal to the industry and above the market. The firm's receivables collection period is

Exhibit 10.8	Walgreen Co. Components of Growth and the Implied Sustainable Growth Rate

Year	(1) Retention Rate	(2) Return on Equity[a]	(3)[b] Sustainable Growth Rate
1982	0.72	18.73	13.49
1983	0.74	19.84	14.68
1984	0.74	20.60	15.24
1985	0.71	19.58	13.90
1986	0.70	18.64	13.05
1987	0.68	16.63	11.31
1988	0.71	18.12	12.87
1989	0.73	18.74	13.68
1990	0.72	18.42	13.26
1991	0.71	18.04	12.81
1992	0.71	17.90	12.71
1993	0.67	16.07	10.77
1994	0.70	17.91	12.54
1995	0.69	17.85	12.32
1996	0.71	18.19	12.91
1997	0.73	18.35	13.40
1998	0.75	17.93	13.44
1999	0.79	17.91	14.15
2000	0.82	18.35	15.05
2001	0.84	17.01	14.29
2002	0.85	16.36	13.91
2003	0.86	16.34	14.05
2004	0.86	16.52	14.21

[a]From Exhibit 10.6.
[b]Column (3) is equal to column (1) times column (2).

substantially less than the S&P Industrials and below the retail drugstore industry. Because the collection period has been fairly steady, the difference is due to the firm's basic credit policy.

Overall, the comparisons indicate reasonably strong internal liquidity. An additional positive liquidity factor is the firm's ability to sell high-grade commercial paper and several major bank credit lines.

Operating Performance

This segment of the analysis considers efficiency ratios (turnovers) and profitability ratios. The major comparison is relative to the industry. Walgreen Co.'s turnover ratios were consistently substantially above those of the retail drug store industry.

Exhibit 10.9 Summary of Financial Ratios for Walgreens, S&P Retail Drugstores, S&P Industrials Index, 2001–2003

	2003			2002			2001		
	Walgreens	Drugstores	S&P Industrials	Walgreens	Drugstores	S&P Industrials	Walgreens	Drugstores	S&P Industrials
Internal liquidity									
Current ratio	1.8	1.82	1.43	1.75	1.81	1.36	1.46	1.58	1.29
Quick ratio	0.62	0.56	1.05	0.48	0.47	0.98	0.27	0.32	0.92
Cash ratio	0.35	0.23	0.37	0.15	0.16	0.32	0.01	0.04	0.26
Receivables turnover	32.95	38.30	4.43	32.72	27.54	4.24	34.86	27.03	4.30
Average collection period	11.08	9.53	82.40	11.20	13.30	86.10	10.50	13.50	84.90
Working capital–sales	0.09	0.07	0.16	0.06	0.09	0.11	0.05	0.08	0.09
Operating performance									
Total asset turnover	3.02	4.01	0.79	3.07	2.8	0.76	3.09	2.69	0.79
Inventory turnover (sales)	6.04	10.07	11.43	8.05	6.68	10.89	7.8	6.29	10.94
Working capital turnover	11.06	14.13	6.43	15.96	11.74	8.88	18.73	13.07	11.34
Net fixed asset turnover	6.82	11.81	2.96	6.42	8.11	2.77	6.34	7.71	2.8
Equity turnover	4.84	6.85	2.48	5.02	5.05	2.38	5.22	4.99	2.32
Profitability									
Gross profit margin	27.07	NA*	NA	26.52	NA	NA	26.70	NA	NA
Operating profit margin	5.81	5.29	9.76	5.71	5.41	12.81	5.78	5.38	10.53
Net profit margin	3.62	2.40	6.35	3.55	3.29	7.07	3.60	2.81	4.89
Return on total capital	10.92	9.91	8.72	10.89	9.54	6.85	11.15	9.01	5.41
Return on owners' equity	17.52	16.47	22.90	17.82	16.64	16.80	18.76	15.86	11.33
Financial risk									
Debt–equity ratio	143.05	16.33	157.03	126.43	17.82	139.93	132.07	16.91	113.6
Long-term debt–long-term capital	58.86	14.09	61.09	55.84	15.12	58.32	56.91	14.46	53.18
Total debt–total capital	66.79	68.55	589.40	63.49	42.17	69.81	65.71	45.7	66.09
Interest coverage	5.77	60.95	6.21	6.45	49.18	6.68	6.47	30.77	5.24
Cash flow–long-term debt	15.33	534.95	40.40	24.09	381.10	36.78	15.37	231.48	37.78
Cash flow–total debt	13.3	22.26	19.20	16.9	26.16	17.11	8.81	25.49	16.92
Growth analysis									
Retention rate	0.86	0.87	0.68	0.85	0.86	0.72	0.84	0.81	0.58
Return on equity	16.34	15.38	13.80	16.36	15.37	17.84	17.01	13.14	11.02
Total asset turnover	2.79	3.78	0.72	2.9	2.69	0.76	2.99	2.59	0.76
Total asset–equity	1.62	1.69	3.02	1.59	1.73	3.3	1.68	1.88	2.96
Net profit margin	3.62	2.40	6.35	3.55	3.29	3.12	3.66	2.81	2.26
Sustainable growth rate	14.05	13.39	9.45	13.96	13.18	12.77	14.24	10.67	6.38

*NA: not available.

The comparison of profitability from sales was mixed. Operating profit margins were about equal to the industry, but net margins beat the industry performance. The strong operating profit margin was in spite of the higher growth rate of new stores relative to the competition, and the fact that new stores require 18 to 24 months to reach the firm's "normal" profit rate.

The profit performance related to invested capital was historically strong. The return on total capital (including capitalized leases) for Walgreens was consistently above both the S&P Industrials and the retail drugstore industry. Walgreens likewise always attained higher ROEs than its industry and the market.

Risk Analysis

Walgreen Co.'s financial risk ratios, measured in terms of proportion of debt, were consistently inferior to those of the industry and the market when both deferred taxes and capitalized leases were included as long-term debt for Walgreens, but it was not possible to do a comparable adjustment for the S&P Industrials or the industry. Such an adjustment would have a significant impact on the industry results. Similarly, the financial risk ratios that use cash flow for Walgreens were below the market and its industry. These comparisons indicate that Walgreens has a reasonable amount of financial risk, but it is not of major concern because the firm has very low business risk based on consistently high growth in sales and operating profit. Notably, there are no specific comparative ratios available for both business and external liquidity risk. Regarding business risk, the analysis of relative sales and EBIT volatility adjusted for growth as demonstrated in the Appendix indicated that this adjusted volatility was very low indicating low business risk. Also, the trading turnover and market value data indicated low external liquidity risk.

Growth Analysis

Walgreens has generally maintained a sustainable growth rate above its industry and the aggregate market, based on both a higher ROE and a consistently higher retention rate. In sum, Walgreens has adequate liquidity; a good operating record, including a very consistent growth record that implies low business risk; reasonable financial risk even when we consider the leases on stores; and clearly above-average growth performance. Your success as an investor depends on how well you use these historical numbers to derive meaningful *estimates* of *future* performance for use in a valuation model. As noted previously, everybody is generally aware of the valuation models, so it is the individual who can provide the best *estimates* of relevant valuation variables who will experience superior risk-adjusted performance.

ANALYSIS OF NON-U.S. FINANCIAL STATEMENTS

As we have stressed several times, your portfolio should encompass other economies and markets, numerous global industries, and many foreign firms in these global industries. However, because accounting conventions differ among countries, non-U.S. financial statements will differ from those in this chapter and from what you will see in a typical accounting course.

While it is beyond the scope of this text to discuss these alternative accounting conventions in detail, we encourage you to examine the sources in the "Suggested Readings" section entitled *Analysis of International Financial Statements.*

THE QUALITY OF FINANCIAL STATEMENTS

Analysts sometimes speak of the quality of a firm's earnings or the quality of a firm's balance sheet. In general, **quality financial statements** are a good reflection of reality; accounting tricks and one-time changes are not used to make the firm appear stronger than it really is. Some factors that lead to lower-quality financial statements were mentioned previously when we discussed ratio analysis. Other quality influences are discussed here and in Palepu, Healy, and Bernard (2004, Chapter 3).

Balance Sheet

A high-quality balance sheet typically has limited use of debt or leverage. Therefore, the potential of financial distress resulting from excessive debt is quite low. Little use of debt also implies the firm has unused borrowing capacity, which implies that the firm can draw on that unused capacity to make profitable investments.

A quality balance sheet contains assets with market values greater than their book value. The capability of management and the existence of intangible assets—such as goodwill, trademarks, or patents—will make the market value of the firm's assets exceed their book values. In general, as a result of inflation and historical cost accounting, we might expect the market value of assets to exceed their book values. Overpriced assets on the books occur when a firm has outdated, technologically inferior assets; obsolete inventory; and nonperforming assets such as a bank that has not written off nonperforming loans.

The presence of off-balance-sheet liabilities also harms the quality of a balance sheet. Such liabilities may include joint ventures and loan commitments or guarantees to subsidiaries, which are discussed in Stickney, Brown, and Wahlen (2004, Chapter 6).

Income Statement

High-quality earnings are *repeatable* earnings. For example, they arise from sales to customers who are expected to do repeat business with the firm and from costs that are not artificially low as a result of unusual and short-lived input price reductions. One-time and nonrecurring items—such as accounting changes, mergers, and asset sales—should be ignored when examining earnings. Unexpected exchange rate fluctuations that work in the firm's favor to raise revenues or reduce costs should also be viewed as nonrecurring.

High-quality earnings result from the use of conservative accounting principles that do not result in overstated revenues and understated costs. The closer the earnings are to cash, the higher the quality of the income statement. Suppose a firm sells furniture on credit by allowing customers to make monthly payments. A higher-quality income statement will recognize revenue using the "installment" principle; that is, as the cash is collected each month, in turn, annual sales will reflect only the cash collected from sales during the year. A lower-quality income statement will recognize 100 percent of the revenue at the time of sale, even though payments may stretch well into next year. A detailed discussion of income items is in Stickney, Brown, and Wahlen (2004, Chapter 5).

Footnotes

A word to the wise: **read the footnotes!** The purpose of the footnotes (that have come to include three or more pages in most annual reports) is to provide information on how the firm handles balance sheet and income items. While the footnotes may not reveal everything you should know (e.g., Enron), if you do not read them you cannot hope to be informed. The fact is, many analysts recommend that you should read an annual report *backward,* so that you read the footnotes first!

THE VALUE OF FINANCIAL STATEMENT ANALYSIS

Financial statements, by their nature, are backward-looking. They report the firm's assets, liabilities, and equity as of a certain (past) date; they report a firm's revenues, expenses, or cash flows over some (past) time period. An efficient capital market will have already incorporated this past information into security prices; so it may seem, at first glance, that analysis of a firm's financial statements and ratios is a waste of the analyst's time.

The fact is, the opposite is true. Analysis of financial statements allows the analyst to gain knowledge of a firm's operating and financial strategy and structure. This, in turn, assists the analyst in determining the effects of *future* events on the firm's cash flows. Combining knowledge of the firm's strategy, operating and financial leverage, and possible macro- and microeconomic scenarios is necessary to determine an appropriate market value for the firm's stock. Combining the analysis of historical data with potential future scenarios allows analysts to evaluate the risks facing the firm and then to develop an expected return forecast based on these risks. The final outcome of the process, as future chapters will detail, is the determination of the firm's current intrinsic value based on expected cash flows, which is compared to its security price. The point is, the detailed analysis of the historical results ensures a better estimation of the expected cash flows and an appropriate discount rate that leads to a superior valuation of the firm.

SPECIFIC USES OF FINANCIAL RATIOS

In addition to measuring firm performance and risk, financial ratios have been used in four major areas in investments: (1) stock valuation, (2) the identification of internal corporate variables that affect a stock's systematic risk (beta), (3) assigning credit quality ratings on bonds, and (4) predicting insolvency (bankruptcy) of firms.

Stock Valuation Models

As we will discuss in the following chapter, most valuation models attempt to derive a value based on one of several present value of cash flow models or appropriate relative valuation ratios for a stock. As will be noted, all the valuation models require an estimate of the expected growth rate of earnings, cash flows, or dividends and the required rate of return on the stock. Clearly, financial ratios can help in estimating these critical inputs. The growth rate estimate for earnings, cash flow, or dividends employs the ratios discussed in the potential growth rate section.

When estimating the required rate of return on an investment (i.e., either the cost of equity, *k*, or the weighted average cost of capital, WACC), recall that these estimates depend on the risk premium for the security, which is a function of business risk, financial risk, and liquidity risk. Business risk typically is measured in terms of earnings variability; financial risk is identified by either the debt proportion ratios or the earnings or cash flow ratios. Insights regarding a stock's liquidity risk can be obtained from the external liquidity measures we discussed.

The typical empirical valuation model has examined a cross section of companies and used a multiple regression model that relates one of the relative valuations ratios for the sample firms to some of the following corporate variables (the averages generally consider the past 5 or 10 years).[18]

Financial Ratios
1. Average debt–equity
2. Average interest coverage
3. Average dividend payout
4. Average return on equity
5. Average retention rate
6. Average market price to book value
7. Average market price to cash flow
8. Average market price to sales

Variability Measures
1. Coefficient of variation of operating earnings
2. Coefficient of variation of sales
3. Coefficient of variation of net income
4. Systematic risk (beta)

Nonratio Variables
1. Average growth rate of earnings

Estimating Systematic Risk

As discussed in Chapter 8, the capital asset pricing model (CAPM) asserts that the relevant risk variable for an asset should be its systematic risk, which is its beta coefficient related to the market portfolio of all risky assets. In efficient markets, a relationship should exist between internal corporate risk variables and market-determined risk variables such as beta. Numerous studies have tested the relationship between a stock's systematic risk (beta) and the firm's internal corporate variables intended to reflect business risk and financial risk.[19] The significant variables (usually five-year averages) included were as follows.

Financial Ratios
1. Dividend payout
2. Total debt–total assets
3. Cash flow–total debt
4. Interest coverage
5. Working capital–total assets
6. Current ratio

---

[18]A list of studies in this area appears in the "Suggested Readings" section at the end of the chapter.
[19]A list of studies in this area appears in the "Suggested Readings" section at the end of the chapter.

Variability Measures
1. Coefficient of variation of net earnings
2. Coefficient of variation of operating earnings
3. Coefficient of variation of operating profit margins
4. Operating earnings beta (company earnings related to aggregate earnings)

Nonratio Variables
1. Asset size
2. Market value of stock outstanding

Estimating the Ratings on Bonds

As discussed in Chapter 3, three financial services assign credit ratings to bonds on the basis of the issuing company's ability to meet all its obligations related to the bond. An AAA or Aaa rating indicates high quality and almost no chance of default, whereas a C rating indicates the bond is already in default. Numerous studies have used financial ratios to predict the rating to be assigned to a bond.[20] The major financial variables considered in these studies were as follows:

Financial Ratios
1. Long-term debt–total assets
2. Total debt–total capital
3. Net income plus depreciation (cash flow)–long-term senior debt
4. Cash flow–total debt
5. Earnings before interest and taxes (EBIT)–interest expense (fixed charge coverage)
6. Cash flow from operations plus interest–interest expense
7. Market value of stock–par value of bonds
8. Net operating profit–sales
9. Net income–owners' equity (ROE)
10. Net income–total assets (ROA)
11. Working capital–sales
12. Sales–net worth (equity turnover)

Variability Measures
1. Coefficient of variation of sales
2. Coefficient of variation of net earnings
3. Coefficient of variation of return on assets

Nonratio Variables
1. Subordination of the issue
2. Size of the firm (total assets)
3. Issue size
4. Par value of all publicly traded bonds of the firm

Predicting Insolvency (Bankruptcy)

Analysts have always been interested in using financial ratios to identify firms that might default on a loan or declare bankruptcy.[21] The typical study examines a sample of firms that

---

[20]A list of studies in this area appears in the "Suggested Readings" section at the end of the chapter.
[21]A list of studies on this topic appears in the "Suggested Readings" section at the end of the chapter.

have declared bankruptcy against a matched sample of firms in the same industry and of comparable size that have not failed. The analysis involves examining a number of financial ratios expected to reflect declining liquidity for several years prior to the declaration of bankruptcy. The goal is to determine which set of ratios correctly predict that a firm will be in the bankrupt or nonbankrupt group. The better models have typically correctly classified more than 80 percent of the firms one year prior to failure. Some of the financial ratios included in successful models were as follows:

Financial Ratios
1. Cash flow–total debt
2. Cash flow–long-term debt
3. Sales–total assets*
4. Net income–total assets
5. EBIT/total assets*
6. Total debt/total assets
7. Market value of stock–book value of debt*
8. Working capital–total assets*
9. Retained earnings–total assets*
10. Current ratio
11. Working capital–sales

In addition to the several studies that have used financial ratios to predict bond ratings and failures, other studies have also used cash flow variables or a combination of financial ratios and cash flow variables for these predictions, and the results have been quite successful. These studies are listed in the "Suggested Readings" section at the end of the chapter. The five ratios designated by an asterisk (*) are the ratios used in the well-known Altman Z-score model (Altman, 1968).

Limitations of Financial Ratios

We must reinforce an earlier point: you should always consider *relative* financial ratios. In addition, you should be aware of other questions and limitations of financial ratios:

1. Are alternative firms' accounting treatments comparable? As you know from prior accounting courses, there are several generally accepted methods for treating various accounting items, and the alternatives can cause a difference in results for the same event. Therefore, you should check on the accounting treatment of significant items and adjust the values for major differences. Comparability becomes a critical consideration when dealing with non-U.S. firms.
2. How homogeneous is the firm? Many companies have divisions that operate in different industries, which can make it difficult to derive comparable industry ratios.
3. Are the implied results consistent? It is important to develop a total profile of the firm and not depend on only one set of ratios (for example, internal liquidity ratios). As an example, a firm may be having short-term liquidity problems but be very profitable—the profitability will eventually alleviate the short-run liquidity problems.
4. Is the ratio within a reasonable range for the industry? As noted on several occasions, you typically want to consider a *range* of appropriate values for the ratio because a value that is either too high or too low for the industry can be a problem.

Many publicly traded companies have Web sites, which, among other pieces of information, contain financial information. Sometimes complete copies of the firm's annual report and SEC filings are on their home page. Since the focus of this chapter has been Walgreen Co.'s financial statements, here are some relevant sites:

http://www.walgreens.com Walgreen Co.'s home page, with financial information available through links from this page. At least four of Walgreen Co.'s competitors have Web sites featuring financial information. These include:

http://www.cvs.com The home page for CVS Pharmacy.

http://www.riteaid.com Rite Aid Corporation's home page.

http://www.longs.com The Web site for Longs Drug Stores.

http://www.duanereade.com Duane Reade's home page.

Commercially oriented and government-sponsored databases are also available through the Web.

http://www.sec.gov The Web home page for the Securities and Exchange Commission allows entrance into the SEC's EDGAR (electronic data gathering, analysis, and retrieval) database. Most firm's SEC filings are accessible through EDGAR, including filings for executive compensation, 10-K, and 10-Q forms.

http://www.hoovers.com Hoovers Online is a commercial source of company-specific information, including financial statements and stock performance. Some data are free, including a company profile, news, stock prices and a chart of recent stock price performance. It contains links to a number of sources, including the firm's annual report, SEC filings, and earnings per share estimates by First Call.

http://www.dnb.com Dun & Bradstreet is a well-known gatherer of financial information. Corporations make use of its business credit reporting services. D&B publishes industry average financial ratios which are useful in equity and fixed income analysis.

SUMMARY

- The overall purpose of financial statement analysis is to help investors make decisions on investing in a firm's bonds or stock. Financial ratios should be examined relative to the economy, the firm's industry, the firm's main competitors, and the firm's past relative ratios.
- The specific ratios can be divided into four categories, depending on the purpose of the analysis: internal liquidity, operating performance, risk analysis, and growth analysis.
- When analyzing the financial statements for non-U.S. firms, analysts must consider differences in format and in accounting principles that cause different values for specific ratios.

- Four major uses of financial ratios are (1) stock valuation, (2) analysis of variables affecting a stock's systematic risk (beta), (3) assigning credit ratings on bonds, and (4) predicting insolvency (bankruptcy).

A final caveat: you can envision numerous financial ratios to examine almost every possible relationship. The goal is not more ratios, but to limit and group the ratios so you can examine them in a meaningful way. This entails analyzing the ratios over time relative to the economy, the industry, or the past. You should concentrate on deriving better comparisons for a limited number of ratios that provide insights into the questions of interest to you.

SUGGESTED READINGS

General

Beaver, William H. *Financial Reporting: An Accounting Revolution*. Englewood Cliffs, NJ: Prentice Hall, 1989.

Bernstein, Leopold A., and John J. Wild. *Financial Statement Analysis: Theory, Application, and Interpretation*, 6th ed. Homewood, IL: Irwin/McGraw-Hill, 1998.

Fridson, Martin, and Fernando Alvarez. *Financial Statement Analysis, 3rd ed*. New York: Wiley, 2002.

Heckel, Kenneth S., and Joshua Livnat. *Cash Flow and Security Analysis*, 2nd ed. Burr Ridge, IL: Business One Irwin, 1996.

Helfert, Erich A. *Techniques of Financial Analysis,* 10th ed. New York: McGraw-Hill, 2000.

Higgins, Robert C. *Analysis of Financial Management*, 5th ed. Chicago: Irwin, 1998.

Peterson, Pamela P., and Frank J. Fabozzi. *Analysis of Financial Statements*. New Hope, PA: Frank J. Fabozzi Associates, 1999.

Analysis of International Financial Statements

Choi, Frederick D. S., Carol Ann Frost, and Gary Meek. *International Accounting.* Englewood Cliffs, NJ: Prentice Hall, 2000.

Iqbal, M. Zafar, *International Accounting: A Global Approach.* Cincinnati: South-Western, 2002.

Rueschhoff, Norlin, and David Strupeck, "Equity Returns: Local GAAP versus US GAAP for Foreign Issuers from Developing Countries," *Journal of International Accounting* 33, no. 3 (Spring 2000).

Saudagaran, Shakrokh, *International Accounting: A User Perspective*. Cincinnati: South-Western, 2001.

Financial Ratios and Stock Valuation Models

Copeland, Tom, Tim Koller, and Jack Murrin. *Valuation: Measuring and Managing the Value of Companies,* 3rd ed. New York: Wiley, 2000.

Damodaran, Aswath. *Damodaran on Valuation.* New York: Wiley, 1994.

Danielson, M. G. "A Simple Valuation Model and Growth Expectations," *Financial Analysts Journal* 54, no. 3 (May–June 1998).

Farrell, James L. "The Dividend Discount Model: A Primer." *Financial Analysts Journal* 41, no. 6 (November–December 1985).

Hickman, Kent, and Glenn Petry. "A Comparison of Stock Price Predictions Using Court Accepted Formulas, Dividend Discount, and P/E Models." *Financial Management* (Summer 1990).

Kaplan, S. N., and R. S. Ruback. "The Valuation of Cash Flow Forecasts: An Empirical Analysis." *Journal of Finance* 50, no. 4 (September 1995).

Penman, S. H. "The Articulation of Price–Earnings Ratios and Market-to-Book Ratios and the Evaluation of Growth." *Journal of Accounting Research* 34, no. 2 (Spring 1996).

Financial Ratios and Systematic Risk (Beta)

Gahlon, James M., and James A. Gentry. "On the Relationship between Systematic Risk and the Degrees of Operating

and Financial Leverage." *Financial Management* 11, no. 2 (Summer 1982).

Mandelker, Gershon M., and S. Ghon Rhee. "The Impact of Degrees of Operating and Financial Leverage on the Systematic Risk of Common Stock." *Journal of Financial and Quantitative Analysis* 19, no. 1 (March 1984).

Financial Ratios and Bond Ratings

Cantor, R., and F. Packer. "The Credit Rating Industry." *Journal of Fixed Income* 5, no. 3 (December 1995).

Fisher, Lawrence. "Determinants of Risk Premiums on Corporate Bonds." *Journal of Political Economy* 67, no. 3 (June 1959).

Gentry, James A., David T. Whitford, and Paul Newbold. "Predicting Industrial Bond Ratings with a Probit Model and Funds Flow Components." *Financial Review* 23, no. 3 (August 1988).

Standard and Poor's Corporation. "Corporate Ratings Criteria," 2005.

Zhou, Chunsheng. "Credit Rating and Corporate Defaults." *Journal of Fixed Income* 11, no. 3 (December 2001).

Financial Ratios and Corporate Bankruptcy

Altman, Edward I. "Financial Ratios, Discriminant Analysis, and the Prediction of Corporate Bankruptcy." *Journal of Finance* 23, no. 4 (September 1968).

Altman, Edward I. *Corporate Financial Distress and Bankruptcy,* 2nd ed. New York: Wiley, 1993.

Aziz, A., and G. H. Lawson. "Cash Flow Reporting and Financial Distress Models: Testing of Hypothesis." *Financial Management* 18, no. 1 (Spring 1989).

Beaver, William H. "Financial Ratios as Predictors of Failure." *Empirical Research in Accounting: Selected Studies,* 1966, supplement to vol. 4, *Journal of Accounting Research.*

Beaver, William H. "Market Prices, Financial Ratios, and the Prediction of Failure." *Journal of Accounting Research* 6, no. 2 (Autumn 1968).

Casey, Cornelius, and Norman Bartczak. "Using Operating Cash Flow Data to Predict Financial Distress: Some Extensions." *Journal of Accounting Research* 23, no. 1 (Spring 1985).

Dumbolena, I. G., and J. M. Shulman. "A Primary Rule of Detecting Bankruptcy: Watch the Cash." *Financial Analysts Journal* 44, no. 5 (September–October 1988).

Gentry, James A., Paul Newbold, and David T. Whitford. "Classifying Bankrupt Firms with Funds Flow Components." *Journal of Accounting Research* 23, no. 1 (Spring 1985).

Gentry, James A., Paul Newbold, and David T. Whitford. "Predicting Bankruptcy: If Cash Flow's Not the Bottom Line, What Is?" *Financial Analysts Journal* 41, no. 5 (September–October 1985).

Gombola, M. F., M. E. Haskins, J. E. Katz, and D. D. Williams. "Cash Flow in Bankruptcy Prediction." *Financial Management* 16, no. 4 (Winter 1987).

Helwege, J., and P. Kleiman. "Understanding High Yield
    Bond Default Rates." *Journal of Fixed Income* 7, no. 1
    (June 1997).
Jonsson, J. G., and M. S. Fridson. "Forecasting Default Rates
    on High Yield Bonds." *Journal of Fixed Income* 6, no. 1
    (June 1996).
Largay, J. A., and C. P. Stickney. "Cash Flows Ratio Analysis
    and the W. T. Grant Company Bankruptcy." *Financial
    Analysts Journal* 36, no. 4 (July–August 1980).

Reilly, Frank K. "Using Cash Flows and Financial Ratios to
    Predict Bankruptcies." In *Analyzing Investment
    Opportunities in Distressed and Bankrupt Companies.* ed.
    Thomas A. Bowman. Charlottesville, VA: Institute of
    Chartered Financial Analysts, 1991.

QUESTIONS

1. Discuss briefly two decisions that require the analysis of financial statements.
2. Why do analysts use financial ratios rather than the absolute numbers? Give an example.
3. Besides comparing a company's performance to its total industry, discuss what other comparisons should be considered *within* the industry.
4. How might a jewelry store and a grocery store differ in terms of asset turnover and profit margin? Would you expect their return on total assets to differ assuming equal business risk? Discuss.
5. Describe the components of business risk, and discuss how the components affect the variability of operating earnings (EBIT).
6. Would you expect a steel company or a retail food chain to have greater business risk? Discuss this expectation in terms of the components of business risk.
7. When examining a firm's financial structure, would you be concerned with the firm's business risk? Why or why not?
8. Give an example of how a cash flow ratio might differ from a proportion of debt ratio. Assuming these ratios differ for a firm (for example, the cash flow ratios indicate high financial risk, while the proportion of debt ratio indicates low risk), which ratios would you follow? Justify your choice.
9. Why is the analysis of growth potential important to the common stockholder? Why is it important to the debt investor?
10. Discuss the general factors that determine the rate of growth of *any* economic unit.
11. A firm is earning 24 percent on equity and has low business and financial risk. Discuss why you would expect it to have a high or low retention rate.
12. The Orange Company earned 18 percent on equity, whereas the Blue Company earned only 14 percent on equity. Does this mean that Orange will grow faster than Blue? Explain.
13. In terms of the factors that determine market liquidity, why do investors consider real estate to be a relatively illiquid asset?
14. Discuss some internal company factors that would indicate a firm's market liquidity.
15. Select one of the limitations of ratio analysis and indicate why you believe it is a major limitation.

PROBLEMS

1. The Shamrock Vegetable Company has the following results.

Net sales	$6,000,000
Net total assets	4,000,000
Depreciation	160,000
Net income	400,000
Long-term debt	2,000,000
Equity	1,160,000
Dividends	160,000

a. Compute Shamrock's ROE directly. Confirm this using the three components.
b. Using the ROE computed in part (a), what is the expected sustainable growth rate for Shamrock?
c. Assuming the firm's net profit margin went to 0.04, what would happen to Shamrock's ROE?
d. Using the ROE in part (c), what is the expected sustainable growth rate? What if dividends were only $40,000?

2. Three companies have the following results during the recent period.

	K	L	M
Net profit margin	0.04	0.06	0.10
Total assets turnover	2.20	2.00	1.40
Total assets/equity	2.40	2.20	1.50

   a. Derive for each its return on equity based on the three DuPont components.
   b. Given the following earnings and dividends, compute the estimated sustainable growth rate for each firm.

	K	L	M
Earnings/share	2.75	3.00	4.50
Dividends/share	1.25	1.00	1.00

3. Given the following balance sheet, fill in the ratio values for 2006 and discuss how these results compare with both the industry average and past performance of Sophie Enterprises.

SOPHIE ENTERPRISES CONSOLIDATED BALANCE SHEET, YEARS ENDED DECEMBER 31, 2006 AND 2007

ASSETS ($ THOUSANDS)	2007	2006
Cash	$ 100	$ 90
Receivables	220	170
Inventories	330	230
Total current assets	650	490
Property, plant, and equipment	1,850	1,650
Depreciation	350	225
Net properties	1,500	1,425
Intangibles	150	150
Total assets	2,300	2,065

LIABILITIES AND SHAREHOLDERS' EQUITY

	2007	2006
Accounts payable	$ 85	$ 105
Short-term bank notes	125	110
Current portion of long-term debt	75	—
Accruals	65	85
Total current liabilities	350	300
Long-term debt	625	540
Deferred taxes	100	80
Preferred stock (10%, $100 par)	150	150
Common stock ($2 par, 100,000 issued)	200	200
Additional paid-in capital	325	325
Retained earnings	550	470
Common shareholders' equity	1,075	995
Total liabilities and shareholders' equity	2,300	2,065

SOPHIE ENTERPRISES CONSOLIDATED STATEMENT OF INCOME, YEARS ENDED DECEMBER 31, 2006 AND 2007 ($ THOUSANDS)

	2007	2006
Net sales	$3,500	$2,990
Cost of goods sold	2,135	1,823
Selling, general, and administrative expenses	1,107	974
Operating profit	258	193
Net interest expense	62	54
Income from operations	195	139
Income taxes	66	47
Net income	129	91
Preferred dividends	15	15
Net income available for common shares	114	76
Dividends declared	40	30

	Sophie (2007)	Sophie's Average	Industry Average
Current ratio	——	2.000	2.200
Quick ratio	——	1.000	1.100
Receivables turnover	——	18.000	18.000
Average collection period	——	20.000	20.000
Total asset turnover	——	1.500	1.400
Inventory turnover	——	11.000	12.500
Fixed-asset turnover	——	2.500	2.400
Equity turnover	——	3.200	3.000
Gross profit margin	——	0.400	0.350
Operating profit margin	——	8.000	7.500
Return on capital	——	0.107	0.120
Return on equity	——	0.118	0.126
Return on common equity	——	0.128	0.135
Debt–equity ratio	——	0.600	0.500
Debt–total capital ratio	——	0.400	0.370
Interest coverage	——	4.000	4.500
Fixed charge coverage	——	3.000	4.000
Cash flow–long-term debt	——	0.400	0.450
Cash flow–total debt	——	0.250	0.300
Retention rate	——	0.350	0.400

4. *CFA Examination Level I (Adapted)*
   (Question 4 is composed of two parts, for a total of 20 minutes.)
   The DuPont formula defines the net return on shareholders' equity as a function of the following components:
   - Operating margin
   - Asset turnover

- Interest burden
- Financial leverage
- Income tax rate

Using *only* the data in the table shown below:

a. Calculate *each* of the *five* components listed above for 2002 *and* 2006, and calculate the return on equity (ROE) for 2002 *and* 2006, using all of the *five* components. Show calculations. (15 minutes)

b. Briefly discuss the impact of the changes in asset turnover *and* financial leverage on the change in ROE from 2002 to 2006. (5 minutes)

	2002	2006
Income Statement Data		
Revenues	$542	$979
Operating income	38	76
Depreciation and amortization	3	9
Interest expense	3	0
Pretax income	32	67
Income taxes	13	37
Net income after tax	19	30
Balance Sheet Data		
Fixed assets	$ 41	$ 70
Total assets	245	291
Working capital	123	157
Total debt	16	0
Total shareholders' equity	159	220

5. CFA *Examination Level II*

Mike Smith, CFA, an analyst with Blue River Investments, is considering buying a Montrose Cable Company corporate bond. He has collected the following balance sheet and income statement information for Montrose as shown in Exhibit 5.1. He has also calculated the three ratios shown in Exhibit 5.2, which indicate that the bond is currently rated "A" according to the firm's internal bond-rating criteria shown in Exhibit 5.4.

Smith has decided to consider some off-balance-sheet items in his credit analysis, as shown in Exhibit 5.3. Specifically, Smith wishes to evaluate the impact of each of the off-balance-sheet items on each of the ratios found in Exhibit 5.2.

a. Calculate the combined effect of the *three* off-balance-sheet items in Exhibit 5.3 on *each* of the following *three* financial ratios shown in Exhibit 5.2.

   i.   EBITDA/interest expense
   ii. Long-term debt/equity
   iii. Current assets/current liabilities (9 minutes)

The bond is currently trading at a credit premium of 55 basis points. Using the internal bond-rating criteria in Exhibit 5.4, Smith wants to evaluate whether or not the credit yield premium incorporates the effect of the off-balance-sheet items.

b. State and justify whether or not the current credit yield premium compensates Smith for the credit risk of the bond based on the internal bond-rating criteria found in Exhibit 5.4. (6 minutes)

Exhibit 5.1	Montrose Cable Company Year Ended March 31, 1999 (US$ Thousands)

Balance Sheet	
Current assets	$ 4,735
Fixed assets	43,225
Total assets	$47,960
Current liabilities	$ 4,500
Long-term debt	10,000
Total liabilities	$14,500
Shareholders' equity	33,460
Total liabilities and shareholder's equity	$47,960
Income Statement	
Revenue	$18,500
Operating and administrative expenses	14,050
Operating income	$ 4,450
Depreciation and amortization	1,675
Interest expense	942
Income before income taxes	$ 1,833
Taxes	641
Net income	$ 1,192

Exhibit 5.2	Selected Ratios and Credit Yield Premium Data for Montrose

EBITDA/interest expense	4.72
Long-term debt/equity	0.30
Current assets/current liabilities	1.05
Credit yield premium over U.S. Treasuries	55 basis points

Exhibit 5.3	Montrose Off-Balance-Sheet Items

- Montrose has guaranteed the long-term debt (principal only) of an unconsolidated affiliate. This obligation has a present value of $995,000.
- Montrose has sold $500,000 of accounts receivable with recourse at a yield of 8 percent.
- Montrose is a lessee in a new noncancelable operating leasing agreement to finance transmission equipment. The discounted present value of the lease payments is $6,144,000 using an interest rate of 10 percent. The annual payment will be $1,000,000.

Exhibit 5.4	Blue River Investments: Internal Bond-Rating Criteria and Credit Yield Premium Data

Bond Rating	Interest Coverage (EBITDA/ interest expense)	Leverage (Long-term debt/equity)	Current Ratio (Current assets/ current liabilities)	Credit Yield Premium over U.S. Treasuries (in basis points)
AA	5.00 to 6.00	0.25 to 0.30	1.15 to 1.25	30 bps
A	4.00 to 5.00	0.30 to 0.40	1.00 to 1.15	50 bps
BBB	3.00 to 4.00	0.40 to 0.50	0.90 to 1.00	100 bps
BB	2.00 to 3.00	0.50 to 0.60	0.75 to 0.90	125 bps

THOMSON ONE | Business School Edition

1. Update the ratio analysis for Walgreens presented in this chapter.
2. In Chapter 7 you made a retail sales stock index using price and share data from Amazon (AMZN), Family Dollar (FDO), J.C. Penney (JCP), Target (TGT), and Wal-Mart (WMT). Now download balance sheet and income statement data into a spreadsheet and sum similar accounting categories to create an industry balance sheet and an industry income statement. Compute the following ratios and compare the performance of Wal-Mart's ratios against the industry ratios:
   a. Current ratio
   b. Inventory turnover
   c. Total asset turnover
   d. Net profit margin
   e. Debt-equity
3. Using common-size financial statements, compare the operating characteristics of a retail firm (Walgreens), a technology firm (Microsoft), and one involved in oil production and distribution (ExxonMobil).
4. Using the firms in Problem 3, compare their returns on equity using DuPont analysis.
5. Find Walgreen Co.'s peers using Thomson One: Business School Edition. Click on "financials" and review the financial ratios of Walgreens and its peers. Comment on the strengths and weaknesses of Walgreens compared to these firms.

APPENDIX
Chapter 10

A. Computation of Present Value of Lease Payments for Walgreens as of September 1, 2004 (Discount Rate of 7%)

Year	PRESENT VALUE ASSUMING 15-YEAR SPREAD OF LUMP SUM		PRESENT VALUE ASSUMING 12-YEAR SPREAD OF LUMP SUM	
	Payment $ Mil.	Present Value of Payment $ Mil.	Payment $ Mil.	Present Value of Payment $ Mil.
2005	1309	1223.4	1309	1223.4
2006	1346	1175.6	1346	1175.6
2007	1309	1068.5	1309	1068.5
2008	1242	947.5	1242	947.5
2009	1215	866.3	1215	866.3
2010	1030.3	686.6	1188.8	792.2
2011	1030.3	641.6	1188.8	740.4
2012	1030.3	599.7	1188.8	691.9
2013	1030.3	560.4	1188.8	646.7
2014	1030.3	523.8	1188.8	604.3
2015	1030.3	489.5	1188.8	564.8
2016	1030.3	457.5	1188.8	527.9
2017	1030.3	427.6	1188.8	493.3
2018	1030.3	399.6	1188.8	461.1
2019	1030.3	373.4	1188.8	430.9
2020	1030.3	349.0	1188.8	402.7
2021	1030.3	326.2	1188.8	376.4
2022	1030.3	304.8		
2023	1030.3	284.9		
2024	1030.3	266.3		
Total		**$11,972.1**		**$12,365.5**

B. Computation of Operating Lease Obligations for Walgreens for 2004, 2003, 2002 (7% Debt Rate, 15-Year Amortization Period)

	2004			2003			2002	
Year	Payment $ Mil.	PV of Pmt. $ Mil.	Year	Payment $ Mil.	PV of Pmt. $ Mil.	Year	Payment $ Mil.	PV of Pmt. $ Mil.
2005	1309.0	1223.4	2004	1188.0	1110.3	2003	898.0	839.3
2006	1346.0	1175.6	2005	1219.0	1064.7	2004	943.0	823.7
2007	1309.0	1068.5	2006	1188.0	969.8	2005	933.0	761.6
2008	1242.0	947.5	2007	1149.0	876.6	2006	914.0	697.3
2009	1215.0	866.3	2008	1082.0	771.5	2007	895.6	638.1
2010	1030.3	686.6	2009	899.4	599.3	2008	710.6	473.5
2011	1030.3	641.6	2010	899.4	560.1	2009	710.6	442.5
2012	1030.3	599.7	2011	899.4	523.5	2010	710.6	413.6
2013	1030.3	560.4	2012	899.4	489.2	2011	710.6	386.5
2014	1030.3	523.8	2013	899.4	457.2	2012	710.6	361.2
2015	1030.3	489.5	2014	899.4	427.3	2013	710.6	337.6
2016	1030.3	457.5	2015	899.4	399.3	2014	710.6	315.5
2017	1030.3	427.6	2016	899.4	373.2	2015	710.6	294.9
2018	1030.3	399.6	2017	899.4	348.8	2016	710.6	275.6
2019	1030.3	373.4	2018	899.4	326.0	2017	710.6	257.6
2020	1030.3	349.0	2019	899.4	304.7	2018	710.6	240.7
2021	1030.3	326.2	2020	899.4	284.7	2019	710.6	225.0
2022	1030.3	304.8	2021	899.4	266.1	2020	710.6	210.2
2023	1030.3	284.9	2022	899.4	248.7	2021	710.6	196.5
2024	1030.3	266.3	2023	899.4	232.4	2022	710.6	183.6
Totals		**$11,972.1**			**$10,633.3**			**$8,374.4**

C. As indicated in footnote 11, when computing the volatility of sales and/or operating earnings it is important to consider the effect of growth on the volatility of a series. For example, if you are analyzing the sales data for a company that is growing at a constant 15 percent a year and you compute the standard deviation of the series, you will derive a large measure of volatility because the deviations are being measured from the overall mean of the series. Therefore, the firm's sales during the initial years will be substantially below the mean and the firm's sales in the latter years will be substantially above the mean. The way to avoid this problem is to examine the deviations from a growth series that takes account of either linear growth or compound growth, as shown in Exhibit 10C.1. Notably, in all three calculations the variability measures are compared to the mean value for the series to derive a relative measure of volatility. As shown with the Walgreen example for sales in Exhibit 10C.1, the coefficient of variation based on the standard deviation from the mean indicates a significant level of sales volatility (42%), in contrast to the volatility assuming linear growth, where the relative measure of volatility declines to 15 percent. Finally, when you compute the firm's sales deviation from a compound growth curve of about 14 percent, the relative volatility is only 5 percent, which indicates fairly low sales volatility when the measurement considers growth.

The results when we measure the volatility of operating earnings (EBIT) are similar. Specifically, the relative volatility is 48 percent when compared to the mean, 17 percent when examined relative to the linear growth curve, and only 5 percent when computed relative to the compound growth curve of almost 20 percent a year. This implies what can be seen in the graphs—the growth rates for sales and operating earnings are fairly high, but they are also quite constant, which means that there is not the uncertainty (risk) implied if the volatility is measured relative to the overall mean.

Exhibit 10C.1	Calculation of Sales and Operating Earnings Volatility for Walgreens from Arithmetic Mean, from a Linear Growth Curve, and from a Compound Growth Curve

Variation Model
Input your sales & EBITDA numbers here by "copy & paste," then change the corresponding year if necessary.

	1993	1994	1995	1996	1997	1998	1999	2000	2001	2002	2003	2004
Sales	8,295.0	9,235.0	10,395.0	11,778.0	13,363.0	15,307.0	17,839.0	21,207.0	24,623.0	28,681.1	32,505.4	37,508.2
EBIT	406.2	455.6	523.7	606.9	712.1	877.1	1,027.3	1,263.3	1,422.7	1,637.3	1,888.7	2.176.3

	1993	1994	1995	1996	1997	1998	1999	2000	2001	2002	2003	2004	
Sales	8,295.0	9,235.0	10,395.0	11,778.0	13,363.0	15,307.0	17,839.0	21,207.0	24,623.0	28,681.1	32,505.4	37,508.2	
Linear	8,295.0	10,950.7	13,606.5	16,262.2	18,918.0	21,573.7	24,229.5	26,885.2	29,541.0	32,196.7	34,852.5	37,508.2	2655.75
Compound Growth	8,295.0	9,514.6	10,913.5	12,518.1	14,358.6	16,469.7	18,891.1	21,668.6	24,854.5	28,508.8	32,700.4	37,508.2	1.15
vs. Mean	51%												
	0	2943782	10313674	20108376	30857823	39271871	40838142	32242162	24186366	12359507	5508665	0	
vs. Linear	19%												
	0	78170	268831	547698	991139	1351766	1106994	213115	53601	29686	38011	0	
vs. C.G.	3%												

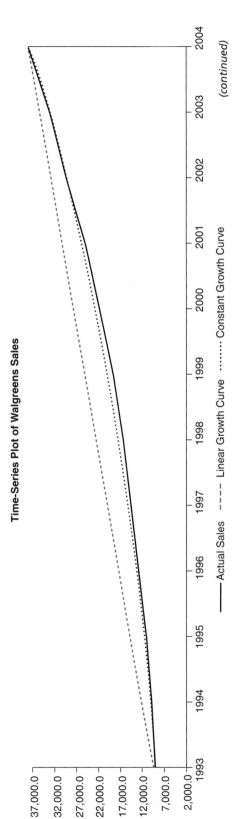

Time-Series Plot of Walgreens Sales

—— Actual Sales   ---- Linear Growth Curve   ······ Constant Growth Curve

(continued)

Exhibit 10C.1 | Calculation of Sales and Operating Earnings Volatility for Walgreens from Arithmetic Mean, from a Linear Growth Curve, and from a Compound Growth Curve (continued)

	1993	1994	1995	1996	1997	1998	1999	2000	2001	2002	2003	2004
EBIT	406.2	455,6	523.7	606.9	712.1	877.1	1,027.3	1,263.3	1,422.7	1,637.3	1,888.7	2,176.3
Linear	406.2	567.1	728.0	889.0	1,049.9	1,210.8	1,371.7	1,532.6	1,693.5	1,854.5	2,015.4	2,176.3
Compound Growth	406.2	473.2	551.2	642.0	747.9	871.2	1,014.8	1,182.0	1,376.9	1,603.9	1,868.3	2,176.3
vs. Mean 55%	0	12436	41753	79555	114090	111350	118618	72537	73357	47160	16048	0
vs. Linear 19%	0	308	754	1234	1279	35	157	6602	2096	1116	416	0
vs. C.G. 3%												

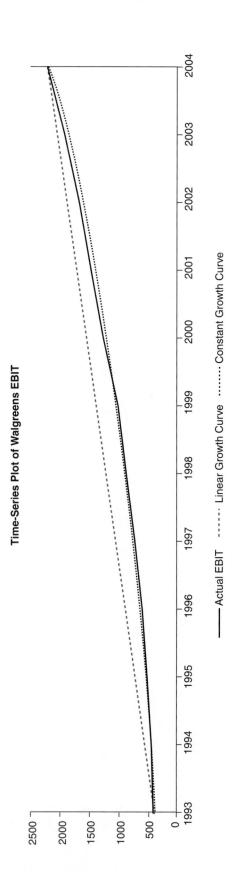

Time-Series Plot of Walgreens EBIT

—— Actual EBIT   - - - - Linear Growth Curve   ······· Constant Growth Curve

Chapter 11

An Introduction to Security Valuation

After you read this chapter, you should be able to answer the following questions:

- What are the two major approaches to the investment process?
- What are the specifics and logic of the top-down (three-step) approach?
- What empirical evidence supports the usefulness of the top-down approach?
- When valuing an asset, what are the required inputs?
- After you have valued an asset, what is the investment decision process?
- How do you determine the value of bonds?
- How do you determine the value of preferred stock?
- What are the two primary approaches to the valuation of common stock?
- Under what conditions is it best to use the present value of cash flow approach for valuing a company's equity?
- Under what conditions is it best to use the relative valuation techniques for valuing a company's equity?
- How do you apply the discounted cash flow valuation approach, and what are the major discounted cash flow valuation techniques?
- What is the dividend discount model (DDM), and what is its logic?
- What is the effect of the assumptions of the DDM when valuing a growth company?
- How do you apply the DDM to the valuation of a firm that is expected to experience temporary supernormal growth?
- How do you apply the present value of operating cash flow technique?
- How do you apply the present value of free cash flow to equity technique?
- How do you apply the relative valuation approach?
- What are the major relative valuation ratios?
- How can you use the DDM to develop an earnings multiplier model?
- What does the DDM model imply are the factors that determine a stock's *P/E* ratio?
- What two general variables need to be estimated in any valuation approach?
- How do you estimate the major inputs to the stock valuation models: (1) the required rate of return and (2) the expected growth rate of earnings and dividends?
- What additional factors must be considered when estimating the required rate of return and growth rate for a foreign security?

At the start of this book, we defined an investment as a commitment of funds for a period of time to derive a rate of return that would compensate the investor for the time during which the funds are invested, for the expected rate of inflation during the investment horizon, and for the uncertainty involved. From this definition, we know that the first step in making an investment is determining your required rate of return.

Once you have determined this rate, some investment alternatives, such as savings accounts and T-bills, are fairly easy to evaluate because they provide stated cash flows. Most investments have expected cash flows and a stated market price (for example, common stock), and you must estimate a value for the investment to determine if its current market price is consistent with your estimated intrinsic value. To do this, you must estimate the value of the security based on its expected cash flows and your required rate of return. This is the process of estimating the intrinsic value of an asset. After you have completed estimating a security's intrinsic value, you compare this estimated intrinsic value to the prevailing market price to decide whether you want to buy the security or not.

This **investment decision process** is similar to the process you follow when deciding on a corporate investment or when shopping for clothes, a stereo, or a car. In each case, you examine the item and decide how much it is worth to you (its value). If the price equals its estimated value or is less, you would buy it. The same technique applies to securities except that the determination of a security's value is more formal.

We start our investigation of security valuation by discussing the **valuation process**. There are two general approaches to the valuation process: (1) the top-down, three-step approach; or (2) the bottom-up, stock valuation, stockpicking approach. Both of these approaches can be implemented by either fundamentalists or technicians. The difference between the two approaches is the perceived importance of the economy and a firm's industry on the valuation of a firm and its stock.

Advocates of the top-down, three-step approach believe that both the economy/market and the industry effect have a significant impact on the total returns for individual stocks. In contrast, those who employ the bottom-up, stockpicking approach contend that it is possible to find stocks that are undervalued relative to their market price, and these stocks will provide superior returns *regardless* of the market and industry outlook.

Both of these approaches have numerous supporters, and advocates of both approaches have been quite successful.[1] In this book, we advocate and present the top-down, three-step approach because of its logic and empirical support. Although we believe that a portfolio manager or an investor can be successful using the bottom-up approach, we believe that it is more difficult to be successful because these stockpickers are ignoring substantial information from the market and the firm's industry.

Although we know that the value of a security is determined by its quality and profit potential, we also believe that the economic environment and the performance of a firm's industry influence the value of a security and its rate of return. Because of the importance of these economic and industry factors, we present an overview of the valuation process that describes these influences and explains how they can be incorporated into the analysis of security value. Subsequently, we describe the theory of value and emphasize the factors that affect the value of individual securities.

Next, we apply these valuation concepts to the valuation of different assets—bonds, preferred stock, and common stock. In this section, we show how the valuation models help investors calculate how much they should pay for these assets. In the final section, we emphasize the estimation of the variables that affect value (the required rate of return and the

---

[1]For the history and selection process of a legendary stockpicker, see Hagstrom (2001) or Lowenstein (1995).

expected growth rate of cash flows). We conclude with a discussion of additional factors that must be considered when we consider the valuation of international securities.

AN OVERVIEW OF THE VALUATION PROCESS

Psychologists suggest that the success or failure of an individual can be caused as much by his or her social, economic, and family environment as by genetic gifts. Extending this idea to the valuation of securities means we should consider a firm's economic and industry environment during the valuation process. Regardless of the qualities or capabilities of a firm and its management, the economic and industry environment will have a major influence on the success of a firm and the realized rate of return on its stock.

As an example, assume you own shares of the strongest and most successful firm producing home furnishings. If you own the shares during a strong economic expansion, the sales and earnings of the firm will increase and your rate of return on the stock should be quite high. In contrast, if you own the same stock during a major economic recession, the sales and earnings of this firm (and probably most or all of the firms in the industry) would likely experience a decline and the price of its stock would be stable or decline. Therefore, when assessing the future value of a security, it is necessary to analyze the outlook for the aggregate economy and the firm's specific industry.

The valuation process is like the chicken-and-egg dilemma. Do you start by analyzing the macroeconomy and various industries before individual stocks, or do you begin with individual securities and gradually combine these firms into industries and the industries into the entire economy? For reasons discussed in the next section, we contend that the discussion should begin with an analysis of aggregate economies and overall securities markets and progress to different industries with a global perspective. Only after a thorough analysis of a global industry are you in a position to properly evaluate the securities issued by individual firms within the better industries. Thus, we recommend a three-step, top-down valuation process in which you first examine the influence of the general economy on all firms and the security markets, then analyze the prospects for various global industries with the best outlooks in this economic environment, and finally turn to the analysis of individual firms in the preferred industries and to the common stock of these firms. Exhibit 11.1 indicates the procedure recommended.

WHY A THREE-STEP VALUATION PROCESS?

General Economic Influences

Monetary and fiscal policy measures enacted by various agencies of national governments influence the aggregate economies of those countries. The resulting economic conditions influence all industries and companies within the economies.

Fiscal policy initiatives, such as tax credits or tax cuts, can encourage spending, whereas additional taxes on income, gasoline, cigarettes, and liquor can discourage spending. Increases or decreases in government spending on defense, on unemployment insurance or retraining programs, or on highways also influence the general economy. All such policies influence the business environment for firms that rely directly on such government expenditures. In addition, we know that government spending has a strong *multiplier effect*. For example, increases in road building increase the demand for earthmoving equipment and concrete

Exhibit 11.1	**Overview of the Investment Process**

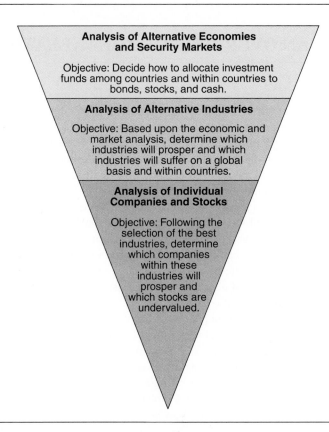

Analysis of Alternative Economies and Security Markets

Objective: Decide how to allocate investment funds among countries and within countries to bonds, stocks, and cash.

Analysis of Alternative Industries

Objective: Based upon the economic and market analysis, determine which industries will prosper and which industries will suffer on a global basis and within countries.

Analysis of Individual Companies and Stocks

Objective: Following the selection of the best industries, determine which companies within these industries will prosper and which stocks are undervalued.

materials. As a result, in addition to construction workers, the employees in those industries that supply the equipment and materials have more to spend on consumer goods, which raises the demand for consumer goods, which affects another set of suppliers.

Monetary policy produces similar economic changes. A restrictive monetary policy that reduces the growth rate of the money supply reduces the supply of funds for working capital and expansion for all businesses. Alternatively, a restrictive monetary policy that targets interest rates would raise market interest rates and therefore firms' costs and make it more expensive for individuals to finance home mortgages and the purchase of other durable goods, such as autos and appliances. Monetary policy therefore affects all segments of an economy and that economy's relationship with other economies.

Any economic analysis requires the consideration of inflation. As we have discussed, inflation causes differences between real and nominal interest rates and changes the spending and savings behavior of consumers and corporations. In addition, unexpected changes in the rate of inflation make it difficult for firms to plan, which inhibits growth and innovation. Beyond the impact on the domestic economy, differential inflation and interest rates influence the trade balance between countries and the exchange rate for currencies.

In addition to monetary and fiscal policy actions, such events as war, political upheavals in foreign countries, or international monetary devaluations produce changes in the business environment that add to the uncertainty of sales and earnings expectations and therefore the risk premium required by investors. For example, the political uncertainty in Russia during 1995–1999 caused a significant increase in the risk premium for investors in Russia and a subsequent reduction in investment and spending in Russia. In contrast, the end of apartheid in South Africa and its open election in 1994 were viewed as positive events and led to a significant increase in economic activity in the country. Similarly, the peace accord in Northern Ireland in the late 1990s caused a major influx of investment and tourist dollars.

In short, it is difficult to conceive of any industry or company that can avoid the impact of macroeconomic developments that affect the total economy. Because aggregate economic events have a profound effect on all industries and companies within these industries, these macroeconomic factors should be considered before industries are analyzed.

Taking a global portfolio perspective, the asset allocation for a country within a global portfolio will be affected by its economic outlook. If a recession is imminent in a country, you would expect a negative impact on its security prices. Because of these economic expectations, investors would be apprehensive about investing in most industries in the country. Given these expectations, the country will be **underweighted** in portfolios relative to its weight based on its market value. Further, given these pessimistic expectations, any funds invested in the country would be directed to low-risk sectors of the economy.

In contrast, optimistic economic and stock market outlooks for a given country should lead an investor to increase the overall allocation to this country (**overweight** the country compared to its weights determined by its relative market value).[2] After allocating funds among countries, the investor looks for outstanding industries in each country. This search for the best industries is enhanced by the economic analysis because the future performance of an industry depends on the country's economic outlook *and* the industry's expected relationship to the economy during the particular phase of the business cycle.

Industry Influences

The second step in the valuation process is to identify global industries that will prosper or suffer in the long run or during the expected near-term economic environment. Examples of conditions that affect specific industries are strikes within a major producing country, import or export quotas or taxes, a worldwide shortage or an excess supply of a resource, or government-imposed regulations on an industry.

You should remember that alternative industries react to economic changes at different points in the business cycle. For example, firms typically increase capital expenditures when they are operating at full capacity at the peak of the economic cycle. Therefore, industries that provide plant and equipment will typically be affected toward the end of a cycle. In addition, alternative industries have different responses to the business cycle. As an example, cyclical industries, such as steel or autos, typically do much better than the aggregate economy during expansions, but they suffer more during contractions. In contrast, noncyclical industries, such as retail food, would not experience a significant decline during a recession but also would not experience a strong increase during an economic expansion.

Another factor that will have a differential effect on industries is demographics. For example, it is widely recognized that the U.S. population is weighted toward "baby boomers" entering their late 50s and that there has been a large surge in the number of citizens over age 65. These two groups have heavy demand for second homes and medical care and the industries related to these segments (e.g., home furnishings and pharmaceuticals).

---

[2]We will show an example of a global asset allocation in Chapter 12.

Firms that sell in international markets can benefit or suffer as foreign economies shift. An industry with a substantial worldwide market might experience low demand in its domestic market but benefit from growing demand in its international market. As an example, much of the growth for Coca-Cola and Pepsi and the fast-food chains, such as McDonald's and Burger King, has come from international expansion in Europe and the Far East.

In general, an industry's prospects within the global business environment will determine how well or poorly an individual firm will fare, so industry analysis should precede company analysis. Few companies perform well in a poor industry, so even the best company in a poor industry is a bad prospect for investment. For example, poor sales and earnings in the farm equipment industry during the late 1980s had a negative impact on Deere and Co., a well-managed firm and probably the best firm in its industry. Though Deere performed better than other firms in the industry (some went bankrupt), its earnings and stock performance still fell far short of its past performance, and the company did poorly compared to firms in most other industries.

Notably, even money managers who are essentially "stockpickers" consider industry analysis important because it determines a firm's business risk due to sales volatility and operating leverage, and its profitability is impacted by the competitive environment in the industry.

Company Analysis

After determining that an industry's outlook is good, an investor can analyze and compare individual firms' performance within the entire industry using financial ratios and cash flow values. As we discussed in Chapter 10, many financial ratios for firms are valid only when they are compared to the performance of their industries.

You undertake company analysis to identify the best company in a promising industry. This involves examining a firm's past performance, but more important, its future prospects. After you understand the firm and its outlook, you can determine its value using one of several valuation models. An important point that will be emphasized is that it is your estimated inputs to the valuation models that are critical, and the quality of these inputs depends on your prior market–industry–company analysis. In the final step, you compare your estimated intrinsic value to the price of the firm's stock and decide whether its stock or bonds are good investments.

Your final goal is to select the best stock or bonds within a desirable industry and include it in your portfolio based on its relationship (correlation) with all other assets in your portfolio. As we discuss in more detail in Chapter 14, the best stock for investment purposes may not necessarily be issued by the best company because the stock of the finest company in an industry may be overpriced, which would cause it to be a poor investment. You cannot know whether a security is undervalued or overvalued until you have analyzed the company, estimated its intrinsic value, and compared your estimated intrinsic value to the market price of the firm's stock.

Does the Three-Step Process Work?

Although you might agree with the logic of the three-step investment process, you might wonder how well this process works in selecting investments. The results of several academic studies have supported this technique. First, studies indicated that most changes in an individual firm's *earnings* could be attributed to changes in aggregate corporate earnings and changes in the firm's industry, with the aggregate earnings changes being more important. Although the relative influence of the general economy and the industry on a firm's earnings varied among individual firms, the results consistently demonstrated that the economic environment had a significant effect on firm earnings.

Second, studies by Moore and Cullity (1988) and Siegel (1991) found a relationship between aggregate stock prices and various economic series, such as employment, income, or production. These results supported the view that a relationship exists between stock prices and economic expansions and contractions.

Third, an analysis of the relationship between *rates of return* for the aggregate stock market, alternative industries, and individual stocks showed that most of the changes in rates of return for individual stocks could be explained by changes in the rates of return for the aggregate stock market and the stock's industry. As shown by Meyers (1973), although the importance of the market effect tended to decline over time and the significance of the industry effect varied among industries, the combined market-industry effect on an individual stock's rate of return was still important.

These results from academic studies support the use of the three-step investment process. This investment decision approach is consistent with the discussion in Chapter 2, which contended that the most important decision is the asset allocation decision.[3] The asset allocation specifies: (1) what proportion of your portfolio will be invested in various nations' economies; (2) within each country, how you will divide your assets among stocks, bonds, or other assets; and (3) your industry selections, based on which industries are expected to prosper in the projected economic environment. We provide an example of global asset allocation in Chapter 12.

Now that we have described and justified the three-step process, we need to consider the theory of valuation. The application of this theory allows us to compute estimated intrinsic values for the market, for alternative industries, and for individual firms and stocks. Finally, we compare these estimated intrinsic values to current market prices and decide whether we want to make particular investments.

THEORY OF VALUATION

You may recall from your studies in accounting, economics, or corporate finance that the value of an asset is the present value of its expected returns. Specifically, you expect an asset to provide a stream of returns during the period of time you own it. To convert this estimated stream of returns to a value for the security, you must discount this stream at your required rate of return. This process of valuation requires estimates of (1) the stream of expected returns and (2) the required rate of return on the investment.

Stream of Expected Returns (Cash Flows)

An estimate of the expected returns from an investment encompasses not only the size but also the form, time pattern, and the uncertainty of returns, which affect the required rate of return.

Form of Returns   The returns from an investment can take many forms, including earnings, cash flows, dividends, interest payments, or capital gains (increases in value) during a period. We will consider several alternative valuation techniques that use different forms of returns. As an example, one common stock valuation model applies a multiplier to a firm's earnings, whereas another valuation model computes the present value of a firm's operating cash flows, and a third model estimates the present value of dividend payments. Returns or cash flows can come in many forms, and you must consider all of them to evaluate an investment accurately.

---

[3]The classic studies that established the importance of asset allocation are Brinson, Hood, and Beebower (1986), followed by Brinson, Singer, and Beebower (1991). A subsequent well-regarded application of these concepts is contained in Cohen (1996).

Time Pattern and Growth Rate of Returns   You cannot calculate an accurate value for a security unless you can estimate when you will receive the returns or cash flows. Because money has a time value, you must know the time pattern and growth rate of returns from an investment. This knowledge will make it possible to properly value the stream of returns relative to alternative investments with a different time pattern and growth rate of returns or cash flows.

Required Rate of Return

$$Ri = Rf + i + RP$$

Uncertainty of Returns (Cash Flows)   You will recall from Chapter 1 that the required rate of return on an investment is determined by (1) the economy's real risk-free rate of return, plus (2) the expected rate of inflation during the holding period, plus (3) a risk premium that is determined by the uncertainty of returns. All investments are affected by the risk-free rate and the expected rate of inflation because these two variables determine the nominal risk-free rate. Therefore, the factor that causes a difference in required rates of return is the risk premium for alternative investments. In turn, this risk premium depends on the uncertainty of returns or cash flows from an investment.

We can identify the sources of the uncertainty of returns by the internal characteristics of assets or by market-determined factors. Earlier, we subdivided the internal characteristics for a firm into business risk (BR), financial risk (FR), liquidity risk (LR), exchange rate risk (ERR), and country risk (CR). The market-determined risk measures are the systematic risk of the asset (its beta), or a set of multiple risk factors that were discussed in Chapter 9.

Investment Decision Process: A Comparison of Estimated Values and Market Prices

To ensure that you receive your required return on an investment, you must estimate the intrinsic value of the investment at your required rate of return and then compare this estimated intrinsic value to the prevailing market price. You should not buy an investment if its market price exceeds your estimated value because the difference will prevent you from receiving your required rate of return on the investment. In contrast, if the estimated intrinsic value of the investment exceeds the market price, you should buy the investment. In summary:

> If Estimated Intrinsic Value > Market Price, Buy
> If Estimated Intrinsic Value < Market Price, Don't Buy or Sell If You Own It.

For example, assume you read about a firm that produces athletic shoes and its stock is listed on the NYSE. Using one of the valuation models we will discuss and making estimates of earnings, or cash flows, and the growth of these variables based on the company's annual report and other information, you estimate the company's intrinsic stock value using your required rate of return as $20 a share. After estimating this value, you look in the paper and see that the stock is currently being traded at $15 a share. You would want to buy this stock because you think it is worth $20 a share and you can buy it for $15 a share. In contrast, if the current market price were $25 a share, you would not want to buy the stock because, based upon your valuation, it is overvalued.

The theory of value provides a common framework for the valuation of all investments. Different applications of this theory generate different estimated values for alternative investments because of the different payment streams and characteristics of the securities. The interest and principal payments on a bond differ substantially from the expected dividends and future selling price for a common stock. The initial discussion that follows applies the discounted cash flow method to bonds, preferred stock, and common stock. This presentation demonstrates that the same basic model is useful across a range of investments. Subsequently, because of the difficulty in estimating the value of common stock, we consider two general approaches and numerous techniques for the valuation of stock.

VALUATION OF ALTERNATIVE INVESTMENTS

Valuation of Bonds

Calculating the value of bonds is relatively easy because the size and time pattern of cash flows from the bond over its life are known. A bond typically promises

1. Interest payments every six months equal to one-half the coupon rate times the face value of the bond
2. The payment of the principal on the bond's maturity date

As an example, in 2006, a $10,000 bond due in 2021 with a 10 percent coupon will pay $500 every six months for its 15-year life. In addition, the bond issuer promises to pay the $10,000 principal at maturity in 2021. Therefore, assuming the bond issuer does not default, the investor knows what payments (cash flows) will be made and when they will be made.

Applying the valuation theory, which states that the value of any asset is the present value of its cash flows, the value of the bond is the present value of the interest payments, which we can think of as an annuity of $500 every six months for 15 years, and the present value of the principal payment, which in this case is the present value of $10,000 to be paid at the end of 15 years. The only unknown for this asset (assuming the borrower does not default) is the required rate of return that should be used to discount the expected stream of returns (cash flows). If the prevailing nominal risk-free rate is 7 percent and the investor requires a 3 percent risk premium on this bond because there is some probability of default, the required rate of return would be 10 percent.

The present value of the interest payments is an annuity for 30 periods (15 years every six months) at one-half the required return (5 percent):[4]

$$\$500 \times 15.3725 = \$7,686$$
(Present Value of Interest Payments at 10 Percent)

The present value of the principal is likewise discounted at 5 percent for 30 periods:[5]

$$\$10,000 \times 0.2314 = \$2,314$$
(Present Value of the Principal Payment at 10 Percent)

This can be summarized as follows:

> Present Value of Interest Payments $500 × 15.3725   = $ 7,686
> Present Value of Principal Payment $10,000 × 0.2314 =   2,314
> Total Value of Bond at 10 Percent   = $10,000

---

[4]The annuity factors and present value factors are contained in Appendix C at the end of the book.
[5]If we used annual compounding, this would be 0.239 rather than 0.2314. We use semiannual compounding because it is consistent with the interest payments and is used in practice.

This is the amount that an investor should be willing to pay for this bond, assuming that the required rate of return on a bond of this risk class is 10 percent. If the market price of the bond is above this value, the investor should not buy it because the promised yield to maturity at this higher price will be less than the investor's required rate of return.

Alternatively, assuming an investor requires a 12 percent return on this bond, its value would be:

$$
\begin{aligned}
\$500 \times 13.7648 &= \$6,882 \\
\$10,000 \times 0.1741 &= \underline{1,741} \\
\text{Total Value of Bond at 12 Percent} &= \$8,623
\end{aligned}
$$

This example shows that if you want a higher rate of return, you will not pay as much for an asset; that is, a given stream of cash flows has a lower value to you. It is this characteristic that leads to the often used phrase that the prices of bonds move in an opposite direction of yields. As before, you would compare this computed value to the market price of the bond to determine whether you should invest in it.[6]

Valuation of Preferred Stock

The owner of a preferred stock receives a promise to pay a stated dividend, usually each quarter, for an infinite period. Preferred stock is a **perpetuity** because it has no maturity. As was true with a bond, stated payments are made on specified dates although the issuer of this stock does not have the same legal obligation to pay investors as do issuers of bonds. Payments are made only after the firm meets its bond interest payments. Because this reduced legal obligation increases the uncertainty of returns, investors should require a higher rate of return on a firm's preferred stock than on its bonds. Although this differential in required return should exist in theory, it generally does not exist in practice because of the tax treatment accorded dividends paid to corporations. As described in Chapter 3, 80 percent of intercompany preferred dividends are tax-exempt, making the effective tax rate on preferred dividends about 6.8 percent, assuming a corporate tax rate of 34 percent. This tax advantage stimulates the demand for preferred stocks by corporations; and, because of this demand, the yield on preferred stocks has generally been below that on the highest-grade corporate bonds.

Because preferred stock is a perpetuity, its value is simply the stated annual dividend divided by the required rate of return on preferred stock (k_p) as follows:

$$
V = \frac{\text{Dividend}}{k_p}
$$

Consider a preferred stock has a $100 par value and a dividend of $8 a year. Because of the expected rate of inflation, the uncertainty of the dividend payment, and the tax advantage to you as a corporate investor, assume that your required rate of return on this stock is 9 percent. Therefore, the value of this preferred stock to you is

$$
V = \frac{\$8}{0.09}
$$

$$
= \$88.89
$$

---

[6]To test your mastery of bond valuation, check that if the required rate of return were 8 percent, the value of this bond would be $11,729.

| Exhibit 11.2 | Common Stock Valuation Approaches and Specific Techniques |

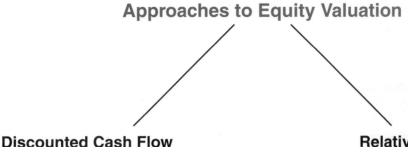

Approaches to Equity Valuation

Discounted Cash Flow Techniques

- **Present Value of Dividends (DDM)**
- **Present Value of Operating Free Cash Flow**
- **Present Value of Free Cash Flow to Equity**

Relative Valuation Techniques

- **Price/Earning Ratio (*P/E*)**
- **Price/Cash Flow Ratio (*P/CF*)**
- **Price/Book Value Ratio (*P/BV*)**
- **Price/Sales Ratio (*P/S*)**

Given this estimated value, you would inquire about the current market price to decide whether you would want to buy this preferred stock. If the current market price is $95, you would decide against a purchase, whereas if it is $80, you would buy the stock. Also, given the market price of preferred stock, you can derive its promised yield. Assuming a current market price of $85, the promised yield would be

$$k_p = \frac{\text{Dividend}}{\text{Price}} = \frac{\$8}{\$85.00} = 0.0941$$

Approaches to the Valuation of Common Stock

Because of the complexity and importance of valuing common stock, various techniques for accomplishing this task have been devised over time. These techniques fall into one of two general approaches: (1) the discounted cash flow valuation techniques, where the value of the stock is estimated based upon the present value of some measure of cash flow, including dividends, operating cash flow, and free cash flow; and (2) the relative valuation techniques, where the value of a stock is estimated based upon its current price relative to variables considered to be significant to valuation, such as earnings, cash flow, book value, or sales. Exhibit 11.2 provides a visual presentation of the alternative approaches and specific techniques.

An important point is that *both of these approaches and all of these valuation techniques have several common factors.* First, all of them are significantly affected by the investor's *required rate of return* on the stock because this rate becomes the discount rate or is a major component of the discount rate. Second, all valuation approaches are affected by *the estimated growth rate of the variable* used in the valuation technique—for example, dividends, earnings, cash flow, or sales. As noted in the efficient market discussion, both of these critical variables must be *estimated.* As a result, different analysts using the same valuation techniques will derive different estimates of value for a stock because they have different estimates for these critical variable inputs. Put another way, you should assume that most investors are aware of the valuation models and it is the *inputs* to the models that make a difference—that is, your estimates of the discount rate and the growth rate of earnings and cash flows. If you are better at estimating these inputs, you will be a superior analyst.

The following discussion of equity valuation techniques considers the specific models and the theoretical and practical strengths and weaknesses of each of them. Notably, the authors' intent is to present these two approaches as complementary, *not* competitive, approaches—that is, you should learn and use both of them.

Why and When to Use the Discounted Cash Flow Valuation Approach

These discounted cash flow valuation techniques are obvious choices for valuation because they are the epitome of how we describe value—that is, the present value of expected cash flows. The major difference between the alternative techniques is how one specifies cash flow—that is, the measure of cash flow used.

The cleanest and most straightforward measure of cash flow is *dividends* because these are clearly cash flows that go directly to the investor, which implies that you should use *the cost of equity* as the discount rate. However, this dividend technique is difficult to apply to firms that do not pay dividends during periods of high growth, or that currently pay very limited dividends because they have high rate of return investment alternatives available. On the other hand, an advantage is that the reduced form of the dividend discount model (DDM) is very useful when discussing valuation for a stable, mature entity where the assumption of relatively constant growth for the long term is appropriate (a good example is the aggregate stock market).

The second specification of cash flow is the *operating free cash flow,* which is generally described as cash flows after direct costs (cost of goods and S, G & A expenses) and after allowing for cash flows to support working capital outlays and capital expenditures required for future growth, but before any payments to capital suppliers. Because we are dealing with the cash flows available for all capital suppliers, the discount rate employed is the firm's *weighted average cost of capital* (WACC). This is a very useful model when comparing firms with diverse capital structures because you determine the value of the total firm and then subtract the value of the firm's debt obligations to arrive at a value for the firm's equity.

The third cash flow measure is *free cash flow to equity,* which is a measure of cash flows similar to the operating free cash flow described above, but after payments to debt holders, which means that these are cash flows available to equity owners. Therefore, the appropriate discount rate is the firm's *cost of equity.*

Beyond being theoretically correct, these models allow a substantial amount of flexibility in terms of changes in sales and expenses that implies changing growth rates over time. Once you understand how to compute each measure of cash flow, you can estimate cash flow for each year by constructing a pro forma statement for each year or you can estimate overall growth rates for the alternative cash flow values as we will demonstrate with the DDM.

A potential difficulty with these cash flow techniques is that they are very dependent on the two significant inputs—(1) the growth rates of cash flows (both the *rate* of growth and the *duration* of growth) and (2) the estimate of the discount rate. As we will show in several instances, a small change in either of these values can have a significant impact on the estimated value. As noted earlier, everyone knows and uses a similar valuation model, but it is the *inputs* that are critical—GIGO: garbage in, garbage out! This is similar to the discussion in Chapter 6 regarding being a superior analyst in a world with an efficient market.

Why and When to Use the Relative Valuation Techniques

As noted, a benefit, but also a potential problem with the discounted cash flow valuation models is that it is possible to derive intrinsic values that are substantially above or below prevailing prices depending on how you adjust your estimated inputs to the prevailing environment. An advantage of the relative valuation techniques is that they provide information about how the market is *currently* valuing stock at several levels—that is, the aggregate market, alternative industries, and individual stocks within industries. Following this chapter, which provides the background for these two approaches, we will demonstrate the alternative relative valuation ratios for the aggregate market, for an industry relative to the market, and for an individual company relative to the aggregate market, to its industry, and to other stocks in its industry.

The good news is that this relative valuation approach provides information on how the market is currently valuing securities. The bad news is that it is providing information on current valuation. The point is, the relative valuation approach provides this information on current valuation, but it does not provide guidance on whether these current valuations are appropriate—that is, *all* valuations at a point in time could be too high or too low. For example, assume that the market becomes significantly overvalued. For example, if you compare the value for an industry to the very overvalued market, you might contend based on such a comparison that an industry is undervalued relative to the market. Unfortunately, your judgment may be wrong because of the benchmark you are using—that is, you might be comparing a fully valued industry to a *very* overvalued market. Alternatively, if you compare an undervalued industry to an aggregate market that is *grossly* undervalued, the industry will appear overvalued by comparison.

Put another way, the relative valuation techniques are appropriate to consider under two conditions:

1. You have a good set of comparable entities—that is, comparable companies that are similar in terms of industry, size, and, it is hoped, risk.
2. The aggregate market and the company's industry are not at a valuation extreme—that is, they are not either seriously undervalued or overvalued.

Discounted Cash Flow Valuation Techniques

All of these valuation techniques are based on the basic valuation model, which asserts that the value of an asset is the present value of its expected future cash flows as follows:

$$V_j = \sum_{t=1}^{n} \frac{CF_t}{(1 + k)^t}$$

where:

V_j = value of Stock j
n = life of the asset
CF_t = cash flow in Period t
k = the discount rate that is equal to the investors' required rate of return for Asset j, which is determined by the uncertainty (risk) of the asset's cash flows

As noted, the specific cash flows used will differ between techniques. They range from dividends (the best-known model) to operating free cash flow and free cash flow to equity. We begin with a fairly detailed presentation of the present-value-of-dividend model, referred to as the dividend discount model (DDM), because it is intuitively appealing and is the best-known model. Also, its general approach is similar to the other discounted cash flow models.

The Dividend Discount Model (DDM)   The **dividend discount model** assumes that the value of a share of common stock is the present value of all future dividends as follows:[7]

$$V_j = \frac{D_1}{(1+k)} + \frac{D_2}{(1+k)^2} + \frac{D_3}{(1+k)^3} + \cdots + \frac{D_\infty}{(1+k)^\infty}$$

$$= \sum_{t=1}^{n} \frac{D_t}{(1+k)^t}$$

where:

V_j = value of common Stock j
D_t = dividend during Period t
k = required rate of return on Stock j

An obvious question is: What happens when the stock is not held for an infinite period? A sale of the stock at the end of Year 2 would imply the following formula:

$$V_j = \frac{D_1}{(1+k)} + \frac{D_2}{(1+k)^2} + \frac{SP_{j2}}{(1+k)^2}$$

The value is equal to the two dividend payments during Years 1 and 2 plus the sale price (*SP*) for stock *j* at the end of Year 2. The expected selling price of stock *j* at the end of Year 2 (SP_{j2}) is simply the value of all remaining dividend payments.

$$SP_{j2} = \frac{D_3}{(1+k)} + \frac{D_2}{(1+k)^2} + \cdots + \frac{D_\infty}{(1+k)^\infty}$$

If SP_{j2} is discounted back to the present by $1/(1+k)^2$, this equation becomes

$$PV(SP_{j2}) = \frac{\dfrac{D_3}{(1+k)} + \dfrac{D_4}{(1+k)^2} + \cdots + \dfrac{D_\infty}{(1+k)^\infty}}{(1+k)^2}$$

$$= \frac{D_3}{(1+k)^3} + \frac{D_4}{(1+k)^2} + \cdots + \frac{D_\infty}{(1+k)^\infty}$$

which is simply an extension of the original equation. Whenever the stock is sold, its value (that is, the sale price at that time) will be the present value of all future dividends. When this ending value is discounted back to the present, you are back to the original dividend discount model.

What about stocks that pay no dividends? Again, the concept is the same, except that some of the early dividend payments are zero. Notably, there are expectations that *at some point* the firm will start paying dividends. If investors lacked such an expectation, nobody would be willing to buy the security. It would have zero value. A firm with a non-dividend-paying stock is reinvesting its capital in very profitable projects rather than paying current dividends so that its earnings and dividend stream will be larger and grow faster in the future. In this case, we would apply the DDM as:

$$V_j = \frac{D_1}{(1+k)} + \frac{D_2}{(1+k)^2} + \frac{D_3}{(1+k)^3} + \cdots + \frac{D_\infty}{(1+k)^\infty}$$

where:

$D_1 = 0; D_2 = 0$

---

[7]This model was initially set forth in Williams (1938) and subsequently reintroduced and expanded by Gordon (1962).

The investor expects that when the firm starts paying dividends in Period 3, it will be a large initial amount and dividends will grow faster than those of a comparable stock that had paid out dividends. The stock has value because of these *future* dividends. We will apply this model to several cases having different holding periods that will show you how it works.

One-Year Holding Period   Assume an investor wants to buy the stock, hold it for one year, and then sell it. To determine the value of the stock—that is, how much the investor should be willing to pay for it—using the DDM, we must estimate the dividend to be received during the period, the expected sale price at the end of the holding period, and the investor's required rate of return.

To estimate the dividend for the coming year, adjust the current dividend for expectations regarding the change in the dividend during the year. Assume the company we are analyzing earned $2.50 a share last year and paid a dividend of $1 a share. Assume further that the firm has been fairly consistent in maintaining this 40 percent payout over time. The consensus of financial analysts is that the firm will earn about $2.75 during the coming year and will raise its dividend to $1.10 per share.

A crucial estimate is the expected selling price for the stock a year from now. You can estimate this expected selling price by one or more of three alternative procedures. In the first, you can apply the dividend discount model where you estimate the specific dividend payments for a number of years into the future and calculate the value of the stock from these estimates. In the second procedure, the earnings multiplier model, you multiply the future expected earnings for the stock by an earnings multiple, which you likewise estimate, to find an expected sale price. We will discuss the earnings multiple model in a later section of the chapter.

In the third method you estimate the firm's future earnings and its dividend payout ratio to arrive at an estimate of its expected dividend at your sale date. Given this dividend and an estimate of the dividend yield on stocks, you can derive a price estimate.

Given the estimated earnings and dividend above (earnings of $2.75, and dividend of $1.10), we can use the earnings multiplier and the dividend yield procedures as follows:

The long-run forward P/E of stocks is between 12 and 16. Using the midpoint of 14, we get an estimated price of:

$$14 \times \$2.75 = \$35.50$$

The long-run dividend yield on stocks has been between 1.50 percent and 5.00 percent, but in recent years (since 1980) it has been 1.50 to 4.00 percent, which implies a midpoint of 2.75 percent. Using this estimate with the $1.10 dividend gives an estimated price of:

$$\frac{\$1.10}{.0275} = \$40.00$$

The average of these two estimates is $37.75, which is rounded to $38.

Finally, you must determine the required rate of return. As discussed before, the nominal risk-free rate is determined by the real risk-free rate and the expected rate of inflation. A widely used proxy for this rate is the promised yield on ten-year government bonds because the typical investment horizon (expected holding period) is 5 to 10 years. You estimate the stock's risk premium by comparing its risk level to the risk of other potential investments. In later chapters, we discuss how you can estimate this risk. For the moment, assume that ten-year government bonds are yielding 7 percent, and you believe that a 3 percent risk premium over the yield of these bonds is appropriate for this stock. Thus, you specify a required rate of return of 10 percent.

In summary, you have estimated the dividend at $1.10 (payable at year end), an ending sale price of $38, and a required rate of return of 10 percent. Given these inputs, you would estimate the value of this stock as follows:

$$V_1 = \frac{\$1.10}{(1 + 0.10)} + \frac{\$38.00}{(1 + 0.10)}$$

$$= \frac{\$1.10}{1.10} + \frac{\$38.00}{1.10}$$

$$= \$1.00 + 34.55$$

$$= \$35.55$$

Note that we have not mentioned the current market price of the stock. This is because the market price is not relevant to you as an investor except as a comparison to the independently derived value based on your estimates of the relevant variables. Once we have calculated the stock's value as $35.55 we can compare it to the market price and apply the investment decision rule: If the stock's market price is more than $35.55, do not buy; if it is equal to or less than $35.55, buy.

Multiple-Year Holding Period   If you anticipate holding the stock for several years and then selling it, the valuation estimate is harder. You must forecast several future dividend payments and estimate the sale price of the stock several years in the future.

The difficulty with estimating future dividend payments is that the future stream can have numerous forms. The exact estimate of the future dividends depends on two projections. The first is your outlook for earnings growth because earnings are the source of dividends. The second projection is the firm's dividend policy, which can take several forms. A firm can have a constant percent payout of earnings each year, which implies a change in dividend each year, or the firm could follow a step pattern in which it increases the dividend rate by a constant dollar amount each year or every two or three years. The easiest dividend policy is to assume that the firm enjoys a constant growth rate in earnings and maintains a constant dividend payout. This set of assumptions implies that the dividend stream will experience a constant growth rate that is equal to the earnings growth rate. Clearly, the important estimate by the analyst is the growth rate of earnings, which will provide the dividend estimates and ending estimates for earnings and the dividends that are used to derive the ending price estimate as above. As before, the estimated intrinsic value is simply the discounted value of these cash flows at your required cost of equity. Finally, compare this estimated intrinsic value for the stock to its current market price to determine whether you should buy it.

At this point, you should recognize that the valuation procedure discussed here is similar to that used in corporate finance when making investment decisions, except that the cash flows are from dividends instead of returns to an investment project. Also, rather than estimating the scrap value or salvage value of a corporate asset, we are estimating the ending sale price for the stock. Finally, rather than discounting cash flows using the firm's cost of capital, we use the individual's required rate of return on the company's equity. In both cases, we are looking for excess present value, which means that the present value of expected cash inflows—that is, the estimated intrinsic value of the asset—exceeds the present value of cash outflows, which is the market price of the asset.

Infinite Period Model   We can extend the multiperiod model by extending our estimates of dividends but the benefits derived from these extensions would be minimal. Instead, we will move to the infinite period dividend discount model, which assumes that investors estimate future dividend payments for an infinite number of periods.

Needless to say, this is a formidable task. We must make some simplifying assumptions about this future stream of dividends to make the task viable. The easiest assumption is that *the future dividend stream will grow at a constant rate for an infinite period*. This is a rather heroic assumption in many instances, but where it does hold, we can use the model to value individual stocks as well as the aggregate market and alternative industries. This model is generalized as follows:

$$V_j = \frac{D_0(1 + g)}{(1 + k)} + \frac{D_0(1 + g)^2}{(1 + k)^2} + \cdots + \frac{D_0(1 + g)^n}{(1 + k)^n}$$

where:

V_j = the value of Stock j
D_0 = the dividend payment in the current period
g = the constant growth rate of dividends
k = the required rate of return on Stock j
n = the number of periods, which we assume to be infinite

In the appendix to this chapter, we show that with certain assumptions, this infinite period constant growth rate model can be simplified to the following expression (referred to as the reduced form DDM):

$$V_j = \frac{D_1}{k - g}$$

You will probably recognize this formula as one that is widely used in corporate finance to estimate the cost of equity capital for the firm—that is, $k = D/V + g$.

To use this model for valuation, you must estimate (1) the required rate of return (k) and (2) the expected constant growth rate of dividends (g). After estimating g, it is a simple matter to estimate D_1, because it is the current dividend (D_0) times $(1 + g)$.

Consider the example of a stock with a current dividend of $1 a share. You believe that, over the long run, this company's earnings and dividends will grow at 7 percent; your estimate of g is 0.07, which implies that you expect the dividend next year (D_1) to be $1.07. For the long run, you expect a nominal risk-free rate of about 8 percent and a risk premium for this stock of 3 percent. Therefore, you set your long-run required rate of return on this stock at 11 percent; your estimate of k is 0.11. To summarize the relevant estimates:

$$g = 0.07$$
$$k = 0.11$$
$$D_1 = \$1.07\,(\$1.00 \times 1.07)$$
$$V = \frac{\$1.07}{0.11 - 0.07}$$
$$= \frac{\$1.07}{0.04}$$
$$= \$26.75$$

A small change in any of the original estimates will have a large impact on V, as shown by the following examples:

1. $g = 0.07$; $k = 0.12$; $D_1 = \$1.07$. (We assume an increase in k.)

$$V = \frac{\$1.07}{0.12 - 0.07}$$
$$= \frac{\$1.07}{0.05}$$
$$= \$21.40$$

2. $g = 0.08$; $k = 0.11$; $D_1 = \$1.08$ (We assume an increase in g.)

$$V = \frac{\$1.08}{0.11 - 0.08}$$

$$= \frac{\$1.08}{0.03}$$

$$= \$36.00$$

These examples show that as small a change as 1 percent in either g or k produces a large difference in the estimated value of the stock. The crucial relationship that determines the value of the stock is the *spread between the required rate of return* (k) *and the expected growth rate of dividends* (g). Anything that causes a decline in the spread will cause an increase in the computed value, whereas any increase in the spread will decrease the computed value of the stock.

Infinite Period DDM and Growth Companies

As noted in the Appendix, the infinite period DDM has the following assumptions:

1. Dividends grow at a constant rate.
2. The constant growth rate will continue for an infinite period.
3. The required rate of return (k) *is greater than the infinite growth rate* (g). If it is not, the model gives meaningless results because the denominator becomes negative.

What is the effect of these assumptions if you want to use this model to value the stock of growth companies, such as Intel, Pfizer, Microsoft, McDonald's, and Wal-Mart? **Growth companies** are firms that have the opportunities and abilities to earn rates of return on investments that are consistently above their required rates of return.[8] You will recall from corporate finance that the required rate of return for a corporation is its weighted average cost of capital (WACC). An example might be Intel, which has a WACC of about 12 percent, but is currently earning about 20 percent on its invested capital. Therefore, we would consider Intel a growth company. To exploit these outstanding investment opportunities, these growth firms generally retain a high percentage of earnings for reinvestment, and their earnings will grow faster than those of the typical firm. You will recall from the discussion in Chapter 10 that a firm's sustainable growth is a function of its retention rate and its return on equity (ROE). Notably, as discussed subsequently, the earnings growth pattern for these growth companies is inconsistent with the assumptions of the infinite period DDM.

First, the infinite period DDM assumes dividends will grow at a constant rate for an infinite period. This assumption seldom holds for companies currently growing at above average rates. As an example, both Intel and Wal-Mart have grown at rates in excess of 20 percent a year for several years. It is unlikely that they can maintain such extreme rates of growth because of the inability to continue earning the ROEs implied by this growth for an infinite period in an economy where other firms will compete with them for these high rates of return.

Second, during the periods when these firms experience abnormally high rates of growth, their rates of growth probably exceed their required rates of return. There is *no* automatic relationship between growth and risk; a high-growth company is not necessarily a high-risk company. In fact, a firm growing at a high *constant rate* would have lower risk (less uncertainty) than a low-growth firm with an unstable earnings pattern.

In summary, some firms experience periods of abnormally high rates of growth for some finite periods of time. The infinite period DDM cannot be used to value these true growth firms because these high-growth conditions are temporary and therefore inconsistent with the

---

[8]Growth companies are discussed in Salomon (1963) and Miller and Modigliani (1961). Models to value growth companies are discussed in Chapter 14.

assumptions of the DDM. In the following section, we discuss how to adjust the DDM to value a firm with temporary supernormal growth. In Chapter 14 we will discuss additional models used for estimating the stock value of growth companies.

Valuation with Temporary Supernormal Growth

Thus far, we have considered how to value a firm with different growth rates for short periods of time (one to three years) and how to value a stock using a model that assumes a constant growth rate for an infinite period. As noted, the assumptions of the model make it impossible to use the infinite period constant growth model to value true growth companies. The point is, in a competitive free enterprise economy, it is not reasonable to expect that a company can permanently maintain a growth rate higher than its required rate of return because competition will eventually enter this apparently lucrative business, which will reduce the firm's profit margins and therefore its ROE and growth rate. Therefore, after a few years of exceptional growth—that is, a period of temporary supernormal growth—a firm's growth rate is expected to decline. Eventually its growth rate is expected to stabilize at a constant level consistent with the assumptions of the infinite period DDM.

To determine the value of a temporary supernormal growth company, you must combine the previous models. In analyzing the initial years of exceptional growth, you examine each year individually. If the company is expected to have two or three stages of supernormal growth, you must examine each year during these stages of growth. When the firm's growth rate stabilizes at a rate below the required rate of return, you can compute the remaining value of the firm assuming constant growth using the DDM and discount this lump-sum constant growth value back to the present. The technique should become clear as you work through the following example.

The Bourke Company has a current dividend (D_0) of $2 a share. The following are the expected annual growth rates for dividends.

Year	Dividend Growth Rate
1–3	25%
4–6	20
7–9	15
10 on	9

The required rate of return for the stock (the company's cost of equity) is 14 percent. Therefore, the value equation becomes (Exhibit 11.3 presents it in a table):

$$V_j = \frac{2.00(1.25)}{1.14} + \frac{2.00(1.25)^2}{(1.14)^2} + \frac{2.00(1.25)^3}{(1.14)^3}$$

$$+ \frac{2.00(1.25)^3(1.20)}{(1.14)^4} + \frac{2.00(1.25)^3(1.20)^2}{(1.14)^5}$$

$$+ \frac{2.00(1.25)^3(1.20)^3}{(1.14)^6} + \frac{2.00(1.25)^3(1.20)^3(1.15)}{(1.14)^7}$$

$$+ \frac{2.00(1.25)^3(1.20)^3(1.15)^2}{(1.14)^8} + \frac{2.00(1.25)^3(1.20)^3(1.15)^3}{(1.14)^9}$$

$$+ \frac{\dfrac{2.00(1.25)^3(1.20)^3(1.15)^3(1.09)}{(0.14 - 0.09)}}{(1.14)^9}$$

Exhibit 11.3	Computation of Value for the Stock of a Company with Temporary Supernormal Growth

Year	Dividend	Discount Factor (14 percent)	Present Value
1	$ 2.50	0.8772	$ 2.193
2	3.12	0.7695	2.401
3	3.91	0.6750	2.639
4	4.69	0.5921	2.777
5	5.63	0.5194	2.924
6	6.76	0.4556	3.080
7	7.77	0.3996	3.105
8	8.94	0.3506	3.134
9	10.28	0.3075[b]	3.161
10	11.21		
	$224.20[a]	0.3075[b]	68.941
		Total value =	$94.355

[a]Value of dividend stream for Year 10 and all future dividends (that is, $11.21/(0.14 − 0.09) = $224.20).
[b]The discount factor is the ninth-year factor because the valuation of the remaining stream is made at the end of Year 9 to reflect the dividend in Year 10 and all future dividends.

The computations in Exhibit 11.3 indicate that the total value of the stock is $94.36. As before, you would compare this estimate of intrinsic value to the market price of the stock when deciding whether to purchase the stock. The difficult part of the valuation is estimating the supernormal growth rates and determining *how long* each of the growth rates will last.

To summarize this section, the initial present value of cash flow stock valuation model considered was the dividend discount model (DDM). After explaining the basic model and the derivation of its reduced form, we noted that the infinite period DDM cannot be applied to the valuation of stock for growth companies because the abnormally high growth rate of earnings for the growth company is inconsistent with the assumptions of the infinite period constant growth DDM model. Subsequently we modified the DDM model to evaluate companies with temporary supernormal growth. In the following sections, we discuss the other present value of cash flow techniques assuming a similar set of scenarios.

Present Value of Operating Free Cash Flows

In this model, you are deriving the value of the total firm because you are discounting the operating free cash flows prior to the payment of interest to the debt holders but after deducting funds needed to maintain the firm's asset base (capital expenditures). Also, because you are discounting the total firm's operating free cash flow, you would use the firm's weighted average cost of capital (*WACC*) as your discount rate. Therefore, once you estimate the value of the total firm, you subtract the value of debt, assuming your goal is to estimate the value of the firm's equity. The total value of the firm is equal to:

$$V_j = \sum_{t=1}^{n} \frac{OFCF_t}{(1 + WACC_j)^t}$$

where:

V_j = value of Firm j

n = number of periods assumed to be infinite

$OFCF_t$ = the firm's operating free cash flow in Period t. The detailed specification of operating free cash flow will be discussed in Chapter 14.

$WACC_j$ = Firm j's weighted average cost of capital. The computation of the firm's $WACC$ will be discussed in Chapter 14.

Similar to the process with the DDM, it is possible to envision this as a model that requires estimates for an infinite period. Alternatively, if you are dealing with a mature firm whereby its operating cash flows have reached a stage of stable growth, you can adapt the infinite period constant growth DDM model as follows:

$$V_j = \frac{OFCF_1}{WACC_j - g_{OFCF}}$$

where:

$OFCF_1$ = operating free cash flow in Period 1 equal to $OFCF_0(1 + g_{OFCF})$

g_{OFCF} = long-term constant growth rate of operating free cash flow

Alternatively, assuming that the firm is expected to experience several different rates of growth for $OFCF$, these estimates can be divided into three or four stages, as demonstrated with the temporary supernormal dividend growth model. Similar to the dividend model, the analyst must estimate the *rate* of growth and the *duration* of growth for each of these periods of supernormal growth as follows:

Year	OFCF Growth Rate
1–4	20%
5–7	16
8–10	12
11 on	7

Therefore, the calculations would estimate the specific $OFCF$s for each year through Year 10 based on the expected growth rates, but you would use the infinite growth model estimate when the growth rate reached stability after Year 10. As noted, after determining the value of the total firm V_j, you must subtract the value of all nonequity items, including accounts payable, total interest-bearing debt, deferred taxes, and preferred stock, to arrive at the estimated value of the firm's equity. This calculation will be demonstrated in Chapter 14.

Present Value of Free Cash Flows to Equity

The third discounted cash flow technique deals with "free" cash flows to equity, which would be derived *after* operating free cash flows have been adjusted for debt payments (interest and principal). Also, these cash flows precede dividend payments to the common stockholder. Such cash flows are referred to as free because they are what is left after providing the funds needed to maintain the firm's asset base (similar to operating free cash flow). They are free cash flows to equity because they also adjust for payments to debt holders and any payments to preferred stockholders.

Notably, because these are cash flows available to equity owners, the discount rate used is the firm's cost of equity (k) rather than the firm's *WACC*.

$$V_j = \sum_{t=1}^{n} \frac{FCFE_t}{(1 + k_j)^t}$$

where:

V_j = value of the stock of Firm j
n = number of periods assumed to be infinite
$FCFE_t$ = the firm's free cash flow to equity in Period t. The detailed specification of free cash flow to equity will be discussed in Chapter 14.

Again, how an analyst would implement this general model depends upon the firm's position in its life cycle. That is, if the firm is expected to experience stable growth, analysts can use the infinite growth model. In contrast, if the firm is expected to experience a period of temporary supernormal growth, analysts should use the multistage growth model similar to the process used with dividends and for operating free cash flow.

RELATIVE VALUATION TECHNIQUES

In contrast to the various discounted cash flow techniques that attempt to estimate a specific value for a stock based on its estimated growth rates and its discount rate, the relative valuation techniques implicitly contend that it is possible to determine the value of an economic entity (i.e., the market, an industry, or a company) by comparing it to similar entities on the basis of several relative ratios that compare its stock price to relevant variables that affect a stock's value, such as earnings, cash flow, book value, and sales. Therefore, in this section, we discuss the following relative valuation ratios: (1) price/earnings (*P/E*), (2) price/cash flow (*P/CF*), (3) price/book value (*P/BV*), and price/sales (*P/S*). We begin with the *P/E* ratio, also referred to as the earnings multiplier model, because it is the most popular relative valuation ratio. In addition, we will show that the *P/E* ratio can be directly related to the DDM in a manner that indicates the variables that affect the *P/E* ratio.

Earnings Multiplier Model

As noted, many investors prefer to estimate the value of common stock using an **earnings multiplier model**. The reasoning for this approach recalls the basic concept that the value of any investment is the present value of future returns. In the case of common stocks, the returns that investors are entitled to receive are the net earnings of the firm. Therefore, one way investors can estimate value is by determining how many dollars they are willing to pay for a dollar of expected earnings (typically represented by the estimated earnings during the following 12-month period or an estimate of "normalized earnings"). For example, if investors are willing to pay 10 times expected or "normal" earnings, they would value a stock they expect to earn $2 a share during the following year at $20. You can compute the prevailing earnings multiplier, also referred to as the **price/earnings (P/E) ratio**, as follows:

$$\text{Earnings Multiplier} = \text{Price/Earnings Ratio}$$
$$= \frac{\text{Current Market Price}}{\text{Expected 12-Month Earnings}}$$

This computation of the current earnings multiplier (*P/E* ratio) indicates the prevailing attitude of investors toward a stock's value. Investors must decide if they agree with the prevailing *P/E* ratio (that is, is the earnings multiplier too high or too low?) based upon how it compares to the *P/E* ratio for the aggregate market, for the firm's industry, and for similar firms and stocks.

To answer this question in a defensible manner, we must consider what influences the earnings multiplier (*P/E* ratio) over time. For example, over time the aggregate stock market *P/E* ratio, as represented by the S&P Industrials Index, has varied from about 6 times earnings to about 30 times earnings.[9] The infinite period dividend discount model can be used to indicate the variables that should determine the value of the *P/E* ratio as follows:[10]

$$P_i = \frac{D_1}{k - g}$$

If we divide both sides of the equation by E_1 (expected earnings during the next 12 months), the result is

$$\frac{P_i}{E_1} = \frac{D_1/E_1}{k - g}$$

Thus, this model implies that the *P/E* ratio is determined by

1. The *expected* dividend payout ratio (dividends divided by earnings)
2. The *estimated* required rate of return on the stock (*k*)
3. The *expected* growth rate of dividends for the stock (*g*)

As an example, if we assume a stock has an expected dividend payout of 50 percent, a required rate of return of 12 percent, and an expected growth rate for dividends of 8 percent, this would imply that the stock's *P/E* ratio should be:

$$D/E = 0.50; k = 0.12; g = 0.08$$

$$P/E = \frac{0.50}{0.12 - 0.08}$$
$$= 0.50/0.04$$
$$= 12.5$$

Again, a small difference in either *k* or *g* or both will have a large impact on the earnings multiplier, as shown in the following three examples.

1. $D/E = 0.50; k = 0.13; g = 0.08$. (In this example, we assume a higher *k* for the stock.)

$$P/E = \frac{0.50}{0.13 - 0.08}$$
$$= \frac{0.50}{0.05}$$
$$= 10$$

---

[9]When computing historical *P/E* ratios, the practice is to use earnings for the past 12 months rather than expected earnings. Although this practice of using historical earnings will influence the level, it demonstrates the changes in the *P/E* ratio over time. Although it may be appropriate to use historical *P/E* ratios for past comparison, we strongly believe that investment decisions should emphasize future or forward *P/E* ratios that use *expected* earnings.
[10]In this formulation of the model we use *P* rather than *V* (that is, the value is stated as the estimated price of the stock). Although the factors that determine the *P/E* are the same for growth companies, this formula cannot be used to estimate a specific value because these firms often do not have dividends, the infinite growth rate assumption is not valid, and the $(k - g)$ assumptions don't apply.

2. $D/E = 0.50$; $k = 0.12$; $g = 0.09$. (In this example, we assume a higher g for the stock and the original k.)

$$P/E = \frac{0.50}{0.12 - 0.09}$$
$$= \frac{0.50}{0.03}$$
$$= 16.7$$

3. $D/E = 0.50$; $k = 0.11$; $g = 0.09$. (In this example, we assume a fairly optimistic scenario where the k for the stock is only 11 percent and there is a higher expected growth rate of dividends of 9 percent.)

$$P/E = \frac{0.50}{0.11 - 0.09}$$
$$= \frac{0.50}{0.02}$$
$$= 25$$

As before, *the spread between k and g is the main determinant of the size of the P/E ratio.* Although the dividend payout ratio has an impact, we are generally referring to a firm's long-run target payout, which is typically rather stable with little effect on year-to-year changes in the *P/E* ratio (earnings multiplier).

After estimating the earnings multiple, you would apply it to your estimate of earnings for the next year (E_1) to arrive at an estimated value. In turn, E_1 is based on the earnings for the current year (E_0) and your expected growth rate of earnings. Using these two estimates, you would compute an estimated value of the stock and compare this estimated value to its market price.

Consider the following estimates for an example firm:

$$D/E = 0.50$$
$$k = 0.12$$
$$g = 0.09$$
$$E_0 = \$2.00$$

Using these estimates, you would compute an earnings multiple of:

$$P/E = \frac{0.50}{0.12 - 0.09} = \frac{0.50}{0.03} = 16.7$$

Given current earnings (E_0) of $2.00 and a g of 9 percent, you would expect E_1 to be $2.18. Therefore, you would estimate the value (price) of the stock as

$$V = 16.7 \times \$2.18$$
$$= \$36.41$$

As before, you would compare this estimated value of the stock to its current market price to decide whether you should invest in it. This estimate of value is referred to as a two-step process because it requires you to estimate future earnings (E_1) and a *P/E* ratio based on expectations of k and g. These two estimates are discussed in Chapter 14.

The Price/Cash Flow Ratio

The growth in popularity of the relative price/cash flow valuation ratio can be traced to concern over the propensity of some firms to manipulate earnings per share, whereas cash flow values are generally less prone to manipulation. Also, as noted, cash flow values are important in fundamental valuation (when computing the present value of cash flow), and they are critical when doing credit analysis where "cash is king." The price to cash flow ratio is computed as follows:

$$P/CF_j = \frac{P_t}{CF_{t+1}}$$

where:

P/CF_j = the price/cash flow ratio for Firm j
P_t = the price of the stock in Period t
CF_{t+1} = the expected cash flow per share for Firm j

Regarding what variables affect this valuation ratio, the factors are similar to the P/E ratio. Specifically, the main variables should be: (1) the expected growth rate of the cash flow variable used, and (2) the risk of the stock as indicated by the uncertainty or variability of the cash flow series over time. The specific cash flow measure used will vary depending upon the nature of the company and industry and which cash flow specification (for example, operating cash flow or free cash flow) is the best measure of performance for this industry.[11] An appropriate ratio can also be affected by the firm's capital structure.

The Price/Book Value Ratio

The price/book value (P/BV) ratio has been widely used for many years by analysts in the banking industry as a measure of relative value. The book value of a bank is typically considered a good indicator of intrinsic value because most bank assets, such as bonds and commercial loans, have a value equal to book value. This ratio gained in popularity and credibility as a relative valuation technique for all types of firms based upon a study by Fama and French (1992) that indicated a significant inverse relationship between P/BV ratios and excess rates of return for a cross section of stocks. The P/BV ratio is specified as follows:

$$P/BV_j = \frac{P_t}{BV_{t+1}}$$

where:

P/BV_j = the price/book value ratio for Firm j
P_t = the price of the stock in Period t
BV_{t+1} = the estimated end-of-year book value per share for Firm j

As with other relative valuation ratios, it is important to match the current price with the future book value that is expected to prevail at the end of the year. The difficulty is that this future book value is not generally available. One can derive an estimate of the end-of-year book value based upon an estimate of net earnings minus the expected dividends (which is added to

---

[11]While there has been a tendency to employ EBITDA as the proxy for cash flow, we do not recommend or encourage this because of the strong upward bias of this series compared to other cash flow measures, as noted in Chapter 10.

retained earnings). The growth rate for the series can be estimated using the growth rate implied by the sustainable growth formula: $g = (\text{ROE})(\text{Retention Rate})$.

Regarding what factors determine the size of the *P/BV* ratio, it is a function of the firm's ROE relative to its cost of equity since the ratio would be one if they were equal—that is, if the firm earned its required return on equity. In contrast, if the firm's ROE is much larger than its cost of equity, it is a growth company and investors should be willing to pay a premium over book value for the stock.

The Price/Sales Ratio

The price/sales (*P/S*) ratio has a volatile history. It was a favorite of Phillip Fisher (1984), a well-known money manager in the late 1950s; his son Kenneth Fisher (1984); and Sanchek and Martin (1987). Recently, the *P/S* ratio has been suggested as useful by Martin Leibowitz (1997), a widely admired stock and bond portfolio manager. These advocates consider this ratio meaningful and useful for two reasons. First, they believe that strong and consistent sales growth is a requirement for a growth company. Although they note the importance of an above-average profit margin, they contend that *the growth process must begin with sales.* Second, given all the data in the balance sheet and income statement, sales information is subject to less manipulation than any other data item. The specific *P/S* ratio is:

$$P/S_j = \frac{P_t}{S_{t+1}}$$

where:

P/S_j = the price to sales ratio for Firm j
P_t = the price of the stock in Period t
S_{t+1} = the expected sales per share for Firm j

Again, it is important to match the current stock price with the firm's *expected* sales per share, which may be difficult to derive for a large cross section of stocks. Two caveats are relevant to the price to sales ratio. First, this particular relative valuation ratio varies dramatically by industry. For example, the sales per share for retail firms, such as Kroger or Wal-Mart, are typically much higher than sales per share for computer or microchip firms. The second consideration is the profit margin on sales. The point is, retail food stores have high sales per share, which will cause a low *P/S* ratio, which is considered good until one realizes that these firms have low net profit margins. Therefore, your relative valuation analysis using the *P/S* ratio should be between firms in the same or similar industries.

Implementing the Relative Valuation Technique

As noted, the relative valuation technique considers several valuation ratios—such as *P/E, P/BV*—to derive a value for a stock. To properly implement this technique, it is essential to compare the various ratios but also to recognize that the analysis needs to go beyond simply comparing the ratios—it is necessary to understand what factors affect each of the valuation ratios and, therefore, know why they should differ. The first step is to compare the valuation ratio (e.g., the *P/E* ratio) for a company to the comparable ratio for the market, for the stock's industry, and to other stocks in the industry to determine how it compares—that is, is it similar to these other *P/Es*, or is it consistently at a premium or discount? Beyond knowing the overall relationship to the market, industry, and competitors, the real analysis is involved in understanding *why* the ratio has this relationship or why it should *not* have this relationship and the implications of this mismatch. Specifically, the second step is to explain the relationship. To do this, you need to understand what factors determine the specific valuation ratio and then compare these factors for the stock versus the same factors for the market, industry, and other stocks.

To illustrate this process, consider the following example wherein you want to value the stock of a pharmaceutical company and, you decide to employ the *P/E* relative valuation technique. As part of this analysis, you compare the *P/E* ratios for this firm over time (e.g., the last 15 years) to similar ratios for the S&P Industrials, the pharmaceutical industry, and specific competitors. This comparison indicates that the company *P/E* ratios are consistently above all the other sets. Following this initial observation, the second part of the analysis considers whether the fundamental factors that affect the *P/E* ratio (i.e., the firm's growth rate and its required rate of return) justify the higher *P/E*. A positive scenario would be that the firm had a historical and expected growth rate that was substantially above all the comparables and it should have a lower required rate of return. This would indicate that the higher *P/E* ratio is justified; the only question that needs to be considered is, how much higher should the *P/E* ratio be? Alternatively, the negative scenario for this stock with a *P/E* ratio above most comparables would be if the company's expected growth rate was equal to or lower than the industry and competitors' while its required *k* was higher than for the industry and competitors. This set of conditions would signal a stock that is apparently overpriced based on the fundamental factors that determine a stock's *P/E* ratio.

In subsequent sections, we discuss how an analyst arrives at estimates for *g* and *k,* and we demonstrate the process in subsequent chapters. At this point, the idea is for the reader to understand the overall process required by the relative valuation technique.

ESTIMATING THE INPUTS: THE REQUIRED RATE OF RETURN AND THE EXPECTED GROWTH RATE OF VALUATION VARIABLES

This section deals with estimating two inputs that are critical to the valuation process irrespective of which approach or technique is being used: the required rate of return (k) and the expected growth rate of earnings and other valuation variables—that is, book value, cash flow, sales, and dividends.

We will review these factors and discuss how the estimation of these variables differs for domestic versus foreign securities. Although the valuation procedure is the same for securities around the world, k and g differ among countries. Therefore, we will review the components of the required rate of return for U.S. securities and then consider the components for foreign securities. Subsequently, we consider the estimation of the growth rate of earnings, cash flow, and dividends for domestic stocks and then for foreign stocks.

Required Rate of Return (k)

This discussion reviews the determinants of the nominal required rate of return on an investment, including a consideration of factors for non-U.S. markets. This required rate of return will be the discount rate for most cash flow models and affects all the relative valuation techniques. The only difference in the discount rate is between the present value of dividends and the present value of free cash flow to equity techniques, which use the required rate of return on equity (k), versus the present value of operating free cash flow technique, which uses the weighted average cost of capital (*WACC*). Notably, the cost of equity is a critical input to estimating the firm's *WACC*.

Recall that three factors influence an equity investor's required rate of return (*k*):

1. The economy's real risk-free rate (*RRFR*)
2. The expected rate of inflation (*I*)
3. A risk premium (*RP*)

The Economy's Real Risk-Free Rate   This is the absolute minimum rate that an investor should require. It depends on the real growth rate of the investor's home economy because capital invested should grow at least as fast as the economy. As noted previously, this rate can be affected for short periods of time by temporary tightness or ease in the capital markets.

The Expected Rate of Inflation   Investors are interested in real rates of return that will allow them to increase their rate of consumption. Therefore, if investors expect a given rate of inflation, they should increase their required *nominal* risk-free rate of return (*NRFR*) to reflect any expected inflation as follows:

$$NRFR = [1 + RRFR] [1 + E(I)] - 1$$

where:

$E(I)$ = expected rate of inflation

The two factors that determine the *NRFR* affect all investments, from U.S. government securities to highly speculative land deals. Investors who hope to calculate security values accurately must carefully estimate the expected rate of inflation. Not only does the *NRFR* affect all investments, but, as shown in Chapter 1, its extreme volatility makes its estimation difficult.

The Risk Premium   The risk premium (*RP*) causes differences in the required rates of return among alternative investments that range from government bonds to corporate bonds to common stocks. The *RP* also explains the difference in the expected return among securities of the same type. For example, this is the reason corporate bonds with different ratings of Aaa, Aa, or A have different yields, and why different common stocks have widely varying earnings multipliers despite similar growth expectations.

In Chapter 1, we noted that investors demand a risk premium because of the uncertainty of returns expected from an investment. A measure of this uncertainty of returns was the dispersion of expected returns. We suggested several internal factors that influence a firm's variability of returns, such as its business risk, financial risk, and liquidity risk. We noted that securities of foreign firms or of domestic companies with significant foreign sales and earnings (e.g., Coca-Cola and McDonald's) have additional risk factors, including exchange rate risk and country (political) risk.

Changes in the Risk Premium   Because different securities (e.g., government bonds and common stocks) have different patterns of returns and different guarantees to investors, we expect their risk premiums to differ. In addition, a fact that is less recognized is that the risk premiums for the same securities can *change over time*. For example, Exhibit 11.4 shows the spread between the yields to maturity for Aaa-rated corporate bonds and Baa-rated corporate bonds from 1974 through 2004. This yield spread, or difference in yield, is a measure of the risk premium for investing in higher-risk bonds (Baa) compared to low-risk bonds (Aaa). As shown, the yield spread varied from about 0.40 percent to 2.69 percent (from less than one-half of 1 percent to almost 3 percent).

Exhibit 11.5 contains a plot of the *ratio* of the yields for the same period, which indicates the percentage risk premium of Baa bonds compared to Aaa bonds. You might expect a larger

Exhibit 11.4	Time-Series Plot of Moody's Corporate Bond Yield Spreads (Baa Yield/Aaa Yield): Monthly 1974–2004

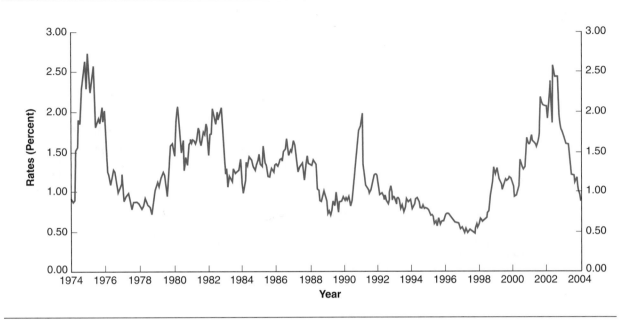

Source: Prepared by authors using data from Lehman Brothers.

difference in yield between Baa and Aaa bonds if Aaa bonds are yielding 12 percent rather than 6 percent. The yield ratio in Exhibit 11.5 adjusts for this size difference. This shows that even adjusting for the yield level difference, the risk premium ratio varies from about 1.06 to 1.56—a 6 percent premium to a 56 percent premium over the base yield on Aaa bonds. This significant change in the credit risk premium over time occurs because either investors perceive a change in the level of risk of Baa bonds compared to Aaa bonds or there is a change in the amount of return that investors require to accept the same risk differential. In either case, this change in the risk premium for a set of assets implies a change in the slope of the security market line (SML) as demonstrated in Chapter 1.

In Chapter 12, we will discuss the controversy regarding estimates of the equity market risk premium and the question of possible changes in the long-run equity risk premium.

Estimating the Required Return for Foreign Securities

Our discussion of the required rate of return for investments has been limited to the domestic market. Although the basic valuation model and its variables are the same around the world, there are significant differences in the values for specific variables. This section points out where these differences occur.

Foreign Real RFR   Because the *RRFR* in other countries should be determined by the real growth rate within the particular economy, the estimated rate can vary substantially among countries due to differences in an economy's real growth rate. An example of differences in the real growth rate of gross domestic product (GDP) can be seen from growth expectations for 2006 real GDP contained in the *IMF World Economic Outlook* as shown in Exhibit 11.6. There is a

| Exhibit 11.5 | Time-Series Plot of Corporate Bond Yield Ratio (Baa Yield/Aaa Yield): Monthly 1988–2004 |

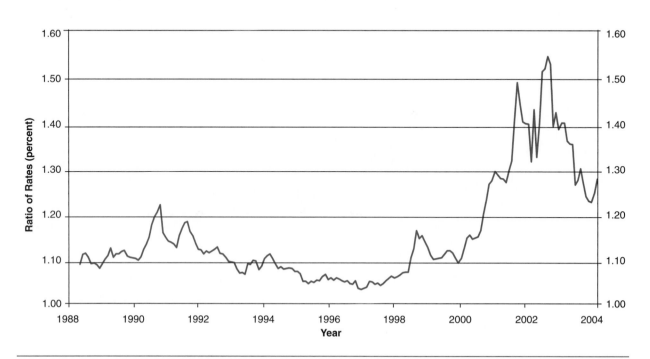

Source: Prepared by authors using data from Lehman Brothers.

range of estimates for 2006 of about 1.6 percent (that is, 1.6 percent for Germany compared to 3.6 percent for the United States with the Euro Zone estimated at about 2.3 percent). This difference in the growth rates of real GDP implies a substantial difference in the RRFR for these countries.[12]

Inflation Rate   To estimate the *NRFR* for a country, you must also estimate its expected rate of inflation and adjust the *NRFR* for this expectation. Again, this rate of inflation typically varies substantially among countries. The price change data show that the expected rate of inflation during 2006 varied from 0 percent in Japan to 2.4 percent in the United States. Assuming equal real growth, this inflation estimate implies a difference in the nominal required rate of return between Japan and the United States of 2.4 percent. Such a difference in *k* can have a substantial impact on estimated values, as demonstrated earlier. Again, you must make a separate estimate for each individual country in which you are evaluating securities.

   To demonstrate the combined impact of differences in real growth and expected inflation, Exhibit 11.6 shows the results of the following computation for four countries and the Euro Area based on the year 2006 estimates:

$$NRFR = (1 + \text{Real Growth}) \times (1 + \text{Expected Inflation}) - 1$$

[12]All the estimates of real growth and inflation are from the *IMF World Economic Outlook* (April, 2005).

Exhibit 11.6 | **Estimates of Year 2006 Nominal RFR for Major Countries**

Country	Real Growth in GDP	Expected Inflation	Nominal RFR
United States	3.6%	2.4%	6.1%
Japan	1.9	0.0	1.8
Germany	1.9	1.8	3.7
Britain	2.6	2.0	4.6
Euro Area	2.3	1.7	4.0

Source: Prepared by authors using data from *IMF World Economic Outlook* (April, 2005).

Given the differences between countries in the two components, the range in the *NRFR* of 4.2 percent is not surprising (6.4 percent for the United States versus 1.9 percent for Japan). As demonstrated earlier, such a difference in *k* for an investment will have a significant impact on its value.

Risk Premium   You must also derive an equity risk premium for the investments in each country. Again, the five risk components differ substantially between countries: business risk, financial risk, liquidity risk, exchange rate risk, and country risk. *Business risk* can vary because it is a function of the variability of economic activity within a country and of the operating leverage used by firms within the country. Firms in different countries assume significantly different *financial risk* as well. For example, Japanese firms use substantially more financial leverage than U.S. or U.K. firms. Regarding *liquidity risk,* the U.S. capital markets are acknowledged to be the most liquid in the world, with Japan and the United Kingdom being close behind. In contrast, some emerging markets are quite illiquid and in such cases investors need to add a significant liquidity risk premium.

When investing globally, you also must estimate *exchange rate risk,* which is the additional uncertainty of returns caused by changes in the exchange rates for the currency of another country. This uncertainty can be small for a U.S. investor in a country such as Hong Kong because the currency is pegged to the U.S. dollar. In contrast, in some countries, substantial volatility in the exchange rate over time can mean significant differences in the domestic return for the country and return in U.S. dollars.[13] The level of volatility for the exchange rate differs between countries. The greater the uncertainty regarding future changes in the exchange rate, the larger the exchange rate risk for the country.[14]

Recall that country risk arises from unexpected events in a country, such as upheavals in its political or economic environment. An example of political and economic disruptions occurred in Russia during 1998 when there was substantial uncertainty about the potential devaluation of the ruble. Similarly, unrest in Indonesia during 1998 led to riots and the eventual resignation of President Suharto. Such political unrest or a change in the economic environment creates uncertainties that increase the risk of investments in these countries. Before investing in such countries, investors must evaluate the additional returns they should require to accept this increased uncertainty.

---

[13]Although we generally refer to these as domestic and U.S. dollar returns, you will also see references to *hedged* returns (for example, domestic) and *unhedged* returns (returns in U.S. dollars). In some cases, the hedged returns will adjust for the cost of hedging.

[14]For a thorough analysis of exchange rate determination and forecasting models, see Rosenberg (1996).

Thus, when estimating required rates of return on foreign investments, you must assign a unique risk premium for each country.

Expected Growth Rates

After arriving at a required rate of return, the investor must estimate the growth rate of cash flows, earnings, and dividends because the alternative valuation models for common stock depend heavily on good estimates of growth (g) for these variables. The initial procedure we describe here is a brief summary of the presentation in Chapter 10, where we used financial ratios to measure a firm's growth potential. Subsequently, we discuss the use of historical growth rates as an input to the estimate.

Estimating Growth from Fundamentals   The growth rate of dividends is determined by the growth rate of earnings and the proportion of earnings paid out in dividends (the payout ratio). Over the short run, dividends can grow faster or slower than earnings if the firm changes its payout ratio. Specifically, if a firm's earnings grow at 6 percent a year and it pays out exactly 50 percent of earnings in dividends, then the firm's dividends will likewise grow at 6 percent a year. Alternatively, if a firm's earnings grow at 6 percent a year and the firm increases its payout, then during the period when the payout ratio increases, dividends will grow faster than earnings. In contrast, if the firm reduces its payout ratio, dividends will grow slower than earnings for a period of time. Because there is a limit to how long this difference in growth rates can continue, most investors assume that the long-run dividend payout ratio is fairly stable. Therefore, our analysis of the growth rate of dividends concentrates on an analysis of the growth rate of equity earnings. Also, as will be shown in Chapter 14, equity earnings are the major factor driving the operating cash flows or the free cash flows for the firm.

When a firm retains earnings and acquires additional assets, if it earns some positive rate of return on these additional assets, the total earnings of the firm will increase because its asset base is larger. How rapidly a firm's earnings increase depends on (1) the proportion of earnings it retains and reinvests in new assets and (2) the rate of return it earns on these new assets. Specifically, the growth rate (g) of equity earnings (that is, earnings per share) without any external financing is equal to the percentage of net earnings retained (the retention rate, which equals 1 – the payout ratio) times the rate of return on equity capital.

$$g = \text{(Retention Rate)} \times \text{(Return on Equity)}$$
$$= RR \times ROE$$

Therefore, a firm can increase its growth rate by increasing its retention rate (reducing its payout ratio) and investing these added funds at its historic *ROE*. Alternatively, the firm can maintain its retention rate but increase its *ROE*. For example, if a firm retains 50 percent of net earnings and consistently has an *ROE* of 10 percent, its net earnings will grow at the rate of 5 percent a year, as follows:

$$g = RR \times ROE$$
$$= 0.50 \times 0.10$$
$$= 0.05$$

If, however, the firm increases its retention rate to 75 percent and is able to invest these additional funds in internal projects that likewise earn 10 percent, its growth rate will increase to 7.5 percent, as follows:

$$g = 0.75 \times 0.10$$
$$= 0.075$$

If, instead, the firm continues to reinvest 50 percent of its earnings but is able to earn a higher rate of return on these investments, say 15 percent, it can likewise increase its growth rate, as follows:

$$g = 0.50 \times 0.15$$
$$= 0.075$$

Breakdown of *ROE*   Although the retention rate is a management decision, changes in the firm's *ROE* result from changes in its operating performance or its financial leverage. As discussed in Chapter 10, we can divide the *ROE* ratio into three components:

$$ROE = \frac{\text{Net Income}}{\text{Sales}} \times \frac{\text{Sales}}{\text{Total Assets}} \times \frac{\text{Total Assets}}{\text{Equity}}$$

$$= \frac{\text{Profit}}{\text{Margin}} \times \frac{\text{Total Asset}}{\text{Turnover}} \times \frac{\text{Financial}}{\text{Leverage}}$$

This breakdown allows us to consider the three factors that determine a firm's *ROE*.[15] Because it is a multiplicative relationship, an increase in any of the three ratios will cause an increase in *ROE*. The first two of the three ratios reflect operating performance, and the third one indicates a firm's financing decision.

The first operating ratio, net profit margin, indicates the firm's profitability on sales. This ratio changes over time for some companies and is highly sensitive to the business cycle. For growth companies, this is one of the first ratios to decline because the increased competition increases the supply of the goods or services and forces price cutting, which leads to lower profit margins. Also, during recessions, profit margins decline because of price cutting or because of higher percentages of fixed costs due to lower sales.

The second component, total asset turnover, is the ultimate indicator of operating efficiency and reflects the asset and capital requirements of the business. Although this ratio varies dramatically by industry, within an industry it is an excellent indicator of management's operating efficiency.

The product of these first two components (profit margin and total asset turnover) equals the firm's return on assets (*ROA*), which reflects the firm's operating performance before the financing impact.[16]

The final component, total assets/equity, does not measure operating performance but, rather, financial leverage. Specifically, it indicates how management has decided to finance the firm. In turn, this management decision regarding the financing of assets can contribute to a higher *ROE*, but it also has financial risk implications for the stockholder.

Knowing this breakdown of *ROE*, you must examine past results and expectations for a firm and develop *estimates* of the three components and therefore an estimate of a firm's *ROE*. This estimate of *ROE* combined with the firm's expected retention rate will indicate its future growth potential. Finally, it is important to note that when estimating growth, it is necessary to estimate, not only the *rate* of growth, but also the *duration* of growth (how long can the firm sustain this rate of growth?). Clearly, the higher the rate of growth the more significant the estimate of the duration of growth to the ultimate value of the stock. Also, a high rate of growth

---

[15]You will recall from Chapter 10 (Exhibit 10.7) that it is possible to employ an extended DuPont system that involves eight ratios. For purposes of this discussion, the three ratios indicate the significant factors and differences among countries.

[16]In Chapter 13, we discuss a study that analyzes why and how alternative industries differ regarding the return on assets and the two components of ROA.

generally implies a high ROE, which is difficult to sustain because numerous competitors want to experience these high rates of return.

Estimating Growth Based on History   Although the authors have a strong bias in favor of using the fundamentals to estimate future growth, which involves estimating the components of *ROE,* we also believe in using all the information available to make this critical estimate. Therefore, we suggest that analysts also consider the historical growth rate of sales, earnings, cash flow, and dividends in this process.

Although we will demonstrate these computations for the market, for an industry, and for a company in subsequent chapters, the following discussion considers some suggestions on alternative calculations. In terms of the relevant period to consider, one is struck by the cliché "more is better" as long as you recognize that "recent is relevant." Specifically, about 20 years of annual observations would be ideal, but it is important to consider subperiods as well as the total period—that is, 20 years, two 10-year periods, and four 5-year periods would indicate the overall growth rate but also would indicate if there were any *changes* in the growth rate in recent periods.

The specific measurement can be done using one or more of three techniques: (1) arithmetic or geometric average of annual percentage changes, (2) linear regression models, and (3) log-linear regression models. Irrespective of the measurement techniques used, we strongly encourage a time-series plot of the annual percentage changes.

The arithmetic or geometric average technique involves computing the annual percentage change and then computing either the simple arithmetic average or the geometric average of these values for the alternative periods. As you will recall from the discussion in Chapter 3, the arithmetic average will always be a higher value than the geometric average (except when the annual values are constant) and the difference between the arithmetic and geometric average values will increase with volatility. As noted previously, we generally prefer the geometric mean because it provides the average annual compound growth rate.

The linear regression model goes well with the suggested time-series plot and is as follows:

$$EPS_t = a + bt$$

where:

EPS_t = earnings per period in Period t
   t = year t where t goes from 1 to n
   b = the coefficient that indicates the average absolute change in the series during the period

It would be very informative to superimpose this regression line on the time-series plot because it would provide insights on changes in absolute growth.

The log-linear model considers that the series might be better described in terms of a constant *growth rate.* This model is as follows:

$$ln(EPS_t) = a + bt$$

where:

$ln(EPS_t)$ = the natural logarithm of earnings per share in Period t
      b = the coefficient that indicates *the average percentage change* in the series during the period

The analysis of these historical growth rates both visually with the time-series graph and the alternative calculations should provide you with significant insights into the trend of the growth rates as well as the *variability* of the growth rates over time. As discussed in Chapter 10 and demonstrated in Appendix 10C, this could provide information on the unit's business risk with the analysis of sales and EBIT growth.

Estimating Dividend Growth for Foreign Stocks

The underlying factors that determine the growth rates for foreign stocks are similar to those for U.S. stocks, but the value of the equation's components may differ substantially from what is common in the United States. The differences in the retention rate or the components of *ROE* result from differences in accounting practices as well as alternative management performance or philosophy.

Retention Rates The retention rates for foreign corporations differ within countries, but differences also exist among countries due to differences in the countries' investment opportunities. As an example, firms in Japan have a higher retention rate than firms in the United States, whereas the rate of retention in France is much lower. Therefore, you need to examine the retention rates for a number of firms in a country as a background for estimating the standard rate within a country.

Net Profit Margin The net profit margin of foreign firms can differ because of different accounting conventions between countries. As noted in Chapter 10, foreign accounting rules allow firms to recognize revenue and allocate expenses differently from U.S. firms. For example, German firms are allowed to build up large reserves for various reasons. As a result, they report low earnings for tax purposes. Also, different foreign depreciation practices require adjustment of earnings and cash flows.

Total Asset Turnover Total asset turnover can likewise differ among countries because of different accounting conventions on the reporting of asset values at cost or market values. For example, in Japan, a large part of the market values for some firms comes from their real estate holdings and their common stock investments in other firms. These assets are reported at cost, which typically has substantially understated their true value. This also means that the total asset turnover ratio for these firms is substantially overstated.

This ratio will also be impacted by leases that are not capitalized on the balance sheet—that is, if leases are not capitalized, both assets and liabilities are understated.

Total Asset/Equity Ratio This ratio, a measure of financial leverage, differs among countries because of differences in economic environments, tax laws, management philosophies regarding corporate debt, and accounting conventions. In several countries, the attitude toward debt is much more liberal than in the United States. A prime example is Japan, where debt as a percentage of total assets is almost 50 percent higher than a similar ratio in the United States. Notably, most corporate debt in Japan entails borrowing from banks at fairly low rates of interest. Balance sheet debt ratios may be higher in Japan than in the United States or other countries; but, because of the lower interest rates in Japan, the fixed-charge coverage ratios, such as the times interest earned ratio, might be similar to those in other countries. The point is, it is important to consider the several cash flow financial risk ratios along with the balance sheet debt ratios.

Consequently, when analyzing a foreign stock market or an individual foreign stock that involves estimating the growth rate for earnings and dividends, you must consider the three components of the *ROE* just as you would for a U.S. stock but recognize that the financial ratios for foreign firms can differ from those of U.S. firms, as discussed in Chapter 10 references. Subsequent chapters on valuation applied to the aggregate market, to various industries, and to companies contain examples of these differences.

The Internet

Investments Online

Several sites that we discussed in earlier chapters contained financial calculators. By inputting the required data, users can determine if it is better to buy or lease a car, calculate returns, and determine how much money they will have if funds are invested at a certain rate of return over time. The sites below all contain financial calculators that may be of use to investors and financial planners.

http://www.leadfusion.com
http://www.jamesko.com/FinCalc
http://www.numeraire.com
http://www.moneychimp.com

SUMMARY

- As an investor, you want to select investments that will provide a rate of return that compensates you for your time, the expected rate of inflation, and the risk involved. To help you find these investments, this chapter considers the theory of valuation by which you derive the value of an investment using your required rate of return. We consider the two investment decision processes, which are the top-down, three-step approach and the bottom-up, stockpicking approach. Although it is recognized that either process can provide abnormal positive returns if the analyst is superior, we feel that a preferable approach is the top-down approach in which you initially consider the aggregate economy and market, then examine alternative global industries, and finally analyze individual firms and their stocks.
- We apply the valuation theory to a range of investments, including bonds, preferred stock, and common stock. Because the valuation of common stock is more complex and difficult, we suggest two alternative approaches (the present value of cash flows and the relative valuation approach) and several techniques for each of these approaches. Notably, these are *not* competitive approaches and we suggest that both approaches be used. Although we suggest using several different valuation models, the investment decision rule is always the same: If the estimated intrinsic value of the investment is greater than the market price, you should buy the investment; if the estimated intrinsic value of an investment is less than its market price, you should not invest in it and if you own it, you should sell it.
- We conclude with a review of factors that you need to consider when estimating the value of stock with either approach—your required rate of return on an investment and the growth rate of earnings, cash flow, and dividends. Finally, we consider some unique factors that affect the application of these valuation models to foreign stocks.

SUGGESTED READINGS

Arzac, Enrique. *Valuations for Mergers, Buyouts, and Restructuring.* New York: Wiley, 2005.

Billingsley, Randall, ed. *Corporate Financial Decision Making and Equity Analysis.* Proceedings of a seminar by the Association of Investment Management and Research. Charlottesville, VA: AIMR, 1995.

Copeland, T. E., Tim Koller, and Jack Murrin. *Valuation: Measuring and Managing the Value of Companies,* 3rd ed. New York: Wiley, 2001.

Damodaran, Aswath. *Damodaran on Valuation.* New York: Wiley, 1994.

Damodaran, Aswath. *Investment Valuation.* New York: Wiley, 1996.

Fogler, H. Russell, ed. *Blending Quantitative and Traditional Equity Analysis.* Proceedings of a seminar by the Association of Investment Management and Research. Charlottesville, VA: AIMR, 1994.

Helfert, Erich A. *Techniques of Financial Analysis,* 10th ed. Burr Ridge, IL: Irwin McGraw-Hill, 2000.

Higgins, Robert C. *Analysis for Financial Management,* 5th ed. Chicago: Irwin, 2000.

Palepu, Krishna, Paul Healy, and Victor Bernard. *Business Analysis and Valuation,* 3rd ed. Cincinnati, OH: South-Western, 2004.

Squires, Jan, ed. *Equity Research and Valuation Techniques.* Proceedings of a seminar by the Association of

Investment Management and Research. Charlottesville, VA: AIMR, 1997.

Squires, Jan, ed. *Practical Issues in Equity Analysis.* Conference proceedings by the Association of Investment Management and Research. Charlottesville, VA: AIMR, 2000.

Stowe, J. D., T. R. Robinson, J. E. Pinto, and D. W. McLeavey. *Analysis of Equity Investments: Valuation.*

Charlottesville, VA: Association of Investment Management and Research; 2002.

Sullivan, Rodney N., ed. *Equity Analysis Issues, Lessons, and Techniques.* Proceedings of a seminar by AIMR, Charlottesville, VA: AIMR, 2003.

QUESTIONS

1. Discuss the difference between the top-down and bottom-up approaches. What is the major assumption that causes the difference in these two approaches?
2. What is the benefit of analyzing the market and alternative industries before individual securities?
3. Discuss why you would not expect all industries to have a similar relationship to the economy. Give an example of two industries that have different relationships to the economy.
4. Discuss why estimating the value for a bond is easier than estimating the value for common stock.
5. Would you expect the required rate of return for a U.S. investor in U.S. common stocks to be the same as the required rate of return on Japanese common stocks? What factors would determine the required rate of return for stocks in these countries?
6. Would you expect the nominal *RFR* in the United States to be the same as in Germany? Discuss your reasoning.
7. Would you expect the risk premium for an investment in an Indonesian stock to be the same as that for a stock from the United Kingdom? Discuss your reasoning.
8. Would you expect the risk premium for an investment in a stock from Singapore to be the same as that for a stock from the United States? Discuss your reasoning.
9. Give an example of a stock where it would be appropriate to use the reduced form DDM for valuation and discuss why you feel that it is appropriate. Similarly, give an example and discuss a stock where it would not be appropriate to use the reduced form DDM.
10. Give an example of and discuss a stock that has temporary, supernormal growth where it would be appropriate (necessary) to use the modified DDM.
11. Under what conditions will it be ideal to use one or several of the relative valuation ratios to evaluate a stock?
12. Discuss a scenario where it would be appropriate to use one of the present value of cash flow techniques for the valuation.
13. Discuss why the two valuation approaches (present value of cash flows and the relative valuation ratios) are competitive or complementary.

PROBLEMS

1. What is the value to you of a 9 percent coupon bond with a par value of $10,000 that matures in 10 years if you want a 7 percent return? Use semiannual compounding.
2. What would be the value of the bond in Problem 1 if you wanted an 11 percent rate of return?
3. The preferred stock of the Clarence Radiology Company has a par value of $100 and a $9 dividend rate. You require an 11 percent rate of return on this stock. What is the maximum price you would pay for it? Would you buy it at a market price of $96?
4. The Baron Basketball Company (BBC) earned $10 a share last year and paid a dividend of $6 a share. Next year, you expect BBC to earn $11 and continue its payout ratio. Assume that you expect to sell the stock for $132 a year from now. If you require 12 percent on this stock, how much would you be willing to pay for it?
5. Given the expected earnings and dividend payments in Problem 4, if you expected a selling price of $110 and required an 8 percent return on this investment, how much would you pay for the BBC stock?

6. Over the long run, you expect dividends for BBC in Problem 4 to grow at 8 percent and you require 11 percent on the stock. Using the infinite period DDM, how much would you pay for this stock?

7. Based on new information regarding the popularity of basketball, you revise your growth estimate for BBC to 9 percent. What is the maximum *P/E* ratio you will apply to BBC, and what is the maximum price you will pay for the stock?

8. The Shamrock Dogfood Company (SDC) has consistently paid out 40 percent of its earnings in dividends. The company's return on equity is 16 percent. What would you estimate as its dividend growth rate?

9. Given the low risk in dog food, your required rate of return on SDC is 13 percent. What *P/E* ratio would you apply to the firm's earnings?

10. What *P/E* ratio would you apply if you learned that SDC had decided to increase its payout to 50 percent? (Hint: This change in payout has multiple effects.)

11. Discuss three ways a firm can increase its *ROE*. Make up an example to illustrate your discussion.

12. It is widely known that grocery chains have low profit margins—on average they earn about 1 percent on sales. How would you explain the fact that their *ROE* is about 12 percent? Does this seem logical?

13. Compute a recent five-year average of the following ratios for three companies of your choice (attempt to select diverse firms):
    a. Retention rate
    b. Net profit margin
    c. Equity turnover
    d. Total asset turnover
    e. Total assets/equity
    Based on these ratios, explain which firm should have the highest growth rate of earnings.

14. You have been reading about the Maddy Computer Company (MCC), which currently retains 90 percent of its earnings ($5 a share this year). It earns an *ROE* of almost 30 percent. Assuming a required rate of return of 14 percent, how much would you pay for MCC on the basis of the earnings multiplier model? Discuss your answer. What would you pay for Maddy Computer if its retention rate was 60 percent and its *ROE* was 19 percent? Show your work.

15. Gentry Can Company's (GCC) latest annual dividend of $1.25 a share was paid yesterday and maintained its historic 7 percent annual rate of growth. You plan to purchase the stock today because you believe that the dividend growth rate will increase to 8 percent for the next three years and the selling price of the stock will be $40 per share at the end of that time.
    a. How much should you be willing to pay for the GCC stock if you require a 12 percent return?
    b. What is the maximum price you should be willing to pay for the GCC stock if you believe that the 8 percent growth rate can be maintained indefinitely and you require a 12 percent return?
    c. If the 8 percent rate of growth is achieved, what will the price be at the end of Year 3, assuming the conditions in Part b?

16. In the *Federal Reserve Bulletin,* find the average yield of AAA and BBB bonds for a recent month. Compute the risk premium (in basis points) and the percentage risk premium on BBB bonds relative to AAA bonds. Discuss how these values compare to those shown in Exhibits 11.4 and 11.5.

THOMSON ONE | Business School Edition

1. Using Ford (F), General Electric (GE), McDonald's (MCD), Nike (NKE), and Walgreens (WAG), find the five-year estimate for net income growth (LTG) dividend yield, *P/E,* Price/Cash Flow, and Price/Book Value ratios. Do a spread sheet listing each of these values for each company and briefly comment on the differences between each item.

2. Assume that the five-year estimates for net income growth for General Electric, McDonald's, and Walgreens are the same as their dividend growth rates—that is, earnings and dividends grow at the same rate.

    a. For each of these three firms, estimate the dollar amount of dividends per share over each of the next five years.

    b. Find the present value of each dividend stream from part a. Use a discount rate of 10 percent for each firm. (This is a simplification; in reality we would need to estimate the required rate of return for each firm.)

    c. For each firm, compare its current stock price with the estimated present value of its dividends over the next five years. Given our assumptions, what proportion of the stock price arises from cash flows *beyond* the next five years?

3. For each of the five firms, using the beta provided, compute the stock's required return on equity (*K*) using the following *SML* equation.

$$E(R) = RFR + \beta_i (R_m - RFR)$$
$$= 0.05 + \beta_i (0.09 - 0.05)$$

4. Knowing that a stock's *P/E* ratio is mainly determined by *K* and *g*, show in a table the following:

Stock	*Current Forward P/E	LTG	K

$$^*\text{Forward } P/E = \frac{\text{Current } P}{EPS_{t+1}}$$

Comment on the stocks that appear to be relatively high priced or low priced and why you label them as such.

APPENDIX
Chapter 11   Derivation of Constant Growth Dividend Discount Model (DDM)

The basic model is

$$P_0 = \frac{D_1}{(1 + k)^1} + \frac{D_2}{(1 + k)^2} + \frac{D_3}{(1 + k)^3} + \cdots + \frac{D_n}{(1 + k)^n}$$

where:

    P_0 = current price
    D_i = expected dividend in Period i
    k = required rate of return on Asset j

If growth rate (g) is constant,

$$P_0 = \frac{D_0(1 + g)^1}{(1 + k)^1} + \frac{D_0(1 + g)^2}{(1 + k)^2} + \cdots + \frac{D_0(1 + g)^n}{(1 + k)^n}$$

This can be written

$$P_0 = D_0\left[\frac{(1 + g)}{(1 + k)} + \frac{(1 + g)^2}{(1 + k)^2} + \frac{(1 + g)^3}{(1 + k)^3} + \cdots + \frac{(1 + g)^n}{(1 + k)^n}\right]$$

Multiply both sides of the equation by $\dfrac{1 + k}{1 + g}$.

$$\left[\frac{(1 + k)}{(1 + g)}\right]P_0 = D_0\left[1 + \frac{(1 + g)}{(1 + k)} + \frac{(1 + g)^2}{(1 + k)^2} + \cdots + \frac{(1 + g)^{n-1}}{(1 + k)^{n-1}}\right]$$

Subtract the previous equation from this equation:

$$\left[\frac{(1 + k)}{(1 + g)} - 1\right]P_0 = D_0\left[1 - \frac{(1 + g)^n}{(1 + k)^n}\right]$$

$$\left[\frac{(1 + k) - (1 + g)}{(1 + g)}\right]P_0 = D_0\left[1 - \frac{(1 + g)^n}{(1 + k)^n}\right]$$

Assuming $k > g$, as $n \to \infty$, the term in brackets on the right side of the equation goes to 1, leaving:

$$\left[\frac{(1 + k) - (1 + g)}{(1 + g)}\right]P_0 = D_0$$

This simplifies to

$$\left[\frac{(1 + k - 1 - g)}{(1 + g)}\right]P_0 = D_0$$

which equals

$$\left[\frac{k - g}{(1 + g)}\right]P_0 = D_0$$

This equals

$$(k - g)P_0 = D_0(1 + g)$$

$$D_0(1 + g) = D_1$$

so:

$$(k - g)P_0 = D_1$$

$$P_0 = \frac{D_1}{k - g}$$

Remember, this model assumes

- A constant growth rate
- An infinite time period
- The required return on the investment (k) is greater than the expected growth rate (g)